AFRICAN ONE-PARTY STATES

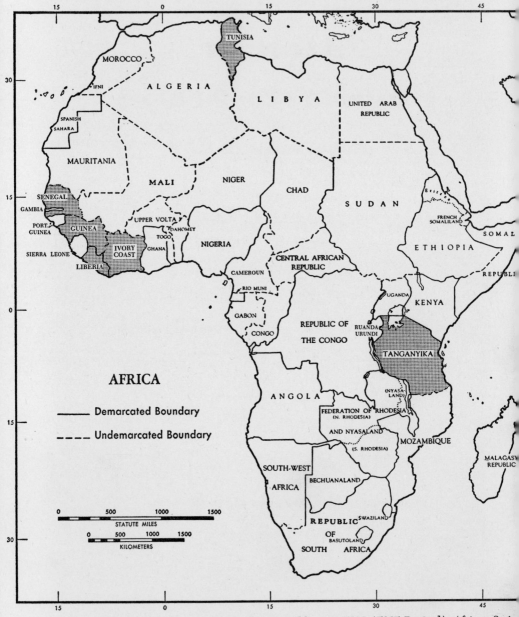

AFRICA

——— Demarcated Boundary

‑ ‑ ‑ Undemarcated Boundary

Adapted from the Department of State Publication 7316 (7067 Revised), African Serie

African One-Party States

EDITED BY

GWENDOLEN M. CARTER

CONTRIBUTORS

CHARLES F. GALLAGHER, ERNEST MILCENT,

L. GRAY COWAN, VIRGINIA THOMPSON,

J. GUS LIEBENOW, *and* MARGARET L. BATES

Cornell University Press

ITHACA, NEW YORK

PREFACE

The fact that within the past few years so many states on the African continent have acquired independence under the control of their indigenous inhabitants has made peculiarly difficult the problem of choice for inclusion in this volume. Two criteria have been used: approximation of the country to the form of a one-party state and lack of comprehensive published accounts in English of its structure and characteristics. On the latter count Ghana, in particular, was excluded.

The final choice for inclusion also aimed at variety. The book includes a section on a North African state, Tunisia, one on an East African state, Tanganyika, and four on West African countries, Senegal, Guinea, the Ivory Coast, and Liberia. Of the six, four have known French colonial rule, one has been under British colonial rule, and Liberia, second only to Ethiopia in its length of time as an independent African state, has been subject to a vague American influence both through the background of its ruling group, the Americo-Liberians, and through intermittent and unsystematic counsel and aid from the United States. By stressing this variety of experience and background, the choice of countries has somewhat complicated the use of the comparative method, but where comparisons can be drawn they may be the more fruitful because they reflect institutions and ideas which spring from the African setting rather than from any particular colonial experience.

Although the contributors to the book did not have the opportunity to meet together to evolve some common approach to the material they handled, they worked from a common outline proposed by the

v

editor and, as far as possible, their sections have been aligned in structure though obviously not in content. To have reduced the rich historical background of Tunisia, for example, to the brief treatment of the precolonial period provided in most of the other sections would have been an arbitrary and stultifying imposition. None of the contributors has seen the work of the others, but all have responded nobly to the critical suggestions of the editor.

The order in which the sections are placed largely results from the contributors' own treatment of their material. The sections on Tunisia and Senegal describe the salient features of the post-World War II evolution of French colonial policy in Africa. The section on Guinea elaborates on the failure of Léopold Sédar Senghor of Senegal and of Sékou Touré to secure African control at the federal level in French West Africa and describes the impact on French Africa of the transition to de Gaulle's Fifth Republic. The section on the Ivory Coast adds to the account of the ill-fated Mali Federation in the Senegalese section the counter—and more successful—efforts of Félix Houphouët-Boigny in the same immediate preindependence period to build the loose association of the Entente. Thus each of these four sections, while a complete entity in itself, gears closely into the others in presenting a coherent background to the achievement of independence by them all.

Explicitly or implicitly all the contributors have commented on the character and prospects of a type of one-party state which should not be confused with the classic totalitarian model. This descriptive material and their analysis, as well as wider reading and personal research, have underlain the comments and ideas brought forward in the Introduction. The editor would like to make it clear that this Introduction is a personal and not group responsibility and that it is intended to suggest lines of thought to those reading the substantive material, not to make judgments or to bring final conclusions. On only one point does the editor feel the right to be dogmatic, and that is to maintain that in Africa today (though not exclusively there) peoples, parties, and leaders are experimenting with new political forms which are influenced strongly, either positively or negatively, by their experience with Western-type institutions but are sufficiently distinctive to be worthy of fresh standards of evaluation. It is sincerely hoped that the book as a whole will help to stimulate the evolution of such standards.

In the interests of finding the closest common denominator com-

patible with clarity, the contributors finally agreed on the present
title of this book. It is only right to point out, however, that in three of
the countries, Tunisia, Senegal, and Tanganyika, there is more than
one party in existence although each has, in practice, a one-party political regime.

Material on such fast-moving events inevitably dates quickly. Moreover, it has not been possible to have the terminal date of writing coincide in all sections although, as far as possible, developments in 1962
have been included. We believe, however, that what is most important
is to provide background, perspective, and trends and to leave it to
our readers to use these in conjunction with whatever news the daily
press provides.

Each of the six contributors of substantive material has had extensive experience in the country on which he or she has written. Nearly
all of them have already published scholarly material based on their
research in these countries. Two were trained primarily in history but
have substantial backgrounds in political science; three others and the
editor are political scientists but with substantial backgrounds in history; one contributor is a practicing journalist who draws on a knowledge of both disciplines.

Charles F. Gallagher is a member of the staff of the American Universities Field Staff. For many years he has alternated between residence in different parts of North Africa and the Middle East and
strenuous periods of lecturing on these areas at the twelve universities that are member institutions of the AUFS. His long series of reports for the AUFS have formed a basic source of information on the
background of contemporary developments in this area as well as on
the events themselves.

Ernest Milcent is editor of *Afrique Nouvelle,* a liberal Catholic
weekly published in Dakar since 1947. He has long been a resident
of Senegal and has traveled widely in French West Africa and attended many conferences and private meetings at which crucial decisions were made. He is a constant contributor to his own and other
newspapers, notably *Le Monde.*

L. Gray Cowan is director of the newly established African program of Columbia University, associate professor of government, and
secretary of the African Studies Association. He has spent extended
periods of research in Guinea in addition to traveling widely throughout other parts of the continent. He is the author of *Local Government in West Africa* (Columbia University Press, 1958).

Virginia Thompson is the author, with her husband, Richard Adloff, of two basic books on French Africa that are the result of extensive field research: *French West Africa* (Stanford University Press, 1958) and *The Emerging States of French Equatorial Africa* (Stanford University Press, 1960). She is lecturer at the University of California in Berkeley and in 1961–1962 was visiting professor in African-Asian studies in the Four-College Program of Amherst, Mount Holyoke, and Smith colleges and the University of Massachusetts.

J. Gus Liebenow is associate professor of government at Indiana University, where he is also chairman of the African Studies Program. He returned recently from fifteen months of field research in Liberia and Sierra Leone. Previously he spent two years in East Africa studying political change in tribal societies.

Margaret L. Bates is professor of history at Goddard College. She has been associate editor of *International Organization* and is now editor of the *African Studies Bulletin*. She has made several extended research trips to Tanganyika, the latest of which was in 1961. Her book on *Tanganyika under British Administration* will be published by Oxford University Press.

The editor is Sophia Smith Professor at Smith College, representative for her college on the Four-College Committee which directs the African-Asian Studies Program, and former president of the African Studies Association. She has made six field trips to different areas of Africa. Her publications include *The Politics of Inequality: South Africa since 1948* (New York: Praeger, 1958), *Independence for Africa* (Praeger, 1960), *Major Foreign Powers: The Governments of Great Britain, the Soviet Union, Germany, and France* (4th ed., New York: Harcourt, Brace and World, 1962; earlier eds., 1949, 1952, 1957), and *Government and Politics in the Twentieth Century* (Praeger, 1961) —the latter two written with John H. Herz. She was coeditor with William O. Brown of *Transition in Africa: Studies in Political Adaptation* (Boston University Press, 1958).

The editor and contributors would like to express their appreciation to the director and staff of Cornell University Press for their tolerance over changing dates in the submission of material and their constructive aid in the preparation of this volume.

GWENDOLEN M. CARTER

Northampton, Massachusetts
May 1962

CONTENTS

IV Guinea, *by L. Gray Cowan* 149

AFRICAN ONE-PARTY STATES

I

INTRODUCTION

By GWENDOLEN M. CARTER

Smith College

Never before have so many countries become independent within so short a space of time as in Africa between 1956 and 1962. Their independence was the culmination of a major movement in human history that is no less significant because of the brevity of its time span and, with rare exceptions (notably in the former Belgian Congo), its lack of violence and basic dislocation. As the result of this movement, some two-thirds of the people of the world's second largest (though most unevenly populated) continent ceased to be part of the last great area of colonial control and came under locally based governments headed by their own leaders.

The emergence of so many newly independent states has had an obvious impact in the realm of international affairs. It should have no less an impact in the fields of theoretical and practical comparative government. Within a few years has been compressed a variety of techniques and practices in the transfer of political power that offers rich opportunities for comparative analysis. So too do the evolving structures and ideologies of the new African states. The concepts of traditional comparative government were developed for the most part out of an analysis of the governments of the United States, Great Britain, western Europe, and the Soviet Union. This led to a theoretical dichotomy between democracy and dictatorship, between the so-called "free world" and that of totalitarianism, whether fascist or Communist, that is more rigid than a rigorous consideration of even

1

these mature political societies can sustain. The wealth of political practice in the developing countries suggests the need of a still more searching reconsideration of fundamental concepts, particularly when the latter are based on governmental structure rather than on practices and attitudes.

The structure and the ideology of a new African state are inevitably affected by its precolonial and colonial background but possibly still more by its leaders' own experiences and their evaluation of their country's particular needs. Thus even those countries that have experienced a common pattern of colonial rule are already diverging widely in their approaches to political decisions, their techniques of control and direction, and their goals, not only internally but also within the continent of Africa and in the international community. To provide interpretation and understanding is, hopefully, one of the contributions of theoretical comparative analysis to the practical conduct of affairs. Thus the consideration of the six states treated in detail in this volume has two purposes: to broaden our knowledge of political practice and the motives underlying such practice and to aid in developing a more general comprehension of the meaning and significance of the new or redesigned forms and the ideas that characterize them.

Few forms of organization have given rise to more differences of opinion than that of the one-party state. In traditional comparative analysis the number of political parties in a country has been considered a sound index to the character of its rule. One-party control is associated not only with dictatorial but also with quasi- or wholly totalitarian rule. This judgment seems to be confirmed by the experience of one-party regimes in Nazi Germany, the Soviet Union, and the "people's democracies" of eastern Europe. Yet the fact that so many of the new states have a dominant or single political party but are clearly not totalitarian suggests a revision of at least this part of the prima-facie argument. Moreover, the representatives of many of these states also claim that they are democratic rather than dictatorial in character since their governments are selected, or at least endorsed, by popular election, they rest on mass party support, and, in addition, there is considerable interplay between groups within these mass parties as well as a broad base of popular participation and consent.

To make a definite choice at this moment between these interpretations of the character of newly developing states may be to do a disservice to them and to ourselves. To term them democratic when they provide little or no chance for an opposition party to play a role within the governmental structure would be to violate a basic criterion of a democratic system—that it institutionalize public criticism of governmental measures and provide a method for the peaceful change of leaders and of ruling groups. Yet to overlook the possibility that such institutional arrangements may develop within their structures may be equally misleading, for their present form is an obvious result of their drive for independence and of their current concentration both on building national unity and on promoting economic development.

In most instances the single or dominant party in a developing state is an outgrowth of the mobilization of persons and groups in the pre-independence period. In the former British territories, the existence of a cohesive political party under a dominant leader was a *sine qua non* for the transfer of political power to local hands. Since the British were empirical, reacting to and through a "process of interrelated pressure," to quote Sir Andrew Cohen,[1] the conditions for extension of local power remained relatively common while the timing differed. In the former French areas, it was the timing of the transfer of powers that was common while local conditions often varied widely. Broad policy decisions, like the passage of the *loi cadre* in 1956 (which made possible the decentralization of power to the territorial assemblies of French African countries and thus to their controlling party groups), and the transformation of the French Union into the Franco-African Community in 1958 through the referendum on the constitution of the Fifth (or de Gaulle) French Republic generalized the change in the *de facto* possession of power and subsequently in status. Nonetheless it was the postwar extension to Africans of representation in the French National Assembly, the Council of the Republic, and the Assembly of the French Union that gave rise to the interterritorial RDA (Rassemblement Démocratique Africain), and within the more advanced units of French West Africa, the local RDA branches also developed in the preindependence period the cohesive party organization and dominant leaders that the British regarded as the passport to responsible government and ultimate independence. Thus both colonial regimes stimulated, though by different means, the mass dominant parties, which form the decisive link between the preindependence and postindependence periods.

Although the single or dominant party under a strong and popular

[1] *British Policy in Changing Africa* (Evanston, Ill.: Northwestern University Press, 1959), p. 41.

leader is closely associated with the progress toward independence in a high proportion of the newly independent states, it has also seemed to provide both stability and continuity after independence. In contrast, a multiplicity of parties in the Sudan and in Pakistan (to take two widely separated countries) and the lack of strong leadership led to impending disorders which gave rise to army rule. It is true that in India and Nigeria the combination of strong linguistic or tribal divisions and a federal structure has provided more pluralistic systems which may well have still greater possibilities of persisting unity than the nonfederal one-party states. But even India has one dominant party, the Congress Party, while Nigeria has a dominant party in each of its regions and one, the Northern Peoples Congress, which can hardly be left out of any federal government coalition.

The stabilizing and, commonly, centralizing role of the dominant party within a new state seems indisputable, but this fact is only one of those which need to be taken into account in evaluating the character of one-party states. At present the existence of a dominant or single political party in a number of states is associated not only with stability but also with mass popular support. Whether this situation is a temporary one or has elements of permanence, whether it is associated only with the first generation of leaders and the early flush of nationalist fervor or can be transmitted through established channels, and whether it can survive in the face of the pressures for rapid economic development are long-range questions whose answers demand a far wider and more long-term investigation than can be attempted in this volume. Even the experience gathered together on these six states suggests, however, that one-party states can differ widely in origin, practice, and objectives and that no one category should encompass this diversity.

Of the six states with which this book is primarily concerned, only one, Liberia, has had a long experience of independence. Liberia also provides an almost classic example of oligarchic one-party rule by the descendants of what was once an alien and remains an unassimilated group, the Americo-Liberians. Liberia is unique on the African continent in the passivity of its majority tribal people who as yet have neither used their numbers to gain local political control, as has happened in what is the most nearly comparable situation of Sierra Leone, nor reacted against local minority control either through violence or by appeals to the United Nations, as have Arabs in Algeria, Africans in Kenya and in the Rhodesias and Nyasaland, and Africans and Asians in South Africa.

The other five countries achieved independence late but under widely varying circumstances, none of which were free from strain. Tunisia had by far the oldest and best-established nationalist movement, one which operated for substantial periods outside the constitutional system and did not win full acceptance by the French until 1954. Houphouët-Boigny's Ivory Coast branch of the RDA was under somewhat comparable restraints between 1949 and 1950, when he made peace with the authorities both within his own territory and in Paris. The Guinea branch of the RDA suffered no such ostracism in its own territory in the comparable period, but subsequently Guinea's decision to vote "no" on the referendum that determined membership in the Franco-African Community and its difficulties in securing acceptance of Guinean independence created a rupture with the former *Métropole* unparalleled in any other transfer of power. Senegal experienced its own particular problems over independence not because of tension with France but because of the breakup of the Mali Federation. The Tanganyika nationalist movement, which began later than any of the others, suffered some slight harassment by colonial authorities, and its leaders had less experience with party organization and political techniques than those of any of these other countries since its first election was held barely three years before independence on December 9, 1961.

Despite these problems, there has been a remarkable degree of continuity between pre- and postindependence periods, not only in local governing groups but also, with the exception of Guinea, in relations with the former *Métropole*. One of the most remarkable features of almost all the former French African states is the degree to which they have continued to depend on French officials (still paid for by France) as administrators and as technical aides and on French subsidies for their economic development. The British, in contrast, have tended to cut off, or sharply to reduce, their economic aid when a former colony becomes independent and to expect the newly sovereign country to assume not only the expense of the salaries of those former colonial officials who become members of local administrative and technical staffs but also to help in providing compensation to those who retire from such services. Nonetheless all the African territories that have graduated from British colonial control have sought to retain a con-

siderable number of the former colonial administrators (though rarely
in as obvious positions as in the French-speaking territories), turn first
to Great Britain for economic aid, and have acquired membership in
the Commonwealth of Nations. Liberia has had something of the same
kind of assistance in technical aid and in financial support from the
United States in the postwar period.

The continuation of these types of contact undoubtedly has some
effect on the character of local rule but far less, it would seem, than
local conditions, organization, and goals. Liberia remains oligarchic,
with only slight and gradual infiltration of tribal peoples into the
governing group. If this process is encouraged by the example of mass
parties in surrounding territories, the latter may have borrowed something from the strongly presidential structure of Liberia. Apart from
Senegal, in which there is both a President and a Prime Minister, all
the French-speaking territories (except the former Belgian Congo)
have centralized the executive authority in a President. So, too, has
Ghana under its new constitution. Tanganyika, Nigeria, and Sierra
Leone, in contrast, have retained the characteristic division of the parliamentary system between the titular and the real executive. None
of these three, as yet, has established a republic although at least the
first two can be expected to do so. In Tanganyika and Sierra Leone
the titular executive has little obvious influence at this stage, but it
seems likely that there is already some division of authority in Nigeria
between the Prime Minister, Sir Abubakar Tafewa Balewa, and the
colorful national leader, Nnamde Azikewe, who became the first
Governor-General. This balance might swing still further toward the
presidential office when the republic is declared. The same might also
become true in Tanganyika, particularly if Julius Nyerere becomes
the first President. If this development should take place in Nigeria
and Tanganyika, the situation of the executive in these countries
would then more nearly approximate that in Senegal, where Senghor
commands the mass support and exercises ultimate authority but
leaves organization and administration in the hands of his Prime Minister, Mamadou Dia.

The political dominance of a single personality is not confined to
developing countries, but it is strongly evident within almost all of
them. In none of the six countries treated in this volume is there so
strong a cult of personality as in Ghana, but Bourguiba, Houphouët-
Boigny, Tubman, and also Senghor have become national symbols as
well as decisive leaders. Sékou Touré's position is somewhat different

because of the Guinean insistence on the primacy of the party, but the role he plays differs less in practice from that of the others than it does in theory. Seemingly most divergent from the pattern is the situation in Tanganyika, where Julius Nyerere stepped down from his office as Prime Minister so shortly after his country achieved independence. It seems possible, however, that in the perspective of the counterpressures among different groups within Tanganyika and the slightness of party cohesion Nyerere can become more of a focus for national unity through his organizational work for the Tanganyika African National Union than through holding a governmental office.

There is an obvious interrelation between the dominance of a single person and the discipline and structure of party organization, but this relationship may take different forms of major importance for the character of the regime. In Mali, but only there, party organization is so dominant and, in a sense, pure that it has excluded the emphasis on personality so obtrusive elsewhere. The intensity of Malian organization and discipline helps to explain why the country was so ill-matched a partner to more pluralistic Senegal. If organization can be a substitute for personal leadership, as in Mali, it is rare, however, that the opposite can be the case. Personal leadership, like that of Houphouët-Boigny and Senghor, may be combined temporarily with a loose party structure. But it is noticeable that much more attention is now being devoted to strengthening the Ivory Coast's party organization than was the case in the period either before or immediately after independence. Bourguiba has found the same need in Tunisia and encountered the same kinds of pressures from younger persons within his party. It is in Senegal and Tanganyika that the dominant party has the least well knit structure, partly because of counterethnic loyalties, group demands, and rural-urban divisions and partly because of lack of dynamic drive. Liberia's True Whig Party does not even seek, much less possess, the mass base of the other parties here described and is content to secure much of its cohesion from personal family relationships.

As long as strong personal leadership continues, mass loyalty (if it exists) tends to be directed to the single figure rather than the party structure. Party orders and party efforts to rouse popular enthusiasm for national or local development plans may suffer in consequence as even Guinea has discovered. The problem of succession is accentuated. Yet the alternative of loyalty to a regime and a country rather than to a person or group of persons requires a national orientation that a

country with the deep roots of Tunisia finds easier to evoke than the
newer entities of sub-Saharan Africa.

None of the new African countries, except Nigeria, places great emphasis on the governmental institutions through which measures are
formally enacted into law. The lack of representation in their assemblies of more than one political party makes opposition highly unlikely
and proceedings dull. Indeed, although Ghana is widely criticized for
its restrictions on the opposition, the nine opposition members still
vocal in its assembly in 1962 made that body far more lively than were
most other African legislative bodies. Not only are discussions rare in
most of these assemblies, but also there is little public interest in what
takes place. Yet there is still a major difference between the insistence
in Guinea that the party ranks higher than any governmental institution and the appearance maintained by the others that the party works
through, but is not above, governmental institutions. By this means,
the framework and an ideology are maintained which leave the way
open for institutionalized opposition that may no longer be considered
dangerous if a national consensus can be achieved.

It will take more than a change in the attitude of the dominant
party, however, to provide the kind of institutionalized interaction between rival political groups which is taken so much for granted in
Western democratic countries. The role of the loyal opposition is a
difficult one to play. No party in newly independent Africa has yet
accepted its discipline. In Ghana, Togo, and elsewhere, at least some
opposition groups have plotted assassination as the means to remove
the ruling figure from office. If frustration over the possibility of gaining power by any other means may help to explain these plots, they
provide the governing group with ample excuse for measures of restraint, arbitrary detention, and exclusion from political activity. None
of these six countries have been wholly free from such dangers, though
Tunisia and Tanganyika have been the least obviously affected by
them. Nowhere among any of them is there any open encouragement
to diversity of political expression.

Moreover, most French-speaking states of sub-Saharan Africa have
adopted an electoral device which effectually shuts out representation
in an assembly by an opposition party. First instituted by Guinea and
then widely copied, this device turns the whole country into an electoral district within which the winning party takes all the seats. Even
a 50.1 per cent of the vote yields 100 per cent representation under
such a scheme, though it must be noted that most of the newly emer-

gent countries, and all five included in this volume, have mass parties which secure a high percentage of the total vote.

But even in those rare African countries where an opposition can still win a few seats in an election, the deprivation involved in their exclusion from a share of the powers and opportunities that are afforded the governing group provides them with a powerful incentive to unity. It is sometimes said facetiously that "the opposition is either in jail or in the government." Increasingly the latter is the case. Most of the dominant African parties have demonstrated a remarkable capacity for absorption of former rival or antagonistic groups and a quite surprising willingness to elevate their leaders thereafter to important government posts.

The result of these mergers in Tunisia, Senegal, the Ivory Coast, and even Guinea has been to develop political parties which are themselves composed of the kind of diverse groups that might be expected in a Western country to form two, or even a series of, political parties. Something of the interaction and compromise hammered out between political parties in the congressional or parliamentary system goes on within these African political parties though without the publicity which is one of the healthiest aspects of public interchanges. These African intraparty debates may even bear some resemblance to that which goes on within the Republican or the Democratic Party. This is not formal, structural democracy, but it can provide for the airing of issues, the awareness by the people at large of the policies that are to affect them, and the consideration by leaders of the sentiments of their followers.

Officially, Guinea has adopted "democratic centralism" as the method of interaction between followers and leaders. Plans can, and indeed must, be discussed widely until decisions have been made. Thereafter no debate and no divergence are permitted. Within these limits, much is being done to bring new ideas and information, particularly to the rural areas. The mass party is looked on in Guinea, as in Tunisia, the Ivory Coast, Senegal, and Tanganyika, as the purveyor of plans and precepts, the stimulator of new projects, the educator of the young and of the peasants, and the emancipator of women. Apart from Liberia, the political party has far more, therefore, than a governing role, for it sees as additional objectives the liberation of the people of its country from poverty, illiteracy, and apathy. In such tasks many Africans feel, with more than a little justification, that there is no room for disagreement or divided efforts.

Many questions remain open both about the character and the future prospects of the regimes described in this book. Some of these questions may be answered by the more detailed material which follows. But on some issues there can be no final answers until there are more experience and data from which to judge and more-refined techniques with which to evaluate. Some people may find this frustrating, but others will feel, as we do, that the search for answers can be as rewarding as their final formulation.

II

TUNISIA

By CHARLES F. GALLAGHER

American Universities Field Staff

Historical Background

Tunisia, the northernmost prolongation of the African continent, is a half peninsula jutting out into the Mediterranean almost midway between Gibraltar and Suez. It is bounded on the north and the east by that sea, on the southeast by Libya, and on the west by Algeria. Although no natural barrier separates Tunisia from Algeria, with which (and including Morocco) it forms a compact geographic ensemble generally known as North Africa in English, and the Maghrib in Arabic, it is cut off by desert and steppe on the south and east. Its double exposure to the sea, its fertile valleys open to the northeast, and its eight hundred miles of coastline have given it at most times a maritime and Mediterranean orientation which distinguishes it from even its closest African neighbors. The nearest large city to Tunis is Palermo in Sicily, and Sardinia lies closer to Tunisia than it does to the European mainland.

If geography has made Tunisia unique in the African setting, it has combined with history and culture to differentiate it still further. The relative openness of the Tunisian national character and the multi-racial makeup of the inhabitants of the country are associated with the ease of access from the sea and the many influences to which Tunisia has been exposed throughout history. Unlike almost all other African countries, save Egypt, Tunisia has a long and distinguished recorded history which has been lived close to the center of the world

stage; and, unique among African states, its civilization is essentially
the fusion of and tension between Asian and European currents which
have alternately entered the country during the last three thousand
years. Indeed, were it not for the rapid development of sentiments of
African solidarity and pan-African consciousness in the most recent
years—which have affected Tunisia as well as other African lands—
it might be questioned whether any of the North African Arab countries has a meaningful place in a work on Africa.

Stone industries dating from the middle Quaternary are found in
Tunisia. This was a time when North Africa was much wetter than
now and the Sahara resembled a steppe. As the area dried gradually,
it was penetrated by a large-boned, white race of hunters and gath-
erers, related to the Cro-Magnons of southern Europe, who were
responsible for the distinctive Capsian stone industry which flourished
here (Capsa is the modern Gafsa in southwest Tunisia). These people
may well have formed a part of the substratum of the stock found in
Tunisia today, but a large contribution seems clearly to have come
from another group which came in, probably from the east, in the
early Neolithic period, bringing with them a knowledge of agriculture,
domestic animals such as the pig and the goat, and improved techniques for polishing stone.

The earliest Phoenician and Greek records of contacts in North
Africa mention a fairly uniform ethnic group throughout the area
from Cyrenaica in the East to Morocco in the West. The Greeks called
them Libyans, the "whites" as opposed to the "black" Ethiopians, and
later in classical times they were also designated by the general name
of *barbaroi,* the barbarians outside Greco-Roman civilization, from
which the modern term "Berber" stems. This indigenous population
used dialects of a common tongue belonging to the Hamitic groups
of languages, whose diffusion area seems to have been northeast
Africa. The language has not been reduced to writing despite an
abortive effort in the second century B.C. in Numidia (a state encompassing parts of what is now western Tunisia and eastern Algeria), where a script was invented called tifinagh, which is still used
by the Tuareg of the central Sahara today.

The Libyans were nomadic shepherds and desert raiders; their
presence on the western frontiers of Egypt is mentioned in chronicles
of the Middle Kingdom. Later they came under Carthaginian influence and are described by Herodotus in the fifth century as practicing
agriculture and living in houses. Their social organization, perpetuated

today by many North African Berber groups, was based on the agnatic family, a clan ruled by a patriarch and in time of danger temporarily allied with other clans in an unstable, defensive confederation. The religious beliefs of these earliest Berbers show considerable connection with those of ancient Egypt, particularly with respect to funerary practices, body position and painting, magic spells and incantations, and the building of dolmens and piles of dry stone something like small pyramids. Associated with these beliefs was a nature cult, stressing places and objects, natural and animal, endowed with a supernatural quality, and the existence of ill-defined spirits of all kinds. Although the Berbers did not place the same emphasis as the Egyptians on a positive life after death, they held a strong belief in these genii and in the power of the dead. This remains a marked characteristic of Berbers at all times and seems to have favored the development of sainthood in early North African Christianity and of Maraboutism in the Islamic period. The persistence of this tendency toward personalization, even after long exposure to these two mono-theistic systems, is a noteworthy element in the North African personality.

The Libyans may not have been the only preclassical inhabitants of Tunisia and the regions immediately adjacent to it. There was much opportunity for other contacts in the Mediterranean. Etruscanlike inscriptions have been found near Tunis, and tombs in northeast Tunisia show analogies with those of the Aegean civilization, as do the attributes of Tanit, the principal Carthaginian goddess who bears a non-Phoenician name. The possibilities are good that Tunisia was influenced during the second millennium B.C. by nearby Sicily, which was itself part of the Minoan world.

In any event, Tunisia enters recorded history as a result of one of the first cases of true colonization known: the founding of Utica (dated by Pliny at 1110 B.C.), the first of the factories and trading posts founded by seafaring Phoenician merchants which were to dot the western Mediterranean in the coming centuries. Nearby were established Hippo, the modern Bizerte, and somewhat to the west, near the present Algerian-Tunisian frontier, Hippo Regius, now Bône. The chain of settlements stretched out to the entrance to the Atlantic, where Gades (Cádiz) flanked one side, Lixus (Larache) the other, and Tingis (Tangier) overlooked the Straits separating Europe from Africa. In the ninth century B.C. Carthage—Qart Hadasht, the "new town" to distinguish it from the "old town" of Utica—was founded on a site exceptionally well designed for defense, as were almost all the Phoenician establishments. These were places chosen by people who had come by sea and traded by sea and, until several hundred years had passed, were encamped on the shore of a hostile hinterland.

Until the middle of the sixth century B.C., Carthage and the other North African towns remained colonies of Tyre. But while the Levantine homeland began to decline through the effects of the troubled times in western Asia which brought the rise of the Assyrian, Babylonian, and Persian empires, the prosperous Punic settlements in the West flourished on their own. Rivalry with the Greeks, who were expanding in Sicily, Magna Graecia, and Marsilia (Marseilles), led the enterprising Carthaginians to the exploration of more distant trading grounds. In the fifth century Hanno completed his famous voyage of discovery along the west coast of Africa, possibly reaching the Gulf of Guinea and establishing an entrepôt station in what is now Río de Oro, while Himilco explored Cornwall to the north. Thus, gold from Africa and tin from Britain were monopolized by the Carthaginian traders whose strongpoints in the western Mediterranean blocked further Greek advances. So began one of the first confrontations of the Orient and the Occident in the Mediterranean.

The consolidation of Carthaginian power in the fifth century B.C. is of prime importance in Tunisian history. After a disaster in Sicily in 480 B.C., Carthage turned to the conquest of the Tunisian hinterland and became for the first time a land power as well as a maritime city-state. Its domain included most of present-day Tunisia, and here for the first time Berber culture mingled with Punic civilization. Carthaginian rule was not easy and taxes were heavy, but on the great estates owned by the Punic patricians a competent dry-farming agriculture was inaugurated which concentrated on cereals, the vine, and the olive tree. Among the important social and political consequences in North Africa of this spread of agriculture throughout the region were a pushing back of the less adaptable and more intractable nomads, the setting up of a long-lasting nomadic-sedentary opposition, and the gradual introduction, through the numerous minor Berber principalities to the west, of the norms of a more stable organized state and government in imitation of the Carthaginian model. What is of immediate concern here is to note that already in the fifth century B.C. Tunisia was effectively governed as a homogeneous entity.

Nevertheless, Carthage remained a tyrannical oligarchy ruling over an insecure backcountry. The weakness of its military position, caused by its reliance on mercenaries and vassal states, had been exposed in 309 B.C. when, by a series of bold attacks, Agathocles and the Syracusans brought the capital to the brink of defeat. What was dangerous laxness with Greek enemies proved to be fatal against a more determined foe. The Romans, during the protracted battles of the Punic Wars (264–241 and 218–202), could depend on the loyalty of the Italian countryside whereas the Carthaginians could not expect anything but infidelity from their own. The final reduction of the Punic metropolis in 146 B.C. was the last step in the conquest of the Orient by a Hellenism which had in fact infiltrated Carthage since the fourth century. It was also the beginning of a long period of Latin civilization in North Africa, particularly in Africa Proconsularis, the heartland of northeastern Tunisia. Punic power had been present for more than eight centuries; the Greco-Roman order would last an equal length of time.

The Roman occupation of Tunisia extended at first only from Tabarka in the northwest to a point south of modern Sfax on the southeast coast. During the Republican century that followed the conquest there was no colonization, and Punic civilization not only persisted in the towns but was spread to Berber areas where it had not previously penetrated. In a somewhat similar way much later the French conquest allowed Arabic to infiltrate Berber regions of Algeria hitherto closed to it.

Under the Empire, Roman Africa was consolidated. Africa Vetus and Africa Nova were united in one province approximately the size of present-day Tunisia, with its capital at Carthage. From Augustan times for some three hundred years there was prodigious development. Prosperous Roman towns grew up, often alongside Punic counterparts, but sometimes fusing with them. Oil factories and olive groves existed where now only arid steppes remain. The Pax Romana provided security for agriculture, and the Empire substituted a more efficient state capitalism for the oligarchic exploitation of the Carthaginians and the privateering land use patterns of the Republic. The great state domains stressed oleoculture—oil was used for food, light, and soap—to the point that Tunisia became the principal producer of the Mediterranean basin. Colonization by army veterans and some Italians began to produce a new bourgeoisie throughout the land after 100 A.D., while even in the more purely Punic cities, such as Maktar, forums were built and the sons of notables frequented gymnasia where they imbibed Hellenistic culture and language.

Greco-Roman literature, thought, and art, though never flourishing,
existed in this unique African atmosphere in a provincial way. The
real African contribution to the times came in the field of religion,
where the ground had been fertilized by the heavy Punic emphasis
on emotional and self-sacrificial ceremonies. It was not surprising that
early Christianity, with its tradition of martyrdom and abnegation,
was so well received by the remnants of Punic sentiment eager to
hearken back to Oriental wellsprings. In the third and fourth centuries A.D., Tunisia was perhaps the most fervent area of Christian
activity, both orthodox and heretical, in the Mediterranean world. The
list of martyrs and saints—Tertullian, Cyprian, St. Monica, and St.
Augustine—is long and distinguished, while the Donatist heresy was
suppressed only by the Vandal invasions in the fifth century, which
brought with them another variant of the faith, Arianism.

The Vandals themselves are of no interest in Tunisian history, except for their failures. As persecuting invaders they remained on
African shores for a century, but in the end as a besieged elite rather
than as a conquering group. Unlike the barbarians in Gaul and
Visigothic Spain, they were unable to merge themselves in a new
society. Africa, no longer an extension of Roman power, was already
too foreign for them, and during the period the Vandals stayed there,
the Berber nomads began slowly and relentlessly to recapture the
frontier lands from which they had been ejected centuries before.

The Vandal collapse came when Justinian landed with Byzantine
armies on the Sahel, the easily accessible eastern shore of Tunisia,
and took Carthage in 534. A brilliant but fragile renaissance of Latin
civilization followed for the next hundred years. It was the last gasp
of classicism, breathed in a restricted coastal area in the north while
the Berbers struck out ever more openly against the sedentary populations of the countryside. Then, in 648, the first Arab raiders from the
East arrived at Sbeitla. Their entry upon the scene permanently
changed the course of Tunisian history.

Following their conquest of Egypt, the Arabs began raiding
Ifriqiya in the mid-seventh century. The outposts of Byzantine Africa
offered little resistance, but the Berber mountaineers were not so
docile. For nearly half a century, their stubbornness slowed the westward Arab march at the gates of North Africa. Around 670 Kairouan
was founded in the central steppes, on the pattern of Kufa and Fustat,
a camp town later to become the sacred Islamic city of Tunisia. A
Berber raid destroyed the town soon after, and intermittent attacks

from the Aures mountain region plagued the western edge of Arab-held territory in Tunisia. It was not until 698 that Carthage fell and was replaced as capital by the new town of Tunis, until then a tiny village sheltered from the sea inside its lagoon. The peninsular fortresses of the Mediterranean, such as Alexandria, Beirut, and Carthage, never appealed to the land-oriented Semitic invaders.

In the first decade of the eighth century, all North Africa was conquered and the Arabo-Berber armies, swelled by local converts to Islam, invaded Spain. Oriental influence began to work, and for thirteen centuries North Africa was lost to Western civilization. Even if one accepts the theory of a Punic preconditioning influence, the success of the Arabs in imposing their language and culture is remarkable, especially in contrast to the failure of the Greco-Romans. It suggests an underlying affinity between the Berbers and Arabs who linguistically are distantly related and were perhaps affected by an early interplay of Hamitic and Semitic cultures. In any case, they seem to have felt a common sense of identity which the indigenous peoples of North Africa had never had in regard to Hellenistic civilization.

For a century North Africa was ruled from Kairouan, with governors, who were titled emirs, installed as representatives of the caliphate in Damascus. But as early as 750, the empire was already loosening its bonds. Spain, Morocco, and parts of Algeria broke away, so that under the Abbasids of Baghdad only Tunisia remained loyal. The continuing relationship between the Arab East and Ifriqiya was important at this time in shaping differences between Tunisia and its western neighbors. Just as Tunisia had maintained Roman civilization in late Roman times, when Morocco and Algeria lay outside its bounds, so it kept contact with the fountainhead of Oriental life and thought in the ninth and tenth centuries, while the farther Maghrib once again slumbered on in ignorance. The population in the cities of Tunisia became more Arab while the Arabization of the countryside was furthered by the arrival of nomadic tribes from the East from the eleventh century on.

Under Aghlabid rule (800–909) the power of the state extended westward to central Algeria and eastward to Tripoli. Descriptions of Kairouan and its region at this time seem unbelievable to one who sees this area now. An atmosphere of general security, the intricate hydraulic works installed by the Arabs, their skillful gardening, and the forested countryside, then unruined by erosion and nomadic devastation, were all important factors in producing a stable and prosperous era.

Early in the tenth century a heterodox (*shi'a*) Muslim group from Kabylia conquered Tunisia and, turning its face eastward, founded a new capital by the sea at Mahdia. They remained in the country for the better part of the century, but when they left in 973 to conquer Egypt they were unmourned, for they had been neither Tunisian, nor orthodox, nor loved.

During the rule of their otherwise undistinguished successors, the Zirids, in the eleventh century, Tunisia suffered the first of a series of Arab nomadic invasions which brought the country to disaster. As first the Banu Hilal, and later the Banu Sulaim, occupied the interior steppes, they forced sedentary civilization back to the Mediterranean littoral. The nomads ruined the irrigation systems, destroyed the forest cover, devastated towns and villages, and established everywhere an air of pillage and insecurity. Within a few generations, however, they completed the Arabization of Tunisia in both language and custom.

Meanwhile the urban culture of maritime Tunisia was itself threatened from the sea by a renascent Europe. Genoese and Pisans ravaged Mahdia, and the Normans, who had just reconquered Sicily from Muslim rule, at one point occupied the Tunisian capital and for a time held a tenuous sovereignty over strong points along the Sahel. Tunisia was saved from this onslaught by a Moroccan dynasty of reforming unitarians, the Almohads (*Muwahhidin*), who briefly unified the Maghrib for the first time since the Arab conquest. The distant power of Marrakesh could not long sustain this unity, however, and exceptional powers of autonomy were eventually given to the governor of Tunis, a descendant of one of the original Almohad henchmen from southern Morocco. With his successors an indigenous Hafsid dynasty which ruled for three hundred years came into existence.

The Hafsids stand out as the first truly national ruling family of Tunisia. They consolidated the territory from Constantine to Tripoli, and gradually a Tunisian way of life began to develop in the coastal cities, stimulated by the first inflow of Andalusian refugees fleeing the *reconquista* in Spain. As craftsmen and artisans in the towns, as gardeners and skilled farmers in the surrounding countryside, they gave a new stamp to the region of northeast Tunisia. Jews also arrived from Catalonia and the Balearics, and in addition Tunis was host to Christian traders in its marketplaces. For the first time since classical days a cosmopolitan culture was developing, closely linked with maritime trade and reorienting Tunisia to the sea.

Tunisia under the Hafsids was already a mirror of the modern state; it made no great or original contribution to civilization or art, but it was a refined, tolerant, mercantile, bourgeois society living in city-states not unlike those originally established by the Greeks. But Hafsid Tunisia was forever engaged in a delicate balancing of power between the threat from a Spartan interior and the menace from overseas. Although the nomads were useful to the rulers as an unofficial auxiliary armed force which could help to control the sedentary population in the countryside, persistent nomadic invasions in the center and south of Tunisia caused constant strain.

By the early sixteenth century Hafsid weakness was an invitation to the powers contending for mastery of the Mediterranean. Levantine pirates were already infesting Tunisian waters, and freebooters, such as Barbarossa and Khaireddin, began to seize cities along the coast of North Africa in the name of the Ottoman ruler. These successes culminated with the taking of Bizerte, La Goulette, and Tunis in 1534. Charles V was forced to reply with force. He briefly recaptured Tunis in 1535 and restored the legitimate ruler, Mulay Hassan, who had called upon him for help. For the next forty years, however, Tunisia was a critical point in the battle for the Mediterranean between the Spanish and the Turks. The Spanish held control of part of the coast, notably Monastir and Mahdia, but they and their local allies were never able to mount an offensive against the interior, which was held by tribes in revolt who were supported by the Turkish garrison at Kairouan. After the defeat of the Ottoman navy at Lepanto (1571), the Spanish position improved temporarily. Don Juan of Austria again took Tunis, which had fallen once more to the Turks, and began the construction of fortifications. Before they were completed, however, the Turks, moving against the city by land and sea, recaptured it in 1574 to end the contest. Turkish control lasted in theory not only until the establishment of the French protectorate in 1881 but down to the Treaty of Sèvres in 1920, when Turkey renounced any claims to the Regency. In fact, Ottoman rule during most of this long period was nominal and grew weaker as time passed. The semi-independent Tunisian rulers for their part continued to play off the Ottoman power against the European states. They sought the protection of the Sultan in Constantinople but at the same time tried to limit his power by engaging in direct negotiations and commercial arrangements with the European states. At the beginning (1590–1640), Tunisia was governed by military chiefs (*deys*) whose position was buttressed by Turkish garrisons. During this time the diversity of the country was further enriched by the final contingents of Andalusians—in 1609–1610 alone nearly 80,000 are said to have arrived—as well as by numerous Christian slaves and renegades who were by-products of the pirate trade.

One such renegade, Moratto (Murad) Corso, began early in the seventeenth century as a tax collector (*bey*) in the army, rose to become first pasha of Tunis, and finally established himself as *de facto* ruler. His successors held power until 1702, when the whole family was killed by an officer of the Turkish garrison, who took simultaneously the titles of bey (chief of the army and collector of taxes), dey (chief of government), and pasha (a title granted by the Ottoman government to its regent in Tunisia). After his successor, Husain Bey, came to power in 1705, a hereditary dynasty was sanctioned by an assembly of local notables. Under the Husainids, Tunisia became a virtually independent monarchy.

The history of the Husainid Regency (*Beylik*) is marked by the growing power and activity of the European states, by increased contact between them and a vulnerable Tunisia, and by the rise of French influence in North Africa. By 1816 the Regency had treaties or conventions with most of the European powers, and in 1819 it wisely accepted the demand of the Congress of Aix-la-Chapelle that it outlaw piracy, thus saving itself from the fate of Algiers which adopted a more intransigent attitude. Not only was the French occupation of the latter city-state in 1830 unopposed by Tunisia, but the Bey sent a note of congratulation to the conquerors.

The reform currents of the nineteenth century, born in Europe and transmitted through Constantinople, where many Tunisians studied, reached the country in mid-century. Ahmed Bey (1839–1855) abolished slavery, discontinued the special regime applied to Tunisian Jews, and allowed the opening of Christian schools. Like his counterparts of the time, in many lands from Egypt to Siam, he was naïvely sincere in his efforts to create a modern state, but he was unable to force the pace of social reorganization. He tried to build an army, establish an officers' school, set up a polytechnical institute, create a fleet, dredge a new harbor at Porto Farina between Bizerte and Tunis, and construct a new Versailles at Muhammadia, near Zaghouan. But the army and navy proved worthless, the new harbor quickly sanded up, the technical institutes lacked candidates, and Muhammadia was never finished. Thus, instead of modernizing the country, he ruined it financially.

The next ruler, Muhammed Bey, continued a policy of liberalization. He granted in 1857 a Fundamental Pact which assured all Tunisians equality with regard to the law and to taxes, guaranteed freedom of belief, provided rights for foreigners (including the holding of property), and abolished state monopolies. He encouraged public works, built roads, installed a telegraph line between Tunis and Sfax, restored aqueducts, and constructed a modern sewer system in the capital. Paradoxically, no one was satisfied. The Tunisians disliked the new taxes which were necessary to pay for the reforms, and the Europeans were unhappy at losing their extraterritorial rights. Taxes were uncollectable, civil servants were unpaid, and the debt rose to a dangerously high level. When an already-unpopular levy was doubled at the beginning of 1864, a general revolt broke out which was mastered with difficulty. Taxes were reduced and the constitution was suspended.

Loans had been contracted abroad because of the difficulties in tax collection, and after the 1864 revolt the interest on foreign debts could no longer be paid. The creditor nations set up a control commission in 1869. One of the last prime ministers, Khaireddin (1873–1877), made a desperate attempt to introduce sound fiscal reforms, while relying politically on Constantinople to save Tunisia from the Europeans, who were now clearly far more dangerous than the ailing Ottoman Empire. It was too late; the intrigues of power politics prevailed, and at the Congress of Berlin in 1878 neither England nor Germany objected to giving France a free hand in Tunisia. It was necessary only to find the appropriate moment, and this occurred in 1881 when some Khoumir tribes in northwest Tunisia crossed the Algerian frontier in a raid. In retaliation, French forces penetrated the Regency in a double expedition by land and sea. It was an almost bloodless affair, for the Bey gave in without a struggle.

THE PROTECTORATE

After the physical occupation of Tunis had been completed, the legal basis for the establishment of a French protectorate was formulated in two agreements made between the French and Tunisian governments. On May 12, 1881, the Treaty of Kassar Said, commonly known as the Bardo Treaty, was signed. Under its terms the Bey of Tunis agreed to the "voluntary limitation" of the external sovereignty of Tunisia for a "temporary but indefinite period." France was empowered to act in a sovereign manner in all external Tunisian affairs and in matters relating to the defense of Tunisia. The Resident-General of France was designated as the sovereign's foreign minister.

This abdication of sovereignty was completed two years later by the La Marsa Convention, under the terms of which the internal sovereignty of Tunisia was placed under French supervision (*contrôle*). At the same time the Bey agreed to introduce such reforms as the French government deemed desirable or necessary in justice, finances, and general administration.

The *contrôle* was effected by setting up a parallel administration to that already functioning in the Tunisian government, which was reduced, however, to two ministers: the Prime Minister, known also as the Grand Vizir, and the Minister of the Pen. The newly established Directions Générales (later Directions) became in practice the ministries of the Tunisian government. These ministries could legally be staffed with either French or Tunisian nationals, but for a long period the upper echelons of the administration were exclusively European.

The Bey remained the titular head of state and preserved his prerogatives as chief of government. In theory, in addition to his supreme executive and judicial functions he continued to act as sole legislator for the country. The Charter of April 28, 1861, which had recognized that the sovereignty of the Tunisian people existed alongside that of the Bey, had been suspended in the disorders of 1864 and was not restored. But in practice a beylical decree would almost always have been proposed by the French-controlled Directions, and in any case it had no authority unless it had the approval of the French government acting through its representative, the Resident-General.

As a direct result of the engagements subscribed to in the agreements with the French government, some internal restrictions on the power of the Bey were gradually developed during the period of the protectorate. In 1922, the Bey agreed to voluntary consultation on public matters with members of the Grand Council; this consultation became obligatory in 1945. The Grand Council, formed in 1922, was an elected advisory body which at first represented taxpayers only but was enlarged in 1945 to provide for limited popular representation. The electors were adult males who paid land and property taxes, or commercial and professional imposts, or were veterans or holders

of certain diplomas. The Muslim, Jewish, and European segments of
the population were all represented, but the "Section française" sat
separately. This introduction of political rights, however limited, for
the European colonists (who were not Tunisian citizens) was the
opening wedge which led to the post-World War II campaign waged
by the settlers for cosovereignty, a campaign which was based upon
the claim that three generations' residence in the country had given
them permanent and continuing rights.

The judicial power of the Bey was also narrowed in 1922 by the
introduction of a corps of magistrates which was empowered to administer secular justice. Thereafter the Bey was left only the power
to judge matters of personal status, inheritance, and the like, in his
capacity as head of the corps of magistrates of the Holy Law (*Sharī'a*).

In 1947 further reforms reduced the arbitrary nature of power in
Tunisia. A Council of Ministers was instituted which could take
decisions that, in the form of ministerial decrees, had the force of
law. The Ministries of Justice, Commerce, Public Health, Labor, and
Agriculture were held by Tunisian nationals. These departments were
balanced by the Ministries of Foreign Affairs and Defense, which were
held by French officials, and the three Directorates of Finance, Public
Works, and Education, which were also headed by French civil
servants. At this time, too, except for the reserved fields of Foreign
Affairs and Defense, the general administration of the state was
placed under the authority of a Tunisian Prime Minister.

These reforms of 1947 in theory delegated a considerable measure
of authority to Tunisian officials at a time when increasing numbers
of young Tunisians were moving into positions of more responsibility
at the middle-echelon levels. This experience which the latter gained
served the country well a decade later when autonomy and independence were granted with relative suddenness. Higher-ranking Tunisian
officials, however, tended to be hand-picked by French functionaries
and were on the whole unrepresentative of the growing national sentiment among the younger generation. And, in the end, much of the
promise of the reforms was lost late in 1951 when a state of emergency was imposed and arbitrary personal rule by a military governor
replaced cabinet responsibility.

In local administration protectorate policy followed the same format
as in national administration. It preserved the traditional local executive, the *qaid*, who continued to be the directly appointed representative of the Bey. To oversee his activities, civil supervisors (*con-*

trôleurs civils) were installed as early as 1884. Their functions at the beginning were to comment on and approve the *qaid's* correspondence, to observe his actions, and to report to the Resident-General. But just as the Directions in the capital tended with the passage of time to become organs of direct administration, so the *contrôleurs* in the countryside gradually usurped the initiative and functions of the local authority. Since the *contrôleur* possessed the ultimate powers of requisitioning the police and using the *gendarmerie* or troops to maintain public order, his popular prestige was also strengthened at the expense of the *qaid*. As *qaidal* functions withered, the institution itself was reorganized. In 1924, for the first time, regular salaries were paid the *qaids* in place of the traditional 5 per cent previously taken out of all sums collected for the government. Assistant and apprentice *qaids* were also appointed. In 1937 the Qaidal Corps was established, and these local administrators became an intrinsic part of the civil service.

Protectorate control throughout Tunisia was strengthened by extending direct administration to the tribes through government-appointed sheikhs. Tribal sheikhs, unlike *qaids*, had not traditionally been government officials but were instead representatives of a fraction of a tribe or a grouping vis-à-vis the administration. In 1905, on the grounds that many tribes were finding it difficult to designate proper representatives, the sheikhs were made civil servants, appointed by the *qaid* with the assent of the *contrôleur*. In 1945 a partial reform of this system, whose abuses were manifold, provided that the sheikhs be named by the Bey from a list of candidates supplied by the electors of the region or grouping in question.

By this kind of reorganization of the government in Tunisia, the French protectorate, whatever its weaknesses and individual abuses, had begun to lay the groundwork of a modern state. It completed this preparation in various other fields. The application of the principles evolved in the Australian Torrens Act to extremely complicated land registration problems was a great step forward, as were the laws establishing the Public Domain in 1885 and the Forest Domain in 1903. French justice was imported to deal with all cases in which a European was at least one party. The restriction of the Shari'a courts to matters of personal law and the introduction of a new Tunisian common-law justice, which was inspired by Western codes, were equally important.

Perhaps the most serious charge that can be made against the protectorate is the insufficient effort made in education. In 1875, six years before the French occupation began, the Sadiqi College, the first indigenous attempt to marry Western technique to the Arabo-Islamic heritage, had been founded in Tunis. Aside from this institution, there existed only traditional Quranic instruction in limited fields of religion, rudimentary mathematics, and archaic science. The protectorate instituted a dual educational system, one part of which was wholly French with standards equated to those in the homeland, the other a mixed Franco-Arab education. The latter was admittedly of lower quality, but in partial compensation were its bilinguality and the fact that it was designed to give the Tunisian a rough background in his own culture. Although there was never segregation of any kind, the spirit behind the unequal duality served to preserve a European minority and to dispense an inferior brand of instruction to the native population. And at the end of seventy-five years of the protectorate—only during the last decade of which a new sense of responsibility had begun to accelerate the slowness of progress—not more than one Tunisian in four of school age was in school, whereas the full educational training of the European colony was taken for granted. The reforms which independent Tunisia has had to make in its educational system since independence in 1956 and the enormous strides it has taken in expanding opportunities despite the difficulties involved in the transfer of power demonstrate clearly the poor French educational record.

It can be argued that a sympathetic tutelage might well have produced a Tunisian renaissance. But if the stultifying effect of direct administration was the principal evil of the protectorate from 1881 on through the next half century or more, at least the 1947 reforms handed back on paper a good deal of political responsibility to Tunisians. Moreover, Paris would have more easily accepted the principle of a total return of the sovereignty which had been surrendered by Tunisia at the beginning of the protectorate had it not been for the political pressure increasingly exerted by the European settlers in the country. Following World War II successive French governments, which were disposed to make concessions to Tunisian national ambitions, found themselves violently opposed by the European minority which was their own creation.

In 1881 there had been only 700 French citizens in Tunisia, as against 11,200 Italians. To protect its interests, the protectorate favored French immigration to the Regency from both metropolitan

France and Algeria. But the poorer Italians, who were attracted from southern Italy, Sicily, and Sardinia by agricultural and economic opportunity in Tunisia, continued to outstrip French growth for some time. By 1911 there were 88,000 Italians to 46,000 French. Special consular prerogatives granted to the Italian colony by an agreement in 1896 remained valid until abrogated by France in World War II. The naturalization of succeeding generations of Italian immigrants and restrictions on Italian entry into Tunisia finally produced a French majority, so that in 1956 out of a total European population of 255,000 (about 7 per cent of the total population) 180,000 were French.

The growing European community, conscious of its economic power and its opportunity for political blackmail, had early demanded the freedoms they had known, however imperfectly, in their land of origin: freedom of speech and association, freedom of the press, and institutions of self-government. This last need was partly satisfied by the creation of municipal councils in the cities—although only that in Tunis was elective—and by the establishment of a European section of the Grand Council, with its control of finances. Increasingly the European minority turned into the Frankenstein of Tunisian politics. It resisted the few Residential attempts at hastening the evolution of the country economically and socially, and either it condemned French governments to halfhearted efforts, or it forced them to break their promises. At the same time, by its very existence and by the threat it posed to the internal homogeneity of the country, it was a paramount factor in the development of a countervailing Tunisian nationalism.

During the first years of the French protectorate a state of somnolent torpor had settled over the Regency. There was not at the beginning, as there was in Algeria and Morocco, a vigorous, country-wide armed resistance to the foreigner. For that Tunisia was too urbane and the focus of its national strength too centered in the *petit bourgeois* culture of the coastal cities. In the later stages of the nationalist struggle the adaptability, intelligence, and political sagacity of leaders issuing from this class were to prove an important asset to the country, but at the start of the French occupation and for a whole generation thereafter it seemed to inhibit direct action.

Tunisia was not completely indifferent, however, to the currents of Pan-Arab awakening during this period. It had the memories of Ottoman reform and its own aborted reorganization in the 1850's and 1860's to look back upon now that liberty had been lost. Turning, as

Arab society is wont to do in time of need, to the Islamic cement that holds it together, the first calls to resistance in 1881 had been issued by the Marabouts, whose cult of personal sainthood, as opposed to the more orthodox manifestations of Islam in the cities, had a strong hold on the masses in the backcountry. A more intellectual Islamic appeal was issued by the famous Egyptian sheikh, Muhammad Abduh, when he visited the country in 1884. The reformist doctrines of his Salafiyah school, which called for a return to the purity of an earlier Islam and denigrated the latter-day governments, scholars, and mystics who had degraded the faith, had a telling effect on Tunisians smarting under the humiliation of occupation by foreign infields. Muhammad Abduh did not oppose the creation of a modern state versed in science and techniques, but he maintained that only true faith could ensure the emergence of such a state among the Arabs.

Salafiyah reform nationalism made an impression in Tunisia, although in the long run not a lasting one. Its usefulness lay rather in the fact that it came so early. But Tunisian nationalism was becoming increasingly secular. By the time of his second visit to the country in 1903, Sheikh Abduh already found the going rougher. The pragmatic Tunisians, by now feeling the influence of Cartesianism, were beginning to search for other methods of advancing toward their goals.

Around the beginning of the century, two divergent tendencies could be seen. The influence of Abduh, and of his disciple, Shekib Arslan, was found in Beshir Sfar, who had been influential in founding the "Bourgeois Movement of Tunis" as early as 1883 and who, in 1895, established the "Khalduniya," an institution named for a famous Tunis-born scholar of the fourteenth century and designed to increase Tunisian knowledge of the rest of the Muslim-Arab world. Not at first directly opposed to this movement, but gradually moving away from it, was the group led by Ali Bash Hamba. The latter was originally a cofounder of the Bourgeois Movement but ended in 1905 by forming with others a group called Young Tunisians, or the "Alumni of the Sadiqi College," that institution which shaped so many modern Tunisian nationalist leaders.

Despite their apparent divergence, both these groups shared a common purpose: they were educating an elite and creating the yeast for a national awakening. Literary and cultural activities, the forerunner of this awakening, increased apace. Four newspapers were then functioning in Tunis. Modernized Quranic schools, a plethora of reviews, and a temporarily revived theater were beginning to shape the middle class of the cities for their coming political role. Recognition of this common goal led to a reconciliation in 1907, when Sfar and Bash Hamba joined forces to form the Evolutionist Party, the first truly political organization in the country, which was made up of lawyers, journalists, civil servants, and intellectuals. With its formation, the first era of the nationalist movement came to a close and political action moved to a more forthright kind of agitation.

As early as the year before, Sfar had addressed demands to the Resident-General that Tunisians be allowed to manage their own affairs. In 1909 a public meeting was held to protest against the wish expressed by Tunisian Jews that they be subject to French jurisdiction. The growing tension between the local population and the European immigrants (who numbered 145,000 by 1911), which was fed by increasing alienation of the land, ended in riots in November, 1911. The ostensible cause of the riots was the forced registration of some religious property, the Djellaz cemetery, and the result was to establish a state of siege, which was not lifted until 1921, and to set the European and Tunisian communities against each other in an openly recognized struggle for political power. In this struggle the Action Committee of the Young Tunisians, which had been organizing a boycott of the streetcars, was severely handicapped when some of its leaders were arrested during the repression of 1912 and others were sent into exile.

At the beginning of World War I, Tunisian nationalism became dormant and remained ineffective for several years. More than 60,000 Tunisians fought on the Allied side, a contribution far outweighing the few tribal revolts in the far south and a certain amount of clandestine activity in the cities. Nationalism was clearly still an incomplete phenomenon at this time. Intellectuals, the bourgeoisie, and most city dwellers had been briefly united during the Djellaz affair in 1911, but they reacted to specific events rather than planning concerted action. After more than thirty-five years of the protectorate, Tunisian nationalism had still not worked out a doctrine and it had as yet no leader with enough charisma to make his voice heard.

GROWTH OF TUNISIAN NATIONALISM

Tunisian nationalism received a new impetus at the end of the war. This impetus came partly from the hope aroused throughout the world by Wilsonian principles and partly through the wartime growth of Arab nationalism in the Middle East which was further stimulated by the disappointments of 1920 when the mandate system was imposed. The Tunisians sent a memorandum to the American President pointing out the relevance of the Fourteen Points to the Tunisian question, and the nationalist leader Sheikh Taalbi published anonymously a booklet entitled "Martyr Tunisia," which became the bible of Tunisian demands through the coming years.

As it gradually became clear to the Tunisians that their hopes would remain unfulfilled, a negative reaction set in. This was accentuated when a new Resident raised the salaries of French civil servants and called for increased European immigration. In order to renew a struggle which had lain fallow for nearly a decade, the nationalists regrouped in February, 1920, to form the Liberal Constitutional Party (*Hizb al Dastur al Hurr,* commonly known as the Destour), whose program called for the separation of powers, the election by universal suffrage of a deliberative assembly, and the establishment of responsible parliamentary government.

The Destour Party remained at the center of the political stage until the mid-thirties, but it had to contend for a decade with a brilliant and complex adversary, Resident-General Lucien Saint, who was appointed in 1921. He carefully interspersed liberal measures, such as ending the state of siege, instituting a new criminal code, and setting up the Grand Council and subsidiary economic consultative bodies, with a policy of dividing and thus controlling the nationalists. When this effort failed, he turned to measures of repression and curtailed public liberties. Finally, the French government was forced to send a commission of inquiry, a step which weakened the authority of the Resident to the point where he had to be recalled. By 1929, however, nearly a decade of time had been lost along with the good will originally engendered at the start of his Residency.

The 1920's had been marked principally by the increasing irritation of the European community, by the concentration of personal power in the hands of the Resident and of the administrative figures around him, and by a progressive loss of contact between Tunis and Paris. The Potemkinization of Tunisia, designed to deceive well-meaning but naïve visiting parliamentary delegations and metropolitan officials, became a commonplace. On the Tunisian side the Destour had been losing support because it had proved unable to advance the nationalist cause; it was too immobile, too proper for public taste, too rigid in principles, and at the same time too compromising in its polite conversations with the protectorate authorities. It had never made the effort to develop mass support from the masses or the younger generation. But a true mass nationalism was soon to come; indeed, it was already being formed by a young lawyer-politician-journalist named Habib Bourguiba.

Habib Bourguiba was born in Monastir August 3, 1903, the youngest of eight brothers and sisters. The son of an officer of the Beylical Army, he belonged to the middle class of the Sahel, the citadel of Tunisian bourgeois tenacity and sobriety. He was sent to Tunis at the age of five and did his primary and secondary schoolwork there. In 1924, having obtained his baccalaureate, he entered the Law Faculty of the University of Paris and the School of Political Science. In 1927 he returned to Tunisia, passed the bar examination, and began his career as a lawyer. Gradually political interests dominated, and in 1930 he began to work with the *Tunisian Voice,* an organ of the Destour. His articles decrying special privilege for Europeans, criticizing rule by decree, calling for general education and freedom of the press and association, and proclaiming the need for women to play a greater role in the nationalist movement soon gave him prominence. He wrote, spoke, and exhorted the country to find itself again. In an article early in 1931 he issued a challenge to the Tunisian people that was to form the nucleus of all later Bourguibist thought.

Is this a country without vitality, a degenerate people which is declining, reduced to be nothing more than a dustbin of individuals, a lump of people . . . ? Or is it, on the other hand, a sound and vigorous people which international competition or a momentary crisis has forced to accept the tutorship of a strong state? Contact with a more advanced civilization has led to a healthful reaction. A true regeneration is being produced [in it] and thanks to a judicious assimilation of the principles and methods of this civilization, Tunisia will inevitably attain by degrees its definitive emancipation.

Tunisian nationalism, in Bourguibist doctrine (for this key idea was repeated often in the *Tunisian Voice*), stemmed then from the original soundness of Tunisian tradition, fortified by interaction with and assimilation of French civilization. To this comprehensive doctrine, despite interim tactical shifts, Bourguiba has always remained faithful. And as Bourguiba's theories evolved in his articles, the neo-Destour was already growing out of and away from the old Destour, just as Tunisian nationalism was being detached from the mainstream of nationalism in other Arab countries, where any idea of assimilation with the Occident was vigorously rejected.

In 1932 Bourguiba founded his own newspaper, *L'Action Tuni-sienne*, which began to voice a new secular nationalism tinged with exasperation at the economic plight of the country and a slight streak of puritanical reformism. This organ called Tunisia a "dumping ground" for colonial products, vilified the courtesans and the old-tie Tunisians clustering around the protectorate, and appealed to new forces in the nation. The generally secular tone of the paper, however, did not prevent tactical attacks which contradicted basic principles. The most famous case was that of the "Naturalization Affair," in which Tunisians who had renounced their Islamic status to take up French citizenship were denied burial in a Muslim cemetery. The Residency obtained a Shari'a tribunal decision reversing this verdict. The nationalists, accusing the naturalized group of being apostates and unbelievers, began a campaign against the decision which led to street violence. In response to this violence, a decree in March, 1933, provided that any individual could be put in a confinement camp by decision (*arrêté*) of the Resident after consultation with the Council of Ministers.

The Destour Party had not followed Bourguiba and his group in the polemic about naturalization, and relations deteriorated between the traditional nationalists and the young men of *L'Action Tunisienne*. For a time the Destour was dissolved and the newspaper suspended, but the arrival of a new Resident, as usual, brought measures of clemency. Now that the party could function once again, the question of which group was to control it became vital. The *Action* group broke with the leaders, ostensibly because of a personal quarrel about expulsions from the party but in reality because the two factions had become fundamentally incompatible. Each represented a separate class and age; each had a style, ideas, and methods of its own.

Bourguiba turned to the masses for popular support, barnstorming the country in a long campaign which bore fruit when a swell of opinion started in favor of calling an extraordinary congress of the Destour Party in order to decide the basic lines of future policy. The meeting was held in Ksar Hellal in March, 1934, but the Destour leaders, who were conscious by now of how much popular backing Bourguiba had, refused to attend. At the congress the Executive Committee was removed and a new one elected which was composed of Bourguibists. The post of secretary-general of the party was given to Bourguiba. Although the Liberal Constitutional Party had not legally changed its name, it was only its title that remained the same. The

neo-Destour, as it was soon popularly known, now took up the battle
of Tunisian nationalism with an activist and realist doctrine, new and
supple tactics, a broad popular base, and leaders from another,
younger generation.

The influence of the neo-Destour upon Tunisian politics and history
since 1934 has been profound and constant. Because of its reduced
activity during World War II, it is convenient to divide the account
of its growth and action into two parts. From 1934 until the outbreak
of the war, the party was being shaped and firmly organized. Bourguiba and several other neo-Destour leaders, including the party president, Dr. Materi, were arrested in the fall of 1934 and sent to camps
in the southern desert. It was not until they were released in the
spring of 1936 that serious organizational work could begin. The party
was structured from its Executive Committee, through local committees, to some 400 sections with about 100,000 members. Supporting
the central organization were youth groups, labor unions, literary and
theatrical associations, and a scouting organization linked with the
Destourian Youth. The party used both languages, publishing *Al
Amal* in Arabic and *L'Action Tunisienne* in French.

The party militants were made up mainly of three groups: *petits
bourgeois*, whose sons were frustrated in their attempt to move up in
the social structure because of competition from Europeans; artisans
and small-scale businessmen, who had suffered through the depression
years of the early thirties and who combined economic grievances with
their newly discovered nationalist sentiments; and the urban workers
and miners, whose employers were usually European and for whom
class solidarity was added to patriotism. These differences in class
structure apparent among the several groups that formed the neo-
Destour in its early period became less sharp through the years. The
party was not only an organ of political liberation; it served also as a
means of social renovation and revolution. The elementary form of
democratic conduct learned by the masses in neo-Destour cells helped
shape new attitudes, and the discussion of national issues gradually
transformed the farmers of Nabeul, the fishermen of Sfax, and the
workers of Gafsa into citizens of a new state with new values. With the
advantage of historical hindsight, it might be said that the most valuable task performed by the neo-Destour was to begin to bridge the
gap between the cultivated Tunisian of the coastal cities and the backward inhabitants of the interior and the steppes.

Neo-Destour activity increased in scope and belligerence through the late thirties, helped considerably by the permissive attitude of the Popular Front government in power in France. But a nationalist general strike toward the end of 1937 followed by continuing civil disobedience finally exhausted Residential patience. Party leaders were arrested in April, 1938; bloodshed followed in Tunis; the neo-Destour was dissolved; and a state of siege was proclaimed. Bourguiba was arrested and held for trial in a military court on a charge of plotting against state security. The trial was never held, however, for the imperatives of the coming war prevailed. Instead, Bourguiba and his associates were transferred to a military prison near Marseilles and held there for nearly four years.

The Allied campaign in North Africa in 1942 and the retaliatory German occupation of Tunisia considerably changed the political situation in that country. Bourguiba had been released to the Italians by the Vichy government at the end of the year and returned to Tunisia in April, 1943. Subsequently he narrowly escaped arrest on unsubstantiated charges of collaboration with the Axis. Before Bourguiba's return, Moncef Bey, acting without Residential permission, had already constituted a ministry, which included representatives of all shades of Tunisian opinion, including both the old and the neo-Destour. After the liberation of Tunis by the Anglo-American forces the Bey was forced to abdicate by Marshal Juin in favor of a more subservient member of his family and was removed to exile in France, where he later died. The provisional French government in Algiers issued a decree delegating to the Secretary-General of the protectorate all powers previously held by the Bey and direct control over the government. This decree remained valid until the reforms of 1947 were introduced.

At the end of the war nationalist sentiment was ready for new steps forward. In February, 1945, all the Tunisian parties (the neo-Destour and the remnants of the old Destour, the Reformist Party, and various independent intellectual groups) banded together to demand internal self-government. The following year a Tunisian National Congress, meeting at the behest of the neo-Destour, called for "integral independence." Bourguiba was not convinced that this path of action would be immediately fruitful. Preferring to gain friends for Tunisia's cause outside the country, he escaped to Libya and ultimately to Cairo, where he spent several years in exile speaking and writing for the Tunisian cause. While the party was reorganized at home under the direction of its then secretary-general, Salah ben Youssef, Bourguiba became a political pilgrim. The wisdom of his choice of action at this moment is debatable. The results he obtained were meager. The Arab Middle East was preoccupied with its own growing pains, Europe was still prostrate from the war, and the world community as a whole had not become conscious of the colonial problem. Moreover, he was to suffer later the effects of having allowed party control to slip into the hands of an ambitious lieutenant.

By 1947 a new air was stirring in Tunisia. The recently appointed Resident, Jean Mons, abolished censorship, and the decrees of 1943 were abrogated. A conservative government was formed under Mustafa Kaak, and reforms in the administration were carried out which proved, as usual, too liberal for the European settlers and insufficient for the Tunisians.

Bourguiba returned to Tunisia in 1949 to canvass popular feeling and was allowed to tour the country and hold political conversations. As a result of these discussions he put forward the next April (1950) his "seven demands" calling for self-government through constitutional reform. No overt mention was made of independence or Pan-Arab nationalism, and French opinion found his appeal not unreasonable. The government of Robert Schumann promised at this time that Tunisia would achieve internal autonomy by stages, and toward this end a government of negotiation headed by Mohamed Chenik was formed in Tunisia. There was further liberalization, as well as an agreement that Tunisians be given priority in the civil service. But the stumbling block remained that the nationalists wanted a parliament elected by universal Tunisian suffrage. The Chenik government went to Paris in October, 1951, but two months later, under the pressure of the European minority which insisted upon participation in any autonomous government, the negotiations failed. The neo-Destour had at first supported the government of negotiation and applauded the reforms of February, 1951, but it now disassociated itself from the government as it came to believe that collaboration was dangerous at this stage where success looked unlikely. The party was thus in a better position to direct the resistance that broke out in the ensuing period.

The breakdown of talks at the end of 1951 ushered in the final act of French oppostion to Tunisian nationalism. A harsh wave of repression descended upon all local political figures. Bourguiba, other political figures, and some members of the Chenik government were arrested and sent into confinement in the desert. Bourguiba was later transferred to a small island off the coast of Tunisia and from there to France.

For the first time since the beginning of the protectorate, armed resistance broke out in the countryside. Bands of guerrilla fighters, the *fellagha,* were tying up as many as 70,000 French troops early in 1954. Terrorism erupted in the cities, engendering a counterterrorism by the European population. Relations between the Tunisians, metropolitan France, and the settlers formed a complex triangle, but gradually there emerged a separation of interest between the two latter groups. At the same time the Tunisian question was being internationalized, with discussions in 1952 and 1953 at the United Nations, accompanied by a more overt sympathy from the eastern Arab states than had been evident a few years before.[1]

A puppet ministry headed by Salaheddin Baccouche was replaced early in 1954 by another of the same stripe. Tunisian civil servants and ministers often delayed and hindered the application of reform decrees which the French were in the ironic position of having to force upon the Tunisians. Extreme pressure had to be put on the Bey to secure his signature on the decrees, and only 8 per cent of the electorate voted in the Tunis municipal elections of May, 1953.

The combination of political impasse in Tunisia and the degeneration of physical security in the end convinced the French government of the need to negotiate seriously. The government of Mendès-France, which had just signed the Geneva agreement in July, 1954, to end the war in Indochina, turned its attention to Tunisia. The Premier made an unheralded flight to Carthage on July 30, 1954, and proclaimed the internal autonomy of Tunisia. Negotiations to this end were opened in September in Paris, and the Tunisian delegation was headed by Mongi Slim, a member of the political Bureau of the neo-Destour. Bourguiba followed the conversations unofficially from his residence in exile in France. A convention was concluded in May, 1955 (signed on June 3), and Bourguiba returned to a triumphal welcome at home.

The short transition period between autonomy (June, 1955) and full independence (March, 1956) was marked by an internal split in the neo-Destour. The secretary-general, Salah ben Youssef, who had escaped to Cairo during the repression of 1952, returned in September

[1] On Dec. 13, 1952, a resolution asking that negotiations be continued between France and Tunisia was approved by the Political Commission (45 votes to 3, with 10 abstentions) and confirmed by the General Assembly on Dec. 18.

to announce his opposition to the autonomy convention as a "step backward." The quarrel between the two neo-Destour leaders became a bitter, personal affair which ultimately resulted in the expulsion of Ben Youssef from the party at the neo-Destour congress held in Sfax in November. Although the party voted its confidence in Bourguiba and the Political Bureau, it also reaffirmed that total independence was the national goal and significantly added resolutions supporting the struggles for freedom of the Moroccan and Algerian peoples.

It was the rapid evolution of the Moroccan problem that in the end hastened Tunisian independence. The Franco-Moroccan accord of La Celle–Saint-Cloud in November, 1955, had agreed to Moroccan "independence within interdependence," a status to be negotiated as soon as convenient. This status went considerably beyond that provided by the Franco-Tunisian conventions and thus upset politically aware Tunisians who considered themselves far more ready for the responsibilities of independence than were the Moroccans. During the winter the French government agreed to consider both cases on an equal footing. When Moroccan independence was announced, on March 2, 1956, Tunisian impatience could no longer be restrained. A protocol of agreement was signed on March 20, "solemnly recognizing the independence of Tunisia" and leaving for further negotiation the modalities of interdependence. After seventy-five years of foreign tutelage Tunisia was again a sovereign state.

Land and People

GEOGRAPHY

Tunisia is shaped something like an elongated quadrilateral. It has an area of approximately 50,000 square miles, its greatest length being 450 miles from north to south and its width varying from 100 to 150 miles. It lies in the Temperate Zone, approximately between the 37th and the 30th parallel north.

The Atlas Mountain barrier, which runs the length of North Africa from Morocco through Algeria into Tunisia, diminishes in altitude as it goes eastward, but its summits (Jebel Shambi, 5,051 ft., is the highest) divide Tunisia into two well-defined regions, a relatively well-watered and fertile Mediterranean north, known as the Tell, and a semiarid plateau region in the south which becomes a desert in the extreme south as it merges with the Sahara.

Four principal regions can be distinguished in Tunisia: the Tell, the steppes, the Sahel, and the desert. The Tell, which is north of the Atlas Mountain dorsal spine, is subdivided into a mountainous north-western part, covered with cork forests and having a rocky coastline on its northern shore, and a north-central part surrounding the Majarda River Valley, the grain and livestock center of Tunisia. Several important towns exist here, among them El Kef, Beja, and Teboursouk, and the good farmlands along the valley attracted the European settlers at the end of the nineteenth century. Rainfall averages 16–24 inches, although it tends to be irregular.

In the northeast, the Tell merges with the Sahel, the coastal plain which extends from Bizerte and Tunis all the way down to Sfax. The northern Sahel, including the Cape Bon region, with about 20 inches of rainfall, is suitable for the production of grain, wine, citrus fruit, and garden products. Farther south an increasing aridity limits cultivation, but around Sfax (which has 8 inches of annual rainfall) olive groves are extensively cultivated. This is the true Sahel. It is not only a center of agriculture but also the seat of ancient towns and civilizations, the cultural heartland of Tunisia. Here are the only true villages in North Africa with a settled peasant life, as well as cities famous for their past, such as Sousse, Monastir, Mahdia, Sfax, and the garden island of Djerba.

The steppes rise from the Sahel, to which they are connected by trade and history, to the frontier of Algeria. They are a pasturage area for flocks of sheep and camels where esparto grass abounds. Dry farming is occasionally practiced but the low (6–12 inch) and uncertain rainfall makes agriculture risky. Finally, in the south, the principal crop of the near-desert area around the Shott Djerid comes from the oases, where dates are grown.

The major climatic influences in Tunisia are the Mediterranean and the Sahara. Summers are long and hot; from May through September rain rarely falls. Winters are mild with moderate rainfall, decreasing from the northwest to the southeast. High humidity along the Sahel coast permits oleoculture despite the low rainfall.

POPULATION AND RESOURCES

According to the census of 1956 the population of Tunisia was 3,782,209, of whom Tunisians constituted 3,441,696, foreign Europeans 255,324, and other (non-European) foreigners 86,189. Since then there has been an influx of more than 100,000 Algerians (mostly refugees, who are not counted in current estimates) as well as the departure of around 150,000 Europeans. Estimates at the end of 1960 gave a population of 3,800,000 Tunisians, 100,000 Europeans, and more than 100,000 other aliens, making a total of just over 4,000,000.

Included in the Tunisian population are about 50,000 Tunisian Jews. The rest of the Tunisians are Muslims. The European population is almost entirely French in nationality, though mixed French, Italian, and Maltese in stock. The birth rate is estimated at around 2 per cent a year, and more than 50 per cent of the total population is under twenty years of age. The rate of population increase is a serious problem for a country which in many years does not produce enough food to feed itself and which hitherto has had an economy unable to absorb the yearly augmentation of the labor force.

Population distribution is uneven and is tending to become more so. About 70 per cent of the inhabitants live in the Tell or the northeast, and the center and the south, already depopulated, are being progressively denuded by emigration to the cities. The metropolitan area of Tunis alone contains 20 per cent of the total population. About one-third of the population was urban in 1956, and the percentage grows each year, despite government efforts to stem the flow and forcibly return immigrants without prospects to their native regions. The Jewish and European minorities are almost completely urban, but the latter category includes some landowners and small farmers. Both minorities occupy a more important place in the Tunisian economy than their number would indicate.

Tunisia is chiefly an agricultural country. The main industry is mining, centered around the extraction of phosphates, iron, zinc, and lead. A small quantity of natural gas exists, but the absence of energy sources has discouraged industrial development. The gross national product, estimated at around $500,000,000, is made up of agriculture (34 per cent), industry (including mining) and handicraft (24 per cent), commerce (23 per cent), governmental salaries (10 per cent), foreign earnings (5 per cent), and miscellaneous (4 per cent).

Agricultural production in normal years provides Tunisia with food crops sufficient for local consumption and an exportable surplus of specialty products. The most important crops are grain, olives, wine, citrus fruits, esparto grass, dates, and cork. The highly variable amount of rainfall, however, makes yields uncertain. Thus surpluses cannot be depended upon to earn foreign currency, and in some years considerable quantities of foodstuffs must be imported.

Durum wheat, soft wheat, and barley are the principal grains, durum wheat forming the staple food and the principal export grain. In 1958 Tunisia, favored by an exceptional crop, was the third largest exporter of olive oil in the world, after Spain and Italy. More than 27,000,000 trees existed in 1956, although not all of these are now producing. The extreme variation in harvests is shown by the fact that although Tunisia produced 135,000 metric tons of oil in 1958 and 132,000 in 1960, a bad year such as 1959 saw the crop reduced to 37,000 tons. This was a heavily contributing cause to the imbalance of trade that year. Most Mediterranean fruits are grown in Tunisia, but only citrus fruits are exported in any quantity. Cultivation and production have expanded considerably in recent years.

Table 1. Tunisian agricultural production, 1955–1959

Sector	Harvest season	1955	1956	1957	1958	1959
				(000 metric tons)		
Wine	Aug.–Sept.	112	130	160	195 *	245 *
Oranges and tangerines	Nov.–May	56	48	52	57	59
Dates	Oct.–Jan.	33	33	28	46	—
Olive oil		24	90	50	135	59
Barley	May–June	81	156	185	282	236
Wheat	June–July	395	477	498	539	525

* Estimated.

Wine is an important export product. In the first nine months of 1960, because of reduced oil exports, wine ranked as the leading export in value accounting for 5,800,000 dinars [2] out of a total of 38.9 million. Grapes are grown at present on more than 40,000 hectares of land, and annual production comes to around 2,000,000 hectoliters, of which less than one-tenth is consumed locally. More than half the production is exported to France for mixing with French wines, and the rest remains for shipment to other countries. Wine production is expected to decline with the gradual departure of the European farmers and the desire of the government to give preference to other crops.

Dates are grown in the southern part of the country, the best quality coming from the oases around the Shott Djerid. About one-third of the crop is exported to Europe. Esparto grass, used in the manufacture of high-quality paper, grows wild in steppe areas of the center-south. State-domain cork forests cover some 500,000 acres; most of the prod-

[2] One dinar = $2.38 at the official rate.

uct is exported raw. Stock raising is an important source of livelihood. Hides are used extensively in the artisan trades, and wool, wool products, skins, and mohair are exported. Unlike most other North African countries, Tunisia has always had a fishing tradition. Small-scale fishing is carried on along the Sahel, in the Gulf of Gabès, and from the Kerkenna Islands, but a sponge fishing industry which formerly prospered is now threatened by plastic products.

The Tunisian extractive industry is dominated by phosphate mining, which accounted in 1958 for 11.5 per cent of all the country's exports. Considerable reserves of iron ore exist in the northern and western regions (estimates range up to 40,000,000 tons), and small amounts

Table 2. Tunisian industrial production, 1955–1960

Sector	Unit (monthly avg.)	1955	1956	1957	1958	1959	1960
Mining (all)	(1953 = 100)	120	113	110	114	104	101
Electricity	(000,000 kwh.)	18.3	19.0	19.8	19.6	21.4	23.0
Iron ore	(000 metric tons)	95.0	97.4	97.9	91.9	81.8	86.1
Calcium phosphate	(000 metric tons)	217	173	172	190	185	175
Cement	(000 metric tons)	31.9	30.0	33.4	28.7	36.8	33.8

of lead and zinc are mined. But Tunisia has always been deficient in sources of energy. The only available solid fuel is a lignite of quite poor quality found on Cape Bon, worth using only when normal sources are shut off. A small field of natural gas exists on Cape Bon, but at present rates of consumption it will be exhausted within a few years. The extensive petroleum fields recently discovered in neighboring Algeria and Libya have not been duplicated in Tunisia. Although to date prospecting has been negative, there are still hopes in official circles that oil may be found.

The desire to obtain a share in Saharan oil output has bulked large in the Tunisian claim (which was ever more vehemently reiterated throughout 1961) to a large part of the eastern Algerian Sahara, including the highly productive Edjele area. A pipeline from this area to the Tunisian coastal port of Skhira was completed late in 1960, and during the first half of 1961 nearly 4,000,000 tons of oil flowed through it. It was closed, however, by the Tunisians following the Bizerte incidents in July, 1961. Losses from royalty revenue were estimated at around $400,000 a month.

Mining is important in the Tunisian economy not only because of the employment it provides (14,000 workers at full capacity) but because it accounts for much of the rail traffic and makes up the bulk of Tunisian exports by tonnage. The mining industry as a whole suffers from small-scale operations, obsolete equipment, and the lack of domestic consumers. The phosphate industry, in particular, having only medium-grade deposits which are relatively far from shipping ports, competes on unfavorable terms with the higher-quality Moroccan product.

Tunisian industry, properly speaking, is very limited. It consists mainly of the processing and canning of some agricultural and fishery products and the production of superphosphates, cement and construction materials, and pig lead. Other small industries provide consumption goods for local use, including textiles, shoes, soap, household wares, foods, wine and beer, plastics, and the like.

The development of heavy industry has been hampered by the absence of local fuels and the scarcity of indigenous capital and entrepreneurial skill on a level higher than the personal or family-type business. Processing industries, on the other hand, were held down by competition from a nearby France whose products until very recently had easy and preferential access to the Tunisian market. The separation of the dinar from the franc at the end of 1958 and the virtual withdrawal of Tunisia from the franc zone during the next two years have somewhat stimulated secondary local industry. Traditional artisanry and handicrafts occupy a large place in the economy, but mostly for local consumption. It is estimated that nearly 600,000 persons live directly or indirectly from the earnings of the handicraft industry.

Internal communications in Tunisia are very good throughout most of the country and excellent in the north and east. The Tunisian National Railways, taken over by the government in 1956 after independence, has 1,529 kilometers of track, of which 483 kilometers are standard gauge connecting Tunis with the main Algerian line and 1,046 kilometers are narrow gauge in the northern and eastern parts of the country. The privately owned Sfax-Gafsa railway, with 455 kilometers of track, is almost exclusively concerned with the transport of phosphate rock. Railroad freight is favored by the government over trucking; thus some products, such as esparto grass, cement, and government-subsidized wheat destined for export must be shipped by rail. The city and suburbs of Tunis are served by an excellent municipal transport system which uses a fleet of modern buses and an electric train line.

The highway network consists of 14,740 kilometers of roads, of which 9,145 are paved. At the beginning of 1959 there were 74,833 motor vehicles, including 18,500 trucks and buses, registered in Tunisia.

Tunis and Bizerte are the principal ports, although the full usefulness of the latter has never been realized because of its restricted function as a naval base occupied by France. In 1955 Tunis and its annex port of La Goulette (Halq el Oued) handled 3,300 ships with a net registered tonnage of 5,300,000 tons. Sfax is actually the second port in tonnage as the chief export center for olive oil and phosphates. There is frequent maritime service for both freight and passengers to Europe, especially France and Italy, and more than twenty weekly air services to metropolitan France alone. The central position of Tunis seems destined to make it an important relay point for aerial traffic between Europe and Africa. In order to handle the expected increased traffic, improvements are being made at El Aouina Airport which are financed in part by United States aid through the Development Loan Fund.

FINANCES

In its international financial relations Tunisia is still a member of the franc zone, although its links to that system have been growing steadily more tenuous. The dinar, officially valued at $2.38, is the basic unit of currency; it was instituted in November, 1958, as the equivalent of 1,000 old Tunisian francs which were then at parity with French francs. However, Tunisia did not follow France in its December, 1958, devaluation of the franc. The dinar was unpegged, and restrictions were applied on transfers of currency to franc zone countries.

Since achieving independence Tunisia has been moving gradually toward a position of lessened dependence on French financial and economic structures. In accordance with this policy the customs union, established by the 1955 convention on internal autonomy, was abrogated and replaced in September, 1959, by a temporary agreement subject to annual renewal. This now regulates Franco-Tunisian trade and financial relations. A new tariff to protect nascent industries and facilitate raw material imports was promulgated in October, 1959. In banking the policy of disengagement has resulted in the creation of a Tunisian Central Bank to which has been given the right to issue bank notes which was formerly reserved to the Banque de l'Algérie et de la Tunisie. Six other financial institutions have been formed with Tunisian juridical status and local capital, among them the National Agricultural Bank, the Tunisian Banking Corporation, and the National Investment Corporation. There are also several other financial institutions which are controlled by foreign nationals and many branches of foreign banks.

Tunisia has been a country with an almost constant imbalance of trade, except in 1958, when an unusually good agricultural season almost eliminated the steady deficit. Imports have always exceeded exports, often by a considerable margin. Until independence in 1956 the deficit was made up by the French treasury, and since 1957 there has been a growing dependence on American financial aid of different kinds (in the period from July, 1960, to June, 1961, it amounted to $41,200,000).

Table 3. Tunisian imports and exports, 1956–1960
(000 dinars)

	1956	1957	1958	1959	1960
Exports	39,293	54,187	63,399	59,585	50,267
Imports	68,000	63,352	64,881	64,202	80,092

Bilateral agreements have lately been negotiated with other countries, including Italy, several Arab states, and some countries of the Communist bloc—Poland, Communist China, Czechoslovakia, and Bulgaria. The Bulgarian commercial agreement made in mid-1961 was on a direct clearing basis without the usual franc area formalities. At the same time the Soviet Union offered a loan of 25,000,000 rubles (12,000,000 dinars) for the construction of five dams in the northern part of the country and a school for agricultural engineers. All these measures are part of the policy of moving away from exclusive independence on France toward an independent economic position more in harmony with the neutralist political tendencies which have been reinforced during the past few years.

SOCIAL ENVIRONMENT

The social originality of Tunisia stems from the great age and importance of its urban life and at the same time from the commercial character and industriousness of its villages along the eastern coastal plains. These elements distinguish it from neighboring Algeria and are unique in North Africa, indeed throughout the continent.

Almost every city is the heir of a Phoenician trading post, itself supplanted by a Roman city and an Arab medina. These towns successfully resisted the nomadic invasions, in part because of their protective ramparts but also because of the strategic maritime location they enjoyed. Turned toward the sea, they lived to a great extent from fishing and from an active artisanry, whose products were exchanged for the goods of the hinterland or traded for the produce of other ports of the Mediterranean. In the most somber periods of Tunisian history the towns have protected civilization behind their walls. They also welcomed and developed the seeds of foreign civilization which drifted across the waters to enrich them. Today, catalyzed by the European-inhabited sections of the cities, which grew up alongside of them, and stimulated by the competitive presence of a commercially oriented Jewish mercantile minority, the medina has adapted itself to a market economy in the modern sense. It is from these centers that a great percentage of the political leaders, students, civil servants, and members of the liberal professions have come.

The center of the traditional town is the great mosque, or cathedral mosque, often, as in Tunis itself, a work of antiquity and beauty. Its annexes contain the religious schools or university attached to the mosque. Around it extends the quarter of the *suqs,* the commercial nucleus which unfolds from the center in a descending scale of luxury, beginning with the dealers in precious goods, jewelers, booksellers, incense makers, and rug merchants and ending with the tanners, butchers, and the more unsavory trades. The middle-class houses of the medina are almost always of two or more stories, their many rooms grouped around a central court which is the Mediterranean atrium, often tiled and decorated with a fountain. Toward the outskirts of town the dwellings are usually more rural in aspect; they tend to be one-storied and more open, with courtyards used as stables. Depending on the region, the character varies: in Sfax, most of the inhabitants own some olive trees and the oil-pressing industry dominates the town; in the small towns along the shores of the Cape Bon Peninsula, the townspeople may possess small citrus groves nearby; and in the coastal towns of the Sahel, such as Monastir, Mahdia, and Sousse, the fishing port is the center around which life revolves.

The towns of northern Tunisia, apart from the capital, are of secondary importance. Bizerte has grown rapidly in this century under the stimulus of foreign naval activity, but with the removal of the French installations it would have to reorient itself considerably. The towns of the interior, such as Beja, Mateur, and El Kef, were opened up only recently, in good measure owing to the influx of European settlers into the region and the effect they had in stimulating the exchange of goods.

With no detraction from the importance of urban civilization in Tunisia, however, it is certainly village life which gives the country its distinctive character. Scattered along the coast or near it, from Bizerte to the Gulf of Gabès, are nearly one hundred smaller towns and villages ranging up to 10,000 in population. Here exists that intermediate life between urban sophistication and rural ignorance upon which Tunisia has so usefully drawn in its development toward a functioning modern state. In these villages, studded with well-built, whitewashed clay or stone houses, which are fitted with blue-painted wooden doors and shutters often ornamented with elaborate iron grillwork, and surrounded by well-tended gardens carefully watered and fenced off, small-town life takes on a special dimension. The villages are usually capped by a mosque and its minaret; they have a steam bath (*hammam*), a regular market place instead of itinerant vendors, and skilled artisans to produce the daily necessities and make ordinary repairs.

The village community recalls the small town of Spain, with its *huerta* of vegetable gardens around it—and it derives historically in large measure from this source. It has much in common with Mediterranean life, from Homer down through the centuries, and little with the harsher African country lying behind it. As one proceeds southward, the fruits, vineyards, and cereal fields give way to the olive orchards which finally engulf the country side around Sfax. In the offshore islands of Kerkenna and Djerba is found a sedentary life mixed with fishing, to which is added an acute commercial sense on Djerba. In a consideration of the difference between the state of civilization in this maritime Tunisia (in whose towns and villages and their immediate surroundings along the coast live nearly two and a half of the four million people of Tunisia) and the backwardness of the rest of the country, historical as well as geographical reasons must be invoked. The coastal strip was spared the nomadic invasions which turned the interior into a wasteland, and the security it enjoyed, however meager and uncertain, was apparently enough at most times to permit a flowering of culture and an activity which managed to keep itself alive through the years.

A good notch below this kind of village life is the environment of the rural sedentary inhabitants of the interior of Tunisia. Here the village is more often a group of houses huddled together, made of mixed clay and straw or of brushwood, encircled by defensive hedges of barbary cactus, and surrounded by pasturage or open fields. The agglomeration may be part of a tribal grouping, but it is often insufficiently attached to this organization just as, on the other hand, it never became an independent, organic, settled community. The appearance of European settlers in some parts of the interior might have been expected to improve social conditions, but in practice the result was only to alienate much good land, to encourage sharecropping and manual contract labor, or to drive the dispirited into the cities in search of a new life.

Varying geographical conditions give different nuances to the social environment of the interior of Tunisia. In the north, dwellings are often more permanent and better constructed and sedentary life more pronounced. South of the Atlas in the true steppe and down to the desert in the extreme south, seminomadism increasingly takes over. Moreover, until recent times, tribal cohesion in this region has been much more clearly maintained. Even here, however, the extension of olive culture has inhibited nomadic movement, just as new opportunities in the mines and ports have tempted some to give up their traditional ways. In the few years since independence, the government has made efforts to fix the nomads on the land with work relief programs, which involve well digging and small-dam construction, and with technical agricultural assistance and gifts of seed and implements, but results cannot yet be judged.

Where the steppe becomes pure desert, the contrast between the date palm groves with their sheltered gardens and the arid sands surrounding them is repeated in the dichotomy between the nomadic cameleers and the docile oasis cultivators. The cameleers were almost always complete masters of the area until the French occupation. Their function as porters of the desert, bringing into the oases the salt, tobacco, and grain needed from outside and exchanging them for the dates and other oasis produce, has been consistently reduced in this century. Likewise, their former relationship of lord and serf with the oasis sedentaries has changed. This double transformation has broken the pride as well as the power of some of the nomads and has sent others into the bulging metropolis of the north looking for food and work.

The Political Process

GOVERNMENT AND CONSTITUTION

Only five days after the signing of the Franco-Tunisian Protocol of March 20, 1956, which established Tunisia as an independent state, national elections were held for a Constituent Assembly. The neo-Destour Party ran on a National Union ticket, along with members of the UNAT (Tunisian National Farmers' Union), UGTT (Tunisian National Labor Union), UTAC (Tunisian Union of Merchants and Artisans), and some independents. There was virtually no opposition, and the National Union won an overwhelming victory. Out of a total of 726,138 registered voters, 616,989 votes were cast, and the Union ticket received some 598,000. The Assembly of 98 members convened on April 8 and elected Habib Bourguiba its first presiding officer. He was succeeded as head of the Constituent Assembly by Djellouli Fares when he resigned shortly thereafter to become Prime Minister of the first independent Tunisian government.

The principal task of the Assembly was to draft a national constitution. During the succeeding year various committees worked on different sections of the document. While they were doing so, pressures began to build up within the Assembly, and within the country as a whole, to hasten the change from a monarchical to a republican system of government. The abolition of the Beylik, for which there was little deep historical sentiment among Tunisians, had long been taken for granted; it was a natural step in the evolution of Tunisian political life, which had been shaped by a mass movement channeled by a widely representative political party enjoying strong leadership. The national hero of the struggle for independence had not been the weak and ineffective Bey but the leader of the neo-Destour Party, Bourguiba.

The first official act of the Assembly, on July 25, 1957, was to pass a unanimous resolution abolishing the monarchy and proclaiming Tunisia a republic. Habib Bourguiba, then President of the Council (Prime Minister), was entrusted with the "duties of head of state in its present form, until the constitution is applied." Sovereignty was expressly said to derive from the people, and the decision to do away with the monarchy was justified in the name of "strengthening the basis of independence and the sovereignty of the people." From then until the general elections of November, 1959, the Tunisian state functioned provisionally under the stewardship of Bourguiba, who exercised the dual functions of President of the Republic and President of the Council.

The salient characteristic of this transition period was the concentration of power in the hands of the President and his cabinet, whose relations with the Constituent Assembly were extremely limited. It is significant that the most important and striking reform legislation which has been enacted in Tunisia since independence came through presidential decree and without legislative review in the period between 1956 and late 1959. Only at the latter time was the provisional regime, established in July, 1957, replaced in accordance with Article 64 of the constitution following elections for the presidency and the National Assembly.

The Constituent Assembly finally approved the draft constitution on June 1, 1959; it was ratified and promulgated on the same date by President Bourguiba. Its preamble contains the basic elements of Tunisian political belief and aspirations. In it, the "representatives of the Tunisian people"

—Proclaim, that this people, who have liberated themselves from foreign domination, thanks to their solidarity and to their struggle against tyranny, exploitation and retrogression, are determined:

—On strengthening national unity and upholding human principles, accepted among peoples who safeguard human dignity, justice and freedom and who work for peace and progress and for a free cooperation between nations,

—On remaining true to the teachings of Islam, to the ideal of a Union of the Great Maghrib, to their membership in the Arab Family, to their cooperation with the African peoples in building a better future and to all peoples struggling for justice and freedom,

—And on the establishment of a democracy, based on the sovereignty of the people, upheld by a stable system and founded on the principle of a division of powers.

We declare that a republican regime is the best guarantee of human rights, of equality among the citizens both in their rights and their duties, that it constitutes the best means for achieving prosperity and the growth of the economy, for utilizing the country's wealth for the good of the people, for protecting the family and for safeguarding the citizen's right to work, health and education.[3]

[3] Official English translation of the Secretariat of State for Information, "The Tunisian Constitution."

The constitution itself is composed of ten chapters encompassing sixty-four articles. The first seventeen articles (Chapter I) define the state ("free, independent and sovereign; Islam is its religion, Arabic its language and the republican system is its regime"), declare the Republic to be a part of the Great Maghrib "working for its unity within the framework of common interests (Article 2), and vest sovereignty in the people (Article 3). The remainder of the chapter is a bill of rights and duties for the Tunisian citizen and guarantees freedom of religion, thought, and expression, of the press and publication, of assembly, and of the right to found organizations and trade unions (Articles 5 and 8). Article 6 establishes the equality of all citizens in rights and obligations and before the law. The inviolability of domicile is guaranteed and also the secrecy of correspondence (Article 9). The accused is considered innocent until proved guilty in court, and punishment is personal and applicable only in accordance with a preexisting law (Articles 12 and 13). The right to property is guaranteed, and all citizens may travel and reside freely within the state; moreover, they may not be exiled from it or forbidden to return to it (Articles 10, 11, and 14). The last three articles (15–17) concern the duty of the individual to defend the homeland and to pay taxes and other public expenses and forbid the extradition of political refugees.

The three succeeding chapters deal respectively with the legislative, executive, and judicial organs of the state. Legislative authority is exercised by the people through a National Assembly, which is elected by direct and secret universal suffrage enjoyed by all Tunisians over twenty years of age who have been citizens for at least five years. Candidates for the Assembly must be born of a Tunisian father and be thirty years of age. Assembly members are elected for five years, but mention is made of the possibility that a national emergency may prevent a regularly scheduled election and require a continuation of the mandate. All deputies represent the country as a whole. Deputies have the usual immunities while in office unless deprived of them by their peers.

The Assembly provides the normal channel for legislation and any deputy may put forward proposals, although those of the President of the Republic take precedence. Exceptionally the Assembly may delegate its legislative powers to the President for a limited time. In addition, during the time it is in recess the President may issue orders in council with the agreement of permanent committees of the Assembly, provided that such decrees are presented to the Assembly for ratification at its next regular session. The President may also take exceptional measures "at times of danger threatening the safety and independence of the Republic, if the ordinary machinery of state is unable to function." The Assembly ratifies and decides the final figures of the national budget.

The head of the executive branch is a President who must be Muslim in religion, of unbroken Tunisian descent in the male line for three generations, and at least forty years of age. He is elected for a period of five years at the same time and in the same way as the Assembly, and he cannot hold office for more than three consecutive terms. The President directs the general policy of the state, appoints the members of his government who are responsible directly to him, is commander in chief of the armed forces, and makes all civil and military appointments. He ratifies treaties and declares war and makes peace with the agreement of the Assembly. The President either signs and promulgates legislation sent him by the Assembly or, if he so chooses, may send bills back for another reading. If a bill is passed again by a two-thirds majority, it must be promulgated and then becomes law within fifteen days.

Chapter IV stipulates that the members of judicial establishment shall be independent, "subject to no higher authority in their judgment but that of the law." Judges are appointed by order of the President of the Republic, after being proposed by the Higher Judicial Assembly.

Chapters V–VIII set up specific organs: a High Court to try members of the government in the event of treason; a Council of State, which comprises both an administrative body to deal with legal disputes between individuals and the state or with those cases where the state exceeds its authority and an Audit Office to verify state accounts; an advisory Economic and Social Council; and municipal and regional councils with local administrative authority. Under the provisions of Chapter IX, the constitution may be amended (providing that nothing alters the republican character of the state) if so proposed by the President of the Republic or one-third of the members of the Assembly and approved by a two-thirds majority of the Assembly registered in two separate readings with an interval of three months.

The Tunisian constitution has several noteworthy features. Perhaps most important is the fact that it was not the first such organic law for the country. The Fundamental Pact of 1857 is considered a historic document by nationalists, and constitutionalism has always had deep roots in Tunisian political thought. The very name of the Destour Party recalls the fact that the demand for a constitution long preceded the call to independence. The considerable period of reflection, a good three years, which the members of the Constituent Assembly allowed themselves, also bespeaks the seriousness of their feelings. There were several occasions when deputies refused to allow themselves to be pushed precipitately into action under pressure from the executive. Tunisia had waited a century for this opportunity to bestow a constitution upon itself; it was considered unseemly to legislate in too great haste.

This concern of the founding fathers for their legislative prerogatives is found in the constitution itself, where the National Assembly emerges as one of the two poles of tension in the body politic. Its powers to consider again and enact legislation over a presidential veto, plus its control of the budget, are safeguards against executive arbitrariness. The choice of a presidential regime gives great power to the head of the state who is at the same time head of the government. But this power is effectively limited in all respects save the ambiguous possibilities presented by Article 32, which grants exceptional powers to the President in a time of crisis, when the only safeguard is that any measures taken by him during this temporary period "are no longer valid once the crisis is over."

In its selection of a presidential regime Tunisia was influenced not only by the need to focus national dynamism and personalize it in a dramatic leader—a need faced by most new states—but by the shadows of contemporary history. The deputies drafting the constitution had grown up under the aegis of the French parliamentary system which crashed in ruins in 1958. A new and more conservative constitution with a greatly strengthened executive was approved in France just before the Tunisian law took final shape. In essence the Tunisian constitution emerges as a subtle compromise between the ideal and the practical, the establishment of a state buttressed by individual liberties, democratic institutions, and checks against the misuse of power which is entrusted in great measure to a dominant leader. It is only with the consolidation and maturing of independent Tunisia in coming years that the effectiveness of this formula can be evaluated. In practice so far the Assembly has tended to be effaced by the President, because of his continuing personal magnetism and because of the constant state of crisis in Tunisian-French relations vis-à-vis the Algerian revolution since independence.

The administrative system is centered around the President, as head of state and chief executive officer, and his cabinet, composed of secretaries of state for the various departments (Foreign Affairs, Agriculture, Commerce, Plan and Finances, Industry and Transport, Information, Interior, Justice, National Education, Postal Services [PTT], Public Health and Social Affairs, Public Works, and Urbanism). Coordination between the secretariats is provided by the Secretary of State to the Presidency, who is in effect the second figure in the administration. This Secretary is also charged with the office of National Defense and in addition supervises the presidential cabinet, or personal office staff, which is headed by a *chef de cabinet*. The *directeur de cabinet* of the President functions, on the other hand, as a personal emissary of the chief of state.

Control of the security forces was transferred from French to Tunisian hands on April 18, 1956, an important step designed to help combat small groups of followers of Salah ben Youssef who were opposing the government as well as to fight a rash of European terrorists, both of whom had been flourishing in the troubled early months of that year. The system now in existence divides the police force into urban police under the control of the director of National Security and a rural *gendarmerie* recruited from the National Guard. Both the director of National Security and the director of the National Guard are attached to the Secretary of State for the Interior.

A small Tunisian army was created in the spring of 1956, formed at first from troops formerly serving in the French army; also incorporated in the nucleus were the Beylical Guard and some members of resistance groups. Since then conscription has been put into effect and the army built up to a force of around 20,000 men. The defense forces include a small naval contingent to patrol coastal waters, a selected group of officer pilots, and a parachutist elite unit. The Tunisian army conducted itself with bravery in skirmishes with French forces in the Remada incidents in southern Tunisia early in 1958 and again during the short, bloody struggle for Bizerte in July, 1961. Most of the officers have been trained either in the French forces or at the French Military Academy at Saint-Cyr, though noncommissioned officers now receive their indoctrination within the country. The close personal relations existing between many Tunisian and French officers made the bitterness of the former after the Bizerte incident even greater than otherwise. In 1960 a Tunisian contingent of more than 3,000 men was dispatched to the Congo as part of the United Nations force operating there. It was withdrawn after the Bizerte battle in order to protect the country, but at the end of 1961 a new, though smaller force was once again sent to Leopoldville as a sign of continuing Tunisian support of United Nations activities. Parallel to military service is a civilian corps to which a part of the annual call-up of trainees is assigned. This corps has played a praiseworthy role in stimulating the unemployed who are engaged in works projects throughout the country as a part of the economic program called the "Battle against Underdevelopment."

The local administration is headed by the governors of the thirteen governorates into which Tunisia is divided. Each governor is assisted by an elected advisory council whose powers are in reality quite limited, although they provide a local sounding board which somewhat reduces the otherwise sweeping powers of the governor.[4] The governor is represented in the various sections of the governorate by delegates. The role of the governor as the spark plug of local development is important. Particularly in the public works programs of the past three years he has played a key part; in these the decentralization of authority, which allows him wide latitude to take administrative decisions without referring them to the capital authorities in Tunis, is balanced by the smallness and homogeneity of the country, which makes it possible for a central control to be exercised over the governors at all times. Frequent conferences with the Secretary of State for the Interior maintain an adequate degree of liaison on the whole without destroying local initiative. Although, because of its physical makeup, Tunisia lends itself to being easily governed, credit should be given both to the supple system which is employed and to the character of the individual appointees, who are usually youngish, enthusiastic members of the neo-Destour.

Municipal institutions remain decentralized as before. Municipal elections, in which women voted for the first time in Tunisian history (women cast 53,895 votes as compared to 197,398 cast by men), were held in May, 1957, and resulted in an overwhelming neo-Destour victory everywhere. Independent opposition slates won in six communes, but even these groups supported the Destourian reform pro-

---

[4] The fiscal and judicial functions exercised by the *qaids* and khalifas under the protectorate have been removed from the governors and transferred to the central government and the new judiciary respectively.

gram. Nearly one hundred cities and towns have municipal councils, which in turn elect their mayor, except in Tunis where the mayor is appointed by the government.

The administration of justice, or more properly its reform, was one of the first concerns of the new Tunisian government. At the time that Tunisia received internal autonomy in 1955 two kinds of modern courts were functioning: French courts that dealt with all matters in which French or European nationals were involved and also with certain categories of cases involving such subjects as civil rights, or external and internal security; and secular Tunisian courts that dealt exclusively with cases involving Tunisians and had enjoyed a relative independence since 1921. In addition, there were the religious Muslim and Jewish tribunals for personal litigation. The Judicial Convention signed in 1955 provided for a twenty-year transition to a unified Tunisian system of justice.

This lengthy wait was manifestly unpalatable to a free Tunisia, and a new agreement was signed in March, 1957, that provided for the abolition of all French jurisdiction by July of that year. Under its terms French magistrates were to be attached to Tunisian courts in civil or commercial cases that involved French nationals or companies more than half French-owned. Moreover, in comparable criminal cases half the members of the jury were to be of French nationality.

At the same time Tunisia had begun reforming its internal judicial structure by promulgating a Nationality Code in January, 1956, and a new Code of Personal Status that went into effect January 1, 1957. The Personal Status Code contained profound innovations for a Muslim state and placed Tunisia in a more progressive position as regards social and familial reform than any other Arab country. Polygamy was abolished and made punishable by both fine and imprisonment. Women were granted full equality before the law. Marriage was made subject to the mutual consent of both spouses and a minimum marriage age was instituted of eighteen for men and fifteen for women, and a legal majority of twenty years was established. Divorce was to be obtainable henceforth only through court action. Repudiation of the wife by the husband was thus invalidated, and equality of access to divorce by either spouse was established. Somewhat later civil marriage rites were instituted and encouraged in preference to the Quranic custom of signing contracts between families. Simultaneously the religious (Shari'a) tribunals for Muslims were abolished and subsequently also the rabbinical tribunals. Thus all citizens were brought under the same secular law. These reform texts were published in a new Civil and Commercial Code, and a new Code of Criminal Procedure was also drawn up to afford the guarantees of modern justice to accused persons.

During this period the machinery of justice was also reformed. Forty cantonal courts, each presided over by a single judge, were established to handle petty cases; more serious matters are dealt with by eleven courts of first instance, each of which has three judges. There is an appeals court in each of the three cities of Tunis, Sousse, and Sfax to review the decisions of the lower courts. Finally, a Court of Cassation at the highest level, designed to assure a uniform and proper application of the law, is the apex of the judicial system.

The Civil Status Law of August 1, 1957, completed the personal status reforms by insisting on a specific identity for each citizen. Registration of births and marriages was made obligatory and, in place of the previous anarchic anonymity that had prevailed because of the custom of using patronymics, everyone was ordered to adopt a true family name. The Tunisian government had wisely recognized that without a fully operative civil state register from which to draw statistical information real progress was impossible. The rapid reform of justice, the emancipation of a large segment of the population from archaic religious law, and the proclamation of the legal equality of all citizens were probably more important than any other moves made by the government in the direction of building a fully functioning modern nation.

THE ROLE OF THE PARTY

No matter how soundly conceived, an administration does not function well without capable leaders. The men who shaped the Tunisian state and provided its constitution were in the main the dour, practical merchants of the Sahelian bourgeoisie, the representatives of the professional classes of Tunis and the coastal cities, and a group of pragmatic intellectuals who had turned to politics. Tunisia is rich in human resources relative to most of the newer countries in the world. The contribution of long-established civilization to forming this social and human material has been one of the keys to the success Tunisia has had in adapting itself to the modern world, a success that is notable in comparison to some of its immediate neighbors who possessed similar geoeconomic backgrounds.

The Destourian militants, who form the overwhelming majority of

the leaders and of the higher cadres of the new state, are the dis-
tillation of this heritage, aged by a generation of struggle in the harsh
school of colonial politics. They form a homogeneous group with a
common educational background (seven of the present ministers are
alumni of the Sadiqi College in Tunis), common social origins, and
common prison experiences. A closed-in, clublike, school-tie atmosphere often prevails among the members of the establishment, among
whom there is genuine personal friendliness and much intermixing.

Heading the group, originally as a *primus inter pares* but increasingly in lofty isolation, is Habib Bourguiba. Of him it can truly be
said that he was first in revolt, first to make peace with France, and
first in the hearts of his fellow citizens. At fifty-eight the eldest statesman of his group, Bourguiba stands out as the founder of the neo-
Destour Party, the organizer of the first government in independent
Tunisia, and the first President of the Republic. In Tunisian eyes he
incarnates the national spirit. To foreigners it has become impossible
to divorce the leader and the country. On occasion it has even seemed
that the Tunisian stage was too small for Bourguiba to perform on,
and he has given much attention to foreign affairs and international
politics.

At all times there is the feeling that Bourguiba has to exhort, cajole,
and prod the people as he unfolds to them in patient explanation his
vision of the future. The charismatic role is always difficult, even when
it appears to be played with gusto; it is tempting to criticize those
politicians who overindulge. But it must be remembered that the
spark which has been lighted in Tunisia is at the moment kept alive
only by the untiring efforts of one man and the emotional contact he
maintains with the masses. Bourguiba's assets are his ability to personalize ideas, the compelling manner of his conversational oratory,
and his mass appeal, so skillfully exploited through the weekly broadcasts that are inspired by the fireside chats of Franklin D. Roosevelt.
There is also Bourguiba's candor, refreshing in any public figure, as
well as his ability to sense popular wants on most issues.

Countering these strong points in Bourguiba are found a certain
inconsistency, which may stem in part from the sheer volume of what
he says in public speeches, broadcasts, and interviews or may be a
studied policy; an authoritarian cast of mind, reinforced in the past
few years and accompanied by a growing sensitivity to criticism; and
—a characteristic common to many natural leaders—a seeming inability to foster the growth of independent-minded, younger figures

around him. The accomplishments of Bourguiba, including the achievement of independence, the social reforms which have distinguished Tunisia, and the resoluteness with which the economic battle against underdevelopment has finally been tackled, must be balanced against his failures on the question of Ramadan and the religious issue, the question of inter-Arab relations, and the problems with France stemming from the Franco-Algerian dispute.

Ranged about Bourguiba are his oldest companions in politics, a group of distinguished men around fifty years of age headed by Mongi Slim, a brilliant lawyer and mathematician, the principal negotiator of the autonomy conventions of 1955, later ambassador to the United States, Tunisian representative in the United Nations, and, in 1961–1962, President of the General Assembly. He is often spoken of as the most capable man in the country and a likely successor to Bourguiba. The Secretary of State to the Presidency, Bahi Ladgham, is a competent but somewhat retiring executive, as is the Secretary of State for Education, Mahmoud Messadi. Two other important figures of the government who have long been close to the President are the Secretary for Foreign Affairs, Sadok Mokaddem, and the governor of the Central Bank of Tunisia, Hedi Nouira.

A decade younger than this elite is a group of men, all in their midthirties, who are characterized by a respect for President Bourguiba but not by a blind obedience to his personalized rule. Each of these men represents some aspect of the new forces which have tended to grow up in the vacuum created around the "Supreme Combatant" in the past several years. Taieb Mehiri, in the key position at the Interior, is a strong and dedicated figure with a personal following built out of the Young Destourians whom he once directed and with a provincial network of influence based upon the governors responsible to him. The most striking figure of the group may be Mohammed Masmoudi, formerly ambassador to France and then Secretary of State for Information. Masmoudi resigned both posts because of quarrels with President Bourguiba. The first time was in 1958 when he supported the *Action* group in its press criticisms of the executive. The two men were later reconciled, but in the fall of 1961 Masmoudi once again fell out with Bourguiba over what he termed the growing authoritarianness of the latter's rule. In return for this criticism, Masmoudi was expelled from the neo-Destour. Masmoudi has always been close to the editors of *L'Action* (now *Jeune Afrique*), who are journalists of the moderate left like Bechir Beni Yahmed, himself Secretary of

State for Information in 1956 at the age of twenty-nine, and Mohamed Ben Smail (presently director of the National Tourist Office), and it is likely that he has considerable influence with them. Another member of the middle group is Ahmed ben Salah, a leading labor figure, who has been in and out of government in recent years. He has argued strongly in the past for a more socialized economy and was at one time eager to head a splinter party. A fourth is Azzouz Rebai, sometime head of the Youth and Sport Secretariat and a Young Destourian leader who is known for his appeal to the crowds and has often espoused a more pro-Arab policy than Tunisia was following at most times.

Except for Masmoudi, these younger men are not in open opposition to Bourguiba. On the contrary, they are still part of the regime and they are cooperating with it, in typically Tunisian fashion, to make the common enterprise succeed. But Tunisian society and expectations are changing, and such figures both reflect a ground swell of greater demands in almost every area and are the opinion molders for even younger lower-echelon officials and students who show some signs of still greater dissatisfaction. To understand why, one must look at the way in which the ruling party has evolved over the years.

Since independence in Tunisia, there has been in the collective national mind only the image of Bourguiba and the ruling elite around him. To the same degree political life has long been dominated by one party, the neo-Destour. Furthermore, its chiefs have been the same men who are the leaders of the government. It was the neo-Destour which awakened national sentiment in the mid 1930's and channeled it into an effective organization for resisting French rule. During this long struggle the neo-Destour learned how to group together the disparate elements of the population—intellectuals, Westernized young Tunisians, the middle classes, villagers, urban masses, and the countryside—into an organic whole manipulable for political action.

This feat is difficult to perform, however, except in time of crisis. Until 1956 the neo-Destour could be all things to many different kinds of men, because the overriding goal was the ending of the protectorate. Destourian leadership, an interlocking group, as has been seen in the description of government leaders, could with tact and subtlety direct groups with divergent aspirations. The very success of the operation worked to cloak differences, which were often slight within the framework of a fundamentally homogeneous country and in any event were played down at the time but which tend to reveal themselves more blatantly as external pressures are removed. The difference between a revolutionary political grouping often operating clandestinely and a formally organized political party closely identified with an authoriarian government has been apparent in many recently emancipated states. The neo-Destour has come off much better than most comparable organizations elsewhere, but it still faces the problems arising from a change of form and of objective. There is much evidence that the party's role vis-à-vis the people and its influence on them, as well as the expectations which the government had for it, have declined in the past few years.

The basic structure of the neo-Destour was set in 1937 after the release of Bourguiba and other leaders from prison. It consisted of a large number of local cells (1,830 in 1956, later increased and then more recently reduced in number) grouped into regional federations (41 in 1956) with committees from each federation elected by the delegates of the various cells. Above them stood the National Council with 73 members: 32 elected by a general vote of the congress plus one representative per federation. The National Congress consisted of one representative from every cell and in theory was the supreme organism of the party, although in practice the Policy Committee, composed of the president and 10 members elected by a general vote of the congress, held the monopoly of power. This organization was sufficient for all needs until independence, and, in fact, the great degree of autonomy accorded the federations in the years of the resistance helped the party to survive after its central leadership was imprisoned or deported.

Soon after independence President Bourguiba and some other top leadership decided that the party organization was too diffuse to serve the interests of a state which increasingly saw itself doing battle on the political, economic, and social fronts. A trend toward increased authoritarianism was noticeable in the summer of 1958, particularly in response to the criticism by *L'Action* of the law on national indignity and the strong governmental reaction to it. As part of a general tightening up, Bourguiba announced the replacement of the elected federation committees by thirteen delegates appointed by central headquarters, one delegate to each governorate, with whom was associated a coordination committee representing the cells of the area. This change was not too enthusiastically received, and there were some charges of railroading.

What is certain is that since late 1958 the neo-Destour has been undergoing a crisis in its history. Many of the most talented party members and militants are in government jobs, dividing their efforts and energies between the two and thus confusing the line which should properly be drawn between governmental authority and political organizations. The government as such has not been able to use the party as a mechanism for enlisting the enthusiasm of the masses; where such enthusiasm has been forthcoming, it has been more often through direct appeal and persuasion by the President. In short, the party has not yet found a new mission clear enough to call forth the kind of support it had during the "evolutionary revolution." This lack shows up in its increasing inability to interest the more modernized young people in those urbanized and coastal areas which originally gave the party its start. When the crisis of the party is placed alongside the strains which seem to be emerging from the aging of the regime and the split between generations, it becomes clear that some kind of renovation must soon be undertaken if the *élan* which has shaped Tunisia is to be preserved through the next decade. The neo-Destour seems at present to have lost a good deal of the meaning of its prefix, and although Tunisians are still wont to remark that everyone of importance in the country is a Destourian, the phrase may now be more often uttered by rote than conviction.

Despite these internal difficulties there is as yet no rival to the party on the horizon. The tactic of submerging minority opponents, both among the independent-minded and more rightist bourgeoisie and the socialist-oriented labor group, in a national front has prevented either group from securing national support for themselves. Early in 1961 there was a slight return onto the scene of the conservatives, who were linked with the old Destour, but it is hard to believe that this group has any future. On the other side, the syndicalists have not yet made any move to split with the neo-Destour. In this connection, the fact that Ahmed ben Salah, a former secretary-general of the Tunisian National Labor Union who had bitterly criticized the government in 1956 for its inattention to the problems of the working classes, is associated with the administration as Secretary of State for the Plan and Finances, seems designed to head off possible discontent from the left. On the extreme left the Tunisian Communist Party remains minuscule and to a large extent dominated by a minority group of Jews. It publishes a journal but has so far made a negligible impression on the bulk of the population.

ASSOCIATED ORGANIZATIONS

Most of the time since World War II, the neo-Destour has functioned not alone but in conjunction with several other groups which have attached themselves to it as part of a "Union of National Organizations." The Destourian Youth is not properly one of these groups since it stems from within the party itself, but it has played a significant role in indoctrinating the young in political behavior and forming them into activist groups for political and social purposes. The so-called national organizations are (1) the Tunisian National Labor Union (UGTT), (2) the Tunisian Union of Merchants and Artisans (UTAC), (3) the Tunisian National Farmers' Union (UNAT), (4) the General Union of Tunisian Students (UGET), and (5) the National Union of Tunisian Women (UNFT).

Of these organizations the UGTT is by far the most important. The history of its development and relations with the neo-Destour Party and the government exemplify the intricacy of shadowy relationships within the well-integrated social framework of Tunisia. The Tunisian trade union movement began in the second decade of this century and received an impetus in World War II when Farhat Hached created free trade unions which, in 1946, merged into the UGTT. The national union soon left the Communist-dominated WFTU (World Federation of Trade Unions) and affiliated itself with the ICFTU (International Confederation of Free Trade Unions). The UGTT functioned both as a labor union and as a subsidiary organ of political action, coordinated with that of the neo-Destour, until the repression which followed the assassination of Hached, presumably by a settler terrorist group, in December, 1952. (The killing provoked a general strike of sympathy in nearby Morocco, which led to the dissolution of the Istiqlal [independence] Party, the exiling of Muhammad V the following year, and the consequent emergence of underground armed resistance to French rule. It can be fairly regarded as the turning point in the North African fight for freedom.) After the Declaration of Carthage by Premier Mendès-France in the summer of 1954, the UGTT was allowed to resume its normal activities, and by the time Tunisia became independent in 1956, it was both a powerful internal force and an institution highly respected in labor circles abroad. Under the leadership of Ahmed ben Salah, its secretary-general after the death of Hached, it began to criticize governmental inertia in dealing with workers' problems and called for nationalization of industry.

Since Bourguiba was now in power, it was embarrassing to have the UGTT express itself openly on political questions, the more so since Ben Salah claimed a separate identity for the union and boasted of a record of nationalism that was second to none. With governmental encouragement, a splinter group broke away from the UGTT at its congress in September, 1956, and established a rival Tunisian Workers' Union (UTT) which shortly thereafter claimed an enrollment of as many as 50,000 workers. The important and sophisticated decision made by the latter's leader, Habib Achour, was that a labor union should concern itself only with questions relating directly to the workers' interests and not deal in political issues. This attitude pleased the neo-Destour government figures who could thus enlist the union under the banner of the state while denying it overt participation in political life. In order to safeguard labor unity, however, Ben Salah relinquished his post as secretary-general of the UGTT in favor of Ahmed Tlili, a member of the Policy Committee of the neo-Destour, and the short-lived schism was healed. Ben Salah was later taken into the government as Secretary of State for Public Health and Social Affairs and, early in 1961, was made responsible at cabinet level for the development program.

The whole story testifies to the gift for compromise possessed by Tunisian statesmen and the power of unifying nationalist pressures, at least in 1956–1957. At the same time the basic issue was never satisfactorily resolved, for Tunisian labor leaders today refuse to admit that the 1956 schism was anything more than a quarrel of personalities. If so, the results are at best a stalemate. The central authority undoubtedly succeeded in confining the UGTT to what it considered the proper field of syndicalist activity, but a counterpoint of some importance is the growing prominence of Ben Salah within the government in a post where he is in a position to carry out many of the reforms he once demanded from outside.

The Tunisian Union of Merchants and Artisans (UTAC), which was founded in 1946 primarily to combat speculation and the black market, is composed of regional unions and trade federations. The UTAC and the Tunisian National Farmers' Union (UNAT), which was organized in 1956 to develop productivity and spread modern agricultural methods, are primarily service organizations which, although closely linked with the neo-Destour, have had little independent political life. Not so, however, is the General Union of Tunisian Students (UGET), clandestinely created in 1953 during the height

of the Franco-Tunisian struggle. It is composed of 35 sections and 4
federations, including one in France which has worked closely with
the Algerian students in Europe. The UGET has also had much international contact as a member of the International Conference of Students and has brought numbers of foreign and particularly African
student groups to Tunisia. In the recent past there is little doubt that
the UGET has become more than a rival for the Destourian Youth
among the several scouting and youth organizations. Its positions have
tended to be more extreme than those of the government, notably on
foreign policy issues. At the time of the death of Patrice Lumumba
early in 1961 the UGET severely criticized the authorities for maintaining Tunisian troops with the UN command and complained that
Destourian Youth groups were using violent means to break up its
meetings. The increasing split between the government and the elite
members of the younger generation may be only a transient phenomenon in view of the Tunisian capacity for accommodation, but it is at
present a trend which needs watching.

Finally, the increasing role played by women in Tunisian society
is reflected in the National Union of Tunisian Women (UNFT),
founded in 1955 under the direct inspiration of Habib Bourguiba, who
has always taken a personal interest in the emancipation of women.
There are now 35,000 UNFT members in Tunis and over 100 local
branches in the major towns and villages outside. These branches serve
as training centers for girls and women who are taught reading and
writing and sewing and embroidery and are given lectures on such
subjects as hygiene, civic responsibilities, and the care of children.
Three subsidiary organizations further the aims of the UNFT: (1) a
National Vestiary where unemployed women are taught to make
clothing, which is then donated to needy children, orphanages, and
the poor; (2) an orphanage for unwanted babies, which is particularly
noteworthy because Tunisia is the only Arab country to have legalized
the adoption of children; and (3) a cultural club, which brings together Tunisian and foreign women.

THE PRESS

The neo-Destour for the past decade has had its own organs of public expression. In 1950 it founded the newspaper, *As Sabah* ("Morning"). When this journal took the side of Salah ben Youssef in his
quarrel with Bourguiba in 1955, the party put out *Al Amal* ("Action"),
which has now become the leading Arabic-language daily in the coun-

try. *As Sabah* was temporarily suspended in 1957 but is now published as an independent newspaper with a slightly greater tendency
to neutralism and Pan-Arabism than the party journal. Freedom of the
press and freedom of expression in Tunisia were guaranteed in the
constitution but are limited by press laws and by a tacit understanding
that one does not criticize the head of state. The excellent French-
language weekly (originally called *L'Action,* later *Afrique Action,* and
now *Jeune Afrique*), founded by one of Bourguiba's former protégés,
Bechir Beni Yahmed, voluntarily suspended publication after it had
crossed swords with the government over the law on national indignity designed to punish those guilty of excessive collaboration during
the protectorate. It has reappeared recently and is now widely read
by North African and French intellectuals, particularly of the left. Its
influence among the younger generation probably exceeds that of any
other journal in the region. One of the greatest difficulties facing the
Tunisian press, however, is the fact that Parisian papers are available
in Tunis the evening of the day of publication. Circulation of *Al Amal*
runs around 25,000, but there are few educated Tunisians in government and business who do not read *Le Monde.*

Contemporary Issues

In dealing with the ensemble of problems facing Tunisian society
on the morrow of independence, the new government was following,
perhaps unconsciously, the outlines of the major reforms in Western
history in the eighteenth and nineteenth centuries. The two main pre-
conditions to progress were the need to free the human resources of
the country for participation in all future activities and the necessity
of using as efficiently as possible all the land resources in a largely
agricultural society. The first issue was handled by the series of reforms in personal status mentioned above, and at almost the same time
the second problem was dealt with by a modernization of property
laws and an agricultural reform program.

Four principal categories of property ownership existed in Tunisia
in 1956: private (*mulk*) holdings by Tunisians, *habous* property, collective lands, and private lands in the possession of European settlers.
Of these, only private Tunisian holdings have continued unaffected by
subsequent reforms. The *habous* are a customary institution of Quranic law, whereby a property is made inalienable and its income
consecrated to pious works or to some generally useful purpose, either
immediately or when the last inheritors of the property have died. In

Islamic history, it has been a successful device for avoiding autocratic despoilation and keeping family property intact from fragmentation resulting from inheritance. Various types of *habous* property (private, *zawiya* intermediate, and public) existed, but all were mortmain lands embroiled in detailed and archaic legislative and administrative complexities. The extent of *habous* land in Tunisia was estimated at 1,600,000 hectares, about one-fourth of the cultivable surface of Tunisia.

Although the protectorate was unable to invalidate a religious institution of this nature, it had helped to undermine *habous* traditions by sanctioning various indirect evasions of the system, involving annual rental or exchange of *habous* property for a consideration. Some *habous* public holdings were also compulsorily allocated to European colonization in violation of Shari'a law. Because of the degradation of the system and its manifestly inefficient management, the independent government was able to move boldly against it. In March, 1956, all public *habous* land was sequestered, and in July, 1957, *zawiya* and private *habous* property were transferred to the state. Public holdings were sold in lots to would-be proprietors, and private holdings were divided or individual title was given as needed.

In September, 1957, collective tribal lands (estimated at 2,200,000 hectares of which roughly one-half was cultivable) were reorganized for division into individual holdings. Simultaneously lands of "unusual fragmentation," arising from the division of property as practiced in Islamic law, were consolidated. The reform in collective lands was associated with the battle against nomadism, under which the Bedouins were encouraged to settle on the land, were supplied with regional dispensaries, schools, and administrative centers, and were helped in various developmental projects, still more intensively when the full-scale works projects program became effective shortly thereafter.

In November, 1958, the Tunisian government announced its intention to repurchase from European settlers all the land in their possession. This caused some dismay, but the settlers were reassured that no one would be expelled from his property without just compensation. The French government has admitted the principle that settler-held land should return to Tunisians hands, and it is likely that within a few years there will be no significant holdings by foreigners. At the height of their position in the protectorate (in 1953), Europeans held 750,000 hectares out of a total of 1,280,000 hectares under modern cultivation and a grand total in cultivation of slightly under 4,000,000 hectares, that is, approximately 20 per cent of Tunisian soil. Late in 1961 it was estimated that Europeans still held about 400,000 hectares, or 2 per cent of the total area.

The parallel between these acts and the reforms of the French Revolution, the Declaration of the Rights of Man, and the sequestration of church property may be coincidental, but the reformers in the neo-Destour had been indirectly schooled in the republican tradition of 1789 and, like their predecessors, aimed at establishing a new society based on an independent peasantry with a new spirit of individual responsibility. The purpose of these major reforms can perhaps best be shown by subsidiary minor changes in the physical and psychological climate fostered by the government, such as the elimination of the hedgerows of cactus and barbary figs which formerly isolated many of the farms and villages. They were replaced, where needed as windbreaks, by rows of trees which did not carry the same air of defensive aloofness as the sharp-spiked hedges. In the cities, the psychological climate was changed by eliminating cemeteries from the centers of town and replacing them with parks and gardens and by opening up new streets and widening avenues, to bring a new breath of air to the closed-in medina. An impressive quantity of newly built housing also stressed openness and permeability to outside influence. All these devices were part of a plan to alter the attitudes of the individual by transforming his life habits, a plan based on the theory that a new Tunisia could not be built without new Tunisians.

With these reforms solidly anchored, the government turned next to the problem of getting all the citizens of the state to work toward shaping their own future. Tunisia was beset by a rapidly growing population, which was increasing at more than 2 per cent a year and adding some 80,000 workers annually to the labor market, by a low per capita income, and by poor productivity. It was estimated that the per capita income for the period 1948–1952 was considerably lower than it had been a generation before, since population growth had far outstripped the rise in national production. Moreover, serious unemployment and underemployment existed; as many as 300,000 potential workers were either without jobs or working sporadically for short periods each year. With 75 per cent of the population engaged in agriculture, some of it highly seasonal, most of the underemployment was rural, but it had resulted in an exodus to the larger cities, principally the capital, in search of work. Here, in the years following World War II, a large, rootless urban proletariat existed on a bare subsistence level by begging, belt tightening, and the exercise of its wits, legally or illegally. The economic problem was equally a social problem in the slum town around Tunis.

Late in 1959 President Bourguiba turned attention to the "Battle for Economic Development." Under a triple format calling for work mobilization, education, and planning, he called for the use of the non-employed labor force in a series of works projects designed to eliminate unemployment at the same time that it changed the face of the country. Since then Tunisia has become a veritable workshop, in which vast numbers of ex-unemployed, removed from the cities and with their slum towns destroyed, have returned to their home provinces. There they are building roads, digging wells, erecting small earthen dams to prevent rain-water runoff, opening irrigation canals, working at reforestation, planting orchard trees, carrying out drainage projects, and undertaking soil conservation and restoration projects. Of the approximately 300,000 unemployed, more than 150,000 have been put to work. The number varies between 100,000 and 200,000 because occasional seasonal agricultural pursuits temporarily divert labor, but the principle is that work is provided for anyone who wants it. Payment is made in cash and in kind; a minimum salary of 200 millimes a day (about $0.48) is provided, to which is added a ration of grain supplied by the United States through its agricultural surplus aid program. In this way potential inflation is held down.

Most observers agree that the Tunisian works program has been eminently successful, especially in comparison to a somewhat similar one attempted in Morocco. One reason for its success may lie in the efficient way it has been administered by the governors at the provincial level. Once a general objective has been determined in consultation with the government, local initiative prevails and paradoxically it is the strength and cohesion of the central government which permits decentralization at lower levels. The political unity of the country and its internal tranquillity also aid the process, as does the work performed by the neo-Destour cell members and those serving in the national civil labor force. The role previously played by the party in enlisting the masses of the countryside in the battle for independence is now bearing fruit in another battle. So too has Bourguiba's decision (taken long ago in other circumstances) to go out to the people and address them directly in the dialect. Both have paid dividends in the confidence accorded the authorities in a program which necessarily involves some coercion and considerable discipline and patience. Finally, the cultural background explains much of the success of the program, the negligible city-country opposition now present in Tunisia, and the existence of a population evolved enough to understand the benefits to be obtained from this kind of cooperation. The enormous drive of Tunisian workers, something noticed by all foreign observers in most recent years, can be explained only by their understanding that the members of a collectivity who dig an irrigation ditch will all eventually profit from it and that the villagers who plant almond trees will one day harvest their crop. If, as Bourguiba once remarked, independence could not have been won without the subtle and elastic support of the people, they seem to be showing the same kind of appreciation of the complexities of the present campaign.

Full employment is planned to lead to better employment through a more careful choice of projects, not merely those which make work but particularly those which create capital and produce the highest future return. As full employment continues, it will also permit increased productivity. In some provinces Western work clothes have been substituted for traditional dress and workers have been forbidden to wear the customary skullcap, innovations which increased the work yield sharply.

The consolidation of the works project regime was undertaken in 1961 with the elevation of the Directorate of the Plan to a Secretariat of State and the elaboration of a ten-year plan for development. At the end of six years of independence, the Tunisian government seemed to have replaced its original hesitation about economic *dirigisme* by a confident vision of an ordered but mixed economy working within the framework of flexible planning.

The Tunisian government has also understood that a necessary adjunct of economic progress is the continuing development of the country's human material. In this area it has not only drawn on the cultural tradition of its own past but has also profited by the reformist zeal of its leaders to make an enormous effort in educational advance, synthesis, and change.

EDUCATION

Independent Tunisia inherited from the protectorate a tripartite educational system which fragmented the concept of cultural unity and favored the immigrant European population. It consisted of (1) a completely French system of instruction based on that employed in the mother country; (2) an "assimilated" or Franco-Arab system (also called "modern" or "Sadiqi" type in secondary schools) in which the Tunisian Muslim was given some instruction in his own culture and language (roughly one-third of the curriculum) but with standards which were admittedly lower than those prevailing in purely French-type schools; and (3) a continuing traditional system of largely religious education, culminating in the university mosque of Az Zeitouna.

In 1954, just before the end of the protectorate, the French-type schools were attended by 59,281 pupils, of whom 29,010 were French, 14,525 Tunisian Muslims, and 12,184 Tunisian Jews. Franco-Arab schools in the same year contained 125,000 pupils, almost all Muslims. A so-called "modern Quranic" type private school system also existed during the protectorate, supported largely by *habous* funds and private donations. These schools attempted an adaptation of Arabo-Islamic studies to the techniques of modern instruction. Around 35,000 Tunisians were attending primary schools of this type at the close of the protectorate. Although only one in four of Tunisian Muslim school age children was receiving instruction, even this figure represented a considerable advance over the past, as can be seen in Table 4.

Table 4. School attendance

Tunisian Muslim children	1920	1925	1930	1935	1940	1945	1950	1955
				(in thousands)				
Of school age	452	467	511	552	623	696	763	840
In school	12	24	35	42	47	66	113	224
Not in school	440	441	476	510	576	630	650	616

In the first years following independence, from 1956–1958, the Tunisian government was forced to move carefully within the existing system, because of extreme shortages of teaching personnel and facilities. It did integrate the archaic Zeitounian religious system into the national education structure, however, by making the university mosque a state institution presided over by a rector appointed by the Minister of Education. Despite trying and makeshift conditions an impressive increase in school attendance was also achieved. By 1958 enough experience had been gained so that the new Minister of Education, Mahmoud Messadi, could undertake a profound reform of the whole school system.

Under the terms of the reform plan, universal primary education will be a reality within ten years, that is, by 1968–1969. An average annual increase in the school population of slightly over 50,000 is to be achieved by eliminating the seventh year of primary education and arranging for two-shift sessions of fifteen hours each for the first two years. From the third to the sixth year twenty-five hours of instruction will be given weekly. By these means primary school enrollment can be sharply augmented and teachers can look after extra classes. The question of the language of instruction has been resolved by giving over the two preparatory years to Arabic and dividing instruction in the next four years into fifteen hours of French and ten of Arabic. Since the language of instruction in secondary and technical education continues to be overwhelmingly French, there exists a *de facto* bilingualism which cannot fail to make a deep impression on Tunisian youth in the coming decade.

Secondary education is subdivided into an intermediate program of three years, essentially of the trade school type, and a full six-year secondary school college-preparatory program. Competitive examinations at the end of primary school determine admission to these programs. The secondary system is envisaged as an elite system, although provision is made for promising intermediate students to transfer into it. The secondary program offers three options—general, technical, and commercial-economic—and includes a strong emphasis on the sciences rather than liberal arts. For the first time a high percentage of the young Tunisians applying for government scholarships have expressed a preference for the natural sciences. A newly established Educational Bureau (*Diwan at Tarbiya*) now deals with technical questions and oversees the preparation and publication in Tunisia of textbooks in both Arabic and French, a move designed to free the country of dependence on materials from Egypt and France.

At the top of the reformed system now stands the new Tunisian University, organized in 1960. So far it is an administrative unification of the previously existing Institute of Higher Studies, the university program of Az Zeitouna, the Higher Normal School, and other formerly separate institutions. Enrollment in the Institute of Higher Studies in 1959–1960 included 1,084 degree candidates, a fivefold increase since 1952. The scientific bent of young Tunisians was confirmed by the number of those in natural sciences (569 in 1959 as against only 47 in 1952). At present there are still more Tunisians following programs of higher education abroad: approximately 1,500 in France in 1959 and 100 in the Middle East.

The first two years of the reformed system showed steady progress toward its goals. In 1960–1961 roughly 50 per cent of the children of primary school age were receiving instruction. There were 439,341 students in primary schools, 18,022 in intermediate, professional, and technical schools, and 27,274 in secondary schools. The proportion of boys to girls was about two to one. The school enrollment for boys in the towns and villages of northern and coastal Tunisia was almost 100 per cent.

Education costs already absorb 17 per cent of the ordinary budget and are scheduled to increase. In 1968–1969 it is estimated that more than $58,000,000 will be devoted to education; apart from that, $122,000,000 will be needed for the ten-year school construction program. The part being played by foreign aid in this development is important. The United States contributed $7,000,000 through 1961, mostly for the construction and equipment of secondary and agricultural schools, and has earmarked funds for assistance to the Tunisian University.

French participation in the Tunisian educational effort is even more extensive and vital, for France provides a large number of teachers for the country. The French government maintains a Mission Universitaire Culturelle in which 1,500 French nationals teach. The mission is primarily for the resident European minority, but it also instructs some 15,000 Tunisian students. In addition, the Tunisian Ministry of Education employs nearly 1,500 French teachers in its own establishments. To teachers in this category the French government contributes salary and allowances which amount to more than one-third of the base figure. It thus encourages recruitment for Tunisia. It is noteworthy that the number of French teachers in Tunisia (3,000) is greater than that in all the former French colonies in Africa south of the Sahara.[5]

SOCIAL PROBLEMS

The plan for universal education in Tunisia is linked with all aspects of economic development, for it presupposes an economy by 1970 that is capable of absorbing four times as many secondary school graduates as at present. It is further an effort to amalgamate the best of both French and Arab culture, while maintaining fundamentally a modern, secular viewpoint heavily impregnated with the Western spirit. It

[5] About 6,000 French teachers are employed in Morocco, and 3,000 in other parts of the world.

represents also a remarkable experiment in bilingualism which may in the end produce a new neo-Cartesian cultural outlook as the thought processes and value systems of the young are molded under its influence. The position of Tunisia with regard to its own cultural future is significantly different from that of the other Arab states. It reflects a determination to be uniquely itself and the hope of constituting a bridge of understanding between the West and the non-West.

In his efforts to shape a new Tunisia, President Bourguiba has found his greatest obstacle in the religious problem. There is an unresolved paradox in Tunisia today in the fact that the constitution declares the state to be Islamic by religion, but the ethic and atmosphere of the government and the principal leaders are strongly secular. The Tunisian government has promulgated laws which no other Arab state has attempted; in direct contradiction with the Quran it abolished polygamy, thereby earning a scathing attack from the leading religious figures in the state. Lay institutions and religious equality have been established as governing principles. Although not actually agnostic, most of the high personalities in the administration are remarkably detached from religious sentiment.

The same cannot be said of the masses, however, among whom flows a powerful current of Muslim solidarity. Tunisian Islam is not on the whole xenophobic, nor is it as completely withdrawn as are Islamic practices in neighboring states. A moderate Malikism (one of the four orthodox schools of Muslim jurisprudence) prevails, tempered slightly by the Hanafi rite introduced in the cities by upper-class Turkish families during the Regency. But a conservative attachment to Islamic tradition cannot be gainsaid, and the tenaciousness with which the average Tunisian clings to his faith has probably been reinforced by the fact that Islam and its tradition have remained the one sure rock in a sea of change and insecurity.

Although the great majority of Tunisians accepted with equanimity the earlier reforms, including the abolition of polygamy and the *habous,* resistance has crystallized around the issue of the fast during the month of Ramadan. The issue was rather suddenly brought up by President Bourguiba early in 1960 just before the fast was scheduled to begin; economic necessity was invoked as the reason. Pointing out that under Islamic law dispensations from fasting were permitted in time of war, during travel, for reasons of health and age, and under various special circumstances, he stressed that the battle against underdevelopment is a form of peaceful competition more vital than

war itself. In his speech of February 18, 1960, he said: "To the extent
that the fast proves incompatible with work, it is essential to take
advantage of the dispensations. One can then break the fast with a
clear conscience. This is my *fetwa* [a religio-legal opinion traditionally
emitted by doctors of Islamic law]."

Although he cited passages from the Quran and the Tradition in
support of his thesis, Bourguiba also attacked the stodginess of "old
professors" who were not modern enough to understand the critical
economic situation. He appealed to reason and logic in preference to
traditional values: "It behooves everyone to turn toward the Good
through his own efforts without bothering himself with learned references." And the speech clearly showed the secular goals to which at
least Bourguiba himself felt attracted: "In order for Africa to attain
the level of strength, culture, and prosperity of Europe or America,
we must work, and vanquish fear, superstition, and social constraint."

The Tunisian public was unprepared for the onslaught, and its relatively strong reaction led Bourguiba to make a second speech a few
days later. It was in effect a retreat from the blunt stand he had at
first taken. He was not trying to weaken religious belief, he explained,
but merely to ensure that it did not interfere with the national productive effort. Even then Bourguiba was not at all widely followed
when the fasting month began in 1960. He was still less heeded the
following year. The pre-Ramadan campaign of 1961 was not so blatant
as that in 1960, but it was significant that in his speech to a relatively
sophisticated body of cadres in February, 1961, the President was applauded only on those occasions when he disclaimed any intention of
tampering with religious thought or activity. It is still true, nevertheless, that state establishments, schools, and the armed forces continued
to serve meals at normal hours during Ramadan, 1960, thus virtually
forcing their members to break the fast. During the Ramadan month
in 1961, Bourguiba left for a rest cure in Switzerland that was punctu-
ated by a state visit to France. The absence of the President from the
country and the publicity surrounding his reception by President de
Gaulle combined to prevent the issue from becoming acute.

The problem persists, however, in chronic form. Many Tunisians
have failed to understand the need for this kind of policy, unless it
camouflages a more fundamental purpose. Telling criticism has come
from other Muslim-Arab states, notably from the Voice of the Arabs
in Cairo, and it may be that the scar of the Ramadan issue will be the
nucleus for other discontent, to the extent that it develops. In all

events, Ramadan with its social and psychological overtones, its deprivation shared by rich and poor alike, and its day-night alternation of abstinence and carnival seems likely to continue to be a necessary factor in Tunisia for some time, just as it is most probable that Tunisian nationalism will need to be supported by a continuing Islamic content. Without this content, nationalism might well not prove a sufficiently stimulating force during the coming period of hard work and social and economic change.

Upon the question of the degree of religious content in Tunisian society turns minority participation in the new state. There are two principal minority groups in the country, the Jews and the Europeans. Despite certain similarities of occupational behavior and the voluntary acculturation of many Tunisian Jews to a European model, they remain distinct in one important respect: the Jews are citizens and, barring catastrophe, represent a permanent minority, whereas the Europeans are recognized by themselves and the Tunisians to be an essentially transient out-group.

The Jewish minority in Tunisia has a place unrivaled in other Arab states. Tunisia has always been a relatively tolerant society, in which anti-Semitism has been no more rampant than in most Western countries. Since independence it has become almost a point of honor not to question Jewish faith in the Tunisian state. At the same time there is little involvement with the Israeli problem and, conversely, little Zionist sentiment among Tunisian Jews. Since 1956 there has been a Tunisian Jew in the cabinet, as well as a more than proportional representation in higher civil service posts. In this respect the government is somewhat ahead of popular sentiment, which does not always accord the same broad acceptance. Tunisian Jews themselves, admitting that they were strong partisans of the protectorate and cool to the idea of independence, have protected themselves with an indrawn feeling which is perhaps natural to any minority. But it is remarkable that leading Tunisian Muslims have created for their own consumption a myth about Jewish participation in the struggle for independence in order to justify the policy of social homogeneity they insist on practicing.

Now, despite new decrees regulating contact with Israel, Tunisian Jews flourish. They obtain passports without difficulty, mingle freely with Muslims, and practice their religion without hindrance (although Jewish schools sponsored by the Alliance Israelite have been nationalized and secularized). If Tunisia continues along the path of secularization, there should be no further problem for them, but if it turns back toward a new religious conservatism, the integration of this minority will be made that much more difficult.

External Relations

The position of the European minority has generally reflected the state of Tunisian-French relations, and these in turn have been molded by the continuing Algerian revolution on Tunisia's border. This fact has created a schizoid split in the Tunisian personality by placing in opposition two of its basic components: its unusual receptivity to French civilization and thought—a quality which has made Tunisia by far the most Gallicized of Arab states—and the sentiments of Arab solidarity and unity which are felt particularly for Algerians, to whom the Tunisians are more closely tied than to other Arabs. Tunisia's bold effort to combine European and Arab culture has been constantly buffeted by the storms of the Algerian conflict.

The first postindependence difficulties arose in October, 1956, when leaders of the Algerian National Liberation Front (FLN) were kidnaped by French forces on their way to a meeting in Tunis with President Bourguiba and King Muhammad V of Morocco. Demonstrations broke out in Tunis, and relations were strained to the point that Tunisia recalled its ambassador from Paris. Tunisia supported the Algerian rebels openly, allowing them to train, equip themselves, and regroup in the shelter of the Tunisian side of the frontier. This caused widespread French indignation, led to numerous protests, and culminated in a suspension of French economic aid to Tunisia in May, 1957. This aid was not subsequently renewed, although France continues to grant Tunisia certain economic and trade privileges.

Frontier incidents were commonplace in 1956–1957, and one of them brought about an international crisis in February, 1958, when French aircraft bombed the Tunisian border town of Sakiet Sidi Youssef, claiming that it was harboring Algerian troops. Casualties among Tunisian civilians were heavy and the Tunisian reaction was heated. A blockade was imposed on French forces in the country, and incidents occurred in a few areas. Tunisia, however, accepted the Anglo-American Good Offices mission later in February. When the French government did likewise in April, the decision was a factor in the May 13 coup in Algiers which brought down the Fourth Republic. After General de Gaulle came to power, an exchange of letters between him and President Bourguiba established a *modus vivendi*.

French troops evacuated all bases in Tunisia except the Bizerte complex; the Tunisian blockade was ended, and the French withdrew without opposition to Bizerte, whose future was left unsettled. Some French nationals were expelled from frontier governorates during the Sakiet crisis, and the European population declined considerably in 1958. The decision of the Tunisian government later that year to repurchase settler-held land and restrictions on foreign nationals holding many categories of jobs hastened the exodus.

After the troubles of 1958, however, a period of relative calm followed and French cultural influence remained strong. Feeling a kinship of personality to de Gaulle, Bourguiba several times declared that the French President should have a reasonable chance to settle the Algerian question, but he simultaneously underlined the need for a speedy agreement and kept trying to bring both sides together, without, however, appearing to seek the role of formal mediator. The official visit of Bourguiba to France in February, 1961, was the high point in Franco-Tunisian cordiality, and it seemed to augur well for the future. But the informal harmony which had been attained in the conversations at Rambouillet was not built into a working structure, and personal agreement failed to produce practical cooperation. By the early summer of 1961 it appeared that France might reach an agreement with the Algerian rebels, an intransigent group which had attained its goals by open hostility toward Paris, while it seemed that France could not be bothered to settle outstanding issues with Tunisia, which had been following a policy of moderation and patience.

Under these circumstances the Tunisian government felt it could no longer justify restraint in pressing what it believed to be its legitimate demands, for it was worried lest Tunisian public opinion construe reasonableness as passivity. These considerations led Bourguiba to renew the call for the "Battle of Evacuation" and announce the blockade of the Bizerte bases. At the same time he reiterated Tunisia's claim to a share in the Sahara by dispatching an army patrol across the disputed southern frontier between Algeria and Tunisia in an unsuccessful attempt to reach Post 233, some 50 kilometers distant.

Events at Bizerte soon escaped Tunisian control. Tunisian forces fired on French aircraft and impeded communications between isolated parts of the base. In a powerful counterattack, French paratroopers dispersed the blockaders, reestablished contact with all units, and occupied part of the city itself. The Tunisians lost over 1,300 men. The shock of the battle was deeply felt throughout the country. It is possible that cooperation with France can never be undertaken on exactly the same basis as before, for there had never been any comparable bloodshed in Tunisia during the years of largely political and verbal skirmishing which led to independence. An agreement to return to the *status quo ante* was later negotiated, after the United Nations by a vote of 66-0 had condemned France. Following his return from the Belgrade Conference in September, 1961, Bourguiba softened his stand somewhat by not insisting for the moment on total evacuation by France. This was interpreted as a sign of his reservations about the extremist positions adopted by some of the states at the neutralist summit meeting. But the President's position was much criticized in some circles and was largely responsible for the resignation of Mohammed Masmoudi from the Secretariat of State for Information. At the end of 1961 negotiations with France were under way on all outstanding issues: evacuation, trade arrangements, and cultural agreements.

The effects of the Bizerte affair continue to be felt in Tunisia in several ways. Diplomatic relations were broken, the pipeline at Skhira was closed, a number of French settlers known for their rightist sympathies were imprisoned, and contact between the two countries came nearly to a halt for several months. Tunisia, feeling rejected by a hitherto benevolent tutor, began to seek ways of reducing its dependence on France and discovered how closely bound, in fact, the two countries were. The agreement under which France bought certain Tunisian exports at premium prices was not renewed, but trade continued on an *ad hoc* basis. The problem of French teachers was handled in the same way; the Tunisian government indicated that it desired contract teachers to come back, and most have done so. It is estimated that more than two-thirds of the Mission teachers also returned, although Tunisian directors were appointed in Mission schools, all but one of which reopened. But the French Cultural Mission was abandoned at the insistence of Tunisian authorities and replaced by the cultural service attached to the French Consulate in Tunis.

In the complex emotional climate which now rules Franco-Tunisian intercourse it is dangerous to predict the future. But it is unlikely that the problem would have been so agonizing to Tunisians were not so much of their own image of themselves at stake. This indicates the degree to which French culture has permeated the country and has become, at least among a large stratum of Tunisian society, a force coequal with the Arab inheritance. It is this depth of French cultural penetration which in the end would seem to assure that, whatever the political passions of the moment, all that has been built up in the past century will not be summarily abandoned.

With the other Arab countries Tunisia's relations since 1956 have been complicated and troubled. They were distorted from the start by the involvement with France, which made Tunisia suspect in the eyes of many orthodox Pan-Arabs. Apart from Algeria (which was itself part of the triangular relationship encompassing France), Tunisia had most in common with Morocco—a joint heritage of Arab culture, a shared colonial past lived out under the same protectorate system, and a coming of age at the same moment. But these have seemingly not been enough to create an effective working comradeship. There are too many cleavages between the homogeneous, open, republican, and disciplined society of Tunisia and the diversified, withdrawn, autocratic atmosphere of Morocco.

The vicissitudes of the Algerian war and the threat it posed to all three countries of the Maghrib, however, led to the forging of a common policy on paper. The Tangier Conference of April, 1958, postulated the concept of a unified North Africa, and the Tunisian constitution makes specific reference to this idea. It is the expression of a vague but strong popular desire for unity and strength through some kind of cooperation which has not yet been thought out in detail. But prospects in recent years have become more elusive while the social structures and the character of each state have grown more disparate. Particularly since the carrying out of its personal and social reforms, Tunisia is vastly different from Morocco in these respects, and in many other ways the two countries are growing still further apart with each passing year.

Relations with Morocco became tense after Morocco failed to support Tunisia in the latter's quarrel with Egypt at the Arab League meeting in October, 1958. In 1960 they came almost to the breaking point when Tunisia cosponsored Mauritania for admission to the United Nations and became the only Arab country to recognize the new state, whose territory Morocco claimed as part of its own. The Moroccan ambassador left Tunis, and violent attacks were made by the Moroccan press and state radio on Tunisia. These were stilled for a time after the funeral of Muhammad V early in 1961, but subsequently they increased again.

Relations with the Algerian nationalists have been cordial on the whole, and Tunisia has sacrificed much for its neighbor. But there have been periods of tension, notably in the summer of 1958 when Tunisia allowed the oil pipeline from Edjele to pass through its territory and was accused by the Algerians of profiting in collusion with France from the natural wealth belonging to the Algerian people. Underneath this sort of quarrel, and that over Saharan boundaries, is a deep division in the philosophies of the two governments. The self-reliant, harsh Algerian leadership distrusts the moderation and elasticity of Tunisian tactics and does not share the generally friendly feelings shown by Tunisia to the West and its ideals. In this regard the Algerians reflect not only the bitterness which their revolution has engendered but more underlying differences in the historical personality of the two countries.

As long as the Algerian war continues, there is little prospect for real stability in inter-Maghribian or Franco-North African relations. Even afterward, the pressures of a socially restless and dynamic Algeria will continue to be felt in Tunisia. The unity of the Maghrib remains an ideal goal, but the realities of the day—different social composition, different rates and paths of socioeconomic progress, incompatible political institutions and habits, and the hardening of innumerable interests into distinct patterns—stand in the way. If Arab history is any lesson, the Maghrib may well repeat the story of the chimera of unity in the Arab Middle East, vociferously but vainly pursued for several decades.

Considering itself the foremost intellectual center of the Arab West, Tunisia has always shown a reserve in its dealings with the Middle East. To Tunisians, the Arab East has not compiled an impressive political record, and the social program of the neo-Destour was inspired exclusively by Western sources. Thus Tunisia thinks itself more progressive and further emancipated than many brother countries in the East who preceded it to independence by as much as a generation.

To these deep-rooted feelings was added a political distrust of Egypt and the policies of the Nasserite regime. This distrust accounted for the long Tunisian delay in joining the Arab League; it did so in September, 1958, only when forced to because of Morocco's decision to adhere. Tunisia left the League almost immediately, however, when the organization refused to consider its complaint against the United Arab Republic for alleged interference in Tunisian internal affairs. Tunisia abstained from all League activity until February, 1961, when it was persuaded to return, partly at the behest of other Arab states seeking a counterbalance to the predominance of the

United Arab Republic and partly because Tunisia itself feared too great a political isolation in the Afro-Arab world, after it had not been invited to the Casablanca Conference in January. Since then it has perfunctorily participated but is perhaps the least engaged of all Arab states in inter-Arab activities. Relations with Egypt, broken in 1958, were resumed in 1961 and have improved considerably on the surface, especially after the Bizerte crisis when Tunisia sought moral support from all possible sources.

If Arabism has at times appeared to be of secondary importance in the Tunisian scheme of international ties, African relations so far have been tertiary. The individual Tunisian still thinks of himself first as a Tunisian (with overtones of being a Muslim depending largely on class), then as an Arab, and only incidentally as an African.

Africanism is quite new. Africa first entered the Tunisian political horizon in 1957 when President Bourguiba went to Accra to take part in Ghana's independence ceremonies. In April, 1958, Tunisia was one of eight independent African countries taking part in the Accra Conference, and in August, 1959, it was present at the Monrovia meeting of African states. About this time a new impetus to Africanism was given by the deteriorating state of its relations with most other Arab countries. A deep impression was made on Tunisian minds when the African People's Congress met in Tunis in January, 1960—significantly no similar Arab group had convened on Tunisian soil. When the United Nations asked African countries to contribute military contingents for service in the Congo in July, 1960, Tunisia responded generously, and it has continued to be a firm supporter of United Nations policies there as elsewhere at all times. The Tunisian force was withdrawn only because it was needed in the country in the Bizerte crisis, but at the end of 1961 a new, smaller force was sent to bolster the international army in the Congo.

Although excluded from the Casablanca group, Tunisia has had good relations with the more moderate African states, notably Nigeria, Togo, Cameroun, and the members of the French Community. Its policy concerning Africa is not excessively ambitious or aggressive, something which gives Tunisia an advantage compared to Morocco or Egypt, both of them regarded somewhat suspiciously because of their past or present territorial ambitions. Plans have been made for an African Research Institute, and elaborate efforts have been undertaken to bring government and student leaders, congresses, youth groups, and trade unionists to Tunis. Many Tunisians think their country can best serve as a culture carrier, transmitter, and interpreter between Europe, primarily France, and Africa. Africanism is strongest among the elite and the student group, but those who believe in it are voluble and dedicated. Some dampening of African solidarity resulted from the Tunisian army's experience in the Congo, where many officers felt a wide gap between the Congolese and themselves and resented the imputation that those who were not black could not be Africans. But, on the whole, the physical atmosphere of sobriety and accomplishment and the example of an efficient, purposeful society in Tunisia have made an impact on thoughtful visiting Africans, as has the spectacle of a Mediterranean Africa, whose orange groves and blue seas proved to be as much of a psychological attraction to visitors from south of the Sahara as the winter sun to Europeans. It is too early to say how far the budding relationship may grow, but under the right conditions Tunisia could become an important factor in coming years as a meeting place for Africans, a way station between cultures, and a window of African intellectual life looking out onto Europe.

In the past few years the United States has developed an increasingly important relationship with Tunisia. Before Tunisian independence America existed in Tunisian minds in an ideal and remote way; since then it has continued to enjoy a place of honor, and the ideal has not been tarnished by any direct act contrary to Tunisian interests or aspirations. Moreover, a general good will toward America is apparent at all levels of Tunisian society, from the political leadership on through ordinary Tunisians everywhere. This band of popular acceptance of the United States is wider than in any other Arab country. There have been disappointments and irritations on both sides as practical relations came into being—and President Bourguiba has never stopped prodding the United States for what he considered its vacillation in taking a stand in favor of Algerian independence—but these have never undermined the over-all sentiment of mutual respect and confidence which has governed relations between the two countries.

The first contact of note was the highly successful visit of Vice-President Nixon in March, 1957. This was followed by the establishment of a United States Operation Mission under the terms of a bilateral agreement signed in March of the same year. Late in 1957, Tunisians were pleased at the joint decision of the British and American governments to sell them a quantity of small arms after France had refused to supply them. Likewise the Good Offices mission sponsored by the United States and the United Kingdom after the Sakiet incident was received with approval in Tunisia. In December, 1959, President Eisenhower was specially requested to stop briefly in Tunisia on his return from South Asia, although his plans had not originally called for a halt in the country. He received a remarkable welcome, which was returned when President Bourguiba visited the United States in May, 1961, as the first head of state to be received in Washington by President Kennedy. Even more notable was the fact that Bourguiba is the only Arab head of state who has made a wholly favorable impression on all sectors of American public opinion; the warmth of the civic reception accorded him in New York was testimony to that. Some of this stems from an appreciation of the Tunisian application of principle to international relations that led Bourguiba to denounce the Soviet Union at the time of the Hungarian revolt in the same terms he used against the Anglo-French-Israeli attack on Egypt. But part of it also stems from an American understanding that Tunisia is less pro-America than it is pro-Tunisia, in the best sense of holding fast to its own principles and its own integrity.

Economic cooperation between the two countries has grown in scope in the past four years. The amount of economic aid furnished by the United States rose from $16,000,000 in 1957 to $25,100,000 in 1958, $31,400,000 in 1959, and $34,400,000 in 1960. Currently it is running at around $40,000,000 a year. Included in these sums are special assistance, technical cooperation, the Development Loan Fund, and Public Law 480 surplus agricultural products which have been used to fight underdevelopment, to supply Algerian refugees, and to feed children. Special assistance funds have been used to finance key commodity imports for Tunisia such as sugar and petroleum. The Tunisian government deposits local currency in amounts equal to the sums involved in a counterpart account which has been used in a variety of projects including reforestation, drainage and irrigation, soil conservation, construction of agricultural schools, improvement of water supply, provision of electric power, road and bridge construction, the establishment of a Revolving Loan Fund for new industries and a Special Revolving Agricultural Fund to make loans to farmers, and so on.

American participation in the development of the Tunisian economy may be much greater in the near future. Under its ten-year development plan in preparation late in 1961, Tunisia will require a commitment of foreign capital approximately twice the amount now furnished by the United States, and American studies are under way to determine the advisability of investing some $800,000,000 in a program aimed at making Tunisia a pilot state for self-development. The clarity of problems in Tunisia, their relatively small and manageable scope, and the good progress already made by efficient use of existing skills and moderate external aid suggest that such a program might produce results beneficial not only to Tunisia itself but to other countries as well.

Unlike many other African states, Tunisia is both a very old and a new country. Drawing on the resources of its prestigious past civilizations and its talented population, it is trying to make up for its shortage of material blessings. Tunisian aspirations recognize that there are physical limitations in the future; the Bourguibist doctrine of a "respectable position among respectable countries" is an indication of this and a sign of the restrained reasonableness inherent in Tunisian thought. The country seems destined, one way or another, to play a more intellectual than material role in the near future, a role heightened by its favorable geographical position through which it participates in three different culture areas.

The problems of building the new Tunisia are in reality those of distilling elements from each such area and combining them smoothly. The new identity being sought may, like a new chemical compound, be quite unlike the original elements which have gone into the formula. It is possible that a purely Tunisian nationalism is in the process of giving way to a more transcendental idea, of which the internationalist viewpoint is only one expression. If Tunisia, buttressed by the empirical, progressive, and tolerant qualities which have long distinguished it, and tempered by a moderate, modernized concept of Islam, can accommodate its religious heritage to the secular synthesis of Western and Arab culture which it is trying to forge, and radiate this in any way to its neighbors, it will have performed a unique and noble service.

A SELECTED BIBLIOGRAPHY

BIBLIOGRAPHIES

Ashbee, H. S. *A Bibliography of Tunisia*. London: Royal Geographical Society, 1889. A detailed bibliography of everything from the earliest times through 1888.

Romeril, Paul E. A. "Tunisian Nationalism: A Bibliographical Outline,"

Middle East Journal (Spring, 1960), pp. 206–215. The most important single bibliography dealing with all aspects of Tunisian political and social development in the past century.

In addition, there are useful critical bibliographies in C.-A. Julien, *L'Afrique du Nord en Marche: Nationalismes Musulmans et Souveraineté Française* (Paris: Juillard, 1953), and in C.-A. Julien, *L'Histoire de l'Afrique du Nord* (2d ed., rev. by Ch. Courtois and Roger Le Tourneau; Paris: Payot, 1956). The bibliography appended to the latter work provides the most comprehensive general coverage to be found.

GENERAL WORKS

Barbour, N., ed. *A Survey of North West Africa (The Maghrib).* London: Royal Institute of International Affairs, 1959. The best general reference work for all of North Africa, including Morocco, Algeria, Tunisia, Libya, Mauritania, and the Sahara. The chapter on Tunisia (pp. 288–340) covers all important happenings in that country through late 1958.

Basset, A., *et al. Initiation à la Tunisie.* Paris: Adrien-Maisonneuve, 1950. Compiled by a group of French scholars as a basic reference work. It contains a summary bibliography.

Despois, Jean. *La Tunisie Orientale; Sahel et Basse Steppe; Etude Geographique.* 2d ed. Algiers: Faculté des Lettres, 1955. The best geographical study of the cultural heartland of Tunisia.

Gautier, E. F. *Le Passé de l'Afrique du Nord.* Paris: Payot, 1952. A study illuminated with daring, subjective, but sometimes brilliant hypothesizing about North African history and its underlying currents, by an outstanding French geographer.

Julien, C.-A. *L'Histoire de l'Afrique du Nord: Tunisie, Algérie, Maroc.* 2d ed. rev. Paris: Payot, 1956. The indispensable historical work for the North African area, even though it covers only the period leading up to the French conquest of Algeria in 1830.

Laitman, Leon. *Tunisia Today.* New York: Citadel Press, 1954. A now dated work useful mainly for a description of Tunisia just prior to independence.

Raymond, A. *La Tunisie.* Paris, 1961. The most recent worth-while study of Tunisian accomplishments and problems.

Sebag, Paul. *La Tunisie.* Paris: Eds. Sociales, 1951. A serious study by Tunisian society and economy by a French leftist who presents a point of view not found among more orthodox scholars.

Tlatli, Salah Eddine. *Tunisie Nouvelle: Problèmes et Perspectives.* Tunis: Sefan, 1957. A well-written and comprehensive study of independent Tunisia by a writer sympathetic to the new regime.

SPECIAL WORKS

Al-Fassi, Allal. *Al-Harakat al-Istiqlaliya fi'l Maghrib al-'Arabi.* Cairo, 1948. Trans. into English by H. Z. Nuseibeh as *The Independence Movements in Arab North Africa* (Washington: Amer. Council of Learned Societies, 1954). An important work on North African nationalist movements from the viewpoint of a participating Arab nationalist.

Bourguiba, Habib. *La Tunisie et la France: Vingt-cinq Ans de Lutte pour une Coopération Libre.* Paris: Juillard, 1954. Gives many insights into the thinking of the founder of the Tunisian nation.

Garas, Felix. *Bourguiba et la Naissance d'une Nation.* Paris: Juillard, 1956. Discusses the nationalist movement and paints a favorable picture of its leader.

Hahn, Lorna. *North Africa: Nationalism to Nationhood.* Washington: Public Affairs Press, 1960. Gives a broad survey but is not free of errors.

Julien, C.-A. *L'Afrique du Nord en Marche.* Paris: Juillard, 1953. The best and fullest account of the nationalist movements in all the North African states.

Two recent portraits of Tunisia and Bourguiba by outstanding journalists are found in R. Stephane, *La Tunisie de Bourguiba: Sept Entretiens avec le Président de la République Tunisienne* (Paris: Plon, 1958), and J. Lacouture, *Cinq Hommes et la France* (Paris: Eds. du Seuil, 1961). In the latter, a section is devoted to Bourguiba (along with Muhammad V, Sékou Touré, Ferhat Abbas, and Ho Chi-Minh) as one of the five men who have successfully struggled against French colonialism.

The best socioeconomic study of modern Tunisia is a small work by G. Ardant, *La Tunisie d'Aujourd'hui et de Demain* (Paris: Calmann-Levy, 1961). A detailed statistical study can be found in J. Vibert, *L'Economie Tunisienne à la Fin de 1955* (Notes et Etudes Documentaires, Tunis, 1956).

The Tunisian Secretariat of State for Information has published a great number of volumes—some of them the equivalent of full-sized books, others pamphlets—dealing with almost all aspects of Tunisian activity. Among the most useful are *Tunisia* (in English; Tunis: S.S.I., 1957); *La Tunisie au Travail* (Tunis: S.S.I., 1960), and *Les Congrès du néo-Destour* (Tunis: S.S.I., 1959). The Secretariat of State for National Education has published its outline for educational reform as *Nouvelle Conception de l'Enseignement en Tunisie* (Tunis, 1958–1959). A complete file of the speeches (usually weekly) of President Bourguiba has also been published, and collections have been made of some of the more important ones.

PERIODICALS AND REVIEWS

The *Middle East Journal* is the most important scholarly review written in English. It has printed many useful articles on Tunisia, and its trimestrial chronology by country is especially valuable. IBLA (Institut des Belles Lettres Arabes) publishes a quarterly periodical in Tunis of great usefulness. Among French periodicals, *Cahiers Nord-Africains* (bimonthly) is noteworthy; it published a special issue entitled *Visages de la Tunisie, 1960.* Also important are *L'Afrique et l'Asie, Les Temps Modernes,* and the liberal Paris weekly, *L'Express.* The Tunisian weekly *Jeune Afrique* is a publication of high quality dealing with political events in Tunisia, the Arab world, and Africa.

Among the dailies, the reputable Paris newspaper *Le Monde* consistently carries the most complete information on Tunisia. In Tunis there are several French and Arabic language newspapers: *Al-'Amal* (Destourian), *As-Sabah,* and *La Dépêche Tunisienne* are the most widely read. The *New York Times* and the *Christian Science Monitor* normally maintain good coverage of Tunisia, as does the reports service, without fixed date, of the American Universities Field Staff.

III

SENEGAL

By ERNEST MILCENT

AFRIQUE NOUVELLE, *Dakar*

Translation by Anne-Marie Foltz *

Historical Background

The name Senegal was originally given to the river which descends from the mountains of Guinea—the Fouta Djallon—flows in a great circle to the northwest, and then empties into the Atlantic Ocean 150 miles north of the present city of Dakar. Later, the river gave its name to the country of Senegal, which is now an independent republic after having been a French colony for more than a century.[1]

Little is known of the history of Senegal prior to the seventeenth century. Until archaeologists uncover more information, there are only tales, legends, genealogies, and the names of a few battles. At most, one can trace for certain only the north-south migrations of the Berbers or "white people" of the desert and a series of confused east-west migrations of the Negroid or Hamitic populations who came originally either from the Soudan or from the Fouta Djallon. Among the people who early established themselves in Senegal were the Tukulor, a Negroid people and a branch of the great Fulani family who settled in the Senegal River Valley. Their kingdom of Tekrur dominated much of the territory of present-day Senegal from the tenth to the

* Mr. Milcent wishes to express his appreciation for Mrs. Foltz's assistance in preparing this section for American publication.

[1] It should be noted that Senegal does not fit exactly under the title of one-party state.

fourteenth centuries. The Tukulor were the first of the Negroid tribes
to be Islamized, and their spiritual leaders today play a great role in
the religious life of Senegal.

During the fourteenth century the Mandingo or Mali Empire, under
the Islamized Keita dynasty, expanded far to the west, governed
Tekrur, and controlled the Senegal and Gambia rivers. The Mandingo
expansion forced the Serer, a non-Islamic people, into the area around
present-day Kaolack, where they live today. In the middle of the fif-
teenth century all the land between the Senegal River and the Cape
Verde Peninsula was consolidated by N'Diadiane N'Diaye into the
Djoloff Empire. This empire gave a unity of language, customs, and
manners to the people it governed, the Wolof. The Bour was the supreme chief of the Empire, which was divided into three autonomous
provinces, Walo, Cayor, and Baol. About one hundred years later
Cayor broke away from Djoloff, and Baol followed suit shortly after;
thus large-scale tribal organization on Senegalese soil was brought to
an end.

THE COMING OF THE FRENCH

The first European to reach the coast of Senegal was the Venetian
Ca da Mosto. Sailing under a Portuguese flag, he arrived at Cape
Verde in 1444. Eleven years later a Portuguese seaman, Diego Gomez,
sailed up the Gambia River which, like the Senegal River, was considered at that time a branch of the Niger River delta. Soon after, the
English, the Dutch, and the French followed along the route pioneered
by the Portuguese.

Among the explorers, it was the French who made the most systematic efforts to establish footholds along this part of the coast,
thereby laying the foundation for their future West African colonial
empire. In 1659, Louis Caullier, a French trader, built Fort St-Louis
(named in honor of his king) on the island of N'Dar in the Senegal
River. This fort was the origin of the city of St-Louis, and it was from
there that the French were to set out on their conquest of the hinterland.

In 1677, the French defeated the Dutch in a naval battle and occupied the island of Gorée (off Dakar). By this means French trading
companies gained the right to trade with the posts of Rufisque, Portu-
dal, and Joal on the coast south of Cape Verde. Two years later Ger-
main Ducasse, a special envoy of the King of France, signed treaties
with the Serer and with the Damal of Cayor which brought the Sene-

galese coast from Cape Verde to the Gambia River, as well as six leagues into the interior, under a French sphere of influence.

The first attempt at European penetration into the interior was not made until the following century and then without much effect. André Bruë, a farsighted Governor, tried to convince the traders on the coast of the advantages for their commerce of controlling the hinterland. He traveled up the Senegal River as far as the mouth of the Falémé River, thus indicating the way for later expeditions to the Soudan. But despite his efforts André Bruë received no support for his ideas. The local traders, attached to their traditional ways, were distrustful of his plans, and France itself had lost interest in Senegal. In any case the resurgence of the war with England put an end to any plans for expansion into the interior.

Not until 1815 and the Treaty of Vienna, by which France regained its Senegalese possessions, did it renew its interest in them. Although the first two governors had plans to promote the extension of French influence, they had scarcely more success than had their pre-1789 predecessors. Local traders continued to distrust attempts to develop a commercial agricultural system and were content with their trade of spices, gum arabic, and other local products. Made wary by their predecessors' failures, the governors that followed—there were 27 in 23 years—tried only to keep their jobs by reconciling as well as possible their "native policy" with the interests of the traders and forgoing any long-range projects. During this period, however, the peanut, which became the basis of Senegal's economy, was introduced. By 1842 Gorée was exporting 853 tons a year of the precious product, with its rich oil content, and in 1850 Senegal produced as much as 5,000 tons.

In the middle of the nineteenth century France, through the efforts of a few vigorous and farsighted men, moved to control the hinterland and thus to consolidate its Senegalese possessions. Outstanding among these men was Louis Faidherbe, who is considered the father of modern Senegal. Soon after his arrival in St-Louis in 1854 Faidherbe set out on a series of military actions to unite the country. His task was made easier by the lack of organized opposition from rival tribal groups. In a few years Faidherbe conquered the valley of the Senegal and Falémé rivers and controlled the coast from Portandick to south of Dakar. He opened a road from Dakar to St-Louis and also developed other roads leading to the Baol, Rip, and Casamance regions. All that remained for Faidherbe's successors to do was to encircle the

Ferlo Desert and to bring the native tribes of that area under French administration.

Faidherbe's role went far beyond that of a mere conqueror. He organized the country's administration and gave it a capital, means of communication, and, most of all, a sense of purpose. Trade profited particularly from his work and from 1848 to 1869 rose in value from 12,000,000 to 37,000,000 francs per year.

Faidherbe created three *arrondissements* in Senegal: St-Louis, Gorée, and Bakel. Then in 1863 he divided the *arrondissements* into smaller units, *cercles.* At the head of each *cercle,* he placed a *commandant* who represented the Governor and exercised local administrative power. Today Senegal is independent. The *commandant de cercle* is now an African, but the organization Faidherbe created remains virtually unchanged. Faidherbe also created schools and improved the judicial system, and in 1857 he formed the first battalion of African troops, the Tirailleurs Sénégalais.

Perhaps most significant of all for the future was Faidherbe's definition of the role of the French in Senegal, a role which was to be quite different from their role in Algeria. In Senegal there was to be no agricultural colonization. The French were to provide technicians, civil servants, and traders, but not planters. A ministerial circular sent around in 1859 [2] made this concept government policy by stating that all land was to be left in the hands of the local inhabitants.

Events moved swiftly thereafter. By 1882 the pacification of the country was sufficiently advanced to permit the appointment of the first civil Governor at St-Louis. In 1895 the colony of Senegal was officially founded with the country's present boundaries. The problem of the relation of Senegal to British penetration along the Gambia River, which had begun almost as early as France's activities along the coast, was settled by an acceptance of British control of the 300-mile navigable section of the Gambia River. Expansion into the interior was creating France's West African empire. Finally, on June 6, 1895, the work of consolidation was crowned when the government-general of French West Africa was established in St-Louis and the Governor of Senegal became its first chief. Thus began the history of modern Senegal, a country which would slowly develop its own characteristic political life and start off at first timidly, then more and more quickly on the road to independence.

[2] André Villard, *Histoire du Sénégal* (Dakar: Maurice Viale, 1943), p. 132.

FRENCH COLONIAL RULE

Senegalese political life began with the extension of French municipal law to Senegal in 1872. Two communes (self-governing municipalities) were created: St-Louis and Dakar-Gorée. A little later,
in 1880, Rufisque was in turn given the same status, and finally, in
1887, Dakar, whose economic importance had continued to grow, was
separated from Gorée. Thus were established the "four old communes"
of Senegal which were to be the only self-governing French West
African municipalities for more than half a century.

The inhabitants of these communes, the *originaires* as they were
called, received a special status. Whereas all the other inhabitants of
the French colonies in Africa were "French subjects," the inhabitants
of these communes were citizens. They elected their own municipal
governments which had the same rights as municipal governments in
France. They also sent a deputy to the French Parliament and representatives to a General Council which legislated on problems involving the four communes.

The Naval Minister, Vice-Admiral Pothau, in a report which foresaw
the creation of this Council wrote that "the experiment that has been
made has led me to believe that even if the people of Senegal do not
yet completely appreciate the advantages of the commune, they have
nevertheless shown a real aptitude for the management of local affairs." [3] Their status reflected the final goal of colonial policy, the
policy of assimilation. Its purpose was to transform slowly the Senegalese into Frenchmen with the same rights and duties as a Frenchman of Lyons or Marseilles.

The civil servants, who were given the task of implementing this
policy in the field, quickly perceived its difficulties and took great
liberties with the directives received from Paris. For them, the purpose of assimilation was to permit a more complete domination of the
country. Thus it is that an official report on municipal reform frankly
states that "the affairs of Cayor and the Senegal River Valley have
shown that native chiefs are difficult to control in the framework of
their local life. Thus, the Franco-Senegalese, absolutely subject to
French law, will be better disciplined and easier to control in body
and soul." [4]

To arrive at their goal of assimilation, the French encouraged the

[3] Villard, *Histoire du Sénégal*, p. 157.   [4] *Ibid.*, p. 152.

development of education. In 1903 there were only twenty-three bush
schools, but their number rapidly increased. A normal school was
founded on Gorée, where it remained for a long time before being
transferred to Sébikotane. In 1910 Governor William Ponty created
the first African secondary school at St-Louis. The school received
boys from all the French territories of Black Africa and became the
most significant training ground for technicians and civil servants.
Today, it is still true that many of the leaders of the French-speaking
states of West Africa are graduates of the William Ponty school.

The French West African Federation, of which Senegal was a
constituent part, was created, as already noted, at the end of the
nineteenth century. The Governor General was installed first in St-
Louis and then after 1902 in Dakar. For this reason his influence on
the life and evolution of Senegal was greater than in the rest of
French West Africa. Moreover, the special status that had been given
to Senegal after the war of 1870 was retained and to a certain degree
independent political life continued there, while it was severely re-
pressed in the other colonies.

Significant in this regard is the fact that in 1914, for the first time,
a black African from Dakar, Blaise Diagne, was elected as deputy to
the French Parliament. Diagne was to maintain this post until his
death in 1934. He rapidly acquired a sizable influence in the French
Parliament, so much so that when, in World War I, France called
for more African troops, Diagne was named in 1916 high commissioner
for the recruiting. Soon, 93,000 Tirailleurs Sénégalais were sent to
join the 110,000 Africans already fighting at the front. In fact, so heavy
was French West Africa's contribution that the French Governor
General, Van Vollenhoven, finally refused to send any more troops to
the front. He even asked to be allowed to go on service himself and
was killed at the front shortly after.

Blaise Diagne obtained some return for the contribution of his
country to the French war effort through the introduction of liberalizing legislation that defined and extended the citizenship rights of the
inhabitants of the four communes. In exchange for compulsory military service, the Law of 1916, called the Diagne Law, stated that "the
natives of the self-governing municipalities and their descendants are
and will remain French citizens." This law did not resolve the problem
of their civil status, however, which was not settled until 1932 when
a decree limited the jurisdiction of the Muslim courts to questions of
personal law.

In 1919 Blaise Diagne was reelected to Parliament, and a short time later he became Undersecretary of State for the Colonies in the French government and thus the first African to hold a ministerial post. Diagne represented only a small part of Senegal, however, that is, the inhabitants of the four communes. In 1936 a Senegalese census listed only 78,000 citizens out of a total population of 1,800,000.

In response to this state of affairs but also in order to limit the power of the four communes, which restricted the colonial government's authority, the General Council was completely re-formed. Where hitherto this body had possessed powers identical to those of a General Council in a French department, it now became a Colonial Council into which representatives from the interior were admitted for the first time. Elected representatives of the communes received twenty seats in the new Council, and the representatives of the chiefs an equal number. At the same time the Senegalese budget was unified, and thereby the distinction between the areas of direct French rule and the protectorate areas was eliminated.

No other significant administrative changes were introduced in Senegal before World War II; in 1937, however, the Popular Front government of Léon Blum extended to all French subjects the right to join labor unions but with the restrictive condition that they must possess a primary school certificate, something rare among Africans at that time. Nevertheless, this measure led in 1937 to the first important strike in Senegal when the railroad workers in Thiès struck for increased wages.

The outbreak of World War II brought up again the problem of recruiting West African troops. The situation differed greatly, however, from that of twenty-five years earlier. Senegal became far more deeply involved in world affairs than had previously been the case. Despite various vicissitudes the impact of the war directly accelerated Senegal's political evolution.

In June, 1940, France was defeated and the "territories of the Empire" had to make the difficult choice between de Gaulle and Pétain. This choice was made by the governors as individuals, however, without consulting the people. While French Equatorial Africa quickly rallied to de Gaulle, the Governor General of French West Africa, Pierre Boisson, adhered to the Vichy government, and Senegal had to submit to his decision. The consequences were immediate and violent. On September 23, 1940, a British fleet appeared off Dakar. A tender brought in General de Gaulle who tried, though in vain, to

convince Boisson to rally to the side of Free France. Thereafter, a
naval battle ensued between the British fleet and a small French
flotilla which had come down from Toulon. Dakar was heavily bom-
barded; this caused a mass exodus of the population, as well as considerable material damage. The fighting lasted for two days, after
which Prime Minister Winston Churchill personally ordered the end
of a battle which in any case could not have had a decisive outcome.

Senegal thus remained within the orbit of Vichy, a circumstance
which was to cause it grave economic difficulties, because of the
Allies' naval blockade. At the same time, the last traces of political
liberty were slowly suppressed. Galandou Diouf, who had replaced
Blaise Diagne in 1934 as deputy from Senegal, died in 1942 and was
not replaced. In any case the French Chamber of Deputies had been
"sent on vacation" in 1940 by Pétain. In Senegal itself various political
councils continued to exist in theory, but they no longer met.

This situation finally ended on November 22, 1942, when the Allies
landed in North Africa and French West Africa rallied to General
de Gaulle. All the measures taken by the Vichy government were
abolished, and Senegal returned to its prewar status. The economic
situation continued to deteriorate until 1944, however, since the war
required more and more men and raw materials.

The year 1944 marked the beginning of a new political period. On
January 30 of that year, all the governors of the French colonies met
in Brazzaville. For all intents and purposes, the war was over, and
the government of General de Gaulle thought it necessary to re-
consider the status of French overseas possessions and even to consider the end of colonial rule. But the officials who met at Brazzaville
remained constant to the traditional line of French thought, and none
of them could envisage an end to colonization that would be other
than complete assimilation.

In opening the Brazzaville Conference, René Pleven, then commissioner for the colonies in the de Gaulle government, declared: "In
Greater France there are no people to liberate, nor is there any racial
discrimination to abolish. There are populations whom we intend to
lead step by step to a more complete individuality, to political freedom, but they will know no other independence than the independence of France." Any idea of separation and self-government, even at
long range, was thus set aside.

Such words sound timid today, but at the time they struck a chord
in all French Africa. When the colonial peoples heard General de

Gaulle affirm at the same Brazzaville Conference, "We are certain that there will be no progress if the peoples who live on their native land cannot profit from it both materially and morally, if this development does not bring them more closely associated with the direction of their own affairs," they concluded, quite legitimately, that they would no longer be treated simply as subjects and that their colonial status was not eternal. Thus new ideas of change matched impending political reforms.

The first formal indication of change came in August, 1945, when the French government called on the colonies to participate in the Constitutional Assembly which was to draw up the new institutions of France and its territories. Their participation, in fact, was very modest. While metropolitan France had 600 deputies for its 40,000,000 inhabitants, French West Africa received only 6 representatives for its 18,000,000 people. What was significant, however, was that for the first time since the beginning of the colonial regime French Africans could participate through their own elected representatives in the elaboration of institutions which would direct their life.

A little later, the Constitutional Assembly drew the logical conclusion from this decision by unanimously voting a law of citizenship by which all inhabitants in the French colonies received the status of citizens of the French Union as of June 1, 1946. The news spread through French West Africa like wildfire. Immediately, workmen toiling at forced labor left their work since "they were citizens." Peasants refused to obey their chiefs. Mass demonstrations of joy were organized everywhere. Lamine Guèye, the sponsor of the law, received hundreds of letters of thanks, many suggesting that June 1 be henceforth a holiday known as "the celebration of the French Union."

In Senegal, as in the other French African territories, the first elections took place on October 21 and November 4, 1945. Two seats in the Constituent Assembly were allotted to Senegal, and the two candidates presented by the local section of the French Socialist Party (SFIO) were elected. One of these men, Lamine Guèye, was already an experienced politician (in 1934 and 1936 he had been a candidate for Parliament); the other, Léopold Sédar Senghor, a professor in France, was still unknown. Both men soon played an important role in the French Parliament of the Fourth Republic and contributed greatly to the texts defining the new status of the colonies.

This status was, in fact, a compromise between the assimilationist tendencies of some members of Parliament and the federalist tendencies of others. The new constitution grouped France and its overseas dependencies in the French Union. Each colony, and thus also Senegal, became an overseas territory represented in the French Parliament which now possessed the legislative power formerly exercised by the Colonial Minister. Immediately less important but in the long run most significant was that each territory was given a territorial assembly; its functions were at first limited, however, to local financial and administrative matters. Finally, the territories of French West Africa remained within a regional federation administered by a High Commissioner, who was advised but not directed by the Grand Council, members of which represented the territorial assemblies.

These new institutions were put into effect in 1946. In Senegal they resulted in another success for the SFIO, which captured the majority of the seats in the territorial assembly. Thus Lamine Guèye was elected its president. A few months later Lamine Guèye, now deputy in the French National Assembly and president of the Senegalese assembly, was also elected president of the Grand Council of French West Africa. Meanwhile, he had been a Secretary of State for several weeks in Léon Blum's ephemeral cabinet.

The speed of this political progress temporarily satisfied everyone. French prestige in Senegal had never been higher. Speaking in Rufisque on December 29, 1946, Lamine Guèye exclaimed: "We can do everything with France, everything with the Republic, nothing without France, nothing without the Republic."

This euphoria was short-lived. At the end of 1946, a number of African deputies, disappointed with the indifference of metropolitan parties toward their problems, decided for the first time to create a party for themselves, the RDA (Rassemblement Démocratique Africain). This new party, which was at first allied with the French Communist Party, saw itself as a large movement "which would be an expression of the masses and at the same time the masses themselves."

RISE AND CHARACTER OF THE SENEGALESE
NATIONALIST MOVEMENT

Senegal remained outside the current of the RDA. The assimilation policy had affected it more than the other French colonies. The four old communes had had opportunities not available elsewhere, and Senegal's political evolution had followed a distinctive course. Tempers did not, moreover, rise as easily there as elsewhere. Nonetheless, on the parliamentary level, certain African representatives, particularly Léopold Senghor, felt uncomfortable within the framework of the French Socialist Party, the SFIO. They had the impression that their French colleagues were losing interest in Africa's problems. On the local level, the SFIO was an urban party representing the interests of the African bourgeoisie. Furthermore, Lamine Guèye, the experienced and much-honored politician, tended to regard his colleague, Senghor, as a "brilliant second."

At the congress of the Senegalese section of the SFIO held in Kaolack in 1947, this uneasiness came to light. While the directors of the party announced their intention of maintaining a strongly centralized local organization, Senghor, supported by a minority of delegates, pronounced himself in favor of a decentralization which would permit the different geographic, economic, and ethnic regions of Senegal to have a more effective representation. This proposal was defeated, but Senghor received permission to found a newspaper, *Condition Humaine,* which would be independent of the SFIO newspaper and in which he could set forth his own ideas.

This ambiguous situation lasted only a few months. In October, 1948, Senghor decided to try his chances alone. He resigned from the SFIO "whose sole aim in Senegal," he declared, "is to establish the personal power of Lamine Guèye"[5] and in France defended only its electoral interests without thinking about the needs of the African territories. He immediately founded a new party, the Bloc Démocratique Sénégalais (BDS), which did not ally itself with any metropolitan party.

The BDS, however, could not remain completely isolated. Senghor thought of fusing it with the RDA of Félix Houphouët-Boigny, but at the time this party was allied to the French Communist Party and he feared it would go more and more toward the Soviet camp. Finally, in November, 1948, he joined a new group created by several overseas representatives in the French Parliament, Indépendants d'Outre-Mer (IOM). Since Senghor's adherence was strictly an individual matter, the BDS maintained its total autonomy.

Five years later the question of fusion with the RDA was again raised but in another context. Everywhere the RDA was losing ground, and association was not attractive. On the other hand, the IOM and its affiliates had gained considerable support during the elections of 1951 and 1952. One of its members, Léon Boissier-Palun, had re-

[5] *Condition Humaine,* Oct. 5, 1948.

placed Lamine Guèye as president of the Grand Council. Senghor had become president of the IOM (a fact which enabled him in 1956 to become a minister of the French Republic in Edgar Faure's cabinet). The IOM therefore organized a congress at Bobo-Dioulasso, where Mamadou Dia, then a Senegalese member of the French Senate, urged that instead of making "an attempt at the coordination of parties by integration at the summit" the IOM itself should become a true *rassemblement* (mass party) based on a doctrine that would be an "African adaptation of the Labour Party concept, a happy mixture of humane socialism and spiritual traditionalism." [6] However, the resolutions of the Bobo-Dioulasso Congress were not carried out, and the mass party never developed.

On the local level, on the other hand, the position of the BDS and of Senghor had been considerably strengthened. When Senghor left the SFIO in 1948, it was generally thought that the next elections would put an end to his political life. The legislative elections of June, 1951, proved these pessimistic expectations to be wrong. In a triumph at which they were as surprised as anyone, the two BDS candidates, Senghor and Abbas Guèye, captured 213,000 votes and thus the two National Assembly seats while Lamine Guèye, who had won only 90,000 votes, lost his seat.

The balloting marked the entrance on the political scene of a new African electoral force whose influence is still great, the peasants of the bush. They voted overwhelmingly for the Serer whom they recognized, in spite of his university degrees, to be one of their sons and against Lamine Guèye, the spokesman for the four old communes. From this point of view the election of June 17, 1951, had great political significance in Senegal, and its consequences are still felt today. It can even be said that this vote of June 17, 1951, presaged Léopold Senghor's ultimate elevation to the presidency of the Republic of Senegal. Senghor's success in June, 1951, was confirmed in March of the following year during the elections for the territorial assembly. The right to the franchise having been extended, there were now 600,000 voters, and the BDS carved out for itself the lion's share of the seats, leaving only 9 (out of a possible 50) seats to the SFIO.

The following years were marked by a lull in the political activities of Senegal and the other overseas territories. It was not until 1956 that progress toward decolonization was resumed. New elections for

[6] *Congrès des Indépendants d'Outre-Mer de Bobo-Dioulasso* (n.p., 1953).

the French Parliament took place on January 2, 1956. In Senegal four lists were presented: the BDS with the names of Senghor and Mamadou Dia; the SFIO under Lamine Guèye and Assane Seck; the MPS, which was the Senegalese section of the RDA; and finally the UDS, an extreme left-wing dissident RDA group which had retained its Communist ties after the parent party had broken them and whose principal leader was Gabriel d'Arboussier. As forecast, the BDS captured both seats without difficulty.

Most of the leaders throughout French West Africa had campaigned on a platform of African unity, and soon after the elections contacts were made in an effort to pass from theory to reality. Senghor met Houphouët-Boigny, the leader of the RDA, for discussion on this subject. According to some stories, the Ivory Coast leader welcomed the Senegalese leader rather coldly and blatantly suggested that he should achieve Senegalese unity before trying to attain African unity.

The anecdote is probably not true, but at least it is certain that Senghor's great objective throughout the year 1956 was to unify Senegal. From May 15 to May 21 the BDS held a congress in Kaolack, where it solemnly urged a general regrouping of all political forces in Senegal. The understanding was that such a regrouping should be made on the basis of a "precise program" between those parties which were in no way dependent upon metropolitan parties. Since the Senegalese SFIO was still part of the French Socialist Party, this statement was both an open call to the electors to desert this party and an attempt to deprive the SFIO of its most dynamic elements in the name of African unity and autonomy.

The SFIO did not dare openly oppose the appeal of the "Senghorists." This was particularly because many young intellectuals, who had at one time thought of forming a third party, had just rallied to the BDS which they considered to be the party of the Senegalese masses. The SFIO therefore agreed to meet on June 13. At this session it was unanimously agreed that the various parties of Senegal should unite "to form one unified party" and that this party would be autonomous with regard to any metropolitan party. However, there is often a large gap between an agreement on principles and their practical realization. Juridically the SFIO could not disband without holding a congress. The party met in St-Louis and without difficulty voted its disaffiliation from the French SFIO. It even stated that "the idea of an SFIO federation in Senegal had been condemned the day the political formula of assimilation died." The

congress did not go any further, however, in response to pressure
from Lamine Guèye, who feared that a fusion of parties would be
certain to work against him.

In the end only the UDS gave a favorable response to Senghor's
appeal for unity. The BDS then announced its own dissolution and
the creation of a new party, the BPS or Bloc Populaire Sénégalais,
which included the former BDS and UDS. The SFIO did not participate in this new alignment but instead formed itself into a new
inter-African party, the MSA, Mouvement Socialiste Africain.

PROGRESSION TO INDEPENDENCE

In France the January, 1956, elections brought into Parliament a
majority much more to the left than previously. Guy Mollet of the
Socialist Party had been chosen Premier and had given the portfolio
for the Overseas Territories to a man known for his liberal ideas,
Gaston Defferre, deuputy and mayor of Marseilles. Defferre recognized
that French Africa was getting restless and that it was necessary to
take new liberal measures to prevent a degeneration of the situation.
He therefore submitted to the French Parliament a *loi cadre,* and this,
as the name indicates, would provide a framework within which the
government received the power to modify by decree the status of the
overseas territories. After much debate Parliament voted the law on
June 23, 1956, by a large majority. The law permitted the government
to increase the power of the territorial assemblies and to establish
executive councils in each territory, changes that were made during
the following months.

In Senegal these reforms were received with a mixture of satisfaction and skepticism. If the masses were pleased to see their territory
acquire a "semiautonomous status" which immediately restored calm
to the country, the leaders were disturbed at the "Balkanization" of
French West Africa which the law would bring about. This was
because the increase in the power of the territorial assemblies was
not accompanied by any reinforcement of power at the federal level
where no cabinet was envisaged. In short, France was on the way
to creating eight independent states and to discouraging any attempts
at federation among them. Senghor, in particular, vigorously denounced this decision which, as he said to the writer in February,
1957, constituted a "regression."

Senghor's point of view did not prevail. The Senegalese leaders
now realized that African unity could not be achieved from the top

down but had to come out of a mass movement. They therefore decided to create their own large inter-African party. During the last months of 1956 Senghor invited all the major politicians of French West and Equatorial Africa to Dakar. A good number of them did not even reply, but all the parliamentary members affiliated with the Indépendants d'Outre-Mer met on January 11, 1957, in Dakar. Together they created a new party, Convention Africaine. The statutes of this party declared that the primary goal was to achieve the unity if not the unification of all African political parties. If necessary, the Convention Africaine itself would disband in order to permit the formation of a larger African party.

A few months later, on March 31, 1957, the elections for the territorial assemblies took place. In accordance with the *loi cadre* this election was held under universal suffrage for the first time. The returns gave 47 seats to the BPS (the Senegalese section of the Convention Africaine) and 13 seats to the PSAS (the Senegalese section of the Mouvement Socialiste Africain of Lamine Guèye). Shortly after, Mamadou Dia formed the first Senegalese cabinet, made up of members of the BPS and one European, André Peytavin, who became Minister of Finance.

Despite this assumption of executive power by the BPS, there were signs that the Senghorists and Laminists were approaching a reconciliation. On May 15, when the Grand Council of French West Africa opened its session in Dakar, the RDA had a majority, thanks to the support of the Mauritanian delegates, and therefore elected a slate of officers to its own liking. The Socialists and members of the Convention Africaine both abstained. Brought together over this issue, these parties held a large joint meeting a few days later in Dakar, and there the two "enemy brothers" were reconciled after ten years of opposition and publicly shook hands before an enthusiastic crowd of 15,000 people.

The MSA and the Convention Africaine swiftly moved to an agreement on essentials, each of them declaring itself ready to be sacrificed on the altar of African unity. Once again it seemed that African unity would be achieved. The occasion for this supreme effort to achieve unity was scheduled to be the interterritorial congress of the RDA which met in Bamako on September 25, 1957. This congress brought together all the leaders of French West and Equatorial Africa, but it did not live up to the hopes that had been placed in it. For one thing, the meeting was almost entirely preoccupied with the quarrel between the "federalists" and the "antifederalists" within the party, and the question of a broader united political party was scarcely mentioned. The congress gave a mandate to its Coordinating Committee to organize a general meeting of African political groups, but it was clear that in the minds of the principal RDA leaders any future fusion would be expected to take place within the framework of the RDA itself. This condition was far from attractive to the other political parties.

Nevertheless, the projected meeting took place in Paris at the beginning of 1958 and, contrary to all expectations, it seemed to succeed. All the participants agreed on a minimum program entailing the transformation of French West and Equatorial Africa into true federations and recognizing that "to handle the relations between France and its former overseas territories federal republics should be established uniting France and the groups of territories . . . on the basis of free cooperation, absolute equality and the *right to independence*." [7]

The practical application of this program was the purpose of another conference held in Dakar on March 26, 1958. But meanwhile the Coordinating Committee of the RDA in Abidjan had decided definitively that any fusion of parties would have to be within the framework of the RDA. Thus as far as its broader program was concerned, the Dakar Conference was doomed to failure from the beginning. The conference resulted nevertheless in the regrouping of all non-RDA parties into the Parti du Regroupement Africain (PRA). This movement also brought together all the Senegalese political parties which now united to form the local section of the PRA, taking the name of UPS (Union Progressiste Sénégalaise).

Other events were taking place, however, that were to affect profoundly the political situation in Africa. On May 13 a significant part of the European population of Algeria, with the support of portions of the French army, rose up against the government. In Senegal, and in general throughout Black Africa, there was little recognition of what the repercussions of the Algerian uprising might be. It was almost with indifference that the Africans watched General de Gaulle return to power. In many of the territories, and particularly in Senegal, people were preoccupied with preparations for the constituent congress of the PRA which was to take place in Cotonou (Dahomey) in July. In June the provisional Directing Committee of the party

[7] *Afrique Nouvelle* (Dakar), Feb. 21, 1958. Italics added.

met in Dakar to reaffirm its support of the program outlined at the February conference in Paris. If the Algerian uprising was mentioned, it was only because General de Gaulle had asked Senghor to participate in his cabinet, something to which the committee gave its assent.

The Cotonou Congress showed, however, that the passive attitude of its political leaders far from pleased the militant among the party members. Senghor's general political report simply advocated the constitution of a French-African federal republic, that is, a vast ensemble in which the Africans would have a greater role to play in the central government. As soon as he had finished speaking, Senghor was subject to the harsh criticism of party members who declared that "the moment for a federal republic is passed. What we want is independence." The militants carried the day, and the conference adopted a motion calling for immediate independence and the formation of a "French African confederation" through negotiations with France conducted as equal to equal.

The participants of the congress were convinced that independence could be obtained without violence and with the agreement of France. The old Senegalese leader, Lamine Guèye, in closing the congress, stated unequivocally while the congress applauded: "This independence—we do not seek it against France." What the Cotonou Congress wanted, in fact, was not so much immediate independence as the right to independence and, moreover, the achievement of this status by gradual steps without a sudden break with the mother country.

The French authorities had difficulty in understanding this reaction. Although they could accept the fact of Africa's interest in obtaining independence, they could not conceive that this independence could be other than directed against France. On August 8, General de Gaulle clearly told the committee, which was drawing up the constitution of the Fifth Republic, that confederation was not possible. The African people would have to choose between secession and federation with France. Finally, however, upon the repeated insistence of Senghor and Lamine Guèye, who were members of the committee, a slightly different option was proposed, that of a state within the Community. This option meant that France conceded the total internal autonomy of those African territories that wanted to retain their association with France.

Now at last, the great majority of militant African politicians decided to go along with France. When de Gaulle made his rapid tour of Africa a few weeks before the referendum, he was well received everywhere except in Conakry and Dakar. Sékou Touré decided that Guinea would vote "no" and would try to make a success of independence. Senghor and Lamine Guèye, on the contrary, had decided to vote "yes" since they believed that this response reflected the general will of the Senegalese people. In their view, Senegal, the oldest French colony in Africa, was not renouncing independence by agreeing to become a member of the Community but avoiding a sudden break with France. Senghor declared on September 21: "The Senegalese option is for independence. Its only desire is that it be achieved in friendship with France, not in conflict."

Certain intellectuals, however, were not of the same opinion as Senghor and decided to vote "no." They left the UPS and formed a new party called PRA-Sénégal under the leadership of Abdoulaye Ly, Mocktar M'Bow, and Assane Seck. Certain conservative circles including a few Europeans and some traditional religious chiefs, on the other hand, although deciding to vote "yes" asked that Senegal become an integral part of France as a department and subsequently created a short-lived party called the Parti de la Solidarité Sénégalaise (PSS).

Despite these differences of view, the result in Senegal was never in doubt. On September 28 the referendum returns showed 870,362 "yes" ballots to 21,901 "no" ballots. Senegal therefore took its place in the French Community.

Less than a month later, on November 25, the Senegalese territorial assembly met in St-Louis to vote, almost unanimously, for the status of a state within the Community. The motion also provided that the new state could federate with other African states that were also members of the Community. The Senegalese leaders thus continued to hope for the formation of a vast West African federation.

In pursuance of this objective, the delegates from Senegal and those from three other states which had adopted identical attitudes—Soudan, Upper Volta, and Dahomey—met in Bamako on December 29, 1958, and decided that each of their countries would delegate powers to a federal constitutional assembly to meet in Dakar.

On January 20, 1959, this assembly adopted a constitution that created the Mali Federation. Shortly after, however, Upper Volta and Dahomey, yielding to external pressures, withdrew from the arrangement and thereby left only Senegal and Soudan to lay the groundwork of the Federation. These two states created a federal Assembly in April which elected Senghor as its president and installed a federal cabinet presided over by Modibo Keita, the Premier of the Soudan. Both states were equally represented in all branches of the federal government.

As soon as it was established, the new federation threw itself into the struggle for independence. Senegalese and Soudanese joined to form a new party, the PFA, Parti de la Fédération Africaine. In July, 1959, at its constituent congress the PFA defined its position in the words of Mamadou Dia: "We want independence in association with France through the establishment of an African community." This idea gained ground, and in increasingly important French circles people began to wonder whether Senghor's policy would not, in the long run, be the wisest way of preserving French interests south of the Sahara.

In September the fifth meeting of the Community's executive council brought together in Paris all the heads of the states of the Community. It was at this meeting that President de Gaulle agreed that the Community had an "evolutionary character." Immediately after the meeting, the two representatives of the Mali Federation made known their intention in the near future to exercise their right to independence. Believing they would receive favorable reactions in France, the PFA leaders immediately returned to Dakar, convoked the Directing Committee of their party, and announced that the Mali Federation was ready to enter into negotiations with France to obtain its independence while remaining within the Community.

Mali's announcement was made in September. France took three months before making known its reply. Taking advantage of the sixth meeting of the Community's executive council which was to be held in St-Louis, General de Gaulle decided to travel first to Mauritania and to Senegal. On December 10 the President of the Fifth Republic, in a speech before the National Assembly of Mauritania, hinted at his reply by presenting the Community simply as a friendly association between peoples who needed one another in a harsh world.

The following day, in St-Louis, de Gaulle announced officially to the other heads of state that Senegal and Soudan had asked to become independent and that the French Republic had agreed to begin the necessary negotiations. But it was in Dakar that de Gaulle chose to make this decision public at an extraordinarily moving meeting on December 13, 1959, at which the Mali federal Assembly received the President of the Community, a meeting which marks an important date in the history of Senegal and even in the history of French-speaking West Africa.

First of all, Senghor welcomed his guest in that elegant and harmonious French which is his own secret. Then a shiver of emotion passed through the audience when, after having repeated his hope that Mali would soon fly with its own wings, the Senegalese leader, turning toward General de Gaulle and paraphrasing the words of the Bible, said: "At this moment when we are asking for independence, 'Stay with us for it grows late.'" General de Gaulle, wearing a simple khaki uniform, rose and pronounced a few banal words of thanks. Suddenly he sat down again because, he said, he would now speak of "certain things." A deathly silence fell in the room. In the galleries as on the floor, everyone knew that the words to be pronounced would be decisive and that upon them would depend the future of French-African relations. President Senghor was later to confess that at that moment he was terribly afraid, not knowing what de Gaulle meant by "certain things." Then, speaking in a conversational manner, the President of the Community gave one of the outstanding speeches of his career. Every person who had the chance to hear him had the impression of living a rare moment of history. It is well known what he said. Not only did de Gaulle confirm that France accepted Mali's independence, but he also added that his country would give the new Mali state all its aid and support. Thus the "Guinean mistake" was not to be repeated. From the other side there would be no secession. Thus the leaders of the Mali Federation received what had been refused to Sékou Touré scarcely a year before.

Despite this agreement, the Franco-Malian negotiations on the form of the new arrangements took several months. They opened in Paris on January 19, 1960. Modibo Keita, Senghor, and Mamadou Dia led the Mali delegation, which included a group of experts under Madeira Keita, the present Minister of the Interior of Mali. Since the negotiations sometimes ran into difficulties, they lasted three months. They ended on April 4 with the signing of an agreement on the transfer of powers from the Community to Mali and of several agreements for cooperation. It had been previously agreed that the two sides would negotiate simultaneously on the agreement permitting Mali's accession to independence and those agreements organizing the cooperation between the new state and France. The latter agreements were not to be definitively signed and ratified until Mali was independent. The leaders of Mali, however, undertook a moral engagement to sign them in the form agreed upon by both sides. The independence of Mali was declared on the night of June 19–20 in the presence of two French ministers, and two days later the accords were signed.

The new federal state, now sovereign, decided of its own free will to remain within the Community as provided for in the agreements. It agreed to coordinate its foreign policy with that of France, to remain within the franc zone, and to sign a common defense agreement with France. The direction and administration of the University of Dakar remained in the hands of the French.

Having achieved its independence without bloodshed or a violent break with France, the new state seemed to have a brilliant future. In fact, succeeding events showed it to be particularly fragile. A federal state cannot be firmly established unless the federal authorities are capable of arbitrating between the federated states. The government of Mali could not play this role, however, because the Federation included only two states and the principle of parity was strictly applied within the institutions of the Federation. Thus any conflict between the states had its repercussions at the summit of the Federation. In other words, there was no possibility of arbitration in case of conflict between Senegal and the Soudan.

Conflict broke out, in fact, almost as soon as the independence of the Federation was recognized. Already it had become apparent that the two partners had different ideas about the structure of the state, the organization of the Federation, and the role of the party and on African and international politics. These differences had become obvious when the partners discussed the principal institutions of the Mali Federation. At the first meeting held on April 16 in Dakar, the Soudanese proposed that the power of the Federation be concentrated in what would be virtually a unitary structure in which the President would be at the same time chief of state, Premier, and Foreign Affairs Minister. Senegal refused this plan, and the discussions continued for three days. When finally it proved impossible to reach a decision, the Directing Committee of the PFA was given the task of finding a compromise.

Following the official proclamation of independence, the officers of the UPS on June 21 publicly proposed the candidature of Senghor for President of the Federation and of Lamine Guèye for president of the Assembly. From that moment relations between the partners worsened. The conflict threatened to break into the open despite at-

tempts to hush it up. At the beginning of July, Modibo Keita took
the floor at the UPS congress in St-Louis and criticized certain Senegalese policies. At the end of the month, Premier Keita named Colonel
Soumaré, Soudanese by birth, as his chief of staff against the advice
of Mamadou Dia, the federal Defense Minister, who supported the
candidature of Colonel Fall, a Senegalese.

Thereafter events moved quickly. At the annual pilgrimage to the
Muslim shrine of Touba, on August 13, Mamadou Dia made a statement that was noticed by everyone: "We are Malians, certainly, but
first of all Senegalese." It is difficult to reconstruct the events of the
crisis when it finally came. What is certain is that when the Soudanese
leaders left Bamako on August 19 to participate in Dakar, on August
27, in the election of the Federation's President, they had decided
under no circumstances to vote for Senghor. Meanwhile the Senegalese leaders decided to hold a meeting on August 21 of the upper
echelons of the party.

During the evening of August 19, Modibo Keita, who had been
warned that great numbers of UPS militants were on their way to
Dakar, became frightened and hastily convoked a special session of
the federal cabinet. From the Senegalese side, only Boubacar Guèye,
Lamine Guèye's nephew, appeared. The cabinet adopted two decrees,
one withdrawing the Defense Ministry from Mamadou Dia and the
other proclaiming a state of emergency and ordering the army to
protect all federal government buildings.

The Senegalese leaders reacted immediately and mobilized their
forces. The French colonel commanding the national police force
(*gendarmerie*) decided to obey the local instead of the federal government. Colonel Soumaré was arrested; the surveillance of public buildings passed to the troops loyal to Senegal; and all the Soudanese
leaders were put under house arrest.

In the middle of the night Mamadou Dia convened first the Senegalese cabinet and then the Senegalese assembly. The latter met at
one o'clock in the morning. Its president, Lamine Guèye, was absent,
but nevertheless 67 out of 80 deputies were in their places. They declared the independence of the Republic of Senegal and its simultaneous withdrawal from the Mali Federation. An hour later the cabinet ministers met again, this time to reshuffle the government. Doudou
Thiam and Abdoulaye Fofana, who had been federal ministers, as
well as Gabriel d'Arboussier, all received ministerial posts. At dawn,
the work of the Senegalese leaders was virtually done.

On the evening of August 21 the Soudanese leaders were escorted under close guard to the railroad station, where they were put on a special train to Bamako. The following day the Senegalese assembly turned itself into a National Assembly. Three days later the constitution was revised to take into account the new circumstances. At the beginning of September, Senghor was unanimously voted President of the Republic while Mamadou Dia and his cabinet received a vote of confidence from the National Assembly.

The Republic of Senegal thus became an independent state. A few weeks later, after some hesitation, Senegal was admitted to the United Nations at the same time as was the Soudan, which had now become the Republic of Mali.

Land and People

The population of Senegal is relatively sparse. According to the economic survey which took place in 1959–1960 under the direction of Father Lebret, the total population in 1959 was no more than 2,700,000.[8] Senegal has only 9 towns of more than 10,000 inhabitants. The average density is about 36 inhabitants per square mile, but there are great variations according to the regions. The population is relatively young with about 40 per cent of the Senegalese under 15 years old and an annual birth rate of approximately 2.4 per cent.

Geographically Senegal can be divided into six regions: the Senegal River Valley, the sylvo-pastoral region, eastern Senegal around the upper Gambia River, the southern region below the Gambia, the peanut-growing area, and the maritime region. Each of these regions has its own characteristic topography and population.

The Senegal River, which extends for 1,060 miles, is a dominant feature of the country. It is formed by the merging at Bafoulabé (in Mali) of the Bafing and Bakoi rivers which flow from the Fouta Djallon in Guinea. The principal tributaries of the Senegal River are the Falémé (which forms part of the boundary with Mali) and the Baoulé and the Gorgol rivers (which are outside Senegal). The Senegal River empties into the sea south of St-Louis after having followed the coast for quite a distance, but its mouth is obstructed by moving sand bars and powerful sea swells, which considerably limit St-Louis' possibilities as a modern port. The river valley has a high density of population—100 inhabitants to the square mile—and includes several

[8] *Rapport Général sur les Perspectives de Développement du Sénégal* (Dakar, 1960).

different tribes, the Wolof, Moor, and Tukulor, all Islamized and still little affected by schooling or Western civilization. Millet is the principal food crop in this area, and fishing constitutes an important resource.

Directly south of this valley lies the sylvo-pastoral region. This region has no hills and no permanent waterways. The population, of which the majority are Fulani, is very sparse—five inhabitants per square mile—and takes little part in the economic and political life of the country.

Eastern Senegal, which is the area of the upper Gambia River, is the only part of Senegal that can be considered mountainous, and it has an altitude varying from 300 to 1,500 feet. The population here is ethnically mixed but mainly Mandingo. The region has always been isolated from the rest of the country and participates very little in its economic life.

The Casamance or southern region which is separated from the rest of Senegal by the British colony, the Gambia, is distinct from the rest of Senegal. Rainfall is more plentiful here than elsewhere, falling for six months of the year. The population density is on the average forty inhabitants to the square mile, but 80 per cent of the region is covered by forests and the inhabitants live along the waterways where rice can be cultivated. The Casamance has three distinct ethnic groups: the Diola, 37 per cent; the Mandingo, 20 per cent; and the Fulani, 27 per cent.

Economically speaking, the most important area of Senegal is the peanut region, which extends from Louga to Kaolack and passes through Diourbel and Thiès. Being choice land for the peanut, which is cultivated alternately with food crops, this area is very densely populated. With only one-seventh of the total land surface, it includes one-half of the total rural Senegalese population. Between the town of Kébémer and the Saloum River, the population density rises to 180 inhabitants per square mile. In this region, the traditional subsistence form of economy has been transformed into a market economy. The inhabitants of the region are 66 per cent Wolof and 25 per cent Serer, many of whom retain the traditions of the ancient historical provinces of Saloum, Sine, Cayor, and Baol.

Finally, from the delta of the Senegal River to the estuary of the Saloum River lies the maritime region, which has a mild climate owing to the *alizés*, breezes that blow from the sea for eight to nine months of the year.

AGRICULTURE AND FISHING

Like all its neighbors, Senegal is an agricultural country. The peasants form over 80 per cent of the population, and they have an extremely low standard of living since Senegalese agriculture is essentially underdeveloped.

A number of factors are responsible for Senegal's agricultural poverty. Most basic of these is climate. Out of Senegal's 19,700,000 hectares, only 5,400,000 have an annual rainfall of more than forty inches. Rain is not only relatively scarce but also badly distributed, falling only during the period called *hivernage* which lasts, according to the particular region, from four to six months. Crops can be cultivated only during this short period with the result that during six to eight months of the year over 1,500,000 Senegalese farmers are idle, left to sit out the dryness and the heat on their useless land.

This is one of the reasons for the low technical level of the Senegalese peasantry. The farmer begins his work period when he is in poor physical condition at the end of a long, hot dry season with little left to eat in his granaries. Moreover, being inactive for the greater part of the year, he has never learned good work habits. He is therefore content to scratch the soil with a few rudimentary tools.

Another hindrance to rural development is the landholding system. There is no individual rural property; the farmer has the right to use the land but without the possibility of alienation since land is not considered the fruit of human labor. Thus he has no ties with the land he cultivates and no incentive to invest or make long-term improvements. Much could be done, in fact, to improve the peasant's lot. For example, although 29.2 per cent of Senegalese land is arable, only 9.4 per cent is being used effectively at the present time.

For the most part Senegalese peasants cultivate an industrial crop, the peanut (which takes up 48 per cent of the land under cultivation), and cereals, millet, sorghum, and rice. For these last three crops (occupying 45 per cent of the land under cultivation) the same techniques are being used today as one or two centuries ago. The yield is very low. Moreover, the peasant grows these crops only to meet his own needs and does not sell them commercially.

Peanut cultivation, carried on mainly in the Kaolack and Diourbel regions, is the principal source of wealth in Senegal. At the beginning of this century, annual production had reached 100,000 tons, and it has regularly increased since then. In 1946 production attained 359,000 tons; in 1952, 448,000 tons; in 1956, 677,000 tons. In 1957 an exceptional crop brought production to 800,000 tons. This crop, which was formerly exported in the shell, is now for the most part processed within the country. The Senegalese oil industry has greatly expanded during the last few years and is now capable of processing about 450,000 tons of peanuts per year.

According to statistics, Senegal has great resources in livestock. For example, the number of cattle is listed as 1,640,000, which gives Senegal a higher density of cattle population than most West African countries. However, although cattle abound, they are not commercially exploited. Cattle farming, as understood in modern countries, does not exist. For the Senegalese owner, his cattle provide a sign of prosperity, a method of hoarding. They are not, or at least very rarely, a speculative venture. His herds wander almost at will, searching for good pasture and water holes. They give little milk, and there is no system of selective breeding. Moreover, Senegalese cattle are subject to numerous diseases, including the dreaded rinderpest. The situation will not change as long as the cattle owner has not been integrated into modern life, that is, as long as he does not understand how he can profit from rationally treated livestock. This is the problem the government is trying to solve by increasing the number of watering places, by continuing research to improve breeding, by developing agricultural extension services, and by establishing cold-storage plants so that the cattle can be bought and slaughtered near where they graze.

Fishing, particularly ocean fishing, in a country with 320 miles of coastline, is another major Senegalese resource. Here again is an activity that uses traditional methods. Nevertheless, a special governmental branch, the Fishing Service, has tried to improve methods in the last ten years. It has worked to modernize equipment, improve the processing of the catch, and develop a more rational system of distribution.

The Senegalese fisherman commonly builds his own boat, a large canoe of a particular shape. Since to replace this homemade fishing boat would mean a head-on clash with tradition, the government has sought first to improve the craft's functioning by adding an outboard motor. This first step has worked out well, for the Senegalese fishermen have readily perceived how much a motor can increase their catch, and some 30 per cent have already put the idea into practice. The next step is to change the boat itself, but this will be much easier now that the technicians of the Fishing Service have won the confidence of the coastal people.

It would not do, however, to increase the yield of fish without finding new markets. The Fishing Service has therefore established fish-drying plants which will turn the fresh fish into a product exportable to the rest of Africa. These plants are cooperative, but each fisherman retains control over his own production as this system seems best to respond to the majority's desires. Indicative of further opportunities for expansion are the recent spectacular developments in tuna fishing, which is done mainly by fishing fleets from outside Senegal, particularly from France.

MINING AND INDUSTRY

Agriculture and fishing are two traditional Senegalese activities, but no efforts were made to exploit Senegal's mineral resources until after World War II. Until now, only two major mineral resources have been discovered. One of these, phosphate, has been found in two regions. The first, an aluminum phosphate deposit, in the region of Lam-Lam, has been marked out and exploitation has begun. Unfortunately this phosphate cannot be directly assimilated by plant life, and it has to be processed before being sold. These difficulties have meant that the mines have scarcely been developed as yet, and they produce only 100,000 tons of raw phosphate per year. The lime phosphate deposit at Taïba, on the other hand, is so pure that a simple rinsing produces a product with 82 per cent calcium phosphate. Industrial exploitation of this deposit began on August 1, 1960, and is expected to produce 600,000 tons annually in the next two to three years.

The second mineral resource, "heavy sand," a product containing ilmenite, rutile, and zircon is found on some of Senegal's beaches. During recent years the industrial center of Djifère has produced about 30,000 tons of these minerals.

Senegal's industry is scarcely more developed than its mineral resources. Nevertheless, in the past few years, the country has begun a modest industrialization, using mainly local products. In 1883, the idea was first proposed that peanut oil should be processed in Senegal itself, but it was not till 1920 that the first refinery was built in Diourbel. By 1933, the Senegalese refineries were already producing 7 tons per day, all reserved solely for local consumption. In 1935 began the first exportation of peanut oil. Today these exports total about

130,000 tons of oil produced by six modern plants. Senegal has also begun to make soap and now supplies all its own needs (11,000 tons).

Aside from the refineries, other food industries—breweries, flour mills, fish canneries, vinegar, biscuit, and candy factories—have been developed. In all there are seventy-eight such enterprises employing 30 per cent of all industrial wage earners.

The textile industry is another significant sector of the economy. The first sisal bag factory was started in 1938 and today there are more than seven important textile plants, representing an investment of five million dollars, which supply 40 per cent of Senegal's needs. There is also a large shoe factory in Rufisque, whose output of 3,000,000 pairs of shoes per year is for the greater part exported. Finally, there are the cement works of Rufisque, whose annual production of 200,000 tons supplies the regions that can be reached by road or rail, and also a match factory and a cigarette factory.

In short, industrialization has begun, almost all of it in the area of Dakar and Rufisque. Much still remains to be done, however, to develop local industry based on local products. For example, the peanut could provide the basis for a chemical industry, the phosphate be turned into fertilizers, and cattle could supply a meat-packing industry.

To pursue its development Senegal is fortunate in possessing a more-developed infrastructure than have most other West African states. The port of Dakar is the foremost port in West Africa. Its geographic position has made it a port of call of prime importance as well as an outlet for goods from Senegal and Mauritania. In 1959, it handled 3,677,356 tons of merchandise, more than twice that of Abidjan.

The airport of Yoff just outside Dakar is also an obligatory transit stop between Europe and South America. Since 1960 it has an 8,000-foot runway for jet airplanes and soon will have the equipment necessary for instrument landings. About fifteen airline companies regularly make flights to Dakar.

These two "entrances" to Senegal are connected to the hinterland by fairly well developed road and rail communications. Until the breakup of the Mali Federation, the railroad, 645 miles long, joined up with the Soudanese network. The line has only a single track, but its bed is excellent and well maintained. In 1958, the railroad handled 900,000 tons of merchandise and 315,000,000 travelers. In the years following the breakup of the Mali Federation, the government of the

Mali Republic refused, however, to let goods use this obvious line of communication and sent them through the Ivory Coast.

The 7,870-mile road system (of which only 500 miles are paved and 6,700 miles are dirt track) is used by the 25,000 cars and trucks of Senegal. This network is obviously insufficient, especially during the rainy season when many of the tracks become strips of mud. Because of this fact, certain areas of the Casamance and eastern Senegal remain isolated from the rest of the country during much of the rainy season.

COMMERCE

The road and rail systems were planned originally for the shipment of the peanut crop, the only product of interest to colonial commerce. The commercial system, or trading economy (*économie de traite*), functioned in the following way. Foreign trading companies would collect at the lowest possible price, sort, and transport to the ports one or two local products (in Senegal the peanut, elsewhere cocoa or coffee), which they would then sell to Europe or America. In return, they would import and sell in the country a few undiversified manufactured items, such as textiles, bicycles, hardware, and sugar. In this system the economic development of the country was conceived of only as a by-product of the metropolitan country's interests or, more precisely, the interests of a few trading companies and metropolitan industries that exported to Africa.

It is natural that the new Senegalese leaders should have a completely different point of view on commerce from this colonially oriented one. They want to develop the country for itself and in order to fulfill its own needs. But the commercial system remains marked by its origins and has not been completely converted, particularly since it is still run largely by Europeans. Moreover, the commercial system is to a certain extent tacked onto the country, not integrated into it. Today, there are two sectors of Senegal's economy which are almost totally unaware of each other's existence: a traditional sector based upon a subsistence economy and a modern sector based on a monetary economy. Each of these sectors obeys its own internal logic. The former is but little involved in monetary exchange, and goods are produced primarily for home consumption; the latter is turned primarily toward the outside world. Senegal's economic dependence on France is the consequence of this state of affairs. Its growth depends for the greater part upon its foreign exchange and the expansion of a sector of the economy whose decisions are dictated from outside the country.

The key to Senegal's economy is the commercial enterprise, which has a double function: to buy and sell in Senegal and to buy and sell in the world market. The commercial structure of Senegal is not adapted to promoting exchanges within the Senegalese economy— Senegal's entry into an exchange economy was not accompanied by a raising of the country's technical level to permit a rise in production but by a substitution of peanut production for production for home consumption. When this took place, the commercial structure completely tied the rural economy to the outside world. As a result, the commercial system increased the disequilibrium in food products by encouraging the peasant to specialize in peanut production. Moreover, it pushed the sale of articles of mass consumption, where the profit margin was greatest, at the expense of the equipment necessary for national development.

It must be noted, however, that this colonial commercial system has been somewhat modified recently. The creation of factories using local products increases the value of the export crops and is thus a factor in Senegal's development. Moreover, the major trading companies have moved toward greater specialization.

Foreign commerce remains dominated, however, by the peanut. For the Senegal-Mali-Mauritania group, the peanut and its derivatives constituted 87 per cent of all exports in 1959 (of which nearly half was in the form of oil). France was practically their only customer, buying 91.5 per cent of their 1959 exports. Statistics show that the group mainly tends to import foodstuffs (two-thirds of total imports). In other words, this group of countries sells a single product to a single customer and imports principally to feed itself and to raise its level of private consumption and not to equip itself for development. Finally, the commercial balance shows a chronic deficit with all monetary zones so that the standard of living is precarious.

Even if one admits that the situation of Senegal is a little better than that of Mali and Mauritania because of its role as redistribution center, foreign commerce statistics reveal the fragility of its economy and its dependence on the outside world, particularly on France.

THE DEVELOPMENT PLAN

From the time of its formation, the Senegalese government has worked to transform the country's economic structure in order to turn Senegal into a modern state. The first step was a systematic and scientific study of the country's economic, social, and human resources. This study was made by the French economist, Father L. J. Lebret, founder of the *économie et humanisme* movement, who directed a team of experts in a vast eighteen-month survey of the country.

Secondly, the government undertook to modernize the system of economic administration by creating economic organs corresponding to each administrative unit in the country. Rural extension centers (*centres d'expansion rurale*) were created at the level of groups of villages (*arrondissements*). At the regional level, development assistance centers (CRAD) were formed, and finally, at the national level, an Agricultural Products Marketing Board (Office de Commercialisation Agricole or OCA) and a development bank (Banque Sénégalaise de Développement) were created.

Most important of all, the government established a four-year development plan with, as Mamadou Dia himself said in his speech of April 4, 1961, five basic objectives:

To increase the sense of responsibility, "that is to say, make each citizen, each group, each community, responsible for the development of the country in proportion to their capacities and the positions they occupy";

To place Africans in control of all essential sectors of the economy;

To mobilize all the forces of the country;

To attract private capital by helping it find its place in the growth operations foreseen by the plan. "Private capital must accept spontaneously to become national capital, that is to say, to participate in constructing our nation." Beyond this "free and trusting cooperation" no further nationalization is envisaged;

To structure the economy by integrating regional activities and growth factors more fully.

From this effort the government expects a rise in the standard of living of 3.5 per cent a year.

The Political Process

POLITICAL AND ADMINISTRATIVE STRUCTURE

The Senegalese constitution states that Senegal is a "lay, democratic, and social" republic and refers expressly to the Declaration of the Rights of Man of 1789 and that of 1948. The sovereignty of the Republic belongs to the people, who exercise their power either directly through referendum or indirectly through their representatives.

In contrast to most West African states, Senegal does not have a presidential regime. The Senegalese President's powers are not as extensive as those of the Guinean President or quasi-dictatorial like those of the President of Ghana. He is elected for seven years by a "congress" made up of the deputies and a delegate from each regional assembly and each municipal council. He cannot hold any other office either public or private. He is chief of the army, presides over the cabinet meetings, and with its approval appoints the upper civil servants and army officers. He promulgates the law. Although he can send a law back to the National Assembly for obligatory further deliberation, he must accede if the Assembly maintains its point of view. He communicates with the Assembly only by notes which are read for him, but he has the right to address the Senegalese people directly. All his acts, except those accomplished "in his capacity of guardian of the people and in exercise of his powers of arbitration" must be countersigned by the Premier.

The Premier is designated by the President, but the Assembly invests him in office only after approving his program. He chooses his own ministers who may or may not be deputies. He has extensive powers: he determines the nation's policy, directs the action of the government, and assures the execution of the laws. He is responsible for national defense, has powers of decree, and directs both the administration and the armed forces. The Senegalese regime is parliamentary. Thus the cabinet, at least in theory, is collectively responsible before the Assembly. While it is said that the President of the Republic represents the nation, the Premier regulates, governs, and administers it.

The deputies of the National Assembly are elected for a period of five years by direct universal suffrage. They hold two regular sessions a year and can be convoked for special sessions. The Assembly votes laws and the budget and ratifies treaties and international agreements. The deputies can initiate laws concurrently with the Premier. They may check on the actions of the cabinet through written or oral questioning and by commissions of inquiry. The Premier can decide in cabinet meeting to pose a question of confidence, in which case the vote must take place within two days. If an absolute majority of the Assembly refuses its confidence, the cabinet must resign. For its part the Assembly can initiate a vote of censure, and if it is passed, the cabinet must also resign.

According to the Senegalese constitution, the judiciary has an authority independent of both the executive and the legislative branches. This independence is guaranteed by the President of the Republic aided by the Superior Council of Magistrates. Magistrates are appointed for life. The Supreme Court passes on the constitutionality of laws and international agreements. Moreover, it is the court of final appeal.

The government organization just described is that outlined in the constitution, but however precise a constitutional text may be, it cannot foresee all the problems posed by day-to-day political life. Therefore, when studying the distribution of power in a specific country, one must generally consider not only the constitutional text as such but also the country's customs and traditions.

The Republic of Senegal is still so young that one can hardly speak of "traditions." Still, it is possible to discern certain general orientations in Senegal's interpretation of its constitution. For example, according to the constitutional text, the power of the President of the Republic is strictly limited. In reality this is not so. The "congress" composed of deputies and representatives from the regional assemblies and municipal councils has elected Léopold Sédar Senghor to the highest governmental post in the country. But Senghor (and this point will be referred to again) is *the* great Senegalese leader. He is political power in Senegal. Moreover, he is secretary-general of the "dominant" party, the UPS. Nothing can be done in Senegal against his open opposition. One can even imagine that with the support of the masses (which he has acquired completely) Senghor imposes his point of view on the other branches of the government. Endowed by the constitution with the feeble powers of a President of the French Fourth Republic, in fact he wields the authority of a de Gaulle.

Nevertheless, the President of the Republic does not govern directly. The country's daily business is directed by the Premier, whose authority no one contests, at least openly. Mamadou Dia is the number two Senegalese politician, and in matters of internal politics he has reserved for himself the key ministerial posts. Mamadou Dia is thus not only Premier but also National Defense Minister, which means he commands the army. Moreover, his office supervises the High Commission for Planning, and this permits him indirectly to control all the economic ministries. Any economic project—whether it has to do with measures for the extension of a crop, the creation of a new industry, or the construction of a road—must be examined by the Planning Commission before being presented to the cabinet. Any tax proposals affecting the economy must also be submitted to the Planning Commission. Even the Minister of the Interior does not escape this indirect supervision, for each region has a "development adviser," and one of the principal roles of the governors themselves is to supervise the plan in their regions. At the third UPS congress held in Thiès in February, 1962, the authority of the Premier was reinforced by his election to the post of deputy secretary-general of the party, thereby making him second only to Senghor in the party as in the governmental hierarchy.

The National Assembly is the constitutional depository of popular sovereignty. Since (with one exception) it is composed solely of deputies belonging to the UPS, one might well wonder if it is not simply a "rubber stamp" for decisions taken either at the cabinet or party level. This is certainly the case in foreign policy, but not in internal politics. In contrast to Guinea, the Senegalese deputies are not elected on a single national list but in large electoral districts that correspond to the administrative regions. They remain, therefore, the representatives of regional interests. Even if the Assembly does not constitute a true political force as such, numerous deputies still hold real political authority at the level of their own regions. They are, therefore, not completely in the government's pocket and do not always blindly accept without protest the government's point of view. Very occasionally at the end of a public debate the cabinet's proposal is defeated, but it is in the closed sessions of the commissions that the real discussions take place and the deputies argue their points of view. At this level, it is not unusual for the debates to be so lively that the cabinet is forced to modify its proposals.

Sometimes the conflict is more muffled. If the deputies do not obtain satisfaction, the president of the Assembly can "forget" to sign a bill that has been voted and thereby prevent its promulgation. This happened to the law establishing the Four-Year Plan in which the cabinet had refused to incorporate a few economic projects (roads, hospitals, schools) that some deputies had promised their electors. Thus, several months went by before the law appeared in the official record.

One of the first acts of the Senegalese government regarding administrative organization was to modernize the administrative structure inherited from the colonial system. Thus, the traditional chiefdoms were practically eliminated, and the 139 cantons which existed from colonial times were replaced by 85 *arrondissements*, each administered by a civil servant who is called the *chef d'arrondissement*. Although reduced in influence in their former spheres, several traditional chiefs were chosen as *chef d'arrondissement*—but never in their "traditional" districts. This fact illustrates the constant concern of Senegalese politics to strike a balance between what is daring and what is prudent.

The *arrondissement* is the basic administrative unit. Immediately above this unit is the old administrative district created by Faidherbe, the *cercle*, whose number has now been increased to twenty-seven. The *commandant de cercle* wields the power of the central government in his area; he is in charge of maintaining order, exercises police power, and has authority over all the civil servants in his district. Independent Senegal has thus retained the French system. The *commandant de cercle* is, in fact, a prefect who, like the French prefect, centralizes in his hands all administrative power. The *cercles* are grouped into seven regions, each headed by a governor appointed by the cabinet. The governor is a kind of superprefect who provides the link between the cabinet and the *cercle*. Each region also has a regional assembly. These assemblies were established in July, 1960, and are each empowered to vote a regional budget financed by self-imposed taxes.

The regions serve two purposes: first, to decentralize the administration and, second, to adapt the administrative structure to the large natural economic regions of the country. Economic development remains one of the government's principal concerns, and therefore administrative reform has been reinforced by a reform of the economic structure. Each governor has two deputy governors: one is in charge of administration, and the other, known as the "development adviser," coordinates the region's economic development.

Each administrative region also has a Centre Régional d'Assistance pour le Développement (CRAD) directed by a president named every four years by the Premier. CRAD is the government's instrument for carrying out the regional development plan. Its responsibilities encompass all rural construction programs. CRAD also assists and advises the rural cooperatives, mainly in matters of administration and accounting. It is in constant contact with the two national economic organs which play the major role in economic development, the Agricultural Products Marketing Board (OCA) and the Development Bank.

The principal urban centers have been set up as self-governing municipalities. Today there are thirty-three of these municipalities, including Dakar, which has a special system of government. To become self-governing a town must have enough resources to balance its budget. Municipalities are directed by councils which are elected by universal suffrage. The Minister of the Interior supervises the municipalities' administration and must give his express approval to certain acts, but this administrative surveillance extends mainly to financial matters.

THE POLITICAL PARTIES

Political life in Senegal is dominated by the governmental party, the Union Progressiste Sénégalaise or UPS, which was created in February, 1959, as already noted, by the fusion of the major Senegalese parties, principally the BPS of Senghor and the SFIO of Lamine Guèye. The UPS considers itself the "governmental party." Created with the achievement of political independence as its principal goal, the party has gone on to lead the cause of economic development.

The UPS considers itself a "socialist" party, but not in the usual sense. It is impossible, said Mamadou Dia, "constantly to retailor the socialist fabric to our reality." A new socialism must be constructed that takes into account African realities. In other words, the socialist method must be applied to the Senegalese context and Senegalese tradition. In developing such a method, the UPS places man at the center of its concern. "Man is our measure," as Senghor so often says.

The basic unit of the party is the village committee or, in cities, the ward committee. According to the report on party life presented by Ousmane N'Gom at the 1962 UPS congress in Thiès, the UPS at the end of 1961 had 2,500 committees throughout the country. These committees are grouped into 400 subsections. According to Article 7 of the party statutes, the subsection includes either several village committees or, in a city, all the committees of the same *arrondissement* or electoral district. At the level above is the section which is formed by the totality of subsections of a city or region. (It is not a question here of administrative regions as discussed above but simply of groups of rural villages.)

The sections of the same *cercle* form the coordinating commission of the *cercle*. At the end of 1961 there were thirty-two of these commissions. (The large cities have their own autonomous coordinating commissions.) The delegates of the coordinating commissions of the same administrative region form the regional union. In fact, at the end of 1961 only five regional unions were operating, those of Dakar and the Senegal River Valley region not yet having been constituted.

At the level of each section exists a conflict commission; this is in charge of settling the differences which may arise between party members, particularly at election time. If the conflict commission cannot solve the difficulty, the question is brought directly before the national organs of the party. In other words, the coordinating commission of the *cercle* and the regional union cannot make decisions but only advise and coordinate action. This is significant because it helps to maintain democratic interaction within the party. No regional leader can impose his authority in his region if he does not have the confidence of the party's local groups, and the section thus retains a good deal of autonomy.

UPS committees function also on the professional and technical levels within numerous industrial and commercial enterprises and in the administrative services. These committees provide a means of reaching UPS members who are not interested in ward politics and are not intended to be substitutes for labor unions.

The Executive Committee [9] and its Executive Bureau direct the UPS at the national level. The Executive Committee, which serves as a party "parliament," includes several hundred elected members who represent all the *cercles* and also a certain number of ex officio members (ministers, deputies, UPS youth delegates, and so on). The Executive Committee elects forty-one members to the Executive Bureau, the supreme organ of the party, which meets once a week. Its members include the political director, Lamine Guèye; the secretary-general, Léopold Senghor; the deputy secretary-general, Mamadou Dia; and the political secretary, Ousmane N'Gom. In contrast to what is found in certain other African countries, the Executive Bureau does not exercise directive power over the executive or legislative branches of the government. It does not dictate to the ministers or other elected officials but supervises their activities.

The deputies are supervised through the UPS parliamentary group meetings, which are held periodically and in which parliamentary strategy is worked out. Supervision of the cabinet is more difficult because the executive branch of the government is not directly under the authority of the party. Nevertheless, according to a kind of gentlemen's agreement, the cabinet customarily submits to the UPS Executive Bureau all important economic and political questions as they arise. These questions are then discussed, and it is seldom hard to find a common position since the principal members of the cabinet are also members of the Executive Bureau.

[9] At the 1962 UPS congress its name was changed to National Council.

Senegal's concept of democratic centralism is thus different from
that of Guinea. In Senegal the party does not direct the totality of the
nation's life; rather the government seeks the participation of the party
militants in developing general policy. The militants can give their
points of view freely through the intermediary of the Executive Committee and the Executive Bureau. But once the decision is made, the
executive branch of the government alone has the right to define the
ways and means to arrive at the proper end. Only the cabinet can
interpret these decisions. The party checks up only after the plan has
been put into effect.

The UPS has its own youth movement, the MJUPS (Mouvement
des Jeunes de l'UPS), but Senegalese youth are not obliged to join.
Senegal at the present time is one of the few independent African
states that permits its youth freedom of association. The structure of
the MJUPS follows that of the UPS itself, with regional unions and
coordinating committees. Moreover, the MJUPS is represented as such
in the national organs of the party.

The opponents of the UPS accuse it of being less well organized
than other African parties such as the PDG of Guinea or the Union
Soudanaise. It is true that for many years the UPS was a federation of
political movements rather than a party properly speaking. The former
parties of Senghor and Lamine Guèye survived within the UPS as two
rival and often opposed clans. Furthermore, in the Senegal River Valley region, for example, family or tribal clans were at constant war
within the party structure. All this conflict has not completely disappeared, but with time this phenomenon is dying out. At the last party
congress in February, 1962, these tendencies were much less evident
than at previous congresses. It must also be noted at the same time
that the Senegalese concept of "dominant" party is marked by a real
concern for democratic discussions and thus comes closer to Western
than to Marxist concepts.

Senegal's major opposition party is PRA-Senegal, whose genesis has
already been mentioned. PRA-Senegal considers its program more
"revolutionary" and more "socialist" in the Marxist sense than is that
of the UPS. Its support is limited to a few intellectual groups and
several areas of the Casamance. The party's freedom of maneuver is
greatly restricted. A government censorship on all newspapers pre-
vents PRA-Senegal from publishing its paper, and it is practically impossible for the party to hold public meetings. Moreover, several of
PRA-Senegal's leaders were arrested during 1961 for implication in an

alleged traffic in illicit arms, a charge which has not as yet been satisfactorily explained.

The third Senegalese party, the PAI (Parti Africain de l'Indépendance), whose principal leader is Majemouth Diop, is today only an underground movement since its dissolution by the government in 1960. Its program is clearly Communist, and several of its leaders have spent much time behind the iron curtain. The PAI has a following among students and some other sectors of Senegal's youth. Its dynamism is demonstrated by its adherents who are ready to give all to "the cause." The party seems, however, to lack a true leader as well as any good political minds.

In 1961, following the Dakar municipal elections, a new party, the Bloc des Masses Sénégalaises (BMS), was formed by Boubacar Guèye, former Minister of Justice of the Mali Federation, Patrice Diouf, and Cheikh Anta Diop. Its program scarcely differs from that of the UPS, and its following seems limited to a few intellectuals and UPS dissidents who once belonged to the SFIO.

All in all, these opposition parties have only a limited following. It is true that they cannot address the voters freely and that they are obliged to carry out most of their activities clandestinely, even though they may not officially be outlawed, but it is also obvious to any impartial observer that at the present time the UPS holds the confidence of the great majority of Senegalese.

THE LEADERS

To this survey of the political and administrative structure must be added a word about the principal leaders. These individuals have greatly contributed to the establishment of the present political structure, and the masses remain more attached to them than to the structure of the state. If tomorrow Senghor decided to change the constitution entirely, it is probable that the great majority of Senegalese people would follow him. One could perhaps even say that Lamine Guèye, Léopold Senghor, and Mamadou Dia are, in Senegal, the very symbols of the nation. They succeeded in leading the country into the Mali adventure, making Senegal renounce part of its sovereignty to the federal government. Then they were able to go back on their decision and in the process arouse the opposition of only a few individuals.

Lamine Guèye is the "dean" of the leaders. In fact, for years he was "*the* Senegalese leader." He represented an era of Senegalese life, the period between the days of traditional colonialism and the advance toward independence. This was the period that began in 1936, reached its apex immediately after World War II, and ended in 1956. It was the era of the SFIO, the incarnation of the assimilation policy and of the political control of the bourgeoisie of the four old communes— Gorée, Dakar, Rufisque, and St-Louis—whose inhabitants then had most of the same rights as the French in France itself.

Lamine Guèye threw himself into politics upon his return from the Antilles (where he had served several years as judge) and ran for election in 1934. Although he was not elected, he at least made himself known. In 1945 he came into his own and was triumphantly elected deputy to the French Parliament in the first postwar election. He even brought into Parliament on his coat-tails his young compatriot, Léopold Senghor. The following year brought the most striking triumph of Lamine Guèye. He was elected mayor of Dakar and shortly after was made a minister in Léon Blum's cabinet. This success, however, was short-lived. In 1948 Senghor broke away from him and founded his own party. Thenceforward the strength of the SFIO in Senegal diminished steadily. The year 1951 brought unexpected and crushing defeat: Lamine Guèye lost his seat as a deputy. Gradually, his adherents drifted away to join the triumphant rival. Many of those around him spoke of a possible "forced retirement." But Lamine Guèye is a true politician. If the times had changed, then he too would have to change. He therefore joined Senghor's party, in full realization that his political future would now depend on his former rival. The UPS showed its gratitude by reinstating him as president of the Assembly. In 1960, at the moment of the Mali Federation's breakup, he hesitated, and this hesitation almost put an end to his political life. The hesitation, however, lasted only a short while. On the morning of August 21 he rallied to Senghor.

Nevertheless, the city of Dakar remained faithful to Lamine Guèye, its mayor, an increasingly annoying state of affairs to the younger UPS members. The administration of the mayor, a combination of traditional solidarity and the classic "old crony" policy of the French SFIO, had led him to be severely criticized. After the Mali Federation's disappearance, Senghor's partisans, taking advantage of the semidisgrace of the Dakar leader, moved to the offensive. A new law reorganized the city of Dakar, dividing it into six boroughs (arrondissements), each governed by a borough mayor, and thus limiting the power of the mayor of the whole city. Once again, Lamine Guèye did not object but accepted a minority position for his partisans on the municipal council. Although he was himself elected to the municipal council, he decided to resign as mayor. The old Senegalese leader says that he no longer has any ambition except to remain the "mentor" of Senegal, the "dean," having only the moral authority of his age and experience. Perhaps this is wise. Lamine Guèye can still continue to play a far from negligible role at this level, for no one contests the good he has done for his country.

Léopold Sédar Senghor had the good fortune to arrive later on the political scene. Future historians will certainly credit much more effect to him than to his predecessor for, in the long run, his influence has been much greater on Africa's political evolution, particularly Africa beyond the borders of Senegal. The career of Lamine Guèye was, before all else, Senegalese. Léopold Sédar Senghor is an African politician.

At first glance nothing would seem to predispose Senghor to such a career. Poetry seems to suit him better than political life. French culture has impregnated and conquered him more than any other African. It was pointed out that Lamine Guèye represented the era of assimilation—but what African is more assimilated to France than the former deputy and mayor of Thiès? Perhaps this fact, however, is precisely the explanation of his political success. As he himself has written, he has assimilated without letting himself become assimilated. His peasant forebears have given this intellectual a healthy distrust of all ready-made systems and ideologies. Senghor, the brilliant intellectual, the frequenter of fashionable Parisian circles, has also known how to maintain contact with the peasants of the bush who see him as one of themselves and have made him their idol. He has remained sensitive to their needs. For example, in 1948, understanding at the right moment how impatiently the people of the bush were straining under the paternalistic tutelage of the big cities, he took the great risk of breaking with the SFIO. Nine years later, when he felt the profound aspirations of the African masses toward unity, he threw himself into a desperate battle against "Balkanization."

In the 1958 referendum, Senghor hesitated before making his decision. The peasant of the interior, in a rather paradoxical way, aspired to self-determination while hoping for close friendly relations with France. At the time this combination seemed contradictory, as General de Gaulle had equated independence with secession. The intellectuals in the Senegalese section of the PRA declared that independence must come before all else. Finally, however, Senghor opted for the people of the bush against the intellectuals, and once again he triumphed. Immediately after the vote in support of the constitution for the Fifth Republic, however, Senghor began the fight for independence and a *communauté* with looser contractual ties. This fight brought him harsh criticism from certain French and African circles, but once more events proved him right, so much so that this poet, whom many claim to scorn, has finally shown himself to be one of the best politicians of West Africa.

Today, Senghor has attained the place of honor. President of the Senegalese Republic, he is also one of the master planners behind the Monrovia group of twenty independent African nations. In spite of this, the "little Serer" has remained simple and unaffected. He is as much at ease under the thatched roof of a Senegalese hut as under the paneled ceiling of a French château. This contact with the peasant is where Senghor's strength lies. Some observers calculate that he has little chance of staying in power, feeling that he represents the Senegal of yesterday. But so long as Senghor remains alert to the needs of the people of the bush, he will remain "*the* Senegalese leader" and no one, in the opinion of the writer, can hope to replace him.

On the intellectual level it is not at all certain that Senghor represents the Senegal of yesterday. Senghor, the intellectual guide of the UPS, is also one of the best political theoreticians of modern Africa. Even the young men who criticize his tactics or laugh at his idiosyncrasies (and who does not have a few?) are forced to reckon with his ideas.

It is impossible in this brief study to present the political thought of Senghor. Such a task would necessitate a book. Nevertheless, one can at least present an outline of his ideas to give the reader a better idea of what is Senegalese policy.

Like most present-day African leaders, Léopold Senghor developed his political thought out of a reaction, the affirmation of *négritude* against white domination, and out of a discovery, Marxism, which taught him humanism. "The essential truth of Marx is to have shown us Man through and beyond the economic history of individual man." [10] Young Senghor, like many others, applied Marx's analysis of Western society to the colonial situation, thereby revealing all its abnormality. But the future Senegalese leader was never tempted by communism as such. It seemed to him to exude a crude, undifferen-

[10] Léopold Sédar Senghor, *Pierre Teilhard de Chardin et la Politique Africaine* (Paris: Edition du Seuil, 1962), p. 23.

tiated cultural imperialism which repelled him. As Senghor said of any ideology devised for western Europe and denying the values of Negro civilization: "We could not adopt it without adapting it." [11] As an African, he could not admit that religion, morality, and art were only reflections of material or economic reality. As a country boy he could not understand why Marx should be interested only in a minority like the working class. Finally, as a Westernized intellectual, he could not accept Marxist thinking that would lead to a denial of individual liberty.

Senghor's discovery of the work of Pierre Teilhard de Chardin provided him with a way out of the impasse to which Marx had led him and a means to answer the questions which Marx did not answer satisfactorily. For the twentieth-century thinker, Teilhard de Chardin, the significant fact of our era is that we are constructing a planetary civilization through socialization and totalization: socialization through the "examination of the conscience by itself" and totalization by the extension of civilization to the whole planet, that is, the opening of each particular civilization to others and through this to the entire world.[12] Moreover, Teilhardian thought is resolutely optimistic. In spite of everything, "socialization and totalization are working in the right direction. . . . Men of good will are arising in greater and greater numbers. . . . They are weaving over the world a denser and denser cloth of horizontal and vertical ties." [13] Suddenly, *négritude* had found its place. It could no longer be condemned as a "racist anti-racism." On the contrary, *négritude* can be considered one of the essential components of the universal civilization which is being built through the "living symbiosis of all particular values, of all civilizations." [14]

Négritude, as Senghor conceives of it at this stage in his intellectual and political evolution, is thus the antithesis of an aggressive reaction. In his words before the 1962 UPS congress:

We can now see clearly what each of us, after having cultivated it in ourselves, must bring to the meeting of the universal and also what we must take away. . . . Europe has taken the word "understanding" and made it into a discursive, organizing reasoning, while Africa has made it into an intuitive reasoning, a creative moistness, an *act of love.*[15]

---

[11] *Ibid.,* p. 26.
[12] Léopold Sédar Senghor, *Rapport sur la Doctrine et la Politique Générale,* presented at the UPS congress, Feb. 4, 1962.
[13] *Ibid.*   [14] *Ibid.*   [15] Italics are the author's.

The third "great" man of Senegal, Mamadou Dia, contrasts sharply with President Senghor. Senghor is university bred to his fingertips. Mamadou Dia is a self-made man. Before going into politics, he was a simple schoolteacher. Senghor is the man of the masses. Since 1945 he has traveled extensively through the country so that his name is known in even the smallest village. Mamadou Dia was for a long time virtually unknown. He made his career in the shadow of Senghor and has never tried to replace him. Senghor is a politician, whereas Dia is a governmental technician, reserved, not easy to approach or to get along with. Senghor is a Catholic and Dia is a fervent Muslim, but both are united in their approach to the problems of today.

Dia was elected to the French Parliament, first as a senator, then as a deputy. Unlike many of his African colleagues, he took advantage of this period in Paris to continue his studies and thus obtained a thorough grounding in economics. This makes Mamadou Dia today the best informed of African leaders on economic problems. Were it absolutely necessary to categorize him, one would say that he represents the Senegalese middle class, that of the African doctors, schoolteachers, and lesser civil servants which in its most serious aspects unites the traditional qualities of Africa with the contribution of Western civilization. This group is attached to the values of yesterday but open to the promise of tomorrow.

Contemporary Issues

Even with its decided advantages—a larger and better-trained elite than most of its neighbors, a more-developed economic infrastructure, and the beginnings of industrialization—Senegal cannot wholly escape the ambiguity of modern Africa. Yet Senegalese nationhood is a reality. Some states which have recently acquired independence are extremely artificial and give the impression that the slightest internal or external crisis would bring their whole structure tumbling down. This is not the case with Senegal. A century of French colonial rule has unified a diversified country under a single administration. Wolof, Serer, and people from the Casamance have learned to live together, to think in common. There are, of course, many holdovers from the past which might surge up again at any moment to create difficulties for the young Senegalese nation, but there is little chance they will jeopardize its existence.

Among these holdovers is the persistence of a certain tribal spirit. This tribal spirit is virtually nonexistent among the elite. A cabinet minister does not surround himself solely with men of his race or ethnic group; a *commandant de cercle* can impose his authority without being from the region. But at the bottom of the social ladder, the spirit still remains. Traditional chiefs, village elders, and all those living off the old animist and fetishist system—magicians, faith healers, and sorcerers—have been marked by the tribal spirit and can erase it only with difficulty. At each Dakar municipal election, for example, appeals are made to the solidarity of the Lébou community, that is, the race that inhabited the region before the city grew up. The caste system has also not completely disappeared. The musicians and the blacksmiths are still handicapped in certain areas of life, while those who belong to the noble castes sometimes continue to use their birth to make their fortunes. But more and more, this tribal spirit tends to yield to a simple regionalism which is found in all countries of the world and which, from many points of view, is not to be condemned.

More serious is the persistence of what one could call a "spiritual regionalism." The great Muslim religious leaders have long played a political and social role of prime importance. During the colonial era, they held extensive political power and the colonial administration relied on them. They were, and still are, closely tied to the traditional Africa, a fact which explains their distrust and occasional hostility to the struggle for independence. In 1958 they even created a "union of Marabouts" which grouped together the great Mouride and Tidjani Muslim brotherhoods and others of lesser importance. But the union failed; at the crucial moment the leaders lost their nerve. Only a few, like the young Tidjane Sy, opposed the government openly. They were defeated at the polls, their leaders were imprisoned, and not a peasant lifted a finger to help them. This incident shows the limits to the power of the religious leaders. Doubtless they retain a great religious following; they are still able to make many of the faithful work for them or upon occasion to block a particular social, economic, or even agricultural reform. No longer, however, can they directly and openly oppose the central government. In a vague manner the peasants sense that the future belongs to the new leaders, and they are not ready to fight to maintain privileges from which they profit little.

This attitude will be reinforced by education. But here is another weakness in Senegal; notwithstanding much recent progress the school system is still little developed. At the end of 1960 it was estimated that only 136,000 pupils (of which 40,000 were girls) were in the primary schools of Senegal. In other words, only a little more than 30 per cent of school-age children were actually in school. Moreover, even this percentage has been attained only very recently so that the older an individual is, the greater is the likelihood that he is illiterate; for instance, less than 10 per cent of those over forty know how to read and write. Yet it is difficult to change old village customs and to modernize the methods of agriculture and of raising livestock if one has to work with an illiterate peasantry. The development of the nation is therefore closely tied to that of the schools. Promising, however, in this regard is the fact that the situation in the secondary schools is proportionately better than on the primary level, for in 1960 there were 8,536 students (of whom 2,090 were girls) enrolled in the high schools.

A fourth weakness of the young Senegalese nation, a weakness that stems directly from the previous one, is the lack of trained African personnel. During the last few years, the government has made a big push toward Africanization in the public service. All the *commandants de cercle* are now Africans, as are the chiefs of the administrative services. But in technical fields Senegal must still rely on foreign experts and technicians. In the secondary schools, for example, only 17 out of 253 teachers are African. This situation in Senegal is not unusual; it exists in all African countries. Even in those countries which maintain that they have Africanized to the maximum, the chief of an administrative service is often helped by a French or British or German or Russian or Czech adviser who is of primary importance because he is the only really trained person there. But can a country be really independent so long as there is such vital dependence on foreign technicians?

In the private sector, Africanization is even less advanced. The majority of the large commercial houses and virtually all the industries have only a tiny minority of trained African personnel. Further, few Senegalese are in business for themselves and run their own affairs. In other words, the key sectors of industry, like foreign commerce, are almost completely under the control of non-Senegalese.

Finally, still another weakness must be noted, one of a different sort, which is not limited to Senegal or even to Africa—the phenomenon of the *mystique* of the leader. This *mystique* has developed to such an extent among certain sectors of the population that one sometimes wonders whether it has replaced a national conscience. One wonders whether, for certain Sengalese, the party spirit—which is generally incarnated in a single man—has taken precedence over the national spirit, whether these Senegalese are not ready to sacrifice everything for the triumph of their leader. When the Senegalese peasants marched on Dakar on August 19, 1960, they did not come to destroy the Mali Federation, or to save Senegal; they came simply because "Senghor had told them to come."

This state of mind constitutes a weakness to the extent that the "charismatic" leader thrust before the crowd may become enamored of his role, taking his own ideas for those of the masses or sacrificing the interests of the country to personal interests. At the stage of development reached by most African states, however, this probably constitutes a necessary stage in the creation of national unity and gives the country needed impetus for its development. This is so true that in states where no real leader has come forth great confusion generally reigns and sometimes serious difficulties arise. Moreover, in most African states, and particularly in Senegal, the public leaders have shown wisdom and realism in their actions and have known how to maintain the indispensable contact with their people. Nowhere in Africa has a real fascist regime appeared, and in Senegal the danger is less than elsewhere. Yet this is not to say that it could not appear in the African context.

THE NATION ORGANIZES

Alongside these weaknesses exist also a certain number of positive factors. To Senegal's credit is the persistence of a genuine sense of democracy. This spirit is rather far removed, of course, from the democracy practiced on the banks of the Thames, but it is also very different from the totalitarianism in vogue behind the iron curtain. In Senegal the party in power does not dominate the whole life of the country; it does not give direct orders to the government on all subjects. Thus it is not an exclusive or totalitarian party. Even though there is a UPS youth movement, the young Senegalese are not obliged to belong. And other youth organizations in the cultural and religious fields are freely permitted to exist.

In addition, the government allows several different trade unions in Senegal. Only the "national" trade union is officially encouraged, but the leaders of the other unions, although minority organizations, can continue to organize meetings, training programs, and seminars. They are received from time to time by the government authorities, and their followers can even parade in the streets, for example, on May Day.

Lastly, a certain freedom of the press persists in Senegal. The cables sent by foreign correspondents are not censored, and the local press can talk about Senegal's opponents without being obliged to describe them as traitors or imbeciles. No opposition newspaper is allowed, but for others the censorship is relatively light, if not always intelligent. One cannot publish a photograph of President Senghor on a bicycle (it would be disrespectful). Nor can one write that Senghor and Houphouët-Boigny do not have the same ideas on Red China (that would imply that there were some differences between them). But one can give an objective account of the Belgrade Conference (to which Senegal was not invited) or describe in detail the meetings of the Casablanca group (the rival of the Monrovia group).

Senegal's opponents, particularly those of the "positive neutralism" group, claim that the survival of Western democratic traditions is a holdover from colonialism and therefore constitutes a weakness. It is true that Senegal does not form a people "pure and hard," a "bloc without fissures," solidly backing its leaders. But to the Western view this fact constitutes a strength, with the persistence of democratic values playing the role of safety valve. It must be remembered that Senegal is one of those rare countries of former French West Africa in which students do not pose a "problem" for the government. The ministers know that the majority of the students belong to the opposition, but they do not believe that this endangers the regime.

The second positive factor is the effort that Senegal has made to elaborate an original type of socialism. All or almost all the African countries call themselves socialist, but their socialism is generally nothing but a copy of European socialism. The Senegalese have tried to go further and to outline a truly African socialism. It is not certain that this attempt will meet with success, but, in any case, it has led the government to study the specific features of Senegal. This was the basis for the vast survey made by Father Lebret. No work of this sort had ever been attempted before in the country, and no other African country has had the courage to undertake a similar study. Thanks to this report, the Senegalese government now has a first-class working tool with which to plan for the future.

In moving to the practical application of their ideas, the Senegalese leaders have demonstrated the same realism. Distrusting pat formulas, they have not set out on immediate collectivization and nationalization of all sectors of the country's life. They have limited themselves to a first phase, mainly in the agricultural sector, and even in this sector they have been prudent and have progressed by stages. The first step was to work on the problem of marketing agricultural products, a process that had earlier given rise to a number of abuses. Then the peasants were grouped into cooperatives. These are not yet obligatory, and the government hopes that they will soon be administered by the peasants themselves.

The reform of the commercial sector is also being undertaken. The sale of certain essential commodities will, at least in the interior of the country, be placed progressively under state organizations. It is also possible that the state will increase its control over foreign commerce. All this has as its goal not the implementation of some theory but the improvement of the lot of the peasants and the urban workers by doing away with the middlemen and moneylenders who exploit them and by eliminating the old harmful trading system.

These reforms are accompanied by a great push toward basic education, particularly the education of the rural population. This constitutes the third positive factor. In his speech outlining his program before the National Assembly on April 4, 1961, Mamadou Dia said: "It is necessary to modify profoundly the social structure itself so that it harmonizes with the framework of a young nation that is forcefully entering on its road to development. It is in taking this goal into account that the people must be mobilized." In contrast to what is happening in other countries, Senegal wants to effect this mobilization while "respecting that freedom of association that we consider an essential aspect of our socialism."

To reach this goal, Senegal is launching, as already mentioned, a vast rural promotion (*animation rurale*) program. By the end of the first Four-Year Plan the entire country should be serviced by a network of 7,000 rural promoters. These promoters are young villagers who take a preliminary three-week training course organized in their region. They then return to their villages, where their work is supervised by trained personnel. They are, in addition, obliged to participate in a series of advanced training courses which will progressively give them the technical competence and civic experience necessary to permit them in turn to provide leadership for their villages. The government counts on these young men to extend the cooperative system, to transform the villages into modern communal societies, and finally to make its socialism a success.

It is important to note the risks involved in this program: through their training the young villagers acquire an entirely new mentality; they discover the modern world. By the same token, they become much more demanding of themselves and of their neighbors. If the government does not keep the promises it has made, if economic development does not produce concrete results, if the peasants' standard of living is not raised, these young people may well become the spokesmen for discontent. The Senegalese leaders believe, however, that there is no other way to get the peasant masses moving and thus develop the country. They believe also that this will probably be the best means of keeping a small urban bourgeois oligarchy from reserving its profits for itself alone. In following this policy, the Dia government remains loyal to its faith in a socialism which has confidence in man, in the African man. This is an original experiment, for most other African states feel that it is not possible to make such methods work and that it is simpler to employ methods more restrictive of individual liberties.

External Relations

The colonial system had not permitted Senegal to enter into contact with the outside world except through the intermediary of the colonial power. Independence, however, has made it possible for Senegal to establish relations with all the other nations of the world. One of the first tasks of its government, therefore, was to develop an international policy, and after almost two years of independence this policy began to appear clearly.

"DECOLONIZATION"

As early as December 8, 1960, in a speech before the United Nations, Mamadou Dia set forth certain principles underlying Senegal's foreign policy. Senegal, he said, takes as its point of departure the fact that its independence was achieved by political means which have permitted it to "maintain intact the friendship between its people and the people of the former colonizing country." Senegal has not broken its connection with France but on the contrary has striven to maintain particularly close relations. For the same reason, it has maintained the agreements which were signed between France and the Mali Federation. (Nevertheless, the government has not found it necessary to submit them to the National Assembly.)

Senegal has adopted this attitude because, as Mamadou Dia has said, its leaders believe that this is the best way of reinforcing its new independence. They feel that a sudden break with the former colonizer would have lead to a Congolike chaos or at the least to the difficulties Guinea had. The Senegalese leaders, after analyzing the international situation, saw realistically that their country did not have a choice between neocolonialism and independence with prosperity but "between one kind of neocolonialism and another," in Habib Bourguiba's expression. On the whole, the neocolonialism of a France reduced to its European boundaries seemed less harmful than that of the two great world powers. Other reasons, such as language, also played a role in the decision. As Senghor said at the 1962 UPS congress, "Our elite has been formed intellectually by France. To change the language would mean fifty years—fifty years' delay." Finally, on August 21, 1960, when Senegal attained its independence it seemed particularly isolated in Africa and in the world. It needed effective and solid support of its sovereignty to be admitted to the United Nations, and France was in the best position to assure this support.

Senegal therefore remains a state within the Franco-African Community, but this formula does not have much meaning today. The Community has no juridical existence and no common institutions. The heads of state of the Community countries hold no meetings. Moreover, the states which officially belong to the Community have no closer ties to France, in fact, than do those like the Ivory Coast and Dahomey which have left the Community. According to Senghor at the 1962 UPS congress, the Community is based on two principles: "to concert our policies and to harmonize our economies." "To concert our policies" is a vague expression and can be interpreted variously. In fact, it has meant a mutual agreement to keep the other partner informed on policy and a desire to avoid coming directly into conflict with each other. When France undertook its atomic-bomb explosions in the Sahara and aroused a wave of reproach in many parts of Africa, Senegal did not criticize France publicly. On several occasions, however, Senegal made known in Paris by discreet diplomatic means its hostility to the tests. So did other French-speaking states. This attitude was worth while. France stopped its nuclear explosions.

The Algerian affair has been a much more delicate subject. The Senegalese as Africans and as former colonized peoples feel great sympathy for the Algerians. They consider that because they themselves have attained independence, nothing can justify keeping the Algerians from theirs. On the other hand, the Senegalese government, as just mentioned, is convinced that it needs French aid to consolidate its independence. Senegal's policy on Algeria has gradually revealed itself as the result of these two positions. Thus, Senegal is a determined partisan of decolonization. It holds that all colonial rule should disappear from the face of the earth and that all should have the right to self-determination. Following this policy, the Senegalese delegation to the United Nations vigorously supported the General Assembly resolution advocating the end of the colonial system. Senegal held that Algeria had the right to independence and in 1960 pronounced itself in favor of an "independent Algerian republic obedient to the laws of the majority." To achieve this decolonization, Senegal proposed a method identical to the one it has used itself, that is, the opening of direct negotiations between the two partners. This is the method Senegal supported before the General Assembly at the end of 1960 despite the disapproval of the majority of the Afro-Asian group.

This attitude, which appears to have become its basic policy, inspired Senegal's position at the time of the Bizerte crisis. In this delicate affair, involving two of its friends, Senegal from the beginning supported Tunisian sovereignty over Bizerte. Since Tunisia had shown its desire to have Bizerte returned to Tunisian control, Senegal held that France should accede to this request. At the same time, Senegal deplored the fact that recourse had been taken to arms to settle the affair, and it did all in its power to favor the opening of bilateral negotiations. This crisis also permitted a clearer definition of Senegal's position on the question of military bases. The Senegalese government considers that any country has the right to yield military bases freely to a foreign power if it deems this necessary for the protection of its independence, but it also supports the right to recover these bases when it so wants and believes the foreign power must then accede to the request.

Senegal does not encourage recourse to violence or direct action (though it admits this may sometimes be necessary) and believes in the virtue of talks and diplomacy. Mamadou Dia has said, "We want peace with justice," and in this respect his attitude is close to that of India or that in "Bourguibism." This explains Senegal's attitude to the nationalists of Portuguese Guinea. It approves of the Guinean nationalist movement and is ready to aid it on the moral, material, and international level. Senegal gives asylum to its leaders but refuses to let Senegalese territory become a point of departure for military operations and has disarmed the troops which had been formed in the Casamance to "liberate" their Guinean "brothers."

Senegal and France have harmonized their military policies. Senegal has agreed to retain temporarily the French military bases of

Dakar and Thiès, but these bases are not of great strategic importance and it is probable that France will evacuate them in the near future. Senegal has also given France priority in equipping and advising its army.

The Senegalese school system at the secondary and university level remains based on the French system. Degrees conferred in Dakar are the same as those conferred in France. The University of Dakar, although under the Senegalese Minister of Education, has a French rector (named jointly by the two governments), and most of its professors, as well as those of the secondary schools, are French.

Senegal has maintained very close economic ties with France. It remains in the franc zone, with France as its major client and supplier. It could scarcely have done otherwise, for its principal product, the peanut, is not easily sold on the world market and a sudden upheaval of the existing system at the time of independence would have had disturbing financial and social consequences which would have made the government's task much more difficult. Nevertheless, the Senegalese leaders are well aware of this indirect dependence on France, and they are trying to diversify their products progressively and to find new buyers for their exports. The exploitation of the Taïba phosphate deposit will help decrease their present dependence. Moreover, in contrast to many other African states, Senegal is free from any direct financial dependence on the former colonial power. Senegal balances its budget through its own resources and does not need to call for outside help to make up a deficit.

Senegal's policy toward the Western countries does not differ markedly from its policy toward France. Senegal hopes that Great Britain will pursue its policy of decolonization of the African countries still under its sovereignty and that this will be done with the agreement of both sides and without a sudden or total rupture. In the same way, Senegal distrusts American capitalism and sympathizes with Cuba when it seems to be the object of an attack fomented in the United States.

Senegal is realistic and understands full well that an underdeveloped country cannot grow without outside aid unless it has extensive resources such as the USSR and China have at their disposal. It has refrained from joining other African countries in condemning a priori any association with the Common Market. Without doubt, say the Senegalese leaders, neocolonialism must be distrusted and the government must at all times maintain its liberty of action, but there is also need of outside capital. It would be foolish to think it possible to obtain sufficient funds without the help of the West. Moreover, the Senegalese leaders believe that capital will require guarantees before investing in Africa and that if these guarantees are not economic or financial, they will be political. Discussions with possible sources of capital deal above all with these guarantees. It is up to the government to fix the limits beyond which it will not go. For example, Senegal considers it dangerous to ask for private investment in the agricultural sector, but it is ready to open its doors in the industrial sector if the investments are in enterprises which it considers useful and which are included in the development plan.

Senegal's attitude to the Communist bloc has been rather reserved. Senegal distrusts any ready-made ideologies or a priori and rigid attitudes. It finds it normal to recognize these countries, for they do in fact exist. It has, therefore, recognized both Red China and North Vietnam, and it also supports Red China's admission to the United Nations. So far, however, it has refused to let these countries open embassies in Senegal because it distrusts their propaganda and intellectual totalitarianism. On the other hand, should the occasion arise, Senegal would not refuse economic or financial aid from these countries as long as this aid in no way jeopardizes its independence.

This complex of attitudes explains the position Senegal has taken on the Gambian question. The Gambia, that minute British colony that reaches like a finger into the interior of Senegal, poses a problem for Senegalese foreign policy. The Gambia cannot live by itself, and its survival is a nuisance to Senegal which is thereby deprived of one of its natural outlets, the lower course of the Gambia River. Some of the Senegalese have wanted to see their country launch a vast movement in favor of a pure and simple annexation, the "return of the Gambia to the mother country," but Senegalese leaders have refused to follow such a policy. They have said that Great Britain must recognize the Gambia's right to self-rule and that then the Gambia will freely determine its own future. Given its geographic situation, they are convinced that the Gambia can do nothing except unite with its neighbor. The Senegalese leaders' behavior on this issue is significant. The Dakar government shuns any spectacular initiatives or demagoguery and considers that the best long-term policy is to act discreetly and prudently.

Senegal's foreign policy is rather unusual in present-day Africa. Senegal's critics at home and abroad, the leaders of "revolutionary

Africa," accuse the Senegalese leaders of being in France's pay and of having sold out to the West. Such statements are absurd. It is true that the Senegalese leaders find themselves closer in viewpoint to the Western than to the Eastern bloc, but they are not prepared to play the role of simple satellite or to adopt automatically the point of view of Paris, London, or Washington. On the other hand, certain rightist extremists in France, for example, have reproached Senegal for being anti-French and, in the last analysis, a tool of communism. This attitude, too, is senseless. Senegal is groping for a truly neutral way but without illusions, knowing full well that no country is ever completely neutral. If one considers that Mali follows a "pro-Eastern neutrality," then one can certainly say that Senegal pursues a "neutrality sympathetic to the West."

THE BUILDING OF AFRICA

Another principle of Senegalese diplomacy is to work for the achievement of African unity. Senegal wants to be African before all else and hopes that in the future it will form part of a much vaster African community. It has been pointed out that in the earlier period the Senegalese leaders were fierce advocates of an African federation. This desire for a larger grouping led to the creation of the Mali Federation, which was, however, too limited and too fragile to survive. Since the unfortunate Mali experience, Senegal has somewhat modified its attitude. Its leaders now realize that even if the desire for unity is universal, the achievement of this goal is hindered by numerous obstacles, mainly the many differences between the peoples and ethnic groups of Africa. Therefore they now believe that unity will be attained not by spectacular political decisions which might be jeopardized by the first storms of dissension but only by the progressive creation of a vast economic and cultural entity whose different parties agree to bind themselves closer and closer together. This concept provides the basis for Senegal's African policy.

Senegal has come to the conclusion (which Guinea held somewhat earlier) that the road to unity lies through the achievement of independence by the former colonial territories within their existing colonial boundaries, artificial as these may seem to be. Thus Senegal vigorously supported Mauritania's independence. It is well known that Morocco claimed that Mauritania was once a part of the Sherifian Empire and therefore should be returned to the kingdom of Morocco. The least one can say is that this argument from history was far from conclusive. Moreover, southern Mauritania is populated with Negroid peoples closely related to the Senegalese. Dakar could also have claimed its share of Mauritanian land, but it refrained from doing so. As soon as Mauritania sought its independence, Senegal staunchly supported it, believing that Africa has greatly evolved since the precolonial period and that to go back to early boundaries —which, moreover, had never been firmly established—would plunge the whole continent into incredible anarchy.

In being faithful to its policy of African unity, Senegal has not denied the natural affinity between Mauritania and Morocco, and it has discreetly tried to bring the two countries together. It is no longer a secret that after Hassan II's accession to the Moroccan throne, contacts between Morocco and Mauritania were made through the intermediacy of the Sengalese Embassy in Rabat and the Moroccan Embassy in Dakar. These efforts did not succeed, it seems, because of the internal situation in Morocco, but there is still hope in the Senegalese capital that one day Rabat will recognize Mauritanian sovereignty in exchange for a treaty of alliance and cooperation.

Finally, Senegal believes that African unity can be achieved only by stages and that its way must be prepared through a coordination of foreign policies and through specific economic, cultural, and defense pacts which will lead the way toward unity. The latter approach has been at the base of the working together of the groups called "Brazzaville" and "Monrovia."

In August, 1960, when Senegal secured its independence after leaving the Mali Federation, it found itself somewhat isolated from other African states. On the one hand, Guinea and Ghana seemed to have more in common with the new Mali (the former Soudan) than with Senegal. On the other hand, the breakup of the Mali Federation had given the advantage to Houphouët-Boigny and the Council of the Entente (formed by the Ivory Coast, Upper Volta, Dahomey, and Niger) which had rejected any idea of African federation. One of the first objectives of Senegalese diplomacy was to emerge from this isolation and to reestablish its close relations with other African states. Senegal soon found a sympathetic listener in Houphouët-Boigny who, now that independence had been acquired and there was no possibility of a federation, shared the same ideas as Senegal on almost all the problems of African and foreign policy.

Thus was born the idea of grouping into a homogeneous body the French-speaking states which had just received independence. Invitations were sent out for a preparatory conference in Abidjan and a decision-making conference in Brazzaville. The latter, held in December, 1960, convened eleven African countries and Madagascar. They agreed on a charter of "African cooperation" based on four principles to which Senegal fully subscribed: a persistent search for peace, noninterference in the internal affairs of other countries, economic and cultural cooperation on a footing of equality among the member states, and, finally, concerted diplomacy.

A few months later, on March 26, 1961, the same chiefs of state met in Yaoundé, the capital of Cameroun, where they then adopted a treaty creating among them the African and Malagasy Organization for Economic Cooperation (OAMCE) similar in spirit to the Organization for European Economic Cooperation of postwar Europe. They also decided to create a common airline company named Air-Afrique. Finally, they agreed on the principle of a political union, (Union Africaine et Malgache), whose organization was to be outlined at a later date but whose members after mutual consultation would adopt an identical policy on important foreign policy questions such as Algeria and negotiations with the Common Market.

All these decisions evidently marked a great step toward African unity, but they also aroused harsh criticism in certain countries. Since the Brazzaville group included only French-speaking countries which (except for Cameroun) had all been members of the Community and which were linked or were going to be linked to France by agreements of cooperation, people in Accra and Conakry disdainfully called them lackeys of France who had, by order from Paris, come together the better to serve French interests. Even though false, this idea received a certain amount of credence among the young people of all African countries and was well developed in the corridors of the United Nations.

In any case, it was obvious that such a regrouping was only partial and that if one really wanted to speak of African unity, it would be necessary to enlarge the circle. To make known the exact policy of the Brazzaville "twelve," Senghor went in person to three English-speaking West African states, Liberia, Ghana, and Nigeria. Everywhere he received a courteous welcome and, as the future was to show, his talks in Lagos and Monrovia were useful. In contrast, those in Ghana bore little fruit, though it must be said that in that country circumstances worked against the Senegalese President since he arrived in Accra the day of the announcement of the murder of Patrice Lumumba, an event that aroused a great deal of anti-West feeling in all Africa.

Nigeria's Prime Minister, Sir Abubakar Tafawa Balewa, had already in March suggested a meeting of all independent African states, and the Brazzaville group enthusiastically supported this idea. It was decided that the meeting should be held in Monrovia, capital of the oldest independent state in West Africa. As it turned out, the followers of "positive" neutralism, the Casablanca group, refused to come to Monrovia, but representatives from twenty countries were present —Nigeria, Sierra Leone, Tunisia, Togo, Somalia, Ethiopia, Libya, the twelve members of the Brazzaville group, and, of course, Liberia. The Brazzaville group thus showed its determination not to confine itself to a purely French-speaking grouping. The conference did not produce spectacular results, but this was scarcely possible in view of the great differences between the participants. The latter agreed, however, on several basic principles for inter-African cooperation, recommending particularly that no African country serve as a haven for subversion against another African country. They decided, above all, to ask their experts to study the means progressively to establish economic and cultural cooperation between their respective countries. In this conference, as well as that of Brazzaville, Senegal played a role of prime importance, showing itself to be one of the master thinkers of the Monrovia group.

Despite this success, the formation of the Casablanca group of Ghana, Guinea, Mali, Morocco, the United Arab Republic, and the provisional government of the Algerian Republic (GPRA) posed particular problems for Senegal. To explain Senegal's attitude it is necessary to define its attitude to each of the countries composing the Casablanca group as well as to the group as a whole.

With regard to Mali, Senegal had hoped after the breakup of the Federation on August 20, 1960, quickly to restore cordial if not friendly relations. That is why Dakar refrained from engaging in polemics with Bamako. Senghor even suggested at the end of August that the railroad line be reopened and commercial and economic relations renewed. But the leaders in Bamako would not listen. In their view it was Senegal, with the aid of the French, which had torpedoed the Mali Federation. The Soudanese felt that in arresting the Soudanese leaders the night of August 19 the Senegalese leaders had done something which definitively discredited them in the eyes of nationalist African opinion. No agreement could therefore be possible as long as the Senegalese leaders remained in power. "One does not discuss with traitors."

With this state of mind, the break was rigorously maintained not only on the political but also on the commercial and economic levels, while the Mali press and radio regularly continued their vigorous attacks on the "Senegalo-French clique" of Dakar. After having kept quiet for a year, Senegal seemed to give up hope that the situation would improve in the near future and began to answer the insults flung from the other side of the Falémé River. Senegalese-Malian relations still remain bad, and nothing indicates that they are likely to improve quickly. Nevertheless, the two former partners conferred several times during 1961 and at least managed to agree on the methods of liquidating the assets of the ex-Federation.

Senegal's relations with Guinea are quite different. They have greatly improved, in comparison to what they were after the 1958 referendum when Guinea chose to break with the French Community. Dakar and Conakry have exchanged ambassadors. They have also signed financial and commercial agreements which permit Guinea to buy again on the Senegalese market and Senegal to obtain Guinean fruits. Without doubt their policies remain very different regarding internal as well as foreign affairs, but the two neighbors have at least normalized their relations.

Senegal maintains diplomatic relations with almost all the other members of the Casablanca group. It has opened embassies in Accra, Rabat, and Cairo and in turn has received their ambassadors. The one exception is Algeria. Senegal has not recognized the Algerian provisional government but is willing to do so when it establishes itself on Algerian soil. Direct contacts have been made on many occasions with the leaders of the FLN, and the Senegalese government is convinced that Algerian independence can be achieved only under the direction of the Algerian "rebels" and their leaders.

With regard to the Casablanca group as a whole, Senegal has never officially expressed its opinion. It has not done so because of its concern for African unity and because it refuses to pronounce words or perform deeds that might irrevocably divide Africa into two hostile camps. The Senegalese are still convinced that the positions of the Monrovia and Casablanca groups are not far apart, and they hope that one day, perhaps sooner than one might expect, the two groups will come together. For the moment, however, Dakar and the Casablanca group propose different methods for solving common problems. In consequence Senegal treats them as strangers and for this reason has opened embassies in Conakry and Accra, but it has not opened any within the Brazzaville group since it considers that its members are not foreign but "brother" countries with which a different form of representation is more suitable.

A word must be said about the attitude of Senegal toward the United Nations. Mamadou Dia, in his speech before the General Assembly, already cited, made a certain number of realistic observations: "The United Nations has become a theater of the cold war. Two great blocs confront each other daily, sometimes with shouting and fury to the point that one wonders if the edifice, still a shield against violence, will not be smashed to pieces; sometimes the competition takes the form of procedural maneuvers." Despite this strife, he added, the United Nations should be the "living image" of the dialogue between peoples and its principal role should be that of "helping to solve difficulties instead of exacerbating them." This, Mamadou Dia concluded, is an extremely important role on which depends the survival of all nations great and small. Therefore Senegal is a confirmed partisan of the United Nations.

AN INDUSTRIOUS AND SERIOUS COUNTRY

Senegal's distinctive domestic policy, combined with its foreign policy which avoids bloc politics and demagoguery and verbal excesses, gives Senegal a particular personality in the Africa of today. Will it be able to maintain these characteristics? Some observers, who expect from Africa only the radical and the excessive, are doubtful. This is not the author's opinion. The colonial period is drawing to an end (except behind the iron curtain). Once Algeria and the countries of British East Africa have reached independence, it seems highly unlikely that the West will long sacrifice its obvious interests in the defense of Portuguese colonialism and South African apartheid. One can also hope that the United States will adopt a more open, understanding, and attentive attitude to the real needs of underdeveloped countries and the aspirations of their people. Under such circumstances nearly all the grievances of the Afro-Asian nations against the Western world will fall of their own weight.

At the same time, it seems likely that these same nations will discover more and more that the USSR is a great power and, as such, is no more understanding of their real problems than any other great power. Africa has greater need of dams, roads, and outlets for its products than of printing presses, travel grants, and ideological literature. It will discover that the Soviet world is even more embedded in its ideological dogmas than America or western Europe. At that time—which will probably come in three or four years—Senegal will appear as one of the African countries which, by ignoring the distractions of the moment, has set off most rapidly on the road to economic and human development.

BIBLIOGRAPHY

The studies on modern Senegal in English are few, although their number has increased notably in the last few years. Following are some major sources, most of which are readily available.

Two general studies of French West Africa containing considerable information on Senegal are Virginia Thompson and Richard Adloff, *French West Africa* (Stanford: Stanford University Press, 1958), and Thomas Hodgkin and Ruth Schachter, "French-speaking West Africa in Transition," *International Conciliation*, no. 528 (New York, May, 1960). The former treats the economic, social, and political evolution of France's West African territories in the decade after World War II. Although marred by occasional inaccuracies, it provides a wealth of varied information and has an excellent bibliography. The Hodgkin-Schachter study analyzes succintly the major political developments in the area through 1960.

Those interested in the colonial background should consult Raymond Leslie Buell's *The Native Problem in Africa* (New York: Macmillan, 1928). Chapters 57 and 58 deal with Senegal, particularly with political life in the four communes. Robert Delavignette, a French colonial administrator, expounds a liberal view of prewar French administrative policy in *Freedom and Authority in French West Africa* (London: Oxford University Press for the International African Institute, 1950).

An excellent study of Senegalese political life which traces in some detail the evolution of political parties is Kenneth E. Robinson's "Senegal: The Elections to the Territorial Assembly, March, 1957," in W. J. M. Mackenzie and Kenneth E. Robinson, *Five Elections in Africa* (New York: Oxford University Press, 1960). Paul Mercier, a French sociologist, relates Senegalese political developments to their social context in "Evolution of Senegalese Elites," *International Social Science Bulletin*, VIII, no. 3 (1956), 441–452, and in "Political Life in the Urban Centers of Senegal: A study of a Period of Transition," *PROD* (Princeton), III, no. 10 (June, 1960), 3–20.

David P. Gamble provides the most comprehensive anthropological study of a major Senegalese ethnic group in his *The Wolof of Senegambia* (London: International African Institute, 1957). Other studies treating particular aspects of modern Senegalese life are Elliot S. Berg, "French West Africa," in Walter Galenson, ed., *Labor and Economic Development* (New York: Wiley, 1959), which traces the role of labor movements under the colonial regime, and J. Spencer Trimingham, *Islam in West Africa* (Lon-

don: Oxford University Press, 1959), which provides a thorough introduction to the dominant religion of Senegal.

Of particular interest to students of politics are two books by Senegalese
political leaders, Léopold Senghor's African Socialism (New York: American Society for African Culture, 1959), and Mamadou Dia's African Nations and World Solidarity (New York: Praeger, 1962). Senghor's book
expounds the intellectual underpinnings of his policies, and Dia's work discusses his government's approach to problems of economic and social development.

Those who read French will find the following books of interest. Jacques
Richard-Molard's Afrique Occidentale Française (Paris: Berger Levrault,
1956) provides a good general introduction to French-speaking West
Africa, with the emphasis on its geographic, economic, and social aspects.
Ernest Milcent traces the postwar development of French West African
politics in L'A.O.F. Entre en Scène (Paris: Edition du Témoignage Chré-
tien, 1958). Alphonse Gouilly discusses the Islamic background in L'Islam
en Afrique Occidentale Française (Paris: Larose, 1952). André Villard's
Histoire du Sénégal (Dakar: Maurice Viale, 1943) is the only general his-
tory of Senegal and contains much of interest although it is essentially a
history of the French in Senegal and modern scholarship has outdated a
good deal of his precolonial background. Karim (Paris: Nouvelles Editions
Latines, 1948), a short novel by Senegal's ambassador to the United States,
Ousmane Socé Diop, provides a penetrating insight into Senegalese society.
Marcel Capet, Traité d'Economie Tropicale: Les Economies d'AOF? (Paris:
Librairie Générale de Droit, 1958), analyzes the economic structure of
French West Africa under the colonial regime. Gil Dugué, Vers les Etats
Unis d'Afrique (Dakar: Lettres Africaines, 1960), is an inside story of the
end of the colonial period and the rise of independent African politics in
French-speaking West Africa, but it is difficult for the uninitiated to follow.

Among the studies to appear in 1962, three are of particular interest.
Michael Crowder's Senegal (London: Oxford University Press) analyzes
modern social, cultural, and political life with special reference to the
heritage of France's assimilationist policies. The chapter on Senegal in
Ruth Schachter's forthcoming Parties of French-speaking West Africa (Oxford University Press) traces Senegalese political developments through
independence. William J. Foltz concentrates on the postindependence
period in his chapter "The Political Parties of Senegal" in James S. Coleman
and Carl Rosberg, eds., Political Groups in Middle Africa (Los Angeles:
University of California Press).

Two weekly publications, Afrique Nouvelle (Dakar) and West Africa
(London), report on major developments in Senegal, the former concentrating on reporting the week's happenings and the latter specializing in
somewhat less topical articles of political and economic analysis.

IV

GUINEA

By L. GRAY COWAN

Columbia University

Historical Background

The Republic of Guinea, which came into existence in 1958, is, like the other independent states of West Africa, the result of the colonial partition of Africa in the nineteenth century. Its present borders were determined by agreement between Great Britain, France, and Germany. Within them is contained a variety of tribal groups which, prior to the period of European contact, were more often at war than at peace. The artificial unity imposed by the colonial administration brought about a suppression of tribal warfare, but the creation of Guinean national unity is the product of the struggle for independence which has marked the postwar period in Africa.

The origins of the people who are today the citizens of Guinea go back beyond the record of history. Very little is known of the coastal peoples except that they were gradually pushed to the ocean by succeeding waves of invaders who descended from the desert to the north and east. The ancestors of the present peoples of the Fouta Djallon plateau figure in the history of the great empires of the Soudan in the sixteenth and seventeenth centuries. Fierce warriors, they long resisted the influence of Islam. According to legend, the first of the Foula peoples to immigrate to the great plateau of northeast Guinea formed four groups—the children of four brothers who bore the names Ba, Sow, Diallo, and Bari. In their modern spellings these surnames are to be found everywhere in northern Guinea today.

THE COMING OF THE FRENCH

Under the influence of powerful teachers or Marabouts of Maure-
tania, a group of converted Foula chieftains launched a holy war in
1725, to convert the pagan peoples of the plateau to Islam. With the
successful completion of the war, the country was divided into nine
provinces or *diwals,* each ruled by one of the leaders of the campaign.
Under the general suzerainty of the descendants of the two major
leaders of the war, who had proclaimed themselves the Almamys of
Timbo, the vast feudal empire lasted until the coming of the French
in the nineteenth century. Although torn by internal strife, the empire
of the Almamys was subjected to a rudimentary form of administration which included the payment of annual tribute from the villages
to the *diwal* chief and the dispensing of a rough justice by courts
whose judges relied on a combination of Koranic and customary law.

From the mid-nineteenth century, European contacts became more
frequent along the coast of the "Rivières du Sud," as the area between
Sierra Leone and Portuguese Guinea was known to the French traders.
Operating from posts in the estuary of the Nuñez River near the
present Boké, French and English expeditions penetrated into the
interior and engaged in trade with the peoples of the Fouta Djallon.
Protectorate treaties were made and broken with both the French and
the English by the coastal chiefs from the middle of the century on,
but it was not until 1887 that French possession of Conakry was
finally assured over the protests of the British who occupied the offshore Los Islands. By 1889, on the conclusion of a convention with
Great Britain recognizing the present border with Sierra Leone and
the occupation of the Fouta Djallon, French rights to the Guinean
colony were finally secured against the claims of rival European
powers.

But the establishment of French hegemony was to be delayed by
the bitter resistance of the last of the great nineteenth-century
Soudanese conquerors, the Almamy Samory Touré, the great-grand-
father of the first President of the new Republic of Guinea. Samory
was born at Sanankoro in northern Guinea, of a middle-class family.
He rapidly acquired a reputation as a warrior and by 1872 had made
himself king of his native town. He extended his control along the
left bank of the Niger until he came in contact with the French military expeditions. Fighting fiercely, his supporters were finally pushed
back into eastern Guinea and northern Ivory Coast. From here he

led a second attempt to conquer the Mossi country as far east as the Black Volta. Repulsed once more by a combination of French and British force, he retired to eastern Liberia, where he was finally captured on September 29, 1898.

Samory was a leader in the great tradition of the Soudanic conquerors of the past. His career was marked by savage violence; to supply his troops he exchanged his captives as slaves for arms from Liberia and Sierra Leone. But at the same time he was an able administrator. He divided his empire into provinces and cantons; each was ruled by one of his faithful appointed representatives. Samory was to be the last of the independent Guineans for more than half a century, but his memory lived on in song and story among the people of upper Guinea. The rise to power of his great-grandson as the leader of resistance against the French colonial regime was regarded by many as a sign of the rebirth of Guinean independence, and public consciousness of Samory's role in Guinean history was to play an important part in the enthusiastic support of Sékou Touré's efforts to organize a Guinean nationalist movement.

French control over Guinea spanned a period of little more than sixty years—two generations. It is not surprising, then, that the memory of the independent states of the Fouta Djallon was by no means effaced by the end of World War II. Samory's campaigns could be recounted by men who were still alive, and his struggle against the French could easily be translated into the setting of the modern day. Both on the coast and in the uplands the precolonial period had been marked by savage intertribal wars and by ruthless violence and pillage, but in this respect Guinea was by no means different from the surrounding West African territories. Perhaps the most powerful and lasting influence of this period was Islam, which spread slowly throughout the country after the seventeenth century and acted as a pole about which those from remote parts of the country could group their mutual interests. Islam came to Guinea more often by the sword than by the book, but nonetheless it provided a unifying tendency which countered the deep tribal cleavages. Even today the peoples of the coast who resisted the religion of the pastoral peoples are rapidly becoming Islamized.

FRENCH COLONIAL RULE

Until the turn of the century, the French were occupied with the pacification of tribal rebellions and with the securing of the Rivières

du Sud against encroachment by the English governors of Sierra
Leone. Guinea was formally created a colony by decree in 1891, and
by 1899 the borders of the present state were finally established
with the addition of the former Soudanese administrative regions of
Kouroussa, Siguiri, Kankan, Beyla, and Kissidougou. One of the early
efforts of the new administration was to create a port to rival Free-
town as a center from which trade with the Niger Valley could be
carried on. Conakry was chosen as the port and the seat of government. At first an autonomous colony, Guinea was joined to the newly
created federation of French West Africa after 1895, and a skeleton
administrative organization, largely under military control, was slowly
erected. Up until World War I the chiefs of the Fouta Djallon were
kept under control only by constant supervision, however, and frequent references are to be found in the reports of the early governors
to incipient rebellions led by the Almamys of the plateau.

The administrative structure of Guinea followed the pattern laid
down by the French elsewhere in West Africa. The country was
divided into 17 *cercles* (and 10 subdivisions), each headed by a *commandant* whose extensive powers made him the virtual ruler of his
domain. Not only was he responsible for law and order and the collection of taxes in his territory, but he sat as a judge in the lower
courts. Until 1946, when the regime of summary disciplinary penalties
known as the *indigénat* was eliminated, the *commandant* had the
power to imprison an African for a period of two weeks without
trial of any kind. The colonial administrative structure was completed
by the central services of government, each with its complement of
French civil servants and a governor at its head. In 1913 there were
168 administrators in Guinea, but by 1926 the number had been
reduced to 100. Even so, during the interwar period the French had
almost three times as many administrators in West Africa as had the
British, though the African population of the French possessions was
much smaller. European personnel was used in many posts where
in the British colonies African clerks were employed. The double
consequence of this system was to produce a top-heavy administrative
machine (which created particular difficulties for the Guineans who
took the place of the French officials immediately upon independence)
and to give relatively few Africans an opportunity for experience in
posts involving any genuine executive responsibility.

Throughout the colonial period until after World War II the French
administration operated on one or another theory of assimilation.

Beginning with a concept of assimilation in which the colonies were considered part of France itself, the theory became gradually modified in succeeding phases into the policies of "association" and "identity" as it became increasingly evident that the African could not be transformed completely into the French mold. From an emphasis on the assimilation of French culture by the entire population, official policy moved toward the limited association of an educated elite which, it was expected, would form a bridge between the administration and the mass of the rural peasantry who remained close to the African traditional way of life. Association was, however, to prove in the end no more successful than assimilation, since the educated group tended to remain part of the rapidly growing urban complexes rather than to return to the villages where their influence would be exerted on the rural population. Education, instead of creating a bridge, became a barrier, since many of the younger men who had been to France or had attended French secondary schools in Africa no longer felt themselves a part of the traditional milieu.

Far from creating a group of *évolués* upon which the administration could depend for support, the education that was offered to an African elite sowed the seeds from which the demand for independence was later to spring. The educated African usually realized that he could no more become a fully accepted member of the French administrative world than he could return to the world of his native village. As Jacques Richard-Molard has pointed out:

Education was oriented in French West Africa under the Third Republic toward the formation not of future citizens as in France, but of subjects, of assistants in the lower ranks of the administration. Those who rose in the service owed it not to the spirit of colonial law but to the personal efforts of a number of European civil servants who did not cease to be republicans just because they were serving overseas. Thus was prepared the basis of the postwar [nationalist] movement.[1]

The French education to which the young African was exposed taught him not only French culture but also the concepts of equality and liberty of Republican France. But when he returned to Africa he found neither social equality nor liberty under a colonial regime.

Apart from the limited opportunity afforded by minor civil service posts, the educated African found little opening for his talents. In the French-controlled business world of the colonies, with rare ex-

[1] *Afrique Occidentale Française* (Paris, 1952), p. 152.

ceptions, the African received no training for positions of management. For a tiny minority a wider horizon might be opened in professional fields such as law and medicine (although in Guinea even these fields were not opened), but little or no encouragement was offered to embark upon a commercial career which might eventually provide competition for the French merchants. In the eyes of many younger African leaders who began to play a political role after 1945, the economic system developed by the French colonial administration was based upon exploitation of African resources and manpower. Whatever efforts the administration made toward African advancement were, in Sékou Touré's words, aimed only at "the utilization of the men and riches of Africa—a utilization considered solely from the point of view of profits and the interests of the colonialists."[2]

The Guinean leaders recognized, of course, that material benefits had been derived from the period of colonial control. French technical services had improved the health of the African peasant by public health controls and had raised his standard of living by introducing new techniques of farming and new forms of marketing. The young nationalists of French-speaking Africa had enjoyed a French education at such institutions as the famous William Ponty school and in the universities of France—an education which was to leave a deeper impress of French civilization than most of them realized. But it was precisely this education which made them aware of the damage to African society done by the colonial relationship. By exposing them to the values of Western civilization, it made them all the more determined to reassert those values which were peculiarly African and upon which the structure of African society rested.

Sékou Touré has reiterated his view that exploitation by the colonial regimes resulted not only in robbing Africa of its resources but in destroying the basic values of African society. The changes which the colonial system brought about in African traditional life undermined the network of mutual obligations which created communal solidarity. For these obligations was substituted individual self-interest, and this in turn worked for the benefit of the colonial administrations since it prevented the Africans from organizing collective resistance against the economic exploitation to which they were subjected. This breaking down of the bonds that held traditional society together was to the Guinean nationalist leaders one of the

[2] *L'Action Politique du Parti Démocratique de Guinée pour l'Emancipation Africaine* (Conakry, 1959), p. 304. Hereafter referred to as *Action*.

greatest sins of the colonial administration, and one that its positive accomplishments, no matter how impressive, could never overbalance.

In the decade prior to the referendum of September, 1958, the governments of the Fourth Republic went far toward loosening the ties that bound the African colonies to the mother country. The territorial assemblies, whose function had been conceived initially to be largely advisory, became by stages parliaments with substantive powers. The number of African voters increased with the procession of decrees liberalizing the franchise, and the power of the African deputies in the French National Assembly became more effective as they were drawn into the party struggles in the declining years of the Fourth Republic. The majority of the present leaders of the independent states of former French West Africa gained invaluable political experience as deputies, members of the Assembly of the French Union, and as members of the Grand Council in Dakar. The culminating stage of these steps toward wider popular participation in government came with the *loi cadre* of 1956, which gave to the Overseas Territories semiautonomy over local affairs and a Council of Ministers responsible to the locally elected assembly.

But even this radical departure from previous policies failed to keep pace with the progress of African nationalism. It is ironic that the *loi cadre*, which was designed to answer the African demand for local autonomy while retaining in French hands those aspects of government (defense, education, and monetary control) that would ensure continued French influence, had in fact the reverse effect. In Guinea the *loi cadre*, under which the Parti Démocratique de Guinée gained effective control of government through its parliamentary majority, provided the African leadership with the final proof (if any were needed) that Africans were capable of running the country. But the speed of political evolution in French Africa had been such that the provisions of the *loi cadre*, however liberal they may have seemed to the colonial administration and to the lawmakers in Paris, were outdated by the time the law had come into operation. Instead of creating the truly independent African governments hoped for by African leaders, the *loi cadre* in effect reaffirmed the continued supremacy of Paris by failing to create a strong federal executive at Dakar and thereby increasing the dependence of individual territories on the direct relationship to the *Métropole*. The battle which was to break out within the Rassemblement Démocratique Africain at the Bamako Conference of September, 1957, over the issue of total independence or a continuing tie to France within the framework of a modified *loi cadre* was to lead directly to the Guinean rejection of the Community in the referendum a year later.

Addressing the assembled *commandants de cercle* of Guinea in July, 1957, Sékou Touré, as President of the Guinean Council of Ministers, clearly expressed his point of view on the *loi cadre:*

> You might say that this *loi cadre* created too high hopes in the peoples of the Overseas Territories and particularly in the Africans. Agreed. It is clear that it did not take into account the degree of their economic and social evolution, but it did take account of their political evolution. . . . In Black Africa there has occurred in recent years a real crisis in the popular conscience, out of which has come a determination to participate more actively in the fulfillment of man's destiny. The trade unions, youth, veterans . . . and the political parties have sought autonomy, not because they denied the necessity of collaboration with similar metropolitan organizations but because they sought to preserve their own originality. . . . This is a political phenomenon which France in its wisdom must take into account.[3]

In many of his speeches since independence, Sékou Touré has returned to this theme of preserving the essentials of African culture against the influences of the French policy of assimilation which was aimed at making Guinea "a military, economic, and cultural extension of France." He has repeatedly emphasized the need for "reconversion" of Guinean society from the mental outlook created by colonialism to the new outlook made necessary by independence. Guinean cultural development within an African milieu had been interrupted by the colonial period; it was necessary now to pick up again the strands of a truly Guinean life where they had been forcibly cut by the intrusion of an alien culture and to work toward a reintegration of African traditional values into the mold required by a modern mechanized civilization.

The French colonial regime contained within itself certain inherent contradictions, in the view of the Guinean nationalists, which would have forced its eventual collapse even without the external pressures of postwar nationalism. These contradictions, existing at every level of society, stemmed from the fact that in this view the colonial administration had never at any time the interests of the African genuinely at heart. Although acknowledging that a small group of Africans may have secured certain benefits from the French regime, the nationalists felt that these were incidental to the further-

---

[3] *Guinée: Prélude à l'Indépendance* (Paris: Présence Africaine, 1958), p. 146.

ing of French objectives. In the course of sixty years the French administrative system perverted the indigenous African feudal system for its own ends by the creation of artificial chiefs. By educating a small elite to the neglect of the masses, the nationalists claimed, the French created severe internal stresses within African society by pitting this group of young intellectuals against the illiterate rural peasantry. In the economy, moreover, the prices of imported goods were fixed at levels which provided French trading companies with exorbitant profits.

There was much justification to the Guinean nationalists' criticism of the French colonial regime. French administration was all too often concerned more with the maintenance of law and order and the collection of taxes than with African advancement. Assimilation, under whatever disguise, was preoccupied with demonstrating the values of French culture, not with preserving the foundations of an African way of life. The difference in living standard between the French who controlled the economy and that of the Africans whose labor created the products which went into French colonial trade was too great to be ignored. But even under these circumstances the ultimate demand for independence might have been avoided had the French been able to erase the psychological scars left by the indignities of the colonial regime. More important, perhaps, than any other causal factor in the rise of African nationalism after 1945 was the growing realization on the part of educated Africans that while the colonial administration lasted they could at best be only second-class citizens. In Sékou Touré's own words, "We have known the brutality and arrogance of a colonialism that treated us not as men but as inferior beings."

Despite the efforts made after 1946 to create juridical equality between the citizens of the *Métropole* and those of overseas France, there remained the barriers of social equality which were bridged by only a handful of French-speaking Africans. Assimilation could never be successful since by definition it required the surrender of the African heritage to a European heritage. The concept of an "African personality," however vague it may be, is basically an emphasizing of those qualities that distinguish the African from the European; it is an attempt to recover that essential ingredient of human dignity which was absent in the colonial relationship of the ruler and the ruled. In the political sphere this ingredient could be supplied only by regaining African independence. Paradoxically the rekindling of the spirit of independence in Africa through the teaching of the Republican principles of liberty and equality may well be the most enduring monument to the French colonial system.

RISE AND CHARACTER OF THE GUINEAN NATIONALIST MOVEMENT

Nationalism in Guinea, as in the other territories of West Africa, had its origins in the political ferment that spread through Black Africa following World War II. The growth of the nationalist movement in French-speaking Africa is indissolubly bound with the growth of postwar African political parties, and in particular, of course, with the Rassemblement Démocratique Africain.

The RDA, which until 1958 was by far the most powerful political movement in French West Africa, sprang from the dissatisfaction of African leaders with the defeat of the first constitution of the French Republic in May, 1946. In an attempt to secure greater concessions toward their demands for equal rights for African citizens with those of metropolitan France, a group of the African representatives at the Constitutional Convention determined to issue a manifesto seeking "the realization of political and social democracy in Black Africa." [4] It is significant that at this period their aims envisaged not the future independence of the African territories but the abolition of legal differentiations between Africans and Frenchmen. The manifesto ended with a call for a congress, which took place at Bamako in October, 1946. Out of this congress emerged the RDA, based upon semiautonomous sections in each territory, under the over-all control of a Coordinating Committee consisting of a president, secretary-general, four vice-presidents, and a representative of each territory. General policy was to be laid down at periodic congresses similar to the Bamako meeting.

Sékou Touré was active in the RDA from the beginning. He was one of the eleven delegates from Guinea at Bamako and was later a member of the Coordinating Committee and a vice-president of the party. Since the French African section of the Socialist Party (SFIO) refused to join this united front of African political movements, the only Guinean who had signed the original manifesto, Yacine Diallo, did not even attend the congress.

It was the task of the delegations to the congress to organize the RDA sections in their own territories. Within Guinea the creation of

[4] *Le RDA dans la Lutte Anti-impérialiste* (Paris, 1948), p. 24.

a unified political movement was hampered by the existence of a variety of small associations, most of which were based upon ethnic or special-interest groupings and some of which had existed as mutual self-help associations prior to 1939. For the most part their political ambition had been limited to their own *cercle* or tribal group. Immediately at the end of the war many of these smaller organizations were absorbed into four larger groupings: the Comité de Basse-Guinée, the Amicale Gilbert Vieillard (for the Fouta Djallon), the Union des Manding, and the Union Forestière. The Guinean delegation attending the Bamako Congress was made up of representatives of some of the larger ethnic groups. But none of these early groups could claim any kind of national support. Moreover, their programs, in as far as they were enunciated, were confined to satisfying the interests of their immediate supporters.

A second factor inhibiting the growth of the RDA's Guinean section was the active support given by the administration to a rival group headed by Yacine Diallo, the Socialist deputy. The Socialist Party in Guinea was organized shortly after 1945 with the support of the European element of the population. There is some question of the degree of organized support it received among the African population, but official pressure plus Diallo's personal following in the Fouta Djallon managed to return him as deputy until his death in 1954. Although it was clear that Diallo could not match the popular appeal of Sékou Touré, his record in support of African nationalist objectives in the French National Assembly was by no means a bad one, and after his death the administration could not produce a candidate who fully took his place.

The formation of the Guinean section of RDA was finally accomplished in May, 1947, but only after seven months of negotiation to bring together into a unified effort the various ethnic groups that had been represented in the delegation to Bamako. At best it was a precarious coalition; certainly it was not capable of withstanding the opposition of the administration plus the internal pressures created by the varying interests of its constituent groups. Thus in this early stage the RDA was far from representing the unified political force necessary to press forward toward nationalist objectives.

Sékou Touré depicts the party at this time as unified for electoral purposes only.

Within the Comité Directéur each ethnic group maintained its own representation, which made the Comité Directéur of the RDA of Guinea a coordinating committee whose organic bases, being those of the former ethnic groups, were never unified and whose actions had to take into account the particular positions of each of these groups. The contradictions existing in the methods and doctrines of the ethnic groups thus persisted inside the RDA, almost robbing it of its real objective of unification. . . . The fragile bases (which, it must be admitted, were purely for electoral purposes) of our new section crumbled under the mutually opposing interests of its own leaders.[5]

In the first three years following the formation of the Guinean RDA the administration's opposition to it was based less on the party's nationalistic aims than on its relationship to the French Communist Party. From its inception the RDA was regarded by the French Communists as a useful tool in the fight against imperialism and, under the expert tutelage of French party members, many of the RDA supporters received training in Leninist techniques of political organization. Particularly through the "Groupes d'Etudes Communistes" many of the young intellectuals received thorough indoctrination in Marxist philosophy. Moreover, the RDA deputies were *apparentés* to the Communists in the National Assembly in the immediate postwar period.

By 1950 the president of the RDA, Félix Houphouët-Boigny of the Ivory Coast, had become aware of the damage the relationship with the French Communists was doing to his ambitions for greater autonomy in the African territories. He broke with the Communist Party in 1951 in an open letter announcing his change in policy and caused Gabriel d'Arboussier to be expelled from his post as secretary-general of the RDA. Even before this formal declaration, however, direct Communist influence had been waning, as had Moscow's interest in the future of the RDA. However, in Guinea the administration still feared a possible Communist-inspired drive by the RDA and placed every possible obstacle in the way of the new party's expansion.

The combination of the pressures of local ethnic groups, the opposition of the administration, and the weakening of the more militant RDA members in the face of the abrupt *volte-face* in Houphouët's policy prevented the RDA from gaining any of the three deputies' seats in the 1951 election or seats in the territorial assembly in 1952. It was only after the reorganization of the Guinean section, when Sékou Touré became secretary-general of the Parti Démocratique de

---

[5] *L'Expérience Guinéenne et l'Unité Africaine* (Paris: Présence Africaine, 1959 [?]), p. 13. Hereafter referred to as *Expérience*.

Guinée in 1952, and the subsequent support it gained of the organized labor movement that the PDG grew into the unified nationalist party that was to lead the country to independence in 1958.

In his *rapport moral* to the party congress in 1958 Sékou Touré attributed the declining fortunes of the party in these years in part to the repressive tactics of the administration. Because of the active campaign carried on against the PDG by the administration, many young men dropped out who were dependent on the government for employment. In the rural areas, the administration could, of course, always count on the salaried *chefs de canton* to counter the appeals of the PDG. In addition, however, Touré emphasized three other major factors which restricted its growth. At that time political ambition in Guinea was limited to creating an organization for the purpose of electing candidates from particular regions; once the election was over, the organization disappeared. Secondly, political organization was in the hands of the intellectuals (largely minor civil servants) whose goal was to use politics as a means of serving their own interests and not those of the mass of the peasants. Lastly, he blamed the lack of contact between the party militants and the masses.

Under Sékou Touré's leadership, the party gained greatly in popular strength within a relatively short time. This was in part due to the rapid growth of trade unionism as the economy developed and to Touré's ability to use for political purposes the growing strength of the labor movement which he headed. In particular, the success in 1953 of the 67-day strike by all organized labor for the 40-hour week made Touré a national figure in his fight against the administration and brought him wide popular support. By 1954 it was estimated that the RDA membership in Guinea had risen to 300,000 or about 13 per cent of the population. This figure must be taken with reservations, as Thomas Hodgkin warns, since whole families rather than voting adults were counted. Nonetheless, he adds, "these and similar figures are not absurd if they are taken as referring to a mental attitude, a sense of party loyalty, rather than to an organized, formal, contributory connection." [6]

As the PDG became increasingly the vehicle of new nationalist sentiment, the power of the older ethnic groups waned correspondingly. Some chiefs whose traditional authority had remained relatively strong sensed the changed direction of public opinion and swung to the support of the PDG. Moreover, the administration's support of

[6] *Nationalism in Tropical Africa* (London: Muller, 1956), p. 166.

its favored candidate, Yacine Diallo (carried in the election of 1951 to the extent of rigging the ballot boxes), aroused strong resentment among the 80,000 new voters who were added by changes in the franchise laws. After Diallo's death in 1954 the protests broke into open violence when Sékou Touré was defeated in the election for Diallo's seat by the candidate of the Rassemblement du Peuple Français (RPF), Diawadou Barry, under circumstances which strongly implicated the administration in falsification of the count.

The PDG thereafter became the undisputed spearhead of the popular nationalist movement, embracing the young intellectuals, a group of the traditional authorities outside the Fouta Djallon, and the only other organized force in the country, the trade unions, which were supported by the French General Confederation of Labor (CGT). The continued unofficial efforts of the colonial regime to retain control over the elections through the use of hand-picked candidates resulted in periodic outbreaks of violence at every election between RDA supporters and those of Diawadou Barry's Bloc Africain de Guinée. Because of Diawadou's position as the son of a prominent Foula chief, the Almamy of Dabola, the Bloc could count on solid support in the plateau region. But the power of the older ethnic groups was waning. In the elections of January, 1956, the PDG candidates, Touré and Saïfoulaye Diallo, were able to carry off two of the deputy's seats while Diawadou barely retained the third. In the elections for the territorial assembly of May 31, 1957, the RDA easily won 57 of the 60 seats, compared to 2 out of 48 in the previous assembly. Moreover, the three opposition seats were won not by Diawadou Barry's party but by the Démocratie Socialiste de Guinée led by Ibrahima Barry (known also as Barry III) who claimed to be the spiritual heir of Yacine Diallo. Thus by mid-1957 the stage was set for the PDG's campaign for independence which was to be secured only a little over a year later.

ACHIEVEMENT OF INDEPENDENCE

By an overwhelming vote of "no" to the constitution of the Fifth French Republic on September 28, 1958, Guinea received its independence more dramatically than has any other African state. But the decision of Sékou Touré and the PDG leadership to call for a negative vote from their followers was not entirely a sudden shift in policy. Touré's own position had been made clear in party meetings almost a year before; as the time for the referendum approached, he publicly reiterated those conditions which France must fulfill in order to make the Community acceptable to the PDG and to the other RDA sections.

Sékou Touré's stand was based on his firm conviction that the Franco-African Community, as conceived by de Gaulle, offered no genuine independence for its African members. In addition, by breaking up the old federations of French West Africa and French Equatorial Africa, the Community placed insurmountable obstructions in the way of future union of African states.

On both counts Touré believed that the proposed constitution of the Fifth Republic did nothing to correct the shortcomings of the *loi cadre* but rather reaffirmed them. The *loi cadre* of June, 1956, had finally established full adult suffrage for elections in French Africa (a step of no great political consequence since the suffrage had been successively widened since 1947 and this provision added only a small number of new voters to the rolls) and gave virtually full parliamentary powers over local affairs to the territorial assemblies and their executive organs, the Executive Councils (Conseils de Gouvernement). By thus establishing autonomous governments in the territories, the *loi cadre* radically altered the existing relationships between the *Métropole*, the territories, and the centers of the two federations at Dakar and Brazzaville. The measure stripped the federal administrations of many of their powers, drastically reduced the powers of the governors general, and left the federal legislatures, the Grand Councils, little more than debating societies. Both the elective body and the administrative services at the federal level became merely coordinating bodies controlling only a few interterritorial services. Thus the emphasis under the *loi cadre* was almost exclusively on the direct relationships of the territory to France without the intervening stage of control emanating from the group level.

Despite its provision for territorial autonomy, the *loi cadre* was soon condemned by a group within the RDA leadership because its failure to support the federal government not only implicitly denied the conception of African unity but, through the destruction of federal power, also paved the way for continued French control over the individual territories. In a speech made shortly before independence, Sékou Touré stated the case in these terms:

The *loi cadre*, by dividing the federations into separately administered territories, by refusing even to consider a coordinating government among the territories, sowed the seed in Africa of the breakup of the federations. And it was not by chance that French West Africa was given eight autonomous governments instead of a single one. It was part of a nefarious scheme to continue the metropolitan control over underdeveloped but potentially rich territories. It was to perpetuate colonialism in a less apparent but nonetheless efficient form, in the final analysis to continue the exploitation of the men and riches of Africa, who were to be rendered the more vulnerable by this "balkanization." [7]

Only a few months after the inauguration of the changes under the *loi cadre* it became clear that the question of the future relationship of the African territories to France was a threat to the unity of the nationalist movement represented by the RDA. Two opposing points of view quickly developed. One, espoused by Houphouët-Boigny, favored a federal relationship between the Metropole and the eight territories by which France would become one of a group of states united by a common federal parliamentary structure in which members from France would be elected on an equal basis with those from overseas. Under this arrangement the existing federations in Africa would be largely, or wholly, bypassed. The other position, for which Sékou Touré was the chief spokesman, supported a strong federal structure in Africa itself which would consist of an elected parliament at the federal level and an Executive Council (as in the territories). This arrangement would imply independent status for the two African federations, and the continuing relationships with France would be worked out from this level, probably on a confederal basis.

These two positions regarding the form of the federal structure met head-on at the Bamako Congress of the RDA in September, 1957. It was already evident that the outcome of the clash between Sékou Touré and Houphouët-Boigny over this issue was to be a decisive factor in the future of the independence movement in French West Africa. From its somewhat inauspicious beginning in 1946 the RDA had become in a decade by far the strongest political force in West Africa. RDA sections were in control of the government in the Soudan, Guinea, and Ivory Coast; more than half the members of all the territorial assemblies of French West Africa belonged to the movement. Compared to the RDA, the opposing Mouvement Socialiste Africain had 62 assembly members and the Convention Africaine had 52 (47 of whom were in Senegal alone). In the popular vote for the elections of April, 1957, the RDA was in the majority for the Federation as a whole. In addition, the members of the largest supraterritorial force

[7] *Expérience*, p. 168.

outside the political parties, the trade unions of the left, were predominantly RDA supporters.

The congress was torn between the imperative need to maintain
unity within the RDA and the desire of the more militant younger
delegates to support the views on federalism favored by Sékou Touré.
Loyalty to its first president, Houphouët-Boigny, conflicted with the
more popular stand in favor of independence. The delegates argued
bitterly for four days. The resolution which finally emerged clearly
expressed the majority view but sought to save Houphouët-Boigny
from the appearance of decisive defeat:

The congress gives its mandate to its parliamentarians to propose a law
for the erection of a federal state, composed of autonomous states, with a
federal government, the supreme organ of a unitary state. Conscious of the
economic, political, and cultural ties that bind the territories together and
mindful of the future destiny of the African community, the congress gives
its parliamentarians full powers to propose a law looking toward the democ-
ratization of the existing federal executive organs.[8]

The congress was, however, careful to refrain from specifying whether
the federal state should be at the level of a Franco-African Community
or at the level of a purely African federation. Sékou Touré, in his
closing address, emphasized the early role of Houphouët-Boigny in
the nationalist struggle and the necessity of continued party unity
under Houphouët's command. He added, however, speaking directly
to the Ivory Coast delegates, "We know that despite appearances to
the contrary, you are, as we all are, in favor of a federal executive."
Speaking prior to the referendum a year later, he did not hesitate to
point out that "at the Bamako Congress, the victory of the revolutionary forces who represent the real wishes of the masses, and who think
first about Africa, was sacrificed on the altar of party unity." [9]

Despite the form of unity achieved at Bamako the 1957 congress
resulted in practice in a serious split within the ranks of the RDA, the
ultimate outcome of which was to be the withdrawal of the PDG from
the movement shortly after Guinea voted for independence. Houphouët's position on federalism stemmed in part from the peculiar
interests of the Ivory Coast which he represented and in part from
his personal rivalry with Léopold Senghor of Senegal for leadership

---

[8] The resolution is quoted in full in André Blanchet, *L'Itinéraire des Partis
depuis Bamako* (Paris: Plon, 1958), pp. 187–189.

[9] *Expérience*, p. 171.

in French-speaking West Africa. Houphouët's desire for a direct federal relationship with France reflected the fact that Ivory Coast with its greater resources and higher stage of economic development than other French West African territories would benefit from both French markets and French technical aid in a direct federal structure. On the other hand, in a purely African federation, the Ivory Coast would be expected to contribute heavily to the development of the less-favored members of the Federation at the price of slowing down the rate of development at home. An additional consideration was undoubtedly his disinclination to build up Dakar as a federal capital, thus adding to the prestige of his rival, Senghor. Since Guinea, being less well developed than the Ivory Coast, would benefit economically from a larger African federation, Sékou Touré had not been loath to make a forceful presentation of the case for an independent federation based on Dakar.

Aware of the serious damage to which the RDA was exposed by the deep divergence of views at the Bamako Congress, the party leadership lost no time in exploring ways by which the breach could be healed. It became clear, however, during the PDG congress in January, 1958, and in the RDA Coordination Committee meetings in February that Houphouët and Sékou Touré were no closer together than before on the federal question. An attempt to form a united front at the federal level between the opposition parties and the RDA failed in April. At the fourth congress of the PDG held in Conakry in June, Sékou Touré's determination to join the proposed Community only on a basis of a multinational federation of sovereign states was fully supported by the delegates. He stated his position flatly in a speech to the territorial assembly on July 28:

The future constitution [of the Fifth Republic] must find fundamental solutions to the lacunae and the contradictions of the present regime by modifying the nature of the legal ties between France and the Overseas Territories. . . . The peoples of Africa . . . will henceforth seek the right to free self-determination, to administer themselves directly, and to manage their own affairs. Having their own parliaments, they no longer want to sit in the French parliament. . . . So far as the constitution is concerned, our position is unequivocal. . . . Whether our relationship with France be called federal or confederal, whether it be called community or association matters little. What matters is the nature of the sovereignty attributed to each state in this multinational body and that this key question be freely agreed to by each interested party.[10]

[10] *Ibid.*, pp. 66–67.

But the constitutional formula devised for the Community under the Fifth Republic was far from satisfying Sékou Touré's requirements. The all-important question of the status of the Community members was unresolved; for those who joined the Community, he felt, the question of future independence was left not in their hands but in those of the Community—in effect, those of France. The members of the Community were not to be sovereign states which had voluntarily renounced control over foreign affairs, defense, and currency matters as Community members. No supranational legislative organs were to be created (even the short-lived Senate of the Community could hardly be considered in this category) so that the French National Assembly was to remain, as in the past, the supreme legislative body. However the vague phrases in the constitution regarding the Community might be construed, the fact remained that ultimate control rested with the *Métropole*. The Overseas Territories were not to be considered as equal members with France in the Community; rather, the Community structure provided a legal umbrella for their integration into a larger metropolitan France.

As the French and African viewpoints on the nature of the Community became more precise, it became all the more obvious to Touré that they were irreconcilable. A federation of states was impossible without a federal governmental structure with real powers. To this France could never consent without itself losing control over the Community since the French Assembly would of necessity be subordinate to the Community legislature. At the same time the African goal of independence could never be attained within a Community in which the supreme authority rested with a parliament elected only by metropolitan Frenchmen and in which French interests were regarded as paramount.

With the visit of General de Gaulle to Conakry on August 25, the choice to be offered to the African territories under the constitution sharpened in Touré's mind. Guinea could vote to join the Community under the terms of the constitution or it could choose independence outside the Community. In his speech of welcome to the General, Sékou Touré restated his conditions briefly. Guinea would vote "yes" in the referendum only if independence and juridical equality were recognized and the rights were secured to free withdrawal from the Community and to equal voice in the management of Community affairs. To this the French President replied curtly and without diplomatic circumlocutions:

France proposes this Community; nobody is obliged to join it. You have talked of independence. I say here even more loudly than I have elsewhere that independence is up to Guinea. It can have it on September 28 by voting "no" to the proposal, and I guarantee the *Métropole* will make no objection. There will, of course, be some consequences for Guinea, but there will be no obstacles in the way. Your country can do what it wants the way it wants to and can follow any course it likes. If Guinea says "yes"—that is, if it freely, spontaneously, of its own accord accepts the constitution—and if France on its side says "yes," then the African territories and the *Métropole* can work together for mutual profit.[11]

General de Gaulle's uncompromising statement of the choice between the Community and independence came as a shock not only to Guineans but to the other RDA sections in French West Africa. The campaign for a "yes" or "no" vote began in furious earnest after his African trip, and the split between the extreme and the moderate nationalists grew deeper during the month of September. The French territorial administrations were accused of applying pressure at every point for an affirmative vote. Speaking to the territorial conference of the party on September 14, Sékou Touré stated that it was known that 3,500,000,000 francs had been voted for propaganda by the French, and he advised the militants of the party to take whatever money was offered them for their votes, while voting "no" anyway. To stave off the impending disaster Touré hoped to persuade Houphouët-Boigny to call a meeting of the Coordination Committee of the RDA at Bobo-Dioulassou. When Houphouët refused, Sékou Touré, in anger, declined to leave Guinea to attend the funeral of Ouezzin Coulibaly of Upper Volta, an old companion in the RDA who had died suddenly in Paris. In a vain effort to persuade him to change his mind, Mamadou Dia of Senegal visited Conakry; unfortunately Senegal was itself so torn by internal dissension over the referendum that Dia's arguments could have little weight. Any possible chance of a change in the direction chosen by Guinea was removed by the final resolution of the territorial conference of the PDG in September which stated that, in view of the choice offered by de Gaulle, "no dependent people would hesitate for a moment between independence and the proposed Community." The conference therefore decided to choose independence by voting "no" and launched an appeal to all French-African organizations "to do everything possible to save the future of Africa by the triumph of 'no' throughout French-speaking Africa."

[11] *Ibid.*, p. 83.

Within Guinea the remarkably efficient organization of the PDG went into full operation to urge a "no" vote in every community down to the smallest and most remote villages. The opposition leaders swung into line, bringing the majority of their followers with them; none dared to stand against the issue of independence. The French administration at first doubted that the Guineans would dare to vote against de Gaulle. When it became clear that this was not the case, parachute troops were brought in "to maintain order" during the election and incidentally as a display of French force. But the time had passed when the flag could be effectively shown, and the troops made little or no impression on the populace.

The vote on September 28 showed the overwhelming support of the Guineans for the stand of Sékou Touré and the PDG. Out of a total of 1,405,986 voters on the lists, 1,200,171 voted. Of these, 1,130,292 voted "no," 12,920 ballots were spoiled or left blank, and 56,959 voted "yes." Of the slightly over 5 per cent of the voters in the 26 *circonscriptions* who voted "yes," the numbers ranged from zero in Forécariah, a southwestern Guinea town, to 27,140 in Labé, an opposition stronghold in the northeastern Fouta Djallon plateau. The fact that almost half of the "yes" vote came from this single *circonscription* reflected the traditional antagonism between the Foulas and the coastal peoples rather than a desire of the plateau people to retain the colonial regime. Of the eight territories of French West Africa, Guinea was alone in a majority of "no" votes. It was charged, however, that the number of "no's" in other territories might have been larger had the administration not been responsible for counting the votes.

True to his word, General de Gaulle created no obstacles to Guinean independence; on the contrary, it appeared that France acted to recognize at least the *de facto* independence of the new nation with almost indecent haste. On the day of the referendum a communiqué was handed to the Guinean leaders by the chief of the French mission stating that since Guinea had failed to adopt the constitution it would henceforth be separated from the other territories of French West Africa, that its representation in any organ of the Community no longer existed, that French administrative and economic assistance was at an end, and that French responsibilities in Guinea would undergo complete revision.

Guinea thereupon proceeded to take its first steps as a sovereign state. On October 2 a special session of the territorial assembly was convened to listen to the proclamation of independence which turned it into a Constituent Assembly, to accept the resignation of Sékou Touré's government, and to adopt the new name of the Republic of Guinea. In a gesture of unity a former opposition leader, Diawadou Barry, was seated next to Sékou Touré during the ceremony. Touré was promptly reelected unanimously to the post of President of the Republic, and the Assembly proceeded to pass laws establishing a committee to work out the text of a new constitution and to pronounce measures of clemency for those in prison. The new republic had begun to function.

AFTER INDEPENDENCE

The mounting political tension that had accompanied the preparation for the referendum in Guinea had tended to obscure the nature of the problems Guineans had to face immediately upon the dawn of independence. Primary among these was the maintenance of a functioning administrative machine. The continuation of the day-to-day operation of government at the highest level was greatly aided by the fact that under the *loi cadre* there had existed a legislature and a responsible cabinet from whose ranks experienced ministers could be drawn to head up the departments of government. In the period since May, 1957, when Sékou Touré first assumed responsibility in the Council of Ministers, measures had been taken, including suppression of the traditional authorities and the establishment of local government organs, which prepared the way for independent administration. Moreover, the task of keeping law and order was made immeasurably easier by the internal political unity achieved during the referendum campaign and by the high degree of discipline that could be counted on in the lower echelons of the party hierarchy.

Despite these favorable factors, however, the problems confronting the party leadership were staggering. With very rare exceptions the bureaucratic structure of the country at the executive level had remained in French hands. Relatively few Africans had been given responsible administrative posts; those who had such posts tended to be concentrated in the capital. In consequence administration in the rural areas was almost entirely directed by French career administrators. In addition, the educational structure of Guinea depended upon French teachers, and technical services and transportation were French-supervised.

Even under the best of circumstances replacements for many of the key French civil servants would have been hard to find. But the situation in Guinea was made all the more difficult in the months following independence by the unsympathetic attitude adopted by France toward the new country. Despite General de Gaulle's expansive statements, the metropolitan government and the local French administration were by no means reconciled to the result of the referendum. Their pride stung to the quick, the French engaged in punitive actions which comprise one of the sorriest chapters in French postwar colonial administration.

By the agreement made immediately upon independence, French administrators and technicians were given a period of ten months during which they were to hand over their responsibilities to their African successors and to familiarize the newcomers with the details of the work as best they could. Instead, the majority of the administration departed from the country as rapidly as possible. In their pique, French officials made it more difficult for Guineans to operate the administrative machine by destroying vital files in some cases and in others taking them as part of their baggage. Excesses such as destruction of telephone instruments and plumbing facilities were not uncommon. Sékou Touré has claimed that circulars from the French mission in Conakry indicated that this administrative sabotage had official concurrence. A group of eighty French teachers en route to Guinea by ship for the opening of the school year was halted at Dakar, despite Guinean assurances that seniority rights would be respected. Guinean students attending schools in Dakar and Bamako on scholarships that were valid until December 31, 1958, under provisions of the Grand Council budget, were immediately dismissed and sent home.

At the intergovernmental level, France delayed *de jure* recognition of the new government for some months, on the pretext that such recognition was dependent on the negotiation of an agreement regarding Guinean membership in the franc zone. But the government in Paris made it clear that negotiations would be undertaken only on the basis of proposals made by Guinea; by implication, the legal existence of the Guinean government was made dependent on an agreement with France. Sékou Touré rejected the French note, declaring that "in international life there is no example of the recognition of the independence of a people or of its sovereignty being made the object of bargaining; however important the conditions they seek to impose on us may be, any condition imposed a priori is incompatible with our national dignity." France, in turn, ignored the Guinean request for "association" under the terms of Title XIII of the constitution of the Fifth Republic.

Meanwhile Guinea did not lack recognition on the broader international scene. Immediately upon the announcement of Guinean independence the new nation was recognized on October 2, 1958, by its African neighbors, Ghana and Liberia. The Soviet Union and the members of the Eastern bloc promptly followed suit. The first recognition from the NATO countries was that by Great Britain on October 30, made in the face of strong French disapproval. The following day the German Federal Republic, not to be outdone by the German Democratic Republic, announced recognition of Guinea. By the end of the year, sixty countries, including both the Chinas and the United States, had recognized the new state. In the American case, however, there had been sufficient hesitation for consultation with France to convince the Guineans that Franco-American relations were clearly regarded in Washington as being more vital to American interests than were Guinean-American relations.

Guinea promptly sought and received membership in the United Nations on December 13, sponsored by Japan and Iraq and supported by Ghana and Haiti. To Guinea's disappointment, France not only found itself unable to sponsor the new member but was the only nation in the Assembly to abstain from the vote, since there was no official French cognizance of Guinea's existence. The French government finally agreed on January 7, 1959, to sign protocols with Guinea covering technical aid and cultural relations, but the Guinean ambassador in Paris was not granted accreditation until January 21. Meanwhile Guinea lost no time in establishing diplomatic ties in Washington and Moscow and in entering into cultural and economic agreements with Eastern bloc countries and the Soviet Union. At the end of 1958 Sékou Touré's new government could pride itself that its international status was secure.

At home, offers of aid poured in from a variety of sources. Teachers and administrators came voluntarily from other French-speaking African territories, and Guineans who had been serving in other territories were called home. In the emergency, many Guineans were moved from minor posts to those essential to maintain government services. Members of the legislative assembly were pressed into service either in Conakry or in the interior, on the assumption that they had had at least some experience in government and a minimum of education. European teachers and technicians who were personally in sympathy with the Guinean cause offered their services from France and elsewhere; a few French officers stayed on, abandoning their careers in the French overseas service. Within six months after independence it was clear that Guinea had weathered the initial shock and that the foundations of the wider revolution envisaged by the PDG had been laid. Speaking to the Tass correspondent early in 1959, Sékou Touré posed as Guinea's major problems the acceleration of mass education, the reconversion of the economy from a colonial pattern to that of an independent state, and the improvement of agricultural production. In the political sphere, he stressed the completion of the revolution by constant improvement of the party as a tool for the expression of the popular will. The blueprints were drawn; it was the task of the party to build from them.

Guinea and the Guineans

Of the independent French-speaking states of West Africa, Guinea enjoys the distinction of having the most varied geographical features and consequently of being among the most picturesque. Topographically the country falls into four reasonably clearly marked divisions, the coastal region (Lower Guinea), the Fouta Djallon plateau, the pre-Soudanic zone (Upper Guinea), and the forest zone. The four regions are demarcated by climatic changes and variations in vegetation which have been determining factors in the social and political organization of the people.

The coastal area of Lower Guinea is largely a plain, giving way at its eastern borders to low hills and cut by deep river valleys which in turn lead up to the higher escarpment of the Fouta Djallon. Lower Guinea stretches from 30 to 60 miles inland from the ocean and covers an over-all expanse of slightly over 16,000 square miles. As a result of direct exposure to the moisture-laden ocean breeze, the rainfall is exceptionally heavy during the rainy season from June to November, and even during the dry season (December to May) there continue to be high humidity and occasional rains. The temperature in this region varies only about 10 degrees throughout the year. The tropical climate produces heavy vegetation and rapid growth; it is ideal for banana and pineapple plantations as well as for the ubiquitous oil palm and the staple diet crop of rice. Conakry, the capital, is situated on a volcanic island, connected to the mainland by an artificial causeway; the site of the city is typical of the low, marshy islands and peninsulas along the coast, which is deeply indented by brackish estuaries and dotted with the mangrove swamps that form the mouths of the many rivers that gave Guinea its earlier name of Rivières du Sud.

From the coastal plain the land rises through a succession of low hills to the savannahs of the Fouta Djallon. Apart from the absence of heavy forest (except in the river valleys) the most marked feature of the plateau is the broad depression, from 5 to 10 miles in width, which divides it into two sections. Through this depression the rail line to the interior has been laid, and along it are small centers of urban concentration—Dabola, Kindia, and Mamou. Varying in altitude from 1,500 to over 3,000 feet, the plateau savannahs are covered with short grass, interspersed with occasional clumps of brush, baobabs, and even pines. Here the rainfall is much less than at the coast, and the dry season is more marked. The plateau people are the pastoralists of Guinea; crop raising is confined to the valleys and is usually the work of small settlements of coastal peoples.

Upper Guinea, the eastern portion of the country, is an extension of the plateau region shading off into the basin of the Upper Niger. Beyond Kouroussa and Kankan stretch the Soudanese plains, where an ample water supply permits rice cultivation.

To the south and east the forest zone begins, marked by sharply rising hills toward the Liberian border. Near the frontier south of N'Zérékoré, mountains are found over 5,000 feet high, including Mount Nimba, a rich source of iron ore. The forest areas are exploited for timber, and important plantations of quinine have been established.

Within Guinea's 95,000 square miles live a wide variety of tribal groups. Recent (1959) figures put the total population at 2,665,000, an increase of almost 230,000 since 1954. The major urban center is Conakry, with 78,500 people; no other cities approach this size. Heavy concentrations of rural population occur in the southwest and in particular around Labé in the Fouta Djallon, where over 257,000 people live in an area of 3,000 square miles. The population of the plateau is over 750,000; the explanation usually offered for overpopulation in this area is that almost one-third of the people represent the descendants of slaves captured by the Fulani in their attacks on the surrounding peoples of central and coastal Guinea. As in other African countries there has been a significant move over the past decade from the rural communities to the city. Migrant labor has descended from the plateau to work on the plantations near the coast, and the development of industry has drawn a surplus of labor to the capital. With the departure of some foreign firms the urban unemployment situation has become so serious that Sékou Touré has appealed to the local party sections to discourage further migration from upcountry villages.

From a numerical point of view, the most important tribal group of Guinea is the Fulani.[12] Some 800,000 occupy the northeastern section of the country. They are part of one of the most widespread of African peoples; Fulani are to be found as far west as the Senegal coast and as far east as Lake Tchad. Originally light-skinned, they have intermarried with Negroid stock over the centuries so that today they are largely indistinguishable from their neighbors. In general, they are pastoralists, counting their wealth in cattle, although a few subgroups (such as the Ouassoulounké in Guinea) have become sedentary agriculturalists. Much of the early history of the areas which are now Guinea, Mali, and Senegal was made by the Fulani conquerors, who reigned as feudal lords over their subject peoples. From these peoples came the strict hierarchies of the slave castes who performed the tasks of the artisans. The acquisition of slaves tended to turn the conquerors away from the pastoral pattern so that former nomads became suzerains over the lands they controlled. They remained a proud, independent people, secure in the superiority they felt was theirs by virtue of their Islamic inheritance.

Of the Soudanic Negroid groups which preceded the Fulani in the area of Upper Guinea, the largest group today is the Malinké.[13] Originally found along the Niger from Kankan to Bamako, they probably number about 450,000 in Guinea and are centered around Beyla, Kankan, and Kouroussa, although occasional colonies are found in Lower Guinea. The great early empire of Mali of the thirteenth century was formed by Malinké conquerors. They are for the most part agriculturalists, living traditionally in multidwelling compounds in enclosed villages. Because of their early mastery of the upper Soudan, Malinké language and customs have spread widely. Originally animists, they have been gradually converted to Islam, and some (notably Samory, the last great empire builder) were violent proselytizers of the new religion.

The Soussou, who occupy the areas around Forécariah, Kindia, and Dubreka, are the largest subgroup of a broader ethnic grouping which probably had its origins in the Niger Valley but was pushed to the coast by successive waves of Fulani invaders. Many became slaves of the Fulani; today the 250,000 Soussou have adapted their way of life

[12] The tribal name appears in many variations and spellings. French authors commonly use "Peul(h)."
[13] This version of the name is current in the Upper Niger Valley; they are also known as Mandinkas or Mandingos.

to the swampy coastal areas, where they are growers of rice. In general, the traditional Soussou social structure was based on the independent, fully autonomous villages. Smaller segments of these formerly Soudanic peoples include the 60,000 Dialonké around Faranah and the 40,000 Kouranko near Kissidougou. Toward southeastern Guinea in the heavy forest areas live the Kpelle or Guerzé (115,000 around N'Zérékoré), the Kissi (140,000 around Guékédou), and the Loma (80,000 around Macenta). These are sub-Guinean groups which have developed in the forest milieu forms of traditional political organization differing markedly from those of the coastal peoples.

There remain to be mentioned only the much smaller tribes which are part of the south-Soudanic groups. They are to be found in northwest Guinea (the Coniagui, numbering some 12,000, live near Youkounkoun; the Bassari and the Badaranké are among them). Excellent farmers, they have developed new techniques of tilling the relatively poor soil and a tsetse-resistant breed of cattle. In addition to these more prominent ethnic divisions, there exist a wide variety of tribal and linguistic subgroups.

The vast majority of Guineans are Muslims, although in some areas the practice of Islam has many animist overtones. A recent estimate places the number of Christians at 45,000 in a population of over 2,500,000. Catholic and Protestant missionaries have worked in the Guinean field for many years, but their greatest success has been in the urban areas. The animists of the high forest area have long resisted Islam with the same determination that the Fulani of the Fouta Djallon have shown in their resistance to Christianity. The forest, with its discrete village communities, presented not only a physical but also a psychological barrier to penetration by conquering Muslim warriors. The people of the forest live close to the forces of nature, and their religion has maintained a vitality born of this relationship.

Sékou Touré's government has made no direct attempt to interfere with the freedom of religion, but where religious bodies stand in the way of the party's political objectives, there is no hesitation in pushing them aside. Increasing difficulties have been put in the way of the work of European missionaries. A major political crisis threatened in mid-1961 when the French head of the Guinean Catholic Church, Monsignor de Milleville, was expelled by the government and the church was required to replace him with a Guinean. In Guinea the natural rejection of Christianity by a Muslim community is strengthened by the fact that Christianity is identified with the former colonial regime and consequently its missionaries are open to suspicion as anti-revolutionary agents.

The Political Process

ROLE OF THE PARTI DÉMOCRATIQUE DE GUINÉE

The Parti Démocratique de Guinée in the short period since independence has become a dominating influence at virtually every level of human activity in Guinea. A body of doctrine and theory has been developed which establishes the party as the motivating force behind the operation of Guinea as a national community. Sékou Touré has frequently reiterated this fundamental principle of party supremacy. "The PDG has not hesitated to say that more than ever it will retain its supremacy over all other institutions in the country. Only through the party can we . . . raise ourselves to the level of great responsibilities." [14] Since the party represents a national movement, not the action of individuals, he has declared that "political power must control the life of the country, at the financial, social, and cultural level." [15] Because of its all-embracing nature, the PDG is not, in Sékou Touré's view, to be regarded as a party in the European (or American) sense of the term. "It is a vast movement for African emancipation, whose mission it is to gather all Africans of good will under the banner of anticolonialism and progress." [16]

The party, then, is the supreme organ, occupying a role that is higher than the government itself. Within its hands are concentrated political, technical, economic, and judicial powers. Members of the party, by direct suffrage, elect the President, who is head of the state. In the view of the Guinean party leadership, this method of electing the chief of state is further proof that the PDG ought not to be regarded as a party since, by definition in European political theory, a party can represent only a part of the people. Sékou Touré insists that the Guinean regime is not a single-party system; the regime is itself the party, and no distinction can be made between the two. "All our people are mobilized in the ranks of the PDG; that is to say that the common will derives not from the summit but from a base of the popular will. Authority rests not with the government but with the people." [17]

[14] *Expérience*, p. 341.
[15] *Texte des Interviews Accordées aux Représentants de la Presse par le Président Sékou Touré* (Conakry, 1959), p. 57. Hereafter referred to as *Texte*.
[16] *Expérience*, p. 375.   [17] *Texte*, p. 118.

The PDG sees as its major tasks in Guinea the preservation of national unity and the mobilization of the national energies in a program of economic and social development to raise living standards as rapidly as possible. To enable this transformation to take place a complete psychological reconversion of the people must be achieved. The inherent contradictions of a colonial economic structure designed to benefit only the European must be removed and with them the attitudes of submission bred into the people. To accomplish these tasks the party needs the full support of the mass. Since the people are agreed on the goals to be gained, there is in the party's eyes no place for an opposition party whose tactics would serve only to divert popular energies from the tasks at hand. The PDG comprehends at all times the interests of all the people; it is also at this point that it must, Sékou Touré points out, be distinguished from a European party.

The PDG does not represent itself as the political instrument of any given social class. . . . European parties express the contradictions of class interest, and each has a socially defined base corresponding to precise class interests. . . . European parties base their action on strategies and tactics corresponding basically to the requirements of the class they represent. According to whether this class is or is not in power in the nation, the European class party supports or combats the regime in power. . . . It is easy to understand that none of these parties could satisfy the present situation in Black Africa.[18]

It follows from the claim of the party to represent the interests of all Guineans that its organization must be in effective contact with the largest possible segment of the population as much of the time as is possible. The RDA learned early from its French Communist teachers that the cellular party structure along classic Marxist-Leninist lines was one of the most efficient means of achieving this goal. Today the PDG in Guinea remains probably the best example in former French West Africa of the tightly organized, highly disciplined hierarchic party toward which all sections of the RDA strove in the preindependence period.

STRUCTURE AND ORGANIZATION OF THE PARTY

"The Parti Démocratique de Guinée is a mass party created to defend the interests of the people and to speed the movement for the emancipation of Africa." This key sentence, taken from the introduction to a report on party activity presented to the fifth party congress

[18] *Expérience*, pp. 375–376.

in 1959, gives two important clues to the nature of Guinea's only political party. The leaders of the PDG regard the party not only as the chief instrument of political decision within Guinea but also as a weapon which is to be used in the struggle for African independence anywhere on the continent.

Sékou Touré has said that the fundamental principle upon which the party is organized is democratic centralism, so that "from top to bottom and bottom to top all decisions of whatever nature take into account the will of the majority of its members." Democratic centralism, as it is understood by the leaders of the PDG, includes election of leaders at all levels of party organization, periodic reports by all party organs to the electors, and obligatory acceptance of all decisions of higher party organs by those organs lower in the hierarchy. The decision-making process within the party structure must take into account these principles; hence "decisions of the party will not be debated by the mass until the competent assemblies, bureaus, and committees have had the opportunity to discuss them. Resolutions laid down by the party congress must be executed fully, even though a part of the members of the lower organs do not approve them."

It is evident that the procedure for decision making which revolves around prior discussion by the next highest organizational level within the party requires a tightly knit, cohesive, and highly disciplined party structure. Toward this end the PDG has bent much of its effort since its inception. In the early years of the party before the vertical organization was as complete as at present, there existed a number of parallel party committees at the urban level which were essentially tribal in membership. But as soon as the party felt itself strong enough, these tribal committees were eliminated, so that each unit in the chain of command could direct its full efforts toward reaching the mass.

The present (1962) foundation of the PDG rests on the 7,164 village and urban local committees which are the point of articulation between the party and the mass of the Guinean population. Upon the executive (*bureau*) of these committees falls the responsibility for the organization of mass support and for carrying out the decisions made by the upper echelons of the party. It is the task of the *bureau* of these committees to explain the directives issued by the Bureau Politique to the people and to initiate and report upon village discussions of the questions addressed to the village committees by the Bureau Politique and by the section committees.

The executive of the village committee is elected once a year by the party members of the village which include in theory (and largely in practice) all eligible voters in the community. A committee executive consists of 10 members: 4 men, 3 women (who are the three chief officers of the local women's group of the party), 2 representatives of the party youths' group, and the mayor of the village. The election is carried out at a "general assembly" of the village party members, by direct universal suffrage. The village committee is required, at least a week prior to the election, to establish a definitive list of party members (that is, those who hold party cards and have therefore paid their dues; no one is in theory permitted to buy or renew a party card during the intervening week before the election). Only those on the list may vote. The only stated prerequisite for candidacy in the election is that of having been an active party member for a minimum of three preceding years.

The committees are expected to call meetings of the village membership at least once a week, at which village, regional, and national affairs are discussed. The village meetings within a party section usually take place at the same hour on the same day. Thus in the course of moving from village to village the visitor may watch the gathering in the marketplace, which lasts from one to three or more hours. Many of these meetings will be discussing identical topics, as required by the communications from Conakry.[19]

The village and quarter committees are grouped, at the next level of the party, into 43 sections. The members of the section congress are the 10 bureau members of each village committee within the section. The section congress meets twice annually to discuss the administration of the section and to hear instructions from the party leadership. At the head of each section is the Comité Directeur. The 15 members of this committee are elected by the section congress from among its own membership; 2 of these must be women. The 2 chief officers of the regional youth group executive sit on the Comité Directeur ex officio. Each member of the Directing Committee is assigned a specific post. In addition to the usual secretary and treasurer, there are secretaries for politics, organization, administration, and propaganda, as well as three financial supervisors (*comissaires des comptes*). The head of the committee is the secretary-general, who is directly responsible to the Bureau Politique for the affairs of the section.

Within the Directing Committee are a number of working subcom-

---

[19] Cf. here the description of the village meeting given by Fernand Gigon, *Guinée, Etat-Pilote* (Paris: Plon, 1959), pp. 43 ff.

mittees (political or economic affairs, finance, and organization) which may in turn co-opt noncommittee members to assist them. These committees are required to study and report to the Comité Directeur as a whole on problems which may be submitted to them from the village committees below. Much of the time in the meetings of the Comité Directeur is taken up with discussion of the circulars emanating from the national headquarters. These *mots d'ordre* are received by the permanent secretary, who, after discussion with the secretary-general and the political secretary, fixes the agenda for the committee meetings. After discussion, the *mots d'ordre*, with further comment by the Comité Directeur, are distributed to the village committees for discussion by the members as a whole. Circulars of the Bureau Politique have dealt with such diverse subjects as the preeminence of the party, the role of the party youth organization, the functions of the Comités Directeurs, family allowances, responsibilities of the labor unions, reason for financial contributions to the party, the necessity for popular education to maintain mass enthusiasm, and respect for religious convictions. The latter circular also dealt, incidentally, with "the struggle against all mystification, fraud, and exploitation of the masses under the cover of religion."

The Comité Directeur of the section holds a crucial position since here is the point of articulation between the national leadership of the party and the village committees. Thus the Political Bureau regards the semiannual section meetings as of key importance in pushing forward the party program. Repeatedly party directives have inveighed against the dangers of political apathy at the section level, since such apathy may in turn be felt by the mass through the village committees.

At the section level, a horizontal aspect of the party structure is to be found in the semiannual regional conferences which bring together all the Comités Directeurs of the sections within a single administrative region. To these party officers are added delegates of the village committees, the *commandant de région*, the chiefs of administrative posts, the managers of regional cooperatives, the local trade union heads, and the regional military commanders. The regional conference is designed not only to bring together the regional section committees but to provide a link between the administration and the party at the administrative rather than at the party level. Comparable national conferences of delegates of the sections and the national party leaders are held annually.

The largest formal gathering of the PDG is the party congress, held every third year. The most recent (fifth) congress took place from September 14 to September 17, 1959, in Conakry. The tasks of the congress are primarily to fix party policy for the forthcoming triennium, to receive reports from the secretary-general on the activities of the party (the fact that governmental and party activities are identical means that in effect the secretary-general's report becomes very roughly the equivalent of a State of the Union message), and to elect the members of the national executive of the party, the Bureau Politique. Voting in the congress is by section (one vote per section regardless of the number of delegates), and each section is free to bring up for discussion in the meeting any question of policy it may desire.

The fifth congress was attended by nearly 2,000 delegates, civil servants, and private individuals, Guinean and foreign. In addition to the members of Comités Directeurs in each section, members of the government, senior administrators and civil servants, national inspectors of the youth section, members of the executive committee of the labor federation, and senior military officers were part of the congress.

A breakdown of the 717 members of the Comités Directeurs of the sections, who were delegates to the congress, gives some indication of the cross section of the Guinean population who form the militants of the party. Eighty of the 717 were women, ranging in age from 15 to 65, with an average age of 37. Sixty-eight of these female delegates were housewives, 5 were civil servants, 6 were artisans, and one was in business. The 637 male members were between 18 and 75 years old, with an average age of 37. The largest group (249) was between 31 and 40, the second largest (198) between 27 and 30. Only 42 of the male members were 51 or over, and 35 were between 18 and 25. To an even greater degree than in the case of parties elsewhere in West Africa the PDG in Guinea is the party of youth.

An analysis of the professions of the male members indicated a predominance of civil servants (314), but a wide range of other employment was also included: 132 peasants, 72 merchants, 32 artisans, and 50 laborers. Peasants and laborers greatly outnumbered the members of the "liberal professions"; in contrast to other African party congresses, only one lawyer and one clergyman were listed among the delegates.

As secretary-general of the party and President of the Republic, Sékou Touré has used the party congresses as occasions to present a lengthy *rapport moral* which, in addition to outlining the accomplishments of the party, lays down the political philosophy upon which the party acts. To a greater extent than most other African parties the PDG has developed a coherent body of theory which is intended to provide the rationale for the day-to-day decisions of the party's executive, the Political Bureau.

Since the party is regarded as the motive force behind all political, social, and economic activity in the state, the Political Bureau, in whose hands the ultimate decision-making power is concentrated, is the focus of power both in the party and in the nation. Nine of its 17 members are ministers of government, and all the remaining members hold other responsible posts, including the presidency of the National Assembly, head of the Guinean armed forces, and chief inspector of education. The powers of the bureau over the party and the government are for all practical purposes unrestricted. No decision of a political nature can be taken in any department of government without prior discussion by the bureau, and from it emanate all directives to the lower party echelons.

Each member of the bureau is responsible for a particular aspect of the party's organization. Sékou Touré is secretary-general and head of the party; the political secretary, El Hadj Saïfoulaye Diallo, occupies a position second only to that of Sékou Touré. There are three organizational secretaries (Moussa Diakité, Ismael Touré, and N'Famara Keita), an administrative secretary (Damantang Camara), a permanent secretary (Daouda Camara), and a treasurer (Mamadou Fofana). The interests of the women's section of the party are represented by Mmes Mafory Bangoura and Loffo Camara, and the party youth group is under the direction of Jean Tounkara and the trade union movement of Mamadi Caba, secretary of the Guinean labor organization. Thus, virtually every organized group in the country—the army, youth, women, and labor—is directly related to the party through the presence of their heads in the Bureau Politique. In addition, there are four national inspectors of the party whose job it is to see that the sections and local committees carry out the orders of the bureau.

Internally the bureau is divided, as are the Comités Directeurs of the sections, into three major committees: organization, financial control, and conflicts. The Committee on Organization is concerned with the party congress, preparation of the party budget, and youths' and women's organizations. The Comission des Conflits is given the task of settling internal conflicts between party groups at the lower levels. There are a number of technical committees on which nonmembers of the bureau may serve, but all are headed by bureau members. Finally, a committee for the recruitment of junior party officers is in charge of the short courses offered periodically as part of the training for potential leaders.

The bureau's position as the executive body of the party requires that its members make decisions on an extremely wide variety of questions. There are regular fortnightly meetings of the bureau, but it may also be called into special session at the request of the secretary-general. The agenda for the meetings is prepared by the permanent secretary from dossiers forwarded by the members, but other questions may also be raised for which dossiers have not been prepared. Decisions appear to be made by general debate among the members, but it is clear that the opinions of a small inner group directly surrounding Sékou Touré carry the most weight, particularly on the more important questions. Since the civil service has still far from enough technically trained officers, there is little opportunity for extensive staff work or the preparation of detailed position papers; thus decisions are liable to be made on the basis of the accumulated knowledge of the members. As might be expected under the circumstances, the necessity of funneling so many decisions through the Political Bureau meant that, particularly in the first year after independence, the bureau became an administrative bottleneck. No one group of men can possibly handle the entire business of government. Consequently many urgent matters have had to be deferred for lack of time, or decisions have been made too rapidly on an inadequate basis of information and therefore had later to be rescinded or altered.

In its composition the bureau reflects the youthful makeup of the party congress. The average age of its members in 1960 was thirty-eight; the *doyen* of the group, Abdourahmane Diallo, was born in 1902. They bring to their posts in the party a variety of experience. The majority were civil servants under the colonial administration, having been employed as court clerks, pharmacists, and accountants in various territories. Most have secondary school education; among them are several graduates of the William Ponty school. One of the most common elements in the earlier training of the bureau members is their trade union experience; they learned, as did so many other leaders of the RDA sections, the techniques of organization and agitation through participation in the trade union movement under the leadership of the French CGT. All have been party militants from the earliest period, and at least two began their interest in politics as members of the ethnic groups which preceded the formation of the PDG.

An important part of the program of the PDG since its inception has been the emancipation of Guinean women. The women's organization has played a key role in the growth of the nationalist movement since independence. Today, the women's wing of the the party is included in every level of party activity from the village to the Bureau Politique by a system of interlocking representation. Parallel with the main party organization there exists a complete structure of women's groups, each of which elects representatives to the village and section committees and to the national congress.

As early as 1947 women began to join the PDG, and the early organization of the party, particularly in N'Zérékoré and Macenta, owes much to their activity. Many were militants of the party before their husbands. The women's groups encouraged the men to take part in the national strike of 1953, and some women threatened to divorce their husbands if they failed to join the strikers. The women's section of the PDG was formally organized in 1954 into village and section committees, and by 1956 the women were actively campaigning in most parts of Guinea for the election of PDG deputies. Early in 1955, M'Balia Camara, a prominent militant, died as a result of wounds inflicted by a *chef de canton* and became the first female martyr of the Guinean revolution. Women were a major force in marshaling the vote at the referendum, and in some areas the overwhelming vote of "no" was undoubtedly due to the solid support of the women and the pressure they applied to hesitant males.

Since independence the women's wing of the party has continued to insist on social and cultural liberation for its members. More specifically its program has sought equal wages with men for equal work and the reorganization of the traditional marriage system, with the fixing of the minimum marriage age at seventeen, civil ceremony for all marriages, and the abolition of polygamy. The party leadership has repeatedly paid homage to the role of the women in party organization and to their contribution to the revolution, but men have not, apparently, always been in complete agreement with the women's demands. Sékou Touré was constrained to point out: "If we have encountered difficulty in emancipating our sisters, it is because most men refuse to create those conditions which will permit us to emancipate their wives and daughters. There are still marriage practices which must disappear, without regard to the egoistic and reactionary attitudes of the men." [20]

[20] *Action*, p. 428.

In extending its control over Guinean society the PDG has also paid great attention to the organization of youth. Like the women's wing, the Jeunesse du Rassemblement Démocratique Africain is represented in each organ in the party hierarchy by an elected member so that the youth group has a voice everywhere in the party's activities. At the level of the Bureau Politique one member is assigned to supervise the JRDA and to see that its actions are coordinated with the broader policy goals of the adult group.

The JRDA is now the sole youth organization in Guinea. Within it are incorporated the former student groups and sporting and artistic federations. Its membership includes youths up to the age of 25, at which point it is compulsory to leave the youth organization to join the adult party. Younger children up to the age of 14 are members of the "Pioneers," an integral part of the youth organization. The JRDA is not considered a body separate from the party but an internal division of the PDG through which the youth of Guinea is to play a part in the national effort to develop the nation. In creating a single national youth organization, the PDG made it clear that it intended Guinean youth to be molded in conformity with party theory. Sékou Touré has written:

We do not take as an example the false conception that several of us have of liberty and democracy. In fact, a goodly number of our comrades believe that liberty consists in letting everyone do and say what he pleases, in letting every class of youth organize as it wishes and take what initiative it pleases. Well, the party does not agree. For the party . . . liberty is only a tool, a tool for organizing and orienting our activities to conform with the popular will. Democracy should not be mistaken for disorder and anarchy.[21]

The JRDA was at the outset headed by a national committee composed of the magic number of seventeen members, including *inter alia* secretaries for sports and artistic and cultural and student questions, for the Pioneers, and for *la jeunesse féminine*. The committee was elected for two years by the national youth congress, and its day-to-day work was supervised by inspectors designated by the party. In 1961 the committee was replaced by a Ministry of Youth at cabinet level. Two main sections make up the JRDA's activities, the sporting section (including the major sports federations) and the general section which has charge of the Pioneers and of cultural and scholastic affairs. Part of this activity is concerned with the management of sum-

[21] *La Liberté*, no. 151 (April 10, 1959), p. 4.

mer camps and short courses in a variety of subjects, including indoctrination in party philosophy and the "reconversion" of youth from a colonial to a nationalist psychology.

With the formation of the women's and youth organizations the PDG became the most comprehensive and most disciplined of all the West African parties, although in this respect the party in Mali is not far behind. Inevitably also the PDG broke its ties with the RDA. It became clear shortly after independence that the PDG could not continue to remain a section of the party which acknowledged Houphouët-Boigny of the Ivory Coast as its president. By his support of a direct federal relationship to France, Houphouët had betrayed, in the Guinean view, a cardinal principle of RDA policy, the unity of West Africa. In failing to insist on a strong federal structure at Dakar, Houphouët had renounced independence for the mess of pottage which was the Community. Under these circumstances, then, Guinea's only choice was to break with the RDA, particularly in the face of what the Guinean leaders interpreted as Houphouët's attempts to isolate them after the referendum. Accordingly, on October 19, 1958, the Bureau Politique voted unanimously to break away from the old RDA because of "the manifest incompatibility between its conception of the personality, dignity, and real aspirations of Africa and membership in the RDA." The bureau added, however, that it would consider itself the natural ally of any section of the RDA or of any other party which shared its view that the independence of Africa was inseparable from national independence for the individual colonial territories. Sure of the solid support of the Guinean people based upon effective organization and a series of simply defined and popular goals, the PDG proceeded to harness the full national energies in pursuit of the goal of a completely independent Africa.

POLITICAL THEORY OF THE PARTI DÉMOCRATIQUE DE GUINÉE

The PDG differs from most other African parties in its possession of a body of theory from which its actions stem. The chief and almost the only source of this theory is the secretary-general, Sékou Touré. In his reports to party congresses, in statements to the press, and in radio broadcasts he has adumbrated and repeated the major points of the political philosophy which he has created for the party.

In broad outline, the party philosophy draws heavily on Marxist-Leninist doctrines of political organization and the role of the party in the state. But mixed with Marxism are strands of Rousseau and other

European theorists. Finally, there is an element of African traditionalism which fills in the pattern where European theory fails to provide those aspects of doctrine that Touré believes are required to meet the specific needs of Guinea.

The first and most basic tenet of PDG philosophy is the supremacy of the party over every aspect of the life of the individual and the state. The party is regarded as the repository of the popular will; the real organ of decision making is neither government nor parliament but the party—which he approximates to the people.[22] It is through the organs of the party that the general will of the people is expressed, and in the party that unity of purpose is achieved. Sékou Touré admits that within this system the conception of personal liberties will be different from that in more-developed countries. In Africa, however, at this stage of economic development, individual liberty becomes meaningful, Touré believes, only in terms of the liberty of Guinean society in relationship to the outside world. To become part of this modern world requires a complete transformation of society.

We seek the independence of our society; the prisoner does not consider the liberty he enjoys inside the walls of his jail but only his liberty in relationship to the outside world. Socially we consider ourselves prisoners in relationship to the developed nations, and it is this liberation we seek. In such a perspective individual liberty loses a good deal of its savor and attractiveness.[23]

In Sékou Touré's view, this liberation of society can be accomplished for Africa only by the total mobilization of the energies of the people under the direction and guidance of the party. To this end, the party is prepared to use those methods of political organization which have already been found effective in underdeveloped countries outside Africa; most of these are derived from Marxist-Leninist theory. But Sékou Touré has repeatedly pointed out that he regards Marxism as a means, not an end.

We have used certain parts of the Marxist doctrine to organize rational foundations for African trade unionism. We have adopted from Marxism everything that is true for Africa. We have not sought to make of this science an end in itself, but like all sciences we have tried to put it to the use of Guinean society. Instead of adapting our society to a science, we have sought the means of applying this science to our society. Thus, although Marxism is applied in its doctrinal entirety by the international working

[22] *Texte,* p. 61.   [23] *Ibid.,* p. 62.

class in the class struggle, we have excised this element from it for our-selves in order to permit all Africans, regardless of class, to engage in the anticolonial struggle.[24]

It is precisely the absence of an urban industrial proletariat and hence of the class struggle which, Sékou Touré believes, makes it im-possible to create a Communist state in Africa. All European parties, including the Communist, are designed to serve the needs of a particu-lar class, he considers, but the PDG makes no class distinctions:

We formally reject the principle of the class struggle, less by philosophic conviction than by desire to save at all costs African solidarity . . . which alone is capable of preserving our originality and of imposing on the world respect for the African. In fact, the new African society cannot depend on European-inspired doctrines if it is to succeed. If we prove that without the class struggle a profound transformation of our country is possible, we will have made our contribution to political science. If we are capable of developing in harmony, we will have demonstrated to the world that it was wrong in underestimating . . . and neglecting the African personality.[25]

But, strongly as he holds this view, Sékou Touré's position would ap-pear in the light of history to rest on very doubtful foundations. As the Soviet Union and the People's Republic of China have amply il-lustrated, the presence of an industrial proletariat is by no means neces-sarily a prerequisite to the establishment of a Communist state.

Touré has maintained, as have other African leaders, that traditional African society was classless, in the modern sense of that term, be-cause no economic distinctions could be made in a society in which everyone depended on subsistence farming for his livelihood. This could possibly have been the case in a legendary golden age of communal village life, but most African societies whose traditional structures have been investigated did, in fact, have marked class dis-tinctions. These distinctions may have been based on ascriptive qualifi-cations rather than an achieved economic status, but the effect was to create a society in which the class struggle was at least potentially present. If, as Touré argues, the class struggle does not exist in Africa today, it would seem that this cannot be attributed to any specifically indigenous quality in African societies but rather that the objective con-ditions for it have not yet been created.

It should be added that Sékou Touré has emphatically asserted that the new states of Africa will also reject communism on religious as well

[24] *Expérience,* p. 402.   [25] *Ibid.,* pp. 393–394.

as theoretical grounds. Africans, be they Christians, Muslims, or animists, are deeply religious peoples, he believes, and hence communism, with its rejection of religion, would be unacceptable to them.

Touré has repeatedly emphasized that he himself is not a Communist. In April, 1960, he stated in an interview:

I refuse to allow the PDG to follow the ideological line of communism. If certain people wish to do so, let them found a Guinean Communist Party, but they must realize the PDG will oppose them under my leadership. Communism is not the way for Africa. The class struggle here is impossible for there are no classes . . . the fundamental basis of our society is the family and the village community.[26]

Speaking before the United Nations in September, 1960, he categorically refused the right of the Russians to speak for Africa because Africans did not share the Communist ideology. Similarly in May, 1961, commenting on the award to him of a Stalin Peace Prize, Sékou Touré indicated that he felt it all the more an honor since, during the visit of the Russian President to Conakry, Touré had made it clear to him that the PDG was not a Communist Party. In December, 1961, Touré accused certain unnamed Eastern satellite governments of fomenting an uprising of student groups against the PDG and warned the militants to be on guard against attempts by any foreign government to subvert the goals of the party.

Touré has never denied, however, that he has found certain aspects of Marxist-Leninism both useful and attractive. He feels that the stress laid by Marx on the collective action of the community is more congenial to the African than is the Western stress on the value of individual initiative. The experiments in social reform carried out in the People's Republic of China may, he feels, provide many lessons for Guinea. But the systems developed for China or Russia are not always relevant to Guinean conditions. What is significant in the Chinese revolution, he has pointed out, is that "it attests to the justice of the principles which have been the motivating force of the Chinese people. And if Guinea, too, finds principles corresponding to its human, social, moral, economic, and administrative realities, it too may have the same success."[27] At least part of the attraction of Marxism for Sékou Touré lies in the fact that it is antithetical to the Western capitalism of the colonial powers. In the eyes of the Guinean leaders capitalism is equated with colonial exploitation, and the elimination of colonialism

[26] Cited in *Le Monde*, April, 1960.   [27] *Texte*, p. 107.

makes the adoption of an economic theory opposed to capitalism all the more desirable.

Before all else Sékou Touré is a Guinean, and his acceptance of Marxism stems not so much from philosophical conviction as from an awareness of its utility as a means of forcing the pace of Guinean economic development. As Brian Crozier has commented regarding Sékou Touré: "Marxism has contracted an emotional and intellectual marriage within him to a dimly felt awareness of African communal traditions. Marxism as he is modifying it is a powerful instrument of government by participation, as distinct from delegation through the ballot box." [28]

Because the language of African nationalism employs the terminology of Marxist-Leninism, Touré's Western critics have frequently overlooked his attempts to develop an interpretation of Marx peculiar to an African context. Thomas Hodgkin has recently pointed out that the Leninist definition of imperialism is employed by colonial nationalists everywhere and that the concepts of democratic centralism which Sékou Touré espouses are shared by nationalist leaders whose identification with Marxism has been much less explicit than that of Touré. In fact, there are very important divergences from orthodox Marxist concepts in the Guinean party theory. The PDG and other African nationalist parties have always insisted that they are mass parties, not Leninist, "small, picked bands of revolutionaries." The importance attached to "*négritude*," the "African personality," and African traditional values clearly differentiates Africans from other peoples and is in direct contradiction to the Marxist internationalism of the working-class revolution. "From a Marxist standpoint," Hodgkin adds, "this insistence . . . is surely characteristic of petty-bourgeois romantic nationalism." [29] Sékou Touré has not hesitated to adapt Marx to the political realities of Africa; orthodox European Marxists have at times found his interpretations more than a little difficult to reconcile with current Marxist dogma.

Touré's definition of democracy revolves about the question of popular participation in the actions of the party. "There are democratic and nondemocratic states, which are distinguished one from the other by the importance of the role played by the masses, by the importance of the participation of the people in the affairs of the state." [30] But this

[28] "Six Africans in Search of a Personality," *Encounter,* XVI, no. 5 (May, 1961), 39.
[29] "A Note on the Language of African Nationalism," *St. Antony's Papers,* no. 10 (1961), p. 36.
[30] *Action,* p. 379.

mass participation does not signify that the state should be without leadership or discipline. So long as the leadership (in this case, the party) is a direct emanation of the people and its decisions are freely consented to by them, then the criteria of democracy are met.

Touré is not reluctant to use the term "dictatorship" in his explanation of the nature of Guinean democracy. If the people have agreed upon the basic objectives, then it follows that they must be directed in order to attain these objectives harmoniously and justly. This fact implies using the authority of the party to direct the people, and therefore the system is a form of dictatorship. But in his words, "According to the way in which it is used, dictatorship may be democratic or antidemocratic. As for us, we say that by according preeminence to the people, by having them participate in all important national decisions, this dictatorship is popular and democratic." [31]

Under these circumstances Sékou Touré does not envisage the development of a two-party or multiparty system in Guinea, although the possibility is not entirely excluded. He argues that for the foreseeable future, however, the single-party system is the only way by which Africa can be led rapidly through the necessary stages from underdevelopment to full flowering. National unity was realized in Guinea by the independence struggle, and it is too important to be dissipated by internal political bickerings. "We do not intend to lose our unity just to adapt ourselves to a political system which would deteriorate and reduce our political strength." [32] What is important to Guinea today is rapid evolution. Touré's view is that the existence of more than one party presupposes stable and long-established political and economic institutions; these Guinea lacks. To compensate for this lack Guinea has the dynamic potentiality created by the anticolonial revolution. The goals to be reached by the revolution are agreed upon by the people as a whole; the existence of more than one party would merely act as a brake on progress toward these ends.

Political opposition is constructive when, by its presence and its action, it increases the dynamism of the party in power. This is true for those countries . . . where all elements which participate in economic development follow a balanced rhythm of natural evolution. . . . These are not at all the conditions in Africa.[33]

In the one-party structure of Guinea, the function of continuous criticism of the actions of the PDG is to be fulfilled from within the

[31] *Le Cinquième Congrès National du Parti Démocratique de Guinée* (Conakry, 1959), pp. 84–85. Hereafter referred to as *Congrès*.
[32] *Texte*, p. 38.   [33] *Ibid.*, p. 38.

party by consultations between the Bureau Politique and the lower echelons, by the annual conferences, and by the triennial congresses. Intraparty disagreements will be resolved at the appropriate level of the section or village committee. The party permits and welcomes criticism, Touré maintains, but only within the framework of the broad policy goals determined by the party congress. This opportunity for criticism does not, however, extend to the point where factions will be permitted to grow up within the party. Guinean experience at an earlier period with parties based on ethnic groups has shown that there are still possibilities of creating a political following for the benefit of one man and for the satisfaction of personal ambition. Within the PDG such personal aggrandizement is forbidden. "I tell you, none of those who surround me have been chosen by me. The first principle of the party is 'Whoever is a candidate for election is excluded.'" The party chooses its leadership, according to this principle, not from among an elite or from among those who seek political office to create for themselves a position of power but rather from among those who have distingushed themselves in the eyes of the mass by their devotion to the work of the party and therefore, by definition, to the good of the people.

It is obvious that Sékou Touré's conception of democracy has little in common with that of the West. Immanuel Wallerstein has pointed out Touré's argument that rather than "democracy" as the correct description of the Guinean system it should instead be "communaucracy." [34] Sékou Touré has often insisted that the political system evolved and adapted for an African country cannot be modeled on that of the West because African society sees the individual only in relationship to the immediate group of which he is a part. He declares:

Africa is essentially communaucratic. Collective living and social solidarity give to African customs a depth of humanism which many people might envy. Because of these qualities an individual in Africa cannot conceive of the organization of his life outside that of the family, village, or clan. The voice of the African people is faceless and nameless. But in those areas contaminated by the colonialists, who has not seen the rise of personal egoism? [35]

The party's task is to seek the development of Guinea without losing those values which give African life its real significance and without

[34] Immanuel Wallerstein, "Political Theory in an African Context," paper delivered at the Third Annual Meeting of the African Studies Association, Sept., 1960.

[35] *Action*, p. 257.

which "we lose sight of the real meaning of our surroundings and even
of the meaning of ourselves." The political systems evolved by both
East and West to preserve their own patterns of social values may offer
some guidelines for material development in Africa, but they can never
be a substitute for an African system in which those values that distinguish Africa from the rest of the world will be reflected.

The Parti Démocratique de Guinée and the Mobilization of Guinean Society

THE RECONVERSION OF SOCIETY

The PDG saw as one of its major duties after independence the
spiritual reconversion of Guinean society in order to remove the psychological as well as the physical traces of colonialism. Although the
success of the nationalist struggle had brought an end to the colonial
administration, nonetheless the Guinean leaders felt that the mental
attitudes bred of colonialism remained, particularly in the intellectuals.
What was needed, Sékou Touré claimed, was "integral decolonization,"
that is, "a total reconversion of the human being who has been taught
a way of thinking foreign to the real conditions of his milieu." Everyone in Guinea was to a greater or lesser degree marked by colonialism,
but the peasantry was least marked and therefore remained closest to
the truly African value structure. Thus Touré advised the civil servants
and the younger educated groups to turn to the peasants to regain the
full expression of their African heritage.

Reconversion for the mass must also mean the acquisition of a new
sense of discipline and moral solidarity. The anarchic acts of the
period of nationalist struggle were approved by the party as long as
they were designed to undermine the colonial regime. But with independence, Touré points out, Guineans must realize that such acts are
harmful to the motherland. Revolution should not be confounded with
revolt, because revolution, whatever form it takes, signifies the passage of a people from a lower to a higher state. Suppression of the
colonial regime meant only that a new stage of the revolution had
arrived in which the goal was to be a complete and radical transformation of the Guinean economy. The first step in this reconversion was the
seizure of political power: "Our economic and cultural liberation comes
as a consequence of political liberation."

An aspect of the reconversion of Guinean society which has created
some attention outside Guinea is the party's program of "voluntary

labor" (*investissement humain*). The third party congress in June, 1958, decided to mobilize the human energies of the people in support of public works programs. The details of the projects were to be left to the initiative of village and section committees of the party. In cases where plans called for the creation of buildings the local committees could call on the government for assistance in buying materials provided the labor was supplied by the people. *Investissement humain* was received with enthusiasm after independence, and in 1959 Sékou Touré could announce that 5,035 miles of roads, 33 schools, 672 bridges, and 15 mosques were among the accomplishments of the program and that schemes based on the Guinean example had been undertaken in Mali, Senegal, and Togo.

Investissement humain was urged upon the people by the PDG for a variety of reasons. The most obvious, of course, was the limited budget of the new country for public works. If the people wanted a road, a bridge, or a dispensary, it was clear that it would have to be built on a self-help basis. Moreover, the people were eager to prove that more could be accomplished under a Guinean government than under the French administration. The energy generated by the national effort that was put into the referendum could most usefully be channeled, in the view of the party leadership, into producing some concrete results of independence in which the people could take pride. It was clear, however, that with the meager skills available in the rural areas and the limited time which could be utilized (in several larger towns people worked at voluntary projects at night under floodlights after their day's work) no large-scale projects could be undertaken. The party encouraged the work program, however, not only because of its economic results but also because "in the political field the campaign would bring other benefits in its wake—first, the feeling of responsibility on the part of everyone and a love of the value of work for its own sake." In Sékou Touré's words, "It demonstrates the preeminence of constructive action over verbal wrangling." [36]

Investissement humain has been an essential part of the party's program to create a unified Guinean society and to reduce what Sékou Touré has called the "contradictions" that existed between the interests of an independent Guinean people and those of a colonial regime. It remains to be seen, however, whether the level of popular support for the donation of free time to unpaid work, no matter how socially desirable, can be maintained indefinitely. In Conakry the local party

[36] *Expérience*, p. 346.

committees can no longer exert enough pressure to bring the people out for street cleaning and other similar work on Sunday. There is no doubt that part, at least, of the support for the program has been a result of social pressure, particularly in the villages. Although a man may be theoretically free to remain aloof from a project upon which the village is engaged, the village is equally free to prevent him from sharing in the results of the common labor—and this has, in fact, been the case in some villages where the recalcitrants have been forcibly prevented from using a road built by *investissement humain.*

ROLE OF THE INTELLECTUAL IN GUINEAN SOCIETY

The reconversion from a colonial to an African mentality will be most difficult, the party feels, for the intellectuals since they will have the greatest problem of adjustment in their return to a genuinely African value pattern. The most deleterious effect of colonialism in Africa, in Sékou Touré's view, was not primarily in the economic but in the cultural sphere. Those who received an education designed not for an African but for a French milieu found, he feels, that they had lost real contact with Africa. "The milieu determines the individual. That is why the village peasant has more authentically African characteristics than the lawyer or the doctor of the cities. In fact, the farmer, who has preserved his personality and the nature of his culture more or less intact, is more aware of the real needs of Africa." [37] The intellectual in contrast had been taught by his extended contact with French education to look down upon his African culture. He had been depersonalized by the universal truths taught him in the process of making him a lawyer or a doctor. He can best integrate himself into the new Africa by ridding himself of the complexes created by colonialism; only in this way can the intellectual hope to be of real help to Africa. Sékou Touré insists that he is not seeking "to put intellectualism on trial" but rather to redefine the place of the intellectual among the elite of Africa. "The African elite," he points out, "is not to be recognized by its diplomas, or by its theoretical or practical knowledge, or by its wealth, but only by its devotion to the evolution of Africa." [38]

The PDG, then, is not a party led by a minority of intellectuals, as were some of the early ethnic group parties in Guinea. Leadership need not depend on education. A man of peasant origin with only a primary school education may, in the party's eyes, have more genuine

[37] *Action*, p. 256.　　　　　　　　　[38] *Expérience*, p. 256.

wisdom than an educated man who plays the role of leader only to
advance his personal interests; the individual demonstrates his wisdom by his devotion to the mass.

The somewhat anti-intellectual attitude adopted by the PDG leadership is consistent with Sékou Touré's theoretical position that the party
must not become the vehicle for the expression of the interests of one
class in society. If the argument that African society is classless is
pursued consistently, then the intellectuals cannot be treated as a class
apart; an attempt by them to distinguish themselves from the mass
serves only to alienate them in greater degree from the people they
should be serving.

To understand the viewpoint of the party on the place of the intellectuals requires some reference to the personal histories of the party
leaders. Prior to the end of World War II there were practically no
university graduates in Guinea, and consequently the intellectual elite
of that time consisted of secondary school graduates. As Wallerstein
has pointed out, the leadership of the PDG during its formative years
and in the period of mass organization was largely in the hands of men
who had no more than primary education but had excellent trade union
experience.[39] They found that they were more effective in their contact with the peasantry than were the intellectuals and hence minimized
the place of the intellectuals in the political movement. But unlike
Ghana, where there has been a continuing degree of alienation of the
intellectuals from the Convention Peoples' Party, the breach in Guinea
has been partially healed since independence. Guinean students in
Paris were not only fully in sympathy with Sékou Touré's aims of independence and African unity but were impatient at what they believed to be his temporizing during the period of the *loi cadre*. After
independence, Guineans with university training who were employed
outside Guinea offered their services to the new government, and many
returned home. The PDG has gradually integrated most of them into
its ranks, but not without some reluctance. The party made it clear
that, although these persons were welcomed into posts of importance
in government where their knowledge and skills were of use, few were
to be included in the inner circle of the PDG leadership. This was the
case in particular with those who had remained outside Guinea (regardless of the validity of their reasons) during the period when the
party was actively combating the French administration. The intel-

[39] See "Guinea and African Unity," *New Leader*, XLIII, no. 21 (May 23, 1960),
20–22.

lectuals made good civil servants, but the party cadres remained in the hands of those with lesser education.

With the formation of the JRDA, the Guinean students' association came to an end as a separate organization within the country although in France it continued as an autonomous organization. To assist in the reconversion of the young intellectuals, they were incorporated into the youth wing of the party where they could be subjected to more rigorous control and to training in the party's ideological outlook. This outlook, it may be noted, was in some senses more conservative than that of the students themselves, many of whom had been members of the more strictly orthodox Marxist Parti Africain de l'Indépendance.

THE PARTY AND TRADITIONAL AUTHORITY

The process of detribalization is being actively encouraged by the PDG. At every level individuals are being urged to consider themselves as Guineans first (and preferably exclusively); distinction as to tribe is regarded as being contrary to the interests of national unity. Within the party structure a man is elected to the village committee ideally because he has been a militant, not because he enjoys a traditional position, however minor. It cannot yet be assumed that tribe is a factor to be disregarded entirely, particularly in the balance of political forces at the national level, but there would appear to be indications that geographical spread is considered at least of equal importance with tribal identification in the choice of top party officials.

Prior to independence the PDG took forceful steps to eliminate traditional power as a focus of personal loyalty. Aware that the traditional authorities constituted a threat, real or potential, to the legitimization of party control, the PDG sought during the period of internal autonomy under the *loi cadre* to sweep aside chieftaincy. This was, of course, also a blow at the colonial administration, since the chiefs had become virtually the paid servants of the colonial regime. The entire question of the future of the chiefs was discussed at length in the territorial assembly in the early part of 1957. Thereafter the views of the new government elected under the *loi cadre* and led by Sékou Touré were thoroughly aired at a conference of *commandants de cercle* and members of the government at Conakry in July.

Opening this meeting, the Minister of the Interior, Fodeba Keita, outlined the party position on the chiefs and pointed out that a distinction must be made between the institution of chieftaincy and the individual who occupied the chief's role. He added that although many of the chiefs were men of experience and judgment in administrative affairs, and therefore highly valuable to the country, the fact remained that chieftaincy and the new forms of popular democracy introduced by the *loi cadre* were basically incompatible. The time for feudal rule had passed, in the party's opinion. "In Guinea the practical role of chieftaincy is in contradiction to the new political role of the people; it is bound to disappear through its own uselessness. . . . Respect for custom and tradition must not be a brake on evolution." [40] Sékou Touré, in his role as President of the Council of Ministers, extended and amplified the theme.

It must be recognized that there is a new element now in African life, particularly in the life of the peasant in the bush. The former feudal organization has lived on in the person of the chief; he was the spiritual director as well as political head of his people. This old organization has given way to a new reality—the peasants are now grouped by political party . . . men's actions will henceforth be determined by the political realities as expressed by their parties. Hence the chief . . . will cease to be the director of the political conscience of our peasants.[41]

The election of *conseils de circonscription,* introduced by Sékou Touré as part of the administrative reforms under the *loi cadre,* and the election of village chiefs were proclaimed by the PDG ministers as first steps toward popular political participation in local affairs designed to replace dependence on tribal authority. The PDG government proceeded in 1957 to publish decrees which suppressed the urban *chefs de quartier* and progressively also suppressed the chiefs of the 247 cantons as the new elected councils came into existence. By the end of the year the party felt itself secure enough to suppress all non-elective chiefs by a decree effective January 1, 1958.

The major arguments advanced by the party as the public justification for this action were that the chiefs were a block to progress and that, as an institution, chieftaincy could not be modernized to cope with the rapid pace of economic development. Those chiefs who were already civil servants were continued as functionaries; the younger chiefs could be retrained, but the older ones would simply have to retire on pension. In the official party view the chiefs were exploiters and abusers of their people, since they had acted as tax collectors for the colonial government and had used the colonial authority behind them to enforce their wishes on the unwilling villagers. The party

---

[40] *Guinée: Prélude à l'Indépendance,* p. 21.　　　　[41] *Ibid.*

(and in fact much of the population) regarded the chiefs as tools of the administration; it was admitted after independence that this was one of the major reasons for suppressing them. Writing in the party paper early in 1959, Ismael Touré stated flatly:

If the Guinean people realized political unity after independence, it was because the so-called traditional chiefs had been eliminated. Chieftaincy constituted an instrument of division and exploitation at the service of the colonialists. By upsetting the chief and suppressing the cantons which had artificially divided the country into a multitude of opposing groups, the PDG dealt a mortal blow to the colonial system whose only access to the rural areas was through docile and subservient chiefs.[42]

The party's arguments for dispensing with the chiefs were generally accepted at face value. No popular outcry was raised against the decrees on chieftaincy since the cantonal chiefs were creations of the administration and in the eyes of the people had never been legitimate traditional authorities. Even those chiefs who enjoyed some measure of traditional power (such, for example, as those of the Fouta Djallon) had so seriously compromised their legitimacy in the eyes of the nationalists by cooperating with the administration that their passing went largely unregretted. In part, of course, the fact that the chiefs had been forced into a position of dependence on the administration for the maintenance of their positions was no fault of their own; they were faced with the alternative of cooperating or being deposed. Even the legitimate traditional authorities could not avoid being tarred with the brush of the *chefs de paille*, and they lost the respect of their people.

There were, it should be added, justified grievances on the part of the people at the activities of some chiefs. The taxation system left collection largely in the chief's hands and part of the chief's salary was paid by the *prime de rendement*, an incentive device to promote early tax returns, based upon a diminishing scale of bonus during the first six months of the year. In some areas the chiefs extracted the tax money by applying heavy pressure at a time before the harvests when the people were least able to pay. Public resentment was aroused also by those chiefs who demanded more than the required tax from illiterate peasants and pocketed the difference.

Although the elimination of traditional authority by the PDG was

[42] *La Liberté*, no. 146 (Jan. 13, 1959), p. 2.

by no means unpopular as an administrative reform, it was designed also to assist the party in building mass strength, particularly in the rural areas. The party argued that the existence of chiefs was incompatible with the theory of a mass party since the chiefs represented a privileged class. It was not surprising, therefore, that many chiefs, in the face of this doctrine, had in the past supported the opposition parties, particularly in the Fouta Djallon. Because the appeal of the PDG was based on a program of liberation and economic progress, the opposition was forced into a position of seeming to support traditional power and therefore the conservative and reactionary elements within Guinean society. The PDG was aware, of course, that a major source of opposition stemmed from those areas where traditional power was strongest and that in consequence any move to break down that power, provided it received popular approval, would be an added element of strength. The elected village councils and the circumscription councils were built-in units of the party's cellular structure. Being composed of members of the party, they could be counted on to support the party program against any recalcitrant remnants of traditional authority.

ROLE OF THE TRADE UNIONS

In building its mass strength in the decade before 1958 the RDA counted heavily on the trade union movement in former French West Africa as an organizational base. In the early years when political parties were either ethnic groups or the personal following of an individual and when mass political recruitment was proscribed by the French administration, the trade unions were the most easily available, and often the only, alternative means of securing organized political support. The trade unions at this period were closely tied to metropolitan French labor groups which in turn were affiliated to French political parties, each of which represented a particular ideological outlook. Sékou Touré has expressed the view that the Communist-oriented trade unionism of the CGT, built upon the class struggle, was unsuited to Africa in the long term. Socialist trade unionism, a form of humanistic materialism, in Touré's terms, was opposed to the revolutionary commitment of the Communists but sought to correct social inequalities through evolution. Christian trade unionism, as represented in the Confédération Française des Travailleurs Chrétiens, tried to accomplish the same ends by divine reason, requiring of the individual an extremely high level of morality. Since each of these types of trade unionism represented a major European political tendency (Communist, Social Democratic, or Christian Democratic) it was inevitable that trade unions should become involved in European politics.

African trade unionism, being an offshoot of the European parent movements, could not escape similar involvement. The early period of trade union organization in Africa was one of struggle between these opposing factions. But it became clear to the African labor leaders by 1956 that this internal struggle was weakening the African unions and helping to maintain the colonial regime. The African labor movement was becoming in effect an extension of an essentially European class struggle. Instead of improving the conditions of the African workers, their trade unions were continually forced to formulate their demands "in the light of the opportunities presented by the metropolitan political struggle." The trade unions in Africa were unable to press their own claims because they lacked local political power.[43] Moreover, the insistence of the European trade union movements that the African unions be integrated completely with the parent bodies was increasingly galling to the African nationalists, who felt that they should be permitted to represent separate African interests at international trade union gatherings, particularly those of the World Federation of Trade Unions.

Sékou Touré's objections to continued association of the African trade union movement with the French CGT (which had always commanded the loyalties of the vast majority of African union members) were, then, both ideological and political since the CGT had made clear its view that African liberation was dependent on a Communist Party victory in France. In January, 1956, Touré was one of the leaders in the breakoff of large sections of the CGT group to form the Confédération Générale du Travail Africain.

The final break with the metropolitan labor movements was made at the Cotonou conference of January, 1957, out of which emerged the Union Générale des Travailleurs d'Afrique Noire (UGTAN). Because of his previous trade union experience (secretary of the Postal Employees' Union and of the Treasury Employees' Union, secretary-general of the territorial section of the CGT, and secretary-general of the Coordinating Committee of CGT Unions of French West Africa), Sékou Touré was elected as one of the secretaries of UGTAN.

The new organization was intended to become not only the vehicle

[43] *Expérience*, p. 384.

for expression of the claims of the workers in French-speaking Africa but also the spearhead of the anticolonial struggle. Of it Touré wrote:

In fact, UGTAN, a specifically African trade union movement, wants to remain specifically African. It refuses any alienation of its freedom of action, any organic limitation which might harm . . . its independence. By elaborating a doctrine specifically adapted to the social and economic conditions of our territories, UGTAN is the authentic expression of African values in general and in particular of the workers . . . UGTAN rejects the class struggle for the anticolonial struggle.[44]

Thus the new labor movement was conceived from the first to have a definite political role in the liberation of Africa. It "declared itself, firmly and unequivocally, for a trade unionism that is revolutionary and is authentically African." The necessity to organize the workers brought the movement automatically into the political realm since in the colonial situation the economy was controlled by non-Africans. Although he affirmed that "the fact of trade unions is firstly, whether one likes it or not, a political fact," [45] the trade union movement was not, in Sékou Touré's view, to be a political party. Rather it threw its strength as an organization on the side of those progressive parties which were in the vanguard of the fight against colonialism. The trade unions must conceive of themselves as an instrument in the African revolution—"trade unionism for its own sake does not exist"—and in consequence are in the midst of the nationalist struggle.

Once independence had been acquired, however, the role of the trade unions was expected to undergo considerable change. They were not to oppose the political thinking of the party in which the people had placed their confidence. Thus Sékou Touré condemns those trade unionists who oppose the political institutions that carry out the will of the party. The PDG has not gone as far as the CPP in Ghana, however, in forcing the trade unions to become an integral part of the party. The PDG recognizes the right of the unions to remain separate entities and to define their own means of action provided they remain within the framework of its larger objectives. At the same time, however, the labor movement has been warned that the party will not tolerate opponents of the regime sheltering behind the façade of trade unionism.

Since independence the unions have, on the whole, cooperated closely with the party; the former secretary of the labor movement is now

[44] *Ibid.*, p. 390.   [45] *Ibid.*, p. 391.

Minister of Labor. Collective bargaining in those industries and services operated by the government does not exist in any real sense. In the private sector the unions are still permitted to call strikes against employers, but the party exercises the right to intervene should it appear that the workers' demands may be injurious to over-all economic development plans. At least some unions have not always agreed with the party line. In November, 1961, it was reported that deaths and injuries resulted from riots in Labé, in the Fouta Djallon, when local leaders of the Teachers' Union were arrested after they had demanded higher salaries. Thus in the long run it seems clear that the labor movement can maintain some semblance of independent existence only so long as it proves to be in the interests of the party for this to continue. In seeking to extend its control over Guinean society the PDG could not permit the exclusion of such a strongly organized segment of society, regardless of how important the support of labor may have been during the tense period of the referendum and the preceding years of struggle against the French administration.

RELATION OF THE PARTY TO OTHER GROUPS

One further aspect of the mobilization of Guinean society deserves brief mention. The veterans of service in the French army posed for the party a particular problem of integration. Numbering about 150,000 (of whom 500 were employed in the civil service), these veterans were dependent upon the French administration for their pensions and therefore could be assumed to be, along with the salaried chiefs, among the most reluctant to see the French depart. For them, the party had little patience. In his report to the party congress in 1959 Sékou Touré declared emphatically:

Before independence, did the veterans go to the Governor and ask for work? No, they took good care not to. . . . Today some say, "If you don't give us work we'll do this or that." Whom do they think they are talking to? They are talking to the Guinean people, the very ones who brought independence to their country. Do they imagine that the people will listen or will let them do what they want? [46]

The veterans represented a special danger to party solidarity since they had received some education and had a pro-French bias. The party faithful were urged to concentrate on their reconversion at the village level. Like the intellectuals, they had to be cured for the virus

[46] *Congrès*, pp. 126–128.

implanted by colonialism; for this, complete immersion in the activities of the party was the only remedy.

The case of the veterans' group illustrates the fact that the process of mobilizing Guinean society could not be accomplished without some internal stress. In the course of a most illuminating address delivered at the end of the national conference of the party in November, 1958, Sékou Touré discussed some other problems mentioned in the reports of the party sections which arose from the reconversion of Guinean society. In particular the secretary-general addressed himself to the complaint that members of some section Comités Directeurs were attempting to use their positions for personal gain by promising to use their influence with individual members of the Bureau Politique. In principle, he pointed out, the Bureau Politique never received delegations from individual sections, except in cases of serious local political difficulties. Moreover, the members of the legislature were forbidden to approach a minister of the government with a local problem unless it had been previously discussed at the section level. The desire to use political influence for individual ends was, he commented, not only a sign of political immaturity but directly contrary to the spirit of the Guinean revolution. To have been a party militant during the independence struggle was in itself meritorious, but it did not give license for continued preferential treatment after independence. Since all parties were now united in the PDG, factional rivalry was harmful.

Basically, the problem lies in the state of mind of some comrades who think that each of our successes should be the signal for a reward to former militants. They believe that the services of veteran party members should be preferred to the utilization of the special skills of former political adversaries. This is an extremely dangerous tendency which must stop. We have always said that what counts at a given moment is not number of years of party membership but ability to perform a particular task.[47]

In making this bow to political unity, Sékou Touré undoubtedly had in mind the fact that former opposition party leaders of the Fouta Djallon had been made ministers, much to the objection of certain section leaders. The overriding necessity for this action stemmed from the opposition shown to the PDG in this area in general and in Labé in particular. In commenting on the "political instability of the Fulani," Sékou Touré emphasized, however, that he blamed not the people of the plateau but the PDG section leaders who had failed to find the

[47] *Expérience,* p. 356.

most efficient methods of educating the masses. It would appear that
the correct methods had not yet been found almost three years later
and that Labé was still, as the President put it, "the gangrene of the
party."

The PDG heads were accused by some delegates at the 1958 national
conference of being "too far ahead of the masses in the use of democracy," and the suggestion was made that the village chief and the village councils should be appointed by the party, not elected by the
people. To this idea, the party leaders reacted strongly, pointing out
that this would be contrary to the fundamental concept of the party as
an emanation and tool of the people. It was, in Sékou Touré's view, impossible to be in advance of the people. "This would be a political error
on our part. We would be making the party a creature of one man or
of the government. . . . If a man is in advance of the people, it is up
to him to bring himself to their level. The people don't have to rise to
his level."

In almost every one of his major policy speeches Sékou Touré returns to this theme of the ultimate connection between the mass and
the leadership: "Nothing can be initiated at the summit that does not
come from the base." Only in this way can the real needs of the masses
be known and the quality of party action be raised. The problems of
organization and accomplishment which beset the party initially derived from the failure of the leadership to explain its action properly.
If this explanation was made correctly, the vast reforms which the PDG
envisaged would, the President claimed, be supported by the mass at
all points.

Guinean Institutions and the Parti Démocratique de Guinée

GOVERNMENT AND THE PARTY

The political theory of the PDG assigns a subordinate role in government to the cabinet, the legislature, and the administration. Since
the party assumes the direction and control in the nation, it follows
that all other organs of government, without exception, must be subordinate to it. Western concepts of the separation of the legislative,
executive, and judicial functions of government do not exist. The tasks
of the cabinet and the legislature are defined clearly; they are to "apply
the decisions and *mots d'ordre* of the party, decisions regularly arrived
at by the party congress, by the national conference, and by the Politi-

cal Bureau. This is clear and unequivocal. Only questions of detail and the making of rules for the application of these decisions are left to the legislature and the executive." [48] The legislature, then, is the ratifying arm of the party and the cabinet and administration its executive arms.

The function of the legislature as a ratifying body for the decisions of the Political Bureau has tended more and more since independence to take on symbolic and ceremonial aspects. Debates in the legislature are purely perfunctory since the question has already been decided, and frequently speeches consist only of eulogies of the wisdom of the party's leaders or public displays of national unity. Even such questions as the national budget are summarily treated; the budgetary session, lasting little more than half an hour, consists of a reading of the budget and a unanimous vote. Since many of the deputies are in any case civil servants, it is hardly to be expected that there would be any real disagreement.

The constitution of the Republic lays down that members of the Assembly shall have the right of initiative of expenditure and the right to debate legislation, whether introduced by the government or by private members. The deputies are protected from arrest, and freedom of debate is guaranteed. According to the actual wording of the constitution, there appears to be little difference between the place of the Assembly in Guinea and that in a Western European state, but the position of the party virtually negates any constitutional provisions regarding the powers of the legislature. Only in one respect are the constitutional clauses unusual. Members of the legislature are elected for a five-year period on the basis of a single national list. (No new election has been held since independence; the term of the present legislature, as the first legislature of independent Guinea, will not expire until November 2, 1963.) Representation of the voters of a constituency is thereby obviated, and the deputies are considered the spokesmen for the interests of all citizens. The party considers that this provision of the constitution symbolizes the unitary nature of the Guinean state. It means also that sectional or ethnic interests can count on no special representation and that, since there is a unified list, no deputy can be elected without the approval of the party.

It has already been pointed out that 9 members of the cabinet are simultaneously members of the Bureau Politique. The remaining 10 cabinet members include two former opposition leaders, Diawadou

[48] *La Guinée et l'Emancipation Africaine* (Paris: Présence Africaine, 1959), p. 92.

Barry and Ibrahima Barry (Barry III). In some cases appointments to the cabinet appear to be made for political reasons, in others because the appointee has the technical knowledge required for a specific department. Since the ministers have no power to make policy decisions except at the technical level, the cabinet serves both the function of providing technical advice to the Political Bureau and that of giving a place of prominence and distinction outside the party councils to potential sources of opposition.

The cabinet is not responsible to the legislature, nor, indeed, may its members be deputies. Appointments to the cabinet are made by the President on his sole responsibility, and the ministers may occupy their posts only so long as the President remains satisfied that they are following the party line closely. He may dismiss any minister without consulting the legislature if the minister has lost the confidence of the party, but the election of a new legislature need not necessarily have any effect on the membership of the cabinet.

Sékou Touré has been at pains to point out that the Guinean presidential regime differs from that of the United States in that the Guinean President is responsible for his policy before the legislature. Ministerial responsibility is to the President only. But so long as the President and the secretary-general of the party remain one and the same person and the philosophy of party preeminence is maintained, the question of responsibility is largely academic. The source of political power is expressly kept outside the provisions of the constitution, and the subordination of all organs of government to the party organization render virtually meaningless the constitutional relationships of these organs to one another.

THE PARTY AND LOCAL ADMINISTRATION

The framework of local government in Guinea is based largely on that established by the French colonial administration in all the territories of the former French West African federation. This structure has been altered only in detail since independence, but important changes had already been made by the PDG during the period of the *loi cadre* when the party was in control of the internal administration of the colony. The series of decrees passed in 1957 and 1958 reorganized rural and urban local councils and suppressed both the *chefs de canton* and the native court system (*tribunaux coutumiers*).

At the base of the local government structure is the village. Each village has an elected chief or mayor and a council of from 5 to 15 members, elected by the villagers on a basis of universal suffrage for five years. The man who receives the most votes becomes the village chief; he may therefore only coincidentally be the traditional village head. The chief's powers include local law and order, public health, minor judicial functions, and the collection of taxes. He is required to accept the advice of his council. The party leaders have repeatedly proclaimed that the village is the heart of local party and administrative organization, and much importance is attached to the efficient working of the chief's functions.

At the next highest level the country is divided into 25 *régions*, each headed by a *commandant de région*, appointed by the President on nomination of the Minister of the Interior. Below the *régions* are the *postes administratifs*, headed by an official named in the same way. Each *région* is provided with a *conseil général* of between 14 and 40 members, depending on the population of the district. The councils' powers are limited to the consideration of local public works and the setting of the rates of the regional tax, the proceeds of which from the council's income for local building. Final approval for any large financial transaction (such as contracting a loan) by the council must come from the Minister of the Interior.

The municipalities are provided with an elected council and mayor having roughly the same functions as the general council. For the country as a whole, it is estimated that there are 40,000 village councilors, 280 municipal councilors, and 526 general councilors.

The existence of this local government framework, which in its present form is the work of the PDG itself, has provided one of the more serious problems of "contradiction" which the party has had to resolve since independence. It will have been evident from the description of the party organization in the preceding pages that a complete line of political authority exists within the party structure from the Political Bureau down to the village. A similar line of authority exists on the administrative side stemming from the Minister of the Interior down to the *commandants de région*, the general councils, and the village chiefs and councils. It was inevitable that clashes would occur between these parallel lines of authority within the society. Where did the authority of the secretary-general of the Comité Directeur of the party section end and that of the *commandant de région* begin? Did, for example, the authority of the president of the general council outweigh that of local party officials? Since decisions at the local level which would, under other circumstances, lie purely in the administrative realm were, under the philosophy of the party, within the political realm, it became increasingly difficult to separate the sphere of control of the party and of the administration. The party leadership had reiterated endlessly that the party controlled every aspect of Guinean life; clearly the intrusion of purely administrative authority presented a dilemma which would require both skill and tact to resolve.

The suggestion was made by some party sections immediately after independence that the question of dual authority could be resolved by eliminating the village and general councils. To this the party leadership reacted negatively; the general councils were, in the view of Sékou Touré, an integral part of the system of political education for responsible government at the local level. Although agreeing with the section delegates' objection to the activities of certain members of individual councils, he pointed out:

If we see only the negative aspect of the councils, to justify their suppression we could, for the same reasons, suppress the National Assembly, certain of whose members dishonor the party by their actions. Then we could suppress the government itself, if we found fault with it. We can't engage in this line of conduct.[49]

The President saw the dividing line between the authority of the administrators and the local party officials as that separating technical authority from the political realm of policy making:

The comrade who is *chef de circonscription* [now *commandant de région*], or head of a health group, whose post depends on his technical knowledge, must not disobey a clerk or peasant who is a party official simply because the latter plays a subordinate role in the administrative hierarchy. . . . Similarly, the comrade in the political cadre ought to be proud to obey the orders given by the *chef de circonscription* in the technical sphere because it is he who has helped to create the authority of the administrator. If he disobeys, he has insulted not the *chef de circonscription* but the party he represents.[50]

Despite the attempts of the secretary-general to resolve the problem by logical argument, the stubborn fact remained that, for the first two years after independence, conflicts arose between local party heads and administrators which were serious enough to require the attention of the Political Bureau. If the two protagonists remained irreconcilable,

[49] *Expérience*, p. 353.   [50] *Ibid.*, pp. 351–352.

the administrator was removed to another post in the majority of cases. However, the party has more recently come to the conclusion that the long-range solution is to attempt so far as possible to remove the dual aspects of authority by making the *commandant* an ex officio member of the party's regional coordinating committee and the heads of the administrative posts ex officio members of the section Comités Directeurs. However, members of the administration may not stand for election to local organs of the party.

The presence of a highly disciplined party organization at the local level has had its positive as well as negative sides. Party pressure can be applied to accomplish administrative ends. During the colonial regime much of the French administrator's time was taken up with problems of tax collection. Now, recalcitrant taxpayers can be brought into line much more rapidly through village and section committees of the party. Similarly, cooperation between the administration and the party has assisted the development of public works projects through party-organized *investissement humain*. Where social pressure can be effectively applied to ensure observance of local government rules, the party has taken over much of what at an earlier period were the regulatory and supervisory functions of the administration.

THE PARTY AND EDUCATION

With its emphasis on total mobilization of society for improvement of living standards, the party has been forced to pay particular attention to the educational system. Under the colonial regime Guinea was not one of the better endowed in educational institutions of the territories of AOF. No attempt was made to provide higher education, and even teacher training was in its early stages at the time of independence. Only 1,500 pupils qualified in 1958 to receive the Elementary School Certificate. Moreover, education was based directly on that in France, the great majority of secondary school teachers was French, and all instruction from the earliest age was given in French. No effort was made to teach African history or African languages since they were not included in the French curriculum.

The party promptly set out to reform the entire educational structure. Apart from a vast increase in the numbers attending school, the major aim was to Africanize the content of education so that there would not "still be children who can write the fables of La Fontaine but know nothing of Africa," as the President put it. It would still be necessary to teach in French, but "French must be used to teach the children African materials first of all." [51] To place Guinea in its African context, the classical humanist tradition of French education was dropped in favor of a broader, non-European historical and cultural approach. To increase communication within Africa, English has been made a compulsory subject of instruction.

One of the primary requirements for the new curriculum has been textbooks. New books were commissioned in geology, zoology, and botany, and a new history of West Africa, written in collaboration by a Guinean historian and a Frenchman, was issued for use in the schools. Specially written books for instruction in English are under consideration.

The shortage of secondary school teachers became acute with the departure of 100 French teachers at independence, but this has been overcome by the recruitment of a similar number of replacements from France under a new Franco-Guinean cultural agreement. Moreover, at the end of 1961 there were 300 teachers of other nationalities in Guinea, over one-third of whom were Yugoslav, Czech, or Egyptian.

The effect of this educational reform on the numbers of children at school has been striking. In 1959 there were 4,000 pupils who had graduated from the elementary schools, and in 1960 a total of 84,000 children were enrolled in these schools. In 1961–1962 more than 6,000 secondary school pupils were attending Guinea's four *lycées* and three teacher-training colleges. A technical institute is being built with Russian help in Conakry. Moreover, the three-year plan now in operation envisages doubling the number of intermediate teacher-training colleges, of which there are now ten offering a four-year (rather than the French seven-year) course.

The party has taken the view that education should be free at all levels, and the state supports most of those at secondary school. The private schools (chiefly in the hands of Catholic and a few Protestant missions) were given notice in 1959 that they could continue to operate for a further three years with state assistance but that at the end of that time the state would take them over under a national universal education scheme. In mid-1961, after the religious crisis that involved the expulsion of the French bishop of the archdiocese of Guinea at Conakry, the state ordered the mission schools discontinued.

An important aspect of the new curriculum is the instruction of youth in party history and doctrine. Sékou Touré has condemned those

[51] *Action,* p. 415.

teachers who disagree with "teaching politics" in the schools. "For them [the teachers] the young must know nothing about politics. As if the facts of politics were not the condensation of economic, social, and cultural facts!" [52] The party sees education not as an end in itself but as a tool for the forging of a new national purpose and for the attainment of those ends which the party and the mass have agreed upon. Education of the mass, therefore, is just as important as is the formation of the new elite with the technical training that is necessary for industrialization and modernization of the economy. The educational revolution in Guinea must be seen as part of that country's larger transformation of society, but in an even wider context it may well illustrate the direction to be taken in education by many other African states.

ADMINISTRATION OF JUSTICE

The PDG was forced to turn its attention to the field of judicial reform immediately after independence. The judicial system in Guinea, as elsewhere in French-speaking Africa, was built upon the model of the *Métropole,* and most members of the Corps of Magistrates were expatriates during the colonial regime. With the other French civil servants, the magistrates left Guinea after September, 1958, and the entire court system threatened to collapse.

Since the law administered by the courts was regarded by the mass of Guineans as French law imposed by the colonial administration, the natural reaction was to suppose that the absence of magistrates meant also the elimination of the restrictions imposed by the legal code. There were rumors current at independence that all courts had ceased to exist and that the individual was no longer bound by any man-made law. This popular impression was further reinforced by the action of the legislature which at its first postindependence meeting voted an amnesty law that freed many of the prisoners held under the laws of the colonial courts. Many who had suffered under the laws imposed by the French connected the court system with the administration and drew the conclusion that without the French magistrate the court and the law no longer existed.

The new government promptly took steps to disabuse the people of this notion. Magistrates were appointed as soon as men with even the most shadowy qualifications could be found. The entire weight of authority in the party leadership was directed toward reinforcing the

[52] *Ibid.,* p. 413.

idea that even if the former magistrates were not there, the courts continued to function as before. The Political Bureau decided that, although certain aspects of the French code had to be adapted immediately to "Guinean realities," the basic principles of French law were to continue as the foundation of Guinean law and, in particular, that the penal code was to remain virtually intact. Changes were instituted, however, to accelerate and simplify the judicial procedure, and party leaders at the section and village levels were instructed to educate the people in the proper use of the courts, in order to avoid useless cluttering of already crowded court calendars. In addition, village councils were encouraged to act as conciliation agencies in minor disputes, and only when they failed to settle the question could it be taken to the courts.

The party was also concerned with changing the popular image of the judge and the law. Party officials were charged by the leadership to use every available method to impress on the mass that the law administered by the courts after independence was now Guinean, not foreign, law. Although it might look like (and was) the same law as before, they emphasized that it now had become the freely accepted law of the Guinean people and, as such, it was the duty of every responsible Guinean to respect the law. Sékou Touré stressed that the magistrates and other court officials must take on the heavy task of remodeling the popular attitude toward the law: "The magistrates have the vitally important duty to our people, who hitherto have regarded 'justice' as a monster ready to pounce on them . . . of transforming and converting the spirit as well as the content of justice. This is the objective of the party in the judicial field." [53]

French law has not, of course, remained intact since Guinean independence. In the process of adapting it to the new Guinea, the party has introduced penalties which are frequently much more severe than those of French colonial law. Theft is now punishable by death, and the sentence has been carried out more than once. The party regards the stealing of another's property as the most heinous of crimes because by theft the individual may be robbed of his livelihood and so may lose his life. Similarly, to kill a person while driving an automobile is also punishable by death since the law regards such an act, however unintentional, as equivalent to murder. The processes of justice have become swifter, but the safeguards of legal procedure have not always been maintained. Minor traffic violators are fined on the spot, and

[53] *Ibid.*, p. 422.

failure to pay results in temporary loss of the vehicle. Major crimes (particularly those against the state) may be judged outside the judicial framework by people's courts, reminiscent of those of the French Revolution.

The political theory of the PDG, as already pointed out, does not accept the separations of judicial and legislative or executive functions. Justice, as with all other aspects of government, is considered the direct emanation of the popular will as expressed through the party. The judiciary is not regarded as independent; on the contrary, party officials are encouraged publicly to denounce judges who fail to follow the party line. In reproving an officer of the party (who was also a magistrate) for stating that judicial decisions must be separated from administrative decisions and that party militants should not interfere in judicial activity, Sékou Touré stated flatly: "The party is interested in every facet of political life without exception. . . . If the attitude of a *procureur* [state attorney] creates a political problem, then it is the duty of the local administrator and party officials to intervene." [54] Judges, simply because they are charged with administering the law, are not above party discipline. They are appointed by the party and therefore, by implication, by the people. When they cease to submit to the popular will, they no longer fulfill the delicate mission with which they are charged, namely, "to substitute themselves for the people, and in the name of the people, to judge and to appreciate." [55] The judiciary, in the eyes of the party, is the guardian of the national conscience, and its acts are judged by the people not in the light of the provisions of the penal code but of the national conceptions of moral and spiritual rectitude. Repeatedly, in talking of the role of the magistrates, Sékou Touré has returned to the theme of the African appreciation of justice which, he argues, has been made all the keener by centuries of exploitation, humiliation, and denial of elementary human freedoms. The conception of the place of the law in Guinea today is far from Western ideas of the rule of law; it can be understood only in the context of the African revolt against the legal norms imposed by alien rule.

PARTY CONTROL OVER THE MEDIA OF COMMUNICATION

The all-embracing grip of the party on Guinean life has resulted in bringing virtually every medium of communication under its direct supervision. Prior to independence, little attempt to develop a Guinean press had been made by the colonial administration. For the resident

[54] *Expérience,* p. 365.   [55] *Action,* p. 422.

French civil servants and the educated Africans, French newspapers sufficed; the illiterate mass had no interest in the press. Although the PDG made early efforts to arouse mass support through a party newspaper, which began publication in 1950, its circulation was restricted by administrative opposition and lack of funds. The paper, *La Liberté*, was exclusively a party organ and made no pretense at dissemination of news.

For some months after independence French newspapers continued to arrive in Conakry, and other foreign publications were easily obtainable. But the only local daily news service was provided by a mimeographed sheet distributed by the representative of Agence France Presse. With the introduction of the Guinean franc, exchange was no longer available for French publications, and the party was forced to provide a substitute which could be locally produced. The party newspaper was dropped, and in its place the official Agence Guinéenne de Presse began to publish in April, 1961, a triweekly paper, *Horoya* ("Dignity"), designed to reflect "the broad lines of Guinean policy." It was anticipated that as new technical facilities became available (through the printing plant being built by the German Democratic Republic as part of a technical assistance plan), *Horoya* would become an illustrated daily. In its early issues, the paper continued to carry some news of local party activities, but the remainder of the space was devoted to coverage of African events and to brief stories of important world news. Extensive articles were devoted to analysis, within the party line, of anticolonial uprisings anywhere in the world. *Horoya* is exclusively an official mouthpiece, and, since the party controls the major printing plant in Conakry, it is doubtful that any competing or privately financed newspaper can be started.

The bookstores of Conakry and other large towns have available a wide selection of literature in French from Eastern bloc sources at prices well below cost. Literature from Europe or the United States is costlier and often almost unobtainable.

Radio Guinée is the official broadcasting outlet. It is on the air several hours a day, in French and the major vernacular languages. In addition, there are frequent programs designed to encourage the independence movement in neighboring Portuguese Guinea.

The spoken and written communications networks in Guinea are as yet in their infancy, but the party is clearly aware of the need for wider outlets, not only to ensure national knowledge of the party's policies but to create in Guineans an awareness of African events and of Guinea's role on the broader stage of African politics.

THE PARTY AND ECONOMIC DEVELOPMENT

A major part of the total reconversion of Guinean society envisaged by the PDG is the change from an economic structure oriented toward the colonial relationship to one in which the means of production and exchange will rest, so far as possible, in Guinean hands. The party leadership recognized from the outset that its political success was in large measure dependent on its ability to produce for the mass of Guineans concrete results of independence in the form of higher living standards. Given the Marxist orientation of the political philosophy of the party and its acceptance of the Leninist explanation of imperialism, it is understandable that a primary objective was to eliminate what it believed to be the exploitation of African resources purely for the benefit of monopolies in the hands of the colonialists. The nature of the economic structure of Guinea at independence made it easy to arrive at such a conclusion. The bulk of commercial and financial operations of the country was in the hands of French firms and banks, as was the distribution system except at the lowest level of the African retailer. Practically no capital was in African hands, and the credit structure of the colonial regime made it difficult, if not impossible, to organize an African enterprise of any magnitude, even if the technical and managerial skills had been available in the African community.

The party leaders were faced in 1958 with a dilemma since shared by the governments of all the other West African states. On one hand, the party desired ardently to see control over the major sectors of the economy in Guinean hands; on the other, the sources of capital which would make this possible could come only from outside. Industrialization was, as elsewhere in the underdeveloped areas of the world, a prime target, not only to reduce Guinean dependence on manufactured imports but also to provide employment and new skills at home. The absence of African entrepreneurs made it necessary for the government to initiate schemes for industrialization, but at the same time place had to be left for much-needed private capital, even if this meant that some industries would, at least temporarily, be in foreign control.

The political theory of the PDG posited the existence of a socialist state in which the major means of production would be in the hands of the people, but the demands of postindependence economic development made the full realization of socialism impossible at this early stage. In consequence the attitude of the Guinean party toward private enterprise has tended to be an uneasy compromise between theory and the realities of the postindependence economic situation. In explanation of the party's attitude, Sékou Touré has emphasized that the approach has been an empirical search for the system which best suited Guinea's economic needs of the moment and that the party theory, although socialist, did not preclude a mixed economy. "We have never excluded cooperation with capital; we have rejected capitalism as a form of social organization only because it does not correspond to our stage of development." [56] Speaking before the Economic Commission for Africa in Addis Ababa, Ismael Touré, the President's half brother, indicated something of the party's realistic approach to the role of private capital: "We know that there is no economic philanthropy. Africa, having no capital for development, cannot expect that development capital will come without a profit motive. We have always emphasized the prime importance of the profit factor. Profit is always possible in Africa today because there is a growing market." [57]

Realizing that certain parts of the economy would have to remain for some time in private hands, the party made an effort initially to control foreign capital by requiring banks and companies doing business in Guinea to establish Guinean corporate headquarters and to invest part of their profits in the country. With the appearance of the inconvertible Guinean franc the transfer of profits and assets was automatically subject to the permission of the government to grant foreign exchange. Apparently these controls did not prove sufficient to satisfy the party leaders because in 1960 and 1961 the assets of foreign banks, insurance companies, and the major public utilities doing business in Guinea were nationalized, as was one major industrial concern, Bauxites du Midi (jointly owned by the French aluminum firm of Peychinet and the Aluminum Company of Canada), which was blamed by the government for failing to carry out an agreed program of expansion. Private firms and banks were also accused of attempting to defeat the government's policy of stabilizing and lowering the prices of consumer goods by arbitrarily raising prices to cover the costs of bank interest on business loans and of transferring their assets

[56] *La Planification Economique* (Conakry, 1960), p. 95. Hereafter referred to as *Planification*.
[57] *Action*, p. 213.

from the country in bank-note form so rapidly that the money in circulation in Guinea dropped by one-half in one year.

As a first step in preventing excessive profits by the French firms which controlled wholesale distribution of consumer products the government took control of all import and export operations through a new organ, the Comptoir Guinéen de Commerce Extérieur, established in February, 1959. The importing of basic consumer needs such as rice, matches, flour, sugar, and cement became the sole prerogative of the Comptoir, and it was empowered to regulate the importing of other goods by licenses issued to private firms. The objective of the Comptoir in its control of consumer necessities was to permit the distribution of these commodities at the same fixed price throughout the country, so that Guineans living in the interior would not be penalized by the high cost of transport from the coast. The Comptoir was to buy by contract and sell at a uniform price which would be established at a level high enough to absorb internal transportation costs and a small overhead but leave no margin for profit.

The conception of the role of the Comptoir was laudable in that Guineans living in the more remote villages of the interior had been forced to pay much higher prices than the people of Conakry for imported necessities when in most cases their cash income was lower than that of the urban dwellers. Unfortunately, however, the operations of the Comptoir were not a success. This was largely because Guineans lacked experience in quantity buying and distribution and particularly in the scheduling of deliveries to correspond with the capabilities of the internal road transport system. The Comptoir made a number of serious and costly mistakes, and members of its staff were accused of inefficiency and corruption. The Comptoir was suppressed in mid-1961, and many of its functions were transferred to the newly created Ministry of Commerce. A variety of *sociétés nationales* were created, which were intended to replace the monopoly over certain imported products formerly exercised by the Comptoir. The scope for private initiative in the import-export field has been continually reduced, however, not only by licensing but by the excessive customs formalities required by government departments for each shipment.

A second reason for the existence of the Comptoir was to enable the government to fulfill more easily the trade agreements signed between the Eastern bloc countries and Guinea during the months after independence. The bulk of certain export crops, particularly bananas, was committed at fixed prices under these agreements so that the government was forced into preclusive buying to meet its obligations. The prices set by the Comptoir for bananas had the effect of eliminating most of the European producers, whose overhead costs were higher than those on African-owned plantations; but even the African producers complained, and attempts were made to renegotiate the agreements.

The effect of the trade pacts with East Germany, Czechoslovakia, Poland, Russia, Hungary, and Bulgaria was to change radically the direction of Guinean trade away from the former French markets in which Guinean products were sold at subsidized prices. These agreements were signed at a time when Guinea had little other alternative to complete economic collapse after the disappearance of its French markets, but they have proved to be an economic disadvantage, particularly as the former channels of trade have gradually reopened.

Perhaps the most serious step, in terms of its long-range consequences, taken by the party in the economic field has been the break with the franc zone and the issue of Guinean currency. At independence the government of the new republic indicated a desire to remain within the franc zone but insisted that any monetary agreement with France be based on a full recognition of Guinean sovereignty. French reluctance to make any such agreement with Guinea on terms other than those made with the Community states forced a stalemate. Sékou Touré pointed out that any further prolongation of a financial arrangement which derived from the colonial relationship would be a serious threat to Guinean sovereignty:

We could never subject our political revolution to such conditions. No more could we align ourselves with the African territories of the Community financially or economically. To continue the *status quo* would have led inevitably to reintegration with the French Community by the back door and the renunciation of our political, social, and economic revolution.[58]

At a conference of the members of the Political Bureau and government officials, held at Dalaba in February, 1960, the decision was made to take Guinea out of the franc zone and to proceed with the issue of the Guinean franc, whose value was set arbitrarily at two old French francs or one franc CFA (the current monetary unit in the rest of French-speaking West Africa). Currency had already been printed, and the francs CFA in circulation were exchanged by the banks for the new bills.

[58] *Planification*, p. 79.

The political reasons for issuing Guinean currency are understandable, but the economic rationale is less easy to appreciate. The foundation for the new currency was neither gold nor another foreign currency but what Sékou Touré called the "national possessions" (*biens nationaux*). In his explanation at the Conference on the Three-Year Plan in April, 1960, Touré argued that Africa had possessed units of monetary exchange (cowry shells) before the Europeans came, the value of which had been determined not by comparison with an absolute standard but by agreement based on custom. African society, he claimed, had in practice ignored the mercantile capitalist system and had continued on a basis of barter exchange. The use of money had merely facilitated this internal exchange of products. He went on to assert that the introduction of the new monetary unit as part of the planned development of Guinean society would result (for reasons which appear to have little foundation in economic theory) in a simultaneous reduction of prices and increase in wages.

Sékou Touré's faith in the national goods as the basis for the currency does not seem to be shared either by foreign creditors or by all his fellow countrymen. The National Bank of Guinea controls all foreign exchange, and the Guinean currency is not permitted to leave the country. The temptation to spend Guinean francs outside the country is slight, however, since they are unacceptable even a few hundred yards beyond the border. Within Guinea there have been reports that in the rural areas peasants have refused to accept the new currency, preferring to withdraw their produce from the market, and that cattle herders have driven beasts across the borders to sell them in francs CFA or West African pounds. Guinea's economic resources are not sufficient to provide a foundation for public faith in its currency. With trade decreasing, the meager supply of foreign exchange is not sufficient to import enough consumer goods to avoid serious shortages.

The Three-Year Plan, with which the new currency was to be integrated, was publicly presented at a national conference of the party at Kankan in April, 1960. In his political report preceding the examination of the plan, Sékou Touré elaborated on the reasons for planning and on the philosophy behind the plan. He was at pains to point out that the planning of the Guinean economy in no way involved the acceptance of communism:

When we announced that we were going to make a plan [at the fifth congress of the party in September, 1959], some said they knew what that meant and labeled us communists under the direction of Moscow or Peking.

. . . We are not a communist regime; we say without false pride that we are too busy seeking our own emancipation . . . to adapt ourselves to one political system or another. . . . Planning is not exclusively a part of socialist or communist regimes; it is the scientific basis for determining economic development.[59]

Planning is necessary, he argued, because

in the economic field we are in a state of national mobilization. We are a nondeveloped, not an underdeveloped, country. This difference must be kept in mind in order to appreciate the objectives of national economic mobilization. . . . Some may say this plan hurts free enterprise. Possibly this plan hurts a certain form of free enterprise, but it is certain too that it destroys some types of competition that under our present circumstances are negative elements in our development.[60]

Economic planning was not to be regarded as an end in itself:

Planning is not done for planning's sake but as a function of the requirements of our social evolution which is itself oriented to our political line.[61]

The presentation of the plan began with a detailed examination of the state of the Guinean economy before and after independence. Recognizing that agricultural products represented 75 per cent of Guinea's exports, the report laid great stress on the reorganization of agricultural production. Despite the fact that tonnage had increased since 1958, not only in many exported products (coffee, pineapple, peanuts, palm kernels, and hides) but in basic cereals as well, there was a pressing need for greater production if the agricultural sector of the economy was to keep up with increasing population and demand.

To accomplish the objectives of the plan, new agricultural production cooperatives were to be organized at the village level. For these 500 new cooperatives three stages were envisaged. The first would involve only the strengthening of existing village cooperatives by improved methods of cultivation. A second stage would create collective farms and collective herds, and the third and final stage foresaw the collectivization of all land in the villages. In addition, for each administrative region a model farm or rural modernization center would be established, as well as several national agricultural production centers to serve as pilot projects. Under this scheme rice production would be increased by 1963 by 45,000 tons, bananas by 70,000 tons, coffee by 4,000 tons, and pineapples by 31,000 tons. The report stressed that membership in a village cooperative would be purely voluntary,

[59] *Ibid.*, pp. 295–297.   [60] *Ibid.*, pp. 316–317.   [61] *Ibid.*, p. 309.

but it is difficult to see how the individual could remain outside if all the village lands were collectivized.

In the mining sector of the economy the report emphasized that the value of mineral exports had tripled between 1958 and 1959 (owing largely to the presence of the free diamond market at Kankan) and that it was expected that it would again double in 1960 when exports of alumina began. Hitherto all mineral exploitation had been in private hands, but it was proposed to create national enterprises for exploitation of the diamond fields. One of the great untouched riches of Guinea is the iron of Mount Nimba, estimated at 250,000,000 tons of high-grade ore. The plan proposed systematic exploitation on a private basis under state supervision.

The plan envisaged in the report was designed also to lay the foundations for the rapid industrialization of Guinea. It would clearly be impossible within its three-year period to create a heavy industry complex since technical knowledge, capital, and skilled manpower were lacking. Rather, the plan sought to concentrate on light and medium industries aimed at using local products either for export or for home consumption. Such industries would include an agricultural tool factory, a kitchen-utensil factory, wood furniture and nail plants, and a number of processing plants for fruit juice and palm and peanut oil. To provide a springboard for this industrialization program the plan proposed to devote 800,000,000 francs to the development of hydroelectric potential. Industrial enterprises, it was assumed, would require 5,000,000,000 francs of state funds to which would be added the investments to be made by private enterprises already in the country. These latter investments "would naturally be decided upon within the framework of the Three-Year Plan and according to Guinean legislative provisions on the operation of private companies"—a requirement scarcely to be interpreted as a bait for substantial private investment.

No mention is made in the report of Guinea's largest private enterprise, the consortium of foreign interests (United States 48.5 per cent, France 26.5 per cent, United Kingdom 10 per cent, Switzerland 10 per cent, and West Germany 5 per cent), which is engaged in developing the bauxite ore at Fria. The Fria company, which came into existence in 1956, plans to develop an alumina plant, the initial capacity of which will be 480,000 tons a year, with the possibility of extending the capacity to nearly 1,500,000 tons a year. The first 6,000 tons of alumina was exported in April, 1960. The town surrounding the alumina plant at Kimbo is expected to accommodate permanently between four and five thousand workers, the vast majority of whom will be Guineans. In view of the extreme importance of Fria to the industrialization of the country, it is doubtful whether the government would attempt to interfere with this enterprise since even if it were nationalized, the marketing of the alumina would be dependent on continued good relations with the present developers.

The costs of the Three-Year Plan were expected to total 38,912,-000,000 Guinean francs. Of this sum, 36 per cent was to be devoted to transport and infrastructure development, 47.26 per cent to agricultural and industrial production, and 16 per cent to social services. The plan was to be financed with approximately 10,000,000,000 francs of local savings, the remaining 75 per cent to come from outside loans and grants such as the 140,000,000-ruble loan which had been extended by the Soviet Union at an interest rate of 2.5 per cent. The lack of confidence in the Guinean franc has caused several parts of the plan to be delayed indefinitely, however, since by the time the plan got under way in July, 1960, the franc was beginning to weaken.

Much of the success of the plan depends on the availability of trained personnel, and this in turn depends on the willingness of the party to have foreign assistance. No technical assistance can be effective if its motives are always in question by the recipients. Since independence Guinea has had ample offers of technical aid, and hundreds of experts in every calling and of every political persuasion have come to the country. Not all these experts have confined their activities to the jobs which they were called upon to do, and it is scarcely surprising that Guinean officials have occasionally suffered from a plethora of advice based on motives which in their eyes were questionable. Nevertheless, it is difficult to understand how the objectives of the plan could have been furthered by the closing of the door to United Nations assistance in February, 1961. Sékou Touré's view that economics is a function of politics may be theoretically justifiable, but serious problems are posed for Guinean development when political policy is allowed to interfere with the clear needs of long-range economic programs.

In economics as in politics, Touré is first of all an African. He sees Guinean development in the framework of a larger African unit, and he has said that Guinea's prosperity depends on close relations with its neighbors. Much of his emphasis on planning would meet with the full approval of other African leaders. Guinea's present position on the fringe of an economically more powerful group of states whose political approach to African unification differs so radically from Touré's own makes more difficult, however, the realization of his hope for the construction of "an economy on an African scale that will no longer be an appendix to the European economies but an economy oriented toward a wider African market, which will then be an entity in itself on the world scene, not opposed to other entities but complementary and capable of aiding the development of the whole." [62]

THE PARTI DÉMOCRATIQUE DE GUINÉE AS A
SINGLE-PARTY SYSTEM

The pattern of the one-party system which has developed in Guinea and in the majority of West African states since independence rests upon a foundation laid by the preindependence nationalist parties dedicated to the goal of independence. The successful completion of the struggle for independence made necessary the mobilization of all the energies of the people, and to this end the nationalist movements evolved highly disciplined, cohesive parties whose roots were solidly fixed in the basic cell of African life, the village. At the top of the party hierarchy emerged the charismatic figure who was to become at once the symbol of the new freedom that independence guaranteed and the link with the traditional past.

The need to mobilize popular support left little room for the growth of opposition parties. In the preindependence period the potential opposition leaders could offer no alternative program; in the postindependence period the popular enthusiasm which carried the successful nationalist party to victory ensured its continuation in office. The institutionalization of opposition was not considered by the mass of the African voters a necessary prerequisite to the successful functioning of the political system. In traditional tribal politics there had been ample room for opposition groups, particularly in disputes over the selection of a chief, but these groups arose in response to a particular issue; when that issue was resolved, the opposition dissolved back into the community. Those who sought to maintain opposition to the legitimate authority accepted by the community were regarded as a threat to the solidarity of the tribe. Something of this view remains in West African politics today. A continuing challenge to the authority of the popularly supported leadership is looked upon as an attempt to undermine the unity upon which the future development of the nation depends.

In Guinea, as elsewhere in French-speaking Africa, the organization

[62] *Action,* p. 208.

of mass support by the ruling party has been aided by the knowledge of Marxist techniques possessed by the leaders. Moreover, Marxism provided an ideology which could be differentiated from that of the Western colonialists; in many senses also it was a modern substitute for the traditional African village democracy which was clearly not adaptable to the demands of modern national government. The Guinean system today is essentially a conscious effort to combine Marxist-Leninist forms of political organization with specific elements of the African traditional political and social structures which themselves resemble socialism. It is perhaps in this sense, more than any other, that Sékou Touré's argument is correct that the African system is basically *communautaire.* The result of this combination is a structure of power in which the role of the mass in decision making is constantly stressed and in which the elements of village democracy are never entirely lost. Touré's goal is the creation of a new and relatively sophisticated system in which the African concepts of the political functions in society (concepts never destroyed by the colonial administration) are blended with a Marxist theory to produce an amalgam that will bear the stamp of the African personality and thus can be identified by the outside world as belonging not to the East nor to the West but to Africa alone.

It has been pointed out that the language of African nationalism, although Marxist in origin, has come to have interpretations in Africa which are markedly at variance with those of orthodox Marxism. In addition, the Leninist organizational structure has also undergone substantial modification. The external framework of the Guinean party remains faithful to the Leninist prescriptions, but the *comité de village,* the heart of the party's relationship to the mass, is in essence the traditional village council meeting. Decisions of the *comité de village* are arrived at in African fashion—that is, by common agreement, after lengthy discussion in which all may, and do, participate and at the end of which no dissident minority elements remain. In such meetings the emphasis is on collective decision, not on majority vote. Once a decision has been made, however, all participants bear equally the burden of its consequences since each feels that he had a share in making it.

The African conception of collective responsibility is evident also in the actions of the Political Bureau of the party. Discussion within the bureau may be most influenced by the views of the stronger personalities among its members, but an almost conscious effort is made to depersonalize the ultimate decision so that it becomes one not only of the bureau but of the party as a whole. Sékou Touré considers himself *primus inter pares,* and his fellow members of the bureau share his inclination to dissociate political decisions from a single individual. It may be argued that, in theory at least, the decisions of the Political Bureau in Moscow are also collective, but the personal element, particularly in the early years of Soviet party rule, played a much greater role than it does in Guinea today.

The depersonalization of the decision-making process in Guinea that extends through the lower party hierarchy and to the ministries has certain practical disadvantages, however, in that it tends to blur the lines of authority and needlessly to complicate the operation of government by making it very difficult to lay the blame for errors on specific individuals. The knotty problem of parallel lines of authority within the party and the administration has been alleviated in part by a conscious integration of party and administrative posts. But in even greater degree the two lines of authority are being erased by the complex, circular, interlocking structure of power that is being created by the party. Reminiscent of African traditional political roles, the new roles of party official and administrator now blend with each other so that they are rapidly becoming indistinguishable.

The degree to which the party leadership responds to the expression of opinion at the village level cannot be satisfactorily measured. Consultation with the village or section committees is not directed toward day-to-day decisions of government or to technical questions upon which the members of these bodies could not be expected to have an informed opinion. Rather, village consultation is aimed at broad policy issues upon which an expression of public views may be useful as a guide to detailed decisions which the bureau must take. The *mots d'ordre* sent from the bureau to the lower party levels are frequently statements of accomplished action which are designed to be used by local leaders as a means of informing the party membership. However, they are also used as "trial balloons" to test public reaction to a proposed policy, and there is some evidence to indicate that the Political Bureau has altered or shelved a prospective decision in the face of a ground swell of adverse comment relayed from the villages and sections. On questions of purely local concern it would appear that a substantial amount of autonomy is left to the sections, provided that all decisions are taken in accordance with the broad policy guidelines laid down by the bureau.

The Political Bureau has concentrated in its own hands the entire power of decision making. In addition to the resultant difficulties already mentioned of making the bureau a bottleneck through which only a limited number of decisions can pass, this concentration has meant that the bureau has a constant tendency to become at one and the same time an executive as well as a policy-making body. The fact that these functions are not clearly divorced gives to party theory a practical flavor that tends to prevent the rise of doctrinal splits based on personal animosities. But it also creates difficulties in long-range planning. The bureau spends much time on trivia of an immediate nature which could otherwise be devoted to a leisurely consideration of broad policy matters. Because the party has not yet felt sufficiently secure in its position to have complete confidence in the ministers and the senior civil servants, the bureau has often been unable to devote time and energy to thinking through the consequences of its decisions. As a result there have had to be frequent shifts of policy on internal matters when unforeseen circumstances rendered some decisions impossible of execution. This has led to confusion at the lower party levels and to requests for more frequent meetings with the bureau members to make certain the exact party line on a particular subject. It is here that the absence of any effective use of the legislature as an arena for debate is most keenly felt; periodic party conferences are no substitute for the concentrated discussion possible in a legislative body. It is probable that the present executive role of the party is a temporary one; the situation in Guinea is reminiscent of that in the smaller Soviets of the USSR at an earlier period. On the basis of the Soviet example it may fairly be assumed that, with time and experience, the bureau will withdraw from immediate participation in government. Decisions now made directly by the party executive will be made eventually in the name of the party, then in the name of the party and the Council of Ministers, and ultimately by the Council of Ministers in its own right.

The concentration by the bureau on political and party questions has inevitably meant that less attention could be given to administrative reorganization. Despite the fact that the French administrative structure was both top-heavy and costly the inclination was simply to replace the French occupants of existing posts with Guineans, particularly in the rural areas, under substantially the same civil service regulations although at lower salaries. To the arguments of outside advisers that the new government should seize the opportunity to make radical changes in the lower administrative echelons, the reply of the government was that the people were accustomed to a certain administrative pattern and that changes would only be a source of confusion. It was evident, however, that the party leadership attached much greater importance to political affairs and found them more congenial to deal with than were the minutiae of administration.

At the initial stages the party received widespread popular support for its reorganization of the Guinean economy. The concrete evidence of change from the colonial regime and the skillful use of propaganda and organizational techniques by the party maintained enthusiasm in the immediate postindependence period. For some sections of the population, however, independence has been a mixed blessing. The stringent economic controls imposed by the party planners have created serious shortages of consumer goods formerly imported from Europe. But the impact of these controls has fallen most heavily on the urban dwellers whose higher income levels had made them more accustomed to a variety of European goods. For the bulk of the Guinean peasants the absence of stocks of European products on the shelves of Conakry stores means relatively little so long as the few staple imports they use remain available. The austerity program affected chiefly the intellectuals and civil servants who were most dependent for their livelihood on the government and who were of lesser concern to the party leadership.

The PDG appears to have survived occasional challenges without major impairment of its authority. Partially as a result of rumors current in April, 1960, in the Fouta Djallon that the new economic plan intended to deprive the cattle owners of their property, there was an exodus of nomadic groups across the neighboring Senegalese and Sierra Leone borders, and there were serious disturbances in northeastern Guinea. These disturbances were put down by the arrest of some 500 people and a number of summary executions by people's courts. In discussing the incidents at a subsequent press conference, Sékou Touré laid the blame for the rumors on "counterrevolutionary elements" who had been encouraged by French agents in Senegal and the Ivory Coast and stated that stocks of arms had been found in border villages that indicated collusion with outside sources. Disturbances taking place in the same area in November, 1961, were laid to unnamed East bloc agents and Guineans who felt that the party was not following the Russian model closely enough. These isolated incidents cannot be interpreted, however, as expressions of widespread dissatisfaction with the regime; they have in any case been centered in that part of the country where support for the PDG was not strong even before the referendum.

Guinea today is not a democracy in the Western sense, nor has there ever been any intention on the part of the PDG that it should be. It is an authoritarian regime which uses a system of democratic centralism to achieve the social and economic reorientation that the party feels is required to throw off the bonds of colonialism. Although there is broad agreement on the major goals of the country, there is not necessarily complete accord at all times on the means by which they are to be achieved. Sékou Touré has maintained that all opinions will be heard up to the point of decision; thereafter acceptance of the party line is obligatory. Organized opposition will not be tolerated since the PDG is the expression of the popular will; no second party could rightfully claim to represent more than the interests of a special group. For Touré, the Western conception of the democratic process as a series of compromises between conflicting interest groups is simply not valid for Guinea at its present stage of development.

If Guinea is not a Western democracy, neither is it a people's democracy on the Eastern model. Marx may have profoundly influenced the Guinean leaders in their theory and practice of politics, but Sékou Touré and the members of the Political Bureau are, in the last analysis, Africans. When the theories of Marx and Lenin have failed to fit the needs of emerging Africa as he sees them, Touré has discarded them as ruthlessly as he has discarded those of the West. The African socialism toward which he is groping is designed to reestablish African dignity and to create respect for the African personality in the eyes of the world. Since an authoritarian, one-party system is needed in his view to achieve this goal, he has not hesitated to impose it. The African states can win their rightful place in the world community, he believes, only by developing political systems that are rooted in the African tradition and modernized by contributions, when they are useful, from both East and West. Sékou Touré's ideas, as they are embodied in the political structure of Guinea, have had a powerful influence on the younger generation of African nationalists. The West cannot afford to ignore them.

External Relations

Within a few months after independence the Guinean posture in foreign policy had been made clear to the world. In interviews with foreign journalists, exchanges with visiting heads of state, and speeches delivered abroad Sékou Touré repeated the principles upon which Guinean foreign policy rested. They could be broadly summarized in two main themes: positive neutrality and African unity.

Touré's stress on neutrality corresponded to the immediate post-independence needs of Guinea. Help of all kinds, both economic and technical, was required to build the new republic, and by a stance of neutrality the President sought to indicate to the outside world that Guinea was prepared to accept all offers of aid, provided they did not imply a permanent liaison with either major power bloc. He insisted, however, on accenting the "positive" aspects of his neutralism; it was not to be assumed that Guinean neutrality meant isolation from the main currents of international politics. He defined his attitude in these terms:

We mean by "positive" neutralism that our neutralism, far from being an isolationist principle, or a negative stand, serves the highest interests of humanity. It is essentially a neutralism in the service of all peoples, which favors the right of self-determination. . . . At the international level we seek to be an element of peace. We ask help and support from all the world, but at the same time full respect for our sovereignty.[63]

Positive neutralism for Sékou Touré had two sides: one, a sincere wish to avoid involving Guinea in the cold war, and the other, a desire to prove to other states that Guinea was genuinely independent and had thrown off the shackles which bound it to a Western colonial system.

The application of this neutrality principle to Guinea's day-to-day relations with the outside world has not always succeeded in creating the impression, at least in the West, that Sékou Touré's statements could be taken at face value. Guinea gradually began to assume a position, particularly in the United Nations, which has been characterized as one of "extreme neutrality" toward the West. In effect, this has meant voting, in the majority of issues, on the side of the East. Guinean support for the Soviet position in the UN must be seen in the light not only of Touré's own Marxist predilections but also of the immediate postindependence attitudes of the Western powers. Guinean pride was deeply hurt by the failure of France to sponsor Guinea's membership in the United Nations, by the reluctance of General de Gaulle to recognize Guinean sovereignty, and by the hesitation of France's allies to disregard the French position. The Eastern bloc, on the other hand,

---

[63] *Texte,* p. 81.

supported the new state quickly and fully, granting not only immediate recognition but also large-scale economic aid. In the light of these circumstances a Guinean bias toward the East was natural. Moreover, the openly anticolonial attitude of the Soviet Union in the United Nations was clearly in consonance with the avowed Guinean aim of independence for all African countries. There was always the lurking suspicion that the West might seek to reassert the former colonial control in the guise of economic aid; the Soviet Union, on the contrary, was looked on as a staunch ally in the fight against neocolonialism, real or imagined.

This Guinean interpretation of positive neutralism tended to alienate the West. In many quarters Guinea was branded as Russia's African satellite and as the first beachhead of communism in Africa; Sékou Touré was himself condemned as a puppet of Moscow. Despite the President's repeated affirmations that the PDG had no intention of surrendering Guinea to the tender mercies of either East or West and that Guinean policy decisions were made according to the circumstances of each particular case, and not to a preconceived formula, the impression gradually gained ground in the West that the Guinean brand of neutralism was simply a disguise for wholehearted accord with the East.

By the end of 1961, however, it was becoming clearer that Sékou Touré's nonalignment was more than a pose. Relations between the Soviet Union and Guinea were badly strained by Soviet support of internal disaffection within the Guinean regime. The Soviet ambassador was accused of taking too much interest in Guinean politics and forced to leave. Soviet economic aid had not proved satisfactory in supplying needed consumer goods, and Guineans were also piqued by the criticism of governmental inefficiency voiced by the Soviet mission. Even a visit by the Soviet Deputy Foreign Minister failed to repair the breach; he was received coldly in Conakry and without the fanfare the party usually accorded visiting dignitaries. The chilling of relations with the East did not necessarily mean that Guinea would turn toward the West; there were no signs of great receptiveness to any outside contacts. Positive neutralism seemed to be leading Guinea toward isolation, from the East and the West and even from Africa. Foreigners of any kind were suspect, and the party militants were urged to avoid any contacts with subversive (that is, foreign) elements.

Guinea's relations with the United Nations have also deteriorated since independence. The aid team, which was to make of Guinea a showpiece of United Nations technical assistance, was frustrated in its efforts and finally forced in February, 1961, to leave the country. The Guineans contributed troops to the UN action in the Congo at an early period, but they were withdrawn when the government became alienated by the failure of the United Nations to support the claim of Antoine Gizenga to be the successor to Patrice Lumumba.

Sékou Touré posited at the outset that the major goal of Guinean foreign policy was the liberation and unification of Africa. Guinean freedom was incomplete, in his view, while any part of Africa remained under colonial control. Guinea was prepared to support without reservation any movement for independence anywhere on the continent. Equally important, in Touré's view, is the long-range goal of unification of the independent states of Africa. The constitution provides for the surrender of Guinean sovereignty to a larger African unit if and when such a unit can be created. Sékou Touré has insisted that separately the African states can never expect to play an important role in world affairs: "The place of Africa in the world will be measured by the degree of its political unity. . . . An Africa politically divided, economically underdeveloped, and socially restricted will never be able to contribute anything to the world." [64] Together, he declares, the African states could present a stronger defense against the fluctuations of world market prices for their products and a much more attractive market for investment.

The first Guinean step toward the creation of a united Africa was taken with the announcement on November 24, 1958, of the Ghana-Guinea Union. The Union, which proposed to create a common legislature, currency, and flag for the two countries, was intended to be the nucleus to which other African states could be joined when they became independent. In token of the new relationship, Ghana loaned £10,000,000 ($28,000,000) to Guinea. At the end of 1960 Mali also became part of the Union, bringing into being the Union of African States.

Despite the forms of close association, the difficulties in the way of uniting two geographically noncontiguous countries with different languages, legal systems, and political institutions have prevented the Ghana-Guinea Union from becoming much more than a theoretical structure. The representatives of the three countries sit as members of the cabinet of the country to which they are accredited, but little else can be observed as concrete evidence of the Union's existence. It is

[64] *Ibid.*, p. 32.

significant, however, that the three members of the Union of African States acted in concert at the Casablanca Conference in January, 1961, in the formation of the loose bloc of extreme neutralists known as the Casablanca group. Guinea, Ghana, and Mali have refused to take part in the meetings of the so-called Monrovia group which includes all the other states of West Africa and a number outside that area. Moreover, along with Ghana, Guinea has been the leader in advocating political unification as a prerequisite to economic union, in contradistinction to the Monrovia group's approach which stresses the development of common economic interests prior to any form of political organization.

Sékou Touré's brand of political Pan-Africanism has wide appeal to the youth of West Africa, but it appears to have little attraction for the present leaders of the countries surrounding his. Guinea's close relationship with the East and its identification with the Soviet line on major international issues, such as disarmament, have caused some misgivings among its neighbors. No one doubts Sékou Touré's sincerity as an African nationalist nor do they disagree with his ultimate goal of African unification, but there has been some question of the soundness of his judgment in committing his country to a stand which, in spite of his posture of neutralism, has appeared to be consistently anti-Western.

Guinea has been an active member of the Afro-Asian bloc in the United Nations, and its representatives have spoken frequently in debates on colonial issues. It has also been a strong supporter of the Afro-Asian Solidarity Conference, and sponsored its second meeting at Conakry in April, 1960. Despite these activities, however, Sékou Touré's role in African politics appeared to be declining by the end of 1961. Relations with the countries on the immediate borders of Guinea, particularly the Ivory Coast, had not been improved by implied accusations in 1959 and 1960 that they had supplied bases from which anti-party elements in Guinea could operate. Internally, Guinea was not developing as rapidly as other countries; indeed, in some areas of the economy there had been retrogression since independence. And although the tight discipline of the PDG was admired for its political effectiveness, there were aspects of Guinean political organization which many African leaders found distasteful. Finally, the decision of the Casablanca powers not to attend the Lagos meeting of the Monrovia group in January, 1962, served further to isolate Guinea from one of the major currents of African politics. Positive neutralism had at the outset been advantageous in that it served to emphasize Sékou Touré's independence of colonial influence. But when it appeared to identify Guinea too clearly with one of the cold war blocs, many of the other states became wary of it. Touré's insistence on prior political unification presented a threat to other leaders who were far from prepared as yet to surrender their position as heads of independent states, however appealing the idea of a United States of Africa might be. It remains to be seen whether Sékou Touré will find that the satisfactions of an independence derived from the extreme neutralist position are sufficient compensation for potential exclusion from an African community which is developing in closer contact with the West than his conception of neutrality permits.

BIBLIOGRAPHY

For the background of the RDA and its role in West African politics, Virginia Thompson and Richard Adloff, *French West Africa* (Stanford: Stanford University Press, 1958), should be consulted. The best general account of political developments in the former French-speaking territories since 1945 is by Franz Ansprenger, *Politik im Schwarzen Afrika* (Cologne and Opladen: Westdeutscher Verlag, 1961). For a detailed preindependence account of the crosscurrents within the RDA and other parties in the former French West Africa consult André Blanchet, *L'Itinéraire des Partis depuis Bamako* (Paris: Plon, 1958), and Gil Dugué, *Vers les Etats-Unis d'Afrique* (Dakar: Editions Lettres Africaines, 1960).

There is little material in English on Guinea or the PDG except for occasional periodical articles. In French, Fernand Gigon has written a brief survey of the PDG immediately after independence in *Guinée, Etat-Pilote* (Paris: Plon, 1959).

Sékou Touré's own political theory may be found in the volumes of *L'Action Politique du Parti Démocratique de Guinée,* published from time to time in Conakry. They contain, in addition to his reports to party meetings, speeches delivered by him on Radio Guinée and a variety of other occasional texts. Some have been reprinted by Présence Africaine in Paris.

Guinée: Prélude à l'Indépendance. Paris: Présence Africaine, 1958. A report of the proceedings of a conference of *commandants de cercle* in Conakry in 1957 which was attended by Sékou Touré in his capacity as President of the Council of Ministers.
L'Expérience Guinéenne et l'Unité Africaine. Paris: Présence Africaine, 1959(?). Incorporates vols. I and II of *L'Action Politique du PDG.*
L'Action Politique du Parti Démocratique de Guinée pour l'Emancipation

Africaine. Vol. III of *L'Action Politique du PDG*. Conakry, 1959. This volume has been reprinted, except for some 20 pages, as *La Guinée et l'Emancipation Africaine* (Paris: Présence Africaine, 1959).

Le Cinquième Congrès National du Parti Démocratique de Guinée. Vol. IV of *L'Action Politique du PDG*. Conakry, 1959.

Toward Full Re-Africanisation. Paris: Présence Africaine, 1959. A translation of Sékou Touré's "Rapport Moral," addressed to the fifth party congress of the PDG.

La Planification Economique. Vol. V of *L'Action Politique du PDG*. Conakry, 1960.

Texte des Interviews Accordées aux Représentants de la Presse par le Président Sékou Touré. Conakry: n.p., 1959.

V

THE IVORY COAST

By VIRGINIA THOMPSON
University of California

Historical Background

The first Westerners to reach the Ivory Coast were navigators from Portugal and from northwestern France. Beginning in the sixteenth century they traded along the coast in slaves and in the ivory that gave its name to the country. About one hundred years later, a handful of French missionaries established themselves at Assinie, also on the Gulf of Guinea, but neither they nor the other Europeans who followed them during the next two centuries penetrated the hinterland. It was not until the eighteenth century in any case that the hinterland began filling up, following the arrival there of the Baoulé and the Agni-Ashanti tribes. When the French traders and missionaries began to appear in force in the nineteenth century, they found dozens of small tribes living in the forest zone and the western part of the coastal region in a state of chronic anarchy. Only by hearsay did they learn from a few travelers' accounts that well-developed kingdoms flourished in the eastern and northern parts of the backcountry.

THE COLONIAL PERIOD

France's first official contacts with the Ivory Coast date from 1842, when a naval officer sent by King Louis Philippe signed agreements with a few coastal chiefs. By their terms a French protectorate was established over that region, and military and trading posts were set up at Assinie, Grand Bassam, and Dabou that were administered by a

Resident responsible to the Governor of Senegal. During the Franco-Prussian War, the French garrisons were withdrawn, but a resident French merchant carried on as representative of the Senegal government until the *status quo ante* was restored. Obviously the next step was the exploration of the interior, and this was done concurrently by Treich-Laplène and L. G. Binger, who made a series of treaties with the hinterland potentates. Subsequently Binger became the first Governor of the Ivory Coast, and he established French posts at Sassandra, Béréby, and Tabou. He also negotiated agreements with Great Britain and Liberia that defined the colony's eastern and western boundaries. It was also Binger who began a military campaign against Almamy Samory, the slave trader who controlled much of the Guinea Gulf area.

Under the terms of the protectorate treaties the local chiefs granted privileges to French traders, and France promised to respect their traditional institutions and to grant them a subsidy, the amount of which varied with the size of the area they controlled. The peoples of Kaya, Tenkodogo, and Koudougou were permitted to retain their rigid social hierarchy under politico-religious chiefs. The eastern region was divided into provinces, corresponding generally to the old fiefs, and were cut up into cantons, but the indigenous populations there also remained under the leadership of their traditional chiefs. It was only in these parts of the Ivory Coast that a leadership survived which was solidly based upon tradition and custom.

In the late nineteenth century Samory's military successes in West Africa and, in 1900, the imposition of a head tax on the Ivoirian population provoked a widespread rebellion. So successful were these revolts, especially those of the Baoulé, that by 1908 only a small strip along the coast remained firmly under French control. The head tax, conceived as a means for financing a public works program, was regarded by the Ivoirians as a violation of the terms of the protectorate and also as a humiliating mark of submission. It was due only to the ability of a remarkable Governor, Gabriel Angoulvant, that the hinterland was gradually subdued, the tribes there forced to accept the abolition of slavery, the interior opened up by roads, and French traders protected. To achieve this result Angoulvant had to use military force, but he also pledged that France would not interfere with local customs and promised specifically not to intervene in the choice of chiefs.

Yet after the territory was pacified, the French soon returned to direct rule. The tribes were disarmed and recalcitrant chiefs removed on the charge that they either were incompetent or had broken their treaty pledges. The French regrouped villages and tribal units and everywhere imposed a uniform, centralized administration. Although this was characteristic of French policy elsewhere in West and Equatorial Africa, circumstances peculiar to the Ivory Coast and its conquest made France's action there exceptionally adverse to the survival of native institutions. This was the least serious in the forest zone, which was singularly devoid of indigenous political organizations. But that area was also lacking in population, and in order to develop plantations and means of communication within it manpower was drained from the north, especially from the region now known as Upper Volta.

Military recruiting, begun in 1912, completed the disaffection of some of the tribes, though the warriors of the north were by no means opposed to such service. Indeed, when World War I broke out, more men volunteered than could be accepted, and some 20,000 Ivoirians served with French troops on the Western front. It was among the more peaceable forest populations, notably the Agni of Assinie, that the prospect of such military service was so alarming that many of them fled to the Gold Coast in 1917. A supplementary war effort demanded of the Ivoirians, which entailed an increase in the output of oleaginous produce, meat animals, and rubber, tended to push the population's living standards still lower and heightened their discontent. Thus the situation in the Ivory Coast was generally propitious to the Turkish anti-French propaganda that infiltrated there from the eastern Sahara, and in 1916 a very serious revolt broke out that required long and costly military operations to quell.

This revolt aroused the French West African federal government at Dakar to decree drastic changes in the Ivory Coast's administration, mainly aimed at reviving the power of the traditional chiefs. But neither this nor other reforms that subsequently emanated from Dakar did much to check the continued division of Ivoirian states into cantons and subdivisions, placed under officials appointed by the central authorities, and the partial transformation of traditional chiefs into functionaries of the French administration. Even the one fundamental accomplishment of this period—the constitution of Upper Volta as a separate colony in 1919—was undone during the world depression. In 1932 Upper Volta was dismembered and its territory divided among the adjacent colonies.

The area of the Ivory Coast was almost doubled by this measure, and it acquired something over 2,000,000 new inhabitants, becoming almost overnight the most populous colony of the Federation. The big European planters of the Lower Coast—the only sizable such group in French West Africa—were delighted by the prospect of drawing on what they supposed to be an inexhaustible labor reservoir in Upper Volta, and the coastal merchants also happily anticipated new outlets for their goods among the populous Mossi tribes. Both hopes turned out to be illusory. Moreover, other difficulties caused by long-distance administration from Abidjan of the newly acquired territory led to the reconstitution of Upper Volta in 1937 as a distinct administrative unit, though not as a separate colony.

Yet in the economic and social domains the interwar period was by no means a retrogressive one for the Ivory Coast. Communications were improved by the opening of the Ebrié lagoon canal, building of the wharves at Grand Bassam and Port Bouët, extension of the Abidjan railroad to the north, and expansion of the road network, and the establishment of agricultural research stations and of more schools and medical centers stimulated the colony's evolution. In 1936 the coming to power in France of the Popular Front government ushered in a period of lessened tensions in the Ivory Coast, as elsewhere in the Federation, and led to the development of a political consciousness that rapidly gained momentum during World War II.

RISE AND CHARACTER OF THE NATIONALIST MOVEMENT

Curiously enough it was a Catholic Baoulé chief and physician, Félix Houphouët-Boigny, who organized the first political party in the Ivory Coast to defend the interests of small African farmers vis-à-vis the big French planters and lumbermen, as well as against the large European commercial firms. In September, 1944, he founded the Syndicat Africain Agricole (SAA) which, by the end of the war, had reportedly acquired some 20,000 members. These were drawn from a wide variety of ethnic and economic groups, but the most active element among them was the peasant component. It was also Houphouët who was the prime mover behind the Rassemblement Démocratique Africain (RDA), an interterritorial movement founded at Bamako in October, 1946, of which the SAA later became the Ivoirian branch under the name of Parti Démocratique de la Côte d'Ivoire (PDCI). Unlike the other territorial branches of the RDA, notably those of Soudan (now Mali) and Guinea, the PDCI's impetus did not come from African wage earners, nor was its program geared to the satisfaction of labor's demands. This fact accounts in part for its divergent evolution. Another cause of the PDCI's distinctive development was the benevolent attitude during its formative years of the Ivory Coast's first post-war Governor, André Latrille, and of his *chef de cabinet*, Lambert. Both men were closely associated with the French Communist Party, which initially sponsored the RDA. It was with their encouragement that the PDCI was early able to organize a thorough pyramidal party structure throughout the territory modeled on the Communist Party.

That Houphouët himself was not a convert to Marxism but was simply utilizing the methods and support of the French Communists was not grasped by Latrille's ultraconservative successor, Péchoux, who by pressure and by the use of force strove to destroy the PDCI and to create organizations opposed to it. Since the Ivory Coast, in common with all the other French Negro territories, was endowed in 1946 with an elected territorial council and empowered to choose its representatives to France's parliamentary bodies, it was the elections for such posts that provided the occasions for the successive trials of strength between Houphouët and the local French administration. In 1949 this tension degenerated into violence. Moreover, electoral defeats of PDCI candidates and the arrest or resignation of many of its militants, caused either by disapproval of its policies or by fear of official reprisals, certainly weakened the Ivoirian RDA. But the elimination or withdrawal of other leaders probably enhanced the personal authority of Houphouët, who continued to be elected to the French National Assembly and to the territorial assembly despite official opposition. It soon became obvious to the administration that no strong opposition force could be created that would undermine Houphouët's popularity and the mass support for the party that he led. An estimate made in September, 1950, by a French journalist that in the Ivory Coast the Independents then numbered 65,000, the Socialists 25,000, the Progressives 20,000, and the Bloc Eburnéen 8,000 was ridiculed (and probably rightly so) by the PDCI leaders as a gross exaggeration.[1]

In any case the number and strength of the PDCI's opponents soon became only of academic concern. Late in 1950 Houphouët decided that the RDA's affiliation with the Communists had now outlived its usefulness and that his movement would fare better if it collaborated with the administration and French business interests while retaining the type of party organization and propaganda methods it had learned from its Communist mentors. This first *volte-face* in Houphouët's basic policy coincided with the completion of the Vridi Canal that made Abidjan a deepwater port. Under the sympathetic administration of

[1] Philippe Diolé, *Le Monde*, Sept. 7–8, 1950.

Governor Pierre Messmer, the new policy ushered in the first honeymoon period of Franco-PDCI relations, during which the Ivory Coast achieved unprecedented prosperity. By late 1956 the Ivory Coast had outdistanced Senegal as the Federation's wealthiest territory. Consequently, under the prevailing system of redistributing federal revenues it was making the heaviest contribution to the budgets of its poorer neighbors. While these developments caused Ivoirians to equate a federal form of government in West Africa with the denial of their right to use all their earnings for their own country's evolution, it also led them to identify their expanding economy with the rule of the PDCI. Not surprisingly that party won all sixty seats in the territorial assembly in the elections of March, 1957, and two months later it was able to form a homogeneous government council under the regime instituted by the *loi cadre* of June 23, 1956.

In 1956 Houphouët had every reason to feel justified in the policy that he had been pursuing. His movement was clearly dominant in French West Africa and was making headway in French Equatorial Africa. His home territory was enjoying unprecedented prosperity, and his party's organization was functioning so smoothly that he could accept a ministerial portfolio in the Mollet government in France and entrust the Ivory Coast's day-to-day administration to his faithful lieutenants there. Houphouët clearly felt that he could afford to devote most of his time in France in 1956 to drafting in collaboration with Gaston Defferre—then Minister of Overseas France—the *loi cadre* that was drastically to alter the relations between the *Métropole* and its overseas dependencies.

This law reflected the views Houphouët then held as to the evolution that that relationship should follow. It was designed to create a Franco-African federal republic in which each component country would have complete internal autonomy while a federal parliament and a federal executive located in Paris would maintain control of the monetary policy, defense, and foreign relations of its members. Although Houphouët laid stress on the forging of close links between each overseas territory and France, his main objective seems to have been to achieve complete economic independence by the Ivory Coast vis-à-vis Paris and, above all, the government-general at Dakar. With a wholly free hand to manage its internal affairs, the Ivory Coast would then be able to devote its expanding revenues to self-development and no longer be compelled to share them with its less well-to-do neighbors.

Absent in Paris for long periods of time, Houphouët failed to recognize that in West Africa the new and powerful forces of independence, federalism, and Pan-Africanism were challenging the static position that he had given the RDA. Moreover, he continued to underestimate the appeal of those forces even after the RDA congress at Bamako in September, 1957, had shown their dynamism and the unpopularity of his own views. Soon after, at a public dinner at Paris, he stated categorically: "We will not fall into the trap made for us by Great Britain in creating independent states in Africa." [2] Deliberately dissociating himself from the new trends, Houphouët permitted Senghor's rival interterritorial movement—the Parti du Regroupement Africain (PRA) —to gather such momentum by capturing the profederalist and pro-independence elements that it split the RDA and jeopardized his leadership of French Negro Africa. Repeated proofs of his complete control over the Ivory Coast and its steadily growing wealth apparently lulled Houphouët into a false sense of security, and he did not perceive the consequences of his territory's increasing political isolation. Twice in the spring of 1958, the Ivory Coast territorial assembly unanimously rejected the federal Grand Council's resolutions favoring an African-controlled primary federation in French West Africa, and in the referendum of September, 1958, on the constitution of France's Fifth Republic only 219 Ivoirians voted against membership in the Franco-African Community which Houphouët had helped to mold.

Although all but Guinea of the French Negro territories also voted overwhelmingly in favor of membership in the Franco-African community, it soon became apparent that the massive affirmative vote in the referendum was not tantamount to acceptance of Houphouët's concept of its nature. A rapid succession of shocks, beginning with the inter-African riots at Abidjan in October, 1958, followed by announcement of the Ghana-Guinea Union and then of the formation of the Mali Federation, began to undermine the confidence that he had placed in his policy. He was still powerful enough to detach—with or without French connivance—Dahomey and Upper Volta from the nascent Mali Federation. But he proved not strong enough to prevent General de Gaulle from accepting the Mali Federation formed by Senegal and Soudan and later from agreeing to its membership as an independent unit in a remodeled confederal Community. Moreover, in his own stronghold of the Ivory Coast, the Ivoirians' resentment against resident foreigners, the defection of the "King" of Sanwi, and a strike by radical

[2] A. Blanchet, *L'Itinéraire des Partis Africains depuis Bamako* (Paris, 1958), p. 109.

labor leaders showed weak spots in his armor that were the more serious because they were also being probed by neighboring countries bent on undermining his authority.

ACHIEVEMENT OF INDEPENDENCE

By the spring of 1959 it became apparent that Houphouët was seriously considering another drastic change in his policies. In April he laid the foundations with Upper Volta and Niger of the Council of the Entente, which Dahomey joined the following month; in June he agreed to enter a customs union with six of the other former French West African territories. Concurrently he was becoming more and more disillusioned with France, particularly after it granted the Mali Federation a seat on the executive council of the Community and replaced the popular Governor of the Ivory Coast, de Nattes, without first consulting him. Yet Houphouët accepted the post of Minister-Adviser to the Debré government in July, and at the Tananarive meeting of the executive council of the Community that same month he gave his approval to French nuclear testing in the Sahara.

At the September, 1959, meeting of the RDA in Abidjan, Houphouët's position remained ambivalent. While he openly criticized the retention of French high commissioners at Brazzaville and Dakar, the politicization of some Community institutions (particularly the Secretariat), and the slowness and insufficiency of French aid to African territories, his tone was one of reasonableness and moderation. He maintained this attitude, at least publicly, even after it became clear that France would acquiesce to Mali's demand for independence within the Community.

However, Houphouët must have decided by this time to strike out in a new direction, though one that would not result in an open break with France. When he led the Entente states along the path to independence outside the Community in mid-1960, he did this without sacrificing his friendship with France. In so doing he utilized the same forces of independence and Pan-Africanism that had made the Ghana-Guinea Union and the Mali Federation, but in an original way that enabled him to outbid the Mali leaders and at the same time avoid jumping on the Nkrumah-Sékou Touré bandwagon. Moreover, although Houphouët has loosened his ties with France and the local French residents, he has managed at the same time to remain on cordial terms with the Paris government and to increase the French subsidies and foreign investments required to stimulate the Ivory Coast's economy.

Undisputed master in his own territory, Houphouët has made a brilliant comeback in the domain of West African foreign relations, for the Ivory Coast is now at least formally on good terms with all its neighbors. Houphouët has succeeded in building up ever-widening groups of countries, many of which acknowledge him to be their unobtrusive leader. The Council of the Entente has proved to be the nucleus of successive, ever-larger groupings which Houphouët is still in the process of constructing.

THE COUNCIL OF THE ENTENTE

Three weeks before the federalist congress at Bamako in December, 1958, had laid the foundations of the Mali Federation, Houphouët let it be known that he was not averse to having economic and technical ties with other French West African states, and he suggested for the first time the formation of such an apolitical Council of the Entente. For some months nothing further was heard of this proposal, but it was certainly not unrelated to the withdrawal of Upper Volta and Dahomey from the embryonic Mali Federation early in 1959. The Ivory Coast with those two states and Niger formed a fairly cohesive geographical group. Upper Volta was linked with the Ivory Coast by the Mossi railroad and its use of Abidjan as the port of its foreign trade. Niger was similarly, though more artificially, linked to Dahomey by Cotonou port and a road-and-rail connection called Opération Hirondelle. Poverty was the common denominator of Niger, Upper Volta, and Dahomey, and with the cessation of federal subsidies following the dissolution of the government-general at Dakar, their impoverishment was bound to increase. The rich Ivory Coast with its well-equipped port and good system of communications offered undeniable attractions. The fact that Houphouët was now willing to use the Ivory Coast's surpluses as the means of luring its poor neighbors into his Entente is a measure of the radical change that was taking place in his political thinking.

Upper Volta and Niger were relatively easy to bring under Houphouët's wing as both had RDA governments whose premiers acknowledged his leadership. Physically the Ivory Coast's closest ties were with Upper Volta, which also had long supplied its plantations with laborers. Not surprisingly, therefore, the first of the series of agreements that created the Entente was signed by Houphouët and the Voltaic Premier, Maurice Yaméogo, on April 4, 1959. Three days later a similar agreement was reached with Niger, whose Premier, Hamani Diori, was one of Houphouët's oldest and most faithful collaborators. Dahomey presented greater difficulties, and its entry into the Entente was delayed for a month. Dahomey was not linked to the Ivory Coast either commercially or geographically, the RDA party in that territory was not in control of the government, and there existed an influential PRA party that favored union with Mali. Houphouët and Hamani Diori wasted a month in courting the Parti Républicain du Dahomey (PRD) and helping its leader, Sourou Migan Apithy, to settle a political crisis, for Apithy was soon replaced by Hubert Maga as head of the Dahomey government and Maga's party had not participated in the initial negotiations. When Maga was finally persuaded to join the Entente in May, he made it clear that he was doing so solely for the practical advantages that such an association would bring to his country. His self-interested attitude contrasted with the personal loyalty to Houphouët expressed by Hamani Diori and Yaméogo, and it was erroneously thought at the time that Dahomey was the weakest link in the new Entente.

With the formation of the Council of the Entente, Mauritania became the only one of the former French West African territories to remain outside any group. Guinea had formed a nominal union with Ghana, Senegal had joined Soudan in the Mali Federation, and the old French West African Federation had now split into two zones—one oriented to Dakar and the other to Abidjan. At the time the Entente was formed, there was no question of its leaving the Community. Indeed, the Entente was proclaimed open to any member state of the Community that cared to join it. Moreover, to show that it had no exclusive character the Entente territories agreed to enter the customs union formed by the former French West African states (except Guinea) in June, 1959. Clearly in the eyes of its founder the Entente was to be a counterpoise to the Mali Federation, but one of a very different, strictly practical and apolitical character. Houphouët in an interview published on April 3, 1959, in *Afrique Nouvelle* had described his conception of the Entente:

It would be the getting together of the premiers of each state, assisted by such of their ministers who deal with affairs common to all members and the presidents and vice-presidents of their legislative assemblies. The Council of the Entente would meet successively in the capital of each state under the chairmanship of that state's prime minister. Decisions would be made either unanimously or by majority vote, and these decisions would have an executive character. In case of grave conflict we would take our case to the

Community court of arbitration. As to the Solidarity Fund, each state belonging to the Entente would pay into it one-tenth of its revenues. A fifth of this fund would be placed in a reserve fund that could serve, for example, to guarantee loans to each state for some project of concern to it.

For a short time the Entente evolved according to this formula. At the first meeting of the Entente premiers held at Abidjan on May 29–30, 1959, the questions discussed were the establishment of a solidarity fund in July, a customs union, methods of jointly combating epidemics and plant diseases, and common legislation regulating the civil service and labor questions. But as the Entente had been founded basically for political reasons—to offset the Mali Federation—though it was nominally only an economic and technical association it gradually changed its character under the pressure of external events and internal friction. The latter was mainly between its two original partners, the Ivory Coast and Upper Volta, and the strains to which the Entente became subject grew as Houphouët attempted to tighten its structure and assert closer controls. Externally the Mali Federation's evolution affected that of the Entente and in turn this development altered the latter's relations with France. Moreover, subsequently the Ghana-Guinea Union deliberately exercised a corrosive effect upon the Entente. But by the time this occurred the Entente, which had never quite got off the ground, had been largely superseded by a succession of wider groupings also engineered by Houphouët, which received organizational form at Yaoundé in March, 1961, as the Union Africaine et Malgache (UAM).

As to the Entente's relations with the Mali Federation, Houphouët's initial public reaction to the latter's creation was one of skepticism. He told members of the PDCI that he did not believe in the efficacy or durability of Mali but added that he was ready to make agreements with its leaders. In May he held out his hand to Mali, asserting that there would be no conflict between its leaders and the Entente. Four months later at the Abidjan Congress of the RDA he repeated this line, paraphrasing Giraudoux's well-known drama:

La guerre du Mali et de l'Entente n'aura pas lieu [The war between Mali and the Entente will not take place], for there are no basic problems that divide those who have joined the Community as groups or as individuals. Today independence is fictitious. If the confederation which the Mali leaders speak about is also a multinational and intercontinental confederation that has a common political and economic organization, we are agreed.

It is not Mali that worries us but the currents that manifest themselves outside the Community.[3]

It was when Mali began clearly to move away from the Community as established in 1958 and, above all, when this change was accepted by de Gaulle the following November that Houphouët's attitude began to alter sharply—but more toward France than toward the Malian leaders. Yet once again Houphouët's remarkable realism and adaptability came to the rescue. At a meeting of the Entente premiers held at Niamey in December, 1959, it was Houphouët who, though not himself present, exerted by phone and through emissaries a moderating influence on the bitterness expressed there by his Voltaic and Nigérien colleagues. Maga did not join the other two premiers in reproaching France for penalizing its staunchest friends and advocates of a "durable" Community, but all of Houphouët's skill was needed to prevent Yaméogo and Hamani Diori from individually voicing their indignation. Houphouët insisted, however, that in all matters the Entente should speak with one voice. He pledged that the Entente as a unit would negotiate with France for a transfer of power and would not find itself consequently in a less-favored position than Mali. But in order that the Entente could speak as one voice, Houphouët had to strengthen its structure, which was being strained by disagreements that had arisen by January, 1960, between the Ivory Coast and Upper Volta.

The first cause of this friction was that the Ivory Coast abolished its local head tax without first consulting its partners, despite their agreement to coordinate the Entente's fiscal policies. Because the head tax supplied only 4 per cent of the Ivory Coast's revenues, that territory could afford to abolish it and thus add notably to the PDCI's popularity. But in Upper Volta the head tax accounted for a fourth of its whole income and could not be eliminated without upsetting that country's economy. In retaliation for Ivory Coast's action, Upper Volta abolished the organization that supplied Mossi laborers for the Ivory Coast plantations on the ground that those migrant workers were maltreated in the south. An even greater source of irritation to the Voltaic leaders was the Ivory Coast's method of dividing the customs duties collected on Upper Volta's imports at the port of Abidjan. Under the former French West African Federation, Upper Volta had been allotted a rebate on these duties gauged on the quantity of merchandise it im-

[3] *Le Monde*, Sept. 5, 1959.

ported for local consumption. Now Raphaël Saller, the Ivory Coast's
Finance Minister, refused to continue this practice and substituted for
the proportionate rebate a flat sum, which Upper Volta's leaders felt
was less than their country's due.

The rising tide of Upper Volta's discontent was obliquely reflected
in a statement made by Yaméogo to his party on January 30, 1960, in
which he stressed the "absolute necessity of preparing the masses for
an eventual transfer of power."[4] This threat of taking independent
action outside the framework of the Entente was perhaps even more
alarming to Hamani Diori in Niger than it was to Houphouët. Upper
Volta provided the physical link between the Entente countries, and
if the Voltaic leader decided to move unilaterally toward independence, Niger would be cut off from direct contact with the Ivory Coast
and its government would become more vulnerable to the opposing
forces that advocated union with Nigeria. This possibility seemed
dangerous enough to precipitate a hurried trip to Ouagadougou by
Hamani Diori, Maga, and Philippe Yacé (president of the Ivory Coast
assembly), whose "good offices" officially smoothed over the differences.
Upper Volta was assured that the Ivory Coast would work out an
equitable arrangement in regard to their fiscal systems, customs duties,
and the treatment of Mossi laborers and would also continue to provide
financial support. The Ivory Coast's sovereign remedy for curing the
ills and ill humor of its partners again proved efficacious, and Yaméogo
quickly denied rumors that he was considering leaving the Entente.[5]
Maga also issued a similar denial, which was apparently considered
essential to quell the growing restiveness of those Dahomeyans who
were still eager to join the Mali Federation.

The centrifugal tendencies manifested by Upper Volta and to a lesser
degree by Dahomey looked serious enough to Houphouët for him to
try to bolster the Entente's structure. It was decided that a small permanent secretariat should be set up at Niamey and that meetings of
the four premiers should be more frequent than in the past, with the
chairmanship of the Entente rotating on a yearly basis among the
partners. But more than such machinery was necessary if Houphouët
was to keep members of the Entente in line.

By the spring of 1960 Houphouët had come to realize that in order
even to maintain his ascendancy over his junior partners of the
Entente, let alone to reassert his leadership of French-speaking Africa,
he must make some spectacular move. This was made especially urgent

---

[4] *Afrique Nouvelle*, Feb. 10, 1960. [5] *Ibid.*, Feb. 17, 1960.

by the imminence of Mali's independence, slated for June 20, 1960.
His first step was to dispatch Hamani Diori in March on a tour of the
equatorial states to sound out the possibility of their joining the Entente
in a "sub-Community of French Africa." But Hamani Diori found
Tchad, the Central African Republic, and the Congo Republic preoccupied with forming their own *Union Equatoriale* and Gabon still
determined to go it alone. Mauritania, the only other former French
African state still uncommitted to any bloc, seemed equally determined
to pursue its own course.

Thus the only way still open for Houphouët to recapture a position
of preeminence was to outbid Mali with a nationalist move. Shortly
before that Federation was to become independent, Houphouët announced that the Entente states would seek their independence from
France and, if necessary, each would hold a referendum on the issue.
As wholly sovereign states, he said, the members of the Entente would
seek admission to the United Nations, and only after they were admitted to that organization would they make agreements with France.
To this demand for independence the French government acceded with
surprising rapidity on June 25, 1960. Indeed, some groups in Paris,
feeling that Houphouët had been unjustly recompensed for his faith-
fulness to France, had apparently been urging him to follow Mali's
example.[6] Both the French government and Houphouët realized that
unless the members of the Entente became sovereign states officially
their applications for membership in the United Nations might be rejected on the ground that they were still satellites of France. And, as
had been the case with Senegal and Soudan, the French were above
all eager to avoid a referendum in any sub-Saharan African country
on the issue of independence from France. At this time it appeared
that no one in Paris took seriously the possibility that the loyal Houphouët would not later agree to reenter the Community. Early in
August, 1960, therefore, all four Entente states became independent,
and, on August 16, their applications for membership in the United
Nations were approved by the Security Council. All of them accepted
French sponsorship for admission to the United Nations, and their
spokesmen warmly voiced their countries' gratitude to General de
Gaulle.

After this hurdle was taken, Houphouët proceeded to reinforce
further the ties between the Entente states. Still without creating any
supranational institutional links he had succeeded, by September,

[6] *The Economist,* June 11, 1960.

1960, in transforming the Entente from its originally economic character into a primarily political grouping. After a meeting at Abidjan, the Entente premiers had agreed to coordinate their administrative, electoral, and fiscal systems, achieve a closer customs union, work out a concerted foreign policy, and accept with only minor variations the same type of constitution. There was only one area in which agreement proved hard to reach and, surprisingly enough, this divided Niger and the Ivory Coast. The latter wanted a strong army and navy, for its relations with neighboring Ghana and Guinea had been deteriorating during the summer of 1960. Niger felt no similar threat and also for reasons of economy preferred a *gendarmerie* to a national army. Committees were named to iron out this difficulty and other practical details and to draft what were to be largely identical constitutions. Late in October the four premiers met again to study and slightly modify the committees' proposals, and the constitutions as finally drafted were subsequently submitted to their respective assemblies for adoption. Obviously the next step to be taken was the negotiation of agreements with France. In this Houphouët continued to lead the Entente, but by the spring of 1961 there were signs that seemed to presage a possible breakdown of the structure that Houphouët had carefully built up, for divergent views in regard to foreign policy were again challenging the Ivory Coast's leadership.

Land and People

The Ivory Coast has roughly the shape of a quadrangle, covering an area of 320,000 square kilometers. It is about three-fifths the size of France and has approximately the same area as New Mexico. Its southern coastline, 550 kilometers long, borders on the Gulf of Guinea. To the west lie Guinea and Liberia, to the east Ghana, and to the north Upper Volta and the Mali Republic.

In the south, a series of lagoons stretching from Fresco to the Ghanaian frontier are separated from the ocean by a narrow sandy bar, and the rest of the coastline from Fresco to the Liberian frontier is hilly and rocky. To the north of the lagoons comes the forest zone; this gives way toward the frontiers with Mali and Upper Volta to a savannah area in which the dense forest is replaced by grassy stretches sparsely dotted with trees. As one moves northward, the climate changes from equatorial to tropical. In the equatorial region of the forest the rainfall is very abundant, and it is divided into two seasons separated by dry periods of uneven duration. The tropical zone has only two seasons, one dry and one rainy, the latter being shorter and less heavy than in the south.

The Ivory Coast forms an eroded plateau in which the land rises gradually and evenly from the Gulf of Guinea to the north, with only a few isolated mountainous areas. In the northeast there is high ground around Man and Odienné; the Grabo chain of mountains rises near the Liberian frontier in the west; east of Tabou there is another range; in Grand Lahou occurs the massif of Kouta; and another mountainous region is to be found in the Baoulé country. The Comoë, Bandama, Sassandra, and Cavally—the Ivory Coast's four main rivers—flow from north to south, and of these the Comoë is the longest. All these waterways are encumbered with rapids and are seasonal in their flow. Although none of them is navigable for more than short distances, they and their tributaries can be used for floating timber in the forest zone.

On December 1, 1958, the population of the Ivory Coast was estimated at 3,088,000, and by 1961 it probably reached about 3,200,000 as the annual rate of growth has been approximately 2 per cent. As of 1921, the Ivoirians numbered only some 1,500,000, so that the total population has doubled in less than forty years. The average density is believed to be 9.6 inhabitants to the square kilometer, but the population is unevenly divided. The most populous *cercles* are those of the Lagunes, Grand Bassam, Bouaké, Gagnoa, Bouaflé, and Agboville, and those with the fewest inhabitants are Tabou, Bondoukou, Sassandra, Odienné, and Katiola. The greatest growth has occurred in the coffee- and cocoa-growing region, culminating in the Abidjan area, which the development of communications has made highly accessible. Of the total population, 12,000 or so are non-Africans, mainly French, Lebanese, and Syrians. The Ivoirians themselves are a very young population, with an exceptionally high birth rate and slightly lower death rate. It is believed that today 43 per cent of the population of the Ivory Coast is under fifteen years of age.

Increase in the urban component has been spectacular even for West Africa. Of the five towns that have a population of over 10,000, the growth of Abidjan is particularly striking. At the beginning of the twentieth century, Abidjan had fewer than 1,000 inhabitants and its location cannot be found on many of the maps of that period. It now has a population of between 250,000 and 300,000 (of whom about 9,000 are non-Africans), and its development has been especially rapid in the past two years. In order of declining importance as urban centers come Bouaké (41,200), Daloa (17,400), Gagnoa (15,000), and Korhogo

(12,100), and there are six other agglomerations with populations ranging between 3,400 and 7,200.

THE ECONOMY

Like all the other French-speaking West African territories except Mauritania, the Ivory Coast is predominantly agricultural. Some 95 per cent of its population derives its livelihood from farming, forestry, fishing, and animal husbandry, which also supply virtually all the country's revenues. Generally speaking, export crops, timber, and fish are produced in the south, whereas livestock and most of the food crops are grown in the north. Already less dependent than Ghana on a single export crop, the Ivory Coast is in the process of further diversifying its agricultural production in order to lessen its dependence on fluctuating world markets. The main cash crops are coffee and cocoa, which together account for 90 per cent of the Ivory Coast's exports. Other major exports are lumber and bananas, and there are great hopes for the future for rubber, pineapples, and fish shipments.

Coffee production remains the key to the Ivory Coast's economy, though the government opposes the expansion of areas planted to coffee and is trying to improve its yield and quality. Coffee cultivation dates only from the 1920's, but it now covers nearly 300,000 hectares, and almost 98 per cent of its output is in the hands of Africans. The main producing *cercles* are Dimbokro, Daloa, Bouaké, Gagnoa, Grand Lahou, Agboville, Bondoukou, and Abengourou, and the principal variety now cultivated is the *robusta*. Research on coffeegrowing is carried on at the Adiopodoumé station of the Organisation de Recherches Scientifiques et Techniques d'Outre-Mer (ORSTOM) and also at the experimental farms of the Institut Français du Café et Cacao at Bingerville, Akandjé, and Abengourou. The work of these stations has effected a marked improvement in yields and quality and has led to a sensational increase in exports. Coffee shipments from the Ivory Coast rose from 37,000 tons in 1945 to a record of 114,500 tons in 1958. This expansion has created grave marketing difficulties, especially since the world price for coffee began to fall toward the end of 1954. In turn this development led to the creation that year of a Price Stabilization Fund and to a search for new markets. Since 1931 the Ivory Coast's coffee has enjoyed protection in the French market, and in recent years France's subsidies in one form or another to Ivoirian coffeegrowers have reached fantastic proportions. The Ivory Coast now supplies 60 per cent of all the coffee that France imports from the

Community countries, and the French market cannot keep pace with expanding Ivoirian production. Ivory Coast coffee planters have been demanding the payment of about 31 cents a pound, and they are reluctant to sell their coffee outside the franc zone where the price is 15 per cent lower and the competition stiffer.

Cocoa is an older local crop than coffee, and it is less threatened by overproduction. Its cultivation began in the Bingerville region about 1895, and initially the colonial administration forced its growth by the local population to compensate for the cessation of wild rubber exports. Soon the cocoa crop proved remunerative enough for the Ivoirians to begin growing it voluntarily, and production expanded particularly in the Indénié region, where conditions were exceptionally propitious for its growth. Today cocoa is planted on some 210,000 hectares, and nine-tenths of the cocoa growers are Africans. Although the research carried on at the Abengourou station, established in 1948, has successfully combated the swollen-shoot disease, production tends to decline. Exports, which had risen from about 30,000 tons in 1946 to over 71,000 tons ten years later, dropped to 63,000 tons in 1959. Responsible for this shrinkage in shipments are the greater attraction of coffeegrowing, which is normally more remunerative and less difficult; the over-age of most of the Ivory Coast's cocoa bushes; and the limited amount of land suited to this crop. To revive exports the government has encouraged replanting and also improvements in the fermentation and drying of beans and has required three-fourths of the country's cocoa shipments to be of superior quality.

Bananas are an even more recent export of the Ivory Coast, the first shipments occurring in 1935 when some 1,700 tons were produced. The coastal zone is admirably suited to this crop, and production has expanded rapidly in the cercles of the Lagunes, Agboville, Sassandra, and Grand Bassam. Exports, which ceased during World War II, revived rapidly thereafter and came to some 54,000 tons in 1959. In part this was due to the substitution of the more resistant poyo for the musa sinensis variety and to cheaper and more efficient packing methods promoted by the Institut Français des Recherches Fruitières, and in part to the creation in 1953 of a local cooperative society, the Cobafruit. Unlike coffeegrowing and cocoa growing in the Ivory Coast, bananas have been grown almost exclusively by European planters. To increase the African share in banana production to half of the total, an Association pour l'Africanisation de la Culture Bananière was founded in 1959, which the local government has encouraged by a loan. This association plans to collaborate with Cobafruit in the sale of its output, and in 1961 it created the first African "banana village" at Poyokro. France buys 15 per cent of its bananas from the Ivory Coast, which is its principal African supplier of that commodity, and the European Economic Community offers the prospect of a much larger market.

Another Ivoirian fruit crop, pineapples, has not yet been greatly developed, but it is hoped that by official encouragement the European market, which is far from glutted, can be greatly enlarged. Land and climatic conditions in the lagoon zone especially around Binger-ville are favorable to pineapple growing. However, production has been confined to less than 350 hectares there, and the amount grown in 1957 came only to about 10,000 tons. Exports are mainly juice and canned fruit—3,600 tons and 4,000 tons respectively in 1959—though the shipment of fresh pineapples is also increasing.

Hevea rubber is considered the most promising of the Ivory Coast's new export crops. With the development of hevea plantations in the Far East, especially during the interwar period, wild rubber exports from the Ivory Coast disappeared, and an attempt to develop plantation rubber during World War II proved to be abortive. In the early 1950's, the war in Indochina induced two of the French companies established there to start plantations in the Ivory Coast, using clones that they brought from the Far East. Their work in West Africa has been encouraged by the French rubber research institute set up in 1956. Two years later the two Indochina companies had planted to hevea over 2,000 hectares of the 20,000 that had been conceded to them in the coastal region of the Ivory Coast, and by 1959 their production of latex amounted to some 800 tons. If these companies' operations fulfill their present promise, the local government intends to promote the growing of hevea rubber by African families and cooperatives.

Since 1908 cotton has been cultivated for local consumption and for export near Bouaké, where an experimental station has been created. Production, however, accounts for only about 5,000 tons of boll cotton, and the local textile industries must buy a large proportion of their raw material supplies from other countries. Such encouraging results have been achieved by the research stations working with selected varieties of seed that, with official encouragement, the area planted to cotton now comprises some 10,000 hectares. If this expansion continues, the government hopes that the Ivory Coast will no longer have to import the cotton required for local consumption.

Other local industries that import raw material supplies which could be grown on a larger scale in the Ivory Coast are those of soap and of margarine. To remedy this deficiency the Ivoirian government is trying to expand the area planted to oil palms to 20,000 hectares and that to coconut palms to 10,000 hectares and also to increase the output of peanuts for eating. Currently the country exports only small amounts of vegetable oil materials—15,000 tons of palm kernels, 520 tons of sesame seed, 100 tons of copra, and 120 tons of shelled peanuts. Other crops now produced in small quantities which the government intends to encourage for local consumption and for export are tobacco, sisal, cola nuts, and sugar cane.

Food crops are produced principally in the northern savannah zone, where 90 per cent of the output is consumed by their growers. Yams are both the largest and the most highly prized local food crop, and in 1959 their output was estimated at 1,300,000 tons. They are followed in order of declining importance by manioc (700,000 tons), plantain bananas (500,000 tons), taros and sweet potatoes (150,000 tons), millet and sorghum (85,000 tons), paddy (75,000 tons), and corn (45,000 tons).

Of the Ivory Coast's total food production, perhaps one-third is sold in local markets by African women. The quality of the commercialized product is usually defective, having often suffered mishaps on its way to market, and the price asked from buyers varies widely with the sellers' estimate made of their income. Some effort is being made to improve the yields and quality of food crops at the agricultural stations of Bouaké and Ferkessédougou, but the Ivory Coast could grow a great deal more and better food crops than it does today. Although Ivoirians have never known a famine and food production has generally kept pace with the population's growth, the country continues to import between 30,000 and 50,000 tons of rice a year, as well as considerable quantities of palm oil. Despite the existence of natural palm groves covering more than 700,000 hectares, the Dabou oil mill has never worked to capacity. If the amount of food produced in the Ivory Coast is fairly adequate, the diet of most Ivoirians is poorly balanced. Tubers have acquired too large a place in their eating habits, and they suffer generally from a lack of fats and proteins.

The Ivory Coast is a big consumer of both sea and fresh-water fish, but the supply is far from equal to the demand. In recent years there has been a considerable development of the industrial fishing of tuna and sardines, and Abidjan has become a major fishing port of the franc zone. In 1960 the catch landed at Abidjan amounted to 50,000 tons, and by 1964 an increase of 20,000 tons is expected. Modern facilities for the industry and a training center for apprentice fishermen are being built at Abidjan, which should stimulate production and also "nationalize" this occupation. At present it is Ghanaian, Togolese, and Dahomeyan fishermen who are responsible for most of the catch brought into Abidjan, and the government wants more Ivoirians—who traditionally are more predisposed to farming—to take up fishing. Another governmental project is to improve the distribution system through the establishment of refrigerated transport facilities for the interior. Currently some 4,000 tons of dried fish from Mopti and Ségou in the Mali Republic are sold every year in the Bouaké market. Also to stimulate fish consumption in the hinterland, family ponds are being built there and stocked with fish (mainly tilapia) produced at the two state-owned hatcheries at Bamoro and Korhogo.

It is officially recognized, however, that any large-scale increase in the Ivoirians' protein consumption depends upon a big expansion of the meat industry. The Ivory Coast has no more than about 270,000 head of cattle. Most of its animals are pigs and poultry. Traditionally, Ivoirian villagers have grown poultry for their own consumption, and it has only been since cooperative societies began to develop in 1955 that chickens and eggs have been produced on a commercial scale. Pigs are also bred for sale and for consumption by their owners. As the great majority of Ivoirians are not Muslims, pork is widely eaten. Only about 20 tons of that meat were imported in 1959. It is estimated that some 55,000 pigs are utilized for their meat each year, although pig slaughtering is not officially controlled. It is beef and mutton that are in shortest supply, and all the *cercles* except Odienné and Korhogo import meat. About 40 per cent of such imports come from Upper Volta and 60 per cent from Niger. As most of these animals are driven south on foot, many perish on the way, and those that arrive in the Ivory Coast reach there in a depleted condition. To satisfy the normal consumer needs of the present population in beef and mutton, the Ivory Coast needs to increase its cattle herds fourfold and those of sheep and goats threefold. As the northern savannah zone offers vast areas of grazing land, there seems to be no reason why the official plan to develop animal husbandry in that area should not be successfully carried out, and the Common Market countries have now provided the funds needed to set up the first of three ranches which will raise the N'Dama and Baoulé cattle that are especially well suited to the country. A big meat industry would find a large and ready local market, especially in view of the Ivory Coast's expanding population, and some of its output could probably also be shipped to nearby coastal countries.

Of the Ivory Coast's established exports, the oldest is timber, shipments of which began in 1880. Indeed, the Ivory Coast has been the only French West African territory to grow commercially valuable woods on a large scale. Although exports have increased rapidly, they have never attained maximum development because of the shortage of local labor, transport difficulties, the instability of the world market for tropical woods, and the dispersed location of valuable species. The future of this industry depends upon the reforestation of an area of approximately 200,000 hectares. Forest reserves now cover over 5,000,000 hectares, but mahogany and iroko are the only two varieties that have given rise to an appreciable export trade. In 1952 the Ivoirian forest industry underwent a grave crisis owing to a sharp fall in the price paid for its exports and to competition in the European market from less costly Ghanaian and Nigerian woods. The territorial assembly came to its rescue by guaranteeing a sizable loan to this industry and by reducing the export duty on its output from 6 per cent to 2 per cent, in return for the foresters' pledge to cut down production costs. Since then exports have risen rapidly and are expected soon to reach a million cubic meters a year. In 1959 there were 88 forest enterprises operating in the country, as well as 28 sawmills with a combined annual capacity of 70,000 cubic meters. The imminent establishment of a paper pulp industry will provide Ivoirian foresters with an important local market to supplement the much smaller one now represented by the two existing plywood factories.

For some years the Ivory Coast, except in the extreme north, has been evolving beyond the stage of a subsistence economy to one of trading in raw and processed agricultural materials. It is now moving rapidly toward industrialization. Industrial activity, in the modern sense of the term, began only in 1952, two years after the opening of the Vridi Canal had permitted a vast development of the port of Abidjan. This development not only encouraged the expansion of exports but also enabled the Ivory Coast to import heavy equipment essential for its industrialization. Further stimulus was given to this process by the passage of an investment code by the assembly on January 22, 1959. This code granted appreciable advantages to investors who created or expanded plants judged to be of primary importance to the country's economy, and the laws, under which long-term concessions have been made, are now serving as models for some other West African countries. Basic company taxes are low, for example, and many companies have paid virtually no taxes at all for a decade. Moreover, the government has not insisted on having any considerable participation in newly organized industries, there are no state-run development corporations, and the officially controlled produce-buying cooperatives have no export organizations and merely sell to private trading firms in Abidjan.[7]

By its special legislation, the range of its natural resources, and the stability of its government, the Ivory Coast has inspired the confidence of private capitalists. Industry has been developing at a rapid tempo, the volume of such business increasing regularly at the rate of 1,500,-000,000 francs a year. By the end of 1958 it reached a total value of 8,500,000,000 CFA francs and was employing some 8,000 workers. (The CFA [Colonies Françaises d'Afrique] franc was worth two metropolitan francs.) Currently, industry is about one-quarter as important as agriculture in the Ivory Coast's economy, and this percentage is growing rapidly. By the end of 1960, the country had approximately 50 industrial enterprises and its industrial turnover came to over 10,000,000,000 CFA francs. Thirty or so of those enterprises did an annual volume of business amounting to over 100,000,000 CFA francs while 7 or 8 of them exceeded 400,000,000. Although most of the country's industries are located in the south in or near Abidjan, Bouaké has also become an important industrial center through its location in the cotton, tobacco, and sisal growing zone. The majority of these industries process local products, either for export or for the domestic market, or both.

Food-processing industries are the oldest and most important of all, accounting for about 40 per cent of the Ivory Coast's total industrial output and an annual volume of business worth about 3,000,000,000 CFA francs. They include plants producing breadstuffs, beer and soft drinks, ice, margarine, refined peanut and palm oil, fruit juice and canned fruit, and tinned tuna fish and cocoa- and coffee-processing enterprises. There are also textile industries, plywood factories, chemical and fats plants, machine and metal industries, as well as a building industry. A large flour mill, four instant-coffee plants, a Renault as-

[7] *West Africa*, Aug. 19, 1961.

sembly plant, and factories producing matches, bicycles, paper pulp, latex, and aluminum sheets are in process of being built. Under consideration is the establishment of industries producing refined sugar, fish meal, and tinned meat.[8]

Mining has been the least-developed industry in the Ivory Coast because large-scale prospecting has been undertaken only in recent years and because the operations of the only two such existing industries have proved discouraging to potential investors. In the regions of the Cavally and Sassandra rivers two companies have been extracting gold and diamonds, but their combined output in 1958 came to only 4.5 kilograms and 157,000 carats respectively. (These figures do not include the unknown amounts of locally produced gold and diamonds that entered into the flourishing contraband trade. The government estimates that over 40,000 persons each year infiltrate the Ivory Coast to prospect clandestinely for diamonds in the Seguéla region, and in November, 1961, a law was passed severely penalizing all those involved directly or indirectly in such fraudulent operations.)

In 1957 the government drew up a large-scale and costly prospecting program in the belief that the Ivory Coast must possess unknown and valuable deposits because of its proximity to mineral-rich Ghana. It was further encouraged by the discovery at the end of 1955 of manganese ore near Grand Lahou. Reserves amounting to 13,000,000 tons are expected to lead to the extraction of about 100,000 tons a year, and in 1960 a private company—the Société Moktar-el-Hadid— began mining operations. Although the manganese of Grand Lahou is of little account, if judged by world standards, and its quality is mediocre (46–48 per cent of manganese), the ore is accessibly located and easy to extract and, above all, its export will help to balance the Ivory Coast's predominantly agricultural economy. Traces of bauxite, iron, copper, and chromite have also been found in various parts of the country, but the search for petroleum has thus far proved disappointing. The Société Africaine des Pétroles is continuing prospecting, but in April, 1960, its American associate, the Plymouth Oil Company, terminated its interest in exploratory drilling operations.

The lack of such sources of power as petroleum and coal has been a serious handicap to the Ivory Coast's industrialization. Costly imported fuel has had to be used in the 9 plants generating limited amounts of

---

[8] For details about the Ivory Coast's industries, especially their location and capacities, see *La République de Côte d'Ivoire*, Nov. 7, 1959, *Marchés Tropicaux*, June 3, 1961, and *Europe-France-Outremer*, Dec., 1960.

electrical power (31,000,000 kwh. in 1958). Late in 1960 a power plant was opened at Ayamé, following construction of a dam across the Bia River, and it is planned soon to expand this enterprise to its potential capacity of 80,000,000 kwh. In June, 1961, the French government agreed to guarantee the financing of this expansion in order to supply the current required by the growth of Abidjan and the industrialization of the Ivory Coast. French private interests are reportedly willing to finance the investment, which it is estimated will cost some 10,000,-000 new francs. If this project materializes, the resulting supply of cheap and abundant electricity should enable Abidjan to replace Dakar as the premier industrial town of French-speaking Negro Africa.

The expansion of the Ivory Coast's internal and foreign trade has naturally been closely linked to the development of its means of communication, particularly that of its seaports. Cutting of the Vridi Canal through the bar that separated the Ebrié lagoon from the Gulf of Guinea, which was completed in 1950, gave an enormous impetus to the whole economy of the Ivory Coast. By transforming Abidjan from a lagoon to a deepwater port the delays and expense involved in utilizing the wharves of Grand Bassam and Port Bouët were eliminated. Indeed, those two wharves are no longer used by ocean-going shipping, and almost all of the Ivory Coast's foreign trade now passes through the port of Abidjan. The ports of Sassandra (34,000 tons a year) and of Tabou (1,600 tons) handle only very limited amounts of cargo, and air freight accounts for but a mere 2,000 or so tons annually of the country's external commerce. Abidjan's importance as a port has grown phenomenally: in 1960 it handled nearly 1,800,000 tons of imports and exports compared with a little over half a million tons ten years before. With the imminent construction of supplementary ore-loading and fishing ports, the role played by Abidjan will be still further enhanced.

Ivoirian roads, airplanes, and railroad have also increased their carrying capacity though they have not expanded so spectacularly as has the port of Abidjan. Between 1947 and 1957, French public funds to the amount of nearly 4,000,000,000 CFA francs were spent on the road network, and in the latter year the Ivory Coast had a total of 8,752 kilometers of roads. Orientation of the highway system was determined by the need to increase communications with adjacent countries and, even more, to facilitate the export of local produce. Inevitably, the forest zone has been the region most favored with roads, and about three-fourths of the Ivory Coast's cocoa and coffee exports are carried by road to the ports of Abidjan and Sassandra. Also largely concentrated in the south are the 15,700 or so private motor vehicles and the nearly 12,000 trucks that have been imported into the country. When the Renault assembly plant enters into full operation, the road network will probably have to be enlarged to meet the additional carrying load.

In 1954, the Abidjan-Niger railroad, which had been begun thirty years before and suffered many delays, was finally extended to the Voltaic capital, Ouagadougou. Of its total length of 1,175 kilometers, about 600 are in the Ivory Coast. This railroad's rolling stock has been increased and modernized: it now comprises 790 passenger and freight cars and (since 1956) it is wholly diesel-powered. Since 1957, the traffic handled by this line has been growing by leaps and bounds, but it still runs at a deficit and the Ivory Coast budget has to pay about 60 per cent of its maintenance costs. The railroad is operated jointly by the governments of the Ivory Coast and Upper Volta following an agreement reached between them on April 4, 1959. As to aviation, Abidjan has an airport that can accommodate jet planes, and there are about sixteen secondary airports in other towns throughout the country.

Among French West African territories, the Ivory Coast has been distinguished by a regularly favorable balance of trade. The relative scale of its external trading and of its people's living standards in the last days of the Federation was shown by the fact that, although the Ivoirians accounted for only 13 per cent of all the federal population, the Ivory Coast was responsible for nearly half of French West African exports and absorbed almost a fourth of its imports. Its foreign trade, which seemed stabilized in 1955–1956, surged ahead following the dissolution of the Federation, and this advance has continued with the expansion and increasing diversification of its production. The change in the structure of the Ivory Coast's exports has been accompanied by a less-marked modification in the range of its clients and provisioners and also in the type of its imports.

The import picture for the Ivory Coast is not a clear one, and further changes may be expected within the next few years if the tempo of its industrialization is maintained and if the government's plan to increase food production is carried out. Imports of all categories have tended to increase in volume and value, but the relative position of consumer and equipment goods has changed from one year to another. Textiles, fuel, and cement have generally topped the list in recent years, while the position of food imports has fluctuated considerably. The importation of alcoholic beverages has increased since the ban on their entry into the country was lifted in January, 1960, and will probably continue to grow. But the imports of flour should decline after the Grands Moulins d'Abidjan enter into full production and a quota is imposed on the shipment of foreign flour into the Ivory Coast. Similarly, fuel importation must dwindle when the Bia hydroelectrical dam is completed, and the quantity of machinery and other equipment goods brought into the country should expand when the new industrial projects already approved by the assembly get under way.

Sources of supply have changed less than the type of imports, for the African clientele is notably faithful to established brands of merchandise. Although 3,000,000 or so Ivoirians represent only a small market for imported goods, the population as well as its living standards are growing rapidly. In 1951 a report of the United Nations estimated the annual income of the average Ivoirian family at 23,000 francs; in 1956 this had increased by an estimated 7,000 francs. By 1960 it approximated 35,000 francs, compared with an average of 10,000 francs for the rest of former Franch West Africa and with less than 5,000 francs in such poor territories as Niger and Upper Volta. Savings bank accounts also reflect the Ivoirians' growing wealth: their total rose from 123,000,000 francs in 1955 to 187,000,000 in 1958. A study of Ivoirian family budgets made in 1957 showed that the lowest-income groups spent two-thirds of their revenues on the purchase of foodstuffs, most of which were grown in the country. Thus it is not surprising that food is the major item of internal trade in the Ivory Coast. Because of the increasing concentration of the southern region on the production of export goods, its population has become a growing market for the food produced in the center and north of the country. This demand has stimulated the expansion and diversification of food crops and has served to introduce a money economy into the savannah zone, which until recently produced exclusively for its own subsistence.

Cola nuts—consumed widely as a stimulant especially by the Muslim populations—are the sole agricultural item which the coastal zone sends to the north. This commodity is believed to represent an annual value of about 1,500,000,000 CFA francs. If they are shipped by road, colas furnish a profitable return freight for trucks bringing dried fish, small animals, yams, and rice to the south. The exact value of this trade in agricultural produce is unknown, but it is large enough to provide a livelihood for many transporters and middlemen. Not all these shipments originate in the Ivory Coast, and most of the livestock and some of the dried fish sold in the country come from Upper Volta, Niger, and the Mali Republic. Of all the internal trade, that in animals is the most remunerative. Between 40,000 and 50,000 sheep and goats and between 30,000 and 40,000 cattle are imported annually and sold in the Ivory Coast to the value of some 2,000,000,000 CFA francs a year. It is believed that this trade could be made far more profitable than it currently is and, at the same time, that better-quality and cheaper meat could be made available to the coastal populations. Such improvements, however, depend upon drastic changes being made in the trading habits and organization of the Dioulas and Peulhs who now control this commerce.

Traditionally, coffee, cocoa, timber, and bananas comprise the bulk of the Ivory Coast's exports, and in terms of value they account for 94 per cent of the total. Those four commodities maintained their pre-eminence, but their relative positions have changed since 1959. Between 1948 and 1958 the volume of exports more than doubled, and in the latter year coffee and cocoa made up about 80 per cent of total exports in value. Coffee production and exports expanded steadily, but those of cocoa began to flag because of poor yields due to adverse climatic conditions and to the over-age of most Ivoirian bushes. Beginning in 1959, a relative decline occurred in those two basic exports that redounded to the improved status of wood and banana exports, which represented that year over 21 per cent of the value of all exports compared with 8 per cent in 1954. Also in 1959, a change began in the orientation of the Ivory Coast's external commerce. France (and the franc zone) still held top rank as the country's chief market, taking 63.5 per cent of total exports in terms of value, but this share was smaller than in 1958 when that country took 73.8 per cent of the whole. Correspondingly, the participation in the Ivory Coast's foreign trade of countries outside the franc zone (as well as their number) rose from 26.7 per cent to 36.5 per cent in 1959. Thus the PDCI government was beginning to achieve success in its efforts to open up new markets without losing the old ones.

The year 1960 saw these trends accentuated. Foreign trade increased, especially exports, which totaled 1,007,598 tons and sold for 37,328,-000,000 CFA francs compared with 35,820,000,000 the preceding year. Coffee exports again increased as regards both tonnage and their proportionate value. The 147,488 tons of coffee shipped out represented over half the value of total exports, whereas in 1959 this percentage came to slightly over 47 per cent. Cocoa exports remained fairly stable as to volume—70,896 tons compared with 63,263 tons in 1959—but their proportionate value declined from 31.3 per cent of the total to 23.3 per cent. The most notable expansion in 1960 occurred in timber and banana shipments. Wood exports amounted to 654,824 tons and 17 per cent of the total value, whereas in 1959 they had come to 444,247 tons or 12.8 per cent of the value of all the Ivory Coast's exports. Banana shipments similarly, though less sharply, increased, rising from 55,995 tons to 72,620 tons. In 1960, those four commodities together still represented—as they had the preceding year—all but 6 per cent of the Ivory Coast's shipments in terms of value, but the appearance of the first manganese ore and latex shipments may soon change this percentage. Palm kernel, diamond, and pineapple exports remain negligible items.

After the Vridi Canal was cut, the trading structure of the Ivory Coast began to undergo a transformation that has become more pronounced in recent years. Until 1950, the country's commerce was in the hands of two main groups of traders. The more important of the two were the big European import-export firms, few in number, which bought most of the local export crops and distributed imported goods throughout the hinterland. The second group comprised a host of European and African traders, whose operations resembled those of the big firms but were much more localized and on a far smaller scale. As of 1953, there were about 300 licensed export-import merchants, of whom only 40 or so did an annual volume of business exceeding 100,-000,000 CFA francs. Since that time the big trading houses, though still solidly entrenched, have tended to restrict their circuits of purchasing and distribution. This has been largely due to the proliferation of middlemen who have been attracted to trading by the country's rapidly growing commerce. Many of these newcomers are alien Africans and some of them are Syrians or Lebanese. Their activities have greatly enlarged the Ivory Coast's commercial network. Another recent development also related to the country's expanding prosperity is the trend in the main urban centers toward commercial specialization, including the birth of a retail trade in luxury and semiluxury items.

The Ivory Coast's outstanding prosperity naturally raises the question as to what degree it has been due to outside aid. Between 1947 and 1957, the country received the equivalent of $109,000,000 from French public funds; in one form or another France has continued to grant it subsidies on a generous scale. The United States is the only other foreign country from which the Ivory Coast has accepted aid, but according to the agreement of May, 1961, the amount granted— only $7,000,000 for all four Entente countries—is comparatively negligible. Since the Ivory Coast has a large dollar surplus from its coffee and cocoa exports to the United States, American aid mainly takes the form of merchandise and of technical service. What most profoundly differentiates the Ivory Coast from other French-speaking African states is the exceptionally large contribution that it has been able to make toward self-development from its own resources.

On July 30, 1957, two months after the setting up of the first PDCI government, its spokesman announced that the cost of personnel would be reduced to 50 per cent of total expenditures and that the funds thus saved would be mainly devoted to development projects. Obviously the conflict that later developed between the party and the civil service was not unrelated to the thoroughness with which this policy of retrenchment was applied. But such a pruning of expenditures produced nothing like so much revenues for development projects as did the fiscal reform that was carried out in 1959. The fiscal concessions then granted to investors and the suppression of the head tax were more than offset by the 25 per cent increase in import duties and, above all, by a sharp rise in income taxes. In January, 1960, the government was able to announce not only that taxes had been more rapidly collected but also that there had been a 20 per cent increase in fiscal revenue. The Ivory Coast's budget naturally reflected the country's accelerated wealth after 70 per cent of its revenues were made dependent upon taxing the incomes of producers. The budget for 1959 came to 21,725,000,000 CFA francs, or double that of 1958. In 1960 the budget totaled 24,718,000,000 CFA francs, and the next year marked another rise to 27,210,000,000—a staggeringly large amount for a French Negro African territory. Although expenditures involved in the Ivory Coast's acquisition of sovereignty have tended to absorb much of this surplus, the government has been able to set aside every year since 1958 about 4,000,000,000 CFA francs for expenditure on its basic equipment.

SOCIAL STRUCTURE

The Ivory Coast is believed to have well over 60 different ethnic groups, but of these only 7 are sizable. The Agni-Ashanti-Baoulé group lives in the southeast and includes, as well, the Appoloniens, Ehoutilé, Essouma, Gnan, and Abro. The Koua-Koua and Krumen group, with the Bété and Bakoué, inhabit the southwest. In the northeast and northwest are to be found the Mandé, who also comprise the Malinké, Marka, Bafing, and Bambara tribes. In addition, they include the Dioulas, who are a mobile people, many of them trading in the main centers. Also in the north live the Senoufos, and in the center reside the Dan and Gourou groups. Finally, there are remnants of such tribes as the Bobos, Lobi, and Peulh, whose main tribal branches are found in other territories. The great majority of these tribes are animists, though the Peulhs, some of the Mandé, and, above all, the Senoufos are Muslims.

The Ivory Coast is fortunate in not being a prey to religious or inter-tribal strife among its indigenous peoples. In part this is due to Houphouët's strong leadership and in part to the absence of basic ethnic conflicts such as those that divide the Soussous and the Peulhs in Guinea. Numerically no single tribe dominates the country, though in terms of enterprise, ability, and education the Baoulé and Agni-Ashanti groups probably lead the others. The PDCI has apparently absorbed or neutralized the various tribal and other organizations that were created by the French administration in the late 1940's as a counterpoise to the RDA. The fact that Houphouët is himself a chief and a Catholic has served to check most of the centrifugal tendencies that might have otherwise developed among such elements, though ethnic separatism is always a latent danger.

It is the relatively recent factor of wealth that has created the present divisions in Ivoirian society, which exist between the coastal and the northern zones and between the indigenous population and the immigrants. The prosperity of the south has had the dual effect of creating a rural bourgeoisie and of attracting foreigners, whose presence has awakened a national consciousness among the Ivoirians. Houphouët has bowed to the strength of this feeling for the sake of national unity. He has eliminated the Togolese and Dahomeyans from Ivory Coast's civil service and has transferred his French collaborators to less conspicuous posts. Since social stratification among Ivoirians is a recent phenomenon, he may be able partially to check its more aggressive aspects by raising the level of the less-privileged elements to that of the coastal zone bourgeoisie.

The socioeconomic group for which Houphouët has shown the least apparent consideration is that of labor. Obviously what he regards as the politically subversive activities of the trade unions and the comparatively privileged situation of their members are responsible for his severe measures toward them. In its efforts to check the fast-rising cost of living in the Ivory Coast, the PDCI government long held out against the unions' demands for increased wages. When some concessions in this domain were finally granted in September, 1960, workers on plantations and forest enterprises who comprised 80 per cent of the country's labor force were excluded from such benefits.

In view of the importance of export crops to the Ivory Coast's economy and also the scarcity of labor in the forest zone, it seems surprising that so little effort has apparently been made either by radical leaders or by the government to organize rural labor or to improve its working conditions. Perhaps the seasonal character of such labor, its geographical dispersal, the difficulty of reaching and then applying agreements with Upper Volta to regulate the immigration and status of Mossi workers, and finally the fact that it is Ivoirian planters who are major employers of rural wage labor explain this apparent oversight.

Although the Ivory Coast, along with Senegal, has for some years paid the highest wages in all French-speaking Negro Africa and has reduced the number of its wage zones from three to two, the cost of living in the country has risen even more rapidly than the wage earners' income. In the first or higher-paid zone, the hourly wage in 1960 for all but agricultural workers was 37 CFA francs (compared with 19.25 in 1953), but the cost of living index had doubled between 1953 and 1960 while wages had not been increased since 1958. In April, 1960, the Ivory Coast Labor Advisory Commission had recommended an increase in the minimum wage, but nothing was done for the next eight months to carry out this suggestion. It was not until the progovernment Union Nationale des Syndicats de la Côte d'Ivoire had protested and asserted that this delay was causing a dangerous malaise in working-class circles that the government finally moved. It then raised the hourly wage by 8 per cent, but only for organized urban workers.

In its relations with labor, the government's main concern has been to control the turbulent civil servants' unions, though it has also readjusted some wage scales, imposed price controls, and drafted collective agreements for certain categories of urban workers. The major labor item on the PDCI agenda has been the organization of a single labor *centrale* in the Ivory Coast, and this has proved to be a time-consuming task. It was not until June 22, 1961, that the conference was held at which a single Union Générale des Travailleurs de la Côte d'Ivoire was finally created. This conference was attended by high government officials, representatives of management, and delegates from the three surviving *centrales* as well as the unaffiliated unions. As the result of careful preparation, all four of the unions' spokesmen agreed to detach their organizations from all international labor movements and to endorse the principle of a unified labor organization that would follow occupational or geographical lines. At almost the same time Houphouët moved to solve the unemployment problem in Abidjan by instituting a modified form of forced labor. With the introduction of compulsory military service in July, 1961, all conscripts were required to devote half of their twelve months' term of duty to carrying out "works of civic construction." Because so many of the basic problems in this domain are similar to those in other French-speaking Negro countries, the policy that Houphouët has evolved bears a striking resemblance to those worked out by Senghor in Senegal and Modibo Keita in Mali. Each of these three leaders has been trying to forge a multipurpose united organization by which he can control union activities and utilize the unemployed or underemployed manpower, especially in urban centers, for execution of projects which he considers essential to economic development.

In his efforts to create national unity in the Ivory Coast, Houphouët has been indirectly aided by the notable absence of religious fanaticism. The great majority of Ivoirians seem to be firmly animist, with Muslims and Christians representing only small minorities. Muslims comprise some 15 per cent of the total population, and for the most part they are concentrated in the north. Those living near the frontiers of Mali and Upper Volta are the descendants of converts made by the conquerors who came down from the Niger Bend area before the French occupation. The residue are largely made up of the Dioulas and their converts who form pockets of Muslims in the Bouaké, Dimbokro, and Agboville regions. Virtually all these isolated groups are surrounded by animists who have apparently resisted the encroachments of Islam. There are said to be only two authorized Koranic schools in the Ivory Coast, and, at most, about fifty Ivoirians a year make the pilgrimage to Mecca. Most Ivoirian Muslims belong to the Tidjaniya sect, though there are some followers of the Qadriya in the northeast. None of these Muslims appears to be fervent proselytizers, and many of the Senoufo and Mandé Muslims are believed also to practice animist rites. Even Yacoub Sylla of Gagnoa, for many years the Ivory Coast's outstanding Islamic leader, who was regarded with suspicion by the French authorities for his alleged contacts with the Arab League, seems to have attracted followers more by his wealth than by his religious or political activities. If Islam as a religious force is superficial in the Ivory Coast, the same can also be said of Christianity. The only recorded spurt of religious zeal in the country was the Harris movement, founded by a Liberian Negro on the eve of World War I. In many ways Harris resembled the founders of the politico-religious sects in Equatorial Africa during the interwar period, and his movement followed much the same course. It spread like wildfire in the region of Fresco and Grand Bassam, but after Harris was exiled in 1915 by the colonial administration, his followers reportedly became either Catholics or Protestants. The revival of what was called Neo-Harrisism after World War II likewise seems to have been a religious flash in the pan.

In the early twentieth century many Ivoirians, like those in other parts of French West Africa, sought the support of the missions vis-à-vis the administration, and they were similarly attracted by the schools and medical centers run by missionaries. After World War II, the Catholic missions strongly opposed the RDA until the latter changed its policy in 1950. Thereafter the PDCI and especially its Catholic leader have collaborated with the missions to the point where the government now grants sizable subsidies to the mission schools. Over 60,000 youthful Ivoirians, or about one-third of all the children attending school in the Ivory Coast, are pupils of the parochial primary schools. Secondary education is also given to about 1,460 students by the missions, which employ in all some 1,500 teachers.

Catholics are more numerous and influential than Protestants, especially in the coastal zone. Of the more than 300,000 baptized Catholics, 123,335 belong to the 24 parishes that comprise the archdiocese of Abidjan. Since April, 1960, an Ivoirian priest—Monseigneur Bernard Yago—has been archbishop of Abidjan, but of the 102 priests who serve under him only 22 are Africans. The small number of indigenous priests has hampered Catholic efforts at evangelization, but a more serious obstacle is the materialism and anticlerical attitude of many Ivoirians. Of all the French-speaking African states except Guinea, it is in the Ivory Coast that there is the strongest demand for laicizing the mission schools. On several recent occasions, various local youth organizations and the teachers in state schools have protested against the government's granting of subsidies to mission education.

Ever since the first school in the Ivory Coast was opened at Assinie in 1882, the administration has been trying to make up for this late start, but it is in the past decade that the greatest such efforts have been made. Under the Ivory Coast's first two plans, most of the funds earmarked for education went to primary schools. In 1947 some 310,000, or only 9 per cent of the children of school age, attended primary schools, and 192 students were being given secondary education in three establishments. By January, 1958, over 22 per cent of the 480,000 children of school age attended primary schools, and secondary instruction was being received by 4,210 students in 11 institutions. Technical education has also been expanded through the establishment of a technical college and of two centers of apprenticeship, with a combined attendance of 750 pupils. That same year, 960 Ivoirians (of whom 220 had state scholarships) were studying at universities in France and 171 at the University of Dakar. Also in 1958 there opened at Abidjan a Center of Higher Studies, whose first class had an enrollment of over 200 students. By the Franco-Ivoirian agreement of May 6, 1961, France is to give both financial and technical aid for the transformation of this Center into a university that will be open to qualified students from all the Entente states and will give degrees and diplomas the equivalent of those granted by analogous French institutions. Currently about a fifth of the Ivory Coast's revenues are devoted to the promotion of education.

Despite this very considerable effort, the progress of education in the Ivory Coast is encountering difficulties. The main obstacles are the uneven distribution of schools and the dearth of qualified teachers. In Korhogo in the extreme north, only 10 per cent of the children of school age—and far fewer girls than boys—are attending school, whereas in Abengourou and Abidjan *cercles* the percentages are, respectively, 87 per cent and 83 per cent. In 1958 teachers in state schools totaled 1,423, but of these only 1,071 were instructors and the majority were monitors. Moreover, the percentage of the latter to the former has been steadily increasing. A major obstacle to any marked improvement in this situation has been the lack of aptitude or unwillingness of young Ivoirians to enter the teaching profession and, above all, to accept an assignment to a northern school. Furthermore, so great is the demand for education and so rapid the growth of population that the government has not been able to keep pace, even in regard to the construction of school buildings and of teachers' housing.

THE PRESS AND OTHER MEDIA OF COMMUNICATION

The Ivory Coast has the distinction of being the first French West African territory to have had a newspaper founded and published by

Africans. This was the *Eclaireur de la Côte d'Ivoire,* first printed in 1935, which was an immediate success with African readers. Its second mark of distinction is its survival, for most of the many papers started in the Ivory Coast have had a very short life span.[9] In common with the press in other French-speaking African countries, the Ivory Coast's newspapers have been characterized by inadequate financing, poor editing, and small circulations. Abidjan cannot yet rival Dakar as a publishing center, as regards either quantity or quality of output. But it does possess some fairly stable journals, notably one belonging to the Breteuil chain (*Abidjan-Matin*) and the PDCI party organ (*Fraternité*). The imminent establishment of an Agence Ivoirien de Presse was announced in May, 1961, to be headed by a committee composed exclusively of Ivoirians. As this committee was to include government officers as well as representatives of the press, its advent may herald the institution of strict official controls.

The small circulation figures of Abidjan newspapers should not be taken as a literal indication of their reading public. In 1954 it was estimated that for every copy of a newspaper purchased in the Ivory Coast there were at least 100 African readers.[10] The Ivoirians are by no means bereft of news, and in the prosperous south many illiterates have their own radio sets through which they can and do listen to broadcasts. Radio-Abidjan, founded in 1951 as a satellite of Radio-Dakar, began broadcasting in four local languages the following year. It has been replaced by a new 100-kilowatt transmitter, which began experimental broadcasting in February, 1961. Radio-Abidjan is now one of the most modern and powerful stations in Africa, and its broadcasts reportedly can be heard in Europe and the United States and in Africa from the Canary Islands to Libya.

The Political Process

THE FORMAL STRUCTURE OF GOVERNMENT

Adopted on October 31, 1960, the current constitution of the Ivory Coast subscribes to the principles of France's Declaration of the Rights of Man, proclaiming the Ivoirian republic to be "one and indivisible, secular, democratic, and social." It also lays down that the official lan-

[9] For a description of the newspapers that have appeared in the Ivory Coast since World War II see F. J. Amon d'Aby, *La Côte d'Ivoire dans la Cité Africaine* (Paris, 1951), p. 61, and Helen Kitchen, *The Press in Africa* (Washington, D.C., 1956), p. 87.

[10] *Vente et Publicité,* July–Aug., 1954.

guage is French and endorses the motto of "Union, Discipline, and Work." Executive power is exercised by the President of the Republic, who is elected for a five-year term by direct universal suffrage. The President is empowered to appoint and dismiss the ministers who are responsible to him, to negotiate treaties, and to command the country's armed forces. Legislative power lies with a seventy-member assembly, also elected by direct universal suffrage and at the same time as the President and for the same term. This assembly votes upon the laws submitted to it either by the President or by one of its members. He may ask for a reconsideration of a bill, which then must be passed by two-thirds of the assembly's members. The President, assisted by a High Council of the Magistracy, guarantees the independence of the judiciary. But a High Court of Justice may try the President for high treason and the members of his government for "crimes and misdemeanors committed in the exercise of their functions, and for conspiracy against the security of the state." In addition, the constitution provides for a Supreme Court made up of four chambers and an Economic and Social Council modeled after that of France.

POLITICAL DYNAMICS

Since World War II, the Ivory Coast and Senegal have been regarded as the most developed territories in French West Africa. In recent years Abidjan has been increasingly challenging the position of Dakar as the economic and political—though not the intellectual—capital of French-speaking Negro Africa. The breakup of the Mali Federation has adversely affected both Senegal's economy and the international influence of its leaders, whereas the Ivory Coast has surged rapidly forward and its leader, Félix Houphouët-Boigny, has regained his preeminence in the West African political scene.

In many respects the Ivory Coast is a country of paradox and contradictions. It was the first French Negro territory to organize a mass party and, with the support of the French Communist Party, to conduct a vigorous campaign against the colonial administration. But beginning in 1950, this policy was completely reversed. On the world stage, the locally dominant party—the Parti Démocratique de la Côte d'Ivoire (PDCI)—broke with international Marxism and moved toward the Western powers. On the local scene, the PDCI cooperated more closely thereafter with the colonial administration and with the resident French business community than any African party in any other French West African territory. By 1958 the Ivory Coast had become the main advocate of close and direct ties with France and of a Franco-African Community that would be a federal republic composed of autonomous but not sovereign states. Then suddenly in 1959, after having firmly and repeatedly rejected the formation of any primary federation in Africa because it would lead to political independence from France, the Ivory Coast became the founder and financier of a group of nearby countries—the Council of the Entente. And finally in 1960, the leader of the Ivory Coast demanded for all members of the Entente independence from France without committing them to remain in the Franco-African Community or even to make any prior agreements of cooperation with the French government. Partially and more gradually, the established policy of Houphouët—that of utilizing Frenchmen as members of the government and of the assembly—has also been modified, as has that of welcoming any and all nonindigenous Africans into the local body politic and economic. In every case these policy shifts have been made in response to the famous "winds of change" in West Africa.

The original but unplanned course that the Ivory Coast has followed is due almost wholly to the leadership of Houphouët-Boigny. His influence is probably more extensive than that of any other West African leader, though he remains comparatively unknown in the world at large. Less flamboyant than Nkrumah or Sékou Touré, his ambitions are no whit less grandiose than theirs. Like Senghor, he has been a force in Paris politics without losing his African touch. But unlike Senghor, he is no savant or creator of an original political philosophy. His approach to politics is wholly pragmatic, and consequently he is more susceptible and sensitive than they to external influences. When he realizes that a policy is ineffective, he has no compunctions about discarding it and substituting a contradictory one. Unity and prosperity for Africa in general and for the Ivory Coast in particular appear to be his main goals, but the trail that he has blazed toward them is a circuitous one, and Houphouët has remained largely a behind-the-scenes operator. He excels at personal diplomacy and at party organization, and only when he has failed by those means to win over his opponents does he use harsher measures. Moreover, force is not only a last resort but usually a temporary one, for almost invariably those to whom it has been applied soon see the light, repent, and are welcomed back into Houphouët's fold. His major decisions are reached after a period of solitary meditation, often in his native village. To carry them out, however, he brings into play all the resources at his disposal. These resources are his persuasiveness, firm grip on the party machinery, and the wealth of the Ivory Coast. An acute observer, André Blanchet of *Le Monde,* wrote of Houphouët early in 1961:

Venerated and protected by his Negro and white entourage as if he were the living Buddha, the object of an adulation which he has never sought but which is lavished upon him by both official and unofficial milieus, Houphouët has not acted either as a dictator or a monarch. To affirm his authority he has no need of the scepter of command, like Nkrumah, of the impressive bearing of a Modibo Keita, or of the sex appeal of a Sékou Touré. He even appears to be timid. Houphouët's magnetism and the respect that he inspires derive from something else—a mysticism expressed in his smile and the persuasive quality of his words. Strongly rooted in his native village of Yamoussoukro, Houphouët feels sufficiently African not to have to wear the Baoulé tribal dress. Following his example, not a single deputy wore his tribal costume when the assembly met on January 3, 1961, whereas tribal dress is almost *de rigueur* in the Ghana parliament. But even in Paris, Houphouët never eats any food but African *foufou* . . . and he is an austere man who neither smokes nor drinks alcohol.[11]

Houphouët's publicly expressed attitude toward an opposition—that he is not in principle opposed to one provided that it is constructive, but that it is an unnecessary luxury—is remarkably close to the views expressed by the leaders of the Union Soudanaise and the Parti Démocratique de Guinée. In reply to a query from André Blanchet in regard to the functioning of democratic institutions in the Ivory Coast, Houphouët said:

It was the colonialists who divided us, playing off one against the other, but we all had the same goal. Now we have no reason to be divided, so it is desirable that all of us should be members of the sole party, just like an African family. . . . We are not going to pay for an opposition just to please the Occident. . . . You French have a phobia about the time limit for a "post of command." You cannot bear to see the same man in power for more than two or three years at the most.[12]

Houphouët feels that through constant contacts and through his party machinery he can keep his fingers on the pulse of the country. That this is a one-way form of control which provides a more limited opportunity for participation by the mass of the population in policy decisions than, say, the PDG appears not to concern him unduly. Houphouët has indeed proved to be responsive to local sentiments and pressures, though he does not always yield to them wholly or im-

[11] André Blanchet, *Nice-Matin,* Jan. 20, 1961.   [12] *Ibid.*

mediately. In the Ivory Coast he has come to accept the forces of local nationalism, just as in West Africa he has adjusted himself to the rising tide of Pan-Africanism—but only to a certain degree. Where he has been outstandingly successful is in his policy of neutralizing or absorbing opposition. As André Blanchet wrote early in 1961, "Today one seeks in vain for an open opponent of Houphouët amid old and young, bourgeois or proletariat, rural or townspeople."

So strongly had Houphouët built up his party machinery in cooperation with the administration and so firmly did he hold the reins of power that early in 1956 he felt free to accept a portfolio in the newly formed Mollet government at Paris. In the Ivory Coast he left in charge of party affairs his long-time collaborator, Auguste Denise, who became in May, 1957, the African head of the territory's first government council. In the solidly PDCI cabinet which Denise headed, the portfolios of Public Works and the Plan were assigned to two Frenchmen, Jean Millier and Raphaël Saller. These two men, along with Georges Monnet as Minister of Agriculture, became fixtures in Ivoirian governments for the next three and a half years. Some of Denise's African ministers, such as Jean Delafosse (Finance), Alcide Kacou (Technical Education), and Loua Diomandé (Civil Service), were all tried and true members of the PDCI, and they were either retained in successive cabinets or assigned to high government posts. These men, along with Mamadou Coulibaly, Philippe Yacé, Aliali, and a few others—sometimes called Houphouët's *bataillon sacré*—come from the same bourgeois class that produced their leader.

When Houphouët returned permanently to Abidjan early in 1959, he took over the controls from Denise, who continued to serve as Minister of State and, occasionally, as envoy extraordinary for his chief. But Denise's post as secretary-general of the PDCI and as Houphouët's main Ivoirian collaborator was assigned to a younger RDA militant, Jean Mockey. Mockey was taken into the cabinet and given the key portfolio of Interior, in accordance with Houphouët's policy of injecting fresh blood into the government. Although Mockey had been criticized for his inept handling of the Abidjan riots of October, 1958, he not only became the number two PDCI leader after Houphouët but was named Vice-Premier as well. Late in 1959, however, Mockey fell from favor and remained in political eclipse for some time. Reportedly his unbridled personal ambition brought about his downfall, though considerable mystery surrounds his maneuverings inside the PDCI.

After Mockey had voiced an opinion critical of the party line at the RDA congress at Abidjan in September, 1959, Houphouët forced his resignation from the cabinet and from his post as secretary-general of the PDCI. Soon afterward he dissolved the municipal council of Grand Bassam of which Mockey had been mayor. Houphouët himself took over the Interior portfolio and reorganized that ministry, particularly the police force that it controlled. Some time later Houphouët, in a typically conciliatory gesture, offered Mockey the post of ambassador to Tel Aviv; but the current heir apparent to Houphouët's crown seems to be Philippe Yacé, long-time president of the Ivory Coast's assembly and a specialist in parliamentary procedure.

Houphouët's decision early in 1959 to return to Abidjan and to active political life in the Ivory Coast was a timely one. During the years that the PDCI had cooperated with the French administration and, more recently, that Houphouët had participated in successive French governments, his party had lost much of its militancy and its organization had become somewhat slack. Between 1957 and 1959, the PDCI had not had to face the challenge of elections and had not met in a national congress. Its local branches, organized along ethnic lines, were operating almost as autonomous units, it was losing its character as a mass party, and only the close collaboration it maintained with the administration enabled it to keep its dominant position.[13] Then, too, the October, 1958, riots at Abidjan had not only jeopardized Houphouët's generous policy of welcoming nonindigenous Africans to the Ivory Coast but also his good relations with Dahomey and Togo, whose nationals had been the main victims. Even more serious, the riots had revealed a dangerous economic situation in Abidjan, which threatened to have serious political repercussions.

On March 29, 1959, at about the time Houphouët returned to his native land, the Ivory Coast assembly adopted the Republic's first constitution, which had been drafted to satisfy his expressed desire for a "strong and stable government." [14] By its provisions, the Premier of the Ivory Coast was to be not only the chief executive but also to have the prerogatives of a head of state. Although he was responsible to the assembly that invested him, a no-confidence vote that overthrew the government would also entail dissolution of the assembly and was therefore not likely to be used lightly. Elections for the 100-man

[13] Aristide Zolberg, *West Africa,* July 30, 1960.
[14] *Marchés Tropicaux,* April 4, 1959.

unicameral legislative assembly were set for April 12, 1959, at the same time as those for the newly created General Councils, each of which was to have 40 members.

These General Councils were established at the four towns of Abidjan, Bouaké, Korhogo, and Daloa, which, by a law of August 28, 1959, became the headquarters of the departments of the southeast, center, north, and southwest respectively. Although the new departments grouped the 19 existing *cercles* into larger units, the structure and organization of the *cercles* and of their 49 subdivisions remained as before. Thus what was called a "decentralization of the administration" did not in fact reach below the departmental level and was confined to the four elected General Councils. This slow and cautious approach has been typical of Houphouët's handling of administrative as well as political problems. It was not until January, 1961, that he carried the reorganization of the local administration one step further. At that time the four departments were divided into 100 subprefectures, each of which was endowed with an elected council of 20 members. The announced aim of this reform was to bring the administration nearer to the people, but it is as yet too soon to tell whether or not this will lead to a wider popular participation in the process of local government or simply become mainly a device for strengthening the grip of the PDCI. That party had increasingly become identified with the Ivoirian bourgeois elite, and in March and April, 1959, convened congresses of the PDCI and its youth sector (JAPDCI) as the preliminary to a long-overdue reorganization and rejuvenation of its leadership.

The principal themes discussed at those congresses were the future of the Franco-African Community, Africanization of the civil service (for which a Centre de Perfectionnement had been set up), the emancipation of women, and the abolition of the matriarchal system. With his flair for scenting actual and potential opposition, Houphouët was particularly attentive to the views expressed by young members of the party and those of the ethnic groups that no longer had any formal organizational vehicle for expressing their aspirations and grievances. Reportedly, it took him forty-eight hours of tense discussions to work out a *modus vivendi* between old-line party members and the new militants. During the three weeks preceding the legislative elections Houphouët received and talked with innumerable delegations and individuals from all over the Ivory Coast. In consequence of these contacts Houphouët seems to have reached several decisions regarding his party. One was to orient the rising tide of nationalist sentiment, felt especially by youthful Ivoirians, to the party as the embodiment of the *patrie,* and another was to enlarge the PDCI's leadership.

"Ivoirian Nationalism" was the title of an article written by Mamadou Coulibaly in *Fraternité,* on July 3, 1959, in which the beginnings of a PDCI myth can be clearly discerned. The party's leaders were portrayed as national heroes: Ouezzin Coulibaly had died on the RDA's field of honor, and Houphouët had gloriously lived and fought for Ivoirian freedom. It was again Mamadou Coulibaly who, five months later, authored another article in the PDCI organ, designed to arouse a patriotic feeling for the country's new flag. Its orange color, Mamadou Coulibaly explained, symbolized the nation's flowering and also recalled the savannah country of the north; its white strip stressed the Ivoirians' "love of peace in the purity and union of our hearts which is the gauge of our success"; and its green stripe showed how strong was the people's hope in the future, and at the same time that color reminded them of the south's luxuriant vegetation, "the primary source of our national prosperity." [15] Such flights of rhetoric were all very well for stimulating patriotic enthusiam in general terms, but Houphouët had to find some more concrete and practical way to strengthen his party. He determined to enlarge its leadership and channel into it all useful elements in the country, including his political opponents, and the device he used was the time-honored one of offering them posts and prestige. In his so doing, the democratic process of government suffered, for elections henceforth became simply a confirmation of the choice of candidates made by himself and his trusted collaborators.

In the elections of April 12, 1959, the PDCI presented a union slate of candidates in the four newly created electoral circumscriptions. But as there were nearly 800 aspirants for the 100 seats to be contested on April 12, the process of selection was a long and delicate one. However, since the new assembly had 40 more seats than its predecessor and 160 new general councilors were to be elected in the rural areas, Houphouët had considerable patronage at his disposal. So firmly did he maintain his principle initiated in 1954 of political collaboration with nonindigenous Africans and old-time European residents that onefourth of the seats in the new assembly were allotted to aliens. This was clearly out of line with the numerical size of those communities and displeasing to nationalistic Ivoirians, but it harmonized with

[15] *Fraternité,* Dec. 11, 1959.

Houphouët's views as to the true nature of the Franco-African Community and also enabled him to associate private capitalists closely with his government. Houphouët has consistently put into practice his belief that officeholding—and ministers and deputies are exceptionally well paid in the Ivory Coast—has a miraculously softening effect upon his opponents, past, present, and potential. He infinitely prefers to persuade such men to join him rather than be forced to beat them. Of those who have proved irreconcilable, some have voluntarily retired from public life, a few were jailed at the times of the 1957 elections and the September, 1958, referendum, and a handful have gone into exile or been expelled. But the great majority of his erstwhile enemies have succumbed, sooner or later, to one form or another of his offers of collaboration.

Aristide Zolberg has aptly described Houphouët's strategy at the time of the April, 1959, elections and cogently commented upon its consequences.

Final composition of the Union lists was announced one-half hour before the deadline for filing. It has been estimated that about 3,000 hopefuls had invaded Abidjan by this time. Because of this timing disappointed office-seekers could not regroup and present opposition lists. Enlargement of the electoral districts meant that small political organizations based on local support had no chance of winning and had to make wide-flung alliances to qualify. Simultaneous elections meant that there was no possibility of re-organizing for a later contest. . . . Thus by preventing the formation of opposition lists, the PDCI, acting through the Union [list], secured complete control over all organs of government in Ivory Coast. Perhaps more important, however, was its success in widening the base of its support throughout the country by accommodating many diverse nonparty elements, each one of which could possibly form a nucleus for opposition activity. With many offices available, faithful party workers could also be re-warded. . . .

The makeup of the current political institutions of the Ivory Coast clearly indicates that the country is ruled by a one party coalition, a heterogeneous monolith.[16]

The 1959 elections represented the culmination of a strategy that Houphouët had perfected over the preceding fourteen years, and in the matter of voter participation they marked a big step forward. Whereas 46 per cent of the registered electorate had failed to vote in the 1957 elections, abstentions were sharply reduced in 1959 to 5.6

[16] *West Africa,* July 30 and Aug. 6, 1960.

per cent. Since the abstainers were largely confined to the Aboisso region where the "King" of Sanwi's attempt to separate his area from the new Ivory Coast republic had been encouraged from Accra, Houphouët probably felt justified in attributing this nonvoting, at least in part, to foreign influences. Other traditional chiefs seem to have given him no trouble, and he has certainly not taken drastic measures against them. Early in September, 1958, Prince Adingra, president of the Ivory Coast Association of Customary Chiefs, called on his colleagues to cast an affirmative vote in the referendum as proof of their confidence in Houphouët.[17] As a chief himself, Houphouët well understands their problems and position, and as the leader of a new republic he must reach a *modus vivendi* with them. Characteristically, Houphouët wants to utilize those among them who are susceptible of "modernization" rather than antagonize them by shearing them of their powers. As he told the RDA congress of September, 1959, at Abidjan, he did not condemn those RDA governments (in Guinea and Mali) that had taken a "much more revolutionary stand than ours against the chieftaincy, for everyone knows that the traditional chieftaincy is a great problem for all the African states. . . . The RDA is a *rassemblement,* not a party, and we [in Ivory Coast] are all partisans of unity in diversity."

Successful as was Houphouët's policy of inducements *cum* appeasement in his relations with the great majority of traditional chiefs and with the rank and file of the PDCI, he did not escape encountering the opposition of extremist forces both inside the party and outside. The Union Progressiste Sénégalaise government of Senegal and, to a lesser extent, the Union Soudanaise government of Soudan likewise suffered from party rifts and from the attacks of extremist youths and labor leaders. Everywhere these elements are eager to take over power from their elders and pursue more radical policies, particularly in the economic domain, and in many cases they have been encouraged in these activities by alien influences. Houphouët's relatively stronger position than that of Senghor and of Modibo Keita was shown by the summary fashion in which he disposed of the opposition. The crisis which the PDCI underwent in September, 1959, as represented by the insubordination of Mockey (and Gaston Fiankan), virtually ended with their dismissal from the cabinet. But the hostility shown to Houphouët by two other sets of opponents—Ivoirian students in France and some labor leaders in Abidjan—proved harder and longer to cope

[17] *Marchés Tropicaux,* Sept. 6, 1958.

with, largely because it was stimulated by foreign sources bent on destroying Houphouët's power.

On a visit to Paris in June, 1959, Houphouët had a brush with some Marxist members of the Union Générale des Etudiants de la Côte d'Ivoire who accused him of behaving like a fascist. Visibly angered, Houphouët retorted that they knew nothing about the "masses" in whose name they professed to speak while living abroad in comparative comfort. And he added that any who demanded independence for the Ivory Coast would be "imprisoned, judged, and condemned." [18] But the students were not intimidated and continued to attack Houphouët and to ally themselves with the Communist-oriented Fédération des Etudiants d'Afrique Noire. This led in the fall of 1959 to dissolution of the Union Générale and to the creation of a more cooperative student association by the Ivory Coast government. Naturally the Union Générale leadership protested energetically against the "measures taken against us because of our political activities . . . and because we are the only organization that has dared to express views contrary to those of the PDCI." [19] After a suitable cooling-down period, Houphouët pursued his usual tactics of offering posts in his government to some of the dissident youths. Included on the PDCI union list for election to the assembly in November, 1960, were Guedé Loregnon and Bissouma Tapé, who only a short time earlier had been officials of the Union Générale and outspoken opponents of the PDCI before making their peace with Houphouët. (Tapé was even accorded a special four-month leave from his duties as deputy in order to permit him to complete his studies in France.) Indeed, "le Vieux" (as Houphouët is sometimes called) now heads what is perhaps the youngest government in West Africa, though he himself is by temperament a traditionalist. And his desire to extract Ivoirian students from Communist influence in France certainly lies behind his insistence upon creating an African university at Abidjan. Houphouët has recently had reason to realize that the Ivoirian students in France have not all been won over to him by the prospect of officeholding upon their return home or by their country's acquisition of independence. In July, 1961, four of them criticized Houphouët so harshly that they were expelled by the French government and offered asylum in Accra.[20] Nor has Houphouët been wholly successful in his dealings with students and teachers in the Ivory Coast itself. It was also in July, 1961, that he reproached them

[18] *Afrique Nouvelle,* June 19, 1959.   [19] *Le Monde,* Jan. 20, 1960.
[20] *Ibid.,* July 9–10, 1961.

with their generally negative attitude toward his government and for some "antinational statements" made at a recent pedagogic conference.[21]

Another more dangerously active and adjacent group of Houphouët's opponents has been some urban labor leaders, whose unions have been affiliated with the Union Générale des Travailleurs d'Afrique Noire (UGTAN), with its headquarters at Conakry. Particularly recalcitrant have been the civil service unions which have resisted his efforts to make them cooperate with the government. In many ways the relationship between government and organized labor in the Ivory Coast duplicates the situation in Senegal. In both countries civil servants have been regarded by the dominant party as an unduly privileged group, whose demands for improved working conditions and pay are unjustified and whose political activities are largely inspired by Guinean leaders bent on disrupting the country's administration. Like the UPS in Senegal, the PDCI government has emerged as the apparent victor in its trial of strength with the orthodox UGTAN unions and subsequently has tried to unite the whole labor movement in a single organization under its control.

In the rural areas there have also been analogies between the labor situation in Senegal and in the Ivory Coast. The development of export crops in both countries has given birth to an indigenous rural bourgeoisie that increasingly employs wage labor, much of it alien and seasonal. But in the Ivory Coast there is no group comparable to the Mouride peanut farmers, and the shortage of labor in the forest zone is so acute that a greater call has had to be made on hired workers not native to the area. Consequently the labor situation in the Ivory Coast has become more involved than that in Senegal in ethnic conflicts, which have come to a head particularly in Abidjan during periods of unemployment. Both as a matter of principle and also as a means of developing the country more rapidly, Houphouët has encouraged the influx of alien Africans, but this has aroused an adverse nationalistic reaction. The upsurge of nationalist feeling has been sharper and more acute—though basically similar—to that which characterized the Senegalese in their resistance to Soudanese attempts to take over the economy and government of the Mali Federation.

During the first postwar decade, cutting the Vridi Canal and then work on the Houphouët-Boigny bridge attracted to Abidjan many laborers, particularly from the less prosperous north. Similarly, the ex-

[21] *Ibid.,* July 29, 1961.

pansion of coffee and cocoa exports created wealth and job opportunities that induced Africans from less-favored territories to settle in the Ivory Coast. This was especially true of Dahomeyans and Togolese whose intelligence and superior education enabled them to fill many of the most remunerative posts in the Ivory Coast, both in trade and in the administration. With the completion of Abidjan's major public works program and the shrinkage of funds from FIDES (Fonds d'Investissements pour le Développement Economique et Social), many Ivoirians in the capital found themselves without work. It was during the summer of 1958, when half the workers in the building trade were idle, that the situation became acute. The restiveness inevitably engendered by unemployment became focused on the resident Dahomeyans and Togolese. Also contributing to the prevailing tension in Abidjan were the conflicting emotions aroused by the imminence of the referendum, emotions which were fanned by the campaign for a negative vote led by the orthodox UGTAN unions.

Organized labor in the Ivory Coast, aside from a group of autonomous unions, was divided into three *centrales*—the Confédération des Travailleurs Croyants de la Côte d'Ivoire (CATC), the Confédération Africaine des Syndicats Libres, and the UGTAN-orthodoxe. Already in March, 1958, the CATC had rejected the UGTAN's policy of injecting political issues into the labor movement.[22] One faction of the UGTAN favored an affirmative vote in the referendum, claiming that the "workers of the Ivory Coast give their confidence to *l'homme prestigieux du 18 juin*," but the orthodox UGTAN leaders campaigned so violently for a negative vote that some of them were jailed or felt obliged to flee the country. Such measures and the massive affirmative vote in the referendum for a time reduced the UGTAN's agitation, but they did nothing to quell the Ivoirians' resentment against the alien jobholders in their midst.

The Ligue des Originaires de la Côte d'Ivoire was the organized form taken by this xenophobic element. It was the leaders of that League who instigated the series of riots directed mainly against Dahomeyans and Togolese that broke out on October 19, 1958, and lasted for 8 days, principally in the Treichville suburb of Abidjan. At least 6 persons were killed, many wounded, 425 lodgings destroyed or damaged, and more than 8,000 Togolese and Dahomeyans immediately forced to take refuge in the old port of Abidjan. The police did little to protect the refugees, and it was obvious that many Ivoirians, though

[22] See *Marchés Tropicaux,* March 22, 1958.

disapproving of the methods that had been used, sympathized with the League's demand that employment in the country should be reserved to its nationals.[23] Although Premier Denise at once claimed that the riots were part of a plot organized against the government from outside the country, the prevailing economic conditions in the southern Ivory Coast sufficed to account for the sudden explosion. In recent years an increasing number of young Ivoirians had been unable to find jobs after graduating from school, and it was principally such youths who had organized the League and the riots. Houphouët, appreciating the seriousness of the situation, returned to Abidjan from Paris to investigate. Eventually arrangements were made with the governments of Lomé and Porto Novo for the compensation and repatriation of their nationals, almost every one of whom was by then eager to leave the Ivory Coast permanently. (By February, 1959, 12,-706 Dahomeyans had returned to their own country.) In December, 1958, the government promised to get rid of all foreign African civil servants within two months, and it recommended to private enterprises in the country that they dismiss their foreign African employees.[24]

The October, 1958, riots dealt an almost fatal blow to a basic tenet of Houphouët's policy and gave ammunition to his detractors and virtually complete satisfaction to the Ligue des Originaires de la Côte d'Ivoire. By the spring of 1959, the employment situation in Abidjan had definitely improved, particularly in the building industry. Yet there still remained many unemployed, principally youths without skills whose number was steadily increased by young men drifting from the rural areas to Abidjan. Although the government tried to check this influx and eventually instituted a form of forced labor related to compulsory military service, its main efforts were now directed to the creation of a single labor union that would be apolitical and independent of the UGTAN.

Transfer of the UGTAN's headquarters to Conakry in January, 1959, naturally aggravated the PDCI's fears lest the local branch of that *centrale* be used increasingly to undermine the Ivory Coast government. Substance was given to this threat by the dispatch to Abidjan of a Guinean labor agitator, Yao Ngo Blaise. In July, 1959, a government-sponsored Union Nationale des Syndicats de la Côte d'Ivoire (UNSCI) was constituted at a congress in which the orthodox UGTAN was reproached for having sounded the call for political in-

[23] *Le Monde,* Nov. 13, 1958.   [24] *Ibid.,* Dec. 27, 1958.

dependence and in which ties between the two labor organizations were broken. The only aspiration voiced by the new union's leaders at this congress was for a more rapid Africanization of the cadres, in both the public and the private sectors. No other significant grievance was expressed, and the new union voted overwhelmingly its confidence in the government.[25] Tension quickly built up between the new union and the local orthodox UGTAN. In mid-August each sponsored its own labor confederation for the Entente states, and each proposed that the headquarters should be located in Abidjan. Such competitive activities, not to mention the very creation of the UNSCI, provoked a strong reaction on the part of the local orthodox UGTAN. Among members of the civil service unions, fuel was added to the flame by the government's concurrent announcement that henceforth family allowances for functionaries would be restricted to six children. All these developments incited the orthodox UGTAN under the leadership of Yao Ngo Blaise to conduct such a vigorous campaign against the UNSCI that, in October, he was arrested and charged with subversive activities. Yao Ngo Blaise had become the secretary-general of the Inter-Syndicat de la Fonction Publique, 18 of whose unions were affiliated with the Conakry UGTAN and 2 with the CATC. In retaliation for his arrest, the Inter-Syndicat launched a warning strike, in which some of its CATC members participated but in which the private sector did not become involved.

Houphouët promptly declared this strike to be illegal, dismissed 184 civil servants who had obeyed the strike order, and expelled Yao Ngo Blaise from the country.[26] For some time there was no letup in the severity of the government's repression of recalcitrant labor leaders, and Houphouët showed little indulgence toward further demands from the civil servants. In reply to their repeated requests for a more rapid Africanization of the Ivory Coast cadres, Houphouët declared dryly in January, 1960, that he was not going to do so before being sure that there were enough qualified Ivoirian functionaries to take over the posts of command.[27] Early the following month, Philippe Yacé called a meeting of civil servants and scolded them for not playing a more enterprising role in party affairs. Those who had not been active during the period of national construction, he said, would be given the chance to redeem themselves during the phase of economic construction. He finished his speech by saying that although the government recognized

[25] Afrique Nouvelle, July 17, 1959.   [26] Le Monde, Oct. 16, 1959.
[27] Afrique Nouvelle, Feb. 3, 1960.

labor's right to strike, it was quite unnecessary for civil servants to use that weapon.[28]

So prolonged was the government's policy of repression against the recalcitrant unions that it elicited protests from the CATC unions, which asked for the restoration of democratic freedoms. Even the docile UNSCI, at its meeting on May Day, 1961, asked Houphouët to amnesty "our comrades, victims of the October, 1959, events." He had, indeed, given seats in the assembly elected in November, 1960, to some repentant ringleaders of the functionaries' strike,[29] but his benevolence did not extend to those who had not yet made their peace with him. Houphouët has often said that there was room in the Ivory Coast for unions working to improve the material welfare of their members but not for those which became instruments of forces hostile to his rule.

Houphouët obviously recognized the danger to his government of a possible alliance between such explosive and revolutionary forces as student extremists and urban proletariat leaders. To prevent this danger he preferred to take the calculated risk of bringing into the assembly men who had shown themselves eager to overthrow his government by force, if necessary. This was a daring if logical step in the execution of his policy of broadening the leadership of his predominantly bourgeois party and of associating the most dynamic elements in the country with the carrying out of his program for the Ivory Coast. To be sure, Houphouët has also given diplomatic posts to former political opponents such as Etienne Djaument, Usher Assouan, Gaston Fiankan, and Jean Mockey, but these men are consequently separated geographically from the Ivoirian political scene. Associating extremist elements closely with his government is certainly more hazardous, and it remains to be seen whether or not they will be content with their role as collaborators. Thus far, their participation has been mainly in the nature of a political initiation, and it seems doubtful that Houphouët is willing to share with them an appreciable slice of power. "So long as the masses have confidence in me," he has said, "there will be an authority [of the state]—a just but an undisputed authority." [30]

In addition to his great personal prestige, Houphouët's authority is sanctioned by the country's constitution. Adopted unanimously by the

[28] *Ibid.*, Feb. 10, 1960.

[29] These were Koné Lancina, secretary-general of the Syndicat des Cheminots; Frédéric Able, secretary-general of the Syndicat des Transporteurs; and Joseph Coffie, president of the Centrale Nationale des Travailleurs Ivoiriens.

[30] *Fraternité*, Sept. 25, 1959.

assembly on October 23, 1960, it places exceptionally wide powers in the hands of the President of the Republic. The elections held on November 27, 1960, marked a fresh triumph for Houphouët who, as candidate for the presidency, received nearly 99 per cent of all the votes cast—1,578,000 out of 1,597,000. Although the PDCI was the only government party in all the Entente states that felt strong enough to face the electorate after adoption of the new constitutions, it did not come off so well in the Ivory Coast as did its leader. The PDCI union list of candidates for the assembly's 70 seats received only 96 per cent of the votes cast. This difference in percentages occurred mainly in regions where there were personal conflicts between former deputies and the local PDCI leaders. Such was the case in the towns of Man and Daloa where, respectively, 15 per cent and 10 per cent of those who voted for Houphouët refused to endorse the whole PDCI list. This evidence of weakness in the rural party organization, not to mention the threat of subversion from external sources and the potentially explosive elements recently taken into the assembly, led to new orders being issued by the PDCI politburo in July, 1961. Henceforth the powers of party secretaries were to be increased to give a more efficient execution of the politburo's directives and also to enable them to "denounce possible enemies of the national revolution and thereby assure the success of our common enterprise." [31] Houphouët's fear of aggression from Guinea and Ghana has led to the creation of Ivory Coast armed forces, with a modest air force and navy and an army of 4,000 conscripts. These armed forces have been assigned the tasks of quelling internal troubles and of aiding economic construction, and inevitably it is Houphouët who has been entrusted by the assembly with responsibility for all defense matters.

This reinforcement of Houphouët's authority and of the party structure has been accompanied, characteristically, by more apparent than real concessions to the pressure of local forces. The scramble for power was so intense among the old party faithfuls and the new elements that it took Houphouët over six weeks following the elections to form a new government that would give the maximum satisfaction to both. A complicating factor was the candidacy of the thirteen Ivoirian ministers in the last cabinet who, now barred by new regulations from holding concurrently the seat of a deputy and a ministerial portfolio, preferred not to run for the assembly on the chance of being invited to join the next administration. Their chances were indeed improved by the drop-

[31] *Le Monde,* July 29, 1961.

ping from the cabinet (and from the assembly) of all French nationals except the Antilles "dictator" of the Ivory Coast's economy, Raphaël Saller, whom Houphouët still regarded as an indispensable member of his government. In regard to his other main French collaborators, Georges Monnet and Jean Millier, he yielded to local nationalist sentiment and regretfully received their resignations as ministers. But by the device of creating the posts of private advisers to the new African ministers, he was able to retain their services without assigning them posts so conspicuous as to offend Ivoirian susceptibilities. Five other Frenchmen were named to the recently created Economic Council, the importance of which was underscored by making its president, Jean Delafosse, the third-ranking official in the country. Thus Houphouët, under cover of a wholly African and Ivoirian government, was able to preserve the services of and good relations with the local French business community and also his policy of economic liberalism. By ensuring in this way that his administration would continue along established lines, Houphouët was now free to turn to external matters, and the importance that he attributed to this domain was shown by his taking over the portfolio of Foreign Affairs himself.

ORGANIZATION OF THE JUDICIARY

The judicial system of the Ivory Coast has been reorganized twice since the *loi cadre* was applied to that territory. By a decree of August 28, 1958, a court of appeal and a court of first instance were set up at Abidjan, and courts of second instance were established at Bouaké and Gagnoa. In addition, there were in the country a Conseil des Prudhommes, justices of the peace, and customary courts. Then on May 10, 1961, the assembly accepted a second court reorganization proposed by the government "in the interests of simplification and of greater efficiency." Henceforth there was to be a single judicial system, with all the courts having competence in civil, criminal, commercial, and administrative cases. The court of appeal at Abidjan was retained, courts of first instance were set up in the main towns, and elsewhere justices of the peace were empowered temporarily to act as courts of first instance. A new feature was the institution of a Supreme Court that could also fill the role of a *cour de cassation*. As before, the independence of the judiciary vis-à-vis the executive power was assured and the High Council of the Magistracy entrusted with matters of internal discipline.

Contemporary Issues

In the economic domain, the Ivory Coast's major weaknesses are its dependence on a few export crops, whose prices fluctuate widely, and on imported labor. Since World War II, concentration on the production for export of coffee, cocoa, wood, and bananas has brought wealth to many southern Ivoirians, but it has led to the neglect of the north. In the latter area the population is only just emerging from a subsistence economy through the sale—albeit poorly organized and not properly remunerative—of its food surplus to the coastal peoples. Overstress on export crops has also led to the importation of labor principally from Upper Volta, and this has contributed to tension between the two countries. Moreover, the sudden expansion of coffee (and of other export commodities to a lesser degree) in the south has had some adverse physical and psychological effects there and also upon the economy of the country as a whole. Creation of new plantations has reduced the forest coverage and increased the dangers of soil erosion in that zone.

The high prices fetched by their agricultural exports have affected the psychology of the southern tribes, whose attitude toward the land already differs from the peasant norm as a result of the matriarchal system that prevails among them. In this society parents often urge their children to seek jobs in towns rather than work the land which will inevitably pass not to them but to the maternal nephews. Furthermore, the habit in the forest zone of renting out vacant land to newcomers, a habit which supplements the large income received from their crops, has made the parents themselves increasingly inclined and able to hire agricultural workers. Consequently the outlook of the southern landowner is becoming more that of the bourgeois rather than of peasants who by their own labor contribute to the creation of wealth.

Development of the south on this basis has had other harmful repercussions on the Ivory Coast as a whole. One of these effects has been its increasing dependence upon France for subsidies of various kinds to Ivoirian exports, particularly after the prices for coffee and cocoa fell sharply in the mid-1950's. Only temporarily can France offer a protected market and high prices to Ivoirian exports, for its powers of absorption of them are not able indefinitely to keep pace with the Ivory Coast's expanding shipments. Adapting themselves to competition in the international market has proved difficult for Ivory

Coast producers, and many of them continue to demand guaranteed sales and higher-than-world prices for their output.

Another deleterious consequence of the foregoing situation has been the attraction exercised by the wealth of the southern population on young men from the hinterland and on alien Africans. The former have flocked to the towns where, because they lack skills, they have often been unable to find jobs and where they have swelled the parasitic element of the urban population. The alien African immigrants, on the other hand, generally possess more education and enterprise than the hinterland Ivoirians, and thus they have readily found employment in the administration or in trade. The result has been the upsurge of nationalist feeling in the indigenous population which, as already noted, culminated in violence against the outsiders.

The inter-African riots of October, 1958, at Abidjan were the most acute local manifestation of the weakness of an economic system inherited from the colonial regime. Many other French-speaking African countries suffer similarly from the uneven development of their population, dependence upon French support, and labor shortages. What distinguishes the Ivory Coast from the others is the larger number and type of its assets and also the practice of a free-enterprise economic policy. For most of the post-World War II period the Ivory Coast has enjoyed a stable and strong government and one that has inspired the confidence of its people as well as that of foreign investors. The country has undeniably prospered under the PDCI administration and, even if its wealth is not evenly distributed, the great majority of Ivoirians have given their overwhelming support to Houphouët as their leader. Moreover, the government's maintenance of a free-enterprise system, under which the Ivory Coast has become outstandingly wealthy, has encouraged private capitalists to invest in the country to a greater degree than anywhere else in French-speaking Negro Africa. Since coming to power, the Houphouët government has been energetically trying to strengthen and diversify the Ivory Coast's economy and, more recently, to give it an African coloring without changing its basic policy.

The Ivory Coast's first two plans originated in Paris, but the most recent one, beginning in 1958, was drawn up at Abidjan principally by two French ministers in Houphouët's cabinet—Raphaël Saller and Georges Monnet. The first four-year plan had concentrated heavily on the country's infrastructure, notably digging the Vridi Canal and expanding the port of Abidjan. The second plan laid more stress on social equipment, though it still devoted considerable sums to improvement of means of communication. By its greatly enlarged scope the Ivory Coast's present plan reflects the government's enhanced self-confidence and its preoccupation with raising the living standards of the population. Some 40 per cent of total expenditures under the third plan are to go toward increasing production, the same percentage to strengthening the infrastructure, and 20 per cent to enterprises of social significance. Estimated to cost the huge amount of 25,810,000,000 CFA francs, the Ivory Coast's current plan depends heavily on French financing but also on large contributions from local resources and possibly recourse to a loan.

As befits a predominantly agricultural country, increased production of crops, livestock, and fish receives top priority under the new plan. Export crops and timber will continue to receive official encouragement and the benefits of research conducted by existing institutions, but production is to be pushed on an intensive rather than an extensive basis. Higher yield, rather than expansion of the area under cultivation, is the method advocated to increase export tonnages. By achieving a better-quality output with lower production costs it is hoped that the Ivory Coast will expand its markets outside the franc zone. But the main stress in this domain is placed on diversifying agricultural exports, notably through developing rubber, oil-palm, and sugar-cane plantations, and even more on expanding food crops. If the goals set for food production are achieved, the Ivory Coast will not only save the foreign exchange it now spends on importing annually some 100,000 tons of foodstuffs but also enable Ivoirians to have a better-balanced diet. The country still has considerable stretches of virgin land, particularly in the west, on which sizable food crops could be grown with comparatively little extra effort. The encouragement of large-scale animal husbandry in the savannah zone is the recognized prerequisite for developing a meat industry.

Although the authorities realize that they must improve the internal distribution system, they have not tried to revolutionize the existing trade network. It is on diversified and increased production that they have laid the greatest emphasis. The means by which this is to be achieved are the stabilization of remunerative prices paid to farmers, herders, and fishermen and their organization into producing cooperatives. As the first step toward changing the Ivoirian farmers' archaic methods of cultivation, the Ministry of Agriculture set up in 1959 the first Centers of Agricultural Coordination and Cooperation, one of which is to be established ultimately in each subdivision, and also the machinery for expanding credit facilities to farmers. The following year it founded the Ivory Coast's first state-run organization for providing technical aid to modernize the country's agriculture. The mass training of agricultural monitors and of selected farmers was begun at the Brimbesso experimental station in 1959, and two years later the first 2,500 trainees started building model farms in a number of villages. It is hoped that cooperative societies of producers will develop through this network of organizations, from which official management can be gradually withdrawn. By these various means the authors of the plan believe that they can develop a taste for farming among the somewhat disaffected Ivoirian peasantry and thereby overcome a major handicap to increased production—the shortage of agricultural labor.

While first place has been accorded to agricultural production, the current plan does not neglect the search for mineral deposits and the need to supply more social equipment. If new ores are discovered, they will provide welcome additions to the Ivory Coast's sources of foreign exchange. Industrialization projects are mainly directed toward supplying the domestic market. To further the well-being of the population in other spheres, more medical centers and schools are being opened up. Here the primary goal is to raise the standards of the northern tribes to the level already reached by those in the south.

In general, the Ivory Coast's third plan represents merely the expansion and intensification of programs already set in motion under the French administration. Houphouët feels that it would be folly to change radically the free-enterprise system under which the economy has flourished. Thus he has resisted the trend toward *planification* that is so marked in neighboring countries. The Ivory Coast's present plan is more in the nature of a list of priority projects than a comprehensive, ideologically oriented plan such as those drawn up by the Guinean and Malian governments. The nearest that Houphouët has come to suggesting such planning was in his speech to the Ivoirian assembly in January, 1961. In that speech he surprised his listeners by decrying individualistic capitalism as it is known in Western countries, advocating a collectivist economy inspired by African traditions, and laying down some new principles. In an interview that he gave the same month to André Blanchet, he elaborated further on his ideas:

We want a constitutional law to require the Ivory Coast state to spend less than it receives. Our society, based on the matriarchal regime and without financial skill, has nevertheless been able to accumulate capital gradually. But this capital is not the property of a single individual but of a collectivity

—the family. The head of the family may or may not increase this capital, but he has no right to touch what he has received from his ancestors. So it is not he alone who is rich but each member of the family. . . .

We will call upon all the population to participate in making a contribution to a national reserve of gold, the amount of which every citizen has the right to know at the end of each year. This is what the Baoulé did when they left the region that is now known as Ghana and by their toil they reconstituted the treasury of the royal family.[32]

As applied to the foreign business community, this policy has not yet effected more than minor changes in the existing situation. Private foreign investors are still protected and favored. They remain free to transfer most of their capital and profits out of the country though they must reinvest a proportion of them locally. The Ivory Coast intends to remain in the franc zone, though jointly with other countries of the Union Africaine et Malgache (UAM) it will probably issue a new currency. The fear expressed by some observers that creation of the Economic Council early in 1961 might be the first step toward economic nationalism has not materialized. Its president, Jean Delafosse, has deprecated state participation in industry and has said that the Council's initial activities would be concentrated on the practical problem of counteracting the overstress placed on export crops.

Thus far it is only in relation to the African population that Houphouët has tried to implement his concept of a collectivist economy. What he calls the "Ivoirian version of human investment" and his government's requirement that no child leave school without having a job or learning a trade have the dual purpose of furthering economic construction and of strengthening national unity. His ideology, if such it can be called, is an economic one, and he has often said that his greatest ambition is to transform the Ivory Coast into a modern state. By this he means not so much a Negro African nation as a united up-to-date country in which every Ivoirian will be "fed, clothed, taught, healed, and housed"—a society in which there is genuine freedom and brotherhood and in which the individual is not sacrificed to the state. In what proportions Houphouët will have to use coercion as compared to persuasion if he is to reach his goal remains to be seen, but there is no doubt of his determination to modernize, strengthen, and unite the Ivory Coast and its inhabitants.

Currently there appear to be no insuperable obstacles lying athwart his path. He is the undisputed master of his party and of his country,

[32] *Nice-Matin,* Jan. 20, 1961.

and opposition to his rule appears to be either nonexistent or ineffective. However, the future depends on the perpetuation of certain phenomena and on elimination of the causes of ethnic cleavages and conflicts. Among the most important of these are Houphouët's physical survival and his ability to keep in close touch with and responsive to local developments without becoming overinvolved in external affairs. Other countries with one-man, one-party governments, of course, share this emphasis on the leader. The Ivory Coast's particular need, however, is the continued expansion of its economy, for without increasing revenues Houphouët cannot hope to raise the underdeveloped regions to the economic and cultural level of the coastal zone. This need may pose more problems, for to assure the expansion of its sources of wealth Ivory Coast will remain dependent for some years to come on outside financial and technical aid.

External Relations

RELATIONS WITH OTHER AFRICAN STATES

So closely has Houphouët been identified with leadership of the Entente (later of the UAM, called alternatively *les douze* or the Brazzaville Bloc) that in many instances it is impossible to distinguish between the foreign policy of the Ivory Coast and those of the various groups that he has dominated. Beginning in 1960, however, and particularly after the Entente states acquired their independence, the relationship of the Ivory Coast to other African countries has been more clearly differentiated, as has been that of its partners. By the terms on which independence from France was granted, each of the Entente countries was able to embark on a foreign policy of its own devising, including the making of agreements with neighboring states. Increasingly their foreign policies toward African states have diverged, with Upper Volta, followed in part by Dahomey, charting a course that has progressively differed from that of the Ivory Coast and Niger.

Early in 1960 the outlook for closer relations between the Entente and the Mali Federation took a turn for the better, but after a year's tension between them progress was necessarily slow. According to Senghor,[33] this *rapprochement* began at Paris in February, 1960, and it developed faster between Senegal and the Ivory Coast than between their respective partners. Although Senghor and Houphouët had long been on opposite sides of the political fence, the issues of a primary

[33] *Le Monde*, March 1, 1960.

federation in West Africa and of independence from France no longer divided them. Much more difficult to establish were cordial relations between Houphouët and his erstwhile lieutenant, Modibo Keita, which had become very tense during the summer of 1959 after the Soudanese leader had left the RDA to link his party with the PRA.

When Houphouët in March, 1960, held out an olive branch to the Mali Federation, the leaders of the latter, however, responded by sending good-will missions to Abidjan. Yet there was a noteworthy difference between the mission sent by Senegal and that from Soudan. The delegation dispatched from Bamako was not headed by Modibo himself but by Jean-Marie Koné, whereas Premier Mamadou Dia himself led the Senegalese mission to the Ivory Coast and while there lavished warm praise on Houphouët. "The Dakar-Abidjan axis is a reality," he said, "and though the dialogue between us has never been broken off we are now going to make a fresh start." [34] Senegal, then on bad terms with Guinea and Ghana and beginning to have friction with Soudan, was obviously eager for the Ivory Coast's support. The *rapprochement* between Dakar and Abidjan rapidly evolved toward a cordial relationship that culminated by the end of 1960 in their common membership in the Brazzaville Bloc.

Houphouët, who was also on bad terms with Nkrumah and Sékou Touré, was equally anxious for closer ties with the Senegalese leaders. The Ghana-Guinea Union had frustrated his plan to isolate Sékou Touré, following the latter's vote for independence in the September, 1958, referendum. At first Houphouët's anger with Sékou Touré and Nkrumah expressed itself in derogatory comments about their union and the unlikelihood of its lasting. In April, 1959, when publicly rejecting any plan for a "great African ensemble because it would not serve the interests of our country," Houphouët added: "The sum total of misery does not create abundance. See today how Sékou Touré is knocking at the door of Nkrumah." [35] Two months later, in reply to a question on the Ghana-Guinea Union at a press conference at Paris, Houphouët declared:

I do not want to interfere in the affairs of other states. . . . Sékou Touré was my friend and some people hope that he will return to the Community. I deeply desire this but I doubt it. I have been accused of being vexed with Guinea. This is an error. In the Ivory Coast we have 75,000 Guineans who have refused to return to their country and want to acquire Ivoirian nationality, and many more continue to come. . . . In 1957 I made a wager

[34] *Ibid.*, May 2, 1960.   [35] *Ibid.*, April 7, 1959.

with Nkrumah, but the bases of that wager were not then clearly enough defined. Today they are clearer. . . . If Guinea can assure its population of an appreciable improvement in its lot, I will have lost the wager. If we do so in the Ivory Coast, we will have won. As to the Guinea-Ghana Union, knowing Sékou Touré and Nkrumah as I do, I cannot believe that either of them wants to play second fiddle to the other.[36]

Obviously Houphouët's initial irritation with Sékou Touré and Nkrumah was gradually giving way to concern lest their union provide a greater pole of attraction for West Africans than did Abidjan, though he still counted on the Ivory Coast's spectacular prosperity to offset it. Moreover, although its location between Guinea and Ghana made its wealth equally apparent to both Sékou Touré and Nkrumah, the Ivory Coast's geographical position also rendered it highly vulnerable to their attacks. Many of such attacks were simply verbal and were also voiced by other members of the Afro-Asian bloc. (The Ivory Coast was the object of derogatory comments at the Afro-Asian meeting in Conakry in April, 1960, where a resolution was passed urging the "establishment of democratic elections in the Entente states and especially in the Ivory Coast." [37]) But by mid-1959, Houphouët had become convinced that his neighbors were deliberately stirring up trouble for his government through their encouragement of extremist labor leaders and other dissident groups.

Nkrumah, more than Sékou Touré, was the object of Houphouët's ire. The two men had not met since making their famous wager in 1957, at which time they seem to have inspired dislike and distrust in each other. Even before that, however, it was noticeable that at Ghana's independence celebrations the Ivory Coast had not been represented except by individual guests, nor subsequently was any official delegation sent from Abidjan to the various conferences held at Accra. In particular, in the spring of 1958, Houphouët chalked up against Nkrumah a specific grievance—his apparent encouragement of the defection of Amon Ndouffou III of Aboisso, the so-called "King" of Sanwi.

Aboisso, which comprises 2.5 per cent of the area and 1.5 per cent of the population of the Ivory Coast, is located on the Ghana frontier and is of economic importance to the country. Its chief, who had vainly protested to Paris against the incorporation of his domain in the Ivory Coast, was arrested with five collaborators near the Ghana frontier. In May, 1958, a few days before his arrest, he had set up in Aboisso a "provisional government," whose other seven members soon sought

[36] *Marchés Tropicaux*, June 13, 1959.   [37] *Ibid.*, April 23, 1960.

refuge in Ghana. After the September, 1958, referendum, Camille Adam, an Ivoirian lawyer who had formed a local branch of the PRA and campaigned for a negative vote, was expelled from the Ivory Coast. After wanderings that reportedly took him as far afield as Peking and Cairo, Adam went to Accra, where he set up a National Committee for the Liberation of the Ivory Coast. In this enterprise he had the cooperation of another refugee from Houphouët's regime, a former schoolteacher named Armand Kadio Attié. Although at their trial at Abidjan in February, 1960, the Sanwi dissidents claimed that they had only sought direct ties with France and denied any connection with the Adam-Kadié committee, Houphouët apparently regarded all these developments as part of a plot hatched by Nkrumah to undermine the PDCI government. That the Aboisso region remained disaffected almost a year after its chief's arrest was indicated by the large percentage of abstentions there in the April, 1959, elections. The fact that Nkrumah was concurrently showing irredentist tendencies in regard to Togo seemed to confirm Houphouët's suspicions of meddling in the Ivory Coast. In June, 1959, these suspicions were clearly stated by the Ivory Coast's Secretary of State for Information:

The so-called kingdom of Sanwi was never respected as such during the colonial regime. The present "king" is a clerk in a trading firm, a man without education who was raised to power by the intellectual elite of Aboisso. The Aboisso region has a large minority of Africans who, together with a sizable Agni element, constitute a majority in favor of integration with the Ivory Coast. . . . The game of that handful of autonomists is clear: they are trying to deceive the *Métropole* and to ally themselves with Ghana. They intend to bring as their dowry to Ghana the wealth which has been created by the totality of Ivoirians, in particular the hydroelectrical plant that the Ivory Coast has built at great expense.[38]

In January, 1960, Houphouët was given positive proof of his surmise that Ghana was definitely encouraging Ivoirian dissidents. Armand Attié's press conference that month at Accra was given wide coverage by the Ghana radio. In it Attié, described as president of the National Committee for Liberation of the Ivory Coast, claimed to represent the 52,000 people living in the Sanwi area who, he said, wanted to join Ghana and also claimed to have received the moral support of the Accra government.[39] Houphouët at once reacted to this statement by touring the frontier area, arming the veterans living there, and broadcasting a vigorous counterblast: "I am obliged to state plainly to Dr.

[38] *Afrique Nouvelle,* June 12, 1959.   [39] *Ibid.,* Feb. 17, 1960.

Nkrumah that he should stop cherishing illusions. He has neither the right nor the means to claim or hope to annex the smallest piece of the Ivory Coast state." [40]

Perhaps Nkrumah was impressed by Houphouët's firmness and also depressed by his failure to intimidate Sylvanus Olympio of Togo. In any case the Ghanaian leader seems to have pulled in his horns, and little more was heard about the Ivory Coast's government-in-exile. Camille Adam, after being refused permission to return to Abidjan to celebrate the Ivory Coast's independence in August, 1960, reportedly went to Nigeria, where he is teaching French. Even Nkrumah wired his congratulations to the Entente states on their acquisition of independence, though he could not resist offering them paternalistic advice in his own patronizing and florid style. He warned them to

be watchful that the independence [granted] is in truth a full and unfettered independence and not a disguised freedom delimited by agreements which accede to the Metropolitan country competence in important spheres of national life. For this is a false freedom dressed in the panoply of sovereignty but lacking the substance of power.[41]

At the end of July, 1960, Nkrumah made his first direct overture to Houphouët by inviting him to make an official visit to Accra. Houphouët did not immediately accept, but he sent Auguste Denise on a good-will mission to Accra and in October announced that Ghana and the Ivory Coast would exchange diplomatic representatives. The improving relations between the two countries received a setback later in 1960 when Nkrumah engineered the Mali Republic into the Ghana-Guinea Union after Houphouët had organized the Brazzaville Bloc. Houphouët must also have looked with a jaundiced eye at Ghana's attempts to woo Upper Volta and Dahomey from the Entente. Nor could he have been pleased when Nkrumah reportedly offered refuge to the Ivoirian students expelled from France in July, 1961, for their violent criticism of Houphouët.[42]

Yet both countries seem determined to established friendlier relations with each other. In August, 1961, Nkrumah repeated his invitation to Houphouët to make a state visit to Accra, and that same month the Ghanaian ambassador at Abidjan categorically denied that his government had ever officially recognized the Sanwi dissidents, and added that Ivoirian exiles in Ghana were a source of embarrassment to his

[40] *West Africa*, Feb. 13, 1960.   [41] *Ibid.*, July 2, 1960.
[42] *Marchés Tropicaux*, July 15, 1961; *Le Monde*, July 9–10, 1961.

government.[43] Four months later Houphouët pardoned both the Sanwi rebels who had taken refuge in Ghana and those whom he had imprisoned in Abidjan. At the same time he laid the cornerstone of a very long bridge that, when completed, will link the Sanwi region more closely with Abidjan. While he also finally agreed to make a state visit to Accra, Houphouët obviously remains skeptical about Nkrumah's overtures, and he is taking no chances on a possible recurrence of Ghanaian irredentism.

Houphouët's relations with Sékou Touré have been on a plane quite different from those with Nkrumah, though Guinea has shown itself to be far from friendly to his regime. Immediately after the September, 1958, referendum, Houphouët's emotions were compounded of anger and grief that Sékou Touré, his old friend and follower, had chosen a path so divergent from his own and had broken up the RDA movement. His annoyance and then his fear of subversion were increased by Guinea's union with Ghana and by their joint aggressiveness toward him and the Entente. In September, 1959, he was so convinced that the Conakry UGTAN was deliberately trying to undermine his government that he expelled the Guinean labor agitator, Yao Ngo Blaise. Six months later he became alarmed lest Guinea, wittingly or unconsciously, serve as a bridge for the spread of communism throughout West Africa. But between the two men the ties of friendship were never wholly severed, and they felt it imperative to meet after the Mali Federation broke up. Early in September, 1960, they met secretly at a place near their common frontier and, in the words of Houphouët, they met not as heads of state but as brothers.[44] But though they then agreed on a common policy toward Senegal and Soudan, basic disagreements largely on foreign policy issues subsequently drove them apart and, in 1961, they entered rival camps.

On a purely personal basis it seems that Houphouët and Sékou Touré might once more have gravitated closer together. Direct relations between them have been marked since late 1958 by a correctness—if not warmth—that contrasts with the sharpness of the attacks made on Houphouët by the Conakry radio. During the summer of 1959 Sékou Touré and Houphouët exchanged telegrams in which each urged the other to follow his own example. "History," said Houphouët moderately at the end of this exchange, "will decide between us." [45] Matters might

[43] *Le Monde*, Sept. 1, 1961.   [44] *Ibid.*, Sept. 6, 1960.
[45] *Ibid.*, Sept. 5, 1959.

have remained at this level of repartee had it not been for Guinea's sponsorship of Ngo Blaise's activities and that country's increasingly close relations with the Eastern bloc. But Houphouët seems to have attributed such moves less to Sékou Touré himself than to the extreme pro-Soviet element in the PDG. At a meeting held in March, 1960, at Ouagadougou, he warned his Entente colleagues that it was through Guinea that Africa was being opened for the first time to communism: "The Russians are in Guinea and the Chinese are with them. The presence of Chinese on the West African coast constitutes a menace on the ideological level and an even greater one in the economic domain."[46]

It may have been such criticism that provoked Sékou Touré into launching an open counteroffensive against Houphouët. When in April, 1960, the Guinean leader announced the uncovering of a "monstrous plot" against his regime, he claimed that the French-backed conspirators had been operating from bases in Senegal and the Ivory Coast.[47] The next month he followed up this attack by wiring a protest to Houphouët, alleging that a Guinean village had been attacked by raiders coming from the Ivory Coast.[48] But Sékou Touré's ire was directed more against Senegal and France than against Houphouët, and in July he went so far as to say that he would be happy to meet Ivory Coast leaders. The face-to-face meeting between Houphouët and Sékou Touré which followed the breakup of the Mali Federation was preceded by a good-will mission from Abidjan to Conakry. This was led by Coffi Godeau, a member of the PDCI politburo, who invited Sékou Touré to the Ivory Coast's independence celebrations. Had it not been for an element in Guinea that was profoundly opposed to Houphouët, it is possible that Sékou Touré might have accepted, and, after the September meeting with Houphouët, closer contacts might have been reestablished between the two men.

The extreme Marxists in the PDG politburo apparently have remained skeptical about Houphouët's basic motives, resentful of his free-enterprise economic policy under which the Ivory Coast has waxed rich, and annoyed that the country—albeit now independent and outside the Community—maintains close and friendly relations with France and with local French residents. Reportedly they believe that the Ivory Coast's economy is still essentially a colonial one, dependent

[46] *Ibid.*, March 12, 1960. [47] UPI dispatch from Abidjan, April 23, 1960.
[48] *Le Monde,* May 26, 1960.

upon French subsidies and the importation of cheap labor from Upper
Volta.[49] Encouraged by the success which PDG militants have had in
the Mali Republic, this group seemed convinced that by exploiting
Upper Volta's grievances against the Ivory Coast it could not only
undermine the latter country's prosperity but also break up the Entente.
And in this endeavor they have enjoyed the cooperation of Guinea's
partners, Ghana and Mali. In the spring of 1961 such efforts to subvert
Upper Volta seemed well on the way to success. The following July it
looked as if Dahomey, too, might be gravitating toward Ghana when
Maga took the road to Accra and made a trade agreement with
Nkrumah. The pressures and attractions that Upper Volta and Dahomey felt in relation to the Mali Federation early in 1959 have reasserted themselves, following formation of the Ghana-Guinea-Mali
Union and the deliberate attempts made by those three partners to
frustrate Houphouët's new bid for leadership.

As to Soudan, it appeared for a time after breakup of the Mali
Federation that Houphouët would be able to improve his relations
with Modibo Keita as he was doing with Sékou Touré. Radio Abidjan
broadcast an impartial account of the Mali crisis, and the large
Soudanese minority in the Ivory Coast made no attempt at reprisals
against the many Senegalese who were living in the main Ivoirian
towns. Houphouët was both sympathetic and discreet: he held out a
helping hand to Modibo, pardoning him for his defection from the
RDA and personal attacks, and he sent a good-will mission to Bamako
headed by Boucoum Adamadou. The Soudanese and Ivoirian premiers
exchanged visits early in September and reached an agreement by
which Abidjan replaced Dakar as the main foreign trading port of the
Mali Republic. Houphouët seemed temporarily to be emerging as
arbiter of the Mali situation. But to retain this ascendancy particularly
over the Soudanese he had to move further to the left. As time was
soon to tell, he could not move far or fast enough to prevent Modibo
from gravitating to the Ghana-Guinea Union, to which the Union
Soudanaise leaders were already strongly inclined ideologically. Houphouët, nevertheless, has remained on fairly cordial terms with Modibo,
and though he himself did not immediately make a state visit to the
Mali Republic the presidents of the legislatures of the two countries
exchanged visits in 1961 in a friendly atmosphere. Moreover, Houphouët, at least outwardly, seems not to have held against Modibo the
ever-closer ties that have been developing between him and Yaméogo.

[49] The Economist, June 25, 1960.

It was Nkrumah, rather than Houphouët's former RDA colleagues in Mali and Guinea, who took the initiative in trying to lure Upper Volta and Dahomey out of the Entente. Moreover, it was the government of Ghana that offered a customs union to Yaméogo on terms more generous than those given by the Ivory Coast. The fact that Upper Volta was now trading more heavily with the Ghana-Guinea-Mali Union than with its Entente partners, that Yaméogo was under internal pressure to shake off the domination of Houphouët and to denounce French policy in Algeria and the Sahara, and, in brief, that the attraction which some Voltaics had felt for the Mali Federation was now increased by concrete advantages, all inclined Yaméogo to accept and to reciprocate Nkrumah's advances.

Yaméogo's insistence on rejecting the military agreements reached with France by the other Entente states did not apparently worry Houphouët unduly, but that the Ivoirian leader should accept in silence Upper Volta's customs union with Ghana surprised many observers. Perhaps Houphouët believed that Yaméogo would never break away wholly from the Ivory Coast, for the Voltaic leader was reputed to be in considerable awe of the personality of *le sage* at Abidjan. In all likelihood, Houphouët either directly or indirectly exercised some behind-the-scenes pressure on Yaméogo, for in August, 1961, Yaméogo announced over Radio Ouagadougou that "those who are eager to see the Entente break up will be disappointed." [50] At Abidjan, a few days later, he felt impelled to state that the agreements he had made with Nkrumah were purely economic and that

at no time was any engagement of a political character undertaken. Upper Volta does not envisage leaving the Entente . . . because that formula appears to be the most supple. It permits the cooperation between states on a basis of perfect equality, without requiring those states [belonging to it] to renounce their own personality.[51]

Similarly, Houphouët has put no visible obstacle in the path of Dahomey's following Upper Volta's example. Probably he feels that those two states are so poor and powerless that he can afford to keep them on a loose leash. In any case he has become absorbed in playing a game for much higher stakes with the UAM and the Monrovia powers. The Entente, seen in this perspective, now appears to be but the first and smallest of a series of concentric circles which have been steadily expanded by Houphouët to include an ever-larger number of

West and Central African states. Although in January, 1961, he did create a ministry to deal with Entente affairs in the Ivory Coast, he now may well feel that the Entente has outlived its usefulness. Its fate is certainly of much less concern to him than in the days when he conceived it as a counterpoise to the now defunct Mali Federation.

THE BRAZZAVILLE BLOC AND THE
UNION AFRICAINE ET MALGACHE

The admission of the Ivory Coast, Upper Volta, Niger, and Dahomey to the United Nations in August, 1960, enabled Houphouët to widen the scope of his activities beyond the restricted circle formed by the Entente states. In particular, the imminence of a debate on Algeria in the United Nations General Assembly provided him with the opportunity to hold a conference at which he could make a new bid for the leadership of French-speaking Negro Africa. The calling of such a conference was no light undertaking, and Houphouët made careful preparations during the weeks that preceded its opening date on October 27. Nigeria's independence celebrations on October 1 gave him the chance to make personal contact with future participants at Lagos. The Senegalese proved to be the most responsive to his proposal, and a few days later Premier Dia came to Abidjan to talk over the final details.

The prudence and caution with which he proceeded were characteristic of Houphouët. If the conference was a success, he could later expand its scope, but he was anxious to avoid publicizing a failure. Therefore who was actually invited to attend has never been exactly known, sessions were held behind closed doors, and the agenda and final communiqué were couched in general terms. No representative of France was present at the conference, in order to underscore the purely African nature of the meeting. In the way in which it combined modernity with African tradition, the conference was also typical of Houphouët. The luxurious cars and receptions given to the delegates, not to mention the setting of Abidjan itself, were ultramodern, but the sessions themselves were planned to be in the nature of an "African palaver of wise men sitting under a village tree." [52]

According to Houphouët, the Abidjan Conference had been convened to find a solution to all problems troubling African heads of state. These were, specifically, Mauritania's admission to the United Nations, the crisis in the Congo, a common market for West African

[52] *Afrique Nouvelle*, Nov. 2, 1960.

countries, and, above all, the Algerian conflict. It seemed that agreement on none of these questions—with the possible exception of support for Mauritania—was likely to be reached and that the conference was foredoomed to failure. The most thorny issue was undoubtedly that of Algeria, for even the most Francophile African leaders were obviously not going to support France unconditionally and the most that could be hoped for was to find some compromise acceptable to General de Gaulle. On the Congo, the orientation that Houphouët seemed likely to give the conference was one unfavorable to Lumumba. This was made doubly certain by the presence at Abidjan of the pro-Kasavubu Premier of the Congo Republic, Abbé Fulbert Youlou, who brought with him Albert Kalondji of South Kasai. Indeed, it was the leadership physically represented at Abidjan that gave the clue to the turn which the conference discussions were likely to take.

That it was Houphouët who called this conference was undoubtedly the decisive factor in determining its attendance. For the Entente countries and, to a lesser degree, for the Equatorial French-speaking nations this was a command performance, and they were all duly represented by heads of state. (François Tombalbaye of Tchad at first refused to come, but he arrived later at the insistence of Houphouët, who feared that his absence might be misinterpreted.[53]) Premier Tsiranana too at first declined, but eventually he changed his mind. He may well have been afraid lest his well-known declaration that Algeria was a purely internal question for France might alienate his African colleagues and permanently isolate Madagascar. Senegal's wholehearted endorsement of the conference was shown by the presence of both Senghor and Dia. Inevitably Mauritania was represented at the highest level, for Premier Daddah had urgent need of African support in the United Nations to refute Moroccan claims. Perhaps most noteworthy of all was the appearance at Abidjan of Ahmadou Ahidjo, which suggested that Cameroun for the first time was going to associate itself closely with the rest of French-speaking Negro Africa. The Mali Republic, at this time not wanting to commit itself firmly in the political sphere and anxious to remain on good terms with both camps, compromised by sending an observer to Abidjan.

As significant as those who came to the Abidjan Conference were the absentees. The presence of Daddah automatically eliminated any representation of Morocco, though probably neither of the Maghreb states was invited to come because of their well-known pro-FLN senti-

[53] *Afrique Action,* Oct. 31, 1960.

ments. But the report that they had not been asked gave Togo's Premier Sylvanus Olympio an excuse to refuse to attend, on the ground that any discussion of the Algerian question would be fruitless without the participation of the two states most cognizant of the problem. Reasonable as this attitude was, it probably did not reflect all of Olympio's thinking. It was said that he had wanted the conference to be held at Lomé, where he might have been able to exercise some control over the proceedings. In any case, he was certainly reluctant to involve Togo, which had heretofore remained aloof from other French African political organizations, in a group whose membership and orientation were both uncertain quantities. In particular, he had misgivings about Houphouët's motives in calling the Abidjan Conference. In this connection, Olympio reportedly said:

Houphouët is a complex person. He is certainly sincere, but that is not the point. He has been for too long a Minister of France, and he loves France though periodically he gets annoyed with her. Once he told me that he no longer believed in France, for the *coup de Mali* was very hard for him to take. France's recognition [of Mali] wounded his pride.[54]

If Olympio was uncertain about Houphouët's current attitude toward France, the Guineans felt no such doubts. Whether or not they were invited to Abidjan, they lost no time in condemning the prospective conference as worse than useless. They implied that Paris was in fact sponsoring the conference. Because of Mali's strong stand in favor of the FLN and Senegal's favoring the admission of Red China to the UN, they thought that Paris was working through Abidjan to forestall an unfavorable vote on Algeria in the General Assembly. Sékou Touré admitted that a discussion of problems common to Africa and of African methods for taking action on them might be useful, but he expressed the fear that under current conditions the Abidjan Conference would "constitute a precedent that might serve as a pretext for sabotaging any true union of African states."[55]

Skepticism or indifference marked the general attitude of the African elite to Houphouët's conference, in part—but only in part—because he was deliberately trying not to raise too high hopes for its success. As it turned out, the conference was a new triumph for the Ivoirian leader. As one delegate was overheard to remark: "The Abbé Youlou has worn his cassock in vain, it is Houphouët who is the pope here."[56]

[54] *Ibid.*, Nov. 21, 1960.　　　　　　　　[55] *Afrique Nouvelle*, Oct. 25, 1960.
[56] *Afrique Action*, Oct. 31, 1960.

When the conference issued its final communiqué, widespread interest
was belatedly aroused, for it was obvious that more had been accomplished at Abidjan than expected and that the nucleus of a new force
in Africa had been born. It was announced that the participants had
agreed to adopt a common stand on world problems, particularly African ones, and that they would so instruct their delegations at the UN.
It was also stated that periodically other such conferences would be
held, first at Brazzaville and then at Yaoundé, and that the membership would be enlarged if possible. Members of the conference then
charged Houphouët, Senghor, and Youlou to inform General de Gaulle
of the decisions taken at Abidjan, especially those concerning Algeria.
In keeping with the discretion that had characterized the whole conference, no official report was published in regard to their talk with
the general. But later, in the General Assembly, it became apparent
that the Abidjan powers had agreed not to support the Afro-Asian proposal for a UN-supervised referendum in Algeria but to urge settlement
of the dispute by means of direct negotiations between France and the
FLN. Furthermore, their wholehearted support of Mauritania's candidacy for admission to the UN, their refusal specifically to condemn
French nuclear testing in the Sahara, and their opposition to Lumumba
in the Congo were clearly opposed to the stands taken by the "nationalist radicals" of French-speaking West Africa—Guinea and Mali.

Houphouët's success in achieving so wide an area of agreement
paved the way for a second conference held at Brazzaville on December 15–19, 1960. Just as the Nigerian independence celebrations had
afforded the sponsors of the Abidjan meeting a chance for preliminary
face-to-face discussions, so the independence celebrations at Nouak-
chott late in November enabled those preparing the Brazzaville Conference to discuss and draft its agenda. Although Houphouët had
intended that this conference study economic questions, it was Abbé
Youlou, the official host, who succeeded in transforming it into a political meeting. Youlou's ambition to be mediator in the Congo conflict
and to promote a Bakongo state under his leadership was well known.
Thus it was not surprising that he invited 18 representatives of all the
Congolese factions to cross Stanley Pool and attend the conference.
Moreover, it was easier for the Congo to be given top billing at the
Brazzaville meeting because an impasse had been reached on the other
main foreign policy issues. The Brazzaville Conference reiterated its
support for Premier Daddah, but Russia's veto of Mauritania's candidacy for admission to the UN had temporarily shelved that question.

And progress toward a solution of the Algerian conflict had to await the outcome of the referendum to be held in France the following month. Present at Brazzaville at the end of 1960 were all 12 of the French-speaking African states represented at Abidjan, with the conspicuous exception of Mali. The "family council of African nations," as Youlou described the meeting, was assembled to help such mutually hostile Congolese leaders as Kasavubu, Tshombe, Kalondji, Kassongo, Kamitatu, and Bomboko work out some acceptable compromise.

In regard to the Congo it looked—briefly—as if the Brazzaville twelve might succeed where more experienced and greater powers had failed. *Les douze* supported Kasavubu's thesis that a peaceful solution of the Congo crisis could be found around a conference table, at which all the warring factions would be represented. By this stand the Brazzaville conferees bowed themselves out of the picture as possible arbitrators of the Congolese situation. Although an observer from the Congo was invited—at the request of the Congolese—to the Tananarive meeting in September, 1961, he did not appear and there was no further question of the Congo's membership in the Brazzaville Bloc. As regards Algeria, the Brazzaville Conference took a stronger position than did its predecessor. Its members insistently asked France to end the war there in 1961 and, after direct negotiations with the Algerians and the exchange of political guarantees, to apply to them fully the principle of self-determination. More positive than the stands taken at Abidjan, those contained in the Brazzaville resolutions were still compromises. They did, however, embody a fundamental principle. This was that both issues were African questions and that they should be solved by Africans alone. For this same reason, the Brazzaville Bloc also opposed Communist intervention in Africa, in both political and economic forms, and its members openly showed a distrust of Russian intervention in the Congo. They declared themselves to be "obstinately dedicated" to the cause of international peace.

Probably the most important achievements of the Brazzaville meeting were the plans it laid for long-term cooperation between its members in the economic and social fields "on the basis of equality and concerted diplomacy." In conformity with Houphouët's views, there was to be no surrender of national sovereignty and no interference in the internal affairs of any member state. No supranational organization was to be set up. There would be only a permanent secretariat which was mainly to handle economic and technical questions of common concern. An agenda covering such matters was drawn up for study by a group of experts that were to meet at Dakar the next month. Another full-scale conference would be held at Yaoundé in March, at which decisions would be taken on the recommendations made by the Dakar experts and the feasibility of a mutual defense pact debated. Thus, *les douze* served notice on the world that they would no longer meet simply to formulate a common stand on specific questions of foreign policy but would deal as a permanently organized body with vital matters affecting their own economic and social development. That the Brazzaville Bloc was not intended to be an exclusive group was shown by its members' expressed wish that they would be joined by any African states that shared their objectives. How far the more radical nationalist Africans were from joining the Brazzaville Bloc was shown a few days later by Mali's adherence to the Ghana-Guinea Union and by formation of the Casablanca group the following month. There is little doubt that both moves were largely stimulated by the work of the Brazzaville Conference.

The meeting of the Brazzaville Bloc's economic experts at Dakar on January 31, 1961, marked another forward step, although their recommendations had no binding force. Here for the first time were discussed by Africans meeting together the major problems posed by their countries' underdevelopment: the fluctuating prices paid for their agricultural exports, the question of how to harmonize the divergencies in their respective fiscal regimes, their attitude toward the Common Market, foreign aid, and the like. The conclusions reached at Dakar were the more solid for representing the consensus of African expert opinion, voluntarily arrived at and not imposed from outside. Reportedly the debates were animated, sometimes tense, particularly in regard to creating a common air-transport company. But the conference, which had opened in an atmosphere of reserve and caution, ended in a kind of euphoria. As had been the case at Abidjan a few months before, greater unanimity was achieved than had been anticipated. It now appeared that a coherent regional group was emerging that would not merely attack the vestiges of colonialism emotionally and negatively but would also try to deal constructively with Africa's most fundamental problems. Certainly a measure of the greater self-confidence that *les douze* had now acquired was shown by their willingness to enlarge the scope of their cooperation by tackling divisive issues of internal policy, particularly in the economic domain.

According to Ernest Milcent, writing in *Le Monde* on February 9, 1961:

Many proposals were voted in regard to justice, nationality, fiscal regimes, revival of the French West African customs union, relations with the [European] common market. . . . The conference did not try to cope with monetary or credit questions in order not to trouble the negotiations currently taking place between France and the Entente. . . . This conference was important in promoting a clear realization of the existence of an African economy. For the first time, twelve African states tried to define the main lines of a union that would be not only political but economic. Their leaders appreciate their countries' underdevelopment and want to unite and coordinate their policies, help each other and their products, and formulate a common attitude toward regional and international organizations. Even if it had not reached any concrete conclusions, this conference would have been significant.

Not only was the draft of an Organisation Africaine et Malgache pour la Coopération Economique (OAMCE) that was worked out at Dakar accepted by les douze, but a political union was also achieved by their leaders meeting at Yaoundé on March 31. This was the Union Africaine et Malgache (UAM), comprising six members of the re-modeled Franco-African Community (Senegal, Gabon, Tchad, the Central African Republic, the Congo Republic, and Madagascar), five other French-speaking states which had made or were in process of negotiating bilateral agreements with France (the Entente countries and Mauritania), and, finally, the Cameroun Republic. Superficially, the UAM appeared to be a supranational organization. But its secretary-general was merely the executive officer who carried out the decisions reached unanimously by the UAM Council, on which each member state was represented and of which the presidency rotated among the members. In the UAM, the principle of national sovereignty was maintained, and the pledge of noninterference in the internal affairs of member states was renewed. "The form taken by the UAM at Yaoundé reflected the ideas of Houphouët more than those of any other African leader." [57]

In some respects, the UAM was not far apart from the group formed at Casablanca on January 7, 1961, by Ghana, Guinea, Mali, Morocco, and the UAR. Those five powers had also recognized the need for united action in facing the problems posed by their common colonial past and by underdevelopment. It was primarily in regard to the form such united action should take and on their approach to foreign policy issues that the two groups were furthest apart. In the eyes of Hou-

[57] Philippe Decraene, Le Monde, April 19, 1961.

phouët the gravest mistake of the Casablanca powers was their insistence on creating a supranational organization, and their cardinal sin was knitting close relations with the Communist bloc. In an interesting article published in *Afrique Nouvelle* on March 22, 1961, Houphouët gave his views regarding the differences between the two groups.

The first African states that became independent joined the Afro-Asian bloc of Bandung, which professes a policy of positive neutrality. This is only a veneer, and one has only to scratch beneath the surface to find China and the Communist world. If we are naïve enough to cut ourselves off from the West, we will be invaded by the Chinese, and Soviet Russia will impose communism on our countries.

Aside from Algeria and South Africa which have large white minorities, the African states cannot claim that they have been invaded by white men and that, during the colonial period, their populations were exterminated. Despite certain mistakes made by the colonizers, we have made progress under colonialism and have emerged from it under the best possible conditions. This is true of the Ivory Coast, and in most of our states the population is larger than it was and we now control production. . . . After achieving independence we were able to organize ourselves on the basis of friendship and of a cooperation [with the *Métropole*] that is profitable to our countries. And we will preserve that most precious possession—the freedom of man. . . .

We see the Soviets at work in Africa. Theirs is a policy of hatred, of sowing discord among Africans, and of terrorism in countries like Cameroun and the Congo. We must choose. The 12 of Brazzaville have chosen the Occidental world. The other group, which calls itself the group of unity, has chosen an alliance with Asia and has given its preference to the East. I do not think that such a choice will lead to unity, for those who make it are isolated. It was attempted between Dakar and Bamako, and it did not work. For many, it means unity around their own persons or their country. If Nkrumah thinks of unity, it is on condition that he should be its leader and his country the capital.

In the group that we form, no one claims a leadership position. It was suggested that I preside over this group and I refused. In the race toward unity, many can think of only one post—the top one. Do you think that Nasser would accept Nkrumah to head up African unity, or vice versa? He who cannot get the top post will abandon the race, and that is why African unity is not possible now. . . .

Two tendencies exist in Africa. The first aims to achieve African unity, but it has never been decided whether this is to be realized from Bizerte to the Cape or is to be limited to sub-Saharan Africa. Nor has it been decided whether it is better to have a federal government and assembly or a single parliament. Another group of Africans exists to which I belong. This group believes that we cannot achieve unity right away, for unity on a continental scale would be extremely difficult. The best formula is a supple one—that of close collaboration between African states. In other words, union must be created within the framework of national diversity and of the personalities of each state. That is why [at Yaoundé] the 12 of Brazzaville intend to lay the foundations of a close cooperation that will not [adversely] affect the independence of the participants.

Subsequently, the UAM has moved steadily forward along the lines of cooperation described by Houphouët, who has remained its self-effacing leader. At Yaoundé the company Air-Afrique was formed, moves toward a customs union made, and a common attitude toward the European Economic Community gradually formulated. Moreover, at the Tananarive Conference of September 6–12, a defense pact was signed which supplemented the defense agreements that most of the UAM's members had made with France. The UAM's structure was reinforced, and its expanding functions were distributed among the member states. Cotonou was selected as administrative headquarters of the UAM and a Dahomeyan named its secretary-general; Ouagadougou was chosen as the site of the newly formed defense organization and a Senegalese officer named to head it; a postal and telecommunications union was set up at Brazzaville; and study committees were formed and placed under the supervision of a Malagasy whose base of operations would be at Yaoundé. To meet the cost of the UAM's operations a budget was established, to which each member state would contribute according to its national revenues.

The firm structure now achieved by the UAM, its businesslike preparation of conferences, the unobtrusiveness of Houphouët's leadership, and, above all, his insistence on a policy of African solutions for African problems to be achieved by direct negotiations kept the UAM from foundering on the foreign policy issues that continued to divide its members. In the UN, Houphouët and Hamani Diori had taken a minority stand on Bizerte, and on the Congo, Abbé Youlou now found himself isolated in supporting the Katanga secessionists. Yet at Tananarive the UAM was able to work out moderately nationalistic and generally acceptable positions on both questions. The conference's final communiqué urged a solution of the Bizerte question in keeping with Tunisia's sovereignty and with the desire to cooperate expressed by both the countries involved. On Algeria, the hope was expressed for a cooperation that would permit the Sahara's wealth to be enjoyed profitably by Algeria, France, and the other African countries directly concerned. In regard to the Congo, the United Nations' "unwarranted interference" in internal Congolese affairs was regretted, but that organization's motive of promoting unity in the Congo was approved.

On a wider range of international problems than had ever before been tackled by the UAM, unanimity was achieved. The UAM not only condemned Russia's veto of Mauritania's application for membership in the UN but also the Soviets' resumption of nuclear testing. It also disapproved of Khrushchev's troika proposal though it did advocate a more equitable and wider geographical distribution of the posts of assistants to the Secretary-General. Britain's application for membership in the European Economic Community was singled out for special praise. The UAM powers stressed the need to avoid an intensification of the cold war in Berlin and Laos, and they urged that the process of decolonization be accelerated. Here, however, they drew a clear-cut distinction between the policies of France and Britain, which they praised, and those of Portugal, Spain, and South Africa, which they strongly denounced. Going one step further, the UAM states declared that decolonization would be ineffective unless the process was accompanied by large-scale aid to newly decolonized countries. They wound up with a general endorsement of democratic solutions that would preserve the inalienable right of Africans to enjoy national independence.

Noteworthy as was the progress being made by the UAM, Houphouët (and also Senghor) still aspired to widen its scope and membership. The UAM's charter specified that it was open to all independent African states whose candidacy for admission was unanimously approved by its existing members. Like the Entente before it, the UAM was in the view of its founder the nucleus of a wider grouping that he hoped would include English-speaking African states and even some members of the Casablanca group. And the conference that met at Monrovia in May, 1961, was largely due to the initiative taken by the UAM's two main leaders. In March, 1961, Houphouët described the steps that he and Senghor had taken as follows:

We have asked all the independent states of Africa to meet together for a general confrontation of our viewpoints. Our group [the UAM] proposed an agenda that included the Congo, Algeria, the Sahara atomic explosions, economic and cultural cooperation, as well as a resolution embodying the principle of noninterference in the internal affairs of other states. Three have replied [to our invitation]. Nkrumah agreed to come if we accepted his theses. Modibo [Keita] asked that the invitation be addressed to him through some neutral personality, so we asked President Tubman to do the inviting. Finally, on the proposal of Nigeria, it was decided that a letter signed by the heads of the states of Liberia, Nigeria, Mali, and the Ivory Coast—and to which Cameroun was added at my request—would be sent to all independent states. Those states would be invited to meet at Monrovia on April 8 with the Congo question as the sole item on the agenda. . . . I think that this conference will enable us to understand each other. We are living through a period of growing pains. We believe that within five years the situation will be normal and that whatever is to be the nature of our friendships then we will have arrived at an understanding.[58]

Houphouët's optimism proved—in part at least—to be justified, for 20 of the 27 nations invited were represented at the conference that opened at Monrovia on May 9. The initial sponsors of this conference reflected a wide range of African opinion. Guinea and Mali represented the Casablanca bloc, the Ivory Coast and Cameroun the UAM; and Togo and Nigeria were uncommitted. But the two Casablanca states failed to send delegations, as did Ghana, Morocco, and the UAR; Sudan refused at the last minute, after it was learned that Mauritania would attend; and Tshombe was asked not to come because of the tension created by Lumumba's assassination. The Casablanca group had asked that the conference be postponed until its members had time to produce their own charter. They also wanted the conference to include on its agenda a debate on the political action that should be taken immediately on the Congo, Angola, Algeria, and South Africa. Although the majority of delegates who came to Monrovia expected to discuss those issues, they wanted the conference to concentrate on the widest possible areas of agreement and on plans for long-term cooperation. The Casablanca powers, after their proposals were turned down, not only refused to go to Monrovia but expressed their disapproval of holding the conference at all.

This negative stand dashed the hope that a reconciliation between the African "reformists and revolutionaries" might take place at Monrovia, but the conference did bring together a remarkable array of outstanding African personalities. Fifteen premiers or heads of state, both French- and English-speaking, attended, and for the first time the leaders of Nigeria, Togo, Somalia, Sierra Leone, Ethiopia, Liberia, and Tunisia conferred with their UAM colleagues. Of the uncommitted

[58] *Afrique Nouvelle*, March 22, 1961.

leaders Sir Abubakar of Nigeria was the most important, and on most of the major issues his views concurred with those of Houphouët and Senghor. Because of such local tensions as those between Cameroun and Nigeria, Ethiopia and Somalia, the Congo Republic and the Leopoldville government, and because of the special relationship between the UAM countries and France, controversial points were avoided or soft-pedaled. All those present approved of imposing penalties on South Africa and of proffering aid to the Angolese nationalists, and France was only mildly censured for its testing in the Sahara within the context of a general condemnation of all nuclear explosions. Algerian independence was favored without wholeheartedly backing the FLN. An appeal was made to Congolese leaders to settle their disputes within the framework of the UN: disapproval of both Tshombe and Gizenga was expressed, but a resolution condemning the assassination of Lumumba was deleted.[59]

Although they realized that such resolutions were bound to displease the Casablanca powers, the Monrovia-group leaders refused to accept the rift between the two blocs as final. At the conference Senghor said that "far from blaming the Casablanca nations [for their absence], we should by the serious nature of our work persuade them of the need to join us in the future." [60] In the summer of 1961, the negotiations being conducted by France with Guinea and with Mali, the trade agreements reached between Guinea and Senegal and between the Ivory Coast and Mali, and the lessening of tension over the Congo that resulted from Adoula's assumption of the premiership, all gave cause for optimism. In his comprehensive tour of West African states in the fall of 1961, Houphouët hoped through the personal diplomacy at which he excelled to persuade the more radical African leaders to attend the second summit conference of the Monrovia bloc that met at Lagos in January, 1962. But again at the last minute the Casablanca powers failed to attend, and once more it was the Algerian issue that provided the excuse for their absence. By calling for another summit conference at an unspecified date of all the independent African nations, which could include Algeria, the delegates at Lagos showed that they did not despair of an eventual reconciliation between themselves and the Casablanca powers. Such perennial optimism seems based on the assumption that it is specific issues which divide the two blocs rather than a more fundamental approach to African and world problems.

By insisting on organized intergovernmental cooperation as opposed

[59] *The Economist*, May 20, 1961.   [60] *Le Monde*, May 17, 1961.

to Pan-African political integration, by refusing to surrender national sovereignty and obliterate present frontiers, by affirming the political equality of all independent African states and their freedom to enter or reject blocs, and by their generally moderate and pro-Western policies, the Monrovia powers conform to Houphouët's views. And in concentrating on economic cooperation prepared at a series of presummit meetings of technical experts and in the structure it is assuming, the Monrovia bloc has followed the pattern set by the UAM. Although the UAM at Tananarive affirmed that it was but a part of the Monrovia group and although Houphouët has willingly shared the limelight with other like-minded African leaders at Monrovia and Lagos, he has been careful to keep the UAM's distinctive organization and his own leadership intact. Since the UAM and the Ghana-Guinea-Mali Union are the only organized groups in their respective blocs, any hope of attaining real unity seems to lie in harmonizing the viewpoints of their leaders. At present there is little indication of any serious willingness on the part of Nkrumah, Sékou Touré, and Modibo Keita to accept Houphouët's views, or vice versa.

RELATIONS WITH NON-AFRICAN STATES AND THE
UNITED NATIONS

In the months that followed the Ivory Coast's achievement of independence and admission to the United Nations, Houphouët used his newly acquired powers to develop the Brazzaville Bloc. Obviously he was in no hurry to start negotiations with France before he had strengthened his hand by building up a new grouping of countries in Africa. This long delay engendered nervousness among the European civil servants and businessmen living in the Ivory Coast. But contrary to reports in the Paris press, it did not lead to any large-scale flight of French capital or mass departures by locally resident Europeans.

When negotiations were finally begun at Paris in January, 1961, Houphouët was under strong internal and external pressures. To refute the charge of his opponents that he was a French stooge and also to further his own leadership ambitions, he had to get the maximum concessions from France. When Houphouët made it plain for the first time that the Entente would not reenter the Community, he ran into the opposition of Premier Debré. Even the group of French officials who had reportedly encouraged Houphouët in the summer of 1960 to seek independence for the Entente were now dismayed and offended by his stand. The next difficulty arose when Houphouët insisted—or so it was said—that French aid be granted to the Entente states in a lump sum and for a long period without France's being able to exercise any control over the use to which such funds would be put.[61] Further disagreement arose over the question of defense, which the French wanted organized on a joint basis. Houphouët, for his part, preferred bilateral agreements in which France would agree to train the new national armies of the Entente states and provide equipment for them without establishing any common defense organization.

For some months negotiations were carried on intermittently, the Entente states holding their own conferences at Ouagadougou and Niamey for the purpose of presenting a united front. The negotiations were prolonged by the determination of Yaméogo and Hamani Diori to associate the youthful radicals of their parties with their decisions. On more than one occasion the patience of all the negotiators was strained to the breaking point, but as time went on a greater spirit of compromise developed on both sides. Houphouët's attitude was doubtless influenced by the Casablanca Conference of January, 1961, which dashed any hopes that he may have had of achieving a reconciliation with Guinea and a *rapprochement* with the Mali Republic. Moreover, his relations with Nigeria, which had promised to become close in the summer of 1960, had perceptibly cooled off as a result of friction said to have developed at the time of the Lagos independence celebrations in October.[62] Houphouët had apparently been disappointed by the small amount of aid offered to the Entente states by the United States. Finally, Houphouët was sincerely and deeply attached to France despite his disillusionment regarding the Community's evolution, as had been shown by his persistent efforts to formulate a compromise Algerian resolution in the United Nations and by his consistent approval of French nuclear tests in the Sahara—even at the price of alienating the Afro-Asian bloc. To avoid further antagonizing that group and, more important, left-wing elements in Africa, he proposed at Paris that regulation of the status of French nationals in the Entente countries be postponed for later discussion. He then abandoned his demand for global aid without strings, even denying that he had ever made such a request.[63]

The French government, for its part, was also willing to compromise. It was anxious to salvage as much as possible of the Community, which had now dwindled by half from its original membership. It realized

---

[61] *Afrique Action*, Feb. 13, 1961.   [62] *Le Monde*, Jan. 1, 1961.
[63] *Nice-Matin*, March 7, 1961.

also that loyalty to General de Gaulle had become a far stronger cohesive force than the Community's structural ties. Above all, it was
eager to avoid any revision of the agreements already reached with
the Community states and any adverse repercussions upon the negotiations just beginning with Mauritania. On most of the crucial points it
acceded to the Entente's demands or reached some compromise. France
agreed to allot funds to each of the Entente states for a five-year period,
and they were given a free hand to spend the money to carry out their
own development plans. However, the Paris officials would have the
right to see that the funds granted were used for the purposes stated
and that, as one commentator put it, money earmarked for a dispensary
would not be spent to build a functionary's villa.[64] France also promised
to open its market to certain Entente exports, permit those states to
issue their own bank notes, finance an African university to be built at
Abidjan, and provide their education services with as many French
teachers as possible. The chief hitch was with Upper Volta, for
Yaméogo balked at the provision permitting France to retain bases in
his territory to which all the other Entente states agreed. Therefore on
April 24, 1961, Upper Volta signed only five of the six agreements made
by France with the Entente states, which were ratified by the National
Assembly in Paris on July 20, 1961.

In the months that followed the signing of those agreements, Houphouët took pains to substantiate his contention that he would remain
as good a friend of France outside as inside the Community and that
it was France—not the Ivory Coast—that had rejected the "marriage"
which he had wanted to arrange between the two countries. To be
sure, he wanted continued French aid for the development of the
Ivory Coast, but in some concrete ways he showed a disinterested attachment to France. He was obviously sincere in regretting the resignation of three French ministers from his cabinet, but he succeeded in
retaining their cooperation with his government. He also retained the
services of 125 French teachers, 25 magistrates, and 47 doctors and
pharmacists, as well as many other technical experts. He has sought
to reassure the resident French by permitting them to continue voting
in Ivory Coast elections and by encouraging them in other ways to
remain in the country. In refusing to vote for the Afro-Asian resolutions
on the Bizerte dispute in the United Nations in August, 1961—and of
the French-speaking states only the Ivory Coast and Niger abstained—
Houphouët showed that he was not mouthing empty words when he

[64] *Europe-France-Outremer*, March, 1961.

said on his official visit to France in June, 1961, that he had come there as a "friend and a brother." [65]

France now better understands Houphouët's circuitous policy and has also shown tangibly that it values his friendship highly. By maintaining its heavy subsidies to some Ivoirian exports, it has recognized the need to contribute to that country's prosperity. Moreover, in September, 1961, it granted the Ivory Coast fresh funds amounting to 876,000,000 CFA francs. In addition to financing the prospective university at Abidjan and Houphouët's palatial residence at Cocody, France has also agreed to guarantee a loan for expanding the Bia hydroelectrical dam. On October 26, 1961, a five-year trade agreement was signed by representatives of both countries in which France undertook to import 100,000 tons of coffee "at a price to be fixed each year and always at a level satisfactory to the Ivory Coast irrespective of world rates"; tariff preferences are likewise given to Ivoirian exports of timber and cocoa; and banana exports will receive the same treatment as those from the Antilles. Moreover, the Ivory Coast is to have complete control of its foreign currency earnings and the right to impose quotas or duties on French imports that compete with Ivoirian industries. In return, the Ivory Coast promised to import from France a total of 22,000,000,000 CFA francs worth of goods.

Relations between the two countries late in 1961 reached a new pitch of cordiality, and the August celebrations of the Ivory Coast's independence seemed indeed to inaugurate a second Franco-Ivoirian honeymoon, following a brief estrangement between the two countries. Not only were hundreds of French merchants, industrialists, and officials brought to Abidjan by plane to enjoy Houphouët's lavish hospitality, but his guests included two such diverse French politicians as Michel Debré and Pierre Mendès-France.

Among the other distinguished guests at the Abidjan independence celebrations in August, 1961, were Robert Kennedy and Mennen Williams, whose very presence was considered as significant as the warm words of praise for Houphouët that they voiced. The American Attorney General even likened Houphouët to George Washington and also described him as "an international statesman whose influence is felt not only in Africa but everywhere that man is free." [66] Kennedy deliberately paid tribute to an outstanding African leader whose country has not only a stable government and trade connections with the United States but also staunchly pro-Western sympathies. Houphouët

[65] *Le Monde*, June 8, 1961. [66] *New York Times*, Aug. 6, 1961.

has given evidence of his intention to enlarge his concept of the Negro-white community, which he failed to achieve with France, to include such Occidental countries as the United States and West Germany. The presence and praise of such important officials seem to have done much to offset the disappointment allegedly felt that American aid to all four Entente states thus far has not exceeded $7,000,000. Some attribute the small amount of this aid to Washington's fear lest a larger sum stimulate Soviet competition, while others believe that the American government saw no need to do more because the Entente states were in any case firmly pro-Western.

The only Russian present at the Abidjan fete was the Soviet ambassador to Guinea, accompanied by a few Czechs. In fact, no other Iron Curtain countries were invited to attend. Houphouët is frankly alarmed by the Communist penetration of Africa, and, unlike other African leaders including Senghor, he is averse to accepting multinational aid. He claims he does not fear the spread of communism per se in the Ivory Coast but rather that those using Communist ideology—not so much the Russians as the Chinese—will bring their surplus populations into the country.[67] He told André Blanchet [68] that "if through misguided and overgenerous hospitality, we let them infiltrate the Ivory Coast, we will wake up too late to a realization of the yellow peril." As to foreign aid, he has commented:

We will ask all nations individually to aid us provided that such aid does not jeopardize our independence. In the first place we will turn to France, but we know that France after its wars in Indochina and Algeria and after being solicited by all its former dependencies cannot satisfy all our needs, so inevitably we must ask help from other countries. We are thinking of turning first to the United States, for that country has the means to aid us, then to West Germany and the other Common Market countries, and then to Israel. In the degree to which the Eastern bloc wants to help us without at the same time exporting its ideology and a foreign population, we might accept—but only after we have knocked at the doors of the other powers and only if the aid they offer us is insufficient. We are not thinking of taking the road to Moscow, Prague, or Peking.[69]

Houphouët is distinguished among contemporary African leaders in feeling that Africans should have no sense of shame or embarrassment in regard to their colonial past or in asking aid of the Western powers. Colonialism he has described as "a necessary evil, if it was an evil," and he has pointed out that the United States, now the greatest of the

[67] *Le Monde*, June 10, 1961.   [68] *Nice-Matin*, Jan. 19, 1961.   [69] *Ibid*.

Occidental powers, was itself once a colony. If Africa's present economic backwardness requires it to ask for a helping hand, this is a temporary and reparable situation for its resources are great. But he is emphatic in wanting only the Western industrial nations, and possibly Israel, to assist Africa in general and the Ivory Coast in particular to realize that potential. Houphouët has often stated his conviction that Africa is the prolongation of Europe, not of Asia, and that the unity of Africans on a continental scale is a dream impossible to realize.[70]

Houphouët's pro-Western outlook certainly comes in part from his attachment to France; it derives, too, from his fear of Asians, and, to a lesser degree, it is also due to his antipathy toward certain Arab leaders. At a Paris press conference in June, 1961, he said that the Ivory Coast feels no need for any "higher African leadership," adding that "Nasser and the king of Morocco should be satisfied with what they have got. . . . As far as Black Africa is concerned, what we desire is to be left alone to look after our own affairs to the best of our ability.[71] He believes that the Ivory Coast has an "inter-African vocation as a promoter of the collaboration between French-speaking Africa and the West." [72] Inevitably such an attitude has aroused the antagonism of the Afro-Asian bloc, which holds Houphouët largely responsible for frustrating its attempts to create a united front on such matters as Algeria, nuclear testing in the Sahara, Mauritania, and the Congo. Houphouët does not believe that an African state must inevitably belong to the Afro-Asian bloc in the United Nations, holding that "our sole link with the Asians is underdevelopment, and what differentiates us profoundly is that they suffer from overpopulation and we from underpopulation." [73]

I personally see no reason why we should link our destiny with the Asians. Can you expect me to mediate between India and Pakistan? African problems need African solutions, and it seems to me paradoxical that some African leaders who claim to be in favor of African unity are still opposed in the United Nations to constituting an African bloc.[74]

And his general skepticism about the efficacy of that international body is shown by this statement to André Blanchet: "I cannot see how the United Nations, composed of countries with different and divergent interests and objectives, could aid another country without there appearing the elements that divide that organization." [75]

Today Houphouët stands out among the French-speaking African

[70] *Le Monde*, June 8, 9, 10, 1961; *Europe-France-Outremer*, Dec., 1960.
[71] *West Africa*, June 17, 1961.   [72] *Le Monde*, June 8, 1961.   [73] *Ibid.*
[74] *Nice-Matin*, Jan. 20, 1961.   [75] *Ibid.*

leaders as the main advocate of a moderate, economically liberal, and generally pro-Western Africanism, as opposed to the militant economic nationalism, Pan-Africanism, and neutralism of the Ghana-Guinea-Mali partners. In many vital respects, Houphouët's policy runs counter to prevailing trends in Africa, and he may once more be forced to modify it. Much depends on the Ivory Coast's continued economic expansion, for without it his present plans for transforming his country into a modern state cannot be fulfilled.

BIBLIOGRAPHY

As yet there is no comprehensive up-to-date book on the Ivory Coast in either French or English, and the student of that territory must consult a fairly wide range of publications to acquire a picture of the contemporary scene there. Periodicals in French which give data on the Ivory Coast in almost every issue are *Afrique, Afrique Nouvelle, Chroniques de la Communauté, Fraternité,* and *Marchés Tropicaux.* Material in English is much scarcer, but occasional articles on the Ivory Coast appear in *Africa Report* and *West Africa.*

OFFICIAL PUBLICATIONS

Ambassade de France, Service de Presse et d'Information. *The Republic of the Ivory Coast.* New York, Nov., 1960.
La Documentation Française, Notes et Etudes Documentaires. *La République de Côte d'Ivoire.* Paris, Nov. 7, 1959.

The first of these pamphlets is a very abridged and popularized version of the second. The latter is a clear factual presentation of recent developments in the Ivory Coast, particularly in the economic field.

BOOKS AND ARTICLES

Aké, Loba. *Kocoumbo, l'Etudiant Noir.* Paris: Flammarion, 1959. The life of an Ivoirian student in Paris, fictionalized though based on personal knowledge of the subject.
Amon d'Aby, F. J. *La Côte d'Ivoire dans la Cité Africaine.* Paris: Larose, 1951. A firsthand account of the political scene in the Ivory Coast during the early postwar years by an African participant who has a wealth of information but strong anti-RDA bias.
Angoulvant, G. *La Pacification de la Côte d'Ivoire, 1908–1915.* Paris: Larose, 1916. An authoritative account of the Ivory Coast on the eve of World War I, by one of the outstanding French governors of that colony.
Badie, Bernard. "Le Sort du Travailleur Noir de Côte d'Ivoire," *Le Tra-*

vail en Afrique Noire. Paris: Présence Africaine, 1952. The author describes the situation of the Ivoirian laborer in Abidjan from a left-wing point of view.

Boutillier, J.-L. *Bougouanou, Côte d'Ivoire.* Paris: Berger-Levrault, 1960. A very detailed study of one area of the country by a French sociologist. A similar socioeconomic study of the Adioukrou region was written in 1958 by the same author in collaboration with Marguerite Dupire for the Office de la Recherche Scientifique et Technique Outre-Mer.

Buell, R. L. *The Native Problem in Africa.* 2 vols. New York: Macmillan, 1928. Contains one of the very few descriptions in English of the Ivory Coast in the first quarter of the twentieth century.

Chailley, M. "Explorateurs de la Côte d'Ivoire," *Encyclopédie Mensuelle d'Outre-Mer.* Paris, July, 1951. The story of the country's early explorers told by an army officer.

Cowan, L. Gray. *Local Government in West Africa.* New York: Columbia University Press, 1958. Scattered references to administrative problems, including those related to the local chiefs in the Ivory Coast.

Hailey, Lord W. M. *An African Survey.* London: Oxford University Press, 1957. A general reference work with some comments on the Ivory Coast.

Holas, B. *Changements Sociaux en Côte d'Ivoire.* Paris: Presses Universitaires de France, 1961. A short but up-to-date description of the sociology, art, and customs of the Ivory Coast by a distinguished staff member of the Institut Français d'Afrique Noire, who has been head of its center at Abidjan.

Kitchen, H. *The Press in Africa.* Washington, D.C.: Ruth Sloan Associates, 1958. A very brief treatment of the press in West Africa, including Ivory Coast newspapers.

Mouëzy, H. *Assinie et le Royaume de Krinjabo.* Paris: Larose, 1953. General Gallieni wrote a preface for the first edition of this work, published in 1942. This is one of the few accounts of the early history of an Ivory Coast kingdom, and the bibliography at the end of each chapter is especially noteworthy.

Platt, W. J. *An African Prophet: The Ivory Coast Movement and What Came of It.* London: British and Foreign Bible Society, 1934. A missionary's emotional evaluation of the sect founded by the "prophet" Harris.

Tricart, J. "Les Echanges entre Côte d'Ivoire et Savannes Soudaniennes," *Cahiers d'Outre-Mer* (Bordeaux), July, 1956. A description of internal trade routes and products.

Zolberg, Aristide R. "The Heterogeneous Monolith," *West Africa* (London), July 30 and Aug. 6, 1960. The best account in English of recent political developments and party organization by an outstanding American authority on Ivory Coast politics.

NEWSPAPERS AND PERIODICALS

Côte d'Ivoire, 1959. Special number of *Marchés Tropicaux.* Paris, April 18,
1959. This issue contains informative articles on different aspects of the
Ivory Coast's economy on the eve of independence.

Fraternité, Abidjan. Official organ of the PDCI.

La Nouvelle Côte d'Ivoire et les Autres Etats de l'Entente. Special number
of *Europe-France-Outremer.* Paris, Dec., 1960. Most of the articles are
on economic matters, with a few on current political developments.

VI

LIBERIA

By J. GUS LIEBENOW

Indiana University

Historical Background

Of the many Western colonial ventures in Africa, few have withstood the wave of nationalism which now seeks to dislodge alien minorities from their positions of political power. In most instances the alternatives open to immigrant communities in the new African states have been either physical withdrawal from the territory or accommodation to a minority or even a neutral role in political affairs. The other alternative—continuation of political domination—has been abandoned by all except the Portuguese in Angola and Mozambique, the Afrikaners in the Republic of South Africa, the British in the Rhodesias, and the Americo-Liberians in Africa's oldest republic, Liberia.[1]

Admittedly, the grouping of Liberia with the foregoing states may be doing an injustice to both the spirit and practice of President William V. S. Tubman's Unification Policy. Nevertheless, despite progress made toward integration in Liberia during the past seventeen years, it is clear that the processes of political, economic, and social change in that country have remained firmly in the hands of an alien minority. It is a minority whose antecedents are more Western than African and who have only belatedly attempted to identify themselves with the destinies of a resurgent Africa. Moreover, it was President Tubman

[1] This chapter is the product of field research conducted in Liberia during 1960–1961. The author is indebted to the Social Science Research Council and to the Indiana University Research Foundation for their generous assistance.

himself who in 1960 acknowledged that the administration of the vast tribal hinterland of Liberia was based upon the colonial pattern.[2]

THE ESTABLISHMENT OF LIBERIA

The founding of Liberia was inspired by a number of prominent white Americans who were concerned with the problems of slavery, the slave trade, and the untenable position of "free persons of color" in the United States prior to the Civil War. They were convinced that an ideal solution would be found to many problems by the establishment of a colony on the west coast of Africa which could serve as a refuge for freed American Negroes who desired to be repatriated to the land of their ancestors. It could provide an answer, too, to the embarrassing question of what was to be done with the Africans taken from slaving vessels intercepted by the American navy following the outlawing of the slave trade in 1808.

It is obvious that there were mixed motivations on the part of those who organized themselves into the American Colonization Society in 1816 and into similar groups in later years. Some saw repatriation as a convenient device for ridding cities both north and south of a class which had only a vague legal status and was a constant source of social friction. The Southern planters, who figured prominently in the re-settlement movement, were even more vitally interested in eliminating a class whose very existence constituted a threat to the institution of Negro servitude. There were other supporters of the Colonization Society, however, who appeared to be moved by more clearly humanitarian objectives. Certainly in this group would belong Jehudi Ashmun, Thomas Buchanan, and other agents of the Society, who literally gave their lives for Liberia by accompanying the settlers and ministering to their many needs during the formative years of the colony.

Whatever the motives of the American founders of Liberia, there was little doubt about their ability ultimately to translate their interest into political reality. This was perhaps to be expected, since the distinguished list of those associated with the work of the American Colonization Society included John Marshall, Henry Clay, Bushrod Washington, Francis Scott Key, and even President James Monroe, for whom the capital of Liberia was named. So successful were these leaders in their endeavors that by 1820 the federal government had agreed to make the Society's agent in West Africa its own agent in the

[2] First Annual Message of William V. S. Tubman, President of Liberia, 44th Legislature, 2d sess., Nov. 22, 1960.

suppression of the Negro slave trade and in the resettlement of captured slaves. Of even greater significance was the appropriation by the American Congress of $100,000—the first of a series of grants—to assist in the purchase of land, the construction of homes and forts, the acquisition of farm implements, the payment of teachers, and the carrying out of other projects necessary to the care, training, and defense of the settlers. Financial and other types of assistance from the United States government were evident in subsequent years. The latter, for example, outfitted ships both for the abortive first attempt at resettlement in Sierra Leone in 1821 and for the more successful effort near the present city of Monrovia the following year. The American navy, moreover, intervened at several critical points in the history of the colony to protect the settlers against attacks by the indigenous tribal people, who either opposed the colonization scheme from the outset or only belatedly realized the full implication of the "sale" of their land to the Americo-Liberian settlers.

Throughout the period of close association, the United States government rigidly avoided extending any official recognition to Liberia as an American political appendage. This attitude of studied aloofness assumed monumental importance in the 1840's. During that period the encroachment of British economic interests operating from Sierra Leone and the refusal of the British government to acknowledge the claims of the American Colonization Society to act in a sovereign capacity threatened the very existence of Liberia. Although the American government indicated to the British its concern for the rights of the settlers in the disputes, it was the Americo-Liberians themselves who resolved the impasse. In 1847 the colonists severed their ties with the founding Society and established Liberia as a sovereign and independent state. Similar action was undertaken by the settlers in Maryland, which had been founded by the Maryland Colonization Society in 1833 and remained an independent republic until its annexation by Liberia in 1857. The almost immediate recognition of the new states by Britain stands in sharp contrast to the long-delayed recognition of Liberia by the United States in 1862. By that time the Civil War had temporarily removed from the scene the prime objectors to the presence of a Negro ambassador in Washington, D.C.

A gradual shift to dependence upon the British became very noticeable in the latter decades of the nineteenth century despite conflict over claims to land in the interior. In 1871, for example, the Liberian government turned to the British for a loan when it found itself in dire financial straits. Unfortunately, the results of this loan were disastrous for the Liberian people, for President Edward J. Roye, who was deposed as a result of having profited personally from the transactions, and indeed for everyone except the London bankers. British-Liberian ties were also manifest in the education of Liberian youth in England and Sierra Leone, in trade relations, and in the financial and other forms of assistance given by the British government in the reorganization of the Republic's administrative services and military forces early in the present century.

The American connection remained strong despite the lack of direct assistance from other than missionary sources during the first half century of independence. The United States government was, indeed, influential in maintaining the independence of Liberia even if it was not prepared to do more than admonish the British and French when they whittled away Liberia's extended claims to territory in the hinterland. In 1909, for instance, an American commission of inquiry, by its very presence and by the nature of its recommendations (never officially accepted by the United States government), served to keep both England and France from taking over the country as a protectorate as a result of Liberia's default on the repayment of loans. Furthermore, the American government in 1915 forestalled British intervention during the uprising on the Kru Coast and provided the Americo-Liberians with arms and military advisers to crush the native rebellion. The official American position in the 1930's relative to the League of Nations investigation of slavery and contract labor in Liberia left many Americo-Liberians in doubt regarding American intentions. Nevertheless, the association of the United States with the League inquiry did undermine the efforts of the European powers to place Liberia under some form of international control. American influence during the past four decades has become very noticeable in other respects, as will become evident in the discussion of contemporary issues.

EXPANSION INTO THE INTERIOR

The principal objective of the American Colonization Society, as previously noted, was the establishment of a refuge for free persons of color and for Africans taken from slave ships intercepted on the seas. The white supporters of the movement as well as the Liberian settlers themselves attempted early to broaden the objectives of the colonizing effort, however, and in the process to extend the influence and control of Liberia beyond the series of coastal and riverine settlements. Many people hoped that Liberia would become a beachhead for the penetration of Christianity into the heart of Africa. Indeed, the colony managed to attract many missionary groups who were interested not only in spreading the Gospel but also in furthering pacifism and prohibition and even in carrying out experiments in communal living, in which commercialism and industrialism were rejected. There were others who were working at cross-purposes to the religious and social reformers and who regarded Liberia as the pivotal point in an expanding trade between America and the interior of West Africa. The United States government, of course, viewed the colony as a significant base for the suppression of the continuing slave trade between Africa and the New World. For the Americo-Liberians themselves, Liberia had a special meaning for all Africans. Clearly borrowing a page from the contemporary American political scene, President Joseph Jenkins Roberts and other Liberian leaders assumed that they had a "Manifest Destiny" to bring civilization to the tribal heathen in the hinterland. There were also less doctrinaire reasons advanced to justify the expansion of Liberian influence and control beyond the original settlements at Monrovia, Buchanan, Harper, and other points. Thus it was argued that the defense and natural growth of the colony demanded that the Liberian state expand beyond its original limits.

It seemed not to disturb many of the Americo-Liberian leaders that such expansion would further intensify their minority position in the country. They already found themselves outnumbered by an indigenous tribal majority having no experience with the New World or Westernized slavery and differing markedly in culture from the immigrant community. Moreover, despite their official motto, "The Love of Liberty Brought Us Here," the Americo-Liberians seemed not greatly disturbed by the fact that the process of expansion brought about a relationship of political dependency between themselves and the citizens of the more than twenty tribal groups native to the Liberian hinterland. It was a relationship similar in most respects to that obtaining between Europeans and Africans in other quarters of the continent. The distinguishing criterion for subordination, however, was not race—even though differences in skin pigmentation remain important in Liberia today. Rather, the dependency relationship was based upon differences in culture and upon the barriers which were erected by the Americo-Liberians to either rapid or widespread assimilation of the dominant culture by the tribal people.

The extension of political control by the Americo-Liberians over the

more than twenty tribal societies constituting the subordinate element
in the dependency situation took place over a very long period, and in
some areas the authority of the settlers and their descendants has been
recognized only during the past three or four decades. In many respects
the extension followed the pattern established by the French, British,
Portuguese, and Afrikaners in enlarging their respective spheres of
political influence in Africa. The initial acquisition of land came
through the purchase of a strip 130 miles long and 40 miles wide in
what is now Montserrado County. The Dei and Mamba chiefs who
"signed" the agreement were paid in muskets, powder, tobacco, um-
brellas, hats, and other commodities. It was largely through outright
purchase, too, that the entire coastal strip and many of the river valley
settlements were added to the Liberian polity between 1821 and 1845.
Similarly much of the disputed area later surrendered to Great Britain
as a part of Sierra Leone had been claimed by the Liberians on the
basis of purchase. Significantly, the authority of chiefs to sell land held
in communal trust was no more questioned here than it had been in
other parts of Africa.

An equally effective method of expansion came through the establishment of a protectorate relationship over certain tribal groups, based
upon agreements negotiated between the chiefs and the American
Colonization Society or the successor Liberian government. In some
instances the instruments were broadly constructed treaties of friendship in which the tribal chiefs agreed to end intertribal warfare, submit
quarrels to the Liberian government for arbitration, ban the use of
poison ordeals, and cooperate with the Liberians in ending the slave
trade. A treaty of this nature was concluded in 1839, for example, following General Joseph Jenkins Roberts' victory over Chief Gatumba
of Boporu, an action which had convinced the chiefs in the area northwest of Monrovia that the Liberian military forces could be effective.
In other instances the tribal groups concerned voluntarily accepted
the protection of the Liberian government in the face of threats from
neighboring tribes or in order to avoid coming under French or British
control. In addition to these broad treaties of friendship and protection,
there were many treaties having only limited objectives, such as the
development of commerce between the hinterland and Monrovia. This
was true of the treaties negotiated in the 1850's between President
Roberts and the Vai, Gola, and Buzi tribes. Nevertheless, whether the
agreements were broad or limited in scope, the settler government
rapidly converted the treaties into Liberian claims of ownership over
the territory of the people involved.

The immigrants also emulated their British and French competitors for control of the interior of West Africa by considering that journeys of exploration provided the sponsoring state with a claim to any territory "discovered" by the traveler. Although a number of European trading firms were commissioned by Liberian presidents to carry out such explorations, some of the most exciting journeys were undertaken by Liberians themselves. The chronicles of Benjamin J. K. Anderson, who visited the western Mandingo city of Musardu in 1868, rank with some of the best literature in this genre. Other Liberians such as Seymour and Ash had earlier explored the area north of the St. Paul River and may even have reached Nimba Mountain and the source of the Cavalla River.

Finally, there were instances in which the Americo-Liberian claims to control were based upon conquest. Many of the military ventures were really minor skirmishes in which the spears and knives of the tribal people proved unequal to the rifles and cannons of the Liberian troops. On occasion, however, the superior fighting skill of the natives and their securing of arms from outside sources tipped the scales temporarily in favor of the tribal element. In such cases Liberian authority was established only after many years of fighting and after a considerable loss of life and property by both sides. The Gola tribe in the early period and the Grebo and Kru tribes even during the present century are outstanding examples of tribal resistance to Liberian occupation.

Tribal resistance was not the only source of opposition to Liberian expansion. During the early colonial period Don Pedro Blanco and other European slave traders recognized the obvious threat to their activities posed by the settlers, the American Colonization Society, and the United States navy. The slavers openly encouraged the Gola, Bassa, and others to attack the infant settlements. Later, as the Liberians directed their attention inland, they came into conflict with another element concerned about its commercial interests—the Mandingo tribesmen. The latter had established a fairly high degree of political suzerainty over the interior tribes, and they had effectively monopolized both intertribal trade and the commerce between the interior and the coast. Although the Liberians eventually won out, the antagonism between the settlers and the Mandingo tribesmen persisted until the third decade of the present century.

Of another character was the opposition to Liberian expansion raised by the British and the French. Sometimes the Europeans accomplished their objectives by providing outright encouragement to tribal resistance. This was certainly the case in the Kolahun District as late as 1911. More frequently, however, the Europeans won their victories at the conference table. Liberia, with only token or moral support from the United States, often found that the rules of the game of "Partition" were being changed at the whim of the European players. The British administration in Sierra Leone followed the rather curious line of not recognizing the authority of the Liberian government to collect customs and otherwise regulate trade in the region west of the Mano River but, on the other hand, of holding the Liberian government responsible for not protecting the property of British traders against tribal raids in the same region. In the Treaty of 1885 the Liberians conceded the struggle for control of that area to the British. Two decades later the British extended their control over portions of the Kolahun District, and only because of protests from the United States was their seizure limited to a small tract which was "exchanged" for a pocket of forest area east of the Mano River.

While the British were active in the west, the French had been pressing their claims in the east. In 1892 the French suddenly annexed to the Ivory Coast the 50-mile stretch of coast between the Cavalla and San Pedro rivers, taking much of the hinterland with it. There were protests from the Liberians that were based upon treaties concluded more than fifty years previously with the tribes of that area; however, the Liberians had difficulties enough with the Grebo tribesmen in Maryland County and were incapable of resisting this French *fait accompli*. Furthermore, a boundary delimitation treaty in 1910 found the Liberians surrendering to the French their historic claims to a vast strip along the Guinea and Ivory Coast borders. In all, the British and French assumed control of more than a third of the hinterland once claimed by the Americo-Liberians.

Not all the opposition to Americo-Liberian expansion was external. There were elements within the settler community which regarded expansion, especially by military means, with alarm. Not only did it curtail commerce and threaten the peace, but also it was recognized that expansion might ultimately threaten the supremacy of the immigrant group in the new state. The intensity of internal opposition led to the resignation of at least one President, William D. Coleman, and forced several others to modify substantially their interior policies. There are still vestiges of this conservative approach found in the opposition of many Americo-Liberians to Tubman's Unification and Open-Door policies, on the grounds that they will open the floodgates and leave the descendants of the settlers swamped in a tribal sea.

MAINTENANCE OF THE DEPENDENCY RELATIONSHIP

The supremacy of the settlers and their descendants over the tribal people has been maintained in a number of ways. Until the present administration the primary emphasis was upon sanctions of a coercive nature. With respect to some tribal groups, such as the Grebo and Kru, this was understandable inasmuch as they accepted Americo-Liberian authority only after the lesson of military superiority had been demonstrated time and again in pitched battles. The superior numbers of the tribal people as well as the bitterness of the conflict forced the Liberian leaders to place heavy reliance upon physical force in securing compliance with their orders.

It was perhaps inevitable that the need to employ force in some areas led to its general use in areas where it was not required. The posting of a contingent of the militia or the Liberian Frontier Force to disturbed areas has all too frequently been a measure of first, rather than last, resort in the maintenance of authority. If the area was not actually disturbed before the arrival of the troops, it was not long before the prophecy of chaos was fulfilled. The remarks of President Arthur Barclay in his 1904 Inaugural Address that the militia was "tending to become a greater danger to the loyal citizen, and his property, which it ought to protect, than to the public enemy" have recent echoes in the pages of *Liberian Age* and the annual reports of district commissioners. The commissioner in Sanniquellie in 1960, for example, complained that the enlisted men because of "lack of leadership, live an inebriated life, undisciplined, and mostly dishonest." [3] It has apparently long been the custom of the Frontier Force to live off the local community to the extent that the traffic will bear.

In addition to direct physical force, obligations have been imposed upon the tribal element vis-à-vis the state which constitute at least a formal recognition of the superiority of the Liberian government. The payment of hut taxes, although only sporadically enforced in the early period, has become a recurrent obligation. Also in the latter category is the service that tribal people are compelled by law to render to the central government and to the chiefs in the construction of roads and in carrying out other community projects. Furthermore, the possibility of forcible recruitment into the Liberian Frontier Force is an ever-present threat to restive individuals within a tribal community.

Besides the legal coercive sanctions there were extralegal exactions imposed upon the tribal people by officials and unofficials alike which

[3] Liberia, Department of the Interior, *Annual Report, 1959–1960,* pp. 26–27.

drove home the point of Americo-Liberian supremacy. President Tubman's executive councils in the hinterland have been effective in bringing to light practices which in the previous administrations had gone unpunished and often unnoticed. The tribal people had previously felt powerless to complain when special unauthorized taxes were levied upon them by the district commissioners or when they were forced to work for little or no pay upon the farms of officials and prominent private Americo-Liberians. They had no recourse, moreover, when officials acquired wives without the payment of dowry. It has only been during the Tubman administration that an attempt has been made to regularize and limit the use of compulsory labor.

Another category of negative sanctions calculated to maintain Americo-Liberian supremacy has been the control over residence and population movements. An extreme example has been the deportation from their home areas of politically restive tribal persons and their confinement in one of the more remote districts of the interior.[4] Of a more general character has been the attempt to restrict intertribal contact by establishing tribal land units under traditional authority, similar to the reserve policy followed by the British in East Africa. A member of the group has a right to land in his tribal area, but a tribal stranger may take up residence only with the permission of the traditional leadership and upon the stranger's acceptance of the local chief's political authority. Also by way of population control, the Liberian government has made it clear that it will not tolerate the mass exodus of a community from its traditional tribal area to avoid obligations or diminish the strength of an unpopular chief. The government has taken steps to discourage the flight from their families and farms by males wishing to take advantage of the windfall opportunities present in the discovery of gold and diamonds during the postwar period. The drift of tribal people to Monrovia and other urban centers has been met by the city courts, which have taken drastic steps to remove tribal vagrants to the hinterland. Further Kru, Bassa and other tribal people in Monrovia are organized into separate residential communities for administrative, and judicial purposes.

In addition to restrictions upon the movement of tribal people, the government attempted in the past to minimize contact between the indigenous population and outside influences. True, it was recognized that the European and Liberian missionaries or the Lebanese traders

---

[4] A recent example of this occurred in Tchien District (Department of the Interior, *Annual Report, 1955–1956*, p. 15; *1956–1957*, p. 16).

could be carriers of certain aspects of the culture the Americo-Liberians had established as the norm for the whole state. Moreover, the establishment of Christian mission stations at Bolahun, Ganta, and other points far in the interior had served as bulwarks against Muslim penetration into Liberia. Nevertheless, it was realized that the teachings and actions of the nontribal stranger could undermine the authority of the Liberian government. This was no idle fear. Disputes between missionaries over proselytizing areas, attacks by the Swedish Evangelical Lutherans upon the Poro and other secret societies, and the antagonism aroused by European commercial interests have posed real problems for the Liberian government in the maintenance of peace and order in the interior during the past century. Although aliens are no longer required to have an authorized pass to enter the provinces, there are still both legal and tacit restrictions upon the residence and activities of aliens in the hinterland.[5]

The settlers and their descendants also hoped to maintain control over the tribal majority through the development of an efficient administrative service. To that end the Department of the Interior was created in 1868 during the presidency of James Spriggs Payne. For many decades, however, the effectiveness of the Department was blunted by the lack of qualified Americo-Liberians interested in living in the hinterland and by the difficulties which geography posed for the systematic supervision of the administrative officers. Moreover, there was clearly an absence of explicit policy regarding both the ultimate goals of the dependency relationship and the means whereby the relationship was to be maintained or transformed. It was only during the administration of Arthur Barclay in the first decade of the present century that the Liberian government acknowledged that the tribal people of the hinterland were to be regarded as citizens of the Republic. Not until then were steps taken to establish a more efficient administrative service. Unfortunately, the stimulus for these policy decisions was the charge of the British and French that historic Liberian claims to territory could not be recognized in the absence of "effective occupation." Had the impetus for change come from within the Americo-Liberian community, the reforms might have been more meaningful.

The administrative system introduced by Barclay was patterned along the lines of "indirect rule"—that is, the utilization of traditional

---

[5] See *Liberian Code of Laws of 1956* (Ithaca, N.Y.: Cornell University Press, 1957), title 15, ch. 12C, secs. 301–303.

tribal authorities as instruments of the central government in the main-
tainance of law and order at the local level. Aside from the savings in
money and personnel, this policy had many advantages. In the first
place, it perpetuated the social division of the hinterland into more
than twenty tribal groups and capitalized upon the existing political
fragmentation of the majority of these tribal groups into relatively
autonomous chiefdoms. Even though the creation of consolidated
paramount chieftainships did reverse the process of fragmentation to a
certain degree, only the Dei, Mende, Bandi, Kisi, and Belle people
have been united under single paramount chiefs. In the other groups,
political authority within a tribe is divided among as many as five
paramount chiefs. Moreover, in drawing district boundaries, little respect was accorded tribal lines. Thus, the Kpelle have been dispersed
among four administrative areas whereas fragments of several mutually
hostile tribes have been incorporated within single districts.

Despite the lack of respect for the integrity of a tribe as a social or
political unit, local government was essentially tribal in character.
Where possible, tribal customs and institutions were to be preserved
and utilized by the district commissioner in carrying out central government objectives. Thus, in many areas a modified form of hereditary
succession to chieftainship has prevailed to the present day. Chiefs
and elders at all levels administer customary law in the settlement of
disputes concerning a wide range of social and economic relationships.
Tribal membership has been further strengthened by the legalizing of
the Poro and other secret societies, which in the early period were
banned as potential political threats to Americo-Liberian rule. Corporate membership in the clan or other tribal unit is emphasized not
only by the system of land tenure but also by the Liberian government's
practice of levying fines against a whole community in the settlement
of certain types of disputes. The political stability which resulted from
the policy of recognizing native traditions even prompted the Americo-
Liberians until 1930 to countenance the institutions of domestic slavery and the "pawning" of persons in the tribal areas. Perhaps it is only
fair to point out that the British, experiencing similar difficulties in
controlling the tribal hinterland of Sierra Leone, did not abolish slavery
in that territory until 1928.

The Liberian commitment to indirect rule has been of a pragmatic
rather than a philosophic nature. No attempt was made, as Sir Donald
Cameron had done in Tanganyika, to regard indirect rule as a morally
best colonial system—that is, as one which did the least damage to the

native personality in the transition from traditional to modern society. Native institutions in the Liberian hinterland have flourished only to the extent that they did not conflict with the interests of the Americo-Liberians. Chiefs, for example, might be chosen in a time-honored fashion. Nevertheless, one became chief only because his election had met with presidential approval, and a chief held office only at the pleasure of the President. Similarly, the Poro has survived only on sufferance. Its political role has been truncated, and the appointment of Tubman as head of all Poro societies in Liberia has placed the secret societies under governmental control but also has provided the President with a traditional support for his authority. The expediency of the Liberian policy is revealed as well in the attitude toward bush schools, in which tribal youth have been instructed in tribal lore and custom. Now that the central government has taken a more active interest in the educational programs of the interior, restrictions are being placed upon the traditional system of tribal indoctrination. The fate of the *zoes* and other practitioners of native medicine likewise will be conditional upon the rate at which programs in modern medicine become extensive in the hinterland.

THE UNIFICATION POLICY OF PRESIDENT TUBMAN

Coercive sanctions and a more effective system of administration were instrumental in bringing most of the tribal people under Americo-Liberian control. This was not the same, however, as securing the acceptance by the tribal people of the legitimacy of Americo-Liberian rule. Relations between the two groups reached their lowest ebb during the administration (1920–1930) of Charles D. B. King. Charges by tribal leaders as well as by opposition elements within the Americo-Liberian community led to League of Nations intervention in Liberian internal affairs. An elaborate investigation was undertaken of domestic slavery, the abuses of the compulsory labor system, and the manner in which employees were recruited by Liberian officials for contract work on the Spanish island of Fernando Po. The indictment by the League Commission of prominent Liberian officials posed a severe crisis for the government. Faced with the threat of impeachment and the withdrawal of American diplomatic recognition and financial support, both President King and Vice-President Allen N. Yancy resigned. The latter had been personally implicated in the forcible recruitment of Liberian laborers. They were succeeded by the Secretary of State, Edwin J. Barclay.

Among the first acts of the Barclay administration was the outlawing of slavery, pawning, and the export of contract labor from Liberia. Of a more positive nature were the creation by the Barclay government of a public health service and the reorganization of the interior service in order to hold the district commissioners more responsible for their acts. As political appointees without any specialized training in administration or knowledge of tribal law and custom, they had in the past been largely left to their own devices. Even where cases of abuse did lead to an official investigation, the offending officer was often fined a token sum rather than dismissed from the service. The Barclay reform measures, however, were to a great extent undermined by the retaliatory steps taken against those who had aided the League Commission in its investigations and by the ruthless manner in which Barclay put down yet another tribal rebellion along the Kru Coast. Many individuals, including the recent Secretary of Public Instruction, Nathaniel Massaquoi, were tried and imprisoned during the Barclay administration for allegedly attempting to overthrow the Americo-Liberian ruling class by force.

The election of William V. S. Tubman in 1943 signaled a change in the spirit as well as the substance of the relationship between the tribal people and the descendants of the settlers. Although Tubman had been Barclay's personal choice as his successor and had been both legal and personal defender of many who were involved in the Fernando Po scandals, he nevertheless had developed a popular following. He was an eloquent lawyer and often took the cases of penniless clients against prominent Americo-Liberian adversaries. Tubman's approach to politics and administration was much more personal than that of his predecessors. For the first time in Liberian history the doors of the Executive Mansion have been open to tribal persons who had suggestions or petitions of grievance to present to the President. Moreover, he has developed in a more systematic fashion the device of personal "diplomacy" in the hinterland initiated in a most sporadic fashion by President King. Tubman has made it a point to visit each of the main headquarters in the provinces during a three-year period. There he holds extended sessions of his Executive Council in which the people and chiefs seek correction of wrongs, request new programs in health or education, secure executive arbitration of boundary disputes, and in other ways solicit the help of the President. Without being burdened by legal restrictions or bound by precedents, the President has meted out a form of substantive justice which has had a tremendous impact upon the tribal people, most of whom had long felt isolated from Liberian politics and had never had the opportunity of seeing a Liberian President. The summary dismissal of errant district commissioners (including a very close relative of the President), the immediate granting of justice, and the promises to extend the benefits of the new economic development to the hinterland have been significant factors in reducing almost to nil the incidence of violent opposition on the part of tribal people to Americo-Liberian rule. Tubman's Executive Council decisions, moreover, have frequently struck at one of the most tender spots in the relationship between the two elements, namely, the illegal acquisition of land in the interior by leading members of the Americo-Liberian community. The stern treatment accorded the latter at the Salala Executive Council in 1945 did much to reassure the tribal people that their traditional land tenure rights would be respected.

There have been other ways, too, in which Tubman has attempted to eradicate the distinctions between the members of the two communities and to indicate that the tribal people have a right to be proud of their traditional heritage. The President often appears in tribal dress on civic occasions, has taken a series of tribal names, and has encouraged the appreciation of native dancing and art forms. The employment of anthropologists to study tribal customs and social organization is also evidence of a new appreciation of the indigenous culture of the Liberian masses.

The various development schemes launched in the postwar period have been calculated as well to bring positive benefits to many tribal areas where the inhabitants had known government officials only as collectors of taxes and recruiters of labor. Roads, bridges, and other public works have done much to bring the people of the hinterland into contact with each other and with the Americo-Liberians of the coast. New roads have made it possible for teachers, medical technicians, agricultural instructors, and others to reach the vast interior of Liberia, where the majority of the people actually live. Roads have also permitted a more rapid exploitation of the natural resources of the interior. With this has come a radical transformation in the way of life of tribesmen who until recently were rigidly wedded to subsistence economies and who were able to afford few of the material luxuries of Westernization.

Politically, too, President Tubman has attempted to provide the tribal people with a sense of participation in the national life of the Republic. A property qualification for voting remains, but it has been

revised downward to extend the ballot to the owner of any hut upon
which taxes have been paid. Suffrage, moreover, is now an individual
right in contrast to the past when a chief, acting in his corporate capacity as the holder of title to tribal land, could register and vote the
members of his community as a unit.[6] Further, during Tubman's administration the vote has been extended to women. Along with the
changes in suffrage qualifications the form of representation for the
tribal people has been altered. In the past any tribe which paid $100
had the privilege of electing one of its members as a delegate to the
House of Representatives. There he had the opportunity to discuss
and vote upon all matters relating to tribal interests. During the past
two decades the regular membership of the House has been increased
to permit the three provinces and tribal areas within the counties to
have regular representation. At the executive and judicial levels as
well, Tubman has publicized the appointment of persons with tribal
backgrounds to positions of prominence.

Perhaps the most promising sign in the entire picture is the sense
of guilt which Americo-Liberians now have when it comes to differentiating in public speeches and writings between themselves and the
tribal element. The dropping of the term "Americo-Liberian" and the
employing of ambiguous expressions such as "the natives and the other
element" or the "civilized people and the other element" constitute
evidence that the self-assuredness of the settler aristocracy has been
undermined. Moreover, frontal attacks have been made by prominent
members of the Americo-Liberian community upon the early settlers.
One speaker was heard by the author to refer to the settlers as the
"ill-prepared, ill-informed, and illegitimate offspring of the union between master and slave." Since Tubman came to power, it has once
again become respectable for someone named Caine to call himself
Kandakai and a Freeman to resort to the tribal form of Fahnbulleh.
This has been very important for Liberian students abroad and for
others who are attempting to emphasize their ties with Africa rather
than the West. Thus, County Superintendent George F. Sherman became G. Flama Sherman upon his appointment as ambassador to
Ghana.

The roots of Tubman's Unification Policy are various, and it would
be grossly unfair to attribute the change solely to a desire on the part
of the Americo-Liberian elite to insulate itself from the wave of na-

[6] George G. Parker, "Acculturation in Liberia" (Ph.D. thesis, Kennedy School
of Missions, Hartford Seminary, 1944), p. 261.

tionalism undermining alien rule in other parts of Africa. Many Liberians had traveled to Europe, America, and other African territories and returned convinced that the lot of the tribal people should be improved. There were many in the upper class, too, who had familial and other personal ties with tribal communities and were sufficiently indignant about tribal discrimination to have advocated reform long before Tubman arrived on the scene. Nevertheless, it was clear that the nationalist unrest mounting elsewhere would one day touch Liberia and that if the settler element did not attempt to lead the tribal people to modernity and to grant them political and social rights, the latter would one day try to achieve these things on their own. Thus, if the Americo-Liberians could not prevent change, they could at least attempt to control it.

What were the forces at work that made change inevitable? Certainly the events of World War II and in particular the presence of over 5,000 American troops—both white and colored—had a marked impact upon the tribal people and the poorer element within the Americo-Liberian community. The free spending as well as the free living of the American troops had a disruptive effect upon the Liberian economy and tribal social codes, but the presence of the Americans also drove home the idea that a life of poverty need not be accepted blindly. Moreover, there was an inevitable introduction of ideas of a political and social character which emerged from this new form of culture contact.

Economic development, which had really been launched in the 1920's when Firestone Plantations Company took over the operation of the abandoned rubber plantations near Monrovia, has had a more sustained impact in breaking down traditional tribal relationships and in creating demands of an economic character which would eventually need political answers. The myth that Firestone punctured regarding the lack of economic motivation on the part of the Liberian tribesmen was dealt its death blow by the iron ore companies and other foreign concessions brought into Liberia by Tubman's Open-Door Policy in the postwar period. The tribesman has taken readily to a money economy and to the new status that material wealth can bring to one in his tribal area as well as in the new urban centers. The influx of foreigners under the Open-Door Policy has also exposed the tribal people to contact with individuals from several continents and reversed the long-standing attempt by the Americo-Liberians to insulate the tribal people against alien influences.

Another sustained contributor to social change has been the education of tribal youth, a responsibility assumed almost entirely by the Christian missionaries prior to the Tubman administration. Education has produced a corps of tribal youths who no longer are satisfied with a second-class status in their own country. Although opportunities for higher education at the University of Liberia or abroad have been largely monopolized by the Americo-Liberians, many tribal youths now are receiving a superior education at the Episcopal-run Cuttington College in the interior or are studying abroad under mission, United States government, and even Liberian government scholarships.

The development of radio and the press have not been as significant instigators of change in Liberia as in other parts of West Africa. It is only recently that the Sudan Interior Mission radio station, ELWA, has been broadcasting in several Liberian dialects and that radio sets have been distributed throughout the tribal hinterland. The Voice of America and the national broadcasting station, ELBC, have also been spreading news of political developments in the rest of Africa. A much older and more effective means of communications remains, of course —the carrying of news by the steady flow of people moving back and forth across the arbitrary boundaries separating Liberia from Guinea, Sierra Leone, and the Ivory Coast. The efforts of Sékou Touré in Guinea and Félix Houphouët-Boigny in the Ivory Coast to organize mass-based parties have not gone unnoticed by the tribal people of Liberia. Of even greater significance to the Americo-Liberians is the chain of events in Sierra Leone which has brought the tribal people to political power. There the Creoles, who have roots similar to the Americo-Liberians as descendants of British slaves, have had to accommodate themselves to a minority role in politics.

Land and People

Liberia is among the smallest of the independent African states, outranking only Togo and Sierra Leone in 1961. Its area of approximately 43,000 square miles makes it only one-twentieth the size of the Republic of the Congo or slightly larger than the state of Indiana. Its location, however, gives it peculiar strategic advantages. It lies astride the southern turn of the great western bulge and is thus closer to the American hemisphere than is any other African state. Sierra Leone, its neighbor to the northwest, is one of the newer members of the Commonwealth of Nations. To the east lies the Ivory Coast, which still retains strong ties with France. Along the intervening boundaries on the north lies the Republic of Guinea, which by 1962 had gone further than any other African state in developing economic and political ties with the nations in the Communist bloc.

The generally low elevation of the country, the long Atlantic coastline, and the proximity to the equator give Liberia a decidedly tropical climate. Rainfall during the period from April to October often exceeds 200 inches along the coast, but it tapers off to about 70 inches in the hinterland. Even during the dry season the high humidity and temperatures ranging in the nineties contribute to a generally enervating effect at the coast. Behind the coastal plain, which extends from 20 to 40 miles inland, is a wider belt of gradually rising country, covered in great part by a high forest. Farther inland is a rolling plateau which averages approximately 800 feet to 1,000 feet in altitude. The plateau is broken occasionally by small ranges of hills and granitic outcroppings and in the northwest by Nimba Mountain, which rises 4,000 feet above sea level.

Although the absence of a national census makes bold statements difficult, it is generally agreed that Liberia is also among the smaller countries of Africa in terms of population. The estimates range anywhere from 800,000 to over 3,500,000, and a combination of practical difficulties and domestic and international political considerations have thus far prevented the taking of an accurate enumeration. The United Nations *Demographic Yearbook, 1958,* however, places the population at 1,250,000.

The population is not evenly distributed over the country. Although it is officially acknowledged that the bulk of the people live in the hinterland, there are vast areas in the high forest of the interior where only a few scattered villages break the dense growth. Some of the greatest concentrations of population are found in the pockets of settlement at the coast and in the areas close to the borders of Guinea and Sierra Leone. There is also a continuous line of settlement in the center of the country along the 130 miles of road from Monrovia to Gbarnga. The largest single complex of population, however, is found within a radius of 50 miles from the capital. A very rough sample survey taken in 1961 by the Bureau of Economic Research placed the population of Monrovia at 80,000. Patterns of populations are undergoing rapid changes in recent years as all-weather roads are being constructed throughout the country and as both orderly development of natural resources and "windfall" economic activities lead to redistribution of the present population, to the immigration of aliens, and to the repatriation of Liberians from neighboring African states.

THE ECONOMY

Despite significant changes in recent years the economy of Liberia remains primarily agricultural in character. Most observers estimate that 90 per cent of the population is engaged in the production of rice, cassava, plantain, and other staples or the production, processing, and marketing of tree crops for export. Rubber has dominated in this latter category since the Firestone Plantations Company started production three decades ago, and it is still the most significant item in the cash economy of Liberia. The Liberian government, with American assistance, has attempted to diversify the cash-crop economy through the expansion of coffee, cocoa, palm kernel, citrus fruit, piassava, and kola nut production. The postwar period has also witnessed the first systematic exploitation of Liberia's mahogany and other fine hardwoods.

The tribal people are still primarily wedded to a subsistence economy. There have, of course, been exceptions. Long before the Americo-Liberians arrived, some of the hinterland tribes had established market centers in which various types of crude currency were employed. There existed also a rather sophisticated form of intertribal production and exchange of arts and crafts. During the past three decades individual tribesmen have been brought into the cash economy in increasing numbers as employees on large estates, as participants in tribal communal enterprises, or even as small farmers. Typically, however, the food that the tribal family consumes is the food that the family collectively produces. There is little left over for exchange. Family plots are small and must be numerous to accommodate the fallow system of rotation and the slash-and-burn technique of bringing new land under the hoe. Farms are normally held under usufructuary right of occupancy, with only a small percentage of the tribal people of the hinterland attempting to acquire private leaseholds.

In contrast to the family organization used in production of subsistence crops, the plantation system is dominant in the production of tree crops. Firestone Plantations, for example, produced 87 per cent of the rubber processed in Liberia in 1960. The remaining 13 per cent was produced on smaller farms by 900 independent Liberian growers. Ten Liberian producers, however, accounted for almost a quarter of this latter figure. The pattern of large plantations under the control of foreign concessionaires or private Liberians is also evident in the production of coffee, citrus, and other tree crops. The number of small-scale farmers, however, is growing. Palm kernels and kola nuts are almost entirely gathered by small producers.

Since the war the relative importance of agricultural production in the Liberian economy has diminished as foreign capital has brought about a rapid exploitation of the country's mineral resources. In contrast to the capricious development of diamonds and gold, there has been a solid development of the vast iron ore deposits by a combination of American, Swedish, German, and Liberian capital. Production in 1960 exceeded 3,000,000 tons, and there is an estimated 300,000,000 tons of ore in reserve. Yet to be exploited are the sizable deposits of manganese, bauxite, lead, and corundum.

The development of manufacturing has also taken place under Tubman, but little of it could be classified as heavy industry. Of long-range significance is the development of a cement factory, sugar refineries, coffee-processing mills, starch-reducing plants, and a fish cannery, which can substantially reduce the protein shortage in the interior. The development of heavy industry must await the harnessing of the country's vast hydroelectric power potential. The construction of a power plant on the St. Paul River is already under way, and other projects are planned for the immediate future.

Economic development, as well as political integration and control, is in many ways dependent upon the development of transport facilities. The construction of artificial harbors at Monrovia, Harper, Buchanan, and Greenville is entirely a product of the past two decades. Previously all passengers and produce brought into Liberia had to be discharged to small surfboats from ships anchored a mile or more from shore. The many rivers of Liberia have not been useful for anything other than small internal trade. The airplane in the postwar period has breached the parochialism of Liberia, and Robertsfield is now a major international airport serving over twenty American, European, African, Middle East, and Latin American airlines. The airplane, however, has not alleviated the problem of internal transportation, especially where bulk commodities are concerned. The exploitation of the iron ore deposits at Bomi Hills, 47 miles from Monrovia, and Nimba Mountain, 200 miles inland, has led to the construction of two major railroads. In road construction Liberia lagged considerably behind its West African neighbors before the war. Now 2,000 miles of highway connect most of the major urban centers with each other. The routes, however, are often devious, and only the small portion which is macadamized is actually all-weather highway. Only since 1960, moreover, has Monrovia been in contact by motor road with all three of its West African neighbors.

In terms of external trade, the United States remains Liberia's most significant partner even though the role of the latter has diminished substantially during the past decade. In 1950, for example, the United States received close to 90 per cent of Liberia's exports. By 1959 this figure had dropped to 61 per cent. For the same period imports from America dropped from 71 to 47 per cent of the total. A much more considerable role is now being played by the United Kingdom, the Netherlands, West Germany, and Japan. Only an insignificant portion of Liberia's foreign trade is with other African states.[7]

Spurred on by the Open-Door Policy of President Tubman, foreign investors are making a substantial contribution to Liberia's economic development. The American share is roughly five-sixths of the estimated $300,000,000 worth of foreign investment, but the role of Swedish, Swiss, Dutch, German, and Israeli firms has been rapidly increasing.[8] Whereas Firestone held the only major concession when Tubman assumed office in 1944, there were twenty-five major investors at the end of 1960.

Liberian economic development in the postwar period has also relied heavily upon United States government aid. The amount of direct aid during the period from 1944 to 1960 passed the $88,000,000 mark. In addition, a good portion of the technical assistance provided by United Nations Specialized Agencies, which amounted to $330,000 in 1960 alone, is contributed indirectly by the United States. Neither of these figures include United States military assistance to Liberia or the estimated $1,000,000 annual contribution to the economy made by missionary societies, most of which are American.

SOCIAL STRUCTURE

The most obvious element in the social structure of Liberia today is the cleavage between the Americo-Liberian elite and the tribal majority. This persists despite seventeen years of Tubman's Unification Policy. A certain amount of integration has taken place, but it is largely

---

[7] Liberia, Bureau of Economic Research, *Foreign Trade Supplement for 1959*, *passim*.

[8] A more conservative estimate puts this figure at $150,000,000 in 1960. See Bank of Monrovia, *Liberia* (New York: First National City Bank, 1960), p. 9.

on Americo-Liberian terms and conditional upon the acceptance by the tribal person of various facets of the settler culture. Thus English rather than one of the twenty-odd tribal dialects must be accepted as the only legitimate medium for communication in official circles, in government schools, and in the national press. Christianity—and specifically a Protestant version of it—is to be preferred before Islam or ancestor worship as the prescribed route for salvation. In the social realm, monogamy takes precedence over polygamy in the organization of the family. There must be an acceptance by the tribal person of the national political and legal institutions, which bear at least a formal resemblance to those obtaining in the United States. There must, of course, be an acceptance of the Americo-Liberian historical myth regarding the role each community played in the founding of the Republic. In the economic sphere the tribal person seeking assimilation must embrace the concept of private rather than communal ownership of property, engage in the cash economy, and assume individual rather than collective responsibility for his own prosperity. In general, too, there must be an acceptance of the foods, dress, art, and architecture of the Americo-Liberians as the legitimate standard for emulation.

The non-African component. Initially, the dependency relationship established between the settlers and the tribal people relied heavily upon the support provided by the white agents of the American Colonization Society, the Christian missionaries, American and European traders, and the contingents of the American navy who assisted in the settlement and defense of the coastal settlements. Moreover, as the foregoing section on the economy of Liberia revealed, the leadership is still dependent upon external forms of assistance in developing the country and maintaining control over the territory of the Republic. The influx of Americans, Europeans, Asians, Latin Americans, and other Africans as a result of the Open-Door Policy has created a new community of more than 7,500 aliens. Although this community is of crucial importance in the educational and economic development of Liberia, it plays no direct role in politics and generally adheres to Americo-Liberian social standards. It exists in the country largely on sufferance of the government. The constitutional provision that only persons of Negro ancestry may become citizens of Liberia automatically excludes most of the Americans, Europeans, Asians, and even North Africans from the enjoyment of political rights. Exclusion from citizenship has the further consequence of denying one the privilege of engaging in certain economic enterprises or even owning real estate in

Liberia, since these are rights reserved to citizens. Finally, revocation of an alien's visa or declaring one *persona non grata* are frequently employed devices for ridding the country of uncooperative foreigners.

The Americo-Liberians. Aside from the early colonial period in Liberia, the settlers and their descendants have borne the major burden of maintaining the dependency relationship. The immigrant group was never very large in relation to the tribal element, and even the present estimate is that it is no greater than a 1 to 20 ratio. Despite publicity given to the settlement scheme, only about 15,000 free persons of color ever took advantage of the opportunity to go to Liberia. Most of the emigration took place prior to 1867, and a good portion of the immigrants were of West Indian rather than American origin. After the Civil War most American Negroes decided to win the battle for equality at home, and they rejected Marcus Garvey and other more recent advocates of a "back to Africa" movement.

In addition to the repatriated slaves, there was a smaller group of alien Negroes, estimated at 5,000, consisting of Africans taken from slaving ships. Although their origins might have been Dahomey, Nigeria, or Ghana, these captured Africans were frequently referred to as "Congoes." For the purposes of protection and education they were usually placed in the care of settler families, who were given subsidies from the United States government for this purpose. The Congoes gradually acquired both the ways and the aspirations of the settlers. By 1870 their passive role in politics was abandoned, and for a considerable time they occupied a crucial position in the factional arguments developing within the Americo-Liberian group. Their affiliation with the True Whig Party eventually brought them to their present position of parity with the descendants of the settlers, and today they have been largely absorbed into the Americo-Liberian ranks.

Further accretions to the superordinate group have taken place as a result of emigration from Ghana, Nigeria, Sierra Leone, and other African territories. This is apparently more than offset, however, by the emigration of Liberians to neighboring states and by the reluctance of immigrant Africans in Liberia to give up their own citizenship. The latter find it difficult to break into the inner circle of Liberian politics, which is almost a *sine qua non* for advancement in other fields. Two former Sierra Leoneans—Representative T. Dupigny-Leigh and Hector Gorgla, chairman of the National Production Council—as well as other well-advertised exceptions to the rule only serve to emphasize the general point.

Furthermore, it must be noted that the exclusion of the indigenous population has never been entirely rigid and that persons with tribal origins have in fact been accepted as members of the "honorable" class. Under the "ward" system, talented tribal youths, who have been given to prominent Americo-Liberian families for care and training, have found one avenue to cultural assimilation. Although there have been instances of abuse in which the ward differs but slightly from a domestic servant, there have also been countless cases in which tribal youths have been adopted in the fullest sense and given all the privileges of education and access to politics afforded a full-fledged Americo-Liberian youth.

A second precursor of Tubman's Unification Policy is found in the liaisons which Americo-Liberian males (and occasionally females) have established with tribal persons—frequently without the benefit of clergy. Fortunately for the offspring of such unions, neither illegitimacy nor the mixed character of one's parentage has much stigma attached to it in Liberia. Indeed, several of the leading members of Tubman's cabinet and of the ambasadorial group find it advantageous to stress the tribal backgrounds of their parents, and at least one is even quite proud of the fact that he is a "wild oat."

A third form of assimilation of tribal persons into the Americo-Liberian elite has come through co-optation of leading tribal personalities who were instrumental in establishing Liberian authority in their respective areas at times in the past century and a half. These tribal leaders have participated in the distribution of patronage available to Americo-Liberians, have been given prominent posts in government, and have had their children educated abroad. Although it has been politically expedient for these individuals to maintain their traditional connections, for all practical purposes they have accepted the settler culture.

The tribal element. At the lowest rung of the social ladder is the tribal majority. The basis for classifying tribal groups in Liberia has varied considerably, and according to whether one employs language, kinship ties, or similarity of political and social institutions the number may range from 16 to 28 distinct groups. There is a considerable range, too, in their degree of contact with, and acceptance of, Americo-Liberian cultural traits. The coastal Kru people, for example, have long accepted the money economy, and several thousand regularly serve as crewmen aboard the European and American freighters plying the West African coast. The Gbunde and Buzi have also reacted positively to Liberian rule and now constitute a considerable portion of the Liberian Frontier Force. On the other hand, the Tchien, Sapa, and Gbande have had their traditional institutions but slightly disturbed by the nominal authority that the Americo-Liberians have exercised over their areas. The Mandingo tribesmen deserve special mention since in many ways they have been made an auxiliary to the Americo-Liberian community despite their early opposition to settler expansion into the interior. Their talent in commercial enterprises has been appreciated by President Tubman, who has encouraged them to emigrate from Guinea and other West African states. They enjoy a privileged position with respect to exemption from compulsory tribal labor, and they are not normally subject to the jurisdiction of tribal courts.

Despite the Unification Policy the low ranking of the tribal people and their unequal treatment is evidenced in a number of ways. There is, for example, a difference in personal status between the Americo-Liberians and tribal persons with respect to marriage contracts, the jurisdiction of courts, the ownership of land in the hinterland, and obligations owed the state. Moreover, as will be shown in the section on contemporary issues below, there is an unequal distribution of income, educational and health facilities, and the other products of postwar economic development. Thus, the economic cleavage between the "honorable" class and the tribal masses has become relatively greater despite the absolute improvement in the material lot of the latter. In addition, advances in the political realm have been largely illusory. The expansion of the suffrage means little when there are few elective offices in the country and the machinery of elections is rigidly controlled by the settler elite. Advancement of tribal people within the True Whig Party or one of the branches of national government takes place only under limited conditions. Furthermore, the possibility of tribal people attacking the political citadel by means short of a frontal assault is remote. There is a tacit proscription against tribal political associations, and the opportunities of the army or of religious, economic, and other types of voluntary association to serve as vehicles for tribal protest are severely limited.

The Political Process

In the formal sense at least the constitution of the Republic of Liberia and the structures of government it sets forths are remarkably similar to those obtaining in the United States. This should not be surprising in view of the American origins of the settlers and the fact that the instrument drafted in 1847 was the handiwork of Professor Simon Greenleaf of Harvard University. The constitution contains the familiar provisions of a presidential form of government with the tripartite functional division of responsibility, a bicameral legislature, a series of checks and balances, a bill of rights, a difficult amending procedure, and other limits upon the powers of government. There was almost a blind adherence to the notion that government must be divided even though the primary concern of the Americo-Liberian community was survival against encroachments from the British and from the tribal masses within their midst.

There is one notable area in which the Liberian system of government deviates from the American pattern. Although the pattern of settlement along the coast and the peculiarities of geography might have led the Liberians to introduce a federal system, they rejected it in favor of a concentration of power in the hands of the national government. As a consequence local initiative and responsibility in government have been remarkably absent. Local offices are appointive rather than elective, there are few independent sources of revenue available to municipalities, and the granting and the withdrawing of powers by the national government are done in a capricious fashion. The counties and provinces have been retained largely for the purpose of legislative representation and the administration of central government programs.

THE PRESIDENCY

The emergence of the President as the dominant figure in Liberian national politics along with the obvious subordination of the other two branches was not foreseen by the founding fathers. This did not actually become a clearly established fact until the present century despite the long tenures of Joseph Jenkins Roberts, Hilary Johnson, and other strong-willed presidents during the first fifty years of independence. The fate of the 17 men who have held the office during 19 separate presidencies reveals that in only 7 cases (Benson, Roberts in 1876, Johnson, Gibson, Arthur Barclay, Howard, and Edwin Barclay) did the incumbent President retire voluntarily. In an eighth case (Cheeseman) the President died in office. Excluding the incumbent, of the remaining 10 instances, 4 (Roberts in 1855, Warner, and Payne in both 1869 and 1877) were defeated in their bids for reelection, one (Russell) lost the support of his party and was not renominated, one (Roye) was forcibly deposed, 3 (Gardiner, Coleman, and King) were compelled to resign upon the implied or explicit threat of impeachment, and one successor (Smith) was forced to accept a truncated term of several months until a new election could be held. In addition to the 10 who lost power, at least one more—Garretson Gibson—was threatened by a mob calling for his resignation. He failed to panic, however.

There are a number of factors accounting for this gradual growth in the powers of the President. Partly it is the result of a series of constitutional amendments to the 1847 provision which required the President to seek reelection every two years. Now, following an initial term of eight years, a President may run for any successive number of four-year terms. This has not only freed the executive from recurrent intraparty struggles and campaigning, but it also permits him to launch long-range programs and to consolidate a personal following in the various branches of government. The President, too, has been one of the prime beneficiaries of the increasing effectiveness of the central government's administrative and military services and the improvement in transportation and communications. As a consequence of the latter developments, the regional appointees of the President are increasingly subject to his control rather than permitted to act as free agents. An elaborate system of surveillance, including the employment of "personal relations officers" who report directly to the President, *ad hoc* reviews of specific situations by the President or one of his subordinates, and the penchant of the present chief executive to scrutinize vouchers of more than $250 have also strengthened the President's hand relative to other personages in the political system.

The expanding dimension of governmental operations in Liberia as a result of foreign investment and United States government aid has also been a significant factor. In a country where few offices are elective, a merit-type civil service system exists largely on paper, and the government is one of the largest employers of personnel, the power of appointment provides the President with a considerable political weapon. The expansion of governmental operations means not only more jobs to distribute but also more perquisites of office which can be dispensed to reward the faithful, seduce the doubtful, and entrap the powerful opponents of the regime. Thus, free housing and automobiles, frequent trips abroad, scholarships for one's children, assignment to plush ambassadorial posts, "forgiveness" of taxes and of payment for governmental services, access to governmental equipment for one's private use, and the privilege of receiving exorbitant tax-free rents on private buildings leased by the government are part of the largess which can be distributed by the President to maintain his regime in office. Moreover, in a country in which the extended family is an important political group, the executive does not limit the use of patronage to entrenchment of his own family. He employs patronage as a device to keep the leading families in a state of equilibrium so that no single group constitutes a threat. This accounts for the "rapidly changing face" of the bureaucracy. At the moment when one contender and his family appear to be gaining in terms of patronage and prestige, the family is actually increasing its vulnerability with respect to the President and other leading families. In this situation the President inevitably becomes almost indispensable in his role as arbiter of inter-dynastic disputes.

The presidency has become an indispensable institution in still another crucial respect. The external and internal threats posed to Americo-Liberian supremacy in the Republic have forced the settler group to accept the solitary leadership of the President rather than that of the multiheaded and locally oriented legislature. Indeed, the resignations of Presidents King (1930), Coleman (1900), and Gardiner (1883) were forced precisely because the actions of the incumbent President exposed the settler community to foreign or tribal enemies. The critical importance of the President to the Americo-Liberian community has become even more apparent during the administration of Tubman. Tubman has felt compelled to emulate some of his West African neighbors by casting himself in the role of a charismatic leader who can breach the social and tribal schisms within Liberia. There is little doubt that he has had greater popularity with the tribal people than any President before him. His accessibility and dispensation of personal justice, his respect for tribal customs, the ceremonial aspects of his Unification Policy, and his informality on public occasions have had a decided appeal to the indigenous element. It is a matter of question whether these things justify the erection of statues of Tubman around the country or whether they are sufficient to offset some of the obvious deficiencies of the Unification Policy. Nevertheless, there is no other Americo-Liberian who has as popular a following among the tribal people, and tribal challengers to the President's leadership have been effectively removed from active politics. Thus, there is no other leader on the scene today who could satisfy both communities. This perhaps accounts for the sense of relief which many felt when he announced in 1961 that he would run for a fifth term in 1963. The Americo-Liberians, moreover, appreciate that their initial fears about the Open-Door Policy have not as yet materialized. The policy has yielded considerable financial benefits for the elite without unduly mobilizing the tribal people in political terms. The descendants of the settlers appreciate, too, that Tubman's approach to international politics has thus far shielded Liberia from the torrents of African nationalism.

Having said that the President is the dominant figure in Liberian national politics does not mean, however, that he is a dictator. A more accurate description would be that he has been the presiding officer of the Americo-Liberian ruling class and that increasingly, under Tubman, the President has become the managing director of a moderate social revolution. Although he may manipulate the leadership of various family, regional, tribal, and other groups, he also depends upon them for support. The continuing problems of transportation and communication and the inefficiencies of administration (especially with respect to postaudits) leave many independent pockets of political power throughout the system. The relative political autonomy of these groups is recognized by the fact that the President must constantly attempt to placate his political opposition. The hand of forgiveness appears always to be extended, and even those removed from office on serious charges or imprisoned for grievous offenses find that the gates of patronage are never completely closed. With luck, after a due period of grace, one may be appointed to an even higher post in government. The President cannot bank too strongly on his personal popularity as a weapon with which to control the political opposition. The insecurity of Tubman's *personalismo* is certainly evidenced by the fact that much of what passes for expressions of popular support is either highly subsidized by government or is the result of legal and unofficial coercion. Any unpopularity is masked by the absence of an independent press and by the severity of the libel, slander, and sedition laws when it comes to criticism of the President or his family.[9]

THE LEGISLATURE

The subordination of the legislative branch to the President has been especially apparent during the administrations of Edwin Barclay (1930–1944) and his successor, William Tubman. None of the author's informants could point to one significant measure which had emerged from the Legislature without presidential approval, nor could they point to any major legislation which failed despite concerted and sustained support from the Executive Mansion. This does not mean that

[9] *Liberian Code of Laws of 1956*, title 27, ch. 3, secs. 52–55.

the House and the Senate are completely under the domination of the President, for the membership of the Legislature includes some of the leading figures in the hierarchy of the True Whig Party. These are men who have bases for political support that are independent of the President. The Speaker of the House, the Vice-President, the president pro tempore of the Senate, as well as the senior men in the county delegations, are powerful figures within their own areas. Consultation behind the scene and surveying the opposition in advance are required to spare the President public political defeat.

The President does not always get his way completely or immediately on any measure he has introduced even though he gets his way eventually and substantially. Individual senators or representatives are permitted to place a personal imprint upon certain types of legislation and even to obstruct the passage of a measure. The expression of independence by the legislators, however, is often illusory. Delay in passage of a bill may actually indicate the lack of presidential intent to do more than publicly espouse a reform which he has no intention of putting into effect at that time. Similarly, the senatorial rejection of a presidential nomination for the Supreme Court may create an impression of legislative independence. The only recent case of this, however, was openly acknowledged as a façade for a change of heart on the part of the President himself. The Senator who led the assault on the presidential nominee was himself immediately nominated for the same post. The subordinate role of the Legislature was clearly expressed in the remarks of the Vice-President to this writer in 1960 at the opening of the Legislature. Mr. Tolbert stated that House and Senate could not consider any measure during the first month inasmuch as the President was still in Europe and "we don't know what his thoughts are." Significantly, the $27,000,000 annual budget introduced on December 23, 1960, was passed into law on the following day, without amendment.

Although as a body the Legislature does not initiate legislation or provide a public check upon presidential power, it does have an educative function to perform. Its debates are lively, even though highly rhetorical in character, and help to educate the local leadership and the general public regarding the significance of a new policy decision. The debates often expose defects or pitfalls in a proposed measure which are helpful to the executive branch in reformulating its proposal and to the drafting committees of the Legislature in presenting a final version of the measure.

The Legislature's representative function is poorly served in view of the tendency to make decisions outside the legislative body and in view of what will be said shortly about the tendency of the True Whig Party to derogate pressure-group activity to a minor role in the political process. Party representation, moreover, exaggerates the strength of the True Whig Party, which has enjoyed a virtual monopoly in the Legislature since the founding of the party. The one modern threat to this supremacy was negated when the Legislature refused to seat the People's Party candidates who had been victorious in the Maryland County elections of 1931.[10]

Ethnic representation is also disproportionate. Until the amending of the constitution in 1944, there was a total denial of representation to the provinces even though any tribe could pay to have a speaker sit in the House of Representatives and participate without a vote. Now, 6 of the 39 members of the House of Representatives are chosen from the three provinces, where the majority of the people live. This under-representation of the provinces is only slightly offset by the fact that a few of the representatives from the counties and territories have tribal backgrounds. The inability of many of the provincial members to understand English makes them ineffective in debate and in committee work. Their assignment to the chairmanships of unimportant committees in the House emphasizes the relatively insignificant role they play in the political process.

Geographic disparities in representation are also apparent in the above remarks. The 10-member Senate represents only the counties. Although President Tubman proposed in 1960 that the county system be extended to the provinces, the delay in putting any plan into effect leaves these areas unrepresented in the upper chamber. The lower house, in addition to overrepresenting the counties and territories, gives Montserrado County almost a fourth of the total membership (9 out of 39 seats), which may or may not accurately reflect its greater population. The creation of the separate territories of Marshall, Sasstown, River Cess, and Kru Coast during the past decade constitutes an attempt to provide more adequate representation in the House to some of the older historic settlements and tribal areas. As far as the Senate is concerned, the True Whig Party itself has attempted to provide better geographic representation by following the practice of nominating candidates who represent "different sides of the river" within each of the counties.

Despite the lack of significant power in the matter of legislation,

[10] *African Nationalist*, Nov. 8, 1941, p. 3.

the post of Senator or Representative is one which is eagerly sought. Membership in the Legislature automatically gives one the title "Honorable" as well as the perquisites which are due to the very few elective officials in Liberia. In addition to the other forms of patronage available to party members in good standing, a high proportion of the legislators receive attorney fees for representing the foreign concessionaires and the more prominent private Liberians. Speaker of the House Richard Henries, for example, has the most flourishing law practice in the country. If one is not a lawyer at the time of election, the fledgling legislator quickly finds himself studying for the bar. The Legislature, moreover, is regarded as a very attractive forum for the establishment of a national reputation. With success a young man may go on to the Supreme Court, an ambassadorship, the cabinet, or even as high as the presidency. It was his performance as Liberia's youngest senator that eventually carried Tubman to the Executive Mansion. In any case, the two-term tradition of the True Whig Party assures the Senator at the end of six years and the Representative at the end of four years that his term of office will be renewed largely without a contest. Some have been able to extend their tenure indefinitely without contest.

THE PARTY SYSTEM AND ELECTIONS

An intense interest in politics and a tendency to organize protest movements have been characteristic of Liberia almost from the establishment of the colony in 1822. The "Remonstrance of December 5, 1823" regarding the question of allocation of lots in the settlement at Mesurado provided the American Colonization Society with concrete evidence that the settlers were not entirely content with paternalistic government. The Remonstrance was effective in compelling the Society to publish the Plan of Civil Government of 1824, which set forth the powers of the Board of Agents with respect to the colonists. During most of the first decade, however, the legitimate political activity of the Americo-Liberians was limited to the right of assembly and petition and to the election of a Vice-Agent and two councilors, who were to advise the Agent in the administration of the colony. The election of settlers to fill these three posts turned largely on the personal qualifications of the candidates.

In the election of 1830, a decided split in the settler community arose between those supporting and those opposing the Colonization Society's administration of the settlements. This tendency of elections to revolve more and more around issues rather than personalities became even more apparent as the number of elective offices was increased. By 1835 a cleavage of interest became manifest between the more conservative agricultural groups in the upper settlements and the more liberal and commercial elements in and around Monrovia. It was not until the Commonwealth period of limited self-government (1839–1847), however, that a rudimentary party system actually emerged. The Reverend John Seys, who had been personally offended by Governor Buchanan's policy on the entry of duty-free goods for missionaries, organized an opposition party which conducted its attack on a number of fronts—in the legislative chamber, in public meetings, and through the columns of Seys's newspaper, *Africa's Luminary.* Joseph Jenkins Roberts, Hilary Teage, and other members of the pro-administration group, however, held a majority of the seats in the Commonwealth Legislature and remained in control during the transition to republic status in 1847.

The True Liberian, or Republican, Party founded by President Roberts and his followers after independence remained in control of the national government until the election of 1869. The Anti-Administration Party, which rallied under the banner of Samuel Benedict in opposition to ratification of the constitution in 1847, never seriously threatened the Republicans. There were, however, divisions arising within the Republican Party itself regarding the alleged domination by Monrovia and Montserrado County over the rest of the country. Curiously enough, the issue which became the most significant divisive force within the Republican Party concerned racial extraction. Roberts, who was an octoroon, was rejected in his bid for a fifth term in 1855 in favor of Stephen A. Benson. The latter was also of mixed ancestry, but he was considerably darker in complexion than Roberts. Benson had the support of the poorer Americo-Liberians and the Congoes, both of which had felt discriminated against by those of "brighter" skin color.[11]

By the election of 1869, the issues of skin pigmentation and ancestry split the solidarity of the Republican ranks and brought to power the True Whig Party, which had been formed to oppose the lighter-skinned aristocracy. The candidate of the True Whigs, Edward J. Roye, was Liberia's first full-blooded Negro President. His birth in America, his superior education, his meteoric rise in Liberian commerce, as well as his distinguished service on the Supreme Court, made him sufficiently

[11] Frederick Starr, *Liberia* (Chicago, 1913), p. 90.

acceptable to the Republicans to bring about a peaceful transfer of party control. Roye, however, was a tragic figure. The personal involvement of the President in the disastrous British loan of 1871 and his attempt that year to extend the term of office from two to four years led to Roye's ouster and to his subsequent death under mysterious circumstances. A Republican junta forced his Vice-President, James S. Smith, to accept a truncated term of office, and the junta brought ex-President Roberts back to the presidency. The Republicans were victorious in the next two elections, but their defeat at the hands of the Whigs in 1877 gave the latter the first of a series of victories which have continued unbroken into the present period. Whig domination was not really assured, however, until the election of Hilary R. W. Johnson in 1883, as Liberia's first "son of the soil" President. Johnson, who had the nomination of both the True Whig and the Republican parties, declared himself a Whig after the election. Thus, during the nineteenth century Liberia arrived at the pattern of one-party rule which is rapidly becoming the political norm in the newly independent states of Africa. The period from 1869 to 1883 represents the only period of intensive interparty competition in Liberia during which the opposition had more than merely a theoretical chance of unseating the ruling party.

The mechanisms whereby the True Whig Party has maintained its dominant position for more than eighty years have been fairly well developed. Patronage is the keystone in the arch. Inasmuch as there is only one elected executive in a highly centralized unitary state, the party which captures the presidency enjoys a monopoly over the distribution of patronage in its various forms. The opposition can make promises, but only the ruling party can actually deliver the rewards to the faithful. In the face of repeated failure at the ballot box and of the constant seduction of the opposition by the True Whig Party, it is difficult for a second party to hold its following together from one defeat to the next. The opposition must rely on the voluntary contributions of the faithful. The True Whig Party, on the other hand, levies a yearly "tax" upon every public employee to the extent of one month of his salary over a two-month period, and there is no public accounting of the party treasury.[12]

There are other unofficial and official devices for blunting the effectiveness of the opposition party. The government-owned *Liberian Age*

---

[12] Doris Duncan Grimes, "Economic Development of Liberia" (M.A. thesis, New York University, 1955), p. 6. Mrs. Grimes is the wife of the Secretary of State and daughter of the former Secretary of Public Utilities.

and the subsidized *Daily Listener*, for example, maintain almost a conspiracy of silence with respect to the opposition and on the eve of the
1959 election did not even mention the name of Tubman's opponent.
The official line of defense for the party is the government's control of
the machinery of elections. Ostensibly the Elections Commission is to
be nonpartisan. The three members, however, are chosen by the President—two from among individuals nominated by each of the political
parties and a chairman selected at the President's discretion. The election laws make it difficult for the opposition candidates to get their
names on the ballot in any case. It became even more difficult, however, in 1955 when the Legislature outlawed the major opposition
group, the coalition Reformation and Independent True Whig Party,
"because of their dangerous, unpatriotic, unconstitutional, illegal, and
conscienceless acts"—to use the language of the law.[13]

The restrictive character of the libel and slander laws makes it difficult for the minority party to criticize the President and other leading members of his party during campaigns. Should the opposition
perservere until election day, there is no assurance whatever that their
adherents will be permitted to vote, that the vote will be counted accurately, or that the Legislature will accept any results which give a
victory to the opposition party. Finally, if all else fails, the leader of
the opposition may be forced to flee the country, as Dihdwo Twe felt
obliged to do before the election of 1951. Persistence in contesting the
results of an election, moreover, has no reward. This ex-President Edwin Barclay discovered in 1955 following his unsuccessful attempt to
recapture the presidency as the candidate of the Independent True
Whig Party. The special session of the Legislature which considered
and rejected his appeal was a piece of high comedy in all respects
except for the $19,000 costs which were assessed against Barclay.

The rancor which followed the election of 1955 and led ultimately
to the assassination attempt against President Tubman, as well as the
subsequent indiscriminate prosecution of members of the opposition, is
rare for Liberian politics.[14] Typically, the True Whig Party attempts to
mend any breach in the ranks of the Americo-Liberian community by
absorbing the opposition leadership after the election. This has been
characteristic of party behavior during most of the present century. In
1912, following a bitterly contested election of the preceding year,

[13] *Liberian Code of Laws of 1956*, title 12, ch. 8, sec. 216.
[14] See Liberian Information Service, *The Plot That Failed* (London: Consolidated Publications, 1959).

President Daniel Howard named his opponent the president of Liberia College and subsequently Chief Justice of the Supreme Court. Tubman, too, during his first administration absorbed some of the leading members of the Unit Whig Party and the People's Party, which had opposed him in the election of 1943.

In view of the preceding remarks, it is perhaps understandable why a sustained opposition movement has not survived in Liberian politics. The persistence of party labels from election to election is deceptive. There was no connection, for example, between the People's Party of 1903 and that of 1923. In terms of organization and financing there was really little continuity between the People's Party which contested the elections of 1923, 1927, and 1943 or between the Independent True Whig Party of 1955 and 1959 even though there was in both cases a carry-over of portions of the leadership. Each campaign finds an opposition element organizing anew around the personality of a leader. In four of the campaigns during the present century, the opposition standard-bearer has been an ex-President attempting to oust his successor.

The results of recent elections should be discouraging enough for any future contestants. The flight of Dihdwo Twe in 1951 gave Tubman a unanimous decision for a second term. In 1955 Edwin Barclay garnered only 1,182 votes against 246,131 for William Tubman. The 530,472 votes that Tubman secured in 1959 were remarkable enough in view of various estimates that the population of Liberia does not exceed 1,000,000. His majority, however, was no more remarkable than the 55 votes received by his opponent, W. O. Davies-Bright. The opposition votes, incidentally, included the ballot of President Tubman himself, who publicly expressed his concern about maintaining a two-party system! [15]

Whatever function elections serve in Liberia, they cannot be regarded as mechanisms for deciding which party is to control the machinery of government. The absence of an effective opposition party in the formal sense, however, does not mean that no political opposition is permitted within the country. What is required is that competition must take place within the confines of the True Whig Party. Factional division along regional and even interest lines has been a common feature of intraparty politics. For the most part dissension is resolved by the leaders behind the scene, in consultation with each other and with the President. As a last resort the national or county conventions of the

[15] *Liberian Age*, May 6, 1959, p. 1.

party will make semipublic decisions regarding candidates when the field has not been narrowed before this stage is reached. Real competition does exist for the few elective offices, and the various claimants to the nomination for Senate or House seats make concerted efforts to get the endorsements of as many local branches as possible before the conventions gather. Even at the national level, when an incumbent President is retiring, the field of presidential hopefuls is seldom narrowed to one before the convention is called. The preconvention jockeying in 1919 and even that in 1943 were fairly lively affairs. There are occasions, too, when it is difficult for the party leaders to control a county convention. A good example of this fact was the Grand Bassa County Convention which met in February, 1959, to name a senatorial candidate. After having made a unanimous choice, it found its decision reversed by the leaders of the national party. A new convention was called the following month to make a "proper" choice.[16]

There is, too, a certain amount of "loyal" criticism permitted in public with respect to policies of government and even with respect to personalities, providing that criticism is not directed against the highest ranks of the political hierarchy. Annual reports of the various departments, for example, are quite frank in their expression of self-criticism as well as in suggesting new policy orientations. Public criticism on a limited scale is also permitted the journalists of the *Liberian Age* and *Daily Listener*, although in many instances legislators and other members of the "honorable" class have been hypersensitive to criticism and have attempted to censure journalists for their actions. Often what are cited as examples of press freedom in Liberia, however, turn out to be attacks upon a policy or an individual already marked for the political graveyard by the President.

Criminal prosecution is possible for remarks made abroad which might be acceptable in Liberia itself. Thus the former Attorney General, C. A. Cassell, found himself disbarred from his legal practice for life for having made criticisms of the Liberian judiciary at the Lagos Conference of Jurists in 1961.[17] His remarks, oddly enough, were less offensive than the indictment hurled against the same judiciary by A. Dash Wilson upon assuming the office of Chief Justice a few years previously. This sensitivity to criticism made outside the country no doubt stems from the trying history of Liberia, in which the Americo-Liberians have had to struggle to survive against the territorial en-

[16] *Ibid.*, March 2, 1959, p. 1; March 13, 1959, p. 10.
[17] *Ibid.*, March 3, 1961, p. 4.

croachments made by Great Britain and France prior to World War I, against the moral indictment of the League of Nations during the 1930's, and against the verbal criticisms of leaders of neighboring African states who long felt that maladministration in Liberia weakened the case for the early achievement of African independence.

Of even greater significance is the opportunity which dissension within the ranks of the Americo-Liberian community affords the members of the tribal majority to undermine the authority of the former. Public disagreement raises the specter of a discontented group within the settler community seeking to tip the political scales in its favor by forming an alliance with the tribal people. In view of both these internal and external dangers, it is perhaps understandable why Tubman in his election-eve speech of 1951 charged that the hands of his political opponent, Dihdwo Twe, were "stained with the blood of treason, rebellion and sedition. He has been unfaithful and recreant to his trust as a Liberian citizen." [18] Similarly, the ban on the coalition Independent True Whig and Reformation parties in 1955 equated opposition to the True Whig Party with treason to the state. The solidarity of the True Whig Party is the prime weapon in the defense of Americo-Liberian supremacy.

The concessions that have been made to the tribal people by way of increased representation in the Legislature and an extension of the suffrage constitute no threat to the Americo-Liberian ruling class. The effective political decisions are still made by the inner circle of the True Whig Party, and this remains firmly in settler hands. Elections provide the Liberian masses with the façade of participation in the national political process and permit the national leaders to explain and popularize their programs. Elections, however, have not provided the tribal people with an instrument of political power.

PRESSURE GROUPS

The possibilities of the tribal element making a frontal assault upon Americo-Liberian supremacy via the party and electoral systems are highly limited. Equally remote at this stage are the prospects of an indirect approach through the medium of pressure-group activity. Politics takes precedence over other interests among the Americo-

[18] Reginald Townsend, ed., *President Tubman of Liberia Speaks* (London: Consolidated Publications Company, Ltd., 1959), p. 99. Twe fled from Liberia in 1951 during the electoral campaign. He remained an exile in Sierra Leone until 1960, when Tubman granted him "pardon and freedom from prosecution" (*Liberian Age*, June 17, 1960, p. 1).

Liberians, and as a consequence pressure groups in the Republic are largely subordinated to the True Whig Party. Manifestly political associations among the tribal people are under tacit proscription even though improvement, credit, and burial groups flourish among the Bassa, Kru, and similar indigenous communities in Monrovia and other urbanized centers. Moreover, the opportunities of tribal people to become effective in the major institutional, associational, and nonassociational interest groups in Liberian society are limited by virtue of the prior domination of these groups by the Americo-Liberians.

Religious associations. The formally organized religious institutions, for example, are controlled by the descendants of the settlers, or the latter are attempting to secure the rapid "Liberianization" of churches which are still supported by foreign missionary efforts. The Bassa Community Church and other nativistic religious groups constitute exceptions to this rule of Americo-Liberian domination, as does the Muslim group, which is very strong in the interior. Nevertheless, it is apparent that the Mandingo and other Muslims have not attempted in recent years to secure political objectives which are at variance with the objectives of the Americo-Liberian community. It is significant that the "Muslim" leader in 1960 who presented a petition to Tubman to run for a fifth term was Momolu Dukuly. Five years previously, when Dukuly was the Liberian Secretary of State, he traveled abroad to represent his country at the Methodist General Conference!

Being a Methodist or Baptist preacher or a senior warden in an Episcopal church may provide one with a personal asset as well as an organizational springboard from which to advance in politics. There are certain churches, such as the First Methodist Church and Trinity (Episcopal) Pro-Cathedral, which are regarded as "political" in the sense that some of the leading figures in the "honorable" class are members. The evidence regarding the relationship between church and politics, however, seems to support the conclusion that leadership in the former comes as a reward to one who has advanced in government, rather than the reverse. William R. Tolbert, for example, was elected president of the Liberia Baptist Missionary and Educational Convention six years after he became Vice-President of the Republic, and Joseph J. Mends-Cole became head moderator of the Presbyterian Church after he was elected to the House of Representatives. The prestige of the church is enhanced by the election of an "honorable" to a post of leadership in the church, but the use of the church by the political leader in consolidating his position in government is incidental.

A similar relationship can be discerned between government and the quasi-religious associations such as the YMCA and the Masonic Order. The last five Worshipful Grand Masters in Liberia were Chief Justice Louis A. Grimes, Vice-President Clarence L. Simpson, President William V. S. Tubman, Attorney General C. Abayomi Cassell, and Speaker of the House Richard A. Henries. During 1960 the international president of the YMCA was Secretary of the Treasury Charles D. Sherman.

The army. In common with most African states the army in Liberia has not yet become an institutional interest group of consequence. The officer class is drawn largely from the Americo-Liberian community and is selected on the basis of patronage. The general lack of professionalism among the officers does not give them any motivation to put the political house in order in the way that the professional officer groups have done in many Asian and Middle Eastern states. Nor does the enlisted group, which is drawn largely from the tribal societies, constitute a discontented element in society. The low salary is more than compensated for by the prestige of the uniform and the carte blanche which members of the Liberian Frontier Force have in exploiting the communities in which they are stationed.

Events of the past few years, however, may bring a decided change in the relationship between the army and politics. The realization that Guinea and Ghana were receiving arms from the Communist bloc, at the very time when the inadequacy of the training of Liberian troops was being demonstrated in the Congo, has alarmed both political and military leadership. There has been a decided tightening of the United States Military Mission's objectives in Liberia, and many observers detect the emergence of a professionally minded officer class in the Republic.

Students. Student and professional bodies generally do not constitute pressure groups in the Liberian political system. There have been strikes and other forms of anomic behavior evidenced by students, more so at Cuttington College and Konola Academy, rather than the University of Liberia, since the tribal students at the former are in a higher ratio to those of Americo-Liberian origin. The President during his series of school commencement speeches in 1960 took pains to point out that political activity on the part of students would not be tolerated. In any case, most graduates find that their rebelliousness evaporates rather quickly once they have been given a government position and the perquisites that go with it. The college graduate is still highly articulate about the need for reform in Liberia, but the higher he advances up the political ladder, the greater is the disparity between his advocacy of reform and his actions as a politician.

Economic associations. One would expect that the rapid development of the Liberian economy would lead to the emergence of economic associations comparable to those characteristic of the political systems of neighboring African states. Such has not been the case. The explanation for this is partly historical. The disdain which the upper ranks of the Americo-Liberian community evidenced toward commerce and industry has almost universally been commented upon by observers of the Liberian scene since the middle of the last century. The paternalism of the American Colonization Society, the attitudes imparted by some of the radical missionary groups, the economic depressions which wiped out hard-earned savings, and the emphasis which the legal defense of the Republic against the Europeans placed upon legal and political education account for much of it. It can also be explained in terms of the inevitable politics of a small state. The system permits the political leadership to control the economy to its personal advantage through its manipulation of tariffs, the granting of franchises and subsidies, and the letting of contracts. The rule then for the ambitious businessman is "Seek ye first the political kingdom." Finally, a more contemporary answer can be provided to explain the absence of economic pressure groups in Liberia. This is the realization that trade unions, cooperatives, and commercial associations undermined colonial rule elsewhere in Africa and that they could undermine the supremacy of the settler group in Liberia as well.

The foregoing explanations seem much more logical to this author in accounting for the absence of a Liberian middle class and of economic associations than those proffered by various governmental officials. The arguments of the latter are that economic development at this stage is highly dependent upon foreigners; that Liberians lack capital and entrepreneural ability; and that small Liberian businessmen are being forced out by competition from the Lebanese, who have very close-knit familial and economic ties. Objectively, however, one can see that it is far safer politically for the Americo-Liberian hierarchy and the Liberian government to rely upon foreigners to provide investment capital, managerial skill, and other elements required for economic development. The non-Negro foreigners cannot become citizens and are therefore barred from participation in politics. They are in the country on sufferance and may be deported if they become troublesome. A native commercial middle class, on the other hand, would become a potential threat to the political supremacy of the Americo-Liberian ruling class. This accounts in great measure for the absolute reduction in the number of small Liberian businessmen and for the political impotency of the Liberian National Businessmen's Association during a period when the Liberian economy is undergoing rapid expansion.

It probably accounts, too, for the curious statement made by President Tubman in the author's presence that "Liberians are simply not ready for cooperatives." Could this not have been the realization that it was the cocoa cooperatives in Ghana and the cotton and coffee cooperatives in Tanganyika that provided much of the organizational leadership for the nationalist movements in those countries? Trade unions, similarly, have not been encouraged. Where they have been permitted, they operate without any real standing. Employers are not legally obliged to engage in collective bargaining with the leaders of the unions. A strike is technically illegal until the dispute has been submitted to a labor court. These courts, however, have yet to be constituted.

To ensure that the incipient trade union movement is kept within bounds, its leadership has been carefully selected. The president general of the Labor Congress of Liberia is T. Dupigny-Leigh, a member of the House of Representatives and the former social secretary to the President. A still greater irony, however, was the recent election of William V. S. Tubman, Jr., as the president of the Congress of Industrial Organizations. It was he who had to present a petition to his father, the President of Liberia, during the general strike of September, 1961. This strike grew out of complaints of discrimination against the management of the Ducor Palace Hotel, which is one of the showpieces of Monrovia. The leaders of the CIO (Liberia), who made the charges, were arrested, and this in turn led to demonstrations on the part of many laborers, walkouts at the water front, and the closing of many shops during several very tense days. The government charged that "foreign influence" was responsible for the general strike, and shortly thereafter Ghanaian and Egyptian diplomats were asked to leave the country.

The family in the political system. The significance of the extended family in the politics of tribal societies in Liberia has been adequately documented in monographs by George W. Harley, James Gibbs, and other scholars. Only suggestions have been given, however, with respect to the significance of the family as a political, economic, and social association within the more Westernized sector of the population. The bilateral family ties which one acquires at birth are supplemented later in life not only by the marriage contracts of the individual himself but also by the marriages of his siblings and his children. The ties impose obligations and also provide the individual with a series of allies upon whom he may rely to support him in time of crisis or to advance his standing in the community. Knowledge of his own ties and the family ties of others is a *sine qua non* for the social and political survival of the individual, for in crucial situations individuals interact not solely as atomized personalities but as representatives of family groupings. On the basis of the affiliations of an acquaintance, one cultivates his friendship, shuns him, or regards him as a political neutral. Knowledge of family ties also play a peculiar role in maintaining the supremacy of the nontribal over the tribal community. Although entry to the Americo-Liberian ruling class is permitted to naturalized Liberians and to Gola, Grebo, and others who have undergone a measure of acculturation, for the most part the preponderance of marriages involving members of the leading national families are on an "in-group" basis. The strained publicity given of late to "mixed" marriages only serves to underscore the generalization.

Romantic love is certainly a factor both in marriage and in the establishment of informal liaisons. Marriages within the "honorable" class are not arranged, in the Oriental sense of the term. Nevertheless, it is apparent from an examination of the genealogies of the leading personalities of the political hierarchy in Liberia that connubial ties constitute an important element in the political advancement of the ambitious individual. Although a certain amount of permissiveness across class lines is permitted in premarital and extramarital situations, the marriages of an "honorable" and of his siblings and children provide political relationships which are undertaken with an eye to the future. Thus, when the son of a cabinet member marries the daughter of a Senator or an ambassador, he is thereby assured two patrons who will be concerned with his political advancement. The corollary to this situation is that divorce and remarriage are as much an instrument of political realignment as they are of social readjustment. There is a strong correlation between the severance of marriage ties and the decline in the political fortunes of the family of one of the parties concerned. Thus, the high incidence of multiple (albeit successive) marriages in a nominally monogamous society is explicable partly in terms of the political culture.

The spread of kinship ties throughout the political system is apparent

Chart 1. Family and politics in the Republic of Liberia, 1960–1961

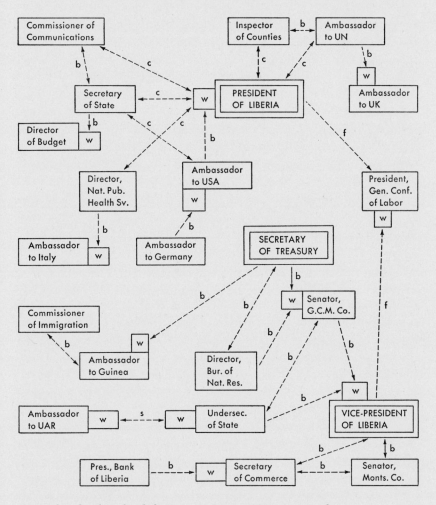

Key: b = brother; f = father; c = cousin; s = sister; w = wife.

at both national and local levels. The Yancy and Wilson families have long been prominent in Maryland County; so have the relatives of the Freemans and Shermans in Cape Mount and the Grigsbys in Sinoe. At the national level the Barclay family has contributed more than its share of presidents, justices of the Supreme Court, and cabinet members—to say nothing of the wives of leading officials. At a lower level in the national picture, the various strands of the Cooper and Dennis families provide significant political linkages. From an examination of the genealogies of the political leadership over a period of years, one is provided with clues regarding both the immediate strength of a given family leader and the upward or downward direction of his political fortunes. Although there were many pockets of strength throughout the national hierarchy, it was clear that three men were strongly entrenched politically in 1960–1961: President William V. S. Tubman, Vice-President William R. Tolbert, and Secretary of the Treasury Charles B. Sherman. In the case of the first two, a significant link was established as a result of the marriage of William V. S. Tubman, Jr., to Wokie Rose Tolbert, the daughter of the Vice-President.

The expansion of the bureaucracy and the creation of diplomatic posts in various quarters of the globe have placed a marked strain upon the monopoly of political office by the leading fifteen families. Inevitably, the need for a particular talent at a particular time permits new entrants to the inner political circle from among the lower strata of the Americo-Liberian community, the immigrant group, or the educated tribal class. The contracting of marital ties by the new entrants with members of the elite families usually takes place, however, at an early date. Thus, the immigrant or tribal person's political status is assured at the same time as the solidarity of the ruling group is restored through this process of co-optation.

ADMINISTRATION

In theory the Republic of Liberia is a highly centralized unitary state. There is relatively little legal autonomy enjoyed by the major political subdivisions—the five coastal counties and the three hinterland provinces—or by the districts, territories, and municipalities into which the counties and provinces are further subdivided. In fact, only the counties and municipalities have a basis in the constitution whereas the other units remain creatures of the Legislature. Administrative officials at all levels are appointed by the President or by the President with the advice and consent of the Senate. Decisions regarding policies, programs, and the expenditure of funds are also made largely at the national level. Revenue collection, moreover, is virtually a monopoly of the central government even though the fines and fees collected by chiefs may be spent for local projects under proper central government supervision. The political division of the country tends largely to be disregarded by the departments of the national government in the planning of programs in agriculture, health, education, and other fields. Thus, the superintendents of counties and territories and the provincial and district commissioners are "chief executives" of their respective areas only with respect to a limited number of government functions. This situation may be altered in the future, particularly if the Rural Area Development Scheme launched in 1961 does in fact strengthen the hand of the district commissioner relative to the technical officers in his area. For the present, however, the counties, territories, and provinces exist largely as electoral areas for the national legislature or, together with the hinterland and coastal districts, as units for the maintenance of order and the collection of taxes.

Unfortunately for the theory of administrative organization, a number of factors have militated against the assertion of central government authority in many areas of the Republic. The most significant factors include the difficulties which geography has posed for the development of an effective system of transport and communications, the historic emergence of satrapies along the coastal strip under the control of leading families, and the resistance of the tribal people as well as the trepidation or indifference of the Americo-Liberians with respect to the establishment of control over the hinterland. As a consequence of these things, there are many areas of the Republic where either little gets done by way of positive governmental programs or what is done is accomplished in a highly inefficient manner with a maximum amount of coercion from the top and scant initiative or enthusiasm emerging from the grass roots.

The new motor roads, the airplane, and the radio at least provide the means for altering the above situation and bringing administrative practices into line with the theory of centralized control over field services. Much more has to be done, however, with respect to improving the system of public administration at both national and local levels. It does no good to insist that the field officer be held responsible for implementing national government policy directives if he has almost no trained staff, is indifferent to the need for adequate reporting and record keeping, and has only sporadic supervision of his work by

officials at a higher echelon. Nor is it of any value to insist upon central
government direction if the executive branch has only recently recognized the value of planning or data collection, if the President ignores
the legal chain of command from chiefs up through the Secretary of
the Interior and insists upon being accessible to all parties, or if rigorous
attention is paid by the President to the preaudit of every expenditure
of more than $250 but almost no attention is paid to postaudit. Indeed,
all the problems of public administration both in developed states and
in other countries of Africa appear to be compounded in Liberia.

Perhaps the heart of the problem is personnel. In terms of per capita
exposure to university training the Liberian upper class is among the
best educated of any African state. The propensity of educated Liberians to regard politics as the preferred profession, moreover, would
seem to give the government of Liberia a decided advantage over
neighboring states where medicine, teaching, and commerce enjoy
relatively high prestige. But this is not actually the case. Partly this
results from the inadequacies of the education received at the University of Liberia or the smaller colleges of the United States. It is also
a function of the overemphasis upon legal and political studies to the
neglect of agriculture, engineering, accounting, business administration, and other subjects which form the substance of governmental
programs or are essential to the efficient operation of government.
Even if a Liberian student does pursue a technical course, however,
there is no guarantee that his talents will be put to the best use. Sheer
inefficiency in allocating personnel, the student's own recognition that
politics will be the most rewarding profession in the long run, and the
operation of the patronage system have all been contributing factors
to the waste of human talent by the government.

Although specific instances of appointment or promotion may be
attributable largely to merit rather than patronage considerations,
this technique of placement is capricious and arises largely when a
particular skill is required in a hurry. The patronage system, on the
other hand, pervades all administrative practices. As the civil service
commissioners have testified in their annual reports, the senior executives regard with scorn such notions as the competitive testing and
certification of candidates, the establishment of impartial criteria for
the promotion or firing of employees, and the need for preservice or
in-service training for posts in government. Only the Department of
State has attempted to regularize its testing and training programs for
foreign service officers and thereby reduce some—but certainly not all

—of the evils of patronage. This effort attests to the critical importance attached by Liberia to good public relations in international politics.

In patronage terms the government employee has a dual obligation. One is to the President and the True Whig Party. This obligation is satisfied by attendance at rallies, by voting, by public displays of loyalty to the President, and by the annual "contribution" to the True Whig Party which is automatically deducted from his salary. The second obligation is to his patron or patrons. This entails his support of the patron in the latter's struggle for power with other influential members of the political hierarchy, including perhaps the employee's administrative superiors. The spread of patronage ties (which are in many cases synonymous with blood and marriage ties) provides the President with a useful mechanism for maintaining control over the political system. There is a built-in watchdog system, with each bloc attempting to report on the sins of omission and commission of the competing bloc. Patronage rivalry, however, takes its toll with respect to administrative boldness in launching new programs and generally plays havoc with the ability of a superior to control his subordinates. A simple executive directive may easily be converted into a contest for power at a higher level in the bureaucracy. Action frequently takes place only by means of indirect communication, and the consequent delay is often fatal for programs.

In addition to its inefficiencies, the Liberian bureaucracy is clearly too large. The expansion of government into areas which might more efficiently be left to private hands is but one of the factors. The lack of planning, the inadequacies of training, and the cultural insistence upon a rigid division of labor also contribute to a multiplication of the number of workers required if administrative programs are to be accomplished at all. The expansion of the bureaucracy increases the need for the general service staff and contributes to a reduction in salary scales at the lower level, which in turn perpetuates the demand for "dash" or petty gifts in return for any service rendered by a public employee.

At the higher levels of the bureaucracy, the inadequacies of training are not so apparent. Although in 1961 several senior members of the government were only high school graduates, this is becoming the exception. A good many of them have advanced degrees from the best universities in America and Europe. Indeed, the ability of Liberian leaders to be articulate about the problems of government is disarming to the outside observer, who later discovers a great chasm between the expressed desire for reform and any positive evidence that administrative and political energies are being directed toward that end. Some of the most vociferous critics of patronage stand at the heart of a vast patronage empire. On the slightest provocation, moreover, agency heads having major responsibilities for new programs undertake extended trips to visit community development schemes in the Negeb Desert or clinics for midwives in the Soviet Union. Often the only time a senior official ventures into the interior of Liberia is to visit his rubber farm or to attend a ceremonial function. There is apparently no notion of a conflict of interest when a government official reaps personal financial profit from his position by securing a monopoly for his company or be receiving retaining fees from foreign concessions. Such behavior is not inconsistent with the moral standards of the nontribal element, and, indeed, it is compatible with the efforts of the ruling class to control economic development to the extent that neither a tribal nor a settler middle class emerges to challenge the existing order. Whether it stimulates or inhibits rapid economic development is an arguable matter. It does compromise the official's objectivity, however, and detracts from the performance of his duties. Ultimately, it may have the unintended result of undermining the very social and political system it is designed to perpetuate.

To compensate for inadequacies of training and to overcome some of the inefficient practices, the Liberian government under President Tubman has placed increased reliance upon foreign advisers from the United States, Great Britain, Israel, and other developed countries. The American Agency for International Development (and its predecessors) and United Nations Specialized Agencies have provided most of the external advisers. The fact that European and American financial and other advisers were imposed upon Liberia at various points in its recent past have made the task of the foreign adviser a difficult one indeed. Some advisers find the inertia and lack of cooperation too much to bear and quit in disgust. Others attempt to deal with their frustrations by welcoming the opportunity of assuming an operational rather than an advisory role. On the whole, the Liberian government does not get its money's worth from its foreign advisers, but it is not sure that the government intended to. In certain cases the foreign adviser is made the unwitting scapegoat for the institution of a new program which encounters public opposition.

THE JUDICIARY

Although the Liberian constitution upholds the principle of the independence of the judiciary, in fact the judges of the Supreme Court and subordinate courts are under the control of the other two branches of the government. The removal of judges by joint resolution of the Legislature is a fairly common occurrence. Two justices of the Supreme Court, for example, were removed in 1957. The occasional display of independence by the judiciary is treated with indifference by the more obviously political branches. A case in point was the classic decision of 1919 in which the Court declared that the existing system of administration in the interior was unconstitutional. Nonetheless that pattern of administration has continued to the present.

The lack of prior judicial experience or even legal training is apparent at all levels of the court system. Chief Justice A. Dash Wilson, upon taking office in 1958, delivered a caustic lecture to the whole judiciary that noted the persistent bias on the part of the judges with respect to litigants, the many improper instructions to juries, and the lack of courage on the part of the courts in dealing with unscrupulous lawyers. Perhaps the greatest problem facing the judiciary is the delay in bringing cases to completion. The first judicial circuit of Montserrado County in 1960, for example, was able to dispose of less than 7 per cent of the 1,297 criminal cases on its dockets.[19] Similar situations prevailed in the other tribunals, especially those dealing with civil cases. For a community which places a high value on litigation, this is indeed a serious problem. Litigation, in fact, is one of the most effective weapons for keeping the politically and socially diffident Liberians in line. The expense, the loss of time from his place of business, the neglect of his family and friends, as well as other by-products of protracted court cases serve to dampen the enthusiasm of the social mischief-maker and the political reformer.[20]

Contemporary Issues

Despite its long history of independence, the Republic of Liberia finds itself beset with many of the same problems facing the leaders of African states only recently emerged from colonial rule. Thus, the primary issues of the Liberian political process are the satisfaction of

[19] Republic of Liberia, *Annual Report of the Attorney General, 1959–1960,* App. B; *Liberian Age,* March 31, 1958, p. 4.
[20] See Parker, "Acculturation in Liberia," p. 270.

the economic demands of the people, the achievement of national unity, the establishment of an efficient and responsible form of government, and the formulation of policies with respect to the new nations of Africa and Asia as well the main protagonists in the cold war. Although the Americo-Liberians may attempt different solutions to the problems they have in common with their newly independent neighbors, they find themselves inevitably being drawn into a common political stream.

THE ECONOMY

To the casual observer, the postwar economy of Liberia generates a great deal of optimism regarding the future of the country. The tall buildings rising along the Monrovia skyline, the crowded docks, the feverish activity at the Bomi Hill and Nimba Mountain iron mines, the steady flow of trucks along the country's new central highway, and the well-stocked shops in Monrovia and other urban centers are all evidence of a surge of economic activity which compares favorably with developments taking place elsewhere in Africa. For a small state Liberia's economic potential is enormous, and under Tubman's Open-Door Policy the rapid exploitation of its resources has poured considerable wealth into the country. There are healthy signs, too, in the efforts of the government to diversify the Liberian economy by introducing a variety of new tree crops as well as encouraging the development of mining, forestry, and light industry. Also during the last decade, the dominant role of the United States in the external trade and capital development of Liberia has diminished as a result of the increased ties being established with Europe and the Middle East.

There are, however, a number of critical problems which have been either ignored or given inadequate attention by the Liberian leadership. The lack of concern with economic planning, for example, has led to a shocking waste of physical resources and human talent. Systematic record keeping is almost an unknown art, and the need for statistical data and comprehensive surveys in carrying out development schemes has only recently become apparent to Liberian officials. Few economic priorities are established, with the result that scarce capital is dissipated on a host of projects that are never completed. Much capital, too, is poured into major prestige items which often lack the necessary supporting infrastructure such as port facilities, roads, and public utilities. The lack of planning, too, has permitted the rechanneling of labor and capital into bizarre economic activities to the neglect of basic production. The outstanding example of this in the past few years has been the need for Liberia to import large quantities of the staple of the country's diet, rice.

Another danger point in the postwar economic picture is the extent to which Americo-Liberians have relied upon foreigners in all phases of the developmental process. Admittedly, a massive infusion of external capital has been required to get development under way. Americo-Liberians are quick to point out that their country did not have the "advantages" of the British Colonial Welfare and Development Act or the comparable French schemes which stimulated postwar economic development in other African states. Nevertheless, the more wealthy and better-educated Americo-Liberians could be investing both their talents and their money to a considerably greater extent in the development of their own country. Few in the latter class are interested in the launching and practical management of new economic enterprises. Although they might be prepared to underwrite foreign management, they are reluctant to lend funds to small Liberian businessmen. Similarly, despite much talk about cooperative societies and a development loan corporation for small businessmen, the Liberian government has not chosen to disperse its patronage among small Liberian businessmen or in other ways to encourage the development of a strong middle class.[21] Furthermore, neither have the major foreign concessionaires felt obliged to train Liberians for management or skilled technical posts in their enterprises as long as the government continues its policy of siphoning off the better-trained personnel. In the long run the failure of the government to insist upon a Liberianization of the economy may react to the detriment of the Americo-Liberian ruling class and the foreign economic interests. It is difficult to see how the country can be insulated against a violent nationalist reaction to this situation by both the tribal element and the lower ranks of the Americo-Liberian community.

The most critical problem—and one related to the previous condition—has been the absence of distributive justice. While economic development has brought wealth to the country and has managed to affect the lives of all except those living in the remotest reaches of the interior, the benefits are dispersed in a highly inequitable fashion. The political elite, drawn largely from the upper ranks of the Americo-Liberian community, enjoys almost a monopoly over the multiple bene-

[21] John P. Mitchell, ed. of United Christian Fellowship Conference of Liberia, *Changing Liberia* (Switzerland, 1959), p. 51.

fits which have come from foreign investment and from intergovernmental aid programs. The standard of living of the "honorable" class has been immeasurably altered as a result of university scholarships, trips abroad at government expense, the use of government housing and transportation, access to government "surplus" equipment at little or no cost, the holding of legal monopolies over certain business enterprises, appointment to bogus offices in government and business, easy acquisition of large-scale landholdings in the interior, and the existence of a very unrealistic tax structure. In themselves, these items do not differentiate Liberia from other countries of the world. What makes them significant is that the benefits accrue to a very close-knit minority while the wages for the tribal people involved in the highly inflated money economy seldom exceed 50 cents a day. Moreover, efforts of the tribal people to enhance their bargaining position through cooperatives and trade unions are not encouraged.

EDUCATION

In the absence of a census and accurate figures on school enrollment, any assessment of literacy rates in Liberia is bound to be impressionistic. The consensus of most observers, however, is not only that Liberia has one of the lowest literacy rates among the independent states of Africa but also that progress in combating illiteracy has lagged considerably behind the efforts of many of the new states which are striving for universal mass literacy. Liberia has a compulsory school attendance law; nevertheless, the optimistic estimate of the Secretary of Public Instruction in 1960 was that 10 per cent of the school-age children were enrolled in either government or mission institutions. The figure was optimistic because one-fourth of the 60,000 students were in kindergarten and the prefirst grade, and only one-half of the total were in classes beyond the fourth grade.

In contrast to the high proportion of the national budget allocated to education in Guinea and Ghana, less than 6 per cent of the 1961 budget of $27,000,000 was allocated to education at all levels. This was approximately $1,000,000 less than Liberia appropriated for the operations of the Department of State, international conferences, and the maintenance of embassies and consulates abroad; and it was roughly a third of the cost of the new Executive Mansion being constructed in Monrovia. A disproportionate share of this amount is allocated to scholarships for study abroad (rather than to the building of firm educational foundations in Liberia itself) and to movie censorship, beauty culture, home arts, sports, and other projects of limited or dubious educational value.

At the primary and secondary school levels there are a number of qualitative and quantitative problems. Despite the fact that Liberia is a developing country, the emphasis in the curriculum is placed upon a classical literary education, and little attention is given to agriculture and the mechanical arts. The one vocational high school in the country, Booker T. Washington Institute, has good facilities and a qualified staff, recruited by Prairie View (Texas) Agriculture and Mechanic College. Unfortunately, the students with better grades and independent finances seldom elect to enroll there. Despite the existence of an ambitious textbook-writing program, the schools generally rely upon American textbooks, which are ill-adapted to the Liberian milieu. There has been, too, a lack of determination to deal realistically with the language diversity of the tribal population. Finally, it must be noted that even the officials of the Department of Public Instruction are quite frank about the generally low standards of teaching in the government schools. Until 1950 over 80 per cent of primary and secondary instruction was in the hands of Christian missions, which have received only token financial support from the government. Although attacks on missionary efforts by the more vocal of the Liberian nationalists have been noted of late, the best education is still provided by these voluntary agencies. In the government schools the patronage element is highly significant in the appointment, promotion, and assignment of teachers, and the post of school supervisor is openly acknowledged as a convenient base for one with political ambitions. Unfortunately, even the students are exploited by the government and their teachers for many purposes unrelated to education.

At the level of higher education the Episcopal-run Cuttington College in the interior and Our Lady of Fatima (Roman Catholic) College in Maryland County are offering instruction of a high quality with a rigid adherence to standards. Their student bodies are drawn largely from the tribal element, and degrees from these institutions lack the political prestige of a degree from a foreign institution or even from the University of Liberia. The latter institution, founded in 1862, in many ways compounds the deficiencies of the Liberian primary and secondary school systems. The report of the Cornell University group which evaluated the University of Liberia in 1960 emphasized the political character of the institution, the lack of professional standards in teaching, and the general inadequacies of the students and the facilities.[22] Nonetheless, undaunted by the inadequacies of the Liberian educational system at the undergraduate level, the Liberian government is negotiating for the establishment of a medical school in Liberia.

NATIONAL UNITY

The most critical problem facing the government of Liberia is that of national unity—the erasing of the legal, political, economic, and social barriers separating the tribal people from the descendants of the settlers. Despite the advances which have been made under Tubman's Unification Policy, there is much evidence indicating that the experiment in cultural assimilation of the two communities is far from complete. The rank discrimination against the tribal people which was so blatant and public during the administrations of Tubman's predecessors is now becoming increasingly rare. Covert discrimination in government employment as well as in social relations continues, however, and the tribal people still tend to regard themselves as Bassa or Kpelle rather than as Liberians. Although the law is purposely vague on the point, it is apparent that a legal distinction has been perpetuated between the members of the two groups in the matter of marriage and divorce, the jurisdiction of tribal and statutory courts, and the occupation of land in the hinterland. Indeed, the Westernized person of tribal origin often finds himself in the frustrating position of having his claims to being a "civilized" person rejected both by the nontribal elite and by his own tribal kinsmen and associates. The latter continue to hold him responsible for traditional obligations to the family and to tribal political leaders despite his superior education, his acceptance of Christianity, and his involvement in the money economy.

Collectively as well, the tribal people find that the cleavages between them and the settler community remain or have become even greater during the postwar period. The unequal distribution of income and other direct benefits of economic development has its counterpart in the maldistribution of educational and welfare facilities under recently launched government programs. For example, the construction and staffing of schools have brought disproportionate gains to the areas where the nontribal population is concentrated. Thus, in the expenditure for salaries of primary and secondary school teachers during 1960–

[22] A. Gordon Nelson and Charles C. Hughes, *University of Liberia: An Appraisal and Recommendations with Observations and Recommendations Relative to Agriculture and Forestry* (hectograph report; Ithaca, N.Y.: Cornell University, 1960).

1961, Montserrado County received twice as much as the three hinterland provinces, where it is assumed that the majority of the population lives. Similarly, in the area of higher education, scholarship preference is still given to the children of the "honorables" and other Americo-Liberians even though the sheer number of awards available has permitted many tribal persons to receive education at home or abroad. In the fields of health, road construction, and the provision of technical services much is being done by the Liberian government, with the assistance of American AID staff and funds, to improve the lot of the tribal people. Here as well, however, a disproportionate share of attention is given the coastal counties relative to the provinces of the interior.

It is the hope of the nontribal community that President Tubman can either sufficiently appease the tribal element with token reform or at the extreme bring about a nonviolent social revolution which leaves the present ruling class with many of its prerogatives. It is extremely doubtful whether the newly educated tribal youth will be satisfied with the appeasement objective, but under the present system of administrative control it appears unlikely that an organized tribal opposition can be brought into existence to threaten the settler dominance. Consequently, about the best that the tribal people can hope for is the gradual program of integration championed by Tubman. Perhaps the additional four years of his fifth term will give him the authority to accomplish what he could not carry through during his first twenty years in office.

EXTERNAL RELATIONS

Liberian-American relations. In view of the history of settlement in Liberia, it was perhaps inevitable that the Republic's external orientation should be stronger toward the United States than toward any other state or dependency. Even during the nineteenth century, when the long-delayed official recognition of Liberia was followed by only token or moral support to the settlers in their disputes with Britain and France, the American connections were firmly maintained through nonofficial channels. Not only did the activities of Protestant missionaries provide organizational and personal ties between Americans and the colonists, but they were also responsible for most of the educational and health programs in the country. On a very personal level, too, the family ties which straddled the ocean remained strong and actually increased as Liberian students and visitors to the United States acquired American spouses.

The twentieth century witnessed the expansion of a variety of nonofficial connections. Firestone Plantations Company, for example, pioneered the economic development of the country, and it has been followed of late by a host of other American investors and commercial firms. American universities, too, have been concerned with Liberia. Only the Nigerians account for a higher percentage of the African students in the United States. Cornell University, Prairie View (Texas) Agriculture and Mechanic College, and Northwestern University have been even more directly involved by providing assistance to the Liberian government and to educational institutions in the country. Other private institutions, such as the Rockefeller Foundation and the Eli Lilly Foundation, have been actively combating the problems of disease, illiteracy, and economic underdevelopment.

At the official level as well, the contacts between the two republics have expanded during recent years. The military assistance the United States gave Liberia in 1915 to quell an uprising on the Kru Coast was continued in a more-or-less sporadic manner until the period following World War II. Now the training and the equipping of Liberian troops by the United States have been put on a permanent basis. In 1959 Liberia became the first—and thus far the only—African state to have concluded a mutual defense pact with the United States. In terms of economic assistance, too, Liberia has been the prime African beneficiary of lend-lease aid, technical assistance programs, loans from the Export-Import Bank, and AID (American International Development) guaranteed loans for private American investors. The entry of Nigeria and other new states into the list of independent countries will alter Liberia's relative standing, but it still expects to receive assistance on an increased scale from the United States.

Liberian officials have been rather ambivalent about the relationship of their country to the United States. On the one hand, they express the opinion that American aid has been too small in relation to need and has been given with "too many strings attached." There is undoubtedly a sincere conviction in the constant repetition of the theme that the United States has a debt to Liberia stemming from its origins as an American colony and from the injustices which the ancestors of the Americo-Liberians suffered at the hands of Southern slaveowners. A more recent debt has been incurred as a result of Liberia's following the lead of the United States in entering both world wars against the Germans. In World War II, Liberia provided the United Nations with land for an important military base, was the major source of natural rubber following the fall of Malaya, and made many sacrifices it need not have made had the country remained neutral. Most recently Liberia has given the United States a considerable advantage in the cold war by permitting the construction of a Voice of America transmitter powerful enough to cover the entire African continent.

At the same time as they stress this theme of American responsibility for Liberia, Liberian officials are becoming very worried about the intensification of relations with the United States. Sensitive to the charge of African and European leaders that Liberia is the "slave and enclave of the dollar," the Liberian government has been attempting to diversify the sources of its foreign investment and to establish a complex of bilateral and multilateral agreements with states in all quarters of the globe. Liberia now has embassies in most countries of Western Europe, Africa, and the Near East as well as Haiti and Taiwan. Despite the lack of formal diplomatic relations, Liberian officials have established contacts with or have actually visited the Soviet Union, Eastern Europe, and Communist China. Liberia is using the facilities of the United Nations to the fullest extent possible to emphasize its independence of action in foreign affairs, and on several occasions the Liberians have found themselves taking an opposing point of view to that of the United States.

Relations with other African states. The development of sustained official relations between Liberia and its African neighbors has been limited largely to the postwar period. The continued dependence of Liberia upon American support was only one of the factors contributing to this isolation. Geography was another, for the rough terrain made it difficult for the Liberians to build roads and bridges connecting Monrovia with its own hinterland let alone reaching the French and British territories beyond. European politics was also a factor inasmuch as Liberia was excluded from the British and French colonial systems which at least had led to some interterritorial cooperation between Nigeria and Sierra Leone, on the one hand, and Senegal and the Ivory Coast, on the other. The attitudes Europeans assumed with respect to the ability of the Americo-Liberians to govern themselves were frequently adopted by African leaders as well.[23] Isolation, however, was also a product of choice by the Americo-Liberians, who rejected their African heritage in favor of an emphasis upon their Western origins.

[23] Nnamdi Azikiwe's *Liberia in World Politics* (London: Stockwell, 1934) is a more contemporary indictment which echoes the criticisms expressed by Dr. Edward Wilmot Blyden.

Such contact as did take place between Liberians and other West Africans was largely personal in character. Family ties, for example, between the Creoles of Sierra Leone and the Americo-Liberians continued to remain strong, as did those among the tribal peoples separated by the arbitrarily drawn international boundaries. The parents of Americo-Liberian youths in many cases recognized the superior standard of schools in the Gold Coast and Sierra Leone and sent them there for education. Better employment opportunities lured the Kru people as well as many Americo-Liberians to Nigeria and Senegal.

The achievement of independence by Ghana in 1957 and Guinea in 1958 had a profound impact upon Liberia. Not only was the Republic permitted for the first time to establish direct official relations with other West African governments, but it was also recognized that the establishment of such ties was a matter of survival. The rising wave of African nationalism posed a threat both to the supremacy of the settler community within the Republic and to Liberia's claim to a major share of the technical and other forms of assistance given through the United Nations to developing countries in Africa. This is a plausible explanation for the almost frenzied efforts of the Liberian government to establish ties with the new states and to assume a role of leadership in the United Nations and at the various conferences of African states. Despite the considerable drain upon its financial resources (roughly one-tenth of the national budget in 1960–1961) and its pool of talent, Liberia has endeavored to establish embassies in each of the new African countries. Exchanges of visits between Tubman and other African heads of state are occurring at rapid intervals and frequently lead to the signing of bilateral agreements on trade, cultural exchanges, and other such activities. During 1959–1960, moreover, Liberian officials attended more than forty international conferences, many of which were devoted to purely African problems. At least five times during the past three years Monrovia has served as the host city for major African conferences. The most historic of these conferences was that of May, 1961, which clearly emphasized the cleavage on various issues between the Casablanca powers and the other African states.

Liberia's claim to speak for other African states in the United Nations was given symbolic recognition in December, 1960, by its selection as the first African state to be given a seat on the Security Council. In both the Security Council and the General Assembly the Liberian delegates have taken vigorous stands in condemning South African apartheid, in opposing Portuguese rule in Angola, and in championing other African causes. From the outset of the Congo operation, Liberia has provided troops for the United Nations effort there and has been active in seeking a peaceable settlement of the Congo's many problems.

Relations between Liberia and the more conservative and pro-Western African states are more cordial than those between Liberia and the members of the Casablanca group, even though Tubman has long insisted that he belongs to no bloc and wants rather to serve as a bridge of understanding between the former British and French territories. The strained relations with Nkrumah were evidenced during the riots of September, 1961, when the second secretary of the Ghanaian Embassy was requested to leave the country for having organized a youth movement to oppose the Liberian government. In October, 1961, the Liberians also asked for the recall of a United Arab Republic diplomat who had challenged the necessity of governmental emergency powers for dealing with alleged subversion.[24] The Americo-Liberians have dealt in a less forthright manner with Guinea, which is a greater threat in view of its proximity and the ties it has developed with the Communist bloc. Conflicting boundary claims and irritations arising out of Guinea's use of Liberia's Free Port of Monrovia and the connecting road, as well as other points of conflict, are constant irritants. To date both countries have preferred to maintain an official attitude of cordiality, however, and Presidents Touré and Tubman have exchanged numerous state visits in the past three years.

The major political difference between Liberia and certain of its neighbors comes over the question of Pan-African unity. This became apparent during the Sanniquellie Conference of 1959, in which Tubman got Sékou Touré and Kwame Nkrumah to agree to the formation of a Community of Independent African States. This was a defeat for Nkrumah, for it put a brake upon his more directly political approach to union at the supranational level in favor of unity based upon an intensification of economic, cultural, social, and scientific cooperation among the governments of independent states. The Monrovia Conference of 1961, from which the Casablanca powers absented themselves, largely endorsed the Tubman approach to Pan-African unity.

APPENDIX

Presidents of the Republic of Liberia

Joseph Jenkins Roberts 1848–1856
Stephen Allen Benson 1856–1864
Daniel Bashiel Warner 1864–1868

[24] *New York Times*, Oct. 5, 1961, p. 14.

James Spriggs Payne 1868–1870
Edward James Roye [1] 1870–1871
James S. Smith [2] 1871–1872
Joseph Jenkins Roberts 1872–1876
James Spriggs Payne 1876–1878
Anthony William Gardiner [3] 1878–1883
Alfred F. Russell [4] 1883–1884
Hilary Richard Wright Johnson 1884–1892
Joseph James Cheeseman [5] 1892–1896
William David Coleman [6] 1896–1900
Garretson Wilmot Gibson [7] 1900–1904
Arthur Barclay 1904–1912
Daniel Edward Howard 1912–1920
Charles Dunbar Burgess King [8] 1920–1930
Edwin Barclay [9] 1930–1944
William Vacanarat Shadrach Tubman 1944–

[1] Deposed.
[2] Succeeded Roye, accepted truncated term of office.
[3] Resigned.
[4] Completed unexpired term of Gardiner.
[5] Died in office.
[6] Completed unexpired term of Cheeseman; elected in own right; forced to resign.
[7] Completed unexpired term of Coleman; elected in own right.
[8] Forced to resign.
[9] Completed unexpired term of King.

BIBLIOGRAPHY

GOVERNMENT DOCUMENTS

Official documents of the government of Liberia have for the most part been either typewritten or mimeographed and have had only a limited distribution abroad. Few complete collections exist even in Liberia aside from the Department of State Archives. For the purposes of this study, the writer found invaluable the annual reports to the Legislature of the following individuals and agencies: the Secretary of the Interior, the Attorney General, the Department of State, the Civil Service Commission, the Treasury Department, the Department of Public Instruction, the Department of Agriculture and Commerce, and the National Public Health Service. Coverage involved the years 1955–1961, for the most part.

The Secretary of the Interior generously made available to this writer the typewritten and mimeographed copies of the "Decisions Rendered by the President of Liberia on Administrative and Other Matters Heard and Determined in His Several Councils of Chiefs." These are important to the understanding of the Tubman Unification Policy and clarify many provisions of the *Liberian Code of Laws of 1956* (Ithaca, N.Y.: Cornell University Press, 1957) regarding the administration of the interior. Also helpful in this latter respect was the mimeographed copy of the "Revised Laws and Administrative Regulations for Governing the Hinterland, 1949," which differ in certain marked respects from the *Code* provisions.

Various publications of the Division of Statistics (formerly in the Department of Agriculture and Commerce but now within the Bureau of Economic Research) were also useful. These include the *Census of Population of Monrovia* (CP Report no. 3-1956), *Census of Population of Greenville* (CP Report no. 1-1958), *Balance of Payments for 1959* (BP Report no. 1-1960), and *Foreign Trade Supplement for 1959* (FT Report no. 1-1960).

Liberia Today, a quarterly bulletin of events and general information, was published by the Department of State through its embassies abroad from 1951 through 1961. The Liberian government has also sponsored the publication of two bimonthly magazines containing information on economic development, trade, and investment opportunities. *Liberia Trade, Industry and Travel*, started in 1958, and *Liberian Agriculture and Commerce*, launched in 1961, are both published by Consolidated Publications, London.

Cornell University Press has been publishing two series on behalf of the Liberian government. Both are the products of the Liberian Codification Project under the direction of Professor Milton R. Konvitz. The first is the *Liberian Code of Laws of 1956*, vols. I–IV (1957–1958) and supplementary vol. V (1960). The second is the *Liberian Law Reports*, of which vols. I–X (1955–1962), containing the decisions of the Supreme Court from 1861 through 1950, have now appeared.

NEWSPAPERS

Although numerous newspapers have been published in Liberia during its history as a colony and republic, political and financial considerations usually gave them brief lives. Files are either incomplete or nonexistent with respect to many of them. A discussion of newspaper sources covering the early period is found in Charles H. Huberich, *The Political and Legislative History of Liberia* (2 vols.; New York: Central Book Co., 1947), II, 1682 ff. Of Monrovia's two current newspapers, the government-owned *Liberian Age* has appeared semiweekly since 1946, and it presents a fair coverage of local and national news. It is available on Library of Congress microfilm. The *Daily Listener* is owned by a local political leader and has a small government subsidy. Although its reporting of national and international news is of dubious quality, it is invaluable as a source of local social items. It is available on microfilm at Indiana University.

Historical Background

There is no single work which can be regarded as the definitive history of Liberia. Much of the story can be pieced together from the several scholarly studies which have the defect, unfortunately, of either being concerned with one narrow segment of Liberia's history or being compendium-like in approach. A great deal of the vital history of the Republic can be obtained only from the exhaustive search of accounts by missionaries, diplomats, merchants, and other observers who were not concerned with the critical separation of fact from fancy or who had a vested interest in altering some aspect of Liberian life.

Among the outstanding scholarly contributions to historical studies of Liberia is the two-volume work by Huberich, cited above, which brings together some of the most significant documents of the pre-1847 period and contains interesting biographical sketches of the pioneers. Aside from its almost exclusive concern with the colonial period, its main limitation is its formal legalistic approach to so exciting a topic. More general scholarly studies which deal with Liberian history (and contain contradictory statements of fact) are Frederick A. Durham, *The Lone-Star of Liberia* (London: E. Stock, 1892); Sir Harry Johnston, *Liberia* (2 vols.; London: Hutchinson, 1906), vol. I; Frederick Starr, *Liberia* (Chicago, 1913); Reginald C. F. Maugham, *The Republic of Liberia* (New York: Charles Scribner's, 1920); Henry F. Reeve, *The Black Republic* (London: H. F. and G. Witherby, 1923); Raymond L. Buell, *The Native Problem in Africa* (2 vols.; New York: Macmillan, 1928), II, 704–890. The Johnston volume, despite its innuendo, is particularly good on the nineteenth-century republican period. Starr's primary asset is his analysis of the early twentieth-century political behavior of the Liberians, which reveals the historical depth of current practices. More superficial but nonetheless informative on the first two decades of the present century are the Reeve and Maugham studies. The work by Buell constitutes one of the best, albeit brief, treatments of the period from the founding of the settlements to the establishment of the Firestone Plantations Company in the 1920's. Other more general studies of Liberia are Hilton A. Phillips, *Liberia's Place in Africa's Sun* (New York: Hobson Press, 1946), which is largely an uncritical hymn of praise to Liberia, and Arthur I. Hayman and Harold Preece, *Lighting Up Liberia* (New York: Creative Age Press, 1943), which is caustic in its comment.

Liberian scholars themselves have attempted to reconstruct their history. One recent effort is *Liberia's Past and Present* (London: Diplomatic Press, 1959) by Nathaniel R. Richardson, the Liberian government printer. Al-

though it is in many ways a mélange of the significant as well as the incon-
sequential, and of historical fact as well as rumor, it is still a very useful
compendium of historic speeches, treaties, and biography. One of the earliest studies by a Liberian is Thomas McCants Stewart, *Liberia, the Americo-
African Republic* (New York: E. O. Jenkins, 1886). One of the most frequently cited works is Abayomi Karnga, *History of Liberia* (Liverpool:
D. H. Tyte, 1926), which makes some original contribution but borrows
heavily from the works of Johnston and other scholars. Two textbooks by
Liberian political leaders for use in civics courses have appeared in recent
years—Ernest J. Yancy, *Historical Lights of Liberia's Yesterday and Today*
(rev. ed.; New York: Jaffee, 1954), and Richard and Doris Henries, *Liberia,
the West African Republic* (New York: Jaffee, 1958). In terms of understanding the process of political socialization and Tubman's Unification
Policy, they are highly informative. Almost no attention is given to the contribution made by tribal people to modern Liberia, and certain historic
events are glossed over or omitted entirely. Yancy's father was Vice-
President at the time of the League of Nations investigation of slavery.

Apart from the general studies, certain works are useful for the under-
standing of particular periods and events in Liberian history. The character
of the colonial period, for example, is well revealed in Jehudi Ashmun,
History of the American Colony of Liberia from December 1821 to 1823
(Washington, D.C.: Day and Gideon, 1826); Ralph R. Gurley, *Life of
Jehudi Ashmun, Late Colonial Agent in Liberia* (Washington, D.C.: J. C.
Dunn, 1835); William Innes, *Liberia* (Edinburgh: Waugh and Innes,
1831); Archibald Alexander, *A History of Colonization on the Western
Coast of Africa* (Philadelphia: W. S. Martien, 1846); J. H. T. McPherson,
"History of Liberia," *Johns Hopkins University Studies in Historical and
Political Science*, 9th ser. (1891), pp. 479–540; and Charles I. Foster, "The
Colonization of Free Negroes in Liberia, 1816–1835," *Journal of Negro
History*, XXXVIII (Jan., 1953), 41–67.

Accounts of Liberian exploration of the hinterland are not very numerous. One classic, however, is Benjamin Anderson, *Narrative of a Journey
to Musardu, the Capital of the Western Mandingoes* (New York: S. W.
Green, 1870), which should rank with the accounts of Stanley, Speke, and
other great explorers. Two other Liberians, Seymour and Ash, penetrated
the northeastern sector of Liberia and are referred to in the Royal Geographical Society, *Proceedings*, IV, no. 4 (1860), 184.

The conflicts between the Americo-Liberians and Great Britain and
France over control of the hinterland are well documented in Johnston, al-
ready cited, and in the other general studies. A significant summary is con-
tained in President Taft's message to the Senate regarding the United States
Commission to Liberia of 1909—"Affairs in Liberia," U.S. Senate, 61st
Cong., 2d sess., Document no. 457 (March 25, 1910).

The controversy with the League of Nations produced a great deal of polemical literature regarding Liberia. Among the more dispassionate coverages of the subject is Raymond L. Buell, "Liberia: A Century of Survival, 1847–1947," *African Handbooks,* no. 7 (Philadelphia: University of Pennsylvania Press, 1947). League of Nations documents which are relevant include *Report by the International Commission of Inquiry into the Existence of Slavery and Forced Labor in the Republic of Liberia* (Geneva, Dec. 15, 1930; c.658.m.272.1930.VI); the monthly *Official Journal,* 1929–1936; and *Annual Report of the Sixth Committee (Slavery) of the Assembly to the Council,* 1929–1936. Official American reactions are chronicled in *Foreign Relations of the United States,* 1929–1936, and Department of State, *Documents Relating to the Plan of Assistance Proposed by the League of Nations* (Washington, D.C.: Superintendent of Documents, 1933). The British reaction is revealed in the British Blue Book, *Papers concerning Affairs in Liberia, December 1930 to May 1934* (London: His Majesty's Stationery Office, 1934), Cmd. 4614. The reaction of an African political leader who is now the Governor-General of Nigeria is contained in Nnamdi Azikiwe, *Liberia in World Politics* (London: A. H. Stockwell, 1934).

The outlines of President Tubman's Open-Door and Unification policies are revealed in Reginald E. Townsend, ed., *President Tubman of Liberia Speaks* (London: Consolidated Publications, 1959), and in Republic of Liberia, Bureau of Information, *The National Unification Program of Liberia* (Monrovia: Department of State, 1954).

Land and People

Descriptions of the geography, economy, and society of Liberia are found in the general historical works cited above. Two postwar volumes which attempt to provide a dispassionate and readable coverage of background material are R. E. Anderson, *Liberia, America's African Friend* (Chapel Hill: University of North Carolina, 1952), and Charles Morrow Wilson, *Liberia* (New York: William Sloan Associates, 1947). A useful compendium of facts about the economy, government, history, and leading Liberian personalities is the *Liberian Yearbook, 1956* (London: Diplomatic Publishing Co., 1956). Its editor, Henry B. Cole, is preparing a revised version for 1962. Also useful is the Liberian Information Service pamphlet, *Liberia: Story of Progress* (London: Consolidated Publications, 1960).

The most significant account of the economic development of Liberia from the 1820's to World War II is George W. Brown, *The Economic History of Liberia* (Washington, D.C.: Associated Publishers, 1941). It is especially valuable for its analysis of Americo-Liberian economic attitudes, of tribal economics, and of the history of the disastrous foreign loans. A more recent discussion of progress in agriculture, transportation, and public development schemes is contained in the series of articles by Harry W.

Yaidoo, "The Basic Economic Development of Liberia," *Liberia Trade, Industry and Travel,* nos. 4–8 (1959–1960). Yaidoo is a staff member of the Bureau of Economic Research, which publishes statistical and other studies. Another staff member, Nathaniel Ejiogu Kevin, wrote an M.B.A. thesis on "Financial Treaties and Foreign Investment in Liberia" (New York University, 1957). Another master's thesis, "The Effects of Foreign Loans and Concessions in Liberia" (School of Public Affairs, American University, 1947) was written by the present Secretary of the Treasury, Charles D. Sherman.

The United States government, in connection with its overseas operations, has produced two documents which assess the agricultural and forestry potential of Liberia: C. R. Orton, *Agriculture in Liberia* (Washington, D.C.: Foreign Operations Administration and Department of Agriculture, 1954), and T. Holsoe, *Forest Progress and Timbering Opportunities in the Republic of Liberia* (Washington, D.C.: International Cooperation Administration, 1955). The Firestone Plantations Company has not been without its vociferous champions and critics. Perhaps the most reasonably objective study of the company's activities is Wayne Chatfield Taylor, "The Firestone Operations in Liberia," *United States Business Performance Abroad,* Case Study no. 5 (New York: National Planning Association, 1956).

The racial and class divisions within Liberia are dealt with by Johnston, Karnga, and other historians. Two scholarly appraisals of the Americo-Liberians which largely avoid adverse conclusions are Richard P. Strong, ed. of Harvard African Expedition of 1926–1927, *The African Republic of Liberia and the Belgian Congo* (2 vols.; Cambridge, Mass.: Harvard University Press, 1930), and D. F. McCall, "Liberia: An Appraisal," *Annals of the American Academy of Political and Social Sciences,* 306 (July, 1956), 88–97. Of quite another character is the highly critical evaluation of Liberian manners, morals, and politics contained in Elizabeth D. Furbay, *Top Hats and Tom-Toms* (Chicago: Ziff Davis Publishing Co., 1943), which has been banned in Liberia. Most revealing of all, perhaps, is the self-analysis conducted by some of Liberia's leading political, social, and religious leaders and set forth in John P. Mitchell, ed. of United Christian Fellowship Conference of Liberia, *Changing Liberia: A Challenge to the Christian* (Switzerland, 1959).

Ethnographic material on Liberia's score of tribal societies is not very abundant. Perhaps the outstanding student of Liberian tribal organization is George W. Harley, whose "Notes on the Poro in Liberia," *Papers of the Peabody Museum,* vol. XIX (1941), and "Masks as Agents of Social Control in Northeast Liberia," *ibid.,* vol. XXXII, no. 2 (1950), are essential reading for the understanding of tribal politics. Additional material by Harley appears in George Schwab, "Tribes of the Liberian Hinterland," *ibid.,* vol. XXXI (1947). The Bureau of Folkways of the Liberian Department of the Interior has issued a series of tribal studies compiled by students of anthropology. Despite the Americo-Liberian social bias there is much information in *Tribes of the Western Province and the Denwoin People* (1955); *Traditional History, Customary Laws, Mores, Folkways and Legends of the Vai Tribe* (1954); and *Traditional History and Folklore of the Glebo* [Grebo] *Tribe* (1957). An excellent monograph on the Kpelle tribal group has recently been presented as a Ph.D. thesis by James L. Gibbs, "Some Judicial Implications of Marital Instability among the Kpelle" (Harvard University, 1960).

The Political Process

The formal structure of government is set forth in the Liberian Information Service, *Liberia: Story of Progress* (London: Consolidated Publications, 1960), and a copy of the constitution with amendments is found in the civics books by Henries and Yancy, already cited. The origins of political controversy and the emergence of political parties in Liberia as a whole and Maryland County in particular are traced in Huberich; Starr; and S. W. Laughon, "Administrative Problems in Maryland in Liberia, 1836–1851," *Journal of Negro History,* XXVI (July, 1941), 325–365.

Biographical sketches of the chief executives of Liberia are fairly numerous although not always informative. Typical of the genre is Thomas H. B. Walker, *The Presidents of Liberia* (Jacksonville, Fla.: Mintz Printing Co., 1915), intended for civics courses. Richardson, cited earlier, is much more useful despite apparent contradictions in facts. The latter volume also contains verbatim accounts of several inaugural addresses. Other presidential messages are listed in the Howard University Library, *Catalogue of the African Collection in the Moorland Foundation* (Washington, D.C.: Howard University Press, 1958). Although to Graham Greene the line between fact and fiction is very thin, an interesting treatment of his meeting with former President Edwin Barclay is presented in the classic *Journey without Maps* (London: William Heinemann, 1936).

Profiles of President Tubman are seldom neutral. Eulogies are found in Thomas P. Melady, *Profiles of African Leaders* (New York: Macmillan, 1961), and in *Liberia's Eighteenth President* (Monrovia, 1946) by Tubman's late cousin, J. Emery Knight. A more objective treatment is the sketch in David Williams, "Profile of a President," *Best Articles and Stories,* IV (April, 1960), 50–53, which was reprinted from *Africa South.* Tubman's philosophy may be extracted in part from the collection of his speeches by Townsend, cited earlier. One phase of Tubman's administration, the assassination attempt of 1955, is covered in the Liberian Information Service, *The Plot That Failed* (London: Consolidated Publications, 1959).

The voice of the opposition to Tubman is partially expressed in a rather pitiful article by the 1951 unsuccessful presidential candidate, Dihdwo Twe, "Liberia: An American Responsibility," *Annals of the American Academy of Political and Social Science*, 282 (July, 1952), 104–107.

The role of churches and other voluntary associations in Liberian social and political life is set forth in the United Christian Fellowship Conference report edited by Mitchell. The significance of the Roman Catholic Church is dealt with at length in Martin J. Bane, *The Catholic Story of Liberia* (New York: D. X. McMullen, 1950). Much of the material on relationships between family and politics has been extracted from the social notices in the *Daily Listener*.

The problems of administration within Liberia can be discerned from an examination of the annual reports of the heads of departments, which are remarkably frank in their self-criticism. A scholarly monograph dealing with the problems of administration in Grand Bassa County is J. Genevray, *Eléments d'une Monographie d'une Division Administrative Liberieenne* (Dakar: IFAN, 1952). A lighter, but nonetheless informative, treatment is the sketch of hinterland administration in Gbarnga District in "Our Far-flung Correspondents: Tubman Bids Us Toil," *New Yorker*, XXXIII (Jan. 11, 1958), 72–91.

For historical purposes, Abayomi Karnga, *A Guide to Our Criminal and Civil Procedure* (Liverpool: D. E. Tyte, 1926), is useful as a general outline of the Liberian legal system. One of the more damning critiques of the Liberian judiciary was delivered at the Lagos Conference of African Jurists in 1961 by C. A. Cassell, a former Attorney General under Tubman.

Contemporary Issues

The role of the American missionaries and philanthropists in the development of the Liberian educational system is revealed in each of the general studies cited earlier. One detailed study of the colonial period from this point of view is Charles A. Earp, "The Role of Education in the Maryland Colonization Movement," *Journal of Negro History*, XXVI (July, 1941), 325–365. Two surveys of educational endeavors during Liberia's first century as a colony and republic are Thomas Jesse Jones, *Education in Africa* (New York: Phelps-Stokes Fund, 1922), and Allen W. Gardner, *The Trustees of Donations for Education in Liberia: A Story of Philanthropic Endeavor, 1850–1923* (Boston: Thomas Todd, 1923). The impact of education upon both tribal and settler cultures was analyzed during the period between the two world wars in James L. Sibley, *Liberia—Old and New* (Garden City, N.Y.: Doubleday, Doran, 1928), and in the postwar period by Thomas Hodgkin, "Education and Social Change in Liberia," *West Africa*, nos. 1907–1911 (Sept. 12–Oct. 10, 1953).

The problems of higher education are dealt with in a straightforward manner in two works, one a Ph.D. thesis by a Liberian student, now dean of administration at the University of Liberia, and the second a report by two Americans. The first is Advertus A. Hoff, "Higher Education for a Changing Liberia" (Columbia University, 1959). The second is A. Gordon Nelson and Charles C. Hughes, *University of Liberia: An Appraisal and Recommendations with Observations and Recommendations Relative to Agriculture and Forestry* (hectograph report; Ithaca, N.Y.: Cornell University, 1960).

The foreign relations of Liberia are chronicled in many works, but it is worth while to single out three of the volumes previously cited: the two by Johnston and Azikiwe and U.S. Senate Document no. 457, "Affairs in Liberia." Two more recent treatments of Liberian-American relations are found in J. H. Mower, "The Republic of Liberia," *Journal of Negro History,* XXXII (July, 1947), 256–306, and Raymond Bixler, *The Foreign Policy of the United States in Liberia* (New York: Pageant Press, 1957). A Liberian interpretation of United States policy with respect to his country is presented in the Ph.D. thesis of the present Secretary of Education, John P. Mitchell—"America's Liberian Policy" (University of Chicago, 1955). A French view which places Liberia more firmly in the category of an American dependency is Pierre and Renée Gosset, *L'Afrique, les Africains* (2 vols.; Paris, 1958), vol. II. Finally, much insight into Liberia's role in world politics is gained through an examination of United Nations documents. During 1961 Liberia was a member of the Security Council, and it has long been active in WHO, ILO, UNESCO, and other Specialized Agencies.

VII

TANGANYIKA

By MARGARET L. BATES

Goddard College

Historical Background

The country now known as Tanganyika, on the east coast of Africa,
offers a number of similarities and a number of contrasts when considered with the West and North African states in this volume. Although it is one of the youngest nations in the world, it is probably one
of the most ancient of inhabited lands; it has passed through two or
even three colonial eras in the last hundred years. It is the largest
African country dealt with in this book, in terms of both area and population, yet it is also one of the most sparsely populated and probably
the poorest. It has a multiracial population, and several political parties
exist, but the term "one-party state" is at the present time an accurate
statement of political reality.*

Tanganyika lies south of the equator; its 351,800 square miles make it
as large as France and Germany combined. Its eastern coast is low and
sandy, broken by many small bays and meandering rivers; mangrove
swamps and coconut palms suggest the equatorial climate which many
Americans associate with Africa. Inland, however, the countryside
changes. The coastal palm belt gives way to a thickly forested strip,

* This chapter is the product of field research conducted in Tanganyika over
a period of years, most recently in 1960–1961. The author is indebted to the
Social Science Research Council for generous assistance on her last trip and to the
Ford Foundation and the United States Educational Commission in the United
Kingdom for earlier support.

and that in turn to a gradually rising plateau of open savannah which stretches, often waterless and treeless, west to the great inland lakes of Nyasa, Tanganyika, and Victoria. The plateau is broken occasionally by a series of mountain ranges, which are better watered and provide a more luxuriant vegetation; in the north Mount Kilimanjaro rises to 19,340 feet, the highest mountain in Africa.

Several facts about this immense inland plateau are of importance. Water is scarce; in many places rainfall is less than twenty inches a year. Much of the country is also infested with tsetse fly, which transmits human and animal sleeping sickness, and hence is uninhabitable. Population is clustered in the well-watered and fertile areas; a study some years ago suggested that two-thirds of Tanganyika's 9,000,000 people lived on one-tenth of its land. Next door to empty acres overcrowding may exist. In the Chagga areas of Mount Kilimanjaro in the northern province, there are more than 600 persons to the square mile. On the plateau the long distances make communication and transport a problem.[1]

THE PRECOLONIAL PERIOD

About the history of this country and its inhabitants there is an incomplete picture, and much of the available information is only educated guessing. Less historical work has been done in the eastern part of Africa than in the west. Geological and archaeological research has in recent years uncovered much evidence of the Stone Age cultures of eastern Africa in early periods, and following Dr. Louis Leakey's discovery of *Homo zinjanthropos* in Olduvai Gorge it now seems possible that Tanganyika may be man's aboriginal home.[2] Knowledge of Tanganyikan history does not automatically improve, however, in approaching the present. It is difficult to speak with any certainty of events or personalities in the interior of the country before 1800.

What is known about the coastal regions is somewhat more certain. The Greeks had some knowledge of eastern Africa, which they called Azania, and contacts existed across the Indian Ocean with Arabia, Persia, India, and possibly China. By the twelfth century, a series of

[1] See the maps appended to Great Britain, *Report of the East African Royal Commission, 1953–1955*, Cmd. 9475 (London, 1955); Clement Gillman, *A Population Map of Tanganyika Territory*, Col. 113 (London, 1936); Walter Fitzgerald, *Africa: A Social, Economic and Political Geography of Its Major Regions* (9th ed.; London, 1961).

[2] Sonia Cole, *The Prehistory of East Africa* (London, 1954); L. S. B. Leakey, *The Progress and Evolution of Man in Africa* (London, 1961).

city-states had been established along the coast from Mozambique north to Somalia; in Tanganyika there were a number of settlements of which Kilwa, Mafia, and Pangani were probably the best known. These were independent Arab principalities, with a Muslim society and architecture, and were based on some trade with the immediate interior, though Arab influence did not at this time penetrate very far inland. The major cities had independent political authorities and their own coinage, and an Arabic history of Kilwa survives. The first European to arrive, the Portuguese Pedro Cabral in 1500, found that the city-states frequently warred among themselves, and the Portuguese soon were able to conquer the coastal cities. Their dominance lasted for over a century, though the extent of their control fluctuated even on the coast, and there is no evidence in Tanganyika that they ever went inland at all. In the seventeenth century the coastal populations gradually reasserted themselves and managed to oust the Portuguese, but their earlier prosperity and influence were not entirely revived.[3]

In the interior, a number of tribes existed. The word tribe is not a very precise one, and its connotations are constantly changing; here it is used to designate a group with some similarities of material culture, language, and spiritual belief. In Tanganyika, at least, the term does not always imply ethnic similarity, for modern tribes have frequently been formed by groups of varying ethnic and geographic origins; nor does it necessarily imply a single political allegiance. It is known that during the last four to five hundred years tribal structure has changed in Tanganyika along with economy, social structure, and physical habitat, though only recently has it become possible to speak at all intelligently of what changes have occurred. Certainly the traditional Western picture of a static African society is practically pure myth.

The interior of Tanganyika in the early nineteenth century probably contained three major ethnic groups. The largest of these was the Bantu, which is really a grouping by linguistic affiliation of many separate tribes. Culturally they tended to be cultivators or mixed farmers, living in relatively small areas with unoccupied bushland separating the tribes. New tribes, in fact, seem to have been formed when one or two families opened up a new section of land; other settlers might arrive, and eventually a separate social and political entity was created. The rate at which these disparate elements coalesced

---

[3] Sir Reginald Coupland, *East Africa and Its Invaders* (Oxford, 1938); J. Strandes, *The Portuguese Period in East Africa* (Berlin, 1899; Eng. trans., London, 1961).

varied considerably; among the Chagga of Mount Kilimanjaro, for instance, it is sometimes still possible, after at least four hundred years, to trace the origins of individual families and clans.

A second group, arriving possibly as late as the eighteenth century, were Nilotic-Cushitic peoples from the north, pastoral nomads who were taller and lighter-skinned and possessed more aquiline features than most of the Bantu. Their progress south was not always peaceful, and Bantu resistance confined them to the northern areas of modern Tanganyika. About the third group very little is known, but they speak click languages and may be related to the Bushmen of South Africa. This group is small, being represented today by only one or two tribes.

In none of these tribes (with minor exceptions) was there a strong, centralized political authority. Groups of families and clans might reside together, but authority tended to be familial and was exercised either by a senior male or by a group of elders acting together. Where a particular clan came to dominate an area, its head might be recognized as chief, or a man who had shown special ability as a leader in war or as a rain maker might gain power and transmit it to his descendants. In Tanganyika, however, this process of gradual coalescence had not often produced one central system, so that a number of chiefs might exist within the same tribe. This fragmentation is an important factor even today. As late as the 1950's the Sukuma, Tanganyika's largest tribe, which totals nearly 1,000,000 persons, had 57 chiefs, each technically independent of the others.[4]

As available information becomes more extensive about the late eighteenth and early nineteenth centuries, these interior societies appear to have been in a disturbed state. Tribal migration occurred on a considerable scale; the Ngoni, an offshoot of the Zulu, traveled all the way north from Natal, while continual Masai pressure came south from Kenya. Among the Tanganyika tribes themselves a series of military leaders appeared, and in Karagwe, Usambara, and Unyamwezi local groups were reorganized into fighting units. At the same time, the ancient slave trade was intensified, to become perhaps the most disruptive element of all.

In 1840, the Sultan of Oman on the Persian Gulf, who had had long contacts with the East African coast, moved to Zanzibar; here, perhaps,

[4] There is no general book available describing tribal structures in Tanganyika. G. F. Murdock, *Africa: Its Peoples and Their Culture History* (New York, 1961), and G. P. Moffett, ed., *Handbook of Tanganyika* (Dar es Salaam, 1958), contain some introductory material.

the history of modern Tanganyika begins. The Sultan's agents soon controlled most of the Tanganyika coast and progressively exerted influence inland. Zanzibari traders penetrated farther and farther each year to obtain the two valuable commodities of slaves and ivory. They traded cotton cloth and cowrie shells and guns in exchange or, forming alliances with some African tribes, warred against others. The effects of the slave trade seem to have been felt most strongly in southern Tanganyika, on the routes to Lake Nyasa. Some of the northern tribes were strong enough to prevent slave raiding in their territories. Much of Tanganyika, however, was so thoroughly fought over and depopulated that by the 1870's the slave raiders had reached west of Tanganyika into the Congo.[5]

European explorers and missionaries, arriving in the 1850's, therefore found anything but a placid and quiescent society. Burton and Speke, traveling to Lake Tanganyika in 1858, and Livingstone a few years later commented extensively on the changing scene of their day: increasing trade and warfare, introduction of new goods and new ideas, and growing intertribal contact.[6]

GERMAN RULE

Whether or not one chooses to speak of Arab rule on the coast and its influence inland as being colonial in character, colonial power was clearly established by the 1880's. The European scramble for Africa in that decade took the form in eastern Africa of a three-way conflict between England, Germany, and France. In Tanganyika, Germany won out. In 1885, it granted a charter for purposes of trade and government to the Society for German Colonization. The Society's founder and agent, Karl Peters, had been active in exploring Tanganyika and had signed treaties with a number of inland chiefs. The German move took Great Britain by surprise, and although it was actively protested by the Sultan of Zanzibar as being a seizure of his territory, no action other than diplomatic protest was taken. The German company established a series of trading posts along the coast.

Relations with the coastal Arabs and the Swahili (that is, coastal Africans who have come under Arab influence and speak the Swahili language, which is of mixed Arabic and Bantu origin) were at first

[5] Sir Reginald Coupland, *The Exploitation of East Africa, 1856–1890* (London, 1939); A. J. Swann, *Fighting the Slave Hunters in Central Africa* (London, 1910).

[6] R. F. Burton, *The Lake Regions of Central Africa* (reprint; New York, 1961); J. H. Speke, *Journal of the Discovery of the Source of the Nile* (London, 1863); Horace Waller, ed., *Livingstone's Last Journals* (London, 1874).

amiable, but in 1888, when the company decided really to exert its military and commercial control, Arabs in the Pangani area rose in rebellion. Other cities and tribes farther south joined in, many asserting their loyalty to the Sultan of Zanzibar, and the company was soon forced to request military and naval assistance from the German government. German troops put down the sporadic outbreaks, but company control was ended. In 1890 a full-fledged German protectorate, administered by the German Foreign Office, came into existence; its boundaries included modern Tanganyika and Ruanda-Urundi.[7]

Penetration into the interior was slow and gradual, and German troops did not reach some sections in the far northwest until as late as 1910. Many of Tanganyika's tribes resisted the German occupation, and the colony's history in its early years was almost entirely one of military campaigns. In the early 1890's, action was taken against the Chagga and Shambaa in the north, then against the Hehe and Bena and Yao of the south. Some tribes tried, as elsewhere in Africa, to utilize the Germans as allies in fighting their own enemies; others recognized the impossibility of resistance to men equipped with machine guns. On the whole, German East Africa was far more a conquered territory than were neighboring Kenya and Uganda, and the destruction of tribal military power, and frequently of tribal chiefs themselves, had considerable consequences for later political development.

As late as 1905, a serious intertribal revolt in the southeast, the Maji-maji rebellion, took the Germans two years to put down and is estimated to have cost 120,000 lives. It was a witchcraft rebellion of the old against the new and atavistic in character; the *maji* (the Swahili word for water) was a medicine designed to make Africans impervious to European bullets. The rebellion was fiercely quelled, and it marked the last Tanganyikan resistance to European control.[8]

Pacification was the first and principal policy of the German administration, which remained predominantly military in tone. The German Empire was new; it had no trained colonial servants and no colonial tradition, and its officials were often army officers drawn from the minor nobility. The *bomas* or administrative headquarters which the Germans built were massive forts, with a clear line of fire around

---

[7] Sir Reginald Coupland, *The Exploitation of East Africa, 1856–1890* (London, 1939); Mary Townsend, *The Rise and Fall of Germany's Colonial Empire, 1884–1918* (New York, 1930).

[8] See Moffett, ed., *Handbook of Tanganyika.* No reliable account of the German period in Tanganyika is yet available.

them, and they indicated plainly the psychology of the men who built them: this was hostile country.

A second strain in early German policy was provided by Germany's interest in economic development. Beginning with the early days of the company, there was much exploration of the resources of the territory: an investigation for minerals, a survey of water supplies, and a search for profitable local plants. With the ending of the slave trade as German authority asserted itself, new trading items were needed. Some economic minerals were found, timber in the north was exploited, and the feasibility of tropical plantations of cotton, coffee, sisal, and rubber was discovered. The German company had already made considerable land grants in the northeast, in the present Tanga province, and encouragement of German settlers was continued by the new administration. In American terminology, these were plantation owners, and their need for an African labor supply resulted in the introduction of forced labor, as well as in increasing population pressure in the fertile mountain areas where German families and firms wished to settle. But German agricultural experimentation also introduced many of the products on which the modern Tanganyika economy is now based. It is difficult to imagine Tanganyika without the sisal plant which was brought over from Mexico in the 1890's and which today provides the largest export crop. As plantations progressed, railroads were built, as well as ports and small commercial towns. In Tanganyika's capital, Dar es Salaam, and in the northeast in Tanga and Arusha, an air of Bavaria still dominates much of the architecture. The conclusion is inescapable that the primary German contribution to Tanganyika was a material one. Modern geologists and agriculturalists, even modern road builders, still work from the old German reports.

In African memories, however, there remains also a vivid impression of the German administrative system and its effects on everyday African life. The military character of the early administration was probably intensified by its weakness (in the entire area the Germans had only seventy-nine administrative officials in 1914), for, as has been pointed out elsewhere, it is frequently the insecure authority which acts most harshly. The German district official, the *bezirksamtmann*, had very wide powers, which were almost unchecked by the central government, and his use of judicial authority made a special impression on the Africans. Judgments tended to be arbitrary, were made with little knowledge of local law and custom, and frequently included corporal punishment or penal labor. The sentence of twenty-five lashes with a rhinoceros-hide whip was so frequently imposed that the phrase *hamsa ishirini* (Swahili for twenty-five) is still a synonym for arbitrary authority.

For the lower echelons of administration Germany adapted an Arab technique of using *akidas* to assist the district officials. *Akidas* were African or Arab assistants, charged with the day-to-day administration of local areas; they were generally appointed because they spoke the local language, could write, and had some organizational ability, but they rarely came from the area which they administered, and they had no role in traditional African society. In some areas the *akidas* proved efficient and useful, but in most sections of Tanganyika the people were soon smarting under their rule. As taxes were introduced, the *akidas* were responsible for their collection, always an unpopular task, and they had also to carry out the recruiting of forced labor. In addition, however, *akidas* had so little supervision that the road to petty tyranny was wide open, and exaction of tribute and bribery in court cases are only two of the accusations made frequently against them. The Maji-maji rebellion seems to have begun, in fact, with action taken against an unpopular *akida* filling a forced-labor quota. Looked at from outside the system, however, the *akida* would appear to be, almost by definition, at the point of severest tension: he was not acceptable to the people whom he had to administer since he had no traditional authority with them, while on the other hand he had little chance of guiding German policy in accordance with his local knowledge.

German pacification of the territory, the introduction of a monetary economy, the building of a rudimentary communication system, the ending of the slave trade—all these factors began to change East Africa markedly. Moreover, missions began to introduce schools and hospitals, the military component in East African administration was materially toned down after 1907, and Germany for reasons of prestige—East Africa was its largest colony and the show place of the Empire—contributed large sums to the territory's budget. Advances were made in the administration of the territory, and its economy was reasonably organized. Little heed was given, however, to the process of social change that was taking place among the Africans or to the problem of political organization. As far as the African population was concerned, political institutions and mechanisms, except as they might still exist unofficially within a tribe, were nonexistent. The *akida* system was really designed to replace the chiefs and elders, and the tribal system was felt by the German administration to be obsolete.[9]

German rule ended with World War I, but in the process the territory was almost wrecked. The decision of the German commander, General Paul von Lettow-Vorbeck, to fight a defensive campaign against invading British and Belgian forces meant long-drawn-out guerrilla warfare, with high casualties and great disruption of African life. Some sections of the territory were fought over three or four times; labor and food supplies were commandeered by both sides; chiefs were shot on accusations of treason. In 1918, influenza struck, and in 1919 the territory suffered its worse recorded famine. Tribes were so dispersed that the Gogo of the Dodoma District, for instance, had almost entirely left that area; remnants of the tribe could be found in five neighboring areas. German records and locomotives alike were buried; rubber and sisal plantations went to seed. The dislocations of the wartime period were to leave their mark for a long time.

BRITISH ADMINISTRATION

The British soldiers and officials who took over Tanganyika from the Germans felt, indeed, that they had to begin again. The first British report on the territory, in 1920, even suggested that the tribes of Tanganyika must again be pacified and that British officials might be killed in the process.[10] Nothing of the sort happened, for as the Swahili proverb puts it, "When elephants fight, it is the grass which is trampled." From the local African's viewpoint, the change of colonial ruler at first made little difference. He was still expected to pay taxes, and there was still a strange authority, sitting above him, to enforce unfamiliar patterns of behavior.

The new regime, however, had some unusual features. Under the provisions of the Treaty of Versailles, the territory was to be administered by Great Britain, as a mandate of the League of Nations, and Britain agreed to abide by a series of principles laid down in the Covenant of the League and in the mandate agreement. These principles were not anticolonial, but were designed instead to provide a paternal, impartial governmental structure which would protect local

[9] Great Britain, *Report to the Council of the League of Nations on the Administration of the Tanganyika Territory from the Conclusion of the Armistice to the End of 1920*, Cmd. 1428 (London, 1921).
[10] *Ibid.*, p. 34.

Africans. The arms trade, forced labor, and liquor traffic were to be outlawed, and the "moral and material welfare" of the inhabitants was encouraged. African lands were guaranteed, use of the territory for military purposes was forbidden, and the equality of nationals of all member states of the League was proclaimed. Britain reported annually on its administration to the Permanent Mandates Commission of the League, and the inhabitants might also send petitions to the commission. The mandate provisions, however, left many questions unanswered about the status of the territory and its inhabitants, and there was long argument in Britain as to whether Tanganyika had become a part of the British Empire. The *Official Gazette,* which in 1920 announced the change of name from German East Africa to Tanganyika, even stated that it was "temporary and until further notice." The uniqueness of Tanganyika's international position and its uncertainties were to influence its development, especially in the 1930's when the possibility arose that the German colonies might be used as bargaining counters to appease Hitler.[11]

Despite its status as a mandate, the constitutional and administrative structure of Tanganyika was made thoroughly British and similar to that of neighboring British colonies. The Tanganyika Order in Council, 1920, established a colonial administration responsible to the British Secretary of State for the Colonies, with a Governor as principal representative of the Crown and an Executive Council of appointed civil servants to assist him. An independent High Court was also created. In this initial instrument there was no provision for a legislative body or for any sort of local representation, the Governor alone promulgating all ordinances until 1926. In that year an appointed Legislative Council was created. Thereafter the constitutional structure of the territory remained unchanged until 1945. This constitutional rigidity contrasts markedly with the rapid change occurring after that date.

In the 1920's three major issues confronted the territory and the new administration (apart from the question of international supervision). The first of these issues was finance; the second was the relations between the Africans and the British; and the third was relations with neighboring territories, particularly Kenya. On these three problems

---

[11] For text of the mandate agreement, see United Nations, *League of Nations Mandates,* Document A/70 (1946). For operation of the mandates system see H. D. Hall, *Mandates, Dependencies and Trusteeship* (Washington, D.C., 1948). C. L. Upthegrove, *Empire by Mandate* (New York, 1954), lists matters concerning Tanganyika discussed by the League.

depended all others, and the answers provided at that time have largely delineated present-day Tanganyika.

The first Governor of the territory, Sir Horace Byatt, arrived to find a financial crisis; indeed, finance remains a major Tanganyikan problem to this day. British imperial thinking favored economic self-sufficiency for each of its colonies, with imperial aid usually granted only for exceptional matters such as defense. Tanganyika was not a wealthy country, and it had recently been the scene of much fighting; nevertheless, it was expected to handle its own economic affairs. A number of policy decisions at the time seem to be traceable to this economic pressure: approval of a customs union with Kenya and Uganda in 1923; high import tariffs; sale of former German farms to a new group of European settlers; encouragement of export crops such as sisal, coffee, and cotton; and native taxation through which to spread a monetary economy inland. In the depression of the 1930's Tanganyika very nearly went bankrupt. As a result the level of government services in such matters as education, agricultural development, communications, and public health was kept very low in comparison with wealthier African states such as Ghana. At the same time Tanganyikan Africans often protested the extent of taxation, which became a source of friction with the British administration. No less important, the necessity of always thinking of budgetary consequences came to dominate the viewpoint of the British administration to the point where few new ideas or improvements seemed possible.

If financial stringency was—and is—an important factor in Tanganyikan history, it was not, however, the major feature of British policy. Throughout Africa and the Commonwealth generally Tanganyika has been famed for the policy usually known simply as "native administration." Although some evidence of its existence in Tanganyika may be found in the Byatt administration, the concept and the system were imported into Tanganyika with Sir Donald Cameron, the second British Governor, in 1925. Cameron was a forceful, energetic man who had been trained by Lord Lugard in Nigeria, and it was Lugard's concept of indirect rule, of using African traditional authorities and institutions as the major factor of administration, which Cameron sought to apply to Tanganyika.

Practically, this system of using African authority to support colonial authority was dictated by lack of men and money on the part of the colonial power, but Lugard in Nigeria and his followers throughout the British Empire elevated the policy into a theory and even a *mystique.* Essentially, the British colonial regime faced the necessity of organizing an administrative system appropriate for an African society that was just coming into contact with the Western world and that confronted mutation or disintegration through the influence of a widely different and technologically superior civilization. A twentieth-century British government found itself unable to leave African society completely as it found it, for ignorance, disease, and even barbarity existed; equally it could not expect to create overnight the patterns of English society. Indeed, it did not wish to remake the African in the European image, and the policy of indirect rule can be regarded as an administrative technique to minimize the social cost of change. But although many enthusiasts of indirect rule spoke of the maintenance of traditional African authority and institutions, they were at the same time engaged in introducing certain features of the European state, such as peace, impartial administration of justice, a monetary economy, health and educational measures, and possibly Christianity, which were changing those institutions and adapting them to the Western world. In basic philosophy this concept was entirely in accord with the mandate provisions of the League of Nations Covenant. In Tanganyika the two strains of paternalism met. Lord Lugard, whose *The Dual Mandate in British Tropical Africa* was published in 1922 and proceeded to influence a whole generation of British colonial administrators, was the following year appointed a member of the Permanent Mandates Commission, from which he helped to supervise the administration of Tanganyika.[12]

Where the Germans had used African personnel (the *akidas* and native troops) to help operate a strictly European system of government, the British thus tried to introduce a system which would be African both in personnel and in concept. In practice this meant discovering what local political structure existed within the various tribes. Because Tanganyika contained so many different African groups, it was axiomatic that many different political structures would be found. When Cameron published in 1927 an official list of recognized tribal authorities, there were found to be no fewer than 679 tribal leaders of

---

[12] For general material on the policy of indirect rule, see F. D. Lugard, *Revision of Instructions to Political Officers on Subjects Chiefly Political and Administrative* (Lagos, 1919) and *The Dual Mandate in British Tropical Africa* (Edinburgh, 1922); Margery Perham, *Native Administration in Nigeria* (Oxford, 1937); Lord Hailey, *Native Administration in the British African Territories* (London, 1950–1953).

major and minor rank, whose traditional powers and tasks differed widely. The nine great chiefs of the Haya, in Bukoba District, had great personal status and prestige as war leaders, judges, and heads of a court hierarchy; the *laibon* of the Masai was almost exclusively a religious leader and rain maker; many tribes in Southern Province recognized no authority higher than the clan head, and for some groups among the Yao the clan head was not to be found in Tanganyika but to the south in Portuguese East Africa. For British officials in Dar es Salaam it was difficult to fit such disparate authorities into a system, while working with some of these small groups was administratively almost impossible. The district officer of Mikindani District found that he had to deal with 156 authorities. To make such authorities efficient agents of local government, and particularly to set up any local financial responsibility, posed vast problems.

A further complication was that the concept of native administration did not go beyond an idea of local government; the chiefs and other authorities were always subject to control at the top. Since tribal institutions remained tribal and there was no provision for consideration of intertribal affairs, African nationalists of a later period have frequently denounced the system of native administration as one of divide and rule; they have been equally critical of the support which the system gave to ancient and often autocratic institutions, whether or not they were any longer appropriate. As anthropologists and historians reveal more about the African background, one discovers as well that the institutions recognized by the British were sometimes not correct and frequently not very traditional, having been established only a few years previous to European control. Equally, the British changed the system just by being there; not even the most powerful chief was independent any longer, and his prestige and his functions gradually altered. Cameron himself envisaged the possibility of one day creating a country-wide Council of Chiefs, which would legislate for all Tanganyika, and he never saw traditional institutions as static: an African authority who administered unchanged native law and custom was a contradiction to the idea of indirect rule. The important point to him was that the initiative ought to be African, a concept which, be it noted, many subsequent British administrators did not share.[13]

A detailed account of the working of native administration in Tanganyika is a fascinating study in social change, both planned and un-

[13] Tanganyika, *Native Administration Memoranda* (Dar es Salaam, 1926–1929); Donald Cameron, *My Tanganyika Service and Some Nigeria* (London, 1939).

planned. Two examples may perhaps illustrate the varying possibilities of the system. Among the Chagga of Northern Province, some nineteen chiefs were at first recognized, a suspicious and mutually jealous group; gradually they were formed into a council, and then three supervising chiefs were chosen. In 1951 the tribe elected a paramount chief and invested him with considerable panoply and power, only to decide several years later that his actions were undemocratic and arbitrary. Power was then turned over to an elected council and an elected chief, who operates in many respects like an American city manager. The changes were not always made easily and were marked by much unrest; the changes in political structure were also accompanied by, and were perhaps the result of, changes in the economic status and educational level of the tribe. The changes did not go beyond the tribe, however, and they probably increased the sense of tribalism of the average Chagga. Or, to use a slightly different and more accurate term, as the Chagga dropped some of the traditional customs associated with the word tribalism, their feeling for the tribe itself, that is, their tribal patriotism, increased. Thus their tribal renascence was not any indication of adjustment or of loyalty to Tanganyika as a whole.[14]

A somewhat different series of changes occurred in the Songea District of Southern Province. There the warrior Angoni tribe, who fought its way north from Zululand in the mid-nineteenth century, had settled down, in the process absorbing several other tribes, principally the Matengo and Ndendeuli. In the early censuses these two tribes appear as Angoni, owing allegiance to one of the two leading Angoni chiefs, whose authority was personal rather than territorial. With peaceful conditions the vassal tribes gradually began again to assert their identity; at the same time there was pressure upon the Angoni to make a chief's jurisdiction territorial in nature and to democratize the structure. As a result the number of African authorities in Songea District tended to increase and fragment.[15]

Other examples could be cited of tribes that came together, perhaps

[14] Material on tribal administration in Tanganyika, although available, is to be found in very scattered sources. For the Chagga, see C. C. F. Dundas, *Kilimanjaro and Its People* (London, 1924) and *African Crossroads* (London, 1955); Chagga Council, *Recent Trends in Chagga Political Development* (Moshi, 1955); Tanganyika, *Annual Reports of the Provincial Commissioners*, various years; P. H. Johnston, "Chagga Constitutional Development," *Journal of African Administration*, July, 1953.

[15] Tanganyika, *Annual Reports of the Provincial Commissioners*, various years; P. H. Gulliver, "A History of the Songea Ngoni," *Tanganyika Notes and Records*, Dec., 1955.

initially through pressures to create a larger financial base (the native treasuries), of changes in inheritance and customary law through the influence of British ideas, or of elected leaders who managed to make their posts hereditary. In a good many cases, the structure broke down, often through lack of adequate African leadership. The demands on a chief or elder were severe. He had to carry out a series of activities that were supposed to be acceptable both to the most isolated tribesman and to the modern colonial administrator. This dualism led on the one side to peculation or apathy and on the other to autocracy. If a chief knew native law, he was not necessarily expert at filling out financial returns or planning new agricultural schemes. Yet his duties in leading his people into the modern world tended to increase. As a district officer in the south wrote in 1929:

The somewhat primitive minded headmen . . . generally reply *iko* (there is) to any query concerning administration or procedure, but give the same old man a complicated inheritance case to decide, involving barter, gift and levy in items varying from drums to dried fish, he will ascend the family tree and descend it by 9 branches and 13 collaterals and a bend sinister to deliver a perfectly equitable judgment in terms of beeswax without looking up from his matutinal porridge; ask him how many court receipts have been issued and he will probably say *iko*.[16]

From the administrator's point of view, the system was successful, on the whole, in keeping the peace and in maintaining good relations with the African population, for although there were points of friction and sometimes removal of chiefs or elders, there was little evidence of serious dissatisfaction. The system worked least successfully in its financial aspects; any idea that the native authorities really managed tax collection or local development funds was, until the 1950's, a polite fiction. In African eyes, the system was not by and large unpopular, as it certainly meant less British interference with the everyday matters of life. Since the African did not usually regard the chief as an executive, any failures in this respect did not worry him, and one important area of action—the native courts—seems generally to have worked very well. Other contemporary African reactions depended often on internal tribal position and politics: a rival clan might be dissatisfied with selection of a chief, or an educated African might object to the decision of illiterate elders. Evidence can be found to support the view that the system was African only in name and personnel and that in fact

[16] Tanganyika, *Annual Reports of the Provincial Commissioners for the Year 1929*, p. 36.

all the policies carried out were British in concept and originated through the local district officer. On the other hand, some chiefs regarded Sir Donald Cameron as a paramount chief ruling over them, and added him to their tribal pantheon. Depending on the assumptions that one makes about the objectives of government, one can reach a whole range of conclusions about the desirability and workability of Tanganyikan native administration.

In retrospect, however, two points seem to be indisputable. The diversity permitted and even encouraged within the system (at least five major categories of native authority could be distinguished by 1935, plus innumerable local variations) was a handicap in the later political development of Tanganyika. Secondly, Cameron's successors in the 1930's and 1940's were not able to maintain the vitality of the system; they emphasized adherence to the idea of traditional authority sometimes to the point of ridiculousness. This static quality was increased by the poverty of the territory and the general "holding-the-line" attitude of administration officials. By the time of World War II the old concepts were out of step with contemporary events. The first signs of serious African dissatisfaction with the system appeared in Chagga in 1937 and in Pare in 1942 and 1944.[17]

One further feature of native administration may be noted. Since the theory was based on the maintenance of native institutions, it came to have implications which went far beyond the field of administration or politics. It was applied to economics, with the use of native authorities to sponsor and even run cooperatives; it determined land policy in many areas; and attempts were even made to run schools on tribal lines. It also affected race relation in a series of way, most simply by separating clearly the legal status and allegiance of African and non-African. Its philosophy and psychology, in fact, dominated Tanganyika for nearly thirty years and helped to decide every territorial question of importance.

Tanganyika also had a non-African population, a group unaffected directly by the policy of native administration. The first non-Africans were the Arabs of the coast, an ancient community which had not entirely coalesced with African society but maintained its ties with Zanzibar and territories across the Indian Ocean. In the nineteenth century Indians also began to arrive, mainly Muslims from Gujerat (in

[17] Great Britain, *Report on the Administration of Tanganyika Territory for 1937*, App. VI; Lord Hailey, *Native Administration and Political Development in British Tropical Africa* (London, 1942).

large part the Ismaili Khoja, followers of the Aga Khan) but also Hindus and other groups including Parsees and Sikhs. They were mainly traders and artisans, who spread widely into the towns and villages of eastern Africa. After 1890, Europeans had come also.

The European group was small during the period of British control, and a large proportion of its members were either civil servants or missionaries, whose residence in Tanganyika was essentially temporary. An economically important commercial and planting community did exist, however, whose principal feature was its heterogeneity. One of the provisions of the mandate (Article 7) was that immigration could not be discriminatory, and nationals of all members of the League of Nations were eligible to reside in Tanganyika. While economic limitations kept the group of entrants low, its membership included numbers of Germans, Greeks, Swiss, and Italians as well as British. The group had many social and economic as well as national variations, and it seldom acted as a unit. Although representatives of both the European and Asian communities were appointed to the Legislative Council after 1926, there was little pressure for political rights or privileges; in contrast to the extremely vocal white settler group in neighboring Kenya, the Europeans in Tanganyika seem actually to have acted as a brake on political development, using their political influence (it would be too extreme to call it power) primarily on matters of taxation. It is probable that they did not press for political change for two major reasons: the heterogeneity of the community itself and the belief that if the Europeans were accorded the vote the Asians would receive it also, again in accordance with Article 7 of the mandate agreement.

From the beginning of British control there existed a movement to unite Tanganyika to Kenya, and this was expanded in the 1920's to include Uganda and the Rhodesias. A British commission reported in 1925 that federation was not yet economically or politically feasible, but the new Secretary of State for the Colonies, Leopold Amery, decided to push the issue. Cameron was violently opposed to such a move, as were most Tanganyikans. They feared the economic and political domination of the Kenya settlers, and a long-drawn-out controversy ensued. With the aid of Lord Lugard, the Permanent Mandates Commission, and some important forces in British political life, the proposal was defeated at the time, only to be revived after World War II. In the process, the policy of "native administration" came to be regarded as the great protector of the African against colonial exploitation, and indeed the only alternative to white settler rule. Although he primarily objected to union because of his objections to Kenya native policy, Cameron used the technicalities of the mandate provisions (which seemed to prohibit political union) as arguments to win his fight. Some of the Tanganyika Europeans, who were inclined to be favorable to a plan which would unite them to a British colony, thus were persuaded that it was not possible under existing international legal arrangements. In the process of the argument Tanganyika Africans were asked for the first time to express an opinion on a territorial political issue. Their widespread opposition to federation, entirely because of fears of Kenya native policy, has had continuing repercussions on interterritorial economic cooperation.[18]

At the opening of World War II, then, Tanganyika had no central political institutions in which Africans were represented and no form of elections, while its system of local government was tending to stultify. Thus it remained the most colonial of territories. Because of the generally undeveloped state of the economy, it was also a territory in which the central colonial administration was a dominant element, making most of the important decisions. Tanganyika as a whole seemed to be run by the civil service mind. It was also primarily still a rural country, with no large towns except the capital, and with new ways being introduced very gradually indeed.

World War II had remarkably little effect on Tanganyika, although supplies were difficult to obtain and many Africans left for war service. Probably the most important local repercussions resulted from the decision at the end of the war permanently to exclude the local German population, a large number of whom had been Nazi sympathizers, and to devote the money from the sale of their property to educational purposes. Even the return of Tanganyikan servicemen after the war had little political effect, a surprising contrast with the servicemen in West Africa who entered the new nationalist movements at an early stage.

THE NATIONALIST MOVEMENT AND
ACHIEVEMENT OF INDEPENDENCE

Somewhere around 1947 Tanganyika entered a new stage in its history. Although as yet there was little territorial consciousness and

[18] No general account of the closer-union controversy has been published. See Cameron, *My Tanganyika Service;* Lord Altrincham, *Kenya's Opportunity* (London, 1955); M. R. Dilley, *British Policy in Kenya Colony* (New York, 1937); Great Britain, *Report of the Commission on Closer Union of the Dependencies in East and Central Africa,* Cmd. 3234 (London, 1929).

no such thing as active politics, outside events and currents began to affect Tanganyika and to remove it permanently from its prepolitical colonial state.

Changes in British colonial philosophy and psychology were evident with the granting of independence to India in 1947, changes that affected at first only the upper echelons of the Colonial Office but that gradually spread to the local administration of the various territories. In a series of memorandums British governors were urged to spur political and economic reform. Perhaps the best known of these documents was a 1947 dispatch from the Secretary of State, Arthur Creech-Jones, recommending an overhaul of the system of native administration to allow democratic local councils and to establish some institutional relationships between central and local government. It is expressive of continuing colonial attitudes that Creech-Jones found it necessary to explain the meaning of the word development to his subordinate officials, in order to urge it upon them.[19]

Some administrative planning had taken place in Tanganyika during the war, and in 1945 the Legislative Council had been enlarged to include the first African members. The Council had first been created in 1926, with 13 official members and 10 unofficials. The racial composition of the Council had never been legally specified, but in practice the unofficial side had always included 7 Europeans and 3 Asians.

These members were chosen by the Governor after consultation with such local interest groups as the Sisal Growers Association, the Northern Province farming community, and the Asian Association, and they frequently spoke for these interests in the Council, though legally they were appointed to the Council in their individual capacities. The Council was not very much inclined to politics; it operated as a small group of advisers to the Governor and opposed him only occasionally on financial matters. In 1945 total Council membership was raised to 29, with 4 new unofficial seats to be reserved for Africans. The first two African members were well-known chiefs; it was another three years before the central government discovered two more persons it considered capable. For the next five years, it would still be accurate to say that the political initiative in Tanganyika came from the Colonial Office and the British administration, but after 1947 there was an increasing degree of local reaction.

Early in that year the Colonial Office published proposals for inter-

[19] Great Britain, Cambridge Summer School on African Administration, *African Local Government*, African 1173 (London, 1947).

territorial cooperation by Kenya, Uganda, and Tanganyika which revived in some respects the federation idea of the 1920's. In the
intervening years the postal services and the customs had been amalga-
mated, and cooperation during the war had been very close; it was now
proposed to create an East African High Commission with a good
many powers in the economic sphere and a Central Legislative Assembly to which the commission would be generally responsible. The
plan was received with mixed reactions in Tanganyika, where it was
opposed by Asians and Africans and favored, somewhat unenthusias-
tically, by Europeans. The fear of Kenya white settlers and of being
run from Nairobi was again evident, and the issue provoked the only
instance on record of straight racial voting in the Tanganyika Legislative Council.[20] The British government was determined to carry
through the measure, which it regarded as essential for the economic
development of East Africa, and in order to placate local opinion it
made at least one offer of political and constitutional change. It did
not expect the results it got, for this controversy stimulated political
thinking and led, gradually but surely, to the formation of Tanganyikan
political parties.

The first of these nascent organizations was a European group known
as the Northern Province Council, which came together in 1948 to
represent the interests of the farming communities of Kilimanjaro and
Meru. Its major concern at first was with Tanganyikan agricultural and
land policy, but in the federation discussions it found itself working
closely with the Kenya Electors Union. In 1948 and 1949 it formed
groups in areas where Europeans were living, changed its name to the
Tanganyika European Council, and attempted to monopolize the formation and representation of European opinion. In this it was not successful, for European opinion did not present a solid front. Many
Tanganyikans regarded the TEC as too close to the Kenya Electors
Union, indeed as dominated by it; others objected to its racial exclusive-
ness. In the years up to 1953, while the TEC was attempting to influence territorial constitutional development, it was perennially split
from within.[21]

At the same time, African resentment against the decisions on closer
union began to channel into the one intertribal organization which

[20] Great Britain, *Inter-Territorial Organization in East Africa*, Col. 210 (London, 1947); Tanganyika Legislative Council, *Proceedings*, 1st extraordinary meeting, 1947, pp. 36–47.
[21] Information on the activities of the Tanganyika European Council is drawn
from its *Bulletin*, its files, and the *Tanganyika Standard*.

existed, the Tanganyika African Association (TAA). This group had been founded in 1930 as a society of urban Africans, mainly those in government employment who had had some Western education. It was in part a mutual benefit society, an educational group, and a purely social association which catered to the needs of the detribalized African; its formation and its general social welfare approach had been encouraged by the government. Its level of activity had fluctuated considerably, the two most active groups being in Dar es Salaam and Tabora, where the one secondary school in Tanganyika was located. Prior to 1948 its occasional representations to government had been very largely concerned with civil service conditions that affected its membership. Almost all the small group of educated Tanganyika Africans belonged as a matter of course to the Tanganyika African Association, including the chiefs who were members of Legislative Council.

The Association had begun to take an interest in local political matters after World War II. It operated mostly through tribal unions, and between 1946 and 1948 it was concerned in several demonstrations urging more modern tribal authorities. It called its first major public meeting in Dar es Salaam to protest association with Kenya and from that time tended more and more toward politics. It was still far from unified, and its branches took an independent line even on territorial matters, but the organizational nucleus for an African nationalist movement now existed.[22]

In 1947 the international status of Tanganyika changed, and it became a trust territory of the United Nations. At the time this event had practically no impact upon territorial opinion except to make a few Britons favor union with Kenya more vigorously. In fact, however, the basic colonial consensus of the mandate had been destroyed in favor of a more radical system. It was the basic assumption of the trusteeship system that territories under tutelage were being groomed for independence, and it was to be the role of the administering authorities to speed them on their way. The Trusteeship Council of the United Nations was also expected to take a more active role regarding the territories for which it was responsible than had the League Permanent Mandates Commission, and it was given more power. The petition system was extended, and the Trusteeship Council acquired the right to send visiting missions to the territory every three years.

In the text of the basic agreement on Tanganyika surprisingly few other changes were made; these included the removal of military re-

[22] *Constitution of the Tanganyika African Association* (Dar es Salaam, 1952).

strictions, the ending of unrestricted commercial privileges for others which had worked out to Tanganyika's disadvantage, and replacement of the word "native" by "inhabitant." The language used to prohibit political union was also made less stringent. In any case, the East African High Commission was a *fait accompli* by the time the Trusteeship Council began to operate.[23] Whatever its potentialities, trusteeship had little immediate impact on Tanganyika. The report of the first mission to Tanganyika, in 1948, was attacked strongly in Great Britain but received little attention in the territory itself; the leading European paper there accepted it as a moderate document. Among other proposals, the report suggested that long-range political plans be formulated. In view of later accusations that the United Nations was encouraging unbridled Tanganyika nationalism this initial apathy is interesting.

In Tanganyika, the British attempts to modernize native administration were proceeding, though the "democratic" of the Creech-Jones dispatch was soon changed to "representative." A series of measures to alter local institutions were tried, some of which reflected African tribal opinion but just as often the enthusiasm of the British district officer. The annual reports on local government in the 1950's are highly technical and confusing documents. Lord Hailey in 1942 had spoken of the heterogeneity of Tanganyika as a danger for its future political growth, but this statement was even more true in later years. In the south, new authorities were established who were called *liwalis* and were without traditional status; elsewhere councils of chiefs were created, or sometimes chiefs were made subordinate executives, responsible to an appointed council. Tribal and district federations were encouraged, while methods of appointment and election varied from tribe to tribe. These new native administrations were pressed to become real units of local government, collecting and using a large proportion of their own revenue and taking over, progressively, as many as possible of the functions of an English town council, from education to poor relief. In some areas, district and provincial councils were mooted, which would be advisory at first and with non-African membership; the link to the Legislative Council was in process of being forged.[24]

[23] For text of the trust agreement see United Nations, *Treaty Series*, VIII (New York, 1947). Hall, *Mandates, Dependencies and Trusteeship*, App. XIII, includes the agreement as well as a useful textual analysis of changes made during negotiation.

[24] Great Britain, *Development of African Local Government in Tanganyika*, Col. 277 (London, 1951).

This political activity was supported and reinforced by economic activity. At the end of the war various delayed public works were undertaken. A rise in crop production and in export prices made more funds available. Tanganyika was chosen as the site of the groundnut scheme, a vast project to increase the availability of edible oils and fats for rationed Britain. From the British viewpoint the project largely failed, but through the scheme some £40,000,000 was poured into the Tanganyika economy, harbors and railways were expanded, and the number of technically trained personnel available was greatly increased.[25]

Into this picture in early 1949 came a new Governor, Sir Edward Twining, the first man since Cameron to serve out a full term in the territory. Sir Edward was a bluff and forthright person, ready to tackle all the problems of the postwar political world. Tanganyika in the next few years became very much the reflection of his image. While continuing political experiments with the native administrations, he moved immediately in the direction of constitutional reform. In December, 1949, Twining appointed the 14 unofficial members of the Legislative Council to a Committee on Constitutional Development and in a document which became famous in Tanganyika as the "cock-shy" suggested a number of reforms. Twining proposed that provincial councils serve as electoral colleges to choose one African and one non-African member from each province to sit on the Legislative Council. Eighteen government (that is, official) members would be appointed, to create a Council of 38 members in all and thus provide an unofficial majority. There would be a Speaker (the Governor still sat as president of the Council), and with immediate local elections the new Council might be established in 1951-1952. But the proposals evoked a storm of protest; the Colonial Office and the Governor were still ahead of Tanganyikan public opinion.

The committee found, indeed, that Tanganyika opinion was really interested in only two matters: a formula for racial representation in the Legislative Council and elections. The committee's unanimous report, made public in August, 1951, concentrated largely on these two issues and suggested new and original constitutional experiments. It rejected an unofficial majority as being premature—though this had been suggested privately at least twice before by the British government—and recommended an enlarged Council, with parity of representation among the three major races. It also accepted the principle of elections but in abandoning the idea of provincial councils as elec-

[25] Alan Wood, *The Groundnut Affair* (London, 1950).

toral bodies left the problem of electoral machinery for further investigation. The committee thought it necessary to suggest that one-third
of the African seats might be reserved for nonchiefs.[26]

The Tanganyika European Council and its Kenya sympathizers announced unceasing opposition to this report and tried to censure the
unofficial Europeans who had signed it; the latter were regarded as
having sold out, not to African interests but to the Asians. Asian and
African associations generally approved, though the TAA made it clear
that it considered parity an interim measure.[27] Although the proposals
did not go as far as his initial recommendations, the Governor eventually accepted most of the committee's report and became an ardent
exponent of both parity and racial equality. It is rather ironic to note
that the committee's long deliberations had slowed down Governor
Twining's timetable and that in one respect the new proposals seemed
retrogressive. The membership of the old Legislative Council had never
been specified constitutionally by race; the new recommendations were
rigid in this respect.

From the time of the committee's report a curious political, or perhaps psychological, process seemed to operate in Tanganyika. Having
taken the first political steps, many of the territory's leaders seemed
reluctant to go further. This may perhaps be explained by the fact
that there were no genuine politicians among them. The members of
the Legislative Council, of whatever race, had previously been public-
spirited businessmen and farmers, similar perhaps to the men who
serve on the School Board of any small American town. The Council
was there to advise the Governor; it operated informally and pater-
nally, and although it felt strongly on matters such as taxation, it
usually bowed to the Governor's wisdom. It was not used to functioning
as an opposition, and it had never paid much attention to outside public
opinion. Indeed, it viewed with consternation the political antics of
neighboring territories, especially Kenya. When a special commissioner
was appointed in 1953 to consider electoral systems and machinery,
Legislative Council members who were to advise him politically shied
away from the idea of elections. As the senior Asian member of the
Council reported later:

When the discussion started and when the realisation dawned on the members of the dangers of elections, Professor Mackenzie stated that he was con-

[26] Tanganyika, *Report of the Committee on Constitutional Development* (Dar
es Salaam, 1951). The unpublished papers of the committee have also been
consulted.

[27] *Tanganyika Standard*, Aug. 5, 1951, and July 12, 1952.

cerned with the mechanics of the thing and nothing more, and, therefore, the committee very nicely and smoothly retired, and we then just had the mechanics of the report and that was all.[28]

The period 1951–1954 was essentially one of marking time and of readjusting ideas. After much internal discussion parity was accepted by the TEC in 1953, and, like the Governor, other European leaders now became advocates of the idea. "The logic of parity" pervaded political and even social life; people began to speak of interracial cooperation in terms of three communities, equal in status and influence. Governor Twining called the concept multiracialism. No one debated in public whether the franchise should be based on a common roll or communal rolls, and the special commissioner's report took it for granted that all of Tanganyika favored a common roll.[29] This issue, which aroused so much debate in other African territories, was not seriously considered in Tanganyika but was accepted as a concommitant, indeed a part of the very idea, of parity and equality.

At the same time that public opinion was readjusting to politics Governor Twining pushed further reform. In 1951 the first African member was appointed to the Executive Council, which already included two unofficial Europeans and one Asian; in 1953 the Governor bowed out of the Legislative Council, and an unofficial European was appointed as Speaker. The Unofficial Members Organization, which included members of all races and which had existed quietly since 1945, was urged to form itself into a government opposition and to become more parliamentary in outlook. In April, 1955, the Governor convened the new Legislative Council of 61 members, 30 of them unofficials. In accordance with the principle of parity, 10 unofficials were appointed from each racial group.

The timing here is interesting, for the year 1954 probably marks the point when the government began to feel political pressure, both externally from the United Nations and internally from the Tanganyika African Association. The 1951 United Nations Visiting Mission had been cautiously impressed by Tanganyika's political plans; the 1954 mission wondered whether African interests were sufficiently protected. The latter mission suggested that the government ought to establish a timetable for political development, with Tanganyika to achieve independ-

---

[28] Tanganyika Legislative Council, *Proceedings*, 29th sess., 1954–1955, p. 75.
[29] Tanganyika, *Report of the Special Commissioner Appointed to Examine Matters Arising Out of the Report of the Committee on Constitutional Development* (Dar es Salaam, 1953).

ence in twenty years' time.[30] This went too far for the Governor, who felt that the mission had interfered with internal Tanganyikan affairs. It was too much also for the Secretary of State, who noted that the British government had almost a "pathological dislike" of timetables. Thus with growing anticolonial pressure in the United Nations, an argument seemed certain when the Trusteeship Council met in February, 1955, and its decision to hear an oral petitioner from Tanganyika increased the friction.

The oral petitioner was Julius K. Nyerere, who in 1954 had become president of the Tanganyika African Association and in July of that year transformed it into a political party, the Tanganyika African National Union (TANU). Nyerere was a Zanaki from Lake Province, a schoolteacher who was one of the few university graduates in Tanganyika; he had returned to Tanganyika from Great Britain in 1952 and had soon come to dominate the organization and outlook of the Tanganyika African Association. Nyerere told the Trusteeship Council that developments were not rapid enough and that unless Africans were assured of greater progress, and especially of more political power than parity implied, they would adopt a more extreme attitude. His appearance and his statement made manifest a growing African political sophistication and also unrest. The period of political transition had lasted too long, and the African members of the Legislative Council, three of whom were chiefs, were no longer representative of advanced African opinion.

At the same time that TANU began to organize strongly in Tanganyika, it discovered the possibility of utilizing United Nations pressure and began systematically to utilize this weapon in an attempt to influence the administration. The 1954 Visiting Mission met TANU delegations all over Tanganyika, and Nyerere impressed the Trusteeship Council itself. The British administration, reacting defensively to public attack, criticized the Trusteeship Council for accepting too easily TANU's claims to represent African opinion and called TANU an extremist racial group. It also accused the American representative, Mason Sears, of going well beyond his official role by advising Nyerere privately. But the British also found it necessary to inform the Council that elections would probably be held in Tanganyika in 1958, before it made the statement in Tanganyika itself. From 1954 on, in fact, the political initiative began to shift from Twining and the British ad-

[30] United Nations Trusteeship Council, *Official Records*, 15th sess., Suppl. 3 (1955).

ministration to TANU, although this was not immediately evident.

The structure and influence of TANU are discussed in detail in a later section, but it is pertinent to speak here of its objectives and position at this time. The policy of TANU was laid down in its constitution in these terms:

I. To prepare the people of Tanganyika for self-government and independence, and to fight relentlessly until Tanganyika is self-governing and independent.

II. To fight against tribalism and all isolationist tendencies amongst the Africans, and to build up a united nationalism.

III. To fight relentlessly for the establishment of a democratic form of government, and as a first step toward democracy, to fight for the introduction of the election principle on all bodies of local and central government.

IV. To achieve African majorities on all bodies of local and central government, and committees, boards or corporations of public service.

V. To fight for the removal of every form of racialism and racial discrimination.

VI. To encourage and organize Trade Unionism and the Cooperative Movement, and to work with Trade Unions and Cooperative Societies and other organizations whose objectives are in harmony with the aims and objects of the Association.

The Union also pledged itself to work for economic and educational advance, to oppose land alienation except with African consent, to fight against any immigration likely to aggravate racial antagonism, and to resist any movement for closer East African federation.[31]

Primarily, TANU thus opposed the government policy of parity, objected to any form of qualitative franchise, and to the extent that it opposed tribalism might also be ranked as opposing the system of native administration. Its aims and objectives were to be achieved by constitutional means, and Nyerere, who had been appointed to fill a temporary vacancy in the Legislative Council in 1954, stressed this approach in replying to a reference by the Governor to irresponsible agitators causing difficulty in the countryside:

I feel sure, sir, that all sensible people, all sensible Africans, are going to support the government. . . . I do not think Africans want trouble in this country, because they have learnt, they have seen what is happening in other places and they know that if trouble were to come to this country

[31] *Constitution of the Tanganyika African National Union* (Dar es Salaam, 1955).

they would be the greatest sufferers. . . . There is a big difference between trouble mongering and criticising Government justifiably. . . . Sometimes I am concerned that the difference may not be very easy to distinguish. . . . I hope that people in the country are not going to take the Governor's warning against trouble-mongers in the country to mean . . . that no criticism of either local government or the Central Government is going to be tolerated. . . . We should not be panicky, sir.[32]

In mentioning local government Nyerere touched on the crux of the problem, for the government was particularly concerned with the effects of political advance on the native authorities. The TANU policy of urging abandonment of tribal institutions was sometimes interpreted very literally by its members, and this fact became both annoying and dangerous when opposition to native-authority orders in such matters as agricultural regulations led to boycotts and demonstrations. The possible involvement of TANU with local grievances, or with local politics through the various tribal unions, was also feared. To a considerable extent this situation involved a basic problem of law and order. Tanganyika under the system of native administration was very lightly policed indeed by Western standards, with the enforcement of law dependent on the authority of the chief. That this problem of security was not invented was demonstrated in late 1955 when serious riots broke out in the Morogoro District. Yet, as Nyerere noted, a colonial government unused to opposition of any sort might easily interpret disagreement as sedition, and there were instances in other African territories of oppression of local opinion. In 1955 and 1956, it was common to hear district officials describing TANU as subversive, though they found it difficult to explain or to justify their use of this term.

While the government was still moving ahead with its own program of constitutional reform and trying to make up its mind how to deal with the phenomenon of a genuine political party in its midst (TEC still existed, but by 1955 mostly on paper), TANU was trying to organize throughout the country. It was circumscribed, to begin with, by two government actions. The first of these was the decision in 1953 that government employees were not to be allowed to join political organizations. Native authorities were advised to follow the same policy. Since almost all educated Africans worked for the government (including, for instance, doctors and schoolteachers), this limited severely the membership of TANU. Although the policy was presumably meant to ensure the impartiality of the civil service, it created the danger that

[32] Tanganyika Legislative Council, _Proceedings_, 29th sess., 1954–1955, p. 64.

African political leadership would be captured by the uneducated and the extremists.

The second relevant government policy was laid down in the Societies Ordinance of 1954, which called for registration with the government of all associations. The government received powers of supervision, especially of finances, and could refuse or revoke registration, at the Governor's discretion, whenever an organization moved outside its stated field of action or its activities were deemed contrary to the public interest. The wording of the measure was so wide that it covered even Sunday school classes. Its political nature soon became apparent. Of 1,300 associations registered by December, 1955, only TANU branches had been refused registration.[33] Enforcement of the ordinance depended on local district commissioners, and their attitudes differed. TANU found special difficulty in meeting financial accounting requirements because of the scarcity of educated members in many upcountry areas. In 1955 and 1956, Julius Nyerere personally spent considerable time touring Tanganyika, checking local books, and as a matter of policy trying to prefer charges in cases of financial irregularity before the administration did so.

Nyerere had left his position as a mission school teacher by 1955 and had become a full-time political organizer; the TANU central staff consisted of him and three other employees. By the end of that year TANU had 17 recognized branches and claimed a membership of 100,000, though the government did not recognize this figure. Its leadership came mainly from commerical employees in the towns, especially Dar es Salaam and Tanga, who were beginning to constitute an African middle class. As an entirely African organization, it faced the same problem which TEC had faced with Tanganyika Europeans: it was trying at one and the same time to represent both a particular policy and all shades of African opinion. By the end of 1955, some members of the old Tanganyika African Association were moving out of TANU on the ground that it was too radical; this was particularly true of the chiefs, who were government employees and who now found themselves in the middle of political argument.

From the administration's point of view, TANU was racialist and dangerously radical, and Governor Twining pushed ahead with the attempt to impose multiracialism, defined politically in terms of parity. He received support from his Legislative Council, for when the first

[33] "Membership of Political Associationss," Tanganyika Government Circular 5 (Aug. 1, 1953); Tanganyika, *Report of the Registrar General, 1955.*

Council appointed according to that formula met in April, 1955, it already knew that it would soon be replaced by an elected body, and it moved into politics itself. After long preliminary negotiations in the Unofficial Members Organization, the majority of unofficial members of all races formed in February, 1956, an interracial political party. The United Tanganyika Party (UTP) quite naturally endorsed the idea of parity. The party was headed by I. C. W. Bayldon, a European member from the Southern Highlands, but its moving spirit was in fact Governor Twining.[34]

The political climate of this period can be indicated by the change in personal relations between Governor Twining and Julius Nyerere. In 1954, the Governor had appointed Nyerere a temporary member of the Legislative Council to advise him, and Nyerere could wander freely in and out of the Secretariat Building in Dar es Salaam. Nyerere personally appealed twice to the Governor to cancel the prohibition on government employees' membership in TANU. On social occasions the two men maintained a joking relationship. Two years later, and particularly after the formation of UTP, this informal relationship no longer existed; the Governor felt that Nyerere was attacking him personally, and TANU from its side moved into straight opposition.

Governor Twining was now firmly committed to replacing the 30 appointed unofficial members of the Legislative Council by elected ones, and in May, 1956, he appointed a committee of 9 members, 6 of them unofficial members of the Council, to examine franchise proposals. In October the committee recommended qualifications which were far from acceptable to TANU. Although the committee, under instruction, was careful to suggest a framework which was expected to produce a majority of African voters in each constituency, it also proposed economic and educational qualifications which would probably enfranchise all adult Europeans, most Asians, and only a small proportion of Africans; it required, for instance, an annual income of £150 or successful completion of Standard VIII, that is, entrance standard for secondary school.[35]

In the subsequent registration, only 59,317 voters were registered in the whole territory. The provision, also, that each voter be required to vote for three candidates, one of each race, provided a hurdle for

[34] The party manifesto appeared in the Dar es Salaam *Sunday News*, Feb. 26, 1956.

[35] Tanganyika, *Report of the Committee Appointed to Study Government's Proposals Regarding the Qualifications of Voters and Candidates for Elections to Legislative Council*, Government Paper no. 1 (1957).

a party of racial composition, since to elect its own candidates it had to support others whom it might not control. It is hardly surprising that TANU attacked the franchise proposals vigorously, saying that they were tailor-made for UTP.

Throughout 1956 and 1957 the two parties devoted themselves to organizational matters in anticipation of the 1958 elections. In this effort TANU seemed the more successful, despite its inability under provisions of the Societies' Ordinance to operate in all areas, notably Sukumaland in Lake Province. Nyerere has spoken frequently of the atmosphere of upcountry political meetings in this period—of a village or district gathering at the local courthouse or under the tribal baobab tree, hearing for the first time of the enchanting possibilities of self-government and independence. Many Africans had then to be convinced that they were indeed capable of running the country's affairs, and it is a tribute to Nyerere's quiet yet persuasive oratory that they found themselves solidly convinced. The African whose first reaction was "independent—me?" indicated the political naïvete which is still present in rural Tanganyika. There were frequently, of course, local disputes or feelings of grievance which contributed to TANU's growth, though as a matter of policy it tried to stay out of local affairs. A provision in its constitution that groups sharing TANU's objectives might affiliate with it was carefully forgotten, for fear of getting into intra-tribal disputes.

UTP organization, in contrast, seemed to concentrate on centers of population and on groups of the higher economic and educational stratum. It hired an organizer from the Conservative Party in Great Britain. Its manifesto accepted parity and multiracialism and stressed the importance of economic goals.[36] It organized a number of branches and by 1957 was claiming a membership that was 60 per cent African. The party had great difficulty, however, in convincing many Tanganyikans that it was not the personal agent of Governor Twining, or at least representative of the wealthier economic groups, particularly after it announced its support of economic and educational requirements for the franchise. It was an elite party, with Governor Twining as patron; TANU, in contrast, was turning into a mass movement.

The period between the determination of voting requirements in early 1957 and the first elections in September, 1958, was one of political seesaw. Since it disagreed so markedly with the franchise arrangements, TANU threatened a number of times to boycott the elections, and long

[36] *Sunday News*, Feb. 26, 1956.

and acrimonious discussion on this issue occurred again and again in
the TANU Executive Committee.[37] It is patent that TANU tried both
to negotiate and to use pressure to change the provision of the electoral law. Nyerere appeared several times before various United Nations groups, and the Trusteeship Council passed a resolution urging
universal franchise in Tanganyika, which the administration flatly
turned down. In early 1957 Governor Twining made a number of
speeches condemning agitation upcountry.[38] Later that year the Secretary of State flew to Tanganyika and made a speech strongly in support of non-African rights. Nyerere was again induced to accept
appointment to the Legislative Council in September but resigned
after several months.

The issue of TANU participation in the elections came before its
annual conference in January, 1958. The majority of the conference,
having discovered that on this particular issue the British administration could not be budged, decided to fight the elections even though
some form of interracial cooperation was thus made necessary. Of
the 15 Legislative Council seats at issue in the first election in September, 1958, only 5 would be African under the system of parity,[39] and
in order not to be a minority TANU would have to gain the support
of non-Africans holding the other 10 seats. It was clear that TANU's
ability to influence African voters might determine the results in a
European or Asian political contest, since Africans were expected to
be a majority of the voters in most constituencies; on the other hand,
TANU had little control over the nomination of non-Africans, since
under the electoral law nomination was largely a racial process. The
party decided to take the risk, but its left wing was alienated by the
decision. Zuberi Mtemvu, who had been party organizing secretary,
withdrew from TANU with a small group of supporters and formed
a new party eventually known as the African National Congress. In
Mtemvu's opinion, TANU was too moderate, especially on racial
questions.

As the electoral campaign proceeded, TANU began to seek European and Asian support. Non-African candidates who were not committed to UTP were approached on the question of cooperation with

[37] Tanganyika African National Union, *TANU and the Vote* (Dar es Salaam,
1956).

[38] Tanganyika, *Address by His Excellency the Governor to Legislative Council
on 30th April 1957* (Dar es Salaam, 1957).

[39] The elections were scheduled to be held in two installments, primarily because
of administrative difficulties.

TANU or sometimes were even endorsed without their previous knowledge. Mrs. Mustafa, one of seven Asian candidates in Northern Province, received word of her adoption as a TANU candidate when she was suddenly asked to appear at a large African political rally; at that time she did not even recognize Nyerere who was sitting next to her. Lady Chesham, opposing the president of UTP in the Southern Highlands, heard over the radio of TANU support of her candidacy. By the end of the campaign, however, many of the non-African candidates receiving TANU support had developed a loyalty to Nyerere and his party. The leading European who moved to support TANU was Derek Bryceson, a farmer from West Kilimanjaro who had previously been an appointed member of the Legislative Council and who had signed the franchise committee report. From their side, the African members of TANU seemed to reciprocate this sentiment of loyalty, and the TANU Executive even began to consider the possibility of admitting non-Africans to membership.

The administration continued to be concerned about TANU action in rural districts, in keeping with its previous strong support of the native administrations. There were some instances during the campaign of local TANU members' usurping a chief's executive and judicial duties; the formation of the TANU Youth League was also held to be dangerous, as the government considered it to be full of young hotheads, and thus a direct-actionist and even a military group. The adoption of a TANU color, a flag, and songs and ceremonials was held to be on the border line of subversion. In July, Julius Nyerere was prosecuted for criminal libel as a result of his comments in the party's newsletter, *Sauti ya TANU*, about bias and discrimination by several district officials. Although on the day before the case went to trial Nyerere personally led an open-air meeting of 10,000 of his followers in pledging themselves to accept any court decision without violence, the situation particularly in Dar es Salaam reached a high point of tension.[40]

Julius Nyerere was found guilty on several counts but was not allowed to win the title of prison graduate so often exploited by nationalist leaders elsewhere in Africa. Instead he was fined, a circumstance usually attributed in Tanganyika to the intervention of the new Governor, Sir Richard Turnbull. Sir Richard had arrived in Tanganyika only a few days previously, and he moved immediately to try to ease the political situation. A quiet, polished man who operated

[40] *Tanganyika Standard,* July 7–12, 1958.

most effectively behind the scenes, Sir Richard proved able to work with Nyerere, so that there were few of the personality conflicts which had marked the last years of Governor Twining's regime.

In the September, 1958, elections, TANU-supported candidates of all races won easily. Three TANU candidates were returned unopposed; in all other constituencies UTP or independent candidates were beaten by large margins. Although no racial breakdown of the voting figures is possible, it was evident that, with the possible exception of the Dar es Salaam constituency, African voters had everywhere carried the elections for TANU. At the opening of the new Legislative Council, Governor Turnbull announced that the next elections would be moved forward from September, 1959, to February, 1959, and that immediately thereafter new steps of constitutional advance could be counted on, including a reexamination of the principle of parity. With its first electoral victories TANU had thus obtained consideration of one of its major grievances, and Nyerere expressed its gratification in the Legislative Council. In February, TANU was unopposed in most constituencies, and the party won easily the three seats in which it was opposed.[41]

After this first series of elections the United Tanganyika Party faded from existence. Earlier suggestions in the press that it combine with TANU were revived for a while, but no institutional action was taken; some individual members gradually began to drift over to support of TANU. The African National Congress, opposing TANU from the left, maintained headquarters in Dar es Salaam, but it had received exiguous support in the elections and had no influence. Outwardly, the nationalist movement was now united; the forum for pressure and negotiations shifted from the electoral field to the Legislative Council.

After the first elections in September, 1958, an Elected Members Organization (TEMO) had been formed, and this began to function as a parliamentary opposition under the leadership of Julius Nyerere, Derek Bryceson, and Amir Jamal of the Asian Association. The political position was unusual, for two-thirds of the elected members were not members of TANU and had no voice in determination of its policy, although they were committed to it. On the whole, TEMO was remarkably successful in welding together an interracial group which worked and thought very largely as a team. Members took care to

[41] Great Britain, *Tanganyika: Report for the Year 1958*, Col. 342 (London, 1959); Tanganyika, *Report on the First Election of Members to the Legislative Council of Tanganyika* (mimeographed; Dar es Salaam, 1959).

speak for their districts, not for their racial groups, and shared each other's constituency work. In TEMO discussions the basic features of policy were hammered out, and decisions were taken on when and how to oppose the government or to push it further. There was a genuine give-and-take relationship between TEMO and the TANU Executive, with the members of both groups acting as liaison. It soon became evident that the elected Europeans and Asians were just as ardent nationalists as the Africans. TANU's outlook on racial matters enabled it to cooperate with non-African members and to urge the appointment of Sir Ernest Vasey, a liberal European formerly Minister of Finance in Kenya, as Minister of Finance. The Executive considered it still premature, however, to admit non-African members to TANU.

In March, 1959, the Governor proposed that a Post Elections Committee be appointed to suggest a new basis for elections and that in the meantime a Council of Ministers be created with five unofficial members. TEMO and TANU were faced with a crucial decision— whether to accept the proposals and work gradually for further legislative and executive control or to refuse to accept them as not going far enough.[42] TANU and TEMO took several days to weigh the pros and cons. Finally, they decided to accept the Governor's offer. Five TANU supporters (three Africans, one European, and one Asian) became ministers in July, 1959, though Nyerere himself chose to stay on the unofficial benches to lead TEMO.

When the Post Elections Committee accepted a number of TANU proposals on the composition of the Legislative Council, the British government also had a crucial decision to make on the manner in which Tanganyika was to go forward to independence. In turn, it took time to make up its mind; a decision due originally in October, 1959, was postponed until December. On December 15, however, Governor Turnbull announced to the Legislative Council the decision to accept most of the committee's proposals, including a substantial widening of the franchise and abandonment of parity in favor of a common roll system with some reserved seats. He proclaimed new elections for September, 1960, to establish a Legislative Council with an unofficial majority.[43] Although TANU regretted the lack of a universal franchise, the governmental proposals were received with jubilation. Parades and dancing took place in the streets of Dar es Salaam.

---

[42] Tanganyika Legislative Council, *Debates*, 34th sess., 1958–1959, pp. 4–6.
[43] *Ibid.*, 35th sess., 1959–1960, pp. 3–7; Tanganyika, *Report of the Post Elections Committee* (Dar es Salaam, 1959).

The tensions of 1959, which had reached high points in the spring and fall, were thus largely resolved by the end of the year. Despite minor friction the way to independence was clear; the nationalist movement would not become more militant or the administration more rigid. TANU now claimed a membership of nearly 1,000,000 persons, and its influence was increasing. On most issues, apart from foreign affairs, finance, and control of the civil service, TANU (in consultation with TEMO) was making policy for some time before it assumed control of the government. Events were moving as rapidly as legal arrangements could be made.

In the 1960 elections, TANU support was so widespread that in 58 out of 71 seats its candidates were unopposed, and it won 12 out of 13 contested districts. There was little formal party opposition; the ANC lost heavily in both districts which it contested. The other electoral contests very largely represented intraparty disputes, on the basis of personality and local issues rather than on lines of party policy. Tribal rivalries appeared in several areas, and the one seat lost by an official TANU candidate, in Mbulu, was due to efforts of the central party headquarters to impose a candidate who did not come from the majority tribe.[44] The election results seemed to sanction a number of TANU statements on the importance of a single independence movement and a strong party that backed the apparatus of the state. Nyerere, who had spoken some time earlier of one-party democracy and its role in new states, now had very much a one-party country to govern.

The last steps to independence were taken smoothly. When the Legislative Council met in October, 1960, *madaraka* (responsible government) was established. Nyerere was made Chief Minister of a cabinet members of which were drawn from all races and which also included several civil service ministers still in office. An orderly pattern of constitutional progress was laid down: a constitutional conference in March, 1961, complete internal self-government in May, and independence in December.[45] Although events in the Congo led to unrest among non-Africans, and a left-wing element in both TANU and ANC was vocal in urging more rapid and extreme measures, Nyerere as Chief Minister was able to calm fears and to lead Tanganyika confidently toward *uhuru* (independence). On December 9,

[44] Tanganyika, *Report on the Second General Election of Members of the Legislative Council of Tanganyika* (mimeographed; Dar es Salaam, 1960).
[45] Great Britain, *Report of the Tanganyika Constitutional Conference*, Cmnd. 1360 (London, 1961).

1961, a beacon flamed atop Mount Kilimanjaro to celebrate the creation of a new nation. In the perspective of the tensions of the past few years and the problems of other African territories, it was notable that local councils all over Tanganyika forbade the brewing of local beer for independence, that no incidents of violence were reported, and that the police force spent its time directing traffic.

EVENTS SINCE INDEPENDENCE

Tanganyika achieved independence while internal change and reform were very much in process. Announcements of new ministries, new schemes, and new ideas continue almost from day to day. Substantively action has been taken to levy a poll tax on women, further to democratize local councils and remove remaining elements of tribalism, to encourage cooperatives and investment, to Africanize the civil service, and to integrate the individual racial school systems formerly operating in the territory.

The major political change has been the resignation of Julius Nyerere as Prime Minister and his replacement by Rashidi Kawawa, a former trade union official, who had been successively Minister of Local Government and Minister without Portfolio. The reasons for Nyerere's resignation have not been entirely clear, and some overseas opinion jumped to the conclusion that he was forced to resign by the more radical wing of TANU, exerting pressure for a wholly African rather than a nonracial regime. Since Kawawa is a close follower of Nyerere and since Nyerere as president of TANU controls the party and through it the making of policy, this interpretation does not provide the full story. Nyerere's public explanation was that he wished to work more closely with the grass-roots structure of TANU, whose dominant party position makes it vitally important in the hard work ahead in turning Tanganyika into a successful modern nation.[46] Both explanations accord with the facts as now known, and since they are not entirely incompatible it may be that both are true.

Formal proposals to change Tanganyika into a republic headed by a President were made public by Prime Minister Kawawa on May 31, 1962. The changes envisaged are considered in the later section on the political process.

[46] Tanganyika Information Services, Press release, Jan. 23, 1962.

Land and People

The preceding section has been mainly devoted to a narrative of political and constitutional events, but a great many other factors are relevant to the present scene. Some of the major issues facing the new Tanganyika may be better understood with a further examination of its land, its people, its social structure, and its economy.

Geographically, Tanganyika consists largely of an elevated plateau, averaging 3,000 to 4,000 feet in height and sloping gently in the east to the Indian Ocean. The central plateau is covered with *miombo* woodland—open forest with grass cover—but it is rarely fertile or well-watered land. This is the open savannah which is the home of Tanganyika's magnificent herds of wild animals, such as antelope and zebra and elephant; the Serengeti plains in the northwest are one of the great game areas of the world. This woodland is sometimes thick enough to provide timber and such forest products as beeswax; in the southwest a large area around Lake Rukwa may contain mineral resources. In the west-central areas the bush has been removed by African cultivators to produce the great cultivation steppe of Sukumaland.

Over many centuries the plateau has shifted to create mountains, especially the Pare and Usambara ranges in the northeast and the Livingstone Mountains and the Southern Highlands of the southwest; Mount Kilimanjaro stands almost alone in the north. The plateau is also cut from north to south by the geological fault known as the Great Rift Valley, which stretches from southern Tanganyika north to the Red Sea. Although this country lies close to the equator, only the low coastal strip in the east has the hot and humid climate of the tropics; inland the height of the plateau produces a more temperate zone, which is no hotter than the American Middle West. Most of Tanganyika's population, however, is concentrated in the relatively more fertile areas on the coast, around the lakes of the interior, and in the mountains. The comment has indeed been made that Tanganyika resembles an inverted saucer, with all the fertile land lying on the saucer's rim. Many of the more progressive tribes live in this area, and it produces a large proportion of Tanganyika's economic crops. This geography, however, immediately suggests problems of communications and transport, difficulties in welding the country together, and differences among the many local groups.

TRADITIONAL SOCIETY

In the last census, 120 tribes were listed in Tanganyika, each speaking its own language, occupying a small area, and separated from its neighbors by well-defined borders. Tanganyika has no single large and dominant tribe; the position of the Baganda in Uganda or of the Kikuyu in Kenya has not been duplicated. The Sukuma, one of the few tribes to move into the *miombo* area, where they both keep cattle and grow cotton, are the largest group, numbering more than 1,000,000 persons. Related to them and living to the south are the next largest tribe, the Nyamwezi. In the more fertile areas of the north live the Chagga of Mount Kilimanjaro, notable for their coffeegrowing and their desire for education, the Shambaa, and the Pare; in the southern mountains are the Angoni, the Hehe, and the Nyakyusa. The Haya of the extreme northwest have been well known for their coffeegrowing and their highly defined hierarchy of tribal chiefs. On the central plateau live the Gogo, cattle keepers who are accustomed to perennial near-famine conditions in their arid homeland; the Masai to the north of them are also cattle keepers and largely nomadic. None of these tribes has more than 300,000 members, and some are much smaller.[47]

This tribal Tanganyika is primarily rural and traditional, based on a subsistence economy. The staples of diet are millet, corn, rice, or bananas according to locality. In central Tanganyika elderly Africans still speak of buying shillings to pay their taxes, and the bride price is payable in cattle, not cash. As late as 1945, one or two areas still reported people wearing skins, and digging sticks were used instead of hoes. Communications have been rudimentary. Yet as the discussion of native administration will have indicated, tribal structure has not been static, and great changes have occurred in this rural environment during the seventy years of colonial rule. The introduction of a monetary economy has brought cash crops and migrant labor to dilute the old subsistence farming. Inheritance patterns have changed in many tribes, and the position of women has improved; more children go to school. Mission schools and mission hospitals have been very important factors in changing tribal society, although their influence has been felt much more strongly in some areas than others. Very nearly a one-to-one correlation exists between mission influence, the cash-crop economy, fertile land, education, and the general desire for prog-

[47] For distribution of tribes, see J. E. Goldthorpe and F. B. Wilson, *Tribal Maps of East Africa and Zanzibar* (Kampala, Uganda, 1960).

ress of the various tribes. Again, in terms of geography, those conditions are usually found on the edges of the country and less often on the central plateau.

Development in the last decade has, however, hastened the pace of change, as roads are built, schools are opened, and new products appear. A list of commodities bought by Africans as they acquire cash is instructive: cotton clothing, tea, sugar, soap, enamel dishes, wooden doors, furniture, a bicycle, a cow, a new wife.[48] Ten years ago it was still true that upcountry shoes were an unusual sight; by 1962 most people wore canvas shoes, made in Dar es Salaam. Styles in clothes, in houses, and in foods are now appearing. Gradually, the countryside begins to blend into the nearest town, which is probably an administrative headquarters, with shops, a TANU office, and a bus service to the main road. The transition is begun to a second, modern Tanganyika. This is urban, with wage earning as the usual economic pattern and with modern transport, education, and attitudes. At its most developed this modern society is seen in Dar es Salaam, the seaport capital, the home of persons from different tribes, and the manufacturing and trading community. It seems both miles and generations removed from the remote areas of Ufipa in the west, still largely unexplored and ridden with tsetse. Many contemporary Tanganyikans have, however, moved from traditional to modern Tanganyika and are part of both worlds. Nyerere spent his early years herding his father's cattle in the area north of Sukumaland; Kawawa began his career some years ago by taking the lead in a movie which pictured the countryman come to town, with all his trials and tribulations.

In the colonial period there were three major ways in which the rural Tanganyikan moved into the new environment: through the growing of cash crops, through migratory labor, and through education. The Chagga and Haya undertook the cultivation of coffee and found themselves immediately enmeshed in the vagaries of a world market. The Angoni of Songea became migrant laborers to the sisal plantations on the coast, while the Nyakyusa preferred to go to the South African gold mines. It became the pattern in both these tribes for young men to fill two or three labor contracts and then to come back and settle down in their homelands with whatever new ideas or material possessions they had garnered. In some instances they did not come back but settled in new areas, and around the sisal planta-

[48] F. C. Wright, *African Consumers in Nyasaland and Tanganyika* (London, 1955).

tions of Tanga it is possible to speak of retribalization, as men of the interior tribes came under coastal Swahili influence.[49]

Both these contacts could be transitory and uneven; a third has had a more lasting influence. Since schools were scarce, all beyond the lower elementary level were boarding schools, and young boys soon met those of other tribes. All were taught in Kiswahili, which was also the language of the administration and which became an important intertribal link. As they left school, the young men looked for white-collar jobs with government or commerce, settling in town away from their original home and subject to transfer from time to time. Since some degree of Western education was necessary for most jobs in the modern economy, or even for the new tasks now assigned to native administration, an elite group began to appear, with a special entry to economic, social, and eventually political power. Although social class had existed in traditional society (in many tribes chiefs and commoners were clearly distinguished), there now appeared many more differentiating factors. The social hierarchy in modern Tanganyika has many subtle steps. While political democracy and economic equality are goals of the Tanganyika government, it could be argued that in fact many more gradations now exist in Tanganyika society than has been true in the past. Not all of them derive from education—traditional descent and religion are two other important factors—but they are frequently associated with it.

RACE RELATIONS AND EDUCATION

This new society is not confined to Tanganyika Africans or even to Africans from neighboring Kenya and Nyasaland; it is interracial. In the towns Indians and Goans have usually been the shopkeepers and artisans; Europeans have staffed the administration, the technical departments such as railways and public health, and the large trading firms which have bought local produce or acquired land for plantation purposes. Small farmers, some of whom have held their land since German days, live in the Northern and Tanga provinces. There are missions throughout the territory. It is not impossible in Tanganyika to find third-generation farmers of Greek descent or Indian traders whose families arrived five generations ago. Numerically, these groups are almost infinitesimal (the 1957 census showed 20,598 Europeans

[49] E. C. Baker, *Report on the Economic and Social Conditions in the Tanga Province* (Dar es Salaam, 1934); J. B. Molohan, *Detribalization* (Dar es Salaam, 1958); P. H. Gulliver, *Labour Migration in a Rural Economy* (Kampala, 1955).

and 95,636 Asians in a total population of 8,788,466), but since they
have had access to the education, the specialized skills, and the capital
necessary in the modern world, their position is considerably more
important than numbers suggest.[50]

In the past, Tanganyika society has been hierarchical in the modern
as well as the traditional sector. The European was on top, though
there were gradations within this community: it carried more prestige
to be an Englishman than a Greek, to work for the government than
in private business, to farm than to be a missionary. Next came the
Asians, with gradations within this community as well, and then the
Africans. This ladder of status had some legal support in terms of
such factors as residential requirements and tax rates, though a strict
legal color bar did not exist. The urban, educated African tried to
climb the ladder, frequently imitating the social habits of groups
higher up the scale. As more educational opportunities have become
available in the last ten years, the hierarchy has become much more
flexible and is dependent on many things other than race. This flexibil-
ity has been stimulated both by the multiracial concepts of Governor
Twining and by the pressures of TANU. The top political status is
now occupied by African ministers and civil servants; this is becoming
true of social status as well, though it is not yet true of the economic
realm.

The statement is frequently made that Tanganyika has the best
race relations in Africa and that these different groups get along well.
It is true that there have been few overt racial difficulties, so that from
a negative point of view there is little to live down. But it is also true
that in the past there has been an absence of racial contact, at least in
any social sense; separate groups tended to lead separate lives, whether
this was due to differences in religion, food patterns, language, or other
factors. It is interesting that Tanganyika writers have tended to see
each of the other two races as being solidly unified and their own as
split from within. One of the effects of multiracial political policies
was at last to bring these groups together, to let them get to know
each other's habits. At first this interaction had its painful aspects and
was undertaken as a matter of official duty; now it is becoming more
natural. Lady Twining, forming the interracial Tanganyika Council
of Women in the 1950's, and Mrs. Nyerere as its president in the 1960's
were both contributing to their husbands' political ideals.

[50] Great Britain, *Tanganyika: Report for the Year 1960*, Col. 349 (1961),
App. I.

For the coming generation this contact may be easier because children of different races will be at school together; the schools will be used to produce good Tanganyikans, as the American school system was used in the nineteenth century to produce good citizens from European immigrants. In the past there have been three separate school systems in the country; few European children learned Kiswahili, and Asian schools were particularly set apart by language and religious differences. For the Africans, a school system had been introduced by the British after 1925, but financial exigencies had kept enrollments minute until after World War II. Curriculum and standards were derived from British practice and were not always pertinent to African needs, a fact of which British educators were aware but with which they never managed to cope very successfully. The system was oriented toward the British universities, so that agricultural education in the villages or technical education in the towns was stunted. So little secondary education was available that Africans could not finish their preparatory work for the university in Tanganyika but had to study elsewhere. Nyerere, in 1949, was a member of the first group of Tanganyika Africans to go to a university overseas. When the country became independent, there were only two African lawyers in Tanganyika, and no engineers.

But the real accomplishments of the educational system, especially in the period since 1945, should not be forgotten. The percentage of children in elementary school has risen from 7.5 per cent in the 1930's to 53 per cent in 1960; the village school is now a part of many communities. Under the current three-year development plan education gets a very high priority, and the number of students receiving secondary education will be multiplied five times between 1960 and 1964.[51] The important role that existing schools have played in creating transtribal ties has been mentioned.

Major problems remain in the educational field. There is still much misunderstanding of standards, so that Africans who have been through the eighth grade fail to understand their lack of qualifications for a course in electrical engineering, or others demand high positions in the civil service because they do not see these jobs as demanding particular skills. It is particularly paradoxical that although in most sections of Tanganyika the demand for schools is greater than the gov-

[51] Betty George, *Education for Africans in Tanganyika* (Washington, D.C., 1961); *Development Plan for Tanganyika, 1961/62–1963/64* (Dar es Salaam, 1961).

ernment can finance and staff, there are still some rural areas where children are kept out of school by their parents. In 1961 there were 13,000 vacant places in the elementary schools of Lake Province.

EMERGING SOCIAL PATTERNS

Africans moving to the towns have created other social patterns not so imitative of non-African forms. In Dar es Salaam and the upcountry towns associations are legion and range from football clubs to mutual benefit societies. It is a good introduction to Tanganyika merely to read the list of those registered under the Societies Ordinance: the Cairo Musical Society, the African Tenants Association, the Bluebird Hospitality Club, the Southern Province Union of Tribal Associations. Some of the groups are religious, others are educational, and some skirt the edges of politics to become pressure groups: they include the tribal associations, the Union of African Traders, the Tanganyika African Parents Association, and the All-Muslim National Union of Tanganyika. Women's groups have been important on the coast and in many towns, and according to some observers, the Old Boys' clubs (alumni associations) of Tabora Secondary School and Makerere College, to which many Tanganyikans have gone, have been powers behind the political throne.

Two of the most influential new associations have been economic in nature: the trade unions and the cooperatives. Tanganyika has approximately 400,000 workers in paid employment, and in the last ten years trade unionism imported from Great Britain and the United States (through the International Confederation of Free Trade Unions) has been growing. A Federation of Labour was founded in 1954 to bring together some twelve territorial unions, but it has not yet been able to build up a strong central authority to control the movement as a whole.[52] Individual unions such as the Railway Workers Union and the Sisal and Plantation Workers Union often go their own way, and strikes have increased in late years. Since trade unionism is an imported concept and is so new, it is difficult to tell what, apart from a demand for higher wages, it may mean to the average worker. It might be expected that unions would appeal most strongly to the skilled workers, but in recent years the dock workers and the plantation workers have shown considerable solidarity. TANU helped to finance the Tanganyika Federation of Labour when it was first founded

[52] The Tanganyika Department of Labour recognizes twenty-seven trade unions; not all of these are members of the Federation (*Tanganyika Report, 1960,* p. 104).

and regards itself as a labor party to which workers logically owe allegiance (in Kiswahili, the word *mtetezi* means both politician and labor leader), but relations between the two groups have recently been acrimonious.[53]

Cooperatives have so far been agricultural marketing societies and based in the rural areas where important cash crops are grown. The British government fostered them in a number of ways as a method of pooling capital and resources, and for most major crops of the territory it has been compulsory to sell through the cooperatives; this element of compulsion differentiates them considerably from the cooperatives of America and western Europe. In many areas cooperatives have been extremely popular, and in 1960 there were 691 societies handling the major production of coffee, cotton, tobacco, and cashew nuts. Among the Chagga and Haya who have grown coffee for many years the cooperatives have practically become part of the tribal structure, and the federation of cooperative unions in Sukumaland after 1954 has probably helped to strengthen tribal structure and spirit. They have frequently been important also in local political terms and, particularly after 1961 when one vast cooperative association was formed for the whole territory, may be expected to influence national politics as well. Several ministers in the first cabinet had long been associated with the cooperative movement, and early in 1962 a Ministry of Cooperative and Community Development was created.

LAND POLICIES AND PROBLEMS

Future development of cooperatives may be particularly important because of conditions of land tenure in Tanganyika. Land tenure is a vitally important matter to most Africans, and if an African were writing this section he would probably begin with it. In most of the tribal systems some form of communal tenure is to be found, and land allocation is a function of the chief or clan head.[54] Freehold land as Americans know it hardly exists in Tanganyika, though various landlord-tenant systems are known. In practice, it is difficult for one African to control a piece of land, for there are always other persons with claims upon it. Thus he may not sell or mortgage the land. In some areas if he puts in permanent crops he acquires title to them, and it may

[53] Julius Nyerere, *African Trade Unions* (mimeographed; Dar es Salaam, 1960). See also issues of the *Tanganyika Standard* for 1961.

[54] A. A. Oldaker, *Interim Report on Tribal Customary Land Tenure in Tanganyika* (Dar es Salaam, 1957).

happen, therefore, that coffee or cashew nuts are owned by persons who do not control the land. The system is so complex (as it is in many other African countries) and the Africans' attachment to the land is so deep and basic that governments of any political hue find it hard to make changes.

Africans also feel very strongly about the amount of land which has been sold or leased to non-Africans, even if this constitutes just over 1 per cent of the total area of Tanganyika.[55] Some years ago the Sukuma people noted that land alienation was their major grievance against the colonial administration, though in Sukumaland only one sizable grant of land had been made, to a diamond mine. This feeling for the land is shared by many town dwellers, who retain their stake in a piece of land to retire to or in case they lose a job. The feeling is similar to that found in France, and it is a factor in drawing Africans together.

THE ECONOMY

The land that has been alienated is extremely important in the territorial economy. Much of it is under sisal, a crop which demands plantation production because of the high costs of machinery and processing, and sisal has been the mainstay of Tanganyikan exports. More than 200,000 tons are now exported annually. The high world price of sisal at the time of the Korean war made possible much recent development, as the government imposed a high export tax. Sisal's major role makes crucial any development concerning the industry, whether it be strikes by the plantation workers or changes in American demand for binder twine. In 1960–1961, when many plantations were seriously affected by drought, there were repercussions on employment and government income.

Other commodities such as tea, coffee, cotton, and tobacco are grown on plantations and contribute substantially to Tanganyika's annual export total of about £55,000,000. Together with the mixed farms of Northern Province, which produce wheat and other food products, the plantations are controlled by non-Africans, who thus constitute a major element in the monetary economy. The per capita gross product in Tanganyika is about £20 or $60, but when this figure is broken down, it appears that the per capita contribution of Asians and Europeans is about £400 and that of Africans about £8. Many African farmers are still mainly subsistence farmers, and in 1960 some

[55] Great Britain, *Tanganyika: Report for the Year 1960*, App. VIII.

40 per cent of the gross national product of Tanganyika was still generated by the subsistence economy.[56]

Tanganyika, in fact, presents almost a classic picture of an under-developed territory. It has tried to produce export crops in order to be able to buy consumer and development goods and has made substantial progress in many areas: sisal exports brought in £15,000,000 in 1960; coffee £7,000,000; cotton £9,000,000. But Tanganyika cannot control fluctuating world prices for these commodities, and even with steadily increasing production over the last ten years the monetary return has varied widely. The territory has at least not been entirely a one-crop economy like so many Latin American countries, and it has tried to vary its exports even further, producing such items as cashew nuts, beeswax, tea, and hides and skins. It cannot expand greatly the acreage under crops unless it can overcome problems of water and tsetse on the central plateau; more intensive farming in the more fertile areas may run into problems of land tenure. Both possibilities also require capital, trained men, and machinery. Even with these the groundnut scheme, investing millions of pounds, was unable to solve the difficult problems of cultivating the central Tanganyikan plain.

Mineral exports now total more than £7,000,000 annually, but most of this income is derived from one large diamond mine in Sukumaland. Gold is found in some quantity, and there are small deposits of tin, mica, and pyrochlore, as well as a coal field in the southern mountains. In comparison with other African countries, however, these deposits are small or uneconomic to work under present world conditions, and no other major mineral reserves are known. Tanganyika cannot quickly, therefore, exploit its own resources. Even the hydroelectric power potential of the country is not high. The one major scheme of river control now under investigation, on the Rufiji River, will be primarily useful for purposes of irrigation rather than power.

With the small internal purchasing power suggested by the low per capita income, there has been small scope for industrial development. Processing industries have recently begun to appear in Dar es Salaam and produce such items as bottled drinks, razor blades, and canvas shoes; a tire factory has been established in Arusha. Industrial development in the past tended to concentrate on Kenya as a better

---

[56] Tanganyika, *The Gross Domestic Product of Tanganyika, 1954–1957* (Dar es Salaam, 1959); *Tanganyika Budget Survey, 1960–61* (Dar es Salaam, 1961), pp. 3–4.

economic proposition, and with free East African trade, under the 1923 customs union, products could be sent to Tanganyika as well. There has been little trade with other African countries except South Africa, owing both to lack of communication and to similarity of product. TANU began a boycott of South African goods in 1960, in protest against its apartheid policies, even though cutting imports of some food items and of hoes for agricultural use may have hurt Tanganyika more than South Africa. The government also stopped South African recruiting of mineworkers. Most Tanganyika exports go to the United States, Great Britain, and India, and these countries lead the import list as well; West Germany and the Netherlands are also important.

The present government introduced in the spring of 1961 a three-year development plan which concentrated particularly on expansion of communications, agricultural extension work, and exploration of further possibilities in mining, forests, and fisheries. With its revenues now about $60,000,000 annually and with many demands for schools and hospitals, the government sees few alternatives to constant hard work. Apart from finances, it also does not have the personnel for rapid development; in the past funds have gone unspent while teachers were recruited or agricultural instructors trained. The territory has received funds regularly from the British Colonial Development and Welfare Fund, in 1961 amounting to about $8,000,000; it has also received some benefit from United Nations agencies such as UNICEF, WHO, and FAO.[57] On independence, it was presented with a number of development gifts, including $10,000,000 from the United States, to be spent, however, on American imported goods. So far Tanganyika has been careful to use outside funds for new capital projects and has kept its regular budget autonomous.

THE PRESS

Two further matters deserve comment in this picture of present-day Tanganyika: the press and the role of religion. A wide variety of newspapers exist, but most of them are published rather irregularly. The leading newspaper for many years has been the *Tanganyika Standard*, published in English, with a territorial circulation of about 9,000.[58] Its coverage is nominally territorial, but it tends to concentrate on Dar es Salaam. Since about 1957 a Swahili press has developed,

[57] Tanganyika, *Development Plan for Tanganyika, 1961/62–1963/64* (Dar es Salaam, 1961); *Tanganyika Budget Survey, 1960–61.*

[58] A separate weekly edition appears as the *Sunday News.*

and *Mwafrika* and *Ngurumo* appear daily, despite considerable editorial and financial problems. The weekly *Uhuru* is the organ of TANU. Several Asian papers appear weekly in Gujerati and English, and a new magazine, *Spearhead,* appeared in Dar es Salaam in late 1961. There are no opposition papers.

Readership is mostly confined to Dar es Salaam and other large towns, and the rural reader depends on newssheets issued by tribal administrations or by missions, plus a monthly long issued by the Department of Education, *Mambo Leo.* Tribal *barazas* for the transmission of news are still held in some areas, though Africans are now tending more and more to listen to the broadcasts of the Tanganyika Broadcasting Corporation.

There are no restrictive press laws, but prosecutions for falsehood and libel have been occasionally threatened and editors warned of their responsibility to "tell the truth." The prosecution against Julius Nyerere, mentioned earlier, and trials by the colonial government of other editors connected with TANU may have boomeranged. The ordinances under which the prosecutions were carried out are still part of the laws of Tanganyika.

RELIGION

In religious affiliation, the majority of Tanganyika Africans are probably still animist. The important social and educational role of Christian missions has been referred to, however, and a considerable indigenous Christian community exists. Churches are now largely Africanized, Protestant churches having local councils in charge and Catholic churches having African bishops. Doctrinal matters have evidently not been very much at issue, and Tanganyika seems exceptional in Africa in having no religious separatist movements of any size. As in the United States, however, religious questions sometimes affect matters of public policy; control of the Catholic mission schools particularly has been at issue. The schools at present are financed by the government but staffed by mission groups. Since Nyerere is a practicing Catholic, this issue may be politely mediated, but the mission school which once called his political activities incompatible with his employment as a teacher must view the present situation rather wryly.

Islam, long traditional at the coast, is now growing rapidly inland as well; for many a rural African the adoption of Islam is the first step out of his traditional environment. The customary law of many tribes has been altered by Muslim influence. There are several schools of

Islamic thought represented in the territory, and a particularly important role has been played by the Indian and African followers of the Aga Khan, the Ismaili Khoja. In recent years Muslims have been concerned that such a very small proportion of their African followers were receiving adequate education, since they would not go to mission schools. This had resulted, in their view, in discrimination against Muslims in public positions, and they have begun to use political influence to press for a more favorable position in Tanganyikan society. Recently they have exercised a major voice in TANU and since 1959 have been active also through AMNUT, the All-Muslim National Union of Tanganyika.

The Political Process

THE STRUCTURE OF GOVERNMENT

When Tanganyika achieved independence on December 9, 1961, it became a parliamentary democracy and a member of the Commonwealth, owing allegiance to the Queen. The formal structure of government was largely inherited from its British colonial past; the Tanganyika (Constitution) Order in Council, 1961, was very British in tone and entirely British in pattern.

As in Great Britain, the backbone of the structure is Parliament, which consisted as the time of independence of the Queen and a National Assembly, which exercises legislative power. The National Assembly has 81 members, 71 of them elected and 10 nominated on the advice of the Prime Minister. This means that Tanganyika now has a far larger assembly than ever before, six times the size of the Legislative Council of ten years earlier.

Amendments to the constitution may be made only by a two-thirds vote; other laws may be passed by a simple majority. The leader of the party that is able to command a parliamentary majority becomes the head of government, that is, the Prime Minister, though the wording of the constitution retains the formal British political terminology which designates the Governor-General as the executive authority on the Queen's behalf. In this sense the Prime Minister constitutionally acts only in an advisory capacity, but the constitution makes it clear that, except in specifically enumerated circumstances such as the choice of a Prime Minister himself, his advice must be followed. Other ministers are appointed on the Prime Minister's advice and thereby constitute a cabinet collectively responsible to Parliament. A High Court is appointed by the Governor-General, who acts upon recommendation of a Judicial Service Commission. In constitutional matters, appeals go directly to the Judicial Committee of the Privy Council; in other cases the pattern of appeal is specified by Parliament.[59]

Universal adult suffrage is established for all Tanganyika citizens at the age of twenty-one, and provision is made for an Electoral Commission, under the chairmanship of the Speaker of the National Assembly, to divide Tanganyika into single-member constituencies. Reserved racial seats will thus disappear at the next election, for though the Electoral Commission may consider geography and means of communication in establishing constituencies, there is no mention of races or of racial questions. It may be presumed that at least some of the ten appointed seats will be kept for non-Africans as a matter of policy.

The constitution also established a Tanganyika citizenship, a matter that had been under consideration for more than forty years but was perennially postponed; previous legislative councils, in consequence, had been elected on the basis of residence rather than citizenship.[60] Tanganyika citizens are now defined as those British citizens or protected persons, born in Tanganyika, of whom one parent had also been born in Tanganyika. This complicated formula seemed to cover virtually all Africans, a fair proportion of Asians, but very few Europeans. Since a question on citizenship had never been asked in the Tanganyika census, this is only a presumption, but the estimate is based on the numbers of local residents who had applied for naturalization as British citizens, a process possible in Tanganyika after the passage of the British Nationality Act of 1948. British citizens or protected persons born in the territory may now register as Tanganyika citizens if they so choose, but other provisions on naturalization are left to later action by Parliament. A heated debate on the citizenship proposals occurred in the National Assembly in October, 1961; although the government proposals were approved on a free vote, strong opposi-

---

[59] Tanganyika (Constitution) Order in Council, 1961, Statutory Instruments, 1961, no. 2274.

[60] The National Assembly elected in 1960 included among its members not only Tanganyika Africans who were British protected persons, but also others of Indian, Goan, Greek, German, Swiss, Swedish, American and British nationality —and perhaps a few more. Earlier assemblies had included Australians, Canadians, Pakistanis, Cypriots, Zanzibaris, and South Africans.

tion to them was voiced by some Assembly members who favored granting citizenship only to persons of African descent.[61]

Three commissions were also created by the constitution: a Public Service Commission, a Judicial Service Commission (already mentioned), and a Police Commission. As their titles indicate, these bodies are primarily concerned with appointments to the judiciary and the civil service; the creation of three groups seemed designed to ensure that no one group attained control over the machinery of government. Members are appointed by the Governor-General on the Prime Minister's advice, and there is an interlocking membership through the chairman of the Public Service Commission. Once appointed, members serve definite terms. Their position may be compared to that of the independent regulatory agencies of the United States.

In other respects, the structure of government remains largely unchanged from that of the colonial period. A cabinet, headed first by Julius Nyerere and then by Rashidi Kawawa, makes major decisions of policy, though Sir Richard Turnbull, as first Governor-General, is the ceremonial head of state. The cabinet ministers at the time of independence were those TANU party leaders and their non-African allies who had been prominent in the independence movement: Oscar Kambona, Minister of Education; George Kahama, Minister of Home Affairs; Sir Ernest Vasey, Minister of Finance; Derek Bryceson, Minister of Health and Labour; and Amir Jamal, Minister of Communications, Power, and Works. On Nyerere's resignation cabinet posts were reshuffled and Sir Ernest Vasey resigned, since he was not eligible for Tanganyika citizenship. The civil service, although increasingly Africanized, has not altered in function. Moreover, despite many changes in local councils and native administrations, which are discussed below, the basic relationship between central government and local authorities has not shifted.

Two fundamental changes in structure were announced by the government for implementation during 1962, however, and several more were suggested. The first change of importance, one which had been suggested more than a year before Tanganyikan independence and probably accepted in principle by the government early in 1961, was the appointment of political representatives in each province, and eventually in each district. As in Ghana, where a similar system exists, this will give the central government greater political representation

[61] Tanganyika National Assembly, *Debates*, 36th sess., 5th meeting, 1960–1961, c. 303–374. The exact vote on the debate was not recorded.

in regions remote from the capital. Provincial and district commissioners remain as administrative officers and as advisers to these political officers. The first appointments to these new political offices, retitled regional commissioners, were announced in February, 1962.[62] Although it was stated that the commissioners were to control local politicians, their relationship to local members of Parliament is not clear.

The second major change was the decision to transform Tanganyika into a republic on December 9, 1962, and to create a President with major executive powers. Constitutional amendments adumbrated by Prime Minister Kawawa in late May are to be implemented at a special meeting of the National Assembly in November. Election of the first President, by universal suffrage, has been scheduled for mid-October, 1962.

The government proposals note that monarchy is essentially a foreign institution in Tanganyika, as prior to independence the Queen was only head of state in the country administering Tanganyika. Since it is highly desirable that "as far as possible Tanganyika's institutions of government must be such as can be understood by the people," the relationship with the British Crown will be broken. The new presidency will be generally modeled on that of Ghana, and some arrangement will be made to link the election of the President with that of the National Assembly. A Vice-President and ministers will be appointed from among members of the Assembly.

The President will inherit the Governor-General's present right to nominate ten members of the Assembly, which he will be able to summon, prorogue, or dissolve. His assent to legislation will be required; if the Assembly by a two-thirds vote passes a law over his veto, he must assent within 21 days or dissolve the Assembly—in effect, ask for a new election. In contrast with the President of Ghana, however, he will have no power to legislate without recourse to parliament. Such provisions "by their very nature subvert democratic principles and inevitably lead to abuse." Aside from a change in the life of the National Assembly from four to five years, no other legislative changes are projected, despite previous speculation in Tanganyika that a consultative second chamber might be established from the Chiefs' Convention, an advisory body which has existed since 1957.

[62] *Ibid.*, c. 98–99; *Ngurumo*, Feb. 3, 1962. From this date, Tanganyika's provinces are to be called regions, though the same substantive names have been kept. Districts will be known as areas.

As chief executive, the President will appoint judges, though the independence of the judiciary will be safeguarded and the Judicial Service Commission will continue to handle disciplinary matters. Appeals to the Judicial Committee of the Privy Council will be discontinued; the Tanganyika High Court will presumably assume the function of constitutional interpretation. The President will also be charged with building "an efficient local civil service capable at all levels of interpreting, and giving effect to, government policy," and he may give directions to the director of public prosecutions. The Public Service and Police Service commissions will act in advisory rather than executive capacities.[63]

Considerable constitutional change is thus envisaged for Tanganyika. A stronger executive may assist the working of the constitutional system, but it is uncertain whether it will solve Tanganyika's principal constitutional difficulty: the fact that the constitutional structure has been designed for a two-party or a multiparty system, whereas Tanganyika is currently operating it with one party. The character of TANU is thus crucial: its party structure and its party philosophy will determine the course of events.

PHILOSOPHY OF THE TANGANYIKA
AFRICAN NATIONAL UNION

The philosophy of TANU has been worked out almost entirely by Julius Nyerere, who has been the one person in TANU consistently concerned with long-range political planning. Many of his ideas have encountered opposition within the party, but they have usually been opposed pragmatically rather than systematically. For purposes of analysis, it may be helpful to regard Nyerere's ideas as the present orthodox strain of TANU thought with several opposition groups in a minority position.

Nyerere's political philosophy has pattern and consistency, though much of it also seems to have a pragmatic basis. His general attitude toward political questions can be adduced from the preamble to the Tanganyika constitution, which he may well have written:

Whereas recognition of the inherent dignity and of the equal and inalienable rights of all members of the human family is the foundation of freedom, justice and peace:

[63] Tanganyika Government Paper no. 1 of 1962; Tanganyika Information Services, Press release, May 29, 1962.

And whereas the said rights include the right of the individual, whatever his race, tribe, place of origin, political opinions, colour, creed or sex, but subject to respect for the rights and freedoms of others and for the public interest, to life, liberty, security of the person, the enjoyment of property, the protection of the law, freedom of conscience, freedom of expression, freedom of assembly and association, and respect for his private and family life:

And whereas the said rights are best maintained and protected in a democratic society where the government is responsible to a freely elected Parliament representative of the people and where the courts of law are independent and impartial:

This Constitution makes provision for the government of Tanganyika as such a democratic society.[64]

In terms of basic philosophical position, Nyerere is thus a believer in the dignity and rights of the individual, as opposed to an overriding emphasis on the party or the state, and is committed to concepts of democracy and equality. In the circumstances of Tanganyika, this view has meant support of African political domination of the country because Africans are numerically the largest group but at the same time has led him to urge a nonracial approach to politics. Multiracialism, he has felt, created an artificial relationship between groups, rather than an understanding among individuals; thus race should be divorced from politics, as also should religion, tribe, sex, or other divisive classifications of humanity. The intensity of Nyerere's feelings and beliefs were movingly indicated in a speech in the Legislative Council in December, 1959, following the government decision to abandon the principle of parity:

Sir, let it not be said by posterity that we were a bunch of hypocrites. Let not the world point a finger at us and say that we gained our freedom on a moral argument—the argument of the brotherhood of man—and then threw that argument overboard and began to discriminate against our brothers on the grounds of colour. I pray, Sir, that Almighty God will save us from committing such a sin against His justice. We have set ourselves a goal. We intend to create a society here happy for everybody. . . . Our duty now is to look to the future and see that the future does not say, "Why did you miss the opportunity to build a better society than the society which you inherited?" [65]

[64] Tanganyika (Constitution) Order in Council, 1961, Statutory Instruments, 1961, no. 2274.

[65] Tanganyika Legislative Council, *Debates*, 35th sess., 1959–1960, p. 39.

This basic belief in the dignity and equality of individuals has led to Nyerere's adoption of the idea of African socialism, as evolved by Senghor and other West African leaders; it also takes him logically to Pan-Africanism, to support of the United Nations, and to a position of positive neutrality in foreign affairs. Nyerere did not originally envisage a one-party state until he was confronted with the practical situation of a TANU monopoly in the Legislative Council; earlier he took the existence of several parties for granted, and he still speaks of the possibility of an eventual emergence of a two-party system in Tanganyika. Since 1958, however, Nyerere has agreed with other African leaders on the necessity of a single independence movement and has justified TANU preeminence as inevitable during the period of anticolonialism and the fight for freedom. By definition, he maintains that there is during this epoch no basis for opposing parties, as all inhabitants of the country are united against an outside power. Within the party, however, there must be wide discussion, and in Tanganyika non-Africans should be allowed to join TANU and to take part in discussions from the inside.

Nyerere has been unwilling to abandon traditional values, whether Western or African; his ethical code is Christian, but he also retains something more than a feeling of nostalgia for tribal values and the role of the chief. It may be from this latter source that he draws his strong belief in personal sacrifice and work for one's country, summed up in an early motto of *uhuru na jasho,* freedom and sweat. This does not imply tribalism or tribal separatism, however, to which Nyerere is unutterably opposed.

As a nationalist, Nyerere has worked against the customs and beliefs he believes deleterious to Tanganyika's achievement of nationhood. In this nationalist fight Nyerere has never had to use violence as a weapon, and he has many times urged his followers to a peaceful course of action. It is notable, however, that Nyerere has never eschewed the use of violence; it is a legitimate weapon in the right circumstances. Here Nyerere stands philosophically in a radical and revolutionary position, but one in which ends clearly dominate means and not vice versa. One can see strands of Western liberalism and socialism joined in Nyerere's thought with borrowings from Gandhi and such West African leaders as Senghor and Nkrumah.[66]

TANU has adopted Nyerere's philosophic position to Tanganyika's

[66] See J. K. Nyerere, "Africa's Place in the World," *Wellesley Symposium on Africa* (Wellesley, Mass., 1960).

political circumstances. The party officially favors nonracialism, involving a removal of reserved seats under the constitution, and an African socialism, which may be described as a nondogmatic belief in equalizing economic opportunity and utilizing Tanganyika's resources for the country as a whole. Cooperatives and trade unions are encouraged as well as other forms of joint economic endeavor. Intraparty discussion is emphasized, and the values of the nation and of nationality are constantly stressed at the expense of more localized or special interests. It is notable, however, that despite some four years of effort Nyerere has never been able to convince TANU that it ought to be more than a racial party; it will not admit non-Africans. Although the party has usually gone his way on matters of policy, it is quite clear that he cannot really dominate it when its opinions are strong.

In opposition to the major views, two schools of thought are now emerging in TANU. One school is inclined to stress African traditionalism and to be sympathetic to tribalism and the role of chiefs; the second and much larger group puts more emphasis on racial questions, regards the non-African inhabitants of Tanganyika as intruders who ought to have no political rights, and urges much faster Africanization of the civil service. The two groups share a strong opposition to non-African ownership of land, and they are now moving also toward opposition to non-African economic ventures of any sort as being necessarily a form of neocolonialism. They dislike government taxation policies while on the whole supporting strong and even authoritarian government. The conventional Western classifications of right and left do not fit these two opposition groups; sometimes their membership as well as their ideas overlap. In today's political context in Tanganyika, in which the major criterion of political position is attitude on race, both groups belong to the radical left, as do two opposition parties, the African National Congress and the All-Muslim National Union of Tanganyika. A third opposition party, the People's Democratic Party, was formed by an ANC splinter group in February, 1962; it seems also to belong to the radical left.

THE PARTY STRUCTURE

TANU has been an open party, the only criteria for membership being membership of the African race and possession of a two-shilling entrance fee. Each member belongs to a branch, organized locally, which elects its own officers; the important roles are those of president and secretary. Branches are grouped into districts, and these in turn into provinces; at each level there exists an executive committee and an annual conference. At the district level, for instance, an annual conference of representatives chosen by the branches will be held; it sets major lines of local policy, approves a budget, and elects a district committee to handle day-to-day business. In turn it elects representatives to a provincial conference.

The culminating point of this hierarchy is the territorial annual conference, which meets in Dar es Salaam usually in February or March; it consists of 2 delegates from each of the 60 districts, 3 delegates from each of the 10 provinces, and the 18 members of the party's Central Committee. The Central Committee is charged with day-to-day administration and is appointed by the TANU president, whom the annual conference elects. Members of the Central Committee serve also on the National Executive, a somewhat larger group (it has a changing membership of about 48 persons, including the Central Committee) which meets four or five times a year to execute the policy decisions of the territorial conference. The Central Committee apparently exists because of the difficulty of quickly convening as large a body as the Executive in a country the size of Tanganyika, but so far as can be determined, major policy decisions are made by the National Executive or the territorial conference. The proceedings of all three groups are closed to the public, except on ceremonial occasions.[67]

In terms of policy, the National Executive is probably the most important body. Nyerere, of course, has occupied an exceptional position. He had been president of TANU since its formation in 1954, but he does not retain the presidency automatically; he is annually reelected. Although he was primarily responsible for building the organization of TANU, he had little time during his period of office to concern himself with party matters except on the highest levels of policy; his recent return to active party work following his resignation as Prime Minister in January, 1962, may foreshadow changes in both policy and administration.

Party decisions have not been imposed on government through any formalized structure or channel; as in other one-party states, decisions are transmitted through personal channels. Most members of the cabinet belong both to the TANU National Executive and to the Central Committee, and almost all important party officials are now

[67] Kasela Bantu, *What T.A.N.U. Is and How It Works* (mimeographed; Dar es Salaam, 1961).

members of the National Assembly or are being prepared to become so. It might be expected that this fact would give the National Assembly an air of unreality. Actually, its first session after TANU moved from the role of opposition into control of the government was disorganized and formless when compared to the discipline that TEMO had been able to impose. At later sessions, however, debate has been animated, and the National Assembly has become a forum for intra-party discussion of policy. Recent debates on the integration of education, on Africanization of the civil service, and on citizenship have constituted a very good introduction to contemporary Tanganyika politics. There has also been some evidence that the cabinet considers itself an independent body and does not automatically accept all the decisions of the TANU Executive.

The administration of TANU is technically the responsibility of the Central Committee, which supervises the headquarters in Dar es Salaam. Appointed officers have included a secretary-general, his deputy, and a group of secretaries in charge of branch affairs, finance, press and publicity, and liaison with government offices. The secretary-general has long been Oscar Kambona, Minister of Home Affairs since the cabinet was reorganized in January, 1962, and he is usually said to control the party apparatus. With a membership of 1,000,000 persons, TANU reaches into almost every hamlet in the territory, and it has extended its hierarchical organization to include even subbranches. Including central office staff, it employs more than 1,500 workers, about one-half of whom are full-time paid employees. Other workers either are paid a living allowance (expressed in the TANU budget in terms of *posho*, African flour, but paid in cash) or receive a percentage of the money they bring into the organization.

TANU activities are far wider than this listing suggests. The party now publishes a weekly newspaper, *Uhuru*. Moreover, it has associated with itself many activities, some of which lie outside what is, to Western eyes, the realm of politics. There are, first of all, several loosely organized groups within TANU itself, especially the TANU Youth League, whose members often appear in the green uniform of TANU. The Youth League is now registered separately under the Societies Ordinance; its branches engage in a variety of activities which range from forming an honor guard at political rallies to cleaning up town streets and building schoolhouses. Originally the League was regarded as a radical group which might become a paramilitary organization, and there have been incidents upcountry in which members of the League interfered with chiefs or local authorities. The TANU government has taken strong disciplinary measures against such action and at the present time appears able to control the League. Some of its members undoubtedly belong to the more radical wing of TANU, but it seems more likely that they will attempt to act through the parent organization itself rather than through the Youth League.

The Youth League has included only youths over eighteen and has not enrolled younger Africans as have the parties in, for instance, Guinea and Ghana. One party faction does favor establishment of teen-age youth groups, but this is not official policy. The League's present president, Joseph Nyerere (who is a younger brother of Julius), provides a personal link with the one TANU operation concerning younger persons—the TANU independent schools. These were started in 1958 in an attempt to provide some education for youngsters for whom the government and mission schools had no room, and they have become one of the most interesting of TANU projects. The schools are usually small mud buildings, frequently TANU offices, or sometimes simply the bare space under a mango tree; the teachers are local TANU officials or former schoolteachers who have lost their teaching licenses.

Classes vary from school to school. Some deal only with the youngest children in Standards I and II, whereas others teach up to Standard VI level. One school in Arusha in 1961 had 78 students and one teacher; another in Dar es Salaam had one teacher and 170 pupils. The children wear green TANU uniforms and learn the party songs; that they also learn more academic subjects is attested by their sporadic but real successes on territorial examinations set by the Department of Education.

In 1960 TANU hired a schools' organizer and attempted to establish a standard syllabus, as well as to inspect the schools and assist the teachers; in the larger towns it was also trying to turn school management over to a group recently established under its aegis, the Tanganyika African Parents Association, or to the local councils. As Tanganyika's school system expands, the TANU schools will eventually disappear, but at the present time they fill a useful purpose. In contrast to the Kikuyu independent schools in Kenya, they have not been used primarily as centers of indoctrination.

The TANU schools grew out of other party activities, primarily the necessity of educating, both politically and generally, the population of the rural countryside. From its founding TANU has run adult literacy classes. Early in its history it started a women's section under Bibi (Mrs.) Titi Mohammed, wife of a Dar es Salaam taxi driver. Bibi Titi organized the women of the Swahili coast not only to attend political meetings but also to take part in classes in reading, cooking, and mother craft; in many areas of Tanganyika the women's section is now one of the most active arms of TANU. An elders' section has also been organized; it operates primarily in coastal areas. Neither section has a separate membership, and both regard themselves as part of TANU.

A number of other associations have worked closely with TANU; these include tribal associations, cooperative marketing societies, trade unions, and groups with such varied purposes as the Tanganyika African Traders Association and the African Study Group, a Dar es Salaam discussion club. The Tanganyika Federation of Labour and the cooperatives send representatives to the TANU Executive. TANU has also encouraged members to form cooperative farming associations to bring bushland under cultivation, though with widely varying results. The party began in 1960 to discourage tribal associations, apparently to de-emphasize any aspects of tribalism; it has been successful in getting a number of these associations to disband. Its relations with the trade unions have fluctuated and seemed in 1962 to be reaching a low ebb, as the unions objected to government wage policies.[68] TANU has tried to work with these varied groups and sometimes to control their policies, but there has been little pressure to bring the groups into TANU in any formal structural manner, such as happened in Ghana. TANU seems to enter those fields of daily life in which it feels action should be taken, but it is not totalitarian as a matter of philosophy.

In organizational terms, TANU is now going through a difficult period. After 1958, when the first TANU government was formed, many TANU officials moved into political office or into the civil service, and few men of ability stayed as party employees. The pressure was intense, since trained people were so rare. The average age of cabinet members in Tanganyika has been in the thirties, and the average age of party officials (even in Dar es Salaam) in the twenties. Many an upcountry official has found himself elected as chairman of the local council; if he did a good job, he would be immediately promoted. Job Lusinde, who at twenty-six was a science teacher in a mission

[68] See the following section below on contemporary issues, which deals with the trade unions in more detail.

school in Dodoma District, became progressively TANU district chairman, chairman of the Ugogo Council, member of the National Assembly, and, at thirty, Minister of Local Government.

The crucial point in TANU organization has been the district. The branches have been too small and widely scattered to employ professional workers; the provinces are too large and spread out to be cohesive units. At the district level, the secretary is a paid official, generally appointed from Dar es Salaam though occasionally a strong district committee appears to have some part in the matter. His rival for local power and also for control of finance is the district president, who is usually a part-time official; he was originally not paid but now receives a *posho* allowance. These two party officials are usually young and of varying educational level; many of them do not speak English. They have in the past provided the chief links between the central headquarters of TANU and the grass roots, and their role in interpreting policy has been vital; this role may change, however, with the appointment of regional commissioners. The district secretaries now meet annually just before the annual conference of the party, and they are cajoled and exhorted by the party leaders at the top. It is hardly surprising to find among their number both dedicated followers of Nyerere and men with a much more radical bent. Nyerere, in attempting to reorganize and revivify the party, will no doubt pay special attention to this group within the party.

Two more organizational aspects of TANU are worthy of comment: finance and external relations. Detailed information on party finance is not available, but the party has generally been able to build itself organizationally through its dues of six shillings a year, and its current budget envisages regular expenditure of about £50,000 annually. It has also developed a system halfway between assessments and voluntary donations to finance a new headquarters building, buy Land Rovers for party traveling, and provide for other special purposes. Voluntary donations have included contributions from many non-Africans who give to party funds as a matter both of policy and of protection. The annual conference approves a party budget in advance, and funds are divided in a set ratio between central and district headquarters.

TANU has not had severe financial problems during its years as an opposition party, though in 1961 after it came to power there were some signs that subscriptions were lagging. In addition to meeting its own needs, it has also financed almost completely the Pan-African

Movement of East and Central Africa (PAFMECA) and supported as well a number of refugee political movements in Dar es Salaam, such as the South African United Front and the Mozambique African Democratic Union. TANU has encouraged these groups as a part of its own anticolonial and egalitarian program. In 1962, as PAFMECA was expanded to cover all southern Africa and moved north to include Ethiopia as well, TANU's influence seemed to be proportionately decreasing. The party has also indicated that it may become stricter with the groups now centered in Dar es Salaam, some of which have seemed in TANU eyes to devote all their time and effort to intrigue.

SOURCES OF POWER

It is very early yet to say much about how TANU will operate in independent Tanganyika, or indeed who its principal leaders will be. Nyerere, as is evident, has been the party's outstanding personality. Prime Minister Kawawa is vice-president of the party, Minister of Home Affairs Kambona its secretary-general. Such non-Africans as Derek Bryceson and Amir Jamal, as members of the cabinet and long-time associates of TANU, have influence in some matters with the TANU Executive but little basis of real political power. The role of other cabinet members, most of whom are members of the National Executive, is harder to assess. Chief Abdullah Fundikira, who is now Minister for Justice, was one of the first chiefs to endorse TANU and occupies a position close to that of elder statesman. A second echelon of TANU leadership is now appearing among members of the cabinet and the National Assembly, led by such men as I. M. Bhoke Munanka, parliamentary secretary in the Prime Minister's office; Amri Abedi, former mayor of Dar es Salaam, who is now regional commissioner for the western region; and Saidi Maswanya, Minister without Portfolio. Behind them comes a third group of younger men, such as R. S. Wambura, regional commissioner for the Lake region; C. S. K. Tumbo, labor leader and member of the National Assembly; and Roland K. Mwanjisi, editor of *Uhuru* and parliamentary secretary to the Ministry of Education and Information Services.

Where these men stand on party policy is very difficult to ascertain. Party discussions are not public, and no one has clearly emerged as leader of an opposition to Nyerere and Kawawa; if a cabal exists, it cannot yet be identified. Kambona is regarded by many Tanganyikans as favoring, with the support of Bhoke Munanka, much more radical policies than those provided by the orthodox TANU line;

Tumbo and Mwanjisi have both taken an extreme position in opposition to citizenship for non-Africans. It would easily be possible to name another 20 or 30 men in the upper echelons of TANU leadership who have differed from Nyerere at one point or another. What is not yet clear is the extent to which this opposition is systematic and united. Tumbo, speaking in the National Assembly on the Citizenship Bill, urged a return to chiefly authority at the same time that he was calling for more extreme action against non-Africans.[69]

The sources of political power and influence are also hard to pinpoint. Despite TANU's consistent opposition to tribalism, tribal affiliations are still important in obtaining local support and thus in taking the first political steps in the party or the state structure. The 1960 elections showed tribal considerations important in areas such as Mbulu and Tukuyu and relatively weaker elsewhere. TANU headquarters was able to impose a number of candidates who did not belong to local tribes, but they were most successful when the candidate came from a distant area; problems arose when a man from a neighboring tribe was nominated. None of the tribes of Tanganyika has been strong enough to move into a position of real territorial political power, though many have tried to act as local pressure groups. Enough political leaders are now arising within different tribes so that no one person is likely to have a monopoly of the backing even of his own tribe, and the tribes themselves will be split on political questions. Chief Abdullah Fundikira, who has sometimes been regarded as the representative of a tribal point of view, is rather spokesman for the Chiefs' Convention and a gradualist approach to politics.

Trade union support was initially important to Kawawa, and co-operative support to several other ministers. Religious affiliation has also played a considerable role and may be even more important in the future; the TANU Executive has a Muslim majority. Most political influence, however, still seems to be based very largely on personal factors, and Nyerere's unassuming appearance, his oratorical skill, and his charismatic quality have probably been more responsible for his rise to power than the other factors mentioned. If TANU develops further internal splits on a systematic, ideological level, political belief may become increasingly important. At the moment, the groups with real political influence are primarily those that are economic in nature,

[69] Tanganyika National Assembly, *Debates,* 36th sess., 5th meeting, 1960–1961, c. 314.

such as the trade unions, the cooperatives, and the sisal industry. The present political counterweights to these special interests are control of the party apparatus and mass support in the rural country-side. Mass support can clearly be seen at present for only three men: Nyerere, Kawawa, and Kambona.

ELECTIONS

One of the reasons it is difficult to assess the relative strength of leaders and policies is the small number of elections which have so far been held; thus one must guess about the role, and the opinions, of the electorate. With fifty-eight unopposed candidates in the 1960 elections, it is evident that political judgments were not made at the polls but in Dar es Salaam when candidates were chosen. Technically the final decision on candidates was made by the district committees; in practice, they were frequently overruled by the TANU Executive and by Kambona as party secretary. Local dislike of this tactic explains some features of the elections. In Mbulu an independent candidate won; in Tukuyu a very small proportion of the electorate voted. In both cases the TANU candidate was not the local first choice.

In early elections, TANU members often ran against each other, and the Executive had to take disciplinary action. Members who did not receive official endorsement were expelled from the party and given to understand that it might be a long time before they worked their way back into party favor. H. E. Sarwatt, who defeated the official TANU candidate in Mbulu and who is a former TANU member, has not been able to secure his readmission to the party. He occupies a lonely position as the one member of the National Assembly not acceptable to TANU.

The machinery of past elections has been similar to that of most other countries in Africa that were under British control. There have been many administrative problems, arising partly from the size of electoral districts (in 1958 all Western Province with its 78,000 square miles was one district) and partly from the inherent difficulties of conducting an election with an inexperienced staff to administer a qualitative franchise law which was capable of many interpretations. In most areas elections had to be spread over several days. At the same time there were few problems either of misunderstanding or of fraud. Coming elections will pose new problems, especially with the illiterate voters. Such techniques as party symbols and colors, though already used in elections so far, will become still more important.[70]

An election is now planned for October, 1962, prior to the acceptance of a republican constitution, and the TANU leadership may find itself facing a new and rather ironic problem. Although the party has been a mass movement and highly popular in the countryside, most of its electoral support has come from the more sophisticated urban areas (the new rather than the traditional Tanganyika) where a larger proportion of Africans could meet the franchise qualifications. In 1960, TANU party membership was still considerably larger than the number of persons qualified to vote. Elections on a universal franchise may thus give a much stronger voice to rural Tanganyika than has been true so far. On the other hand, it seems probable that most differences in viewpoint will be fought out in advance in the party committee rooms and not at the polls. Except for Zuberi Mtemvu of ANC, no prominent member expelled from TANU has yet shown a desire to oppose TANU at the polls, but instead each has tried to work his way back into the party's graces. So long as TANU membership remains unrestricted, it is likely that political battles will occur mainly within the party structure. Some evidence of this comes from the two special by-elections that have been held so far: there was no opposition to the official TANU candidate in Njombe, and in Bagamoyo the opposition candidate, Mtemvu, polled only eighty-nine votes.

ADMINISTRATION

The administration of Tanganyika today is in the hands of the civil service, whose members are appointed by the Governor-General on the advice of the Public Service Commission. As in other governmental matters, the structure has changed little from preindependence days, but the working of the system shows marked differences.

As a territory under British control, Tanganyika was administered by a corps of colonial service officers organized into a general field service (the provincial administration) and specialized technical departments (agriculture, medicine, education, and so on). In early days the technical departments were not well financed or staffed, and

[70] Tanganyika, *Report on the First Election of Members of the Legislative Council of Tanganyika* (mimeographed; Dar es Salaam, 1959); *Report on the Second General Election* . . . (mimeographed; Dar es Salaam, 1960). For a description of elections in conditions similar to those existing in Tanganyika, see W. J. M. Mackenzie and Kenneth Robinson, eds., *Five Elections in Africa* (Oxford, 1960).

the administrators had to be Jacks-of-all-trades, able to collect taxes or decide a court case or build a local road. Officers appointed to the districts (61 at present) worked with the local African chiefs and elders; they were responsible to 10 provincial commissioners, and the provincial commissioners in turn to the Chief Secretary (later the Minister of Provincial Affairs or Local Government) in Dar es Salaam. Prior to the first African appointments to the Legislative Council in 1945, this hierarchical administration constituted the only contact between the colonial government and the African population. The district commissioner's office upcountry became the center of local activity, and the settlements which grew up in the neighborhood frequently became the towns of modern Tanganyika, site of the courthouse, the school, and the Indian shops. This provincial staff also supplied most of the staff for nontechnical positions in the capital.

Originally this administrative service was rigidly structured along racial lines, and only subsidiary clerical jobs were held by Africans or Asians. After 1947, when racial terminology was largely removed from Tanganyika laws, there was pressure to bring local inhabitants into the higher levels of the administration, but this was long resisted by the British government. At the same time, as more money became available and economic and social welfare schemes increased, the size of the administrative corps jumped markedly. Technical personnel also increased, and the non-African establishment of the government of Tanganyika was more than ten times as large in 1960 as it had been in 1920.

In the 1950's when the Tanganyika government finally opened the upper ranks in the administration to Africans, it had difficulty finding personnel; few Tanganyika Africans possessed the required university education. Although this requirement was subsequently modified and training grades were introduced, the entry of Africans was not rapid enough for local opinion. After 1957 in particular, Africanization of the administrative service became a major rallying cry for TANU, and public opinion pressed especially for Africanization in the posts most exposed to contact with the public: the ministries in Dar es Salaam, the district administration, and the police. The number of Africans in senior posts increased from 112 in 1956 to 453 in 1960, out of a total senior service of approximately 3,000 persons. In the district administration upcountry, however, there were in 1960 only 15 Africans in senior posts.[71] After August, 1960, the Public Service Commission was

---

[71] Great Britain, *Tanganyika: Report for the Year 1960,* Col. 349, p. 16.

required to give priority in any available posts to African candidates, and Africanization was speeded up.

Tanganyika is still dependent upon the skills of expatriate officers, however, and will be for some time to come. There has been little pressure on the highly technical branches of the government, such as the geological survey or the medical department, but other areas in which the need of *expertise* is not so immediately obvious have been increasingly pressured to remove their non-African employees. By agreement in late 1960 the United Kingdom government assumed certain financial responsibilities for overseas officers, with the dual motive of encouraging them to stay in Tanganyika while they are needed and of compensating them adequately when they are asked to leave to make way for Tanganyikans. Unlike similar agreements reached between the United Kingdom and its former West African colonies, the Tanganyika terms do not require the officers to leave at a specified time but permit flexible arrangements according to the wishes of the individual officer and the Tanganyika government.[72] In mid-1961 approximately 15 per cent of the overseas officers had decided to leave Tanganyika, but there was a wide variation in this percentage from department to department. After Nyerere's resignation, the general percentage rose.

The impact of this pressure for Africanization can be understood only in the context of the role of the administrative service in Tanganyika. Its position is infinitely more important than that of the civil service in the United States or other Western countries. The administration has many functions which, in the United States, are principally in private hands, such as the health services, or come under control of local government units, such as the schools and the police. In the absence of large private financial resources, government economic activity occupies a predominant place in the territorial economy. Moreover, without developed local governments all functions devolve upon the central administration. Essentially, therefore, Tanganyika is a country run by a bureaucracy, and the bureaucracy's membership, political complexion, efficiency, and training are matters of national importance.

The civil service is at present pro-TANU, but there has been a consistent effort to keep political and administrative matters separate. One of Nyerere's first tasks on becoming Chief Minister was to issue a statement defining clearly the relationship between the civil service

[72] *Ibid.*, p. 26; *Service with Overseas Governments*, Cmnd. 1193 (1960).

upcountry and the new members of the National Assembly. The elected member, wrote Nyerere, is the proper recipient of local grumbles; the civil service is the executor of policy and must not become the target of political antagonism.[73] The recent appointment of regional political commissioners may be a further step toward removing the civil service from political pressures. Early in 1962 the first African permanent secretaries were appointed, and the head of the civil service is now Dunstan Omari, who had been the first African district officer and was more recently Tanganyika's diplomatic representative in London.

In practice, it seems generally admitted that Africanization has affected the efficiency of the Tanganyika civil service, though to what extent remains a matter of debate. So far few questions have been raised about the honesty of the civil service; in the past there have been many cases of peculation among minor officials, but the reputation of the senior service has been good in this respect. Tanganyikans are concerned more about questions of partiality, especially when tribal or racial differences are involved. The civil service has played an important role in breaking down tribalism, partly by its universal use of Kiswahili and partly by its practice of transferring African staff all over Tanganyika. Africans who admired the British senior service nevertheless usually thought that it always supported the European position, and feel that Africans in positions of power will equally guard their own. Local Asians also feel strongly about the present preference accorded Africans on government jobs. The few actions taken by the TANU government which have appeared to favor its own members (for instance, the granting of overseas scholarships) have been taken by ministers against civil service advice and have resulted several times in disputes in the cabinet. It is naïve to expect the civil service to stay entirely removed from politics, but so far the dividing line between administration and politics has been reasonably well observed.

LOCAL GOVERNMENT

In the terms in which local government is understood in the United States, it is difficult to say that it exists at all in Tanganyika today. As the section above has suggested, decisions have always been made

[73] "The Relationship between the Civil Service, Political Parties and Members of Legislative Council," Chief Minister's Circular Letter no. 1 of 1960 (Dar es Salaam, Oct., 1960).

in the past by the local representatives of a central government, and even the old native administration system fitted chiefs and councils into the single governmental hierachy. There have been no local bodies with any independence of action, their own taxation powers, technical personnel supplying local services, or local elected representation. Since 1948, however, the government of Tanganyika has been trying to establish local governments which meet these criteria, and the new independent government has followed very closely, in this respect, the old colonial policy. The guiding line is still the Creech-Jones 1947 dispatch urging democratic local government.

In the early 1950's the British government began a series of experiments in local government in Tanganyika, trying primarily to modernize the native administrations, to make them financially competent, and to introduce some element of popular participation. At one time they tried regionalism, at another provincial councils which would be electoral colleges for the Legislative Council, and at still another the introduction of non-African representation in accordance with ideas of multiracialism. Commoners were added to chiefs' councils, and in some instances the chiefs themselves became elected officials. On the whole, the proper model was held to be the English system of statutory county and district councils, and this concept, together with that of continued experimentation, has been inherited by independent Tanganyika.[74]

Two major steps have changed almost beyond recognition the old native administrations. The first of these steps was the passage of the Local Councils Ordinance of 1953, which provided for representative and eventually elected local councils; the second was the entry of party politics into the field of local government about 1958. As elections have been introduced, TANU and its local officials have begun to take over both local politics and administration, and the TANU district secretary, elected to the council, has sometimes acquired the status and authority of the chief. This has not yet happened where strong tribal units exist, but it has occurred in almost every area of fragmented tribal authority. The chief, in turn, has either been raised to a purely ceremonial position or turned into a chief executive officer. The present Tanganyika government has been willing to move much more quickly

[74] There is a substantial literature on these Tanganyika experiments in local government. See especially Great Britain, *The Development of Local Government in Tanganyika,* Col. 277 (1951), and issues of the *Journal of African Administration.*

on democratizing the councils than the British were able to do, and, in fact, Kawawa, as Minister of Local Government, ordered all local councils to adopt a system of direct elections. He also removed one of the major points of African opposition upcountry by specifying that councils did not have to be interracial; such a provision, indeed, violated TANU's stand in favor of nonracialism. TANU has approved, however, the British habit of co-option, which has made it possible for local African councils to utilize the special talents of local Europeans and Asians in financial or educational matters.

The general structural pattern in Tanganyika remains confusing in its variation. In some areas, such as Uhehe, it seems probable that the present council is only a façade and that the traditional chief still governs. TANU policy on local councils is really one aspect of its anti-tribal feeling, but some councils have also become, as has the Chagga Council, the representatives of a renewed tribal patriotism. Rural councils have frequently been more open to the idea of elections than those of the towns, an attitude which can perhaps be explained by the towns' reluctance to become autonomous and take on many financial burdens previously carried by the central government. Modernization of local government has meant, also, assumption of some powers of taxation and of responsibility for local services as well. This was clearly government policy as it tried to turn the local councils into statutory, independent district and municipal councils, but it has had to move more slowly in this area of development than on elections. In only a few instances, as in Mafia and Newala, has this status been reached. In 1961, the central government announced its intention of turning elementary education over to local councils. On the other hand, it was embroiled in an argument with the municipality of Dar es Salaam, which wanted its own police force. The activities and the financing of local government councils constitute a specialized problem to which administrators all over Africa have had to devote much attention.

The government of Tanganyika has had other problems with local authorities since it came into power. Upcountry, the membership of local councils sometimes parallels exactly that of the local TANU committee, and it is hard to keep the state and the party apparatus separate. As able African personnel has joined the central government, the local administrations have been denuded of staff and unable to find adequate replacements. As councils acquired a feeling of independence, furthermore, some have become more cursory in the performance of their duties. The most serious problem here has concerned the personal tax, which the local councils collect and divide with the central government in accordance with an agreed formula in each district. In many areas a very small proportion of the tax was collected in 1960, sometimes as little as 18 per cent. Local schools were sometimes closed, and local public works projects stopped for lack of finance. Frequently the district commissioner then stepped into the picture and conducted tax raids, a highly unpopular proceeding which consisted of rounding up the men in a village and jailing all those who did not possess a tax receipt. In other instances TANU leaders were called out from Dar es Salaam to pull their party members into line, and in districts like Rufiji this proved very difficult. By 1962 some TANU candidates were being defeated in local council elections and the ANC had won several seats at Tabora. The concentration of both party and government leadership in Dar es Salaam has left local councils open to less-educated and perhaps more extreme local opinion. Such local opinions may well determine the voting pattern of the electorate when new national elections are held.

It is still unclear how the government proposes to deal with some aspects of African life which had been handled by the native administrations but which can hardly be turned over to the local councils. The position of the chief is frequently still anomalous: he possesses traditional authority, he is executive officer of the local council, and he also, in respect to such matters as law and order, is still held to be an employee of the central government and answerable to the district commissioner. His three roles can only too easily overlap and conflict. His judicial powers to deal with native law and custom are gradually being devolved upon persons named court-holders who are appointed by the local councils, but how tribal law can be adapted to fit the new district units which frequently include more than one tribe remains to be seen. It is also uncertain what may happen to the chief's powers concerning allocation of land, and no council can hope to take over the religious or rain-making powers held by many chiefs and still considered an integral part of their authority. With constitutional and political development of the whole territory to be thought of, no one has yet had time to sort out the manifold problems of local administration.

JUDICIAL SYSTEM

The administration of law is particularly interesting in Tanganyika today, as it is in many other parts of Africa. Although a High Court is specified in the constitution of Tanganyika and the independence of the judiciary is safeguarded through the Judical Service Commission, these provisions deal only with one court system. A second system of judicial administration also exists in Tanganyika that is based on the old native courts of Cameron's day, and several different systems of law can be found.

In the early 1920's the British administration had promulgated in Tanganyika a series of laws which seemed appropriate to the circumstances of the territory. Many of these laws were based on Indian or other British colonial ordinances; and the whole of the Indian Penal Code was applied to Tanganyika in 1920. Both the mandate agreement and the 1920 Order in Council, however, required the government also to take native law and custom into account. There were many varieties of local African custom; in addition, Muslim law (sometimes considered in Tanganyika to come under the heading of native law) had to be used for large groups of Asians and Africans. Generally, statute law applied to new aspects of life in urban, modern Tanganyika and also covered such major offenses as murder and the use of witchcraft. Europeans were subject only to the jurisdiction of the British court system which applied statutory law. Asians might, in addition, be subject to the provisions of Muslim law (sometimes as it was applied in India), while Africans, even in the towns, were also responsible for observance of native law and custom. The lines of division between those systems were not always clear; thus there were often controversies over the extent to which individual tribes had adopted Muslim law, for instance, or whether it was illegal for an African Christian to have two wives. It is, indeed, still possible for an African to be prosecuted in one court for carrying out an action required of him by another.

The latter situation arose because there was originally no connection between the courts administering statutory law under the High Court and those in the countryside concerned with native law and custom. Appeals from the native courts, and even from the local town courts presided over by appointed African magistrates known as *liwalis*,[75] did not go to the High Court but to district and provincial administrative officers who possessed magisterial powers, and from them eventually to the Governor's Appeal Board. In 1951 the Local Courts Ordinance widened the jurisdiction of the town courts in particular and

[75] Tanganyika, Local Government Memorandum, 2 (Dar es Salaam, 1953).

[75] This is the same term used of some appointed chiefs under the system of native administration, but two different offices existed. The word *liwali* implies the exercise of judicial power, and both officials possessed this.

also provided for one judge from the High Court to sit on the appeals board for local court cases. Nonetheless, the two systems still remained largely separate. Differences in procedure (local courts did not allow lawyers, for instance) were many, though the British administration was always pressing the African courts to improve their records, adopt modern rules of evidence, and be guided by British judicial principles.[76]

Despite all its structural difficulties and the racial divisions of the court structure, the dual court system has worked surprisingly well. In local courts the chief is now being replaced by a court-holder who has some training in legal principles; Tanganyika has had since 1953 a system of judicial advisers attached to the administration whose function has been to help select and train such men for local court responsibilities. There have been few instances of abuse of local judicial powers through administering cruel or unusual punishments. In the town courts, the difficulty of applying various types of native law has led to a search for basic principles, which might eventually become an African common law. In many cases the statutory courts have adopted a panel of assessors who advise the judge on relevant points of local law or custom, and there has been some attempt to bring British and African legal ideas into line.

The government of independent Tanganyika, however, cannot possibly accept a dual system of law courts for very long. Much African law is still unwritten, and because lawyers are forbidden to appear in local courts, Tanganyika has not developed the African legal cadre found in most West African countries. Magistrates in the local courts are not lawyers trained in British law, and the *liwalis* in the towns are essentially judges applying Muslim law. There has been little public pressure for Africanization of the High Court system, but the government is trying to develop skilled legal officers as soon as possible. The first faculty of the University College of Tanganyika, founded in 1961, was, thus, a faculty of law.

At the present time, the High Court is charged with the interpretation of the constitution, and since provisions of the constitution, requiring a two-thirds vote, cannot be changed as easily as ordinary laws, judicial review may become an important matter. There are no special provisions in the constitution, however, to ensure individual or minority-

---

[76] Tanganyika, *Local Government Memorandum 2* (Dar es Salaam, 1953); J. N. D. Anderson, *Islamic Law in Africa* (London, 1954). Legal problems and developments in Tanganyika are discussed in numerous issues of the *Journal of African Administration* and the *Journal of African Law.*

group rights; the High Court will presumably not enter this realm. The statute books in Tanganyika still include a series of ordinances passed in the colonial period which provide for collective punishment, removal of persons held to be agitators to other parts of the territory, deportation of aliens upon a decision by the Governor, control of meetings by the police, and registration of all societies. The legal basis for autocratic governmental action has thus been left behind by the colonial power. In the early months of 1962 deportation powers were used by the government, but it has not taken any other action based on these ordinances.

It is clear that the next few years in Tanganyika will be years of political adaptation, as both structure and function of government change. The utility of a parliamentary or presidential form of government in Tanganyikan circumstances, the viability of the TANU one-party state, and the survival of a multiracial community are all in question. In this section these problems have been discussed in terms of political process; in the next the more direct and immediate issues which may help to decide them will be given attention.

Contemporary Issues

As in so many newly emergent countries, events in Tanganyika continued to move forward at an almost breakneck pace. With each appearance of the newspaper a new plan for economic development, new ministerial appointments, and new problems concerning schools and trade unions and race relations are set forth. It is hard to keep up with the structure of government, let alone the nuances of its operation. The visitor to Tanganyika has a constant impression of movement and change and social ferment, very different from the quiet and somnolent atmosphere of even ten years ago.

Dar es Salaam still slows down a little in the hot season of January and February, but only a little. The old German buildings are now being replaced; the main street, which was called Unter den Azakien by the Germans and Acacia Avenue by the British, has now become Independence Avenue. In the hotels, the old Swahili term for waiter *boi* is abandoned as derogatory to African dignity. In the western areas of the city, where houses are still built in traditional African style with mud walls and thatch roofs, Julius Nyerere leads TANU officials and members in destroying the worst buildings and erecting new cement houses in their place. In the open space of Mnazi Mmoja, once planned by the British to separate traditional African high-density housing from the business center and wealthier residential areas—and often used for African political meetings—there stand a community center, a clinic, and the TANU headquarters, now housing the University College of Tanganyika. In the middle is a standard with the green, gold, and black flag of Tanganyika.

What are the major problems facing Tanganyika today, those talked of in the streets of Dar es Salaam or in the rural tribal *barazas?* According to the Western point of view, political or economic problems or perhaps those in education would probably be emphasized. Most of the current issues of importance have been mentioned in earlier sections; in this summary it may be useful to try to view problems as a Tanganyikan might.

NATIONAL UNITY

The first and most pressing problem is attainment of national unity. The size of Tanganyika, its lack of communications, and its varied tribal and racial background make it vital to achieve some form of national allegiance and national consensus and to give the country a sense of its common past and its common future. Until a few years ago, there was no way even of saying "Tanganyikan" in Swahili; the words *watanganyika* (the people of Tanganyika) and *wananchi* (the people of the country) had to be invented. The national anthem *Mungu ibariki Afrika* (God bless Africa), the flag, and the ceremony and symbolism used by TANU have all been designed to contribute to this national feeling. Other widely varied policies contribute: the attacks on the British and other colonial powers, which thus become an enemy shared by all; the emphasis in government planning on roads leading *into* Tanganyika instead of toward other countries (the best roads of Northern Province have always led toward Nairobi rather than Dar es Salaam); the development of a national broadcasting system.

The problems and controversies concerned in this creation of national unity have already been mentioned, and indeed it is still uncertain precisely what connotation a word such as *wananchi* will eventually acquire. In the circumstances of Tanganyika, TANU may be the only possible instrument for the creation of genuine national unity, and Julius Nyerere's resignation to return to party work reflects his belief that it is. The National Assembly has interesting debates, but it is too far removed from rural Tanganyika to be significant. The safari around the districts, which resembles greatly the old-fashioned

American political device of whistle-stopping, is much more effective. A political rally in upcountry Tanganyika can indeed be very like an American July Fourth celebration: speeches, refreshments, hot sun, loud music, stray animals, and a milling crowd. TANU has so far been able to act very effectively on this platform. Kambona and Nyerere represent the varying oratorical styles; Kambona is a flamboyant speaker, Nyerere a quiet one. Nyerere uses humor and gestures and holds a rural audience for hours with a simple story in which he compares independent Tanganyika to an African worker who has had a fine time spending this week's wages but soon discovers he has no more money and must go back to work. The open question now is whether Nyerere can swing rural Tanganyika clearly behind his policies or whether either apathy or disaffection will continue.

National unity is in one sense an end in itself, but even more it is urged as a means of attaining other goals. The three chief enemies, say Tanganyikans, are poverty, ignorance, and disease; these can only be defeated in a war in which everyone plays his role and from which will finally result the achievement of African socialism. So much is generally agreed, but differences arise with further definition of the immediate tasks. To the present government, the three-year development plan must be accorded top priority, and local political and economic decisions made in accordance with it; if this entails a firm stand against government wage increases or for the taxation of women, these steps must be taken. Above all, production and exports must increase, and the money found, internally or externally, for development.

In opposition there is not one particular group, but a whole series of specialized interests: the rural population, which prefers to be apathetic about paying taxes but likes more schools and hospitals built with public money; the trade unions, which wish continued wage increases; the politicians, to whom political questions are always more important than economic ones. Where economic special interest happens to coincide with opposition to other policies regarding, for instance, citizenship for all races, a strong internal opposition may be in the making, powerful enough to force its own policies upon the government. Such alignments seem to be the basis of the battle between Nyerere's leadership in TANU and trade union leaders like C. S. K. Tumbo of the Railway African Union who combine a wish for more influence on government policy with a dislike of non-Africans and a desire for a larger slice of the economic pie. Since in former days the economic hierarchy of Tanganyika was the same as the racial hierarchy, it may be inevitable that opposition to one means opposition to the other. Nyerere, in defending his view of racial equality, is put in the position of seeming to defend the European and the Asian business-man against the exploited African. It becomes axiomatic that Nyerere and his followers emphasize the value of cooperative endeavor, because it is automatically African, but their position always appears defensive. The decision in March, 1962, to expropriate freehold land alienated to non-Africans by the Germans is clearly one point where combined economic and racialist pressures forced the government into action that it had previously publicly opposed.

ECONOMIC AND SOCIAL PROBLEMS

The precarious financial status of Tanganyika intensifies the importance of this struggle. Government revenue from the whole territory is approximately £21,000,000 annually, less than what New York City spends on street cleaning. In 1961–1962 nearly £2,000,000 of that sum was absorbed by emergency relief for flood and famine conditions in Central Province and Northern Province, even though considerable assistance came also from the United States and the United Kingdom.[77] Foreign investment may be deterred by internal political developments, and the necessary skilled workers may also leave. In 1961 it was reliably estimated that if more than 30 per cent of the European civil servants chose to leave Tanganyika the three-year development plan would have to be entirely rescheduled. By early 1962, more than 30 per cent had left in some government departments, though the over-all figure was not yet that high.

Closely allied to these economic questions, and really dependent upon them, are solutions to many social and educational problems. Under the three-year development plan, secondary education, in particular, is to be increased to supply educated workers and leaders; yet finance or lack of teaching personnel could bring development to a standstill. It is not unconnected with these issues that Tanganyika has recruited secondary school teachers from the United States (through private groups and the Agency for International Development) and has requested surveyors and nurses from the Peace Corps. The extension of medical services, the decision to ask rural councils to run the elementary schools, and the pace of urbanization (through

[77] *Tanganyika Budget Survey, 1960–61* (Dar es Salaam, 1961); *Development Plan for Tanganyika, 1961/62–1963/64* (Dar es Salaam, 1961).

provision of housing) may all be decided by the basic politico-economic clash.

Other interrelated educational and social issues arise. As Tanganyika moves out of the period of British influence, for instance, how appropriate is a British curriculum in the schools? What role should be assigned to the missions? In what language should children be taught? How well will the integrated school system for children of all races work? And what will happen to the large numbers of children for whom there are still no places available in school? The Tanganyika government, in according priority to increased secondary education for a few, risks the discontent of the countryside where primary education is still not available. In Chagga, for instance, the proportion of children in elementary school has actually gone down in the last few years; population has increased, but the number of schools has not. At the same time, workers drift into the towns; and one of the reasons for militancy by the Tanganyika Federation of Labour is its fear of unemployment.

In the social milieu, as is thus seen, independence may have hastened the pace but has not changed the character of problems already arising in the change from old to new: decline of traditional values, spread of the monetary economy, progressive urbanization, and new patterns of marriage and inheritance and standards of living. In the primarily still rural society of Tanganyika, these problems may be expected to intensify in the next few years. Enough is known of the background of modern revolutions to suggest the potential explosiveness existing in Tanganyika or indeed any other African country; in Tanganyika, in contrast to much of West Africa, however, one still speaks of explosiveness only as potential.

MINORITIES

The other side of the problem of national unity is, of course, the problem of minorities. Most Tanganyikans see these only in racial terms, and if the policy of nonracialism works, there will be no problem. They do not at present examine the issue further. Thus minority rights are not thought of in terms of individual freedom, and although Tanganyika now has an entrenched constitution, a bill of rights has never been publicly mentioned. In the political field, the possible bases for arbitrary action have been mentioned; the Minister of Home Affairs cautions editors and political speakers against statements which could threaten law and order. But Zuberi Mtemvu, after speaking publicly in East Germany of the "repressive" government of Tanganyika, does not hesitate to come home and complain in the newspapers about the state of the roads in Bagamoyo District, which affect his political campaigning.[78]

One problem of civil rights and minorities which may well become pressing is that of religion. Since many schools in the past have been conducted by missions, it is true that Muslim education has been neglected, and the Muslim groups within TANU and AMNUT press for further attention to Muslim rights and prestige. AMNUT at present accuses even Prime Minister Kawawa of being a "yes-man" Muslim who discriminates against his own creed.[79] Religious issues have already entered local politics, and it is entirely conceivable that they will become national issues as well. One of the first actions of the TANU government was to make Idd-el-Fitr, the celebration which occurs at the end of the Muslim month of fasting, a national holiday.

EXTERNAL RELATIONS

The area over which most speculation arises about the future course of events is that of foreign affairs. Until the summer of 1960 TANU had said little on this subject except in regard to East African union, but events in the Congo and South Africa have moved it out of its entirely domestic preoccupations. Tanganyika has virtually no personnel trained in foreign affairs, and while the government has been relatively cautious, therefore, in its public statements, it has also been dogmatic. Foreign policy is seen as the extension of the domestic struggle against colonialism and other antidemocratic forces. Here TANU as an organization takes its most extreme stand; there is no segment of opinion which is moderate in Western terms. This is not unique to Tanganyika, as consideration of the foreign policies of states such as Guinea indicates, and it does not imply agreement within Tanganyika; as in domestic politics, several schools of thought are represented. But the range of opinion as a whole is more radical than would be found in the United States, and this has constantly to be remembered by the outside observer.

The issues which face Tanganyika concern first of all its relationship with other African states. Although, in 1948, the Tanganyika African Association opposed federation of East Africa, it has changed its mind

[78] *Mwafrika,* July 10, 1961; *Ngurumo,* Feb. 5, 1962.
[79] *Mwafrika,* Feb. 5, 1962.

in recent years, as it came to realize that East Africa can be unified under African control rather than European aegis. TANU essentially created and controlled the Pan-African Movement for East and Central Africa, and Nyerere was once willing to defer Tanganyikan independence so that East African federation might be achieved first. Creation of this federation is an essential goal for the Tanganyika government, though ways and means of achieving it have not been worked out. In no other area which would be included in such a federation is there one strong party similar to TANU, and TANU has just begun to realize the complexities involved in bringing together the politicians of Kenya, Uganda, and Zanzibar even if federation is not expanded further. Conversations on union have been conducted with some groups in Ruanda-Urundi, and an interest in association has been shown in the south, especially in Nyasaland and Mozambique but in the two Rhodesias as well. Possible schemes of federation will be constantly discussed for the next few years.

This movement for East African federation may blend into or with the Pan-African movements in West Africa, or it may possibly compete. Tanganyika has taken part officially so far in only one Pan-African meeting, that in Lagos in February, 1962; this action tended to align it with the Monrovia powers. On some other questions as well TANU seems opposed to Ghanaian and Guinean plans. Its trade unionists, for instance, have continued to favor association with the International Confederation of Free Trade Unions in opposition to an all-African trade union movement with no outside ties.

Tanganyika has taken a strong position on several other African issues. TANU boycotted South African products before it formed a government and stated publicly that Tanganyika would not join the Commonwealth so long as South Africa remained a member.[80] Portugese policy in its territories has been sharply criticized, and the Portuguese consul was requested to leave Dar es Salaam. TANU has supported refugee political groups from both areas, and its concern with, and active participation in, southern African affairs will undoubtedly increase. On these two questions, in particular, there is very little internal dissension; most Tanganyikans would like to take still more vigorous action to indicate their dislike for South African and Portuguese policy.

The forum which TANU seems most likely to use to carry forward its ideas is the United Nations. Nyerere and other TANU leaders found

[80] *The Observer* (London), March 12, 1961.

the United Nations helpful during their fight for independence, and they see it as a useful vehicle in pursuing their own policies and as a steppingstone toward the ordered world they wish to see established. They tend to be rather more sympathetic to United Nations problems, therefore, than some other African states.[81] Tanganyikan sympathies were often with Patrice Lumumba in the Congo, but there was very little public criticism of United Nations policy there. In the United Nations, Tanganyika may be expected to pursue the role of positive neutrality, refusing officially to take sides in the cold war, opposing use of nuclear weapons, and calling for further action against colonialist countries. It will urge admission of Communist China to the United Nations, though it favors continued membership for Formosa as well.

The Tanganyika government is, of course, always conscious of its need of funds, and this may determine much of its attitude toward the United Nations and individual member countries. As a member of the Commonwealth, it will be as friendly as possible toward Great Britain, its own former imperial power. It considers itself on good terms with the United States, despite its refusal to take part in the cold war and a considerable dislike of American racial attitudes. It also expects to develop friendly relations with West Germany, the successor of another imperial power, and other countries such as Sweden and Switzerland.

The present government will probably, however, concentrate generally on domestic questions and operate in the world arena only occasionally. Tanganyika has tailored the number of its embassies overseas to meet its purse, for instance, and has established them so far only in New York, London, and New Delhi—even while receiving representatives of other countries including Ghana, China, and the USSR. One section of TANU urges a much more active role in foreign affairs, but this has not so far held much popular appeal.

Even as Tanganyika learns from the experience of older African states, it becomes in turn a symbol of African achievement for other countries. In eastern Africa, as the first country to reach independence, it has taken the lead along a path soon to be followed by Kenya, Uganda, and possibly southern Africa, and continued Tanganyikan initiative may make it the leading member of a new East African federation. As a state with a nonracial philosophy, it now provides a model for all of Africa and indeed a wider world. As a pragmatic country interested in political and economic structure which will work, it becomes a laboratory of social experiment, and it may find new

[81] *United Nations Review*, Jan., 1962.

answers to some of the problems of the twentieth-century world. Tanganyika has an interesting, if perplexing, future ahead.

BIBLIOGRAPHY

The American student searching for further information on the government and politics of Tanganyika is likely to find the task a difficult one. Although a good deal of information on the country has appeared in reports published by the United Kingdom or the United Nations, they have included very little on political structure or political dynamics, and only in the last year or two have books or articles dealt directly with these topics. Most of this section draws on material collected through interviews in Tanganyika or on unpublished sources found there. In view of the scattered and sporadic nature of other materials, a general introductory note on available bibliography on Tanganyika may be helpful.

The starting point for any study of Tanganyika is the annual report issued by the British government, which has appeared under slightly varying titles for 1920–1938 and 1947–1960. The early reports were useful surveys of policy and major events; later ones have tended to bog down in statistical detail. Two giant volumes published by the government of Tanganyika are also extremely useful and cover a variety of subjects, from animal life to history: J. P. Moffett, ed., *Handbook of Tanganyika* (Dar es Salaam, 1958), and J. P. Moffett and J. F. R. Hill, eds., *Tanganyika: A Review of Its Resources and Their Development* (Dar es Salaam, 1955).

The official publications of the Tanganyika government are the most useful source for the interested political scientist. A *Gazette*, published weekly, includes important government notices; supplements contain bills, ordinances, government notices, and law reports. The *Debates* of the National Assembly are reported verbatim and are notable for their frankness and the wide variety of information, especially the answers to parliamentary questions. Government white papers are issued on important matters of policy, but there is as yet no uniform practice on titling or numbering. Some reports from select committees are published, but apparently not all.

Annual reports are issued by all government departments; a list can be obtained from the Government Printer, Dar es Salaam. These vary greatly in size and usefulness. In recent years matter pertinent to political affairs has appeared in the reports of the departments of education, agriculture, labor, and lands and surveys. The *Annual Reports of the Provincial Commissioners*, dealing with events throughout the country, are invaluable. Census data has been collected and issued by the East African Statistical Office; the most recent census returns date from 1957. The Tanganyika unit of this office, now established in Dar es Salaam, prepares an annual *Budget*

Survey and a *Statistical Abstract,* as well as further materials on economic statistics. Various bulletins on trade and commerce appear from time to time, and the Tanganyika Information Services issues reports and press releases and compiled until June, 1962, a daily mimeographed summary of the Swahili press.

Materials on local government, however, exist only in the areas concerned or in government files; more and more of this material is now in Swahili. In the 1950's the central government published an annual report on the development of local government, but this is no longer issued. Ministerial circulars and staff letters issued to the civil service may frequently be consulted in Tanganyika but are not otherwise available. *Law Reports* are published at irregular intervals.

Among the special reports issued by the Tanganyika government in recent years the following are important for political developments:

Report of the Committee on Constitutional Development, 1951.

Report of the Special Commissioner Appointed to Examine Matters Arising Out of the Report of the Committee on Constitutional Development, 1953.

Local Government Memoranda, 1951–1954.

Report of the Committee Appointed to Study Governments' Proposals regarding the Qualifications of Voters and Candidates for Election to Legislative Council, Together with Copies of Despatches Exchanged between His Excellency the Governor and the Secretary of State for the Colonies, 1957.

Report of the Post Elections Committee, 1959.

Report of the Committee on Integration of Education, 1960.

Report of the Salaries Commission, 1961.

Development Plan for Tanganyika, 1961/62–1963/64, 1961.

In addition to the statistical material noted above, the East African Common Services Organisation issues various reports concerning Tanganyika; the *Proceedings* of the Central Legislative Assembly have included political discussions. These publications are listed in Helen Conover, *Official Publications of British East Africa* (Part I, 1960), issued by the Library of Congress. Part II of this publication, compiled by Audrey A. Walker and issued in 1962, now makes available a list of Tanganyika government publications.

Few nonofficial publications of political interest have been issued in East Africa except in periodical form; a recent exception is Sophia Mustafa, *The Tanganyika Way* (Dar es Salaam, 1961), which describes the electoral campaigns of 1958 and 1960. TANU has published its constitution and a few small pamphlets, but most of its material, including its newsletter *Sauti ya TANU* ("The Voice of TANU"), is mimeographed only. Among periodicals, *Tanganyika Notes and Records,* now issued twice a year, contains historical and ethnographic information and occasionally touches on the contemporary scene. In addition to the newspapers mentioned in the section dealing with the press, *The Nation* (daily) and *The Reporter* (bimonthly) cover political events from Nairobi, Kenya. A directory of the local press is available from the Tanganyika Information Services.

Many official British publications refer to Tanganyika; these can be checked through the general monthly publications list or the periodic lists of Colonial Office publications, issued by H.M. Stationery Office. Recent command papers affecting Tanganyika have included the *Report of the Tanganyika Constitutional Conference,* Cmnd. 1360 (1961); *The Future of the East Africa High Commission Services,* Cmnd. 1433 (1961); and the *Report of the East African Economic and Fiscal Commission,* Cmnd. 1279 (1961). Two earlier reports of importance were *Development of African Local Government in Tanganyika,* Col. 277 (1951), and *Report of the East Africa Royal Commission, 1953–55,* Cmnd. 9475 (1955). The Tanganyika constitution, issued as an Order in Council, appears as Statutory Instrument, 1961, no. 2274. Research studies sponsored through the Colonial Office or the East African Institute of Social Research are listed with other publications below. A good short pamphlet, *Tanganyika: The Making of a Nation,* has been published by the British Central Office of Information (London, 1961).

Official publications of the League of Nations and the United Nations include much general information but little specifically on political matters before 1951. The *Minutes* of the Permanent Mandates Commission are voluminous, and the *Official Records* of the Trusteeship Council even more so. In addition to Trusteeship Council discussions, the most helpful United Nations materials are the reports of the five visiting missions (1948, 1951, 1954, 1957, and 1960), which appear as supplements to the *Official Records,* and the series of petitions from Tanganyika. Some of the petitions have been printed, but the complete file is available only in mimeographed form in the T/PET.2/ series of United Nations documents. The UN Department of Social Affairs has published a report entitled *The Population of Tanganyika* (1949), and the economic survey made by the International Bank for Reconstruction and Development has now been published in this country under the title *The Development of Tanganyika* (Baltimore, 1961).

An annotated list of pertinent books and periodical material follows. Aside from a few books dealing with history and ethnography, this list does not cover material published before 1950; the *Handbook of Tanganyika,* already mentioned, may be consulted for further sources.

BOOKS AND PAMPHLETS

Almond, Gabriel, and James S. Coleman, eds. *The Politics of Developing Areas*. Princeton: Princeton University Press, 1960. Discussion of developments in sub-Saharan Africa includes material on Tanganyika politics.

Brown, G. G., and A. B. M. Hutt. *Anthropology in Action: An Experiment in the Iringa Province, Tanganyika Territory*. London: Oxford University Press, 1935. An early, extremely interesting study of Hehe tribal organization and change.

Cairns, J. C. *Bush and Boma*. London: John Murray, 1959. Nostalgic memoirs of a district officer on the Tanganyika coast.

Cameron, D. C. *My Tanganyika Service and Some Nigeria*. London: Allen & Unwin, 1939. The introduction of native administration and other events of Cameron's governorship; probably the best introduction to Tanganyika between the wars.

Chidzero, B. T. G. *Tanganyika and International Trusteeship*. London: Oxford University Press, 1961. A detailed account, based on United Nations and League of Nations documents, of Tanganyika's international status and its effects on the territory, by a Southern Rhodesian.

Cole, Sonia. *The Prehistory of East Africa*. London: Penguin Books, 1954. An excellent technical survey of present knowledge.

Cory, Hans. *The Indigenous Political System of the Sukuma and Proposals for Political Reform*. Kampala, Uganda: Eagle Press for East African Institute of Social Research, 1954. Cory was a Tanganyika government sociologist.

——. *The Ntemi: Traditional Rites of a Sukuma Chief in Tanganyika*. London: Macmillan, 1957.

——, and M. M. Hartnoll. *Customary Law of the Haya Tribe, Tanganyika Territory*. London: P. Lund, Humphries & Co., 1945.

Coupland, Reginald. *East Africa and Its Invaders, from the Earliest Times to the Death of Seyyid Said in 1856*. Oxford: Oxford University Press, 1938. This and the following are two pioneering works in East African history.

——. *The Exploitation of East Africa, 1856–1890*. London: Faber, 1939.

Culwick, A. T. and G. M. *Ubena of the Rivers*. London: Allen & Unwin, 1935. Tribal history and organization in the early days of native administration.

Datta, A. K. *Tanganyika: A Government in a Plural Society*. The Hague: Nijhoff, 1956. An outline of government structure and a listing of current problems, from an Indian point of view.

Dundas, C. C. F. *Kilimanjaro and Its People*. London: Witherby, 1924. A classic account of the Chagga which has greatly influenced their views on their own history.

George, Betty. *Education for Africans in Tanganyika.* Washington, D.C.: Government Printing Office, 1961. An extremely useful introduction issued by the U.S. Office of Education.

Gulliver, P. H. *Labour Migration in a Rural Economy.* Kampala: East African Institute of Social Research, 1955. This and the following are two studies of tribal social change.

——. *Land Tenure and Social Change among the Nyakyusa.* Kampala: East African Institute of Social Research, 1958.

Hailey, Lord. *Native Administration in the British African Territories.* 5 vols. London: H.M. Stationery Office, 1950–1953. The sections on Tanganyika contain much information on the real problems of native administration.

Hill, Martin. *Permanent Way.* 2 vols. Nairobi: East African Railways and Harbours, n.d. The second volume, which deals with the building of the Tanganyika railways, includes much general information on history and economic development.

Hollingsworth, L. W. *The Asians of East Africa.* London: Macmillan, 1960. An elementary account but the only one available.

Leubuscher, Charlotte. *Tanganyika Territory: A Study of Economic Policy under Mandate.* London: Oxford University Press, 1944. A rather limited survey but one of the few available on economic matters.

Malcolm, D. W. *Sukumaland: An African People and Their Country.* London: Oxford University Press for International African Institute, 1953. Natural resources, tribal custom, and native administration among Tanganyika's largest tribe.

Marsh, Z. A., and G. Kingsworth. *Introduction to the History of East Africa.* 2d ed. Cambridge, Eng.: Cambridge University Press, 1961. A basic text which is much more thorough on Kenya than on Tanganyika.

Murray, James N., Jr. *The United Nations Trusteeship System.* Urbana, Ill.: University of Illinois, 1957. A clear and concise account of the mandate and trusteeship systems.

Nyerere, Julius K. "Africa's Place in the World," *Wellesley Symposium on Africa.* Wellesley, Mass.: Wellesley College, 1960. A speech on coming political changes.

Peacock, A. T., and D. G. M. Drosser. *The National Income of Tanganyika, 1952–54.* (Colonial Research Publication 26.) London: H.M. Stationery Office, 1958. A first attempt at basic economic statistics in Tanganyika. Further reporting on gross national product is now undertaken by the Tanganyika Statistical Office.

Prins, A. H. J. *The Swahili-speaking Peoples.* London: International African Institute, 1961. An introduction to coastal ethnography.

Richards, Audrey, ed. *East African Chiefs*. London: Faber, 1960. The changing position of the chief in a number of Uganda and Tanganyika tribes is surveyed in this very interesting work.

Skeffington, Arthur. *Tanganyika in Transition*. London: Fabian Colonial Bureau, 1960. A pamphlet on recent developments by a Labour M.P.

Tew, Mary. *The Peoples of the Lake Nyasa Region*. London: International African Institute, 1950. A general ethnographic survey, similar to the work of Prins.

Wilson, Monica. *Good Company*. London: Oxford University Press for International African Institute, 1957. Villages formed by age groups among the Nyakyusa.

——. *Peoples of the Nyasa-Tanganyika Corridor*. Cape Town: University of Cape Town, 1958. Changing social structure in a group of matrilineal tribes.

Wood, Alan. *The Groundnut Affair*. London: Bodley Head, 1950. Journalistic but reliable.

Wright, F. C. *African Consumers in Nyasaland and Tanganyika*. (Colonial Research Publication 17.) London: H.M. Stationery Office, 1955. An extremely interesting survey of changing social behavior and habits.

Young, Roland, and Henry Fosbrooke. *Smoke in the Hills*. Evanston, Ill.: Northwestern University Press, 1960. Changing tribal structure and agricultural problems, which culminated in a major riot, in Morogoro District. One of the few available accounts of contemporary Tanganyikan politics.

ARTICLES

Current material on Tanganyikan government and politics may be found in such magazines as *Africa Today* (New York), *Africa Report* (Washington, D.C.), and *Africa, Africa Digest, African Affairs, Journal of African Administration, Venture,* and *East Africa and Rhodesia* (all London), in addition to Tanganyikan and East African periodicals listed above. Recent articles of special interest include those listed below.

Africa Today, Dec., 1961. The entire issue is devoted to Tanganyika.

Bates, Margaret L. "Tanganyika: The Development of a Trust Territory," *International Organization*, Feb., 1955.

Carter, G. M. "Multi-racialism in Africa," *International Affairs*, Oct., 1960.

Cox, Richard. "Nyerere Seeks a Middle Way for Africa," *New York Times Magazine*, Dec. 3, 1961.

Fletcher-Cooke, John. "Some Reflections on the International Trusteeship System," *International Organization*, Summer, 1959.

Friedland, William H. "Tanganyika's Rashidi Kawawa," *Africa Report*, Feb., 1962.

Kawawa, Rashidi. "Africanisation," *Africa South*, Oct.–Dec., 1960.

Keith, Robert C. "Rapid Strides in Tanganyika," *Africa Special Report*, Dec., 1958.

Liebenow, J. Gus. "Responses to Planned Political Change in a Tanganyika Tribal Group," *American Political Science Review*, June, 1956.

Loewenkopf, Martin. "Outlook for Tanganyika," *Africa Report*, Dec., 1961.

——. "Tanganyika Achieves Responsible Government," *Parliamentary Affairs*, March, 1961.

McKay, Vernon. "Too Slow or Too Fast? Political Change in African Trust Territories," *Foreign Affairs*, Jan., 1957.

Nyerere, Julius K. "The Task Ahead of Our African Trade Unions," *Labour* (Ghana), June, 1960.

——. "We Cannot Afford to Fail," *Africa Special Report*, Dec., 1959.

——, and C. C. Harris. "Tanganyika Today," *International Affairs*, Jan., 1960.

Pratt, R. C. "Multi-racialism and Local Government in Tanganyika," *Race*, Nov., 1960.

Twining, Lord. "The Last Nine Years in Tanganyika," *African Affairs*, Jan., 1959.

——. "Tanganyika's Middle Course in Race Relations," *Optima*, Dec., 1958.

INDEX